CASES AND MATERIALS ON

EVIDENCE

CASES AND MATERIALS ON

EVIDENCE

Third edition by Simon Cooper

Simon Cooper, MA, LLB
Peter Murphy, MA, LLB, Barrister
John Beaumont, LLM

BLACKSTONE
PRESS LIMITED

First published in Great Britain 1994 by Blackstone Press Limited,
9–15 Aldine Street, London W12 8AW. Telephone 081-740 1173

© Peter Murphy and John Beaumont, 1987
Simon Cooper, Peter Murphy and John Beaumont, 1994

ISBN: 1 85431 279 0

British Library Cataloguing in Publication Data
A CIP catalogue record for this book is available from the British Library

Typeset by Style Photosetting Ltd, Mayfield, East Sussex
Printed by Ashford Colour Press, Gosport, Hampshire

CONTENTS

(A) Relevance, admissibility and weight — (B) Improperly or illegally obtained evidence: judicial discretion — *(i) The approach before the Police and Criminal Evidence Act 1984, s. 78(1)* — *(ii) The Police and Criminal Evidence Act 1984, s. 78(1) and after*

(A) The burden of proof — *(i) Civil cases* — *(ii) Criminal cases* — (B) The standard of proof— *(i) Criminal cases* — *(ii) Civil cases*

(A) Terminology — (B) Particular presumptions — *(i) Presumption of legitimacy* — *(ii) Presumption of marriage* — *(iii) Presumption of death* — *(iv) Presumption of regularity* — *(v) The presumption of negligence – res ipsa loquitur* — (C) Conflicting presumptions

PREFACE

The predecessor of this book, *Evidence: Materials for Discussion*, last appeared in 1987, shortly after the Police and Criminal Evidence Act 1984 came into force. Since then, the law of evidence has changed significantly in a number of areas. The Police and Criminal Evidence Act alone has generated a huge volume of case law, particularly in respect of s. 78(1) and the exercise of judicial discretion. Parliament has contributed to the changes with the Criminal Justice Act 1988 and the Criminal Justice Act 1991 dealing, *inter alia*, with hearsay, corroboration and competence. Even at the time of writing, more legislation is on the way. The Criminal Justice and Public Order Bill 1994, proposes further reform of the law relating to corroboration and to the defendant's right of silence. I have included the Bill's proposals at the appropriate points and attempted to illustrate the impact they will have on the existing law, although any legislative reform inevitably carries with it a degree of uncertainty. The book has of course been thoroughly updated with all significant case law developments.

In producing this new edition, I have changed the format and style to that more traditionally associated with a casebook. The hypothetical cases of *R* v *Coke*; *R* v *Littleton* and *Blackstone* v *Coke* have been removed. This has enabled me to include some new topics not dealt with in earlier editions, and expand on other important areas. Accordingly, this edition has been titled *Cases and Materials on Evidence* to better reflect the new style and format.

I wish to express my thanks to Peter Murphy and John Beaumont who were solely responsible for the production of *Evidence: Materials for Discussion*. Much of their original book has survived to emerge in this edition. I am extremely grateful to my friend and colleague Michael J. Allen who read the manuscript and made many helpful suggestions. I also wish to thank my wife Deborah, who helped me to compile the table of cases and statutes. Lastly, it is a pleasure to thank the publishers, particularly Alistair MacQueen and Heather Saward. They, together with their former colleague Jonathan Harris, made the task of producing the manuscript a genuine pleasure.

Simon Cooper
May 1994

ACKNOWLEDGMENTS

The authors and publishers would like to thank the following for permission to reproduce copyright material:

A. Ashworth and R. Pattenden: 'Reliability, Hearsay Evidence and the English Criminal Trial' (1986) 102 *Law Quarterly Review* 292
P.S. Atiyah: '*Res Ipsa Loquitur* in England and Australia' (1972) 35 *Modern Law Review* 337
D. Birch: 'Children's Evidence' [1992] *Criminal Law Review* 262
D. Birch: 'The Pace Hots Up' [1989] *Criminal Law Review* 95
N. Bridge: 'Presumptions and Burdens' (1949) *Modern Law Review* 273
A.T. Denning: 'Presumptions and Burdens' (1945) 61 *Law Quarterly Review* 379
P. Healy: 'Proof and Policy: No Golden Threads' [1987] *Criminal Law Review* 355
P. Mirfield: 'Similar Facts — *Makin* Out?' [1987] *Cambridge Law Journal* 83
J. Temkin: 'Sexual History Evidence — the Ravishment of Section 2' [1993] *Criminal Law Review* 3
Oxford University Press for permission to reprint an extract from the following book: A.A.S. Zuckerman, *The Principles of Criminal Evidence* (1989)
Butterworth & Co. (Publishers) Ltd: extracts from the All England Law Reports
Incorporated Council of Law Reporting for England & Wales: extracts from the Law Reports and the Weekly Law Reports
Jordan Publishing Ltd: extract from the Family Law Reports
Sweet & Maxwell Ltd: extracts from the Criminal Appeal Reports

TABLE OF CASES

TABLE OF STATUTES

Statutes, and sections thereof, which are set out in full or in part are shown in heavy type. The page at which the statute or section is printed is shown in heavy type.

1   PRELIMINARY MATTERS

The law of evidence serves two main purposes. First it decides what is or is not admissible as evidence for the purpose of proving or disproving facts in issue. Secondly, it determines how, if at all, the admissible matter may or must be presented to the court.

The types of evidence which may be adduced in order to establish the facts in issue may be classified into one of a number of categories such as, for example, testimony, hearsay, documentary, real or circumstantial. But perhaps the single most important rule of evidence is that *irrelevant* evidence is never admissible. It does not follow that *relevant* evidence is always admissible. Evidence which is relevant may be ruled inadmissible, and indeed much of the law of evidence is concerned with those rules which exclude relevant evidence.

This chapter is concerned with some of the basic concepts which underpin the whole of the law of evidence and will then go on to consider the exercise of judicial discretion as it relates to improperly or illegally obtained evidence.

(A)   Relevance, admissibility and weight

Evidence is considered to be relevant if it renders the existence of a fact in issue more or less probable. For example, in a criminal case, if D is charged with dangerous driving contrary to s. 2 of the Road Traffic Act 1988, the prosecution must prove that D:

(a)   drove a mechanically propelled vehicle;
(b)   dangerously;
(c)   on a road or other public place.

D's defence might be that the incident took place on private property and not on a road or other public place. Any evidence which renders the finding of the incident having taken place on a road or other public place either more or less likely, would be considered relevant.

However, merely because evidence is relevant to an issue, it does not mean it will be admitted. There are many occasions where the law sees fit to exclude relevant evidence. For example, hearsay evidence, opinion evidence and evidence of the defendant's character in a criminal case may, or perhaps must, be excluded.

Once the judge has ruled that the relevant evidence may be admitted, the *weight* to be given to that evidence becomes a matter for the trier of the facts. It is for the trier of the facts to evaluate the cogency of the evidence and, ultimately, to decide whether the evidence is accepted or rejected.

Stephen's Digest of the Law of Evidence
12th ed., art. 1

The word 'relevant' means that any two facts to which it is applied are so related to each other that according to the common course of events one either taken by itself or in connection with other facts proves or renders probable the past, present, or future existence or non-existence of the other.

Stephen, 'A General View of the Criminal Law of England'
1st ed.

Any specific facts or sets of facts, employed for the purpose of inferring therefrom the existence of any other fact, is said to be evidence of that fact. Suppose the question is whether John Smith is living or dead; A says, 'I knew John Smith, and I saw him die.' B says, 'I knew John Smith. I saw him in bed; he looked very ill. I shortly afterwards heard he was dead, and saw a funeral procession, which I attended, and which every one said was his funeral, leave his house and go to the chuchyard, where I saw a coffin buried with his name on it.' C says, 'Z told me that he heard from X that John Smith was dead.' D says, 'I had a dream that John Smith was dead.' Each of these facts, if used for the purpose of supporting the inference that John Smith was really dead, would be evidence of his death. The assertions of A and B would, under ordinary circumstances, be convincing; that of C far from satisfactory, and that of D altogether idle, except to a very superstitious person. This would be usually expressed by saying that the assertions of A and B would be good evidence, that of C weak evidence, and that of D no evidence at all of the fact of the death. But this is not quite a correct way of speaking: whether one fact is evidence of another, depends on the way in which it is used. If people usually believed in dreams, the assertion that a man had dreamt of John Smith's death would be evidence of his death. Whether or not it would be wise to allow it to be evidence of his death, would depend on the further question, whether in point of fact the practice of inferring the truth of the dream from the fact of its occurrence, usually produced true belief.

The mode of testing this is by throwing the matter under discussion into the form of a syllogism, of which the evidence forms the minor, and by seeing whether the major which it implies is one, the truth of which the person drawing the conclusion is prepared to assert. The inverted syllogism in the case supposed would stand thus:

John Smith is dead (conclusion),

for
D dreamed that he saw him dead (minor),
  and
Whenever one man dreams that another is dead, he is dead.

The major might also be, 'Whenever D dreams that another person is dead, that other person is dead;' or, 'Whenever D *under certain circumstances*,' etc. But unless the person engaged in considering whether Smith is dead or not, is prepared to make one or other of these general assertions, D's dream is no evidence to him. If he is prepared to do so, it would be evidence. To a person who believes in spirit-rapping, the noises which he hears are evidence of the truth of what he supposes them to assert. That this is the true view of the nature of evidence, appears from the consideration that otherwise there could be no such thing as evidence in favour of a false proposition. Two witnesses falsely swear that they saw A accept a bill of exchange. Are not their oaths evidence that he did accept it? Yet, as the assertion is false in fact, they must imply a false major usually believed, or they would not produce belief.

In the particular instance the false major would be, 'Probable stories affirmed by credible witnesses are true;' and the error would arise from not stating that one of the many exceptions to this rule which would adapt it to the particular instance.

These illustrations show the true nature of evidence. The general observations which men make on the world in which they live — the world of things, and the world of men — are embodied, more or less expressly and consciously, in a number of general assertions. These general assertions from the major propositions (tacit for the most part) of the conclusions which it is one greater business of our lives to draw; and whatever is capable of being made into a minor corresponding to one of these general propositions, is evidence of the truth of the conclusion. The major propositions are of very different degrees of authenticity. Many of them are false. Few of them, except those which relate to comparatively simple phenomena, such as the relations of space and number, are perfectly explicit, and almost all require qualifications and reservations which are seldom expressed, and, indeed, are far from being clearly understood.

This may be illustrated by a few examples. The most important of all the major propositions referred to, in reference at least to the administration of justice, is, that men when put upon their oaths, usually speak the truth as to matters of fact within their knowledge. It is this general conviction which makes the explicit statement — 'I saw such a thing occur,' — evidence that the thing really did occur; but the qualifications to the general proposition in question are so numerous, so intricate, and of such vital importance, that few things are more difficult than to say what degree of credit ought to be attached to the bare assertion of an unknown person that such and such an event did occur. It is evidence of the truth of the event: that is, it is one of a class of facts usually connected in the way of cause and effect with such facts as the one alleged to exist; but that is all that can be said on the subject.

Contrast this with a major proposition of another kind. The question is, whether the moon had risen at a given time on a given night. An almanack is produced which affirms that it had. Here the conclusion is — the moon had then risen. The minor — the almanack, says that it had risen. The major — whatever the almanack says about the time of the moon's rising is true. The connection between the minor and the conclusion here is not more direct and explicit than in the case of the direct assertion of the eye-witness. But the major is affirmed with infinitely stronger conviction and with fewer qualifications, and hence the evidence is far more convincing that in the other case. It thus appears that the question, What is evidence? and the question, What is the probative force of evidence? are distinct, though nearly connected.

Anything is evidence which is a particular case of a general rule which the judge of the question is prepared to affirm to be true. The probative force, or the weight of evidence, depends to a great extent upon the degree of confidence with which he is prepared to affirm the truth of the general rule, and the clearness and fulness with which it is expressed.

Director of Public Prosecutions v Kilbourne
[1973] AC 729
House of Lords

LORD SIMON OF GLAISDALE: Your Lordships have been concerned with four concepts in the law of evidence: (i) relevance; (ii) admissibility; (iii) corroboration; (iv) weight. The first two terms are frequently, and in many circumstances legitimately, used interchangeably; but I think it makes for clarity if they are kept separate, since some relevant evidence is inadmissible and some admissible evidence is irrelevant (in the senses that I shall shortly submit). Evidence is relevant if it is logically probative or disprobative of some matter which requires proof. I do not pause to analyse what is involved in 'logical probativeness', except to note that the term does not of itself express the element of experience which is so significant of its operation in law, and possibly elsewhere. It is sufficient to say, even at the risk of etymological tautology, that relevant (i.e., logically probative or disprobative evidence is evidence which makes the matter which requires proof more or less probable. To link logical probativeness with relevance rather than admissibility (as was done in *R* v *Sims* [1946] KB 531) not only is, I hope, more appropriate conceptually, but also accords better with the explanation of *Sims* given in *Harris* v *Director of Public Prosecutions* [1952] AC 694, 710. Evidence is admissible if it may be lawfully adduced at a trial. 'Weight' of evidence is the degree of probability (both intrinsically and inferentially) which is attached to it by the tribunal of fact once it is established to be relevant and admissible in law (though its relevance may exceptionally, as will appear, be dependent on its evaluation by the tribunal of fact).

Exceptionally evidence which is irrelevant to a fact which is in issue is admitted to lay the foundation for other, relevant, evidence (e.g., evidence of an unsuccessful search for a missing relevant document, in order to lay the foundation for secondary evidence of the document). Apart from such exceptional cases no evidence which is irrelevant to a fact in issue is admissible. But some relevant evidence is nevertheless inadmissible. To cite a famous passage from the opinion of Lord Herschell LC in *Makin* v *Attorney-General for New South Wales* [1894] AC 57, 65:

> It is undoubtedly not competent for the prosecution to adduce evidence tending to show that the accused has been guilty of criminal acts other than those covered in the indictment, for the purpose of leading to the conclusion that the accused is a person likely from his criminal conduct or character to have committed the offence for which he is being tried. On the other hand, the mere fact that the evidence adduced tends to show the commission of other crimes does not render it inadmissible if it is relevant to an issue before the jury and it may be so relevant if it bears upon the question whether the acts alleged to constitute the crime charged in the indictment were designed or accidental, or to rebut a defence which would otherwise be open to the accused.

That what was declared to be inadmissible in the first sentence of this passage is nevertheless relevant (i.e., logically probative) can be seen from numerous studies of offences in which recidivists are matched against first offenders, and by considering that it has never been doubted that evidence of motive (which can be viewed as propensity to commit the particular offence charged, in contradistinction to propensity to commit offences generally of the type charged) is relevant. All relevant evidence is *prima facie* admissible. The reason why the type of evidence referred to by Lord Herschell LC in the first sentence of the passage is inadmissible is, not because it is irrelevant, but because its logically probative significance is considered to be grossly outweighed by its prejudice to the accused, so that a fair trial is endangered if it is admitted; the law therefore exceptionally excludes this relevant evidence: whereas in the circumstances referred to in the second sentence the logically probative significance of the evidence is markedly greater. (See also Lord Molton in *R* v *Christie* [1914] AC 545, 559, 560.)

Not all admissible evidence is universally relevant. Admissible evidence may be relevant to one count of an indictment and not to another. It may be admissible against one accused (or party) but not another. It may be admissible to rebut a defence but inadmissible to reinforce the case for the prosecution. The summing up of Scrutton J in *R* v *Smith (George Joseph)* (1915) 11 Cr App R 229 ('The Brides in the Bath' case: see the report in the *Notable British Trials* series, at pp. 276-278) was a striking example; the jury was directed to consider the drowning of other newly-wedded and well-insured wives of the accused for the purpose only of rebutting a defence of accidental death by drowning, but not otherwise for the purpose of positive proof of the murder charged. (See also Lord Atkinson, Lord Parker concurring, in *R* v *Christie* [1914] AC 545, 553.)

Hollingham v Head
(1858) 27 LJCP 241
Court of Common Pleas

The plantiff was in the habit of travelling about to different market towns selling an artificial manure caled 'Rival guano'. He met the defendant, a farmer, and persuaded him to buy a quantity of this guano which turned out to be worthless. The plantiff sued him for the price of the guano. The defence was that this guano was a new kind, which the plaintiff, being anxious to introduce onto the market, and in order to induce the defendant to become a purchaser, had sold to him at £7 a ton, on condition that if it was not equal to Peruvian guano, the price of which was £14 a ton, the defendant was not to pay for it. In order to establish this defence the defendant wished to call witnesses to prove that the plaintiff had made contracts with other persons for the sales of his guano upon the same evidence. The trial judge held this evidence to be inadmissible and the jury returned a verdict for the plaintiff. The defendant moved for a new trial.

WILLES J: I am of opinion that the evidence was properly disallowed, as not being relevant to the issue. It may be often difficult to decide upon the admissibility of evidence, where it is offered for the purpose of establishing probability, but to be admissible it must at least afford a reasonable inference as to the principal matter in dispute. No doubt the rule, confining evidence to that which is relevant, is one of greater importance; not only with regard to the particular case in which it has to be applied, but with reference to saving the time of the Court, and preventing the minds of the jury being prejudiced, and distracted from the point in issue. The rule is nowhere more clearly laid down than in the very valuable work by Mr Best, on *Evidence*, (2nd ed., p. 319), where he says, 'Of all rules of evidence the most universal and most obvious is this — that the evidence adduced should be alike directed and confined to the matters which are in dispute, or form the subject of investigation.' And the same learned author, in another part of his book, speaks of the admissibility of evidence, which shows the affirmative of the issue to be more probable than the negative. It appears to me that the evidence, which was proposed to be given in this case, would not have shown that it was probable that the plantiff had made the contract, which the defendant contended he had made; for I do not see how the contract, which the defendant contended he had made; for I do not see how the fact, that a man has once or more in his life acted in a particlar way, makes it probable that he so acted on a given occasion. The admission of such evidence would be fraught with the greatest inconvenience. Where, indeed, the question is one of guilty knowledge or intent, as in cases of uttering forged documents, or base coin, such evidence is admissible as tending to establish a necessary ingredient of the crime. But if the evidence were admissible in this case, it would be difficult to say that in any case, where the question was whether or not goods had been sold upon credit, the defendant might not call evidence to prove that other persons had received credit from the plantiff; or in an action for an assault, that the plantiff might not prove that the defendant had assaulted other persons generally, or persons of a particular class. To obviate the prejudice, the injustice, and the waste of time to which the admission of such evidence would lead, and bearing in mind the extent to which it might be carried, and that litigants are mortal, it is necessary not only to adhere to the rule, but to lay it down strictly. I think, therefore, the fact that the plaintiff had entered into contracts of a particular kind with other persons on other occasions could not properly be admitted in evidence, where no custom of trade to make such contracts, and no connexion between such and the one in question, was shown to exist.

(BYLES J and WILLIAMS J gave concurring judgments.)

Rule refused.

Joy v Phillips, Mills and Co. Ltd
[1916] 1 KB 849
Court of Appeal

The father of the deceased claimed compensation for himself and other dependants under the Workmen's Compensation Act 1906. The deceased, who was employed as a stable boy by the respondents, was found in their stable in a dying condition, suffering from a kick behind the ear from one of their horses. There was no direct evidence as to how the accident happened. There was evidence that when the boy was found he was clutching in his hand a halter; that at the time when the accident hapened the boy had nothing to do with the halter and had nothing to do in the stable; and that the horse was a quiet horse. There was also evidence that the foreman of the respondents' yard had some time previously had occasion to speak to the boy about hitting the horses with a halter and teasing them. The county court judge held that the boy must have done something to the horse, which was a quiet one, to make it kick out, and that at the time of the accident the boy's duties in the stable were over, and accordingly that the accident did not arise out of his employment. The father of the deceased appealed.

LORD COZENS-HARDY MR: It seems to me that in a case like this the habits of the deceased cannot be disregarded. It is utterly impossible to do so. If the question was whether a man was drowned in a stream in one circumstance or another, could you not ask whether the man was in the habit of going to his work by the side of the stream and then crossing over a bridge? It seems to me that you could. Otherwise you would be shutting your eyes altogether to facts necessary for drawing the proper inferences. So it is here. I cannot disregard the fact that this lad had on more than one occasion been remonstrated with for teasing the horses. On one occasion he was remonstrated with by the foreman for teasing the horses with a halter, and when his body was found a halter was found clutched in his hand, and that was close to the rear of a very quiet horse.

In my opinion we cannot say that the judge was not entitled to find as he did on a question of fact which was for him, and I think we cannot interfere with his finding.

PHILLIMORE LJ: Wherever an inquiry has to be made into the cause of the death of a person, and, there being no direct evidence, recourse must be had to circumstantial evidence, any evidence as to the habits and ordinary doings of the deceased which may contribute to the circumstances by throwing light upon the probable cause of death is admissible, even in the case of a prosecution for murder. Especially in these cases under the Workmen's Compensation Act the books are full of cases where evidence as to the habits or practice of the deceased or even of his class has been admitted both in favour of the applicant and against him or her, both to contribute towards the conclusion that the accident to the deceased arose out of and in the course of the employment, and to contribute towards the opposite result.

SARGANT J: In a case of this sort where an accident has happened, when no one but the deceased was present, the Court necessarily has to deal with an estimate of probabilities; but an estimate of probabilities is not necessarily the same as mere conjecture. Here in estimating the probabilities it seems to me as relevant to admit evidence that the boy was mischievous as to admit evidence that the horse was quiet.

Woolf v *Woolf*
[1931] P 134
Court of Appeal

On an undefended petition by a wife for dissolution of marriage by reason of the adultery of her husband, the evidence was that the husband passed two nights in a bedroom at an hotel with a woman. He then informed his wife of the fact, but disclosed no name or address of the woman in question either to his wife or to her solicitors or to the King's Proctor to whom the papers in the case had been sent by the Court, although both the solicitors and the King's Proctor applied to him for these particulars. As the result of inquiries by the King's Proctor there was no evidence of any association of the husband with a woman other than his wife, still less of illicit association. The judge held that adultery was not proved and dismissed the petition. The wife appealed.

LORD HANWORTH MR: In *Loveden* v *Loveden* (1810) 2 Hagg Cons 1, Sir William Scott said that it was not necessary to prove the direct fact of adultery, for 'if it were otherwise, there is not one case in a hundred in which that proof would be attainable: it is very rarely indeed that the parties are surprised in the direct fact of adultery. In every case almost the fact is inferred from circmstances that lead to it by fair inference as a necessary conclusion; and unless this were the case, and unless this were so held, no protection whatever could be given to marital rights.' That passage has been quoted with approval in the Court of Appeal by Lopes LJ in *Allen* v *Allen* [1894] P 248, where he says: 'To lay down any general rule, to attempt to define what circumstances would be sufficient and what insufficient upon which to infer the fact of adultery, is impossible. Each case must depend on its own particular circumstances.'

It seems to me that, human nature being what it is, adultery must be inferred here. The husband was twenty-five, and no more, and he had been married, and there is no reason to assume that his sexual appetite was less than that of a normal healthy man. I think that to say that an adulterous inclinaton should be proved is to lay an unjustifiable burden on the petitioner. The case is one of an innocent woman proving opportunity for adultery, and the fact that the parties spent two nights in the same bedroom. In my opinion in this case the Court ought to be satisfied that adultery has been proved.

(LAWRENCE LJ and ROMER LJ delivered concurring judgments.)

Appeal allowed and decree *nisi* granted.

Questions
1.   D is charged with the rape of P. Which of the following facts is relevant and why?

(a)   D and P were living together until shortly before the alleged rape.
(b)   P was working as a prostitute at the time of the alleged rape.
(c)   D has a previous conviction for rape.
(d)   D has a previous conviction for indecent assault on a male.
(e)   D has a previous conviction for theft.
(f)   D refused to answer any questions put to him by the police.
(g)   D refused to give evidence at his trial.
(h)   At the time of his arrest, D was in possession of a carrier bag which contained copies of *Playboy, Mayfair* and other girlie magazines.
(i)   Statistics published by the Home Office show that rape is on the increase.
(j)   Traces of a fibre identified as coming from D's sweater were found on P's dress.

2.   What is the distinction between the terms relevance, admissibility and weight when used in the law of evidence?

(B)   Improperly or illegally obtained evidence: judicial discretion

The common law provides the criminal courts with discretionary power to exclude relevant evidence in order to ensure that the accused receives a fair trial. The common law discretion to exclude evidence has now been supplemented by the statutory power contained in s. 78(1) of the Police and Criminal Evidence Act 1984. This provision has generated a huge number of cases in the Court of Appeal and it has not proved an easy task to draw from those cases a set of rational and coherent principles.

The question of whether or not evidence should be excluded as a matter of discretion, has often arisen where the authorities have gathered evidence by using improper, unfair or even illegal methods. Should the court exclude that evidence as a means of showing its disapproval, hopefully encouraging better standards of conduct in the future? Some jurisdictions have answered that question with a resounding 'Yes', but the answer given by the English courts has generally been 'No'.

The following cases look at the position both before and after the Police and Criminal Evidence Act 1984.

(i) The approach before the Police and Criminal Evidence Act 1984, s. 78(1)

Kuruma, Son of Kaniu v The Queen
[1955] AC 197
Privy Council

The appellant was charged with the unlawful possession of two rounds of ammunition contrary to emergency regulations in Kenya. He had been stopped and searched illegally in that the searchers were not of the rank of assistant inspector or above. The ammunition was alleged to have been found during the search and evidence of this was given at the trial. The appellant was convicted and appealed on the ground that evidence of the finding was inadmissible because of the manner in which it was obtained.

LORD GODDARD LJ: In their Lordships' opinion the test to be applied in considering whether evidence is admissible is whether it is relevant to the matters in issue. If it is, it is admissible and the court is not concerned with how the evidence was obtained. While this proposition may not have been stated in as many words in any English case there are decisions which support it, and in their Lordships' opinion it is plainly right in principle. In *R v Leatham* (1861) 8 Cox CC 498, an information for penalties under the Corrupt Practices Act, objection was taken to the production of a letter written by the defendant because its existence only became known by answers he had given to the commissioners who held the inquiry under the Act, which provided that answers before that tribunal should not be admissible in evidence against him. The Court of Queen's Bench held that though his answers could not be used against the defendant, yet if a clue was thereby given to other evidence, in that case the letter, which would prove the case it was admissible. Crompton J said: 'It matters not how you get it; if you steal it even, it would be admissible.' *Lloyd v Mostyn* (1842) 10 M & W 478 was an action on a bond. The person in whose possession it was objected to produce it on the ground of privilege. The plantiff's attorney, however, had got a copy of it and notice to produce the original being proved the court admitted the copy as secondary evidence. To the same effect was *Calcraft v Guest* [1898] 1 QB 759. There can be no difference in principle for this purpose between a civil and a criminal case. No doubt in a criminal case the judge always has a discretion to disallow evidence if the strict rules of admissibility would operate unfairly against an accused. This was emphasised in the case before the Board of *Noor Mohamed* v *The King* [1949] AC 182 and in the recent case in the House of Lords, *Harris* v *Director of Public Prosecutions* [1952] AC 694. If, for instance, some admission of some piece of evidence, e.g., a document, had been obtained from a defendant by a trick, no doubt the judge might properly rule it out. It was this discretion that lay at the root of the ruling of Lord Guthrie in *HM Advocate* v *Turnbull* [1951] SC(J) 96. The other cases from Scotland to which their Lordships' attention was drawn, *Rattray* v *Rattray* (1897) 25 Rettie 315, *Lawrie* v *Muir* [1950] SC(J) 19 and *Fairly* v *Fishmongers of London* [1951] SC(J) 14, all support the view that if the evidence is relevant it is admissible and the court is not concerned with how it is obtained.

No doubt their Lordships in the Court of Justiciary appear at least to some extent to consider the question from the point of view whether the alleged illegality in the obtaining of the evidence could properly be excused, and it is true that Horridge J in *Elias* v *Passmore* [1934] 2 KB 164 used that expression. It is to be observed, however, that what the judge was there concerned with was an action of trespass, and he held that the trespass was excused. In their Lordships' opinion, when it is a question of the admission of evidence strictly it is not whether the method by which it was obtained in tortious but excusable but whether what has been obtained is relevant to the issue being tried. Their Lordships are not now concerned with whether an action for assault would lie against the police officers and express no opinion on that point. It is right, however that it should be stated that the rule with regard to the admission of confessions, whether it be regarded as an exception to the general rule or not, is a rule of law which their Lordships are not qualifying in any degree whatsoever.

Appeal dismissed.

Jeffrey v *Black*
[1978] QB 490
Divisional Court

The defendant was arrested by two police officers of the drug squad for stealing a sandwich from a public house. The officers then quite improperly searched his home and found cannabis and cannabis resin. He was charged with possession of those drugs. The justices ruled that evidence obtained during the seach was inadmissible and dismissed the informations. The prosecutor appealed.

LORD WIDGERY CJ: It is firmly established according to English law that the mere fact that evidence is obtained in an irregular fashion does not of itself prevent that evidence from being relevant and acceptable to a court. The authority for that is *Kuruma* v *The Queen* [1955] AC 197, and I need only refer to one passage to make good the proposition which I have already put forward, and that is at p. 203 and reads: 'In their Lordships' opinion the test to be applied in considering whether evidence is admissible is whether it is relevant to the matters in issue. If it is, it is admissible and the court is not concerned with how the evidence was obtained. While this proposition may not have been stated in so many words in any English case there are decisions which support it, and in their Lordships' opinion it is plainly right in principle.' There one has that pronouncement from the Privy Council, and I have not the least doubt that we must firmly accept the proposition that an irregularity in obtaining evidence does not render the evidence inadmissible. Whether or not the evidence is admissible depends on whether or not it is relevant to the issues in respect of which it is called.

At this point it would seem that the prosecutor ought to succeed in his appeal because at this point what he appears to have shown is that the justices were wrong in failing to recognise the law as stated in *Kuruma* v *The Queen* [1955] AC 197. But that is not in fact the end of the matter because the justices sitting in this case, like any other tribunal dealing with criminal matters in England and sitting under the English law, have a general discretion to decline to allow any evidence to be called by the prosecution if they think that it would be unfair or oppressive to allow that to be done. In getting an assessment of what this discretion means, justices ought, I think, to stress to themselves that the discretion is not a discretion which arises only in drug cases. It is not a discretion which arises only in cases where police can enter premises. It is a discretion which every judge has all the time in respect of all the evidence which is tendered by the prosecution. It would probably give justices some idea of the extent to which this discretion is used if one asks them whether they are appreciative of the fact that they have the discretion anyway, and it may well be that a number of experienced justices would be quite ignorant of the possession of this discretion. That gives them, I hope, some idea of how relatively rarely it is exercised in our courts. But if the case is exceptional, if the case is such that not only have the police officers entered without authority, but they have been guilty of trickery or they have misled someone, or they have been oppressive or they have been unfair, or in other respects they have behaved in a manner which is morally reprehensible, then it is open to the justices to apply their discretion and decline to allow the particular evidence to be let in as part of the trial. I cannot stress the point too strongly that this is a very exceptional situation, and the simple, unvarnished fact that evidence was obtained by police officers who had gone in without bothering to get a search warrant is not enough to justify the justices in exercising their discretion to keep the evidence out.

(FORBES and CROOM-JOHNSON JJ agreed.)

Appeal allowed.

R v *Sang*
[1980] AC 402
House of Lords

Two defendants were charged with conspiracy to utter counterfeit United States banknotes. They alleged by counsel that they had been induced by an informer, acting on the instructions of the police to commit an offence that they would not have committed otherwise. As it was then clear law that the existence of entrapment, even if established, would not have been a ground to exclude evidence of the offence as a matter of law, counsel sought to investigate the issue in a trial within a trial, with a view to persuading the trial judge to exclude that evidence in his discretion. The trial judge, taking the view that he had no such discretion to exclude admissible prosecution evidence, ruled accordingly after hearing argument on the hypothetical basis that the defendants' allegations were true. The Court of Appeal dismissed an appeal against conviction, but certified the following point of law of general public importance: 'Does a trial judge have a discretion to refuse to allow evidence — being evidence other than evidence of admission — to be given in any circumstances in which such evidence is relevant and of more than minimal probative value.' One of the defendants appealed to the House of Lords.

LORD DIPLOCK: I understand this question as inquiring what are the circumstances, if there be any, in which such a discretion arises; and as not being confined to trials by jury. That the discretion, whatever be its limits, extended to whoever presides in a judicial capacity over a criminal trial, whether it be held in the Crown Court or in a magistrates' court, was expressly stated by Lord Widgery CJ in *Jeffrey* v *Black* [1978] QB 490, an appeal by the prosecution to a Divisional Court by way of case stated from magistrates who had exercised their discretion to exclude evidence of possession of drugs that had been obtained by an illegal search of the accused's room by the police. The Divisional Court held that the magistrates had exercised their discretion wrongly in the particular case; but Lord Widgery CJ, while stressing that the occasions on which the discretion ought to be exercised in favour of excluding admissible evidence would be exceptional, nevertheless referred to it as applying to 'all the evidence which is tendered by the prosecution' and described its ambit in the widest terms, at p. 498:

> ... If the case is such that not only have the police officers entered without authority, but they have been guilty of trickery or they have misled someone, or they have been oppressive or they have been unfair, or in other respects they have behaved in a manner which is morally reprehensible, then it is open to the justices to apply their discretion and decline to allow the particular evidence to be let in as part of the trial.

One or other of the various dyslogistic terms which Lord Widgery uses to describe the kind of conduct on the part of the police that gives rise to judicial discretion to exclude particular pieces of evidence tendered by the prosecution can be found in earlier pronouncements by his predecessor Lord Parker CJ, notably in *Callis* v *Gunn* [1964] 1 QB 495, 502, where he adds to them false representations, threats and bribes; while unfairness and trickery are referred to in *dicta* to be found in a judgment of the Privy Council in *Kuruma* v *The Queen* [1955] AC 197, 204, the case which is generally regarded as having first suggested the existence of a wide judicial discretion of this kind. What is unfair, what is trickery in the context of the detection and prevention of crime, are questions which are liable to attract highly subjective answers. It will not have come as any real surprise to your Lordships to learn that those who preside over or appear as advocates in criminal trials are anxious for guidance as to whether the discretion really is so wide as these imprecise expressions would seem to suggest and, if not, what are its limits. So, although it may not be strictly necessary to answer the certified question in its full breadth in order to dispose of the instant appeal I think that your Lordships should endeavour to do so.

Before turning to that wider question, however I will deal with the narrower point of law upon which this appeal actually turns. I can do so briefly. The decisions in *R* v *McEvilly* (1973) 60 Cr App R 150 and *R* v *Mealey and Sheridan* (1974) 60 Cr App R 59 that there is no defence of 'entrapment' known to English law are clearly right. Many crimes are committed by one person at the instigation of others. From earliest times at common law those who counsel and procure the commission of the offence by the person by whom the *actus reus* itself is done have been guilty themselves of an offence, and since the abolition by the Criminal Law Act 1967 of the distinction between felonies and misdemeanours, can be tried, indicted and punished as principal offenders. The fact that the counsellor and procurer is a policeman or a police informer, although it may be of relevance in mitigation of penalty for the offence, cannot affect the guilt of the principal offender; both the physical element (*actus reus*) and the mental element (*mens rea*) of the offence with which he is charged are present in his case.

My Lords, this being the substantive law upon the matter, the suggestion that it can be evaded by the procedural device of preventing the prosecution from adducing evidence of the commisson of the offence does not bear examination. Let me take first the summary offence prosecuted before magistrates where there is no practical distinction between a trial and a 'trial within a trial'. There are three examples of these in the books, *Brannan* v *Peek* [1948] 1 KB 68; *Browning* v *JWH Watson (Rochester) Ltd* [1953] 1 WLR 1172; *Sneddon* v *Stevenson* [1967] 1 WLR 1051. Here the magistrates in order to decide whether the crime had in fact been instigated by an agent provocateur acting upon police instructions would first have to hear evidence which *ex hypothesi* would involve proving that the crime had been committed by the accused. If they decided that it had been so instigated, then, despite the fact that they had already heard evidence which satisfied them that it had been committed, they would have a discretion to prevent the prosecution from relying on that evidence as proof of its commission. How does this differ from recognising entrapment as a defence — but a defence available only at the discretion of the magistrates?

Where the accused is charged upon indictment and there is a practical distinction between the trial and a 'trial within a trial,' the position, as it seems to me, would be even more anomalous if the judge were to have a discretion to prevent the prosecution from adducing evidence before the jury to prove the commission of the offence by the accused. If he exercised the discretion in favour of the accused he would then have to direct the jury to acquit. How does this differ from recognising entrapment as a defence — but a defence for which the necessary factual foundation is to be found not by the jury but by the judge and even where the factual foundation is so found, the defence is available only at the judge's discretion.

My Lords, this submission goes far beyond a claim to a judicial discretion to exclude *evidence* that has been obtained unfairly or by trickery; nor in any of the English cases on agents provocateurs that have come before appellate courts has it been suggested that it exists. What it really involves is a claim to a judicial discretion to acquit an accused of any offences in connection with which the conduct of the police incurs the disapproval of the judge. The conduct of the police where it has involved the use of an agent provocateur may well be a matter to be taken into consideration in mitigation of sentence; but under the English system of criminal justice it does not give rise to any discretion on the part of the judge himself to acquit the accused or to direct the jury to do so, notwithstanding that he is guilty of the offence. Nevertheless the existence of such a discretion to exclude the evidence of an agent provocateur does appear to have been acknowledged by the Courts-Martial Appeal Court of Northern Ireland in *R* v *Murphy* [1965] NI 138. That was before the rejection of 'entrapment' as a defence by the Court of Appeal in England; and Lord MacDermott CJ in delivering the judgment of the court relied upon the *dicta* as to the existence of a wide discretion which appeared in cases that did not involve an agent provocateur. In the result he held that the court-martial had been right in exercising its discretion in such a way as to admit the evidence.

I understand your Lordships to be agreed that whatever be the ambit of the judicial discretion to exclude admissible evidence it does not extend to excluding evidence of a crime because the crime was instigated by an agent provocateur. In so far as *R* v *Murphy* suggests the contrary it should no longer be regarded as good law.

I turn now to the wider question that has been certified. It does not purport to be concerned with self incriminatory admissions made by the accused himself after commission of the crime though in dealing with the question I will find it necessary to say something about these. What the question is concerned with is the discretion of the trial judge to exclude all other kinds of evidence that are of more than minimal probative value.

Recognition that there may be circumstances in which in a jury trial the judge has a discretion to prevent particular kinds of evidence that is admissible from being adduced before the jury, has grown up piecemeal. It appears first in cases arising under proviso (f) of section 1 of the Criminal Evidence Act 1898, which sets out the circumstances in which an accused may be cross-examined as to his previous convictions or bad character. The relevant cases starting in 1913 with *R* v *Watson* (1913) 109 LT 335 are conveniently cited in the speech of Lord Hodson in *R* v *Selvey* [1970] AC 304, a case in which this House accepted that in such cases the trial judge has a discretion to prevent such cross-examination, nowithstanding that it was strictly admissible under the statute, if he was of opinion that its prejudicial effect upon the jury was likely to outweigh its probative value.

Next the existence of judicial discretion to exclude evidence of 'similar facts,' even where it was technically admissible, was recognised by Lord du Parcq, delivering the opinion of the Privy Council in *Noor Mohamed* v *The King* [1949] AC 182, 192. He put the grounds which justified its exercise rather more narrowly than they had been put in the 'previous conviction' cases to which I have been referring; but in *Harris* v *Director of Public Prosecutions* [1952] AC 694, 707, Viscount Simon, with whose speech the other members of this House agreed, said that the discretion to exclude 'similar facts' evidence should be exercised where the 'probable effect' (sc. prejudicial to the accused) 'would be out of proportion to its true evidential value'.

That phrase was borrowed from the speech of Lord Moulton in *R* v *Christie* [1914] AC 545, 559. That was neither a 'previous conviction' nor a 'similar facts' case, but was one involving evidence of an accusation made in the presence of the accused by the child victm of an alleged indecent assault and the accused's failure to answer it, from which the prosecution sought to infer an admission by the accused that it was true. Lord Molton's statement was not confined to evidence of inferential confessions but was general in its scope and has frequently been cited as applicable in cases of cross-examination as to bad character or previous convictions under the Criminal Evidence Act 1898 and in 'similar facts' cases. So I would hold that there has now developed a general rule of practice whereby in a trial by jury the judge has a discretion to exclude evidence which, though technically admissible, would probably have a prejudicial influence on the minds of the jury, which would be out of proportion to its true evidential value.

Ought your Lordships to go further and to hold that the discretion extends more widely than this, as the comparatively recent *dicta* to which I have already referred suggest? What has been regarded as the fountain head of all subsequent *dicta* on this topic is the statement by Lord Goddard delivering advice of the Privy Council in *Kuruma* v *The Queen* [1955] AC 197. That was a case in which the evidence of unlawful possession of ammunition by the accused was obtained as a result of an illegal search of his person. The Board held that this evidence was admissible and had rightly been admitted; but Lord Goddard although he had earlier said at p. 203 that if evidence is admissible 'the court is not concerned with how the evidence was obtained,' nevertheless went on to say, at p. 204:

No doubt in a criminal case the judge always has a discretion to disallow evidence if the strict rules of admissibility would operate unfairly against an accused. This was emphasised in the case before this Board of *Noor Mohamed* v *The King* [1949] AC 182, and in the recent case in the House of Lords, *Harris* v *Director of Public Prosecutions* [1952] AC 694. *If, for instance, some admission of some piece of evidence, e.g., a document, has been obtained from a defendant by a trick, no doubt the judge might properly rule it out.*

Up to the sentence that I have italicised there is nothing in this passage to suggest that when Lord Goddard spoke of admissible evidence operating 'unfairly' against the accused he intended to refer to any wider aspect of unfairness than the probable prejudicial effect of the evidence upon the minds of the jury outweighing its true evidential value; though he no doubt also had in mind the discretion that had long been exercised in England under the Judges' Rules to refuse to admit confessions by the accused made after the crime even though strictly they may be admissible. The instance given in the passage I have italicised appears to me to deal with a case which falls within the later category since the document 'obtained from a defendant by a trick' is clearly analogous to a confession which the defendant has been unfairly induced to make, and had, indeed been so treated in *R* v *Barker* [1941] 2 KB 381 where an incriminating document obtained from the defendant by a promise of favours was held to be inadmissible.

It is interesting in this connection to observe that the only case that has been brought to your Lordships' attention in which an appellate court has actually excluded evidence on the ground that it had been unfairly obtained (*R* v *Payne* [1963] 1 WLR 637) would appear to fall into this category. The defendant, charged with drunken driving, had been induced to submit himself to examination by a doctor to see if he was suffering from any illness or disability, upon the understanding that the doctor would not examine him for the purpose of seeing whether he were fit to drive. The doctor in fact gave evidence of the defendant's unfitness to drive based upon his symptoms and behaviour in the course of that examination. The Court of Criminal Appeal quashed the conviction on the ground that the trial judge ought to have exercised his discretion to exclude the doctor's evidence. This again, as it seems to me, is analogous to unfairly inducing a defendant to confess to an offence, and the short judgment of the Court of Criminal Appeal is clearly based upon the maxim *nemo debet prodere se ipsum*.

In no other case to which your Lordships' attention has been drawn has either the Court of Criminal Appeal or the Court of Appeal allowed an appeal upon the ground that either magistrates in summary proceedings or the judge in a trial upon indictment ought to have exercised a discretion to exclude admissible evidence upon the ground that it has been obtained unfairly or by trickery or in some other way that is morally reprehensible; though they cover a wide gamut of apparent improprieties from illegal searches, as in *Kuruma* v *The Queen* itself and in *Jeffrey* v *Black* [1978] QB 490 (which must be the high water mark of this kind of illegality) to the clearest cases of evidence obtained by the use of agents provocateur. Of the latter an outstanding example is to be found in *Browning* v *JWH Watson (Rochester) Ltd* [1953] 1 WLR 1172 where Lord Goddard CJ remitted the case to the magistrates *with a direction that the offence had been proved,* but pointedly reminded them that it was open to them to give the defendant an absolute discharge and to award no costs to the prosecution.

Nevertheless it has to be recognised that there is an unbroken series of *dicta* in judgments of appellate courts to the effect that there is a judicial discretion to exclude admissible evidence which has been 'obtained' unfairly or by trickery or oppressively, although except in *R* v *Payne* [1963] 1 WLR 637, there never has been a case in which those courts have come across conduct so unfair, so tricky or so oppressive as to justify them in holding that the discretion ought to have been exercised in favour of exclusion. In every one of the cases to which your Lordships have been referred where such *dicta* appear, the source from which the evidence sought to be excluded had been obtained has been the defendant himself or (in some of the search cases) premises occupied by him; and the dicta can be traced to a common ancestor in Lord Goddard's statement in *Kuruma* v *The Queen* [1955] AC 197 which I have already cited. That statement was not, in my view, ever intended to acknowledge the existence of any wider discretion than to exclude (1) admissible evidence which would probably have a prejudicial influence upon the minds of the jury that would be out of proportion to its true evidential value; and (2) evidence tantamount to a self-incriminatory admission which was obtained from the defendant, after the offence had been committed, by means which would justify a judge in excluding an actual confession which had the like self-incriminating effect. As a matter of language, although not as a matter of application, the subsequent *dicta* go much further than this; but in so far as they do so they have never yet been considered by this House.

My Lords, I propose to exclude, as the certified question does, detailed consideration of the role of the trial judge in relation to confessions and evidence obtained from the defendant after commission of the offence that is tantamount to a confession. It has a long history dating back to the days before the existence of a disciplined police force, when a prisoner on a charge of felony could not be represented by counsel and was not entitled to give evidence in his own defence either to deny that he had made the confession, which was generally oral, or to deny that its contents were true. The underlying rationale of this branch of the criminal law, though it may originally have been based upon ensuring the reliability of confessions is, in my view, now to be found in the maxim *nemo debet prodere se ipsum*, no one can be required to be his own betrayer or in its popular English mistranslation 'the right to silence'. That is why there is no discretion to exclude evidence discovered as the result of an illegal search but there is discretion to exclude evidence which the accused has been induced to produce voluntarily if the method of inducement was unfair.

Outside this limited field in which for historical reasons the function of the trial judge extended to imposing sanctions for improper conduct on the part of the prosecution before the commencement of the proceedings in inducing the accused by threats, favour or trickery to provide evidence against himself, your Lordships should, I think, make it clear that the function of the judge at a criminal trial as respects the admission of evidence is to ensure that the accused has a fair trial according to law. It is no part of a judge's function to exercise disciplinary powers over the police or prosecution as respects the way in which evidence to be used at the trial is obtained by them. If it was obtained illegally there will be a remedy in civil law; if it was obtained legally but in breach of the rules of conduct for the police, this is a matter for the appropriate disciplinary authority to deal with. What the judge at the trial is concerned with is not how the evidence sought to be adduced by the prosecution has been obtained, but with how it is used by the prosecution at the trial.

A fair trial according to law involves, in the case of a trial upon indictment, that it should take place before a judge and a jury; that the case against the accused should be proved to the satisfaction of the jury beyond all reasonable doubt upon evidence that is admissible in law; and, as a corollary to this, that there should be excluded from the jury information about the accused which is likely to have an influence on their minds prejudicial to the accused which is out of proportion to the true probative value of admissible evidence conveying that information. If these conditions are fulfilled and the jury receive correct instructions from the judge as to the law applicable to the case, the requirement that the accused should have a fair trial according to law is, in my view, satisfied; for the fairness of a trial according to law is not all one-sided; it requires that those who are undoubtedly guilty should be convicted as well as that those about whose guilt there is any reasonable doubt should be acquitted. However much the judge may dislike the way in which a particular piece of evidence was obtained before proceedings were commenced, if it is admissible evidence probative of the accused's guilt it is no part of his judicial function to exclude it for this reason. If your Lordships so hold you will be reverting to the law as it was laid down by Lord Moulton in *R* v *Christie* [1914] AC 545, Lord du Parcq in *Noor Mohamed* v *The King* [1949] AC 182 and Viscount Simon in *Harris* v *Director of Public Prosecutions* [1952] AC 694 before the growth of what I believe to have been a misunderstanding of Lord Goddard's *dictum* in *Kuruma* v *The Queen* [1955] AC 197.

I would accordingly answer the question certified in terms which have been suggested by my noble and learned friend, Viscount Dilhorne, in the course of our deliberations on this case. (1) A trial judge in a criminal trial has always a discretion to refuse to admit evidence if in his opinion its prejudicial effect outweighs its probative value. (2) Save with regard to admissions and confessions and generally with regard to evidence obtained from the accused after commission of the offence, he has no discretion to refuse to admit relevant admissible evidence on the ground that it was obtained by improper or unfair means. The court is not concerned with how it was obtained. It is no ground for the exercise of discretion to exclude that the evidence was obtained as the result of the activities of an agent provocateur.

(VISCOUNT DILHORNE, LORDS SALMON, FRASER of TULLYBELTON and SCARMAN delivered speeches agreeing with LORD DIPLOCK's answer to the certified question.)

Appeal dismissed.

Question
In answering the certified question, what does Lord Diplock mean when he refers to 'evidence obtained from the accused after commission of the offence'?

R v *Apicella*
(1985) 82 Cr App R 295
Court of Appeal

The defendant was charged, *inter alia*, with the rape of three girls, each of whom had contracted an unusual strain of gonorrhoea after the attack. The defendant was remanded in custody to await trial. While on remand awaiting trial, a doctor took a sample of the defendant's bodily fluid. The sample was taken for the sole purpose of diagnosing the defendant's condition and then treating it. The doctor assumed the defendant had consented to the taking of the sample. In fact, the defendant had consented only because a prison officer had told him that as a prisoner he had no choice in the matter. The sample showed the defendant to be suffering from the same unusual strain of gonorrhoea as the three girls. The defendant was convicted and appealed on the ground, *inter alia*, that the evidence of the gonorrhoea strain should have been excluded. It was the equivalent to an oral confession which had been extracted from the accused without consent.

LAWTON LJ: ... Miss Goddard's main submission can be stated in these terms. A body fluid was taken from the appellant without his consent. It should not have been. On examination it provided evidence which the prosecution relied on strongly to prove that the appellant was guilty. Out of his own body, if not out of his mouth, he had provided evidence to condemn himself. It was the physical equivalent of an oral confession. The short answer is that it was not. The rules relating to the admission in evidence of confessions have an historical origin dating back to the time when a prisoner on a charge of felony was not entitled to give evidence in his own defence with the result that he could not contradict what he was alleged to have said in an alleged confession. The admission of evidence as to what has been seen or found is not connected in any way with the rules relating to the admissibility of confessions.

The relevant law is to be found in *Sang* (1979) 69 Cr App R 282; [1980] AC 402. In that case the House of Lords was primarily concerned to decide what were the limits to the exercise of judicial discretion to exclude evidence and particularly whether a judge had a discretion to exclude evidence which had been unfairly obtained. All the relevant authorities seem to have been considered, in particular what Lord Goddard had said in *Kuruma, Son of Kaniu* [1955] AC 197, 204. Lord Diplock delivered the leading speech in *Sang* and said at p. 289 and p. 435, respectively

> In every one of the cases to which your Lordships have been referred where such dicta appear, the source from which the evidence sought to be excluded had been obtained had been (from) the defendant himself or (in some of the search cases) premises occupied by him; and the dicta can be traced to a common ancestor in Lord Goddard's statement in *Kuruma, Son of Kaniu (supra)*, which I have already cited. That statement was not, in my view, ever intended to acknowledge the existence of any wider discretion than to exclude (1) admissible evidence which would probably have a prejudicial influence upon the minds of the jury that would be out of proportion to its true evidential value; and (2) evidence tantamount to a self-incriminatory admission which was obtained from the defendant, after the offence had been committed, by means which would justify a judge in excluding an actual confession which had the like self-incriminating effect.

Later in his speech Lord Diplock widened what he had said at p. 289 and p. 435 respectively see p. 291 and 437) so that what he had said under (2) became: 'Save with regard to admissions and confessions and generally with regard to evidence obtained from the accused after commission of the offence, he has no discretion to refuse to admit relevant admissible evidence on the ground that it was obtained by improper or unfair means.' Viscount Dilhorne said at p. 292 and p. 439 respectively:

> I referred in *Selvey v DPP* (1968) 52 Cr App R 443, 461; [1970] AC 304, 341, to the overriding duty of the judge to ensure that a trial is fair. His discretion to control the use of relevant admissible evidence is exercised in the discharge of this duty. It is the use of the evidence, not, save in relation to confessions and admissions by the accused, the manner in which it has been obtained with which he is concerned.

Lord Salmon said at p. 297 and p. 444:

> I consider that it is a clear principle of the law that a trial judge has the power and the duty to ensure that the accused has a fair trial. Accordingly, amongst other things, he has a discretion to exclude legally admissible evidence if justice so requires: see Lord Reid's speech in *Myers v DPP* [1965] AC 1001, 1024.

These *dicta* have to be considered against the basic principle of the law of evidence, namely, that evidence which is relevant should be admitted unless there is a rule of law which says that it should not be. The evidence derived from the appellant's body fluid was relevant, as Miss Goddard accepted it was. There is a rule of law which says that most forms of hearsay should not be admitted. Another says that confessions and admissions should not be admitted without proof that they were made voluntarily. We know of no rule of law which says that evidence of anything taken from the suspect, be it a body fluid, a hair or an article hidden in an orifice of the body, cannot be admitted unless the suspect consented to the taking.

In our judgment the law of evidence should not stray too far from commonsense. It would be likely to do so if Miss Goddard's submission were to be upheld. It might have been possible to diagnose that the appellant was suffering from this strain of gonorrhoea by examining his underpants or his urine passed in the ordinary way. It would be odd if on the facts of this case the evidence obtained from his body fluid was rendered inadmissible because of his silence when Dr Barrow asked him to give a sample of urine or passed an instrument into his urethra. Miss Goddard accepted that in the past, evidence of articles hidden in the orifices of the body had always been admitted, albeit the suspect did not consent to an examination. She sought to draw a distinction between such cases and evidence of body fluids taken in the course of what she called intimate examinations without consent. We do not accept that there is such a distinction. Nor do we accept that evidence is inadmissible solely because it has been obtained as a result of a crime, such as assault, or a tort. Anyway, as Mr Mitchell for the prosecution pointed out, on the facts of the case, Dr Barrow when examining the appellant probably did not assault him as he believed that the appellant was consenting. It is now well established law that the way evidence has been obtained has no relevance to its admissibility. Its intended use in a trial by the prosecution may, however, call for the exercise of judicial discretion to exclude it. It follows that the evidence of the taking of the sample of body fluid was admissible.

The pertinent question in this case is whether the intended use of that evidence was likely to make the trial unfair. The appellant was not tricked into submitting to the examination in the way which led to this Court's predecessor in *Payne* (1963) 47 Cr App R 122; [1963] 1 WLR 637 to exclude evidence. In our judgment the prosecution's use of the evidence derived from the appellant's body fluid, taken in the circumstances it was, was not unfair. The judge was right in the exercise of his discretion not to exclude it.

For the sake of completeness we wish to add, first, that we have dealt with this case as the law of evidence is at present and, secondly, we have not considered whether the prison medical officer, acting on behalf of the prison governor, would have been entitled to take a sample of a body fluid from the appellant in order to treat him for a disease which, if left untreated, might have been communicated to other prisoners.

The appeal against conviction is dismissed.

Question
Would the decision in *Apicella* have been different if the doctor had deliberately told the accused that he could not refuse the taking of the sample?

(ii)   The Police and Criminal Evidence Act 1984, s. 78(1) and after

Police and Criminal Evidence Act 1984

78.   Exclusion of unfair evidence
(1)   In any proceedings the court may refuse to allow evidence on which the prosecution proposes to rely to be given if it appears to the court that, having regard

to all the circumstances, including the circumstances in which the evidence was obtained, the admission of the evidence would have such an adverse effect on the fairness of the proceedings that the court ought not to admit it.

(2)   Nothing in this section shall prejudice any rule of law requiring a court to exclude evidence.

82.   Part VIII — Interpretation

(3)   Nothing in this part of this Act shall prejudice any power of a court to exclude evidence (whether by preventing questions from being put or otherwise) at its discretion.

R v Christou
[1992] 1 QB 979
Court of Appeal

The defendants were charged with offences of burglary and, in the alternative, handling stolen goods. Undercover police officers purported to be shopkeepers who bought and sold jewellery. Hidden cameras recorded all the transactions which took place between the defendants and the officers. The defence argued that the evidence from the undercover operation should be excluded, *inter alia*, under s. 78(1) of the Police and Criminal Evidence Act 1984. The trial judge admitted the evidence.

LORD TAYLOR OF GOSFORTH CJ ... The submissions on this appeal are essentially those rejected by the judge. Mr Thornton argued first that the whole concept of Stardust Jewellers involved a deceit or trick by the police designed to deprive visitors to the shop of their protection or privilege against self-incrimination. By their words and conduct in the shop, including their production of the goods and signing of the receipts, they were expressly or impliedly incriminating themselves. They were tricked into doing so because, although in a sense they entered voluntarily, they would not have entered had they known the true nature of the shop and its managers. Accordingly, the evidence ought to have been excluded either (a) pursuant to the common law principles enunciated in *Reg.* v *Sang* [1980] AC 402, or (b) pursuant to section 78 of the Police and Criminal Evidence Act 1984 ...

... Before considering these arguments, it is convenient to summarise those findings of the judge which are not in dispute. The police were clearly engaged in a trick or deceit. However, they did not themselves participate in the commission of any offence; nor did they act as 'agents provocateurs' or incite crime. The offences charged had already been committed before the appellants entered the shop and the police, so far from having any dishonest intent, were concerned to return the property to its rightful owners and bring offenders to justice. The police referred daily to the current price of gold announced by Johnson Matthey and pitched the prices they offered appropriately to the form of dealing in which they purported to be engaged. So, no market was provided which would not have been available elsewhere.

The officers had grounds to suspect each appellant of having committed an offence by the time the first of the sales in which he was involved was transacted. No caution was administered by Gary or Aggi. That was in accordance with instructions they were given.

The first limb of Mr Thornton's first submission depends strongly on the speeches in *Reg.* v *Sang* [1980] AC 402. The House of Lords held unanimously that there is no defence of entrapment in English law. However, the existence of a discretion in the judge to exclude legally admissible evidence, so as to secure the fairness of the trial, was recognised as extending further than merely the exclusion of evidence more prejudicial than probative. Mr Thornton relies particularly on the speeches of Lord Diplock and Lord Scarman.

Lord Diplock cited dicta of Lord Goddard CJ in *Kuruma* v *The Queen* [1955] AC 197, 204, of Lord Parker CJ in *Callis* v *Gunn* [1964] 1 QB 495, 502, and of Lord Widgery CJ in *Jeffrey* v *Black* [1978] QB 490, 498. Lord Diplock also pointed out that the only case brought to their Lordships' attention in which an appellate court had actually excluded evidence on the ground that it had been unfairly obtained by a trick was *Reg.* v *Payne* [1963] 1 WLR 637. There a defendant, charged with drunken driving, had been induced to undergo a medical examination to see if he was ill on the understanding that the doctor would not test his fitness to drive. However, the doctor gave evidence based on his examination that the defendant was unfit to drive and the Court of Criminal Appeal quashed the conviction. On that decision Lord Diplock commented [1980] AC 402, 435:

> This again, as it seems to me, is analogous to unfairly inducing a defendant to confess to an offence, and the short judgment of the Court of Criminal Appeal is clearly based upon the maxim *nemo debet prodere se ipsum*

The passage relied upon by Mr Thornton is where Lord Diplock said, at pp. 435-436:

> Nevertheless it has to be recognised that there is an unbroken series of dicta in judgments of appellate courts to the effect that there is a judicial discretion to exclude admissible evidence which has been 'obtained' unfairly or by trickery or oppressively, although except in *Reg.* v *Payne* [1963] 1 WLR 637, there never has been a case in which those courts have come across conduct so unfair, so tricky or so oppressive as to justify them in holding that the discretion ought to have been exercised in favour of exclusion. In every one of the cases to which your Lordships have been referred where such dicta appear, the source from which the evidence sought to be excluded had been obtained has been the defendant himself or (in some of the search cases) premises occupied by him; and the dicta can be traced to a common ancestor in Lord Goddard's statement in *Kuruma* v *The Queen* [1955] AC 197 which I have already cited. That statement was not, in my view, ever intended to acknowledge the existence of any wider discretion than to exclude (1) admissible evidence which would probably have a prejudicial influence upon the minds of the jury that would be out of proportion to its true evidential value; and (2) evidence tantamount to a self-incriminatory admission which was obtained from the defendant, after the offence had been committed, by means which would justify a judge in excluding an actual confession which had the like self-incriminating effect.

Finally, Lord Diplock said, at p. 436:

> the function of the judge at a criminal trial as respects the admission of evidence is to ensure that the accused has a fair trial according to law. It is no part of a judge's function to exercise disciplinary powers over the police or prosecution as repects the way in which evidence to be used at the trial is obtained by them.

Lord Scarman also referred to the judge's duty to ensure that the defendant has a fair trial. In a passage he himself acknowledged was obiter, he said, at p. 456:

The test of unfairness is not that of a game: it is whether in the light of the considerations to which I have referred the evidence, if admitted, would undermine the justice of the trial. . . . For the conviction of the guilty is a public interest, as is the acquittal of the innocent.

After referring, as did Lord Diplock, to the dicta of Lord Goddard CJ, Lord Parker CJ and Lord Widgery CJ, Lord Scarman went on, at pp. 456-457:

The dicta of three successive Lord Chief Justices are not to be lightly rejected. It is unnecessary for the purposes of this appeal, to express a conclusion upon them. But, always provided that these dicta are treated as relating exclusively to the obtaining of evidence from the accused, I would not necessarily dissent from them. If an accused is misled or tricked into providing evidence (whether it be an admission or the provision of fingerprints or medical evidence or some other evidence), the rule against self-incrimination . . . is likely to be infringed. Each case must, of course, depend on its circumstances. All I would say is that the principle of fairness, though concerned exclusively with the use of evidence at trial, is not susceptible to categorisation or classification and is wide enough in some circumstances to embrace the way in which, after the crime, evidence has been obtained from the accused.

In view of the terms of those dicta, the paucity of cases in which the discretion has been exercised so as to exclude legally admissible evidence is not surprising. In the present case the judge decided that, since the evidence from Stardust Jewellers had admittedly been obtained from the appellants by a trick and after the offences charged had been committed, he had a discretion to exclude the evidence if its admission would prejudice a fair trial. He also considered the alternative submission that, pursuant to section 78 of the Act of 1984, he ought to exclude the evidence because, in the words of section 78:

having regard to all the circumstances, including the circumstances in which the evidence was obtained, the admission of the evidence would have such an adverse effect on the fairness of the proceedings that the court ought not to admit it.

The judge held that the discretion under section 78 may be wider than the common law discretion identified in *Reg.* v *Sang* [1980] AC 402, the latter relating solely to evidence obtained from the defendant after the offence is complete, the statutory discretion not being so restricted. However, he held that the criteria of unfairness are the same whether the trial judge is exercising his discretion at common law or under the statute. We agree. What is unfair cannot sensibly be subject to different standards depending on the source of the discretion to exclude it.

In the result the judge concluded that to admit the challenged evidence would not have an adverse effect on the fairness of the trial. He said:

Nobody was forcing the defendants to do what they did. They were not persuaded or encouraged to do what they did. They were doing in that shop exactly what they intended to do and in all probability, what they intended to do from the moment they got up that morning. They were dishonestly disposing of dishonest goods. If the police had never set up the jewellers shop, they would, in my judgment, have been doing the same thing, though of course they would not have been doing it in that shop, at that time. They were not tricked into doing what they would not otherwise have done, they were tricked into doing what they wanted to do in that place and before witnesses and devices who can now speak of what happened. I do not think that is unfair or leads to an unfairness in the trial.

Putting it in different words, the trick was not applied to the appellants; they voluntarily applied themselves to the trick. It is not every trick producing evidence against an accused which results in unfairness. There are, in criminal investigations, a number of situations in which the police adopt ruses or tricks in the public interest to obtain evidence. For example, to trap a blackmailer, the victim may be used as an agent of the police to arrange an appointment and false or marked money may be laid as bait to catch the offender. A trick, certainly; in a sense too, a trick which results in a form of self-incrimination; but not one which could reasonably be thought to involve unfairness. Cases such as *Reg.* v *Payne* [1963] 1 WLR 637 and *Reg.* v *Mason (Carl)* [1988] 1 WLR 139 are very different from the present case or the blackmail example. In *Reg.* v *Mason* as in *Reg.* v *Payne* [1963] 1 WLR 637, the defendant was in police custody at a police station. Officers lied to both the defendant and his solicitor. Having no evidence against the defendant, they falsely asserted that his fingerprint had been found in an incriminating place in order to elicit admissions from him. After advice from his solicitor, the defendant made admissions. This court quashed his conviction.

In the present case the argument was at one stage canvassed that requesting the receipt with the consequent obtaining of fingerprints, should be regarded separately from the main issue, that it amounted to a separate trick within a trick. However, Mr Thornton made clear that in his submission requesting the receipt was merely an incident in the operation of the shop. The whole operation was a single trick, all the fruits of which should be excluded. We agree that the operation should be considered as a whole. In the end, the judge treated the receipts as 'part of the general deceit concerning the dishonest jewellers, the general pretence by them that it was a proper jeweller's shop'. It was not unfair. He gave, as a further reason, that had no request been made for a receipt, fingerprints could easily have been obtained in other ways, e.g., by dusting the counter. For this he relied upon *Reg.* v *Apicella* (1958) 82 Cr App R 295 and *Director of Public Prosecutions* v *Marshall* [1988] 3 All ER 683.

The judge's exercise of his discretion could only be impugned if it was unreasonable according to *Wednesbury* principles (*Associated Provincial Picture Houses Ltd* v *Wednesbury Corporation* [1948] 1 KB 223): see *Reg.* v *O'Leary* (1988) 87 Cr App R 387, 391. In our judgment, not only can the judge's conclusion on this issue not be so stigmatised; we think he was right.

Appeal dismissed.

R v *Smurthwaite*
[1994] 1 All ER 898
Court of Appeal

LORD TAYLOR OF GOSFORTH CJ: On 27 July 1993 we dismissed these two appeals against conviction. We now give our reasons and deal also with appeals against sentence.

The two cases were heard together since they had a number of features in common. In each, the appellant was convicted of soliciting to murder, Smurthwaite to murder his wife, Gill to murder her husband. In each case, the person solicited was an undercover police officer posing as a contract killer. Arising from that situation, there was argument on each appeal as to the admission of the undercover officer's evidence of what was said by each appellant.

It is convenient first to consider the legal arguments advanced by Mr Worsley QC on behalf of both appellants and then to apply the law to the facts of each case separately.

Mr Worsley's principal aim was to establish the breadth of the judge's powers, under s. 78 of the Police and Criminal Evidence Act 1984, to exclude prosecution evidence where that evidence has one or more of three features: (a) it includes an element of entrapment, (b) it comes from an agent provocateur or (c) it is obtained by a trick.

Mr Worsley's starting point was the decision of the House of Lords in *R* v *Sang* [1979] 2 All ER 1222, [1980] AC 402. Briefly, his thesis was that certain rulings in that case have now in effect been reversed by the provisions in s. 78. The principles enunciated in *R* v *Sang* are to be found in the final paragraph of Lord Diplock's speech, with which all of their Lordships agreed, as follows ([1979] 2 All ER 1222 at 1231, [1980] AC 402 at 437):

> (1) A trial judge in a criminal trial has always a discretion to refuse to admit evidence if in his opinion its prejudicial effect outweighs its probative value. (2) Save with regard to admissions and confessions and generally with regard to evidence obtained from the accused after commission of the offence, he has no discretion to refuse to admit relevant admissible evidence on the ground that it was obtained by improper or unfair means. The court is not concerned with how it was obtained. It is no ground for the exercise of discretion to exclude that the evidence was obtained as the result of the activities of an agent provocateur.

The decision in *R* v *Sang* thus made it clear that there is no substantive defence of entrapment or agent provocateur in English criminal law. Their Lordships held that a judge had no discretion to exclude otherwise admissible evidence '*on the ground* that it was obtained by improper or unfair means'.

However, they also made it clear that a judge does have an overall discretion to exclude evidence in order to secure a fair trial. Thus, Lord Diplock said ([1979] 2 All ER 1222 at 1230, [1980] AC 402 at 436):

> . . . the function of the judge at a criminal trial as respects the admission of evidence is to ensure that the accused has a fair trial according to law. It is no part of a judge's function to exercise disciplinary powers over the police or prosecution as respects the way in which evidence to be used at the trial is obtained by them. If it was obtained illegally there would be a remedy in civil law; if it was obtained legally but in breach of the rules of conduct for the police, this is a matter for the appropriate disciplinary authority to deal with. What the judge at the trial is concerned with is not how the evidence sought to be adduced by the prosecution has been obtained but with how it is used by the prosecution at the trial.

Similarly, Viscount Dillhorne said ([1979] 2 All ER 1222 at 1234, [1980] AC 402 at 441):

> Evidence may be obtained unfairly though not illegally but it is not the manner in which it has been obtained but its use at the trial if accompanied by prejudicial effects outweighing its probative value and so rendering the trial unfair to the accused which will justify the exercise of judicial discretion to exclude it.

Similar dicta are to be found in the speeches of Lord Salmon, Lord Fraser and Lord Scarman (see [1979] 2 All ER 1222 at 1237, 1241, 1243, 1245, 1247, [1980] AC 402 at 445, 450, 452, 454, 456).

Section 78 of the 1984 Act provides as follows:

> (1) In any proceedings the court may refuse to allow evidence on which the prosecution proposes to rely to be given if it appears to the court that, having regard to all the circumstances, including the circumstances in which the evidence was

obtained, the admission of the evidence would have such an adverse effect on the fairness of the proceedings that the court ought not to admit it.

(2) Nothing in this section shall prejudice any rule of law requiring a court to exclude evidence.

Section 82(3) of the 1984 Act provides:

Nothing in this Part of this Act shall prejudice any power of a court to exclude evidence (whether by preventing questions being put or otherwise) at its discretion.

It was submitted that, since s. 82(3) preserves the judge's common law discretion to exclude evidence so as to ensure a fair trial, s. 78 must introduce a wider power. Mr Worsley emphasised the phrase 'including the circumstances in which the evidence was obtained'. He sought to apply it specifically to evidence obtained by entrapment, by an agent provocateur or by a trick and argued that the section altered the law as laid down in R v Sang so as to enable evidence obtained in those ways to be excluded. Whilst at some stages of his argument he accepted that there is still no substantive defence of entrapment or agent provocateur, at others he contended that, in effect, s. 78 afforded such a defence.

In R v Harwood [1989] Crim LR 285 at 286 the court stated, albeit obiter, that s. 78 has not abrogated the rule that neither entrapment nor agent provocateur afford a defence to a criminal charge: 'The rule that entrapment was no defence could not be evaded by the procedural device of preventing the prosecution adducing evidence of the commission of the offence.' In R v Gill [1989] Crim LR 358 some reservations were expressed as to the correctness of those dicta in R v Harwood.

In our judgment, s. 78 has not altered the substantive rule of law that entrapment or the use of an agent provocateur does not per se afford a defence in law to a criminal charge. A purely evidential provision in a statute, which does not even mention entrapment or agent provocateur, cannot, in our view, have altered a substantive rule of law enunciated so recently by the House of Lords. Had Parliament intended to alter the substantive law, it would have done so in clear terms.

However, that is not to say that entrapment, agent provocateur or the use of a trick are irrelevant to the application of s. 78. The right approach to the 1984 Act, a codifying Act, is that stated in R v Fulling [1987] 2 All ER 65, [1987] QB 426 following the principles laid down in Bank of England v Vagliano Bros [1891] AC 107 at 144, [1891–4] All ER Rep 93 at 113. That is simply to examine the language of the relevant provision in its natural meaning and not to strain for an interpretation which either reasserts or alters the pre-existing law. Viewed in that way, the phrase emphasised by Mr Worsley clearly permits the court to have regard to 'the circumstances in which the evidence was obtained' and to exclude it, but only if it 'would have such an adverse effect on the fairness of the proceedings that the court ought not to admit it'. Thus, the fact that the evidence has been obtained by entrapment, or by agent provocateur, or by a trick, does not of itself require the judge to exclude it. If, however, he considers that in all the circumstances the obtaining of the evidence in that way would have the adverse effect described in the statute, then he will exclude it. (See also R v Governor of Pentonville Prison, ex p Chinoy [1992] 1 All ER 317 at 331–332 to the same effect.) 'Fairness of the proceedings' involves a consideration not only of fairness to the accused but also, as has been said before, of fairness to the public (see for example R v Sang [1979] 2 All ER 1222 at 1246–1247, [1980] AC 402 at 456 per Lord Scarman).

In exercising his discretion whether to admit the evidence of an undercover officer, some, but not an exhaustive list, of the factors that the judge may take into account are as follows. Was the officer acting as an agent provocateur in the sense that he was enticing the defendant to commit an offence he would not otherwise have committed? What was the nature of any entrapment? Does the evidence consist of admissions to a completed offence, or does it consist of the actual commission of an offence? How active or passive was the officer's role in obtaining the evidence? Is there an unassailable record of what occurred, or is it strongly corroborated? In *R* v *Christou* [1992] 4 All ER 559, [1992] QB 979 this court held that discussions between suspects and undercover officers, not overtly acting as police officers, were not within the ambit of the codes under the 1984 Act. However, officers should not use their undercover pose to question suspects so as to circumvent the code. In *R* v *Bryce* [1992] 4 All ER 567 the court held that the undercover officer had done just that. Accordingly, a further consideration for the judge in deciding whether to admit an undercover officer's evidence is whether he has abused his role to ask questions which ought properly to have been asked as a police officer and in accordance with the codes.

Beyond mentioning the considerations set out above, it is not possible to give more general guidance as to how a judge should exercise his discretion under s. 78 in this field, since each case must be determined on its own facts (see *R* v *Samuel* [1988] 2 All ER 135 at 146, [1988] QB 615 at 630, *R* v *Parris* (1988) 89 Cr App R 68 at 72 and *R* v *Jelen*, *R* v *Katz* (1989) 90 Cr App R 456 at 465 and other cases cited in *Archbold's Pleading Evidence and Practice in Criminal Cases* (44th edn, 1993) para 15-364.)

[His Lordship then considered the facts of the case and dismissed the appeal.]

Note
A more detailed discussion of the operation of s. 78(1) and its relationship to confession evidence appears at Chapter 10. The rule in civil cases is essentially the same as that in criminal cases, i.e., the court will not concern itself with how relevant evidence was obtained. In a civil case, the court does not have a discretion to exclude evidence which has been unfairly or illegally obtained (but see *ITC Film Distributors* v *Video Exchange Ltd* [1982] Ch 431).

Questions
1.   'A room is searched against the law, and the body of a murdered man is found. If the place of discovery may not be proved, the other circumstances may be insufficient to connect the defendant with the crime. The privacy of the home has been infringed and the murderer goes free.' (*People* v *Defoe* 242 NY 413 (1926), per Cardozo J.) Does this justify the English approach to the question of the admissibility of improperly obtained evidence?
2.   How, if at all, does s. 78(1) of the Police and Criminal Evidence Act 1984, differ from the rule in *Sang*?
3.   Should there be a distinction between illegally obtained evidence and unfairly obtained evidence?

Further Reading
P. Murphy, *A Practical Approach to Evidence*, 4th ed. (1992), Ch. 1
R. Eggleston, *Evidence, Proof and Probability*, 2nd ed. (1983), Ch. 6
A. A. S. Zuckerman, *The Principle of Criminal Evidence*, (1989), Ch. 4

2 THE BURDEN AND STANDARD OF PROOF

(A) The burden of proof

The term 'burden of proof' has two recognised meanings and is used in two different senses. The first of these is known as the legal burden. The legal burden of proof is sometimes known as the 'persuasive' burden or the 'ultimate' burden. It is often said that if the party who bears the legal burden of proof fails to discharge it by the end of the case then he will lose. This is a useful generalisation, but to understand the term in its proper sense, it is necessary to relate it to a particular issue in a case rather than to the whole case itself. We might therefore say that in a criminal case, the prosecution bear the legal burden of proof which, if not discharged, will result in the defendant being acquitted. However, the defendant who runs a defence of insanity will bear the legal burden of proving that defence and, if the burden is not discharged, his defence will fail (see (A)*(ii)(a)* below). Any trial, whether criminal or civil, is likely to contain several issues, and in respect of each of those issues the legal burden of proving an issue may be cast upon either party. In this sense then, the legal burden of proof means the duty of the prosecution or plaintiff to persuade the trier of the facts by the end of the case of the truth of certain propositions. If, at the end of the case, the trier of the facts is genuinely undecided between the parties, whoever bears the legal burden will fail.

The second sense in which burden of proof arises is known as the evidential burden. This burden is sometimes known as 'the burden of passing the judge' and is most evident in cases tried by a judge and jury, although it applies equally to those cases tried by a judge alone. This burden demands that the judge be satisfied that there is sufficient evidence on any particular issue to justify his allowing the trier of the facts to consider it. If this burden is not discharged, then the judge will refuse to allow the trier of the facts to consider the issue. In a criminal case, this might entail the judge directing the jury to acquit the defendant without even needing to give him the opportunity to answer the allegations made. Similarly, in a civil case, the judge would direct himself (as he is usually the trier of the facts) not to consider any issue raised by a party who has failed to discharge the evidential burden on that issue.

It is obviously important to determine which party bears which burdens and as to what issues. The general principle is that the legal burden of proving facts on any particular issue lies on the party that asserts them, and usually (but not always), the legal and evidential burdens lie in the same place. In criminal cases, it is the prosecution who bears the burden of proving the defendant's guilt beyond reasonable doubt, although there are some occasions where statute places a burden on the defendant (see (A) *(ii)* *(b)* below). In civil cases however, matters can become much more involved and complex, often because it is difficult to determine who is alleging what particular issue. It has been suggested that where a 'negative state of affairs' has to be proved by one party, this should result in placing the burden of proof on the other.

(i)   *Civil cases*

Abrath v Northern Eastern Railway Co.
(1883) 11 QBD 440
Court of Appeal

The plaintiff, a surgeon, had attended one M for injuries alleged to have been sustained in a collision upon the defendants' railway. M brought an action against the defendants, which was compromised by the defendants paying a large sum for damages and costs. Subsequently the directors of the defendants' company, having received certain information, caused the statements of certain persons to be taken by a solicitor; these statements tended to show that the injuries of which M complained were not caused at the collision, but were produced wilfully by the plaintiff, with the consent of M, for the purpose of defrauding the defendants. These statements were laid before counsel, who advised that there was good ground for prosecuting the plaintiff and M for conspiracy. The defendants accordingly prosecuted the plaintiff, but he was acquitted. In an action for malicious prosecution, an issue arose as to whether the burden of proving absence of reasonable and probable cause as well as the prosecution lay on the plaintiff. The Divisional Court held that it did and ordered a new trial. The defendants appealed.

BOWEN LJ: Whenever litigation exists, somebody must go on with it; the plaintiff is the first to begin; if he does nothing, he fails; if he makes a *prima facie* case, and nothing is done to answer it, the defendant fails. The test, therefore, as to the burden of proof or onus of proof, whichever term is used, is simply this: to ask oneself which party will be successful if no evidence is given, or if no more evidence is given than has been given at a particular point of the case, for it is obvious that as the controversy involved in the litigation travels on, the parties from moment to moment may reach points at which the onus of proof shifts, and at which the tribunal will have to say that if the case stops there, it must be decided in a particular manner. The test being such as I have stated, it is not a burden that goes on for ever resting on the shoulders of the person upon whom it is first cast. As soon as he brings evidence which, until it is answered, rebuts the evidence against which he is contending, then the balance descends on the other side, and the burden rolls over until again there is evidence which once more turns the scale. That being so, the question of onus of proof is only a rule for deciding on whom the obligation of going further, if he wishes to win, rests. It is not a rule to enable the jury to decide on the value of conflicting evidence. . . .

Now in an action for malicious prosecution the plaintiff has the burden throughout of establishing that the circumstances of the prosecution were such that a judge can see no reasonable or probable cause for instituting it. In one sense that is the assertion of a negative, and we have been pressed with the proposition that when a negative is to be made out the onus of proof shifts. That is not so. If the assertion of a negative is an essential part of the plaintiff's case, the proof of the assertion still rests upon the plaintiff. The terms 'negative' and 'affirmative' are after all relative and not absolute. In dealing with a question of negligence, that term may be considered either as negative or affirmative according to the definition adopted in measuring the duty which is neglected. Wherever a person asserts affirmatively as part of his case that a certain state of facts is present or is absent, or that a particular thing is insufficient for a particular purpose, that is an averment which he is bound to prove positively. It has been said that an exception exists in those cases where the facts lie peculiarly within the knowledge of the opposite party. The counsel for the plaintiff have not gone to the length of contending that in all those cases the onus shifts, and that the person within whose knowledge the truth peculiarly lies is bound to prove or disprove the matter in dispute. I think a proposition of that kind cannot be maintained, and that the exceptions supposed to be found amongst cases relating to the game laws may be explained on special grounds. . . .

Who had to make good their point as to the proposition whether the defendants had taken reasonable and proper care to inform themselves of the true state of the case? The defendants were not bound to make good anything. It was the plaintiff's duty to show the absence of reasonable care.

Appeal dismissed.

Joseph Constantine Steamship Line v Imperial Smelting Corporation
[1942] AC 154
House of Lords

The charterers of a ship claimed damages from the owners for failure to load. The defendants pleaded that the contract had been frustrated by the destruction of the ship owing to an explosion, the cause of which was unclear. Such frustration would have concluded the case in favour of the defendants in the absence of any fault on their part. Atkinson J held that the onus of proving that the frustration was induced by the defendant's default lay upon the charterers. The Court of Appeal reversed this decision and the defendants appealed to the House of Lords.

VISCOUNT SIMON LC: The question here is where the onus of proof lies; i.e., whether, when a supervening event has been proved which would, apart from the defendant's 'default' put an end to the contract, and when at the end of the case no inference of 'default' exists and the evidence is equally consistent with either view, the defence fails because the defendant has not established affirmatively that the super-vening event was not due to his default.

I may observe, in the first place, that, if this were correct, there must be many cases in which, although in truth frustration is complete and unavoidable, the defendant will be held liable because of his inability to prove a negative — in some cases, indeed, a whole series of negatives. Suppose that a vessel while on the high seas disappears completely during a storm. Can it be that the defence of frustration of the adventure depends on the owner's ability to prove that all his servants on board were navigating the ship with adequate skill and that there was no 'default' which brought about the catastrophe? Suppose that a vessel in convoy is torpedoed by the enemy and sinks immediately with all hands. Does the application of the doctrine require that the owners should affirmatively prove that those on board were keeping a good look-out, were obscuring lights, were steering as directed, and so forth? There is no reported case which requires us so to hold. The doctrine on which the defence of frustration depends is nowhere so stated as to place this onus of proof on the party relying on it ...

In this connection it is well to emphasise that when 'frustration' in the legal sense occurs, it does not merely provide one party with a defence in an action brought by the other. It kills the contract itself and discharges both parties automatically. The plaintiff sues for breach at a past date and the defendant pleads that at that date no contract existed. In this situation the plaintiff could only succeed if it were shown that the determination of the contract were due to the defendant's 'default', and it would be a strange result if the party alleging this were not the party required to prove it.'

VISCOUNT MAUGHAM: I think the burden of proof in any particular case depends on the circumstances under which the claim arises. In general the rule which applies is *'Ei qui affirmat non ei qui negat incumbit probatio'*. It is an ancient rule founded on considerations of good sense and it should not be departed from without strong reasons. The position as to proof of non-responsibility for the event in such a case as the present is not very different from the position of a plaintiff in an action for negligence where contributory negligence on his part is alleged. In such a case the plaintiff must prove that there was some negligent act or omission on the part of the defendant which caused or materially contributed to the injury, but it is for the defendant to prove affirmatively, if he so contends, that there was contributory negligence on the part of the person injured, though here again the onus may easily be shifted ...

LORD WRIGHT: The appeal can, I think, be decided according to the generally accepted view that frustration involves as one of its elements absence of fault, by applying the ordinary rules as to onus of proof. If frustration is viewed (as I think it can be) as analogous to an exception, since it is generally relied on as a defence to a claim for failure to perform a contract, the same rule will properly be applied to it as to the ordinary type of exceptions. The defence may be rebutted by proof of fault, but the onus of proving fault will rest on the plaintiff. This is merely to apply the familiar rule which is applied, for instance, where a carrier by sea relies on the exception of perils of the sea. If the goods owner then desires to rebut that *prima facie* defence on the ground of negligence or other fault on the part of the shipowner, it rests on the goods owner to establish the negligence or fault.

(LORDS RUSSELL of KILLOWEN and PORTER delivered concurring judg-ments.)

Appeal allowed.

Levison and another v Patent Steam Carpet Cleaning Co. Ltd
[1978] QB 69
Court of Appeal

The defendants were guilty of the unexplained loss of a Chinese carpet which had been delivered to them for cleaning and which belonged to the plaintiffs. A clause in the contract signed by the plaintiffs would have exempted the defendants from liability for negligence, but not for any fundamental breach. The plaintiffs sued the cleaners for the loss of the carpet. The county court judge gave judgment against the cleaners who appealed.

LORD DENNING MR: This brings me to the crux of the case. On whom is the burden of proof? Take the present case. Assuming that clause 2(a) or clause 5, or either of them, limits or exempts the cleaners from liability for negligence: but not for a fundamental breach. On whom is the burden to prove that there was fundamental breach?

Upon principle, I should have thought that the burden was on the cleaners to prove that they were not guilty of a fundamental breach. After all, Mrs Levison does not know what happened to it. The cleaners are the ones who know, or should know, what happened to the carpet, and the burden should be on them to say what it was. It was so held by McNair J in *Woolmer* v *Delmer Price Ltd* [1955] 1 QB 291; and by me in *J Spurling Ltd* v *Bradshaw* [1956] 1 WLR 461, 466, and by the East African Court of Appeal in *United Manufacturers Ltd* v *WAFCO Ltd* [1974] EA 233. A contrary view was expressed by this court in *Hunt & Winterbotham (West of England) Ltd* v *BRS (Parcels) Ltd* [1962] 1 QB 617, 635. And there is a long line of shipping cases in which it has been held that, if a shipowner makes a *prima facie* case that the cause of the loss was one of the excepted perils, the burden is on the shipper to prove that it was not covered by the exceptions: see *The Glendarroch* [1894] P226 and *Munro, Brice & Co.* v *War Risks Association Ltd* [1918] 2 KB 78. To which there may be added *Joseph Constantine Steamship Line* v *Imperial Smelting Corporation Ltd* [1942] AC 154 on frustration.

It is, therefore, a moot point for decision. On it I am clearly of the opinion that, in a contract of bailment, when a bailee seeks to escape liability on the ground that he was not negligent or that he was excused by an exception or limitation clause, then he must show what happened to the goods. He must prove all the circumstances known to him in which the loss or damage occurred. If it appears that the goods were lost or damaged without any negligence on his part, then, of course, he is not liable. If it appears that they were lost or damaged by a slight breach — not going to the root of the contract — he may be protected by the exemption or limitation clause. But, if he leaves the cause of loss or damage undiscovered and unexplained — then I think he is liable: because it is then quite likely that the goods were stolen by one of his servants; or delivered by a servant to the wrong address; or damaged by reckless or wilful misconduct; all of which the offending servant will conceal and not make known to his employer. Such conduct would be a fundamental breach against which the exemption or limitation clause will not protect him.

The cleaning company in this case did not show what happened to the carpet. They did not prove how it was lost. They gave all sorts of excuses for non-delivery and eventually said it had been stolen. Then I would ask: By whom was it stolen? Was it by one of their own servants? Or with his connivance? Alternatively, was it delivered by one of their servants to the wrong address? In the absence of any explanation, I would infer that it was one of these causes. In none of them would the cleaning company be protected by the exemption or limitation clause.

(ORR LJ AND SIR DAVIS CAIRNS agreed.)

Appeal dismissed.

Questions

1. In *Abrath* v *Northern Eastern Railway Co.*, Bowen LJ states that during the course of a trial, the onus (or burden) of proof shifts. Is this statement accurate?

2. P brings an action against D for breach of contract, alleging that D has failed to deliver 500 silk shirts. D claims that the shirts were destroyed in a fire at his warehouse, the cause of the fire being unknown. Consider the incidence of the burden of proof.

(ii)   Criminal cases

Woolmington v DPP
[1935] AC 462
House of Lords

The defendant was charged with the murder of his wife from whom he was separated. He gave evidence to the effect that whilst endeavouring to induce her to return to live with him by threatening to shoot himself, he had shot her and killed her accidentally. The jury were directed that, once it was proved that the defendant shot his wife, it was for him to prove the absence of malice, although malice was an essential element of the charge of murder. The defendant was convicted of murder and appealed unsuccessfully to the Court of Criminal Appeal. He further appealed to the House of Lords.

VISCOUNT SANKEY LC: If at any period of a trial it was permissible for the judge to rule that the prosecution had established its case and that the onus was shifted on the prisoner to prove that he was not guilty and that unless he discharged that onus the prosecution was entitled to succeed, it would be enabling the judge in such a case to say that the jury must in law find the prisoner guilty and so make the judge decide the case and not the jury, which is not the common law. It would be an entirely different case from those exceptional instances of special verdicts where a judge asks the jury to find certain facts and directs them that on such facts the prosecution is entitled to succeed. Indeed, a consideration of such special verdicts shows that it is not till the end of the evidence that a verdict can properly be found and that at the end of the evidence it is not for the prisoner to establish his innocence, but for the prosecution to establish his guilt. Just as there is evidence on behalf of the prosecution so there may be evidence on behalf of the prisoner which may cause a doubt as to his guilt. In either case, he is entitled to the benefit of the doubt. But while the prosecution must prove the guilt of the prisoner, there is no such burden laid on the prisoner to prove his innocence and it is sufficient for him to raise a doubt as to his guilt; he is not bound to satisfy the jury of his innocence ... Throughout the web of the English Criminal Law one golden thread is always to be seen, that it is the duty of the prosecution to prove the prisoner's guilt subject to what I have already said as to the defence of insanity and subject also to any statutory exception. If, at the end of and on the whole of the case, there is a reasonable doubt, created by the evidence given by either the prosecution or the prisoner, as to whether the prisoner killed the deceased with a malicious intention, the prosecution has not made out the case and the prisoner is entitled to an acquittal. No matter what the charge or where the trial, the principle that the prosecution must prove the guilt of the prisoner is part of the common law of England and no attempt to whittle it down can be entertained. When dealing with a murder case the Crown must prove (a) death as the result of a voluntary act of the accused and (b) malice of the accused. It may prove malice either expressly or by implication. For malice may be implied where death occurs as the result of a voluntary act of the accused which is (i) intentional and (ii) unprovoked. When evidence of death and malice has been given (this is a question for the jury) the accused is entitled to show, by evidence or by examination of the circumstances adduced by the Crown that the act on his part which caused death was either unintentional or provoked. If the jury are either satisfied with his explanation or, upon a review of all the evidence, are left in reasonable doubt whether, even if his explanation be not accepted, the act was unintentional or provoked, the prisoner is entitled to be acquitted. It is not the law of England to say, as was said in the summing-up in the present case: 'If the Crown satisfy you that this woman died at the prisoner's hands then he has to show that there are circumstances to be found in the evidence which has been given from the witness-box in this case which alleviate the crime so that it is only manslaughter or which excuse the homicide altogether by showing it was a pure accident.'

(LORDS ATKIN, HEWART, TOMLIN and WRIGHT concurred.)

Appeal allowed.

(a)   Defences

Daniel M'Naghten's Case
(1843) 10 Cl & F 200
House of Lords

The defendant, intending to murder Sir Robert Peel, killed the statesman's secretary by mistake. He was acquitted of murder on the ground of insanity. The verdict was made the subject of debate in the House of Lords and it determined to take the opinion of all the judges on the law governing such cases. The judges attended and five questions were put to them:

TINDAL CJ: Your Lordships are pleased to inquire of us, secondly:

What are the proper questions to be submitted to the jury when a person alleged to be afflicted with insane delusion respecting one or more particular subjects or persons is charged with the commission of a crime (murder, for example), and insanity is set up as a defence?

And, thirdly:

In what terms ought the question to be left to the jury as to the prisoner's state of mind at the time when the act was committed?

As these two questions appear to us to be more conveniently answered together we have to submit our opinion to be that the jurors ought to be told in all cases that every man is to be presumed to be sane and to possess a sufficient degree of reason to be responsible for his crimes until the contrary be proved to their satisfaction, and that to establish a defence on the ground of insanity it must be clearly proved that, at the time of committing of the act the party accused was labouring under such a defect of reason, from disease of the mind, as not to know the nature and quality of the act he was doing, or, if he did know it, that he did not know he was doing what was wrong.

Bratty v Attorney-General for Northern Ireland
[1963] AC 386
House of Lords

The appellant was convicted of the murder by strangulation of an 18-year-old girl. Two of his defences were insanity and automatism. He appealed to the Court of Criminal Appeal in Northern Ireland and the House of Lords against the trial judge's refusal to put the defence of automatism to the jury.

VISCOUNT KILMUIR LC: Where the defence succeeds in surmounting the initial hurdle (see *Mancini* v *Director of Public Prosecutions* [1942] AC 1), and satisfies the judge that there is evidence fit for the jury to consider, the question remains whether the proper direction is: (a) that the jury will acquit if, and only if, they are satisfied on the balance of probabilities that the accused acted in a state of automatism, or (b) that they should acquit if they are left in reasonable doubt on this point. In favour of the former direction it might be argued that, since a defence of automatism is (as Lord Goddard said in *Hill* v *Baxter* [1958] 1 QB 277) very near a defence of insanity, it would be anomalous if there were any distinction between the onus in the one case and in the other. If this argument were to prevail it would follow that the defence would fail unless they established on a balance of probabilities that the prisoner's act was unconscious and involuntary in the same way as, under the M'Naughten Rules, they must establish on a balance of probabilities that the necessary requirements are satisfied.

Nevertheless, one must not lose sight of the overriding principle, laid down by this House in *Woolmington's* case [1935] AC 462, that it is for the prosecution to prove every element of the offence charged. One of these elements is the accused's state of mind; normally the presumption of mental capacity is sufficient to prove that he acted consciously and voluntarily, and the prosecution need go no further. But if, after considering evidence properly left to them by the judge, the jury are left in real doubt whether or not the accused acted in a state of automatism, it seems to me that on principle they should acquit because the necessary *mens rea* — if indeed the *actus reus* — has not been proved beyond reasonable doubt.

I find support for this view in the direction given by Barry J to the jury in *R* v *Charlson* [1955] 1 WLR 317. In that case the prisoner was charged on three counts, namely, causing grievous bodily harm with intent to murder, causing grievous bodily harm with intent to cause grievous bodily harm, and unlawful wounding. The defence raised the issue of automatism and called medical evidence in support of it. The learned judge, on the basis — which has aroused some discussion — that insanity did not come into the case, after directing the jury that on each of the first two charges the prosecution must prove the specific intent, went on to deal with the third charge, that is, unlawful wounding, in these words: 'Therefore, in considering this third charge you will have to ask yourselves whether the accused knowingly struck his son, or whether he was acting as an automaton without any knowledge of or control over his acts. ... If you are left in doubt about the matter, and you think that he may well have been acting as an automaton without any real knowledge of what he was doing, then the proper verdict would be "not guilty". ...'

I am also supported by the words of Sholl J in *R v Carter* [1959] VR 105 when he said: 'It must be for the defence in the first instance genuinely to raise the issue, but if the defence does raise the issue in a genuine fashion then the Crown, which of course may call rebutting evidence on the matter, is bound in the long run to carry the ultimate onus of proving all the elements of the crime including the conscious perpetration thereof.'

My conclusion is, therefore, that once the defence have surmounted the initial hurdle to which I have referred and have satisfied the judge that there is evidence fit for the jury's consideration, the proper direction is that, if that evidence leaves them in a real state of doubt, the jury should acquit.'

LORD DENNING: In the present case the defence raised both automatism and insanity. And herein lies the difficulty because of the burden of proof. If the accused says he did not know what he was doing, then, so far as the defence of automatism is concerned, the Crown must prove that the act was a voluntary act, see *Woolmington's* case. But so far as the defence of insanity is concerned, the defence must prove that the act was an involuntary act due to disease of the mind, see *M'Naghten's* case. This apparent incongruity was noticed by Sir Owen Dixon, the Chief Justice of Australia, in an address which is to be found in 31 Australian Law Journal, p. 255, and it needs to be resolved. The defence here say: Even though we have not proved that the act was involuntary, yet the Crown have not proved that it was a voluntary act: and that point at least should have been put to the jury.

My Lords, I think that the difficulty is to be resolved by remembering that, whilst the *ultimate* burden rests on the Crown of proving every element essential in the crime, nevertheless in order to prove that the act was a voluntary act, the Crown is entitled to rely on the *presumption* that every man has sufficient mental capacity to be responsible for his crimes: and that if the defence wish to displace that presumption they must give some evidence from which the contrary may reasonably be inferred. Thus a drunken man is presumed to have the capacity to form the specific intent necessary to constitute the crime, unless evidence is given from which it can reasonably be inferred that he was incapable of forming it, see the valuable judgment of the Court of Justiciary in *Kennedy v HM Advocate* (1944) SC(J) 171 which was delivered by Lord Normand. So also it seems to me that a man's act is presumed to be a voluntary act unless there is evidence from which it can reasonably be inferred that it was involuntary. To use the words of Devlin J, the defence of automatism 'ought not to be considered at all until the defence has produced at least *prima facie* evidence', see *Hill v Baxter* [1958] 1 QB 277, 285; and the words of North J in New Zealand 'unless a proper foundation is laid', see *R v Cottle* [1958] NZLR 999, 1025. The necessity of laying the proper foundation is on the defence: and if it is not so laid, the defence of automatism need not be left to the jury, any more than the defence of drunkenness (*Kennedy v HM Advocate*), provocation (*R v Gauthier* (1943) 29 Cr App R 113) or self-defence (*R v Lobell* [1957] 1 QB 547) need be.

What, then, is a proper foundation? The presumption of mental capacity of which I have spoken is a provisional presumption only. It does not put the legal burden on the defence in the same way as the presumption of sanity does. It leaves the legal burden on the prosecution, but nevertheless, until it is displaced, it enables the prosecution to discharge the ultimate burden of proving that the act was voluntary. Not because the presumption is evidence itself, but because it takes the place of evidence. In order to displace the presumption of mental capacity, the defence must give sufficient evidence from which it may reasonably be inferred that the act was involuntary. The evidence of the man himself will rarely be sufficient unless it is supported by medical evidence which points to the cause of the mental incapacity. It is not sufficient for a man to say 'I had a black-out': for 'black-out' as Stable J said in *Cooper* v *McKenna, Ex parte Cooper* 'is one of the first refuges of a guilty conscience and a popular excuse'. The words of Devlin J in *Hill* v *Baxter* should be remembered: 'I do not doubt that there are genuine cases of automatism and the like, but I do not see how the layman can safely attempt without the help of some medical or scientific evidence to distinguish the genuine from the fraudulent.' When the only cause that is assigned for an involuntary act is drunkenness, then it is only necessary to leave drunkenness to the jury, with the consequential directions, and not to leave automatism at all. When the only cause that is assigned for it is a disease of the mind, then it is only necessary to leave insanity to the jury, and not automatism. When the cause assigned is concussion or sleep-walking, there should be some evidence from which it can reasonably be inferred before it should be left to the jury. If it is said to be due to concussion, there should be evidence of a severe blow shortly beforehand. If it is said to be sleep-walking, there should be some credible support for it. His mere assertion that he was asleep will not suffice.

Once a proper foundation is thus laid for automatism, the matter becomes at large and must be left to the jury. As the case proceeds, the evidence may weigh first to one side and then to the other: and so the burden may appear to shift to and fro. But at the end of the day the legal burden comes into play and requires that the jury should be satisfied beyond reasonable doubt that the act was a voluntary act.

LORD MORRIS of BORTH-Y-GEST: The 'golden' rule of the English criminal law that it is the duty of the prosecution to prove an accused person's guilt (subject to any statutory exception and subject to the special position which arises where it is given in evidence that an accused person is insane), does not involve that the prosecution must speculate as to and specifically anticipate every conceivable explanation that an accused person might offer. The evidence of the commission of certain acts may suffice to prove that they were intentional. In a charge of murder, malice may by implication be proved where death occurs as the result of a voluntary act of the accused which is (i) intentional and (ii) unprovoked. When evidence of death and malice has been given an accused person may, however, either by adducing evidence or by examining the circumstances adduced by the Crown, show that his actions were either unintentional or provoked. In such a situation the continuing and constant obligation of the prosecution to satisfy the jury beyond any reasonable doubt is in no way abated (see *Woolmington* v *Director of Public Prosecutions*). In the conceivably possible case that I have postulated (of a violent act committed by a sleep-walker) it would not necessarily be the duty of the prosecution in leading their evidence as to the commission of the act specifically to direct such evidence to negativing the possibility of the act having been committed while sleep-walking. If, however, during the trial the suggested explanation of the act was advanced and if such explanation was so supported that it had sufficient substance to merit consideration by the jury, then the onus which is upon the prosecution would not be discharged unless the jury, having considered the explanation, were sure that guilt in regard to the particular crime charged was established so that they were left in no reasonable doubt. The position would be analogous to that which arises where a defence of self-defence is raised. Though the onus is upon the prosecution to negative that defence, the obligation to do so only arises effectively when there is a suggestion of such defence (see *R v Lobell* [1957] 1 QB 547).

Before an explanation of any conduct is worthy of consideration such explanation must be warranted by the established facts or be supported by some evidence that has been given by some witness. Though questions as to whether evidence should or should not be accepted or as to the weight to be attached to it are for the determination of the jury, it is a province of the judge to rule whether a theory or a submission has the support of evidence so that it can properly be passed to the jury for their consideration. As human behaviour may manifest itself in infinite varieties of circumstances it is perilous to generalise, but it is not every facile mouthing of some easy phrase of excuse that can amount to an explanation. It is for a judge to decide whether there is evidence fit to be left to a jury which could be the basis for some suggested verdict.

Appeal dismised.

Homicide Act 1957

2. Persons suffering from diminished responsibility

(1) Where a person kills or is party to the killing of another, he shall not be convicted of murder if he was suffering from such abnormality of mind (whether arising from a condition of arrested or retarded development of mind or any inherent causes or induced by disease or injury) as substantially impaired his mental responsibility for his acts and omissions in doing or being a party to the killing.

(2) On a charge of murder, it shall be for the defence to prove that the person charged is by virtue of this section not liable to be convicted of murder.

Note

Where the defendant bears the legal burden of proving a defence (e.g., insanity, insane automatism or diminished responsiblity), it is to the standard normally associated with civil cases, namely, a preponderance or balance of probabilities (see (B)(*i*) below).

A number of other defences impose an evidential burden on the defendant.

R v Lobell
[1957] 1 QB 547
Court of Criminal Appeal   •

The appellant was convicted of wounding with intent to do grievous bodily harm. At the trial the sole defence was that in inflicting the wound the appellant was acting in self-defence. The trial judge directed the jury that it was for the defence to establish that plea to the jury's satisfaction.

LORD GODDARD: The onus was clearly put in the summing-up on the defendant. There is no doubt that in so doing the judge had the support of *R v Smith* (1837) 8 C & P 160 where Bosanquet J apparently with the approval of Bolland B and Coltman J, charged the jury that before a person can avail himself of this defence he must satisfy the jury that the defence was necessary, that he did all he could to avoid it, and that it was necessary to protect his own life, or to protect himself from such serious bodily harm as would give a reasonable apprehension that his life was in immediate danger. In that case the judge said that the accused would be justified. He no doubt had in mind the provisions of 9 Geo. 4, c. 31, s. 10, now replaced and re-enacted by section 7 of the Offences against the Person Act 1861, which enacts that no punishment or forfeiture shall be incurred by any person who shall kill another by misfortune or in his own defence, or in any other manner without felony. This passage from the summing-up has for many years appeared in *Archbold's Criminal Pleading and Practice* as the proper direction to be given in such cases and certainly puts the onus of establishing a defence of killing *se defendendo* on the accused. It is a defence of justification, or, to put it in terms of pleading, a confession and avoidance. In civil cases this plea is always to be proved by the party setting it up; and it is perhaps not altogether easy to see why it should not be so in a criminal case, more especially as when self-defence is set up the facts must often be known only to the defendant who relies upon it.

But in the opinion of the court the cases of *Woolmington* v *Director of Public Prosecutions* [1935] AC 462 and *Mancini* v *Director of Public Prosecutions* [1942] AC 1 establish that in murder or manslaughter the rule that the onus is on the prosecution permits of no exception except as to proof of insanity. In the recent case of *Chan Kau* v *The Queen* [1955] AC 206 this was stated in terms by Lord Tucker, who referred to *R* v *Smith* and said that the passage from the summing-up quoted in Archbold clearly needed some modification in the light of modern decisions. It must, however, be understood that maintaining the rule that the onus always remains on the prosecution does not mean that the Crown must give evidence-in-chief to rebut a suggestion of self-defence before that issue is raised, or indeed need give any evidence on the subject at all. If an issue relating to self-defence is to be left to the jury there must be some evidence from which a jury would be entitled to find that issue in favour of the accused, and ordinarily no doubt such evidence would be given by the defence. But there is a difference between leading evidence which would enable a jury to find an issue in favour of a defendant and in putting the onus upon him. The truth is that the jury must come to a verdict on the whole of the evidence that has been laid before them. If on a consideration of all the evidence the jury are left in doubt whether the killing or wounding may not have been in self-defence the proper verdict would be not guilty. A convenient way of directing the jury is to tell them that the burden of establishing guilt is on the prosecution, but that they must also consider the evidence for the defence which may have one of three results: it may convince them of the innocence of the accused, or it may cause them to doubt, in which case the defendant is entitled to an acquittal, or it may and sometimes does strengthen the case for the prosecution. It is perhaps a fine distinction to say that before a jury can find a particular issue in favour of an accused person he must give some evidence on which it can be found but none the less the onus remains on the prosecution; what it really amounts to is that if in the result the jury are left in doubt where the truth lies the verdict should be not guilty, and this is as true of an issue as to self-defence as it is to one of provocation, though of course the latter plea goes only to a mitigation of the offence.

Appeal allowed.

R v *Johnson*
[1961] 1 WLR 1478
Court of Criminal Appeal

The appellant was convicted of robbery with violence. At his trial he denied taking part in the robbery and put forward an alibi, calling witnesses to support it. The trial judge, in summing up, indicated that the appellant had assumed the burden of proof when he put forward his defence of alibi.

ASHWORTH J: The main ground of appeal is based on an alleged misdirection by the judge in regard to the answer which the appellant put forward in the shape of the alibi. As Mr Skellhorn submits, an alibi is commonly called a defence, but it is to be distinguished from some of the statutory defences, such as the defence of diminished responsibility under the Homicide Act 1957, where Parliament has specifically provided for a defence, and has further indicated that the burden of establishing such a defence rests on the accused. It may be that the true view of an alibi is the same as that of self-defence or provocation. It is the answer which a defendant puts forward, and the burden of proof, in the sense of establishing the guilt of the defendant, rests throughout on the prosecution. If a man puts forward an answer in the shape of an alibi or in the shape of self-defence, he does not in law thereby assume any burden of proving that answer. So much, in the opinion of the court, is plain on the authorities.

Appeal allowed.

R v Gill
[1963] 1 WLR 841
Court of Criminal Appeal

At his trial on two counts charging him with conspiracy to steal and larceny pursuant to that conspiracy the defendant gave evidence admitting that he had participated in the conspiracy but said that he had repented of that decision soon afterwards and decided not to carry out the theft; that his fellow conspirators had threatened violence to his wife and himself if he failed to carry out his part of the plan; and that it was for fear of that violence that he was compelled, against his will, to commit the theft. He thus relied on duress as a defence to the larceny. The trial judge directed the jury that it was for the defendant to satisfy the jury that he was acting under duress. The defendant appealed against his conviction.

EDMUND DAVIES J: The issue of duress was left to the jury in the present case, and that may well have been the prudent course. Having been left, did the burden rest upon the Crown conclusively to destroy this defence, in the same way as it is required to destroy such other defences as provocation or self-defence? Or was the accused required to establish it, on the balance of probabilities? For the latter view, reliance was placed on the judgment of Lord Goddard CJ in *R v Steane* [1947] KB 997, in the course of which he said: '... before any question of duress arises, a jury must be satisfied that the prisoner had the intention which is laid in the indictment. Duress is a matter of defence and the onus of proving it is on the accused. As we have already said, where an intent is charged on the indictment, it is for the prosecution to prove it, so the onus is the other way.' On the other hand, in *R v Purdy* [1946] 10 J Crim Law 182, where a British prisoner of war was charged with treason, Oliver J, directing the jury on the defence of duress, said: 'If you believe, or if you think that it might be true, that he only did that because he had the fear of death upon him, then you will acquit him on that charge, because to act in matters of this sort under threat of death is excusable.' Similarly, in *R v Shiartos* (unreported, September 29, 1961, CCA), where duress was relied upon by an accused charged with arson, Lawton J directed the jury that: 'If, in all the circumstances of this case, you are satisfied that what he did he did at pistol point and in fear of his life, he is entitled to be acquitted. If, although you are not satisfied, you think it might well be that he was forced at pistol point to do what he had to do, then again you should acquit him, because the prosecution would not have made you feel sure that what he did he did maliciously.'

In our judgment, the law on this matter is to be found correctly stated in Dr Glanville Williams' *Criminal Law*, 2nd ed (1961), p. 762, in this way: '. . . although it is convenient to call duress a "defence", this does not mean that the ultimate (persuasive) burden of proving it is on the accused. . . . But the accused must raise the defence by sufficient evidence to go to the jury; in other words, the evidential burden is on him.' The Crown are not called upon to anticipate such a defence and destroy it in advance. The defendant, either by the cross-examination of the prosecution witnesses or by evidence called on his behalf, or by a combination of the two, must place before the court such material as makes duress a live issue fit and proper to be left to the jury. But, once he has succeeded in doing this, it is then for the Crown to destroy that defence in such a manner as to leave in the jury's minds no reasonable doubt that the accused cannot be absolved on the grounds of the alleged compulsion. It is true that this approach appears to conflict with the literal reading of the passage from Lord Goddard CJ's judgment in *R v Steane*. It is to be observed, however, that that passage was *obiter* in that the real decision there was that it was for the Crown to prove the specific intent laid and that in the particular circumstances of that case an inference could not be drawn that the prisoner intended the natural consequences of his act. We agree with Dr Glanville Williams that the *dictum* must be read as relating only to what the author calls the 'evidential' burden cast upon the accused, and not to the ultimate (or 'persuasive') burden placed upon the Crown of destroying the defence of duress where it has been substantially raised.

Appeal dismissed. (The court stating that the passages complained of must be read in the light of the whole summing-up, which was impeccable.)

Questions
1.   Is there any rational distinction between those cases where the defendant bears an evidential burden of raising an issue and those where the legal burden of proving some issue is cast upon him?
2.   D is charged with an offence and raises two defences, sane automatism and insanity. How should the judge direct the jury on the burden of proof?

(b)   Statutory provisions

Note
Numerous statutes (in addition to the Homicide Act 1957 mentioned above) affect the incidence of the burden of proof. Some deal expressly with the issue, whereas others impose a burden by necessary implication.

Prevention of Corruption Act 1916

2.   Presumption of corruption in certain cases
Where in any proceedings against a person for an offence under the Prevention of Corrupton Act 1906, or the Public Bodies Corrupt Practices Act 1889, it is proved that any money, gift, or other consideration has been paid or given to or received by

a person in the employment of His Majesty or any Government Department or a public body by or from a person, or agent of a person, holding or seeking to obtain a contract from His Majesty or any Government Department or public body, the money, gift, or onsideration shall be deemed to have been paid or given and received corruptly as such inducement or reward as is mentioned in such Act unless the contrary is proved.

Prevention of Crime Act 1953

1. Prohibition of the carrying of offensive weapons without lawful authority or reasonable excuse
(1) Any person who without lawful authority or reasonable excuse, the proof whereof shall lie on him, has with him in any public place any offensive weapon shall be guilty of an offence, . . .

Magistrates' Courts Act 1980

101. Onus of proving exceptions, etc.
Where the defendant to an information or complaint relies for his defence on any exception, exemption, proviso, excuse or qualification, whether or not it accompanies the description of the offence or matter of complaint in the enactment creating the offence or on which the complaint is founded, the burden of proving the exception, exemption, proviso, excuse or qualification shall be on him; and this notwithstanding that the information or complaint contains an allegation negativing the exception, exemption, proviso, excuse or qualification.

R v Edwards
[1975] QB 27
Court of Appeal

The defendant was convicted of selling intoxicating liquor without a justices' licence contrary to s. 160(1)(a) of the Licensing Act 1964. He was unrepresented at the trial and did not give evidence, but made an unsworn statement denying the occupation of the premises. He appealed against conviction on the ground that, since the prosecution had access to the register of licences under s. 34(2) of the Act, the prosecution should have called evidence to prove that there was no justices' licence in force.

LAWTON LJ: Mr Leonard, on behalf of the prosecution, submitted that section 81 [of the Magistrates' Courts Act 1952, the precursor of s. 101 of the Magistrates' Courts Act 1980] is a statutory statement of a common law rule applicable in all criminal courts. If it were not, the law would be in an unsatisfactory state, because the burden of proof in summary trials would be different from that in trials on indictment.

Mr Underhill, for the defendant, submitted, however, that at common law the burden of proving an exception, exemption, proviso, excuse or qualification only shifts when the facts constituting it are peculiarly within the accused's own knowledge and that they were not in this case because section 30(1) of the Licensing Act 1964 requires the clerk to the licensing justices for a licensing district to keep a register of licences, containing particulars of all justices' licences granted in the district, the premises for which they were granted, the names of the owners of those premises, and the names of the holders of the licences. It follows, submitted Mr Underhill, that the Brixton police had available to them in their own area a public source of knowledge which they could go to at any reasonable time: see section 34(2). If the rule about shifting the onus of proof only applies when the facts initiating the operation of the exception are peculiarly in the accused's own knowledge, there is much to be said for Mr Underhill's submission.

Mr Underhill accepted that there are three exceptions to the fundamental rule of our criminal law that the prosecution must prove every element of the alleged offence. The first relates to insanity and the second to those cases in which a statute expressly imposes a burden of proof upon an accused. The third exception has been under consideration in this appeal and questions have arisen as to its nature and the circumstances in which it applies.

The phrase which Mr Underhill used in making his submission, namely, 'facts peculiarly within the accused's own knowledge' has been used many times in textbooks and judgments: for example, per Lord Goddard CJ in *John v Humphreys* [1955] 1 WLR 325, 327; *Phipson on Evidence*, 11th ed (1970), p. 108 and *Cross, Evidence*, 3rd ed (1967), p. 81. It has been taken from the judgment of Bayley J in *R v Turner* (1816) 5 M & S 206, 211. If the rule only applies when the facts constituting exculpation are peculiarly within the defendant's own knowledge, we would have expected to have found reported cases giving some help as to how the courts were to decide this. If a query arises, should the judge or the jury decide who had what knowledge? Should evidence be called on this issue? If not, why not? In the century and a half since 1816 the defendant is unlikely to have been the first defendant wishing to query the extent of the prosecution's knowledge. Counsel brought no such cases to our attention and we have found none for ourselves. Despite the many times in the cases and textbooks reference has been made to the words used by Bayley J in *R v Turner*, we thought it necessary to examine that case carefully in its historical setting. For many decades before *R v Turner* there had been much discussion amongst lawyers as to how negative averments were to be pleaded in informations and indictments.

By the end of the 17th century a pleading distinction was drawn between a proviso in a statute and an exception: see *Hale's Pleas of the Crown* (1800 ed), vol. 2, pp. 170-171 (which was written about 1650) and *Jones v Axen* (1696) 1 Ld Raym 119. Exceptions had to be pleaded and disproved whereas there was no need either to plead or disprove provisos. In *R v Jarvis* (1754) 1 East 643 and referred to in *R v Stone* (1801) 1 East 639, 646, Lord Mansfield CJ stated the rule as follows:

> For it is a known distinction that what comes by way of proviso in a statute must be insisted on by way of defence by the party accused; but where exceptions are in the enacting part of a law, it must appear in the charge that the defendant does not fall within any of them.

In some cases, however, it was difficult to decide whether provisions in the enacting part of a statute were in the nature of a proviso. This is shown by the cases arising on *certiorari* out of the notorious game laws. These laws, which were statutory, prohibited those without certain qualifications (some 10 in number set out in the statute 22 & 23 Car 2, c. 25) from keeping a gun or being in possession of game. The problem for those drafting informations under these laws and conducting prosecutions was whether the defendant's alleged lack of qualification should be pleaded and proved. By the end of the 18th century it seems to have been accepted that in actions for penalties under the game laws lack of qualifications did not have to be proved: see *R v Stone* (1801) 1 East 639, 646, 650, 654. The problem of what had to be proved in a criminal case came before the King's Bench on *certiorari* in *R* v *Stone*. Before the justices the prosecution had not proved the defendant's lack of qualification. The court was equally divided, two of the judges (Lord Kenyon CJ and Grose J) being strongly of the opinion that the prosecution had to prove lack of qualification, whereas the other two (Lawrence and Le Blanc JJ) were of the contrary view. The court being equally divided, the conviction stood.

The approach to the problem by all four judges was substantially the same: to wit, their understanding of the rules of pleading. In the course of argument counsel adverted to the difficulty of proving negative averments and there was some discussion about this. Lord Kenyon CJ thought that some general evidence should be given from which lack of qualification could be inferred, whereas Lawrence J thought that proof of the act forbidden by the statute was enough to place the burden on the accused to show that he was qualified to do it. Lord Kenyon CJ's judgment is the foundation of the submissions which have been made in recent years that even when the prosecution seeks to rely upon the exception to the burden of proof rule which is said to derive from *R* v *Turner*, 5 M & S 206, it can only do so after having given some evidence, albeit slight, from which no lawful excuse can be inferred: see *R* v *Putland and Sorrell* [1946] 1 All ER 85 and *Buchanan* v *Moore* [1963] NI 194; both these cases will be discussed later in this judgment. The opinions of Lawrence and Le Blanc JJ were in accord with what was said in *Hawkins's Pleas of the Crown*, 7th ed (1795), vol. 4, bk. 2, c. 25, s. 113, p. 68:

> It seems agreed, that there is no need to allege in an indictment, that the defendant is not within the benefit of the provisos of a statute whereon it is founded; and this hath been adjudged, even as to those statutes which in their purview expressly take notice of the provisos; as by saying, that none shall do the thing prohibited, otherwise than in such special cases, etc. as are expressed in this act.

He cites a number of authorities starting with *Southwell's Case* (1595) Poph 93, where, in the enacting clause, the wording was 'otherwise than in such special cases ... expressed in this Act'. An illustration of how Serjeant Hawkins envisaged this rule would apply appears from a passage in *Pleas of the Crown*, 7th ed., vol. 2, c. 89, s. 17, p. 460, which was noted and approved in *R* v *Oliver* [1944] KB 68, 74. He was commenting on the form of indictment alleging an offence under the statute 9 & 10 Will. 3, c. 41, which enacted that no warlike naval stores should be made by any person

> ... not being a contractor with or authorised by the principal officers or commissioners of our said Lord the King, of the navy, ordinance, or ... victualling office, for the use of our said Lord the King, ...

It was his opinion that the indictment should allege that the prisoner was not an authorised person but he went on to say

> yet it is not incumbent on the prosecutors to prove this negative averment, but that it is incumbent on the defendant to show, if the truth be so, that he is within the exception in the statute.

These passages indicate first that by Serjeant Hawkins's time the old distinction between provisos and exceptions was becoming blurred, secondly that he, like the judges, based his opinion upon rules of pleading and thirdly that he did not associate the rule with the fact that the positive of a negative averment would, or might be, peculiarly within the defendant's own knowledge.

In our judgment *R* v *Turner*, 5 M & S 206 must be considered against this historical background. The point for discussion was the same as in *R* v *Stone*, 1 East 639. The information had alleged that the defendant, a carrier

> 'not . . . qualified or authorised by the laws of this realm' had had in his custody and possession pheasants and hares 'the same not being sent up or placed in [his] hands . . . by any person or persons qualified to kill game, . . .'

No evidence was called by the prosecution to prove want of qualification. The defendant's case on *certiorari* was argued by Scarlett, probably the most able advocate of his generation. He took two points: the first was technical as to the way the conviction had been drawn up; the second was an echo of what Lord Kenyon CJ had said in *R* v *Stone* about the need for *prima facie* evidence. The leading judgment was delivered by Lord Ellenborough CJ. He commented on the difficulty which would rest upon the prosecution of proving the lack of qualification and the ease with which the defendant could show he was qualified; but towards the end of his judgment he referred to Lord Mansfield CJ's opinion expressed in *Spieres* v *Parker* (1786) 1 Term Rep 141, as to the burden of proof resting on the defendant in actions upon the game laws and gave his own which was that he saw no reason why the same rule should not be applied to informations as well as actions. He ended at p. 211 as follows:

> I am, therefore, of opinion, that this conviction, which specifies negatively in the information the several qualifications mentioned in the statute, is sufficient, without going on to negative, by the evidence, those qualifications.

We read Lord Ellenborough CJ's judgment as being based on common law concepts of pleading, rather than on difficulties of proof, such difficulties being the reason why the rule of pleading had developed as it had. The second judgment was delivered by Bayley J. He started by referring at p. 211 to rules of pleading, namely:

> 'I have always understood it to be a general rule, that if a negative averment be made by one party, . . .' and added descriptive words qualifying the negative averment, 'which is peculiarly within the knowledge of the other, . . .'

As far as we have been able to discover from our researches this was the first time the rules of pleading which had been applied for so long were qualified in this way. The qualification cannot apply to all negative averments. There is not, and never has been, a general rule of law that the mere fact that a matter lies peculiarly within the knowledge of the defendant is sufficient to cast the onus on him. If there was any such rule, anyone charged with doing an unlawful act with a specified intent would find himself having to prove his innocence because if there ever was a matter which could be said to be peculiarly within a person's knowledge it is the state of his own mind. Such rule as there is relating to negative averments in informations and indictments developed from the rules for pleading provisos and exceptions in statutes and is limited in its application. No doubt the reason why the rules developed as they did was the common sense of the matter to which Lord Ellenborough CJ referred. In our judgment what Bayley J was doing was to state the reason for the rule as if it was the rule. The third judge, Holroyd J, at p. 213 used the phrase 'peculiarly within the knowledge of the party' but did so in order to demolish the argument that this case was an exception to the general rule of pleading.

It seems likely that practitioners in the decades which followed *R* v *Turner* did not regard Bayley J's words of qualification as a limitation upon an established rule. Thus in *Apothecaries' Co.* v *Bentley* (1824) Ry & M 159, which was an action for penalties under the statute 55 Geo. 3, c. 194, for practising as an apothecary without having obtained a certificate from the Society of Apothecaries of the City of London as required by that Act, no evidence was called by Scarlett, who appeared for the plaintiffs, to prove that they had not issued the defendant with a certificate or that he was exempted from the statute by the fact that he had been in practice before August 1815. Brougham, who was to become Lord Chancellor six years later, is reported at p. 160 as having put his argument as follows:

> The distinction he conceived was this, that where an exception was created by a distinct clause, the burden of showing that he was within it lay upon the defendant; but here the exception was introduced to qualify the penal clause in its very body, the negative therefore must be both stated and proved by the plaintiffs.

There was no submission that as a statutory corporation charged with the duty of examining apothecaries and issuing certificates to those qualified to practise, the plaintiffs would have known whether the defendant had obtained a certificate from them or had been in practice before the commencement of the Act so that the necessary qualification, or lack of it, was not peculiarly within his knowledge. *R v Turner*, 5 M & S 206 was cited to the court by Scarlett in answer to Brougham's submission. Abbott CJ's ruling was that the onus was on the defendant to prove he had a certificate and was based on concepts of pleading, not on the plaintiffs' opportunities of knowing. In our judgment it is most unlikely that an experienced advocate such as Brougham would have failed to appreciate that *R v Turner* only applied when the facts showing exception were peculiarly within the defendant's knowledge. *Starkie's Law of Evidence*, 2nd ed. (1833), vol. I, p. 365, states the rule in these terms:

> And in general, where it has been shown that the case falls within the scope of any general principle or rule of law, or the provision of any statute, whether remedial or even penal, it then lies on the opposite party to show by evidence that the case falls within an exception or proviso.

In 1848, by the Summary Jurisdiction Act 1848 (Jervis's Act), 11 & 12 Vict. c. 43, Parliament consolidated, amended and extended various statutes which had conferred summary jurisdiction on justices. The modern courts of summary jurisdiction came into being. The Act provided a statutory framework for the conduct of proceedings in those courts at all stages. Section 14 of the Act dealt with proceedings at the trial stage. It is clear that what Parliament was trying to do by this section was to adapt proceedings on indictment to the new type of court. The section had a proviso to the effect that if the information or complaint should negative 'any exception, proviso or condition' the prosecutor or complainant need not prove such negative, but the defendant might prove the affirmative. In our judgment the object of the proviso to section 14 was to apply the common law relating to exceptions and provisos to the new courts. After 1848 the courts put a restricted meaning on the word 'exception' in this proviso: see *Taylor v Humphries* (1864) 34 LJMC 1 and *Davis v Scrace* (1869) LR 4 CP 172. Parliament stopped this restricting tendency by the terms of section 39(2) of the Summary Jurisdiction Act 1879 as Lord Pearson said in *Nimmo v Alexander Cowan & Sons Ltd* [1968] AC 107, 135:

> ... these show an intention to widen the provision and to direct attention to the substance and effect rather than the form of the enactment to which it is to be applied.

Section 39(2) of the Act of 1879 was repeated by the Magistrates' Courts Act 1952 and replaced by section 81 of that Act. In our judgment section 81 of the Magistrates'

Courts Act 1952 sets out the common law rule in statutory form. Paragraph 5(2) of Schedule 1 to the Indictments Act 1915 contained a similar provision relating to the form of an indictment. This is now rule 6(c) of the Indictment Rules 1971, which provides as follows:

> It shall not be necessary [when charging an offence created by or under any enactment] to specify or negative an exception, exemption, proviso, excuse or qualification.

If it is not necessary to specify or negative exceptions and the like in a count, it is difficult to see on principle why it should be necessary to prove an element in the offence charged which has not been set out in the count.

Since 1816 there are a number of cases in the reports illustrating the shifting of the onus of proof on to the defendant to prove either that he held a licence to do an act which was otherwise prohibited by a statute or that he was exempted in some way. Thus in *R v Scott* (1921) 86 JP 69 the question arose whether the prosecution should have proved, which they did not, that the defendant, who was charged with an offence under the Dangerous Drugs Act 1920, was not authorised to supply specified drugs. That Act provided that no person should supply any of the specified drugs unless he was licensed by the Secretary of State to do so. Swift J held that if the defendant was licensed, it was a fact which was peculiarly within his own knowledge and there was no hardship on him in being put to the proof. We can see no difference between that case (which was approved by the Court of Criminal Appeal in *R v Oliver* [1944] KB 68 and cited by Lord Pearson with approval in *Nimmo v Alexander Cowan & Sons Ltd* [1968] AC 107) and this. There would have been no difficulty whatsoever in calling someone on the Secretary of State's staff to say that the defendant had not been licensed to supply the drugs.

The statutory prohibition of acts otherwise than under licence granted by a government department was a commonplace of life during the war years 1939 to 1945 and for some time afterwards. The problem as to who was to prove lack of a licence was considered fully in *R v Oliver* [1944] KB 68, 69–70. The appellant had been convicted on an indictment charging him with supplying sugar otherwise than under the terms of a licence, permit or other authority granted by the Ministry of Food, contrary to regulation 55 of the Defence (General) Regulations 1939 and Article 2 of the Sugar Control Order 1940. The prosecution did not prove that he had not been granted a licence and he appealed on that ground. Mr Slade, for the appellant, submitted that the rule shifting the onus to the defendant to prove he came within an exception did not apply 'as the information could easily have been obtained by the prosecution from official sources': see p. 69. The Solicitor-General who appeared for the prosecution, put his case in these terms, at p. 70:

> If a statute lays down that an act is prohibited except in the case of persons who are excepted, the onus is on the defendant to prove that he is within the excepted class.

The Court of Criminal Appeal accepted this submission; and in his judgment Viscount Caldecote CJ dealt with two points which Mr Slade had put forward in support of his main submission. Both had been canvassed in the 18th century and had echoed through the courts in the 19th; first, that although there was no need for the prosecution to prove that a proviso in a statute did not apply, this was not so with an exception; and secondly, the prosecution should have given *prima facie* evidence of the non-existence of a licence. As we have sought to show in this judgment, the old distinction between provisos and exceptions had been moribund, if not dead, for well over a century, although some life had been injected into it by Lord Alverstone CJ in *R* v *James* [1902] 1 KB 540, 545. As to this, Viscount Caldecote CJ said in *R* v *Oliver* [1944] KB 68, 73:

> With the greatest respect to the judgment of Lord Alverstone in *R* v *James*, it seems to us to be very difficult to make the result depend on the question whether the negative is of a proviso or of an exception. We think it makes no difference at all that the order was drafted as it now appears instead of being in a form which absolutely prohibits the supply of sugar except as thereinafter provided, with a later clause providing that if a person is supplied under a licence he should be excused.

As to the second point Viscount Caldecote CJ said plainly that the prosecution were under no necessity of giving *prima facie* evidence of the non-existence of a licence. As this point had been raised we infer that the court did not consider that the availability of evidence to the prosecution was a relevant factor in shifting the burden of proof.

R v *Oliver* was cited to the House of Lords in *Nimmo* v *Alexander Cowan & Sons Ltd* [1968] AC 107, which was concerned with the onus of pleading and proving in cases under section 29(1) of the Factories Act 1961 that it was not reasonably practicable to make and keep working places safe. Where the onus lay would, of course, be the same in both civil and criminal cases brought under that Act, although the standard of proof would be higher in criminal cases than in civil. None of their Lordships criticised *R* v *Oliver;* Lord Pearson clearly approved it. Not everyone has done so; for an example, see *Glanville Williams, Criminal Law*, 2nd ed [1961], pp. 901-904. In *R* v *Putland and Sorrell* [1946] 1 All ER 85 some judicial doubt was expressed as to how far *R* v *Oliver* went. The appellants were charged with having conspired to acquire, and having acquired, rationed goods, namely, silk stockings, without surrendering the appropriate number of coupons, in contravention of the Consumer Rationing Order 1944. No evidence was called by the prosecution to prove that coupons had not been surrendered. *R* v *Oliver* was cited, but Humphreys J, who delivered the judgment of the court, distinguished that case by stating that there was a very broad distinction between a statutory prohibition against doing an act, in which case it was for the defendant to prove that he might do it lawfully, and a statutory prohibition against doing an act otherwise than in a particular way, as for example by surrendering coupons, in which case it was for the prosecution to give *prima facie* evidence that the specified lawful way had not been followed. We have been unable to appreciate the difference between the two types of case. The court had clearly been impressed, as had Lord Kenyon CJ, 150 years before in *R* v *Stone*, 1 East 639, by the argument that the shifting of the onus of proof could be oppressive; but under the Defence (General) Regulations the only difference between a wholesaler of sugar called upon to justify his trade in that commodity and a man wearing a new shirt (one of the examples given by Humphreys J) called upon to prove that he had acquired it lawfully might be that one could do so more easily than the other. We find this difference not substantial enough to justify distinguishing *R* v *Oliver*.

In *John* v *Humphreys* [1955] 1 WLR 325 the Divisional Court had to consider the problem of the onus of proof in a case of a defendant who had been charged with driving a motor vehicle on a road without being the holder of a licence. He did not appear at the hearing before the justices and no evidence was called other than to prove that he had driven a motor vehicle along a road. The justices were of the opinion that mere proof of driving (that not being in itself an unlawful act) was not enough to support the charge and that before the burden of proving that he was the holder of a licence passed to the defendant the prosecution should have established a *prima facie* case. They dismissed the information. The prosecutor appealed. Before the justices he had argued that the burden of proving the holding of a licence lay on the defendant since it was a fact peculiarly within his knowledge; as indeed it was. It would have been impracticable for the prosecution to have proved that no licensing authority had issued a licence. It follows that this case is of little help on the question whether *R* v *Turner* (1816) 5 M & S 206 applies when the prosecution can prove a defendant's lack of qualification or lawful excuse. The court decided that there was no need for the prosecution to establish a *prima facie* case. Ormerod J expressed some hesitation on this point but concluded that the court was bound by the decision in *R* v *Oliver*. . . .

In our judgment this line of authority establishes that over the centuries the common law, as a result of experience and the need to ensure that justice is done both to the community and to defendants, has evolved an exception to the fundamental rule of our criminal law that the prosecution must prove every element of the offence charged. This exception, like so much else in the common law, was hammered out on the anvil of pleading. It is limited to offences arising under enactments which prohibit the doing of an act save in specified circumstances or by persons of specified classes or with specified qualifications or with the licence or permission of specified authorities. Whenever the prosecution seeks to rely on this exception, the court must construe the enactment under which the charge is laid. If the true construction is that the enactment prohibits the doing of acts, subject to provisos, exemptions and the like, then the prosecution can rely upon the exception.

In our judgment its application does not depend upon either the fact, or the presumption, that the defendant has peculiar knowledge enabling him to prove the positive of any negative averment. As Wigmore pointed out in his great *Treatise on Evidence* [1905], vol. 4 p. 3525, this concept of peculiar knowledge furnishes no working rule. If it did, defendants would have to prove lack of intent. What does provide a working rule is what the common law evolved from a rule of pleading. We have striven to identify it in this judgment. Like nearly all rules it could be applied oppressively; but the courts have ample powers to curb and discourage oppressive prosecutors and do not hesitate to use them.

Two consequences follow from the view we have taken as to the evolution and nature of this exception. First, as it comes into operation upon an enactment being construed in a particular way, there is no need for the prosecution to prove a *prima facie* case of lack of excuse, qualification or the like; and secondly, what shifts is the onus: it is for the defendant to prove that he was entitled to do the prohibited act. What rests on him is the legal or, as it is sometimes called, the persuasive burden of proof. It is not the evidential burden.

When the exception as we have adjudged it to be is applied to this case it was for the defendant to prove that he was the holder of a justices' licence, not the prosecution.

Appeal dismissed.

Questions
1.   Can this decision be reconciled with the speech of Lord Sankey LC in *Woolmington* v *DPP*, above.
2.   Do you agree with Lawton LJ's statement that the burden of proof had to be placed on the accused 'to ensure that justice is done both to the community and to defendants'?

3. If D is charged with driving a motor vehicle without having appropriate insurance, who will bear the burden of proof?
4. Would (or should) it make any difference if D were charged with driving a motor vehicle without having an appropriate driving licence?

R v Hunt
[1987] AC 352
House of Lords

The Misuse of Drugs Regulations 1973, as amended, provide by reg. 4(1) that the Misuse of Drugs Act 1971, ss. 3(1) and 5(1), which prohibit the importation, exportation and possession of controlled drugs, do not have effect in relation to the controlled drugs specified in Sch. 1 to the regulations.

The appellant was convicted of possessing a controlled drug contrary to the 1971 Act, s. 5(2). A quantity of white powder had been found at his house which, when analysed, was found to contain morphine mixed with caffeine and atropine. On appeal it was held that the burden of proving that the preparation of morphine fell within the exceptions contained in the 1973 Regulations rested on the appellant. He appealed to the House of Lords arguing, *inter alia*, that *R v Edwards* [1975] QB 27 had been wrongly decided.

LORD GRIFFITHS: I propose first to consider the argument based upon *Woolmington* v *Director of Public Prosecutions* [1935] AC 462. The starting point is the celebrated passage in the speech of Viscount Sankey LC, at pp. 481-482:

> Throughout the web of the English criminal law one golden thread is always to be seen, that it is the duty of the prosecution to prove the prisoner's guilt subject to what I have already said as to the defence of insanity and subject also to any statutory exception. If, at the end of and on the whole of the case, there is a reasonable doubt, created by the evidence given by either the prosecution or the prisoner, as to whether the prisoner killed the deceased with a malicious intention, the prosecution has not made out the case and the prisoner is entitled to an acquittal. No matter what the charge or where the trial, the principle that the prosecution must prove the guilt of the prisoner is part of the common law of England and no attempt to whittle it down can be entertained.

The appellant submits that in using the phrase 'any statutory exception' Lord Sankey LC was referring to statutory exceptions in which Parliament had by the use of express words placed the burden of proof on the accused, in the same way as the judges in *M'Naghten's Case* (1843) 10 Cl & Fin 200 had expressly placed the burden of proving insanity upon the accused. There are, of course, many examples of such statutory drafting of which a number are to be found in this Act — see section 5(4): 'In any proceedings for an offence under subsection (2) above in which it is proved that the accused had a controlled drug in his possession, it shall be a defence for him to prove — ...' (see also section 28(2)(3)). Examples in other Acts are to be found conveniently collected in *Phipson on Evidence*, 13th ed (1982), p. 51, note 68.

The appellant also relies upon a passage in the speech of Viscount Simon LC in *Mancini* v *Director of Public Prosecutions* [1942] AC 1 in which he said, at p. 11:

Woolmington's case is concerned with explaining and reinforcing the rule that the prosecution must prove the charge it makes beyond reasonable doubt, and, consequently, that if, on the material before the jury, there is a reasonable doubt, the prisoner should have the benefit of it. The rule is of general application in all charges under the criminal law. The only exceptions arise, as explained in *Woolmington's* case, in the defence of insanity and in offences where onus of proof is specially dealt with by statute.

It is submitted that the use of the word 'specially' indicates that Lord Simon LC considered that the reference in *Woolmington* [1935] AC 462 was limited to express statutory burdens of proof.

From this premise, it is argued that as it is well settled that if a defendant raises any of the common law defences such as accident, self-defence, provocation or duress and there is evidence to support such a defence the judge must leave it to the jury with a direction that the burden is on the prosecution to negative that defence, so it must follow that if a defendant raises any statutory defence the same rule must apply, and provided there is evidence to support such a defence the burden lies on the prosecution to negative it, the only exceptions to this rule being those cases in which the statute has by express words placed the burden of proving the defence upon the defendant.

However, in *Woolmington* the House was not concerned to consider the nature of a statutory defence or upon whom the burden of proving it might lie. The House was considering a defence of accident to a charge of murder and were concerned to correct a special rule which appeared to have emerged in charges of murder whereby once it was proved that the defendant had killed the deceased a burden was held to lie upon the defendant to excuse himself by proving that it was the result of an accident or that he had been provoked to do so or had acted in self-defence. This in effect relieved the prosecution of the burden of proving an essential element in the crime of murder, namely the malicious intent and placed the burden upon the accused to disprove it. It was this aberration that was so trenchantly corrected by Lord Sankey LC in the passage already cited [1935] AC 462, 481-482. In *Mancini* the House dealt with the duty of the judge to lay before the jury any line of defence which the facts might reasonably support and they also dealt with the particular nature of the defence of provocation. In neither appeal was the House concerned with a statutory defence and no argument was addressed on the nature or scope of statutory exceptions.

Before the decision in *Woolmington* [1935] AC 462 there had been a number of cases in which in trials on indictment the courts had held that the burden of establishing a statutory defence fell upon the defendant although the statute did not expressly so provide: see for example *R* v *Turner* (1816) 5 M & S 206, a decision under the Gaming Acts, and *Apothecaries' Co.* v *Bentley* (1824) 1 C & P 538 and *R* v *Scott* (1921) 86 JP 69, decisions in which it was held that the defendant had the burden of proving that he was licensed to perform an otherwise prohibited act.

I cannot accept that either Viscount Sankey LC or Lord Simon LC intended to cast doubt on these long-standing decisions without having had the benefit of any argument addressed to the House on the question of statutory exceptions. I am, therefore, unwilling to read the reference to 'any statutory exception' in *Woolmington*, at p. 481, in the restricted sense in which the appellant invites us to read it. It is also to be observed that Lord Devlin in *Jayesena* v *The Queen* [1970] AC 618, a decision of the Privy Council, commenting upon *Woolmington* said, at p. 623:

> The House laid it down that, save in the case of insanity or of a statutory defence, there was no burden laid on the prisoner to prove his innocence and that it was sufficient for him to raise a doubt as to his guilt.

Lord Devlin does not appear to restrict a statutory defence to one in which the burden of proof is expressly placed upon the defendant.

In *R v Edwards* [1975] QB 27, the defendant had been convicted in the Crown Court of selling intoxicating liquor without a justices' licence contrary to section 160(1)(a) of the Licensing Act 1964. Section 160(l)(a) provides:

> Subject to the provisions of this Act, if any person — (a) sells or exposes for sale by retail any intoxicating liquor without holding a justices' licence or canteen licence authorising him to hold an excise licence for the sale of that liquor ... he shall be guilty of an offence under this section.

The prosecution had called no evidence that the defendant did not have a licence and he appealed on the ground that the burden was on the prosecution to establish the lack of a licence. The Court of Appeal held that the burden was on the defendant to prove that he held a licence and that as he had not done so he was rightly convicted.

After an extensive review of the authorities the Court of Appeal held that the same rule applied to trials on indictment as was applied to summary trial by section 81 of the Magistrates' Court Act 1952 which provided:

> Where the defendant to an information or complaint relies for his defence on any exception, exemption, proviso, excuse or qualification, whether or not it accompanies the description of the offence or matter of complaint in the enactment creating the offence or on which the complaint is founded, the burden of proving the exception, exemption, proviso, excuse or qualification shall be on him; and this notwithstanding that the information or complaint contains an allegation negativing the exception, exemption, proviso, excuse or qualification.

(Section 81 of that Act has now been repealed and re-enacted in identical language in section 101 of the Magistrates' Courts Act 1980.)

A study of the old cases and practitioners' books led the court to conclude that when Parliament established a new system of summary jurisdiction by the Summary Jurisdiction Act 1848 (Jervis's Act), (11 & 12 Vict. c. 43) and enacted in section 14, which deals with proceedings on the hearing of complaints and informations, the following proviso:

> Provided always, that if the information or complaint in any such case shall negative any exemption, exception, proviso, or condition in the statute on which the same shall be framed, it shall not be necessary for the prosecutor or complainant in that behalf to prove such negative, but the defendant may prove the affirmative thereof in his defence, if he would have advantage of the same

they were there stating the common law rule as to proof that the judges then applied to trials on indictment.

Mr Zucker in a most interesting argument has challenged that conclusion and submitted that the common law rule at that time was that an exception contained in the same clause of the Act which created the offence had to be negatived by the prosecution but if the exception or proviso were in a subsequent clause of a statute or, although in the same section, were not incorporated with the enabling clause by words of reference it was a matter of defence. From this general rule Mr Zucker submits that there were but two exceptions, namely, the burden on a defendant under the gaming laws to show that he was qualified to keep guns, bows, dogs, etc., and, secondly, that where an act was prohibited unless done pursuant to a stipulated licence or authority the defendant had to prove that he possessed the necessary licence or authority.

The authorities certainly show that a rule of pleading had evolved by the beginning of the last century, and probably well before that, in the form of the general rule stated by Mr Zucker. One of the more celebrated statements of the rule is Lord Mansfield CJ's *dictum* in *R* v *Jarvis* (1754) 1 East 643, 645n:

> For it is a known distinction that what comes by way of proviso in a statute must be insisted on by way of defence by the party accused; but where exceptions are in the enacting part of a law, it must appear in the charge that the defendant does not fall within any of them.

However, as Mr Zuckerman demonstrates in his learned article 'The Third Exception to the *Woolmington* Rule' (1976) 92 LQR 402 the judges did not always regard the rules of pleading and the rules as to the burden of proof as being the same. In *Spieres* v *Parker* (1786) 1 Durn & E 141 Lord Mansfield CJ said, at p. 144, that the prosecutor must 'negative the exceptions in the enacting clause, though he threw the burden of proof upon the other side.' And in *Jelfs* v *Ballard* (1799) 1 Bos & Pul 467, 468 Buller J said: 'The plaintiff must state in his *scire facias* everything that entitles him to recover; but it is a very different question what is to be proved by one party and what by the other.'

Sometimes, however, the judges do appear to have applied the old pleading rules to determine the burden of proof. In *Taylor* v *Humphries* (1864) 17 CBNS 539, a publican was charged with opening his premises on a Sunday before 12.30 in the afternoon otherwise than for the refreshment of travellers. The question for the court was upon whom the burden of proof lay to show that those found drinking in the premises at 11.20 in the morning were 'travellers.' In the course of giving judgment Erle CJ, referring to the argument on behalf of the publican, said, at p. 549:

> He further contended, that, as the exception of refreshment to a traveller is contained in the clause creating the prohibition, the burden of proving that the prohibition has been infringed, and that the case is not within the exception, is cast on the informer ... In this argument we think the appellant is well founded, and that the statute ought to be construed on the principles that he has contended for.

In *Davis* v *Scrace* (1869) LR 4 CP 172 a publican had been prosecuted under the Metropolitan Police Act 1839 (2 & 3 Vict. c. 47) for selling liquor before one in the afternoon on a Sunday. The Act provided, by section 42: no licensed victualler or other person shall open his house within the metropolitan police district for the sale of wine, spirits [etc.] on Sundays, Christmas Day, and Good Friday before the hour of one in the afternoon, except refreshment for travellers.

The court held that they were bound to follow *Taylor* v *Humphries*, 17 CBNS 539. Brett J said, at pp. 176-177:

> It is quite impossible to distinguish this case from *Taylor* v *Humphries* ... They seem to have held that, though the word 'except' is used in 11 & 12 Vict. c. 49, s. 1, it is not in truth an exception within the meaning of the proviso in section 14 of 11 & 12 Vict. c. 43 [Summary Jurisdiction Act 1848] and that therefore that proviso had no application to the case in hand. I think we must adopt the same construction here.

It seems likely that these cases played their part in leading Parliament to repeal section 14 of the Act of 1848 and to replace it by section 39(2) of the Summary Jurisdiction Act 1879 (42 & 43 Vict. c. 49) which was in substantially the same language as the present section 101 of the Act of 1980. As Lord Pearson pointed out in *Nimmo* v *Alexander Cowan & Sons Ltd* [1968] AC 107, Parliament was here emphasising that it was the substance and effect as well as the form of the enactment that mattered when considering upon whom it was intended that the burden of proof should lie under any particular Act.

It seems to me that the probabilities are that Parliament when it enacted section 14 of the Act of 1848 was intending to apply to summary trial that which they believed to be the rule relating to burden of proof evolved by the judges on trials on indictment. It seems unlikely that Parliament would have wished to introduce confusion by providing for different burdens of proof in summary trials as opposed to trials on indictment. Looking back over so many years, this must, to some extent, be speculation and I bear in mind that whereas the defendant could give evidence on his own behalf in a summary trial it was not until 1898 that he was allowed to do so in a trial on indictment which might be a reason for placing a heavier burden of proof on the prosecution in trials on indictment.

However, my Lords, the common law adapts itself and evolves to meet the changing patterns and needs of society; it is not static. By the time the Act of 1879 was passed there were already many offences that were triable both summarily and on indictment. This list of offences has been growing steadily and the very crime with which we are concerned in this appeal is such an example. It is conceded that in the case of exceptions within the meaning of section 101 of the Act of 1980 the burden of proving the exception has been specifically placed upon the defendant. The law would have developed on absurd lines if in respect of the same offence the burden of proof today differed according to whether the case was heard by the magistrates or on indictment. I observe that there would be no possibility of presenting such a submission in respect of a crime triable in Scotland for the Criminal Procedure (Scotland) Act 1975, by sections 66 and 312(v), applies the same rule as to the burden of proof in respect of exceptions to both trials on indictment and summary trials. Although the language of sections 66 and 312(v) is slightly different from section 101 of the Act of 1980 it is to the like effect.

There have been a number of cases considered by the Court of Appeal since *Woolmington* v *Director of Public Prosecutions* [1935] AC 462 concerning the burden of proof in licensing cases both on indictment and on summary trial. There is no indication in any of these cases that the court considered that there should be any difference of approach to the burden of proof according to whether the case was tried summarily or on indictment: see *R* v *Oliver* [1944] KB 68, *R* v *Putland and Sorrell* [1946] 1 All ER 85, *John* v *Humphreys* [1955] 1 WLR 325, *Robertson* v *Bannister* [1973] RTR 109; see also *R* v *Ewens* [1967] 1 QB 322 in which it was held that the Drugs (Prevention of Misuse) Act 1964 on its true construction placed an onus on the defendant to show that he was in possession of a prohibited drug by virtue of the issue of a prescription by a duly qualified medical practitioner.

Mr Zucker relied upon three recent decisions of the Court of Appeal which he submitted support his submission that a statutory defence only places an evidentiary burden on the defendant to raise the defence and that if this is done the burden remains on the prosecution to negative the defence. They are *R* v *Burke* (1978) 67 Cr App R 220, *R* v *McPherson* [1973] RTR 157, *R* v *Cousins* [1982] QB 526. In none of these cases was *R* v *Edwards* [1975] QB 27 either cited in argument or referred to in the judgment. In each case the Court of Appeal construed the relevant statutory provision as requiring the burden of proof to be discharged by the prosecution. I do not regard these cases as intending to cast any doubt upon the correctness of the decision in *R* v *Edwards,* or as support for the proposition for which they were cited.

Whatever may have been its genesis I am satisfied that the modern rule was encapsulated by Lord Wilberforce in *Nimmo* v *Alexander Cowan & Sons Ltd* [1968]

AC 107, 130, when speaking of the Scottish section which was then the equivalent of the present section 101 of the Magistrates' Courts Act 1980: 'I would think, then, that the section merely states the orthodox principle (common to both the criminal and the civil law) that exceptions, etc., are to be set up by those who rely on them.'

I would summarise the position thus far by saying that *Woolmington* [1935] AC 462 did not lay down a rule that the burden of proving a statutory defence only lay upon the defendant if the statute specifically so provided: that a statute can, on its true construction, place a burden of proof on the defendant although it does not do so expressly: that if a burden of proof is placed on the defendant it is the same burden whether the case be tried summarily or on indictment, namely, a burden that has to be discharged on the balance of probabilities.

The real difficulty in these cases lies in determining upon whom Parliament intended to place the burden of proof when the statute has not expressly so provided. It presents particularly difficult problems of construction when what might be regarded as a matter of defence appears in a clause creating the offence rather than in some subsequent proviso from which it may more readily be inferred that it was intended to provide for a separate defence which a defendant must set up and prove if he wishes to avail himself of it. This difficulty was acutely demonstrated in *Nimmo* v *Alexander Cowan & Sons Ltd* [1968] AC 107. Section 29(1) of the Factories Act 1961 provides:

> There shall, so far as is reasonably practicable, be provided and maintained safe means of access to every place at which any person has at any time to work, and every such place shall, so far as is reasonably practicable, be made and kept safe for any person working there.

The question before the House was whether the burden of proving that it was not reasonably practicable to make the working place safe lay upon the defendant or the plaintiff in a civil action. However, as the section also created a summary offence the same question would have arisen in a prosecution. In the event, the House divided three to two on the construction of the section, Lord Reid and Lord Wilberforce holding that the section required the plaintiff or prosecution to prove that it was reasonably practicable to make the working place safe, the majority, Lord Guest, Lord Upjohn and Lord Pearson, holding that if the plaintiff or prosecution proved that the working place was not safe it was for the defendant to excuse himself by proving that it was not reasonably practicable to make it safe. However, their Lordships were in agreement that if the linguistic construction of the statute did not clearly indicate upon whom the burden should lie the court should look to other considerations to determine the intention of Parliament such as the mischief at which the Act was aimed and practical considerations affecting the burden of proof and, in particular, the ease or difficulty that the respective parties would encounter in discharging the burden. I regard this last consideration as one of great importance for surely Parliament can never lightly be taken to have intended to impose an onerous duty on a defendant to prove his innocence in a criminal case, and a court should be very slow to draw any such inference from the language of a statute.

When all the cases are analysed, those in which the courts have held that the burden lies on the defendant are cases in which the burden can be easily discharged. This point can be demonstrated by what, at first blush, appear to be two almost indistinguishable cases that arose under wartime regulations. In *R* v *Oliver* [1944] KB 68 the defendant was prosecuted for selling sugar without a licence. The material part of the Sugar (Control) Order 1940 (SR & O 1940 No. 1068) by article 2 provided: Subject to any directions given or except under and in accordance with the terms of a licence permit or other authority granted by or on behalf of the Minister no ... wholesaler shall by way of trade ... supply ... any sugar.

The Court of Criminal Appeal held that this placed the burden upon the defendant to prove that he had the necessary licence to sell sugar. In *R v Putland and Sorrell* [1946] 1 All ER 85, the defendant was charged with acquiring silk stockings without surrendering clothing coupons. The material part of the Consumer *Rationing (Consolidation) Order* 1944 (SR & O 1944 No. 800) article 4 provided: A person shall not acquire rationed goods ... without surrendering ... coupons. The Court of Criminal Appeal there held that the burden was upon the prosecution to prove that the clothing had been bought without the surrender of coupons. The real distinction between these two cases lies in the comparative difficulty which would face a defendant in discharging the burden of proof.

In *Oliver's* case [1944] KB 68 it would have been a simple matter for the defendant to prove that he had a licence if such was the case but in the case of purchase of casual articles of clothing it might, as the court pointed out in *Putland's* case, be a matter of the utmost difficulty for a defendant to establish that he had given the appropriate number of coupons for them. It appears to me that it was this consideration that led the court to construe that particular regulation as imposing the burden of proving that coupons had not been surrendered upon the prosecution.

In *R v Edwards* [1975] QB 27, 39–40 the Court of Appeal expressed their conclusion in the form of an exception to what they said was the fundamental rule of our criminal law that the prosecution must prove every element of the offence charged. They said that the exception: 'is limited to offences arising under enactments which prohibit the doing of an act save in specified circumstances or by persons of specified classes or with specified qualifications or with the licence or permission of specified authorities.'

I have little doubt that the occasions upon which a statute will be construed as imposing a burden of proof upon a defendant which do not fall within this formulation are likely to be exceedingly rare. But I find it difficult to fit *Nimmo v Alexander Cowan & Sons Ltd* [1968] AC 107 into this formula, and I would prefer to adopt the formula as an excellent guide to construction rather than as an exception to a rule. In the final analysis each case must turn upon the construction of the particular legislation to determine whether the defence is an exception within the meaning of section 101 of the Act of 1980 which the Court of Appeal rightly decided reflects the rule for trials on indictment. With this one qualification I regard *R v Edwards* as rightly decided.

My Lords, I am, of course, well aware of the body of distinguished academic opinion that urges that wherever a burden of proof is placed upon a defendant by statute the burden should be an evidential burden and not a persuasive burden, and that it has the support of the distinguished signatories to the 11th Report of the Criminal Law Revision Committee, Evidence (General) (1972) (Cmnd. 4991). My Lords, such a fundamental change is, in my view, a matter for Parliament and not a decision of your Lordships' House.'

(The House held that on its true construction regulation 4(1) of the 1973 Regulations dealt not with exceptions to what would otherwise be unlawful but with the definition of the essential ingredients of an offence; and that, as it was not an offence to possess morphine in one form but an offence to possess it in another form, it had been for the prosecution to prove that the morphine in the possession of the appellant had been in the prohibited form, which it had not done, and no burden had fallen on the appellant.)

(LORDS KEITH of KINKEL and MACKAY of CLASHFERN agreed with LORD GRIFFITHS. LORDS TEMPLEMAN and ACKNER also delivered a judgment in favour of allowing the appeal.)

Appeal allowed.

P. Healy, 'Proof and Policy: No Golden Threads'
[1987] Crim LR 355, pp. 361–3

Woolmington in eclipse?

Lawton LJ's assertion in *Edwards* of a third exception was problematic on its face because he also said that such exceptions existed by virtue of a common-law rule of statutory interpretation. Did this mean a common-law or statutory exception to the rule in *Woolmington*? This ambiguity is aggravated in *Hunt*. It might be claimed that implied statutory exceptions find their source in the statute, coming to light only with the divining skills of the court; alternatively, it could be argued with equal force that the rule by which the courts discern implied statutory exceptions, being not a statutory rule, exists only at common law. The resolution of this point is largely moot because the significance attaching to either alternative is the same: the range of exceptions is open to expansion for flexible reasons of policy.

There is no conclusive authority that restricts the category of common-law exceptions to insanity, even if it might be thought that such a restriction was contemplated by Viscount Sankey. The reasons of the majority in *Hunt* suggest that there is nothing to prevent a subsequent court from concluding that reasons of policy militating in favour of an implied statutory exception might likewise warrant other deviations from the principle in *Woolmington* and an expansion of the exceptions at common law.

Wigmore was of the view that there is no rule of general application that governs the allocation of the burden of proof:

> The truth is that there is not and cannot be any general solvent for all cases. It is merely a question of policy and fairness based on experience in the different situations.
> . . .
> There is, then, no one principle, or set of harmonious principles, which ensure a sure and universal test for the solution of a given class of cases. The logic of the situation does not demand such a test; it would be useless to discover or invent one; and the state of the law does not justify us in saying that it has accepted any. There are merely specific rules for specific classes of cases, resting for their ultimate basis upon broad reasons of experience and fairness.

In the past, of course, it has been claimed that there are clear rules concerning the allocation of the burden of proof, such as the 'rule' against proof of a negative or the requirement of proof of facts peculiarly within the knowledge of a party. These are clearly not rules, however, but examples of expedient reasons of policy that may impel the legislature or a court to allocate the onus of proof to one party or the other. These reasons may be found among many others, including ease or difficulty of proof, the probability or improbability attending to the fact in issue, positive or negative averments, the jeopardy of the accused, and 'the most desirable outcome in terms of social policy in the absence of proof of the particular fact.' With regard to the allocation of a legal burden to the accused, it has been proposed that the accused should not have to discharge any obligation more onerous than an evidential burden. It could equally be argued that there are compelling reasons for standardising defences by requiring that the accused discharge a legal burden in respect of, say, any affirmative defence, whether it be a common-law or statutory defence.

After *Hunt*, however, the position in England is now quite incoherent. There is no class of issues or cases to which a discrete and cogent body of principles applies to justify an exception to the rule in *Woolmington*. There are only sufficient reasons of policy in instant cases. According to the majority, a judge faced with ambiguous legislation may determine the allocation of the inculpatory and exculpatory elements of an offence, and the allocation of the legal burden, by asking whether there are overriding considerations of policy or practical convenience to compel the conclusion that Parliament must have intended to imply a statutory defence on which the accused should bear a legal burden. To say that this approach is warranted in law by *Nimmo* is only to erect implied legislative intent as a conceit or fiction for judicial policy-making and judicial legislation. Moreover, the majority's analysis defies formulation in prescriptive terms for the guidance of trial judges, prosecutors and defending counsel.

The majority was undoubtedly daunted by the practical consequences that would follow from overruling *Edwards*, particularly in conjunction with regulatory offences. Prospective affirmation of *Edwards* can thus be seen as an unarticulated major premise in their Lordships' approach to the issue. This may be criticised as a policy that is inconsistent with the principles enunciated in *Woolmington* and as an approach to decision-making that can only be handled consistently or coherently by appellate courts. Although the legislature is notoriously inconsistent with regard to the form and substance of exceptions to the rule in *Woolmington* and with regard to the reasons for deploying such exceptions, Hunt raises some cause for alarm because it suggests that the appellate courts should not be reticent to complete what Parliament failed to do clearly.

Questions
1. Does the decision in *Hunt* confuse or clarify the law?
2. Can the decision in *Hunt*, as Healy suggests, be explained on policy grounds?
3. The Misuse of Musical Equipment Act provides:

> 1 It shall be an offence to play any personal radio or cassette while on public transport or in any other public place to the annoyance of another.
> 2 No offence is committed under s. 1 above if the radio or cassette in question is constructed or adapted so as to restrict its noise output to a maximum of 10 decibels.

D is charged with an offence under this Act following complaint from a passenger on a train. Consider any issues which might arise concerning the burden of proof where:

(a) the radio/cassette emits a noise level of 15 decibels;
(b) D states he relied on the manufacturer's claim that the radio/cassette is incapable of producing a noise level in excess of 10 decibels;
(c) D claims he removed an internal part of the radio/cassette so it could only emit a maximum noise level of 8 decibels.

(B) The standard of proof

Where a legal burden is placed on a party to prove an issue, the question arises as to the degree of proof necessary to satisfy the trier of fact on that issue. The standard of proof refers to how much more, or better quality, evidence needs to be adduced in order to persuade the trier of the facts to find in his favour. The most apparent difference which exists is that between civil cases and criminal cases. In civil cases, the standard of proof is said to be satisfied on 'a balance of probabilities', whereas in criminal cases the standard of proof is satisfied only where the prosecution adduce evidence demonstrating guilt 'beyond any reasonable doubt'. It is the degree of importance attached to the liberty of the subject which is usually cited as the main justification for demanding a higher standard of proof in criminal cases than in civil cases. Despite this, some judges and writers have argued that there is no need for differing standards of proof, taking the view that if a matter is proved, it is proved. Yet, as the learned editor of *Cross on Evidence* puts it, 'it can hardly be doubted that there are degrees of probability. If this much is conceded, the law can intelligibly require that a very high degree must be established by the prosecution at a criminal trial'.

Further, what should happen if one party to a civil case alleges criminal conduct has been committed by another party in the case? Does this mean that although the matter is being litigated in the civil courts, some degree of proof higher than that normally required in civil matters applies?

(i)   Criminal cases

Miller v *Minister of Pensions*
[1947] 2 All ER 372
King's Bench

The applicant's husband served in the army from 1915 until his death in 1944. He served in the Middle East from 1940 until 1944, when he became hoarse and found difficulty in eating. He reported sick and he was diagnosed as having cancer of the gullet. He died within a month of reporting sick. The tribunal rejected the applicant's claim for the higher pension granted to widows of soldiers whose death was due to war service. The applicant appealed on the ground that the tribunal had not properly directed itself as to the burden of proof.

DENNING J: [T]he degree of cogency ... required in a criminal case before an accused person is found guilty ... is well settled. It need not reach certainty, but it must carry a high degree of probability. Proof beyond reasonable doubt does not mean proof beyond a shadow of a doubt. The law would fail to protect the community if it admitted fanciful possibilities to deflect the course of justice. If the evidence is so strong against a man as to leave only a remote possibility in his favour which can be dismissed with the sentence 'of course it is possible, but not in the least probable,' the case is proved beyond reasonable doubt, but nothing short of that will suffice. . . .

R v *Hepworth and Fearnley*
[1955] 2 QB 600
Court of Criminal Appeal

LORD GODDARD CJ: The appellants were convicted before the recorder of Bradford of the offence of receiving wool, an offence which is by no means uncommon in Yorkshire. I have no doubt that for the most part, at any rate, juries drawn from the citizens of Bradford know perfectly well what their duty is in trying offences of that description. They have to find and feel sure that the goods have been stolen, that they have got into the possession of the accused persons and that the accused knew that they were stolen.

Having read the evidence in this case one is not surprised that the jury found these men guilty, but complaint is made in the case — and the jury were certainly out a very long time before they arrived at their verdict — that the recorder in summing up did not give the jury any direction with regard to the burden of proof, and did not give them a sufficient direction with regard to the duty of a jury and how they were to regard the evidence and the degree of certainty they were to feel.

First, with regard to the burden of proof, it is always desirable that a jury should be told that the burden of proof is on the prosecution. I have no doubt that, in most cases, they know it, but it is desirable that they should be told that it is for the prosecution to prove the case. It is also most desirable that emphasis should be laid upon that in a receiving case. In such a case it is generally desirable, although there may be circumstances in the particular case which would not render it necessary, to remind the jury first, that the burden of proof remains on the prosecution; secondly, to tell them that if an explanation for possession of the goods is given by the accused, although the jury may not be convinced that it is true, if they think that it may be true it would mean that the prosecution have not proved the case because the jury would remain in some degree of doubt. It is not necessary to use on all occasions the formula which was used in R v Schama and Abramovitch (1914) 11 Cr App R 45 because that case, which is constantly cited in these matters relating to receiving, as I have said more than once in giving judgment in appeals, lays down no more than this: if the explanation given by the accused persons which, when they have given it becomes part of the sum of evidence in the case, leaves the jury in doubt whether the accused honestly or dishonestly received the goods, they are entitled to be acquitted because the case has not been proved. A case is never proved if any jury is left in any degree of doubt.

Another thing that is said in the present case is that the recorder only used the word 'satisfied'. It may be, especially considering the number of cases recently in which this question has arisen, that I misled courts because I said in R v Summers (1952) 36 Cr App R 14 — and I still adhere to it — that I thought that it was very unfortunate to talk to juries about 'reasonable doubt' because the explanations given as to what is and what is not a reasonable doubt are so very often extraordinarily difficult to follow and it is very difficult to tell a jury what is a reasonable doubt. To tell a jury that it must not be a fanciful doubt is something that is without any real guidance. To tell them that a reasonable doubt is such a doubt as to cause them to hesitate in their own affairs never seems to me to convey any particular standard; one member of the jury might say he would hesitate over something and another member might say that that would not cause him to hesitate at all. I therefore suggested that it would be better to use some other expression, by which I meant to convey to the jury that they should only convict if they felt sure of the guilt of the accused. It may be that in some cases the word 'satisfied' is enough. Then, it is said that the jury in a civil case has to be satisfied and, therefore, one is only laying down the same standard of proof as in a civil case. I confess that I have had some difficulty in understanding how there is or there can be two standards; therefore, one would be on safe ground if one said in a criminal case to a jury: 'You must be satisfied beyond reasonable doubt' and one could also say: 'You, the jury, must be completely satisfied,' or better still: 'You must feel sure of the prisoner's guilt.' But I desire to repeat what I said in R v Kritz [1950] 1

KB 82, 89: 'It is not the particular formula that matters: it is the effect of the summing-up. If the jury are made to understand that they have to be satisfied and must not return a verdict against a defendant unless they feel sure, and that the onus is all the time on the prosecution and not on the defence,' that is enough. I should be very sorry if it were thought that these cases should depend on the use of a particular formula or particular word or words. The point is that the jury should be directed first, that the onus is always on the prosecution; secondly, that before they convict they must feel sure of the accused's guilt. If that is done, that will be enough.

Comment has been made on the use by the recorder of the word 'satisfied' only, and we have come to the conclusion that the summing-up was not satisfactory; but again I emphasise that this is a case of receiving and in such a case it is always important that the onus of proof should be emphasised and explained. The jury should be told that the possession of goods recently stolen calls for an explanation, and if none is given, or one is given which the jury are convinced is untrue, that entitles them to convict. But if the explanation given leaves them in doubt as to whether the accused received the goods honestly or dishonestly the prosecution have not proved the case and they should acquit.

For the reasons I have endeavoured to give — I hope it will not be thought that we are laying down any particular form of words, but we are saying it is desirable that something more should be said than merely 'satisfied' — we think that the conviction should be quashed.

Appeal allowed.

Question
Is there any difference between 'beyond reasonable doubt' and 'feeling sure of guilt'?

Walters v R
[1969] 2 AC 26
Privy Council

The petitioner was charged with murder. In the course of his summing up the trial judge sought to explain the phrase 'a reasonable doubt' as follows: 'Sometimes it is put this way, that a reasonable doubt is that quality and mind of doubt which, when you are dealing with matters of importance in your own affairs, you allow to influence you one way or the other.' The Court of Appeal of Jamaica confirmed the conviction and refused the petitioner leave to appeal against his conviction for murder. The petitioner applied to the Privy Council for special leave to appeal.

LORD DIPLOCK: At the trial of the petitioner the judge thought it desirable to explain to the jury what was meant by the time-honoured phrase 'a reasonable doubt'. In the course of doing so he said: 'a reasonable doubt is that quality and kind of doubt which, when you are dealing with matters of importance in your own affairs, you allow to influence you one way or the other.'

It has for many years been a common practice of judges in England and other common law jurisdictions when directing the jury on the onus of proof to expand the bare expression 'reasonable doubt' by using this or a similar analogy. On behalf of the petitioner, however, it was contended that a direction in terms such as these is erroneous because it invites the jury to apply a 'subjective' test instead of an 'objective' one. A similar contention had been upheld in *Ramroop* v *The Queen* (1963) 6 WIR 425 by the Court of Appeal of Trinidad and Tobago, where the actual words used at p. 429 were: 'It is better ... merely to look at it as being satisfied, as you have to be in some important matter concerning yourselves.'

That court considered that an explanation in these terms would: 'suggest no particular standard' — (of proof) — 'because whereas one juryman might feel satisfied from certain facts to act in a particular way in some matter of importance to him another on the same facts might feel differently.'

Ramroop v *The Queen* was followed by the Court of Appeal of Jamaica in *R* v *Bromfield* (1965) 8 WIR 273 where the phrase used was 'such a standard of proof or state of mind as you would act upon in a matter of great consequence in your own affairs', and subsequently in *R* v *Powe* (1985) 8 WIR 395 and *R* v *Plinton* (1965) 9 WIR 44 where almost identical phraseology had been used. In *Lesmond* v *The Queen (No. 1)* (1967) 10 WIR 252, however, the Court of Appeal of the West Indies Associated States approved as part of a 'proper and adequate' direction the phrase 'such a doubt as would weigh with you in your own important affairs of everyday life'. The court distinguished these words from those condemned in *R* v *Bromfield* on the grounds that the latter did whereas the former did not equate 'the standard of proof itself with the personal standards of conduct of individual jurors'.

In their Lordships' view the correctness or otherwise of a direction to a jury on the onus of proof cannot depend upon such fine semantic distinctions. No jury, whether in the West Indies or England, as it listens to an oral summing-up by the judge is capable of appreciating them. As Lord Goddard CJ said in *R* v *Kritz* [1950] 1 KB 82, at p. 89:

> It is not the particular formula that matters: it is the effect of the summing-up. If the jury are made to understand that they have to be satisfied and must not return a verdict against a defendant unless they feel sure, and that the onus is all the time on the prosecution and not on the defence, then whether the judge uses one form of language or another is neither here nor there.

The expressions 'objective test' and 'subjective test' are currently in popular use among lawyers, sometimes in contexts in which they are helpful in indicating a meaningful contrast. But in the context of 'doubt', which cannot be other than personal to the doubter, it is meaningless to talk of doubt as 'objective' and otiose to describe it as 'subjective'. It is the duty of each individual juror to make up his own mind as to whether the evidence that the defendant committed the offence with which he is charged is so strong as to convince him personally of the defendant's guilt. Inevitably, because of differences of temperament or experience some jurors will take more convincing than others. That is why there is safety in numbers. And shared responsibility and the opportunity for discussion after retiring serves to counteract individual idiosyncrasies.

By the time he sums up the judge at the trial has had an opportunity of observing the jurors. In their Lordships' view it is best left to his discretion to choose the most appropriate set of words in which to make *that* jury understand that they must not return a verdict against a defendant unless they are sure of his guilt; and if the judge feels that any of them, through unfamiliarity with court procedure, are in danger of thinking that they are engaged in some task more esoteric than applying to the evidence adduced at the trial the common sense with which they approach matters of importance to them in their ordinary lives, then the use of such analogies as that used by Small J in the present case, whether in the words in which he expressed it or in those used in any of the other cases to which reference has been made, may be helpful and is in their Lordships' view unexceptionable. Their Lordships would deprecate any attempt to lay down some precise formula or to draw fine distinctions between one set of words and another. It is the effect of the summing-up as a whole that matters.

Petition dismissed.

R v Ching
(1976) 63 Cr App R 7
Court of Appeal

The defendant was charged with theft from a supermarket. After retiring, the jury returned to the court and the foreman asked the judge to give further directions about the standard of proof. The judge gave a further direction in these terms: 'It is the duty of the prosecution to prove the charge on the whole of the evidence beyond a reasonable doubt. A reasonable doubt, it has been said, is a doubt to which you can give a reason as opposed to a mere fanciful sort of speculation such as 'Well, nothing in this world is certain, nothing in this world can be proved.' It is sometimes said the sort of matter which might influence you if you were to consider some business matter. A matter, for example, of a mortgage concerning your house, something of that nature.' The jury convicted the defendant who appealed.

LAWTON LJ: Mr Latham accepted that when this Court comes to consider the effect of the final direction which the judge gave to the jury, it must be looked at against the whole background of the case, and in particular against the whole of the summing-up. That has been said time and time again in this Court. If any authority is required for the proposition it is to be found in *R v Hepworth and Fearnley* (1955) 39 Cr App R 152; [1955] 2 QB 600. There Lord Goddard CJ said:

> But I desire to repeat what I said in the case of *R v Kritz* (1949) 33 Cr App R 169; [1950] 1 KB 82: 'It is not the particular formula of words that matters; it is the effect of the summing up. If the jury are charged whether in one set of words or in another and are made to understand that they have to be satisfied and must not return a verdict against a defendant unless they feel sure, and that the onus is all the time on the prosecution and not on the defence,' that is enough. I should be very sorry if it were thought that cases should depend on the use of a particular formula or particular word or words.

The task therefore for us has been to consider what was the effect of the summing-up as a whole, including the final direction. Mr Latham attacked that final direction on three grounds. He said that it was unsatisfactory for a judge to define a 'reasonable doubt' as one for which a reason could be given; he pointed to a criticism of that phrase which was made by Lord Justice Edmund Davies (as he then was) in *R v Stafford and Luvaglio* (1968) 53 Cr App R 1. Edmund Davies LJ, sitting with Fenton Atkinson LJ and Waller J said at p. 2: 'We do not, however, ourselves agree with the trial judge when, directing the jury upon the standard of proof, he told them to "Remember that a reasonable doubt is one for which you could give reasons if you were asked," and we dislike such a description or definition.' So do we. It does not help juries. But that is not the problem in this case. The problem is whether its use made this conviction unsafe.

The next ground of complaint was that by using the mortgage of a house analogy, the learned judge was doing something which had been condemned a number of times in this Court. Counsel called our attention to two recent decisions. One was *R v Gray* (1973) 58 Cr App R 177. In that case the phrase which was disapproved of was 'doubt which might affect you in the conduct of your everyday affairs.' The other, even more recently, is the decision of this Court, on January 13, 1976, in *R v Knott*, unreported. In that case the phrase 'the sort of doubt that can influence you as prudent men and women in the conduct of your everyday affairs.' In the past this Court has criticised trial judges for using that kind of analogy. The use of any analogy is to be avoided whenever possible.

The final criticism was that when giving the direction of which complaint is made, the judge did not emphasise once again that the jury had to be sure. But we have no doubt that by the time the jury retired for the last time, they must have appreciated that they had to be sure before they could return a verdict of guilty.

Nevertheless, in most cases — but not in this one — judges would be well advised not to attempt any gloss upon what is meant by 'sure' or what is meant by 'reasonable doubt'. In the last two decades there have been numerous cases before this Court, some of which have been successful, some of which have not, which have come here because judges have thought it helpful to a jury to comment of what the standard of proof is. Experience in this Court has shown that such comments usually create difficulties. They are more likely to confuse than help. But the exceptional case does sometimes arise. This is the sort of case in which, as I have already pointed out, the jury possibly wanted help as to what was meant by 'doubt'. The judge thought they wanted help and he tried to give them some. He was right to try and that is all he was doing. He seems to have steered clear of the formulas which have been condemned in this Court such as 'such doubt as arises in your everyday affairs or your everyday life'; or using another example which has been before the Court, 'the kind of doubts which you may have when trying to make up your minds what kind of motor car to buy.'

Mr Latham said that the judge did not stress that the relevant doubts were those which have to be overcome in *important* business affairs. What he did was to pick an example, which for sensible people would be an important matter. We can see nothing wrong in his so doing.

In conclusion we invite attention to what was said in *Walters v The Queen* [1969] 2 AC 26, where the Board had to consider the kind of problem which is now before us. In that case the trial judge in Jamaica gave the jury a long explanation as to what was meant by 'reasonable doubt'. That explanation was criticised upon the same lines as the final direction given by the trial judge in this case was criticised by Mr Latham. The Privy Council considered the criticisms. It objected to certain phrases which had been put forward in the course of argument, and the opinion of Lord Diplock, at p. 30 ended as follows:

By the time he sums-up the judge at the trial has had an opportunity of observing the jurors. In their Lordships' view it is best left to his discretion to choose the most appropriate set of words in which to make *that* jury understand that they must not return a verdict against a defendant unless they are sure of his guilt; and if the judge feels that any of them, through unfamiliarity with court procedure, are in danger of thinking that they are engaged in some task more esoteric than applying to the evidence adduced at the trial the common sense with which they approach matters of importance to them in their ordinary lives, then the use of such analogies as that used by Small J in the present case, whether in the words in which he expressed it or in those used in any of the other cases to which reference has been made, may be helpful and is in their Lordships' view unexceptionable.

That opinion is the opinion of this Court.

There is no reason for saying in this case that the verdict was unsafe. As I said earlier, and I repeat, this is one of a large number of cases which have come before this Court in recent years, raising fine points about the terms in which judges have directed the jury as to the standard of proof. We point out and emphasise that if judges stopped trying to define that which is almost impossible to define there would be fewer appeals. We hope there will not be any more for some considerable time.

Appeal dismissed.

Ferguson v *R*
[1979] 1 WLR 94
Privy Council

The defendant was charged with murder. The trial judge directed: '. . . it is required to satisfy you beyond reasonable doubt that from the evidence before you . . . the defendant is guilty of murder . . . If you entertain the kind of doubt, which might affect the mind of a person in the conduct of important affairs, then you entertain a reasonable doubt . . .' The defendant was convicted of murder and appealed on the ground, *inter alia,* that the judge misdirected the jury as to the intent necessary to establish the crime of murder.

LORD SCARMAN: It is submitted that the judge encouraged 'too subjective' an approach by telling the jury that the doubt must be such as 'might affect the mind of a person in the conduct of important affairs.'

Their Lordships were told and accepted that in certain Commonwealth jurisdictions some judges avoid this formulation. It is criticised as being unhelpful and possibly dangerous, in that questions arising in the conduct of important affairs often have little resemblance to the issues in a criminal trial and individual jurors may well decide such questions by applying standards lower than satisfaction beyond reasonable doubt and analogous, if to anything, to the civil standard of the balance of probabilities. In *Walters* v *The Queen* [1969] 2 AC 26 their Lordships had to consider a direction almost identical in part with that in this case. Delivering the judgment in that case (which was not an appeal, but an application for special leave to appeal) Lord Diplock pointed out that a distinction between 'objective' and 'subjective' tests is not apt in this context. The Board expressed the view in that case that the formula used in summing up does not matter so long as it is made clear to the jury, whatever words are used, that they must not return a verdict against a defendant unless they are sure of his guilt. Their Lordships' Board agree with these comments with one reservation. Though the law requires no particular formula, judges are wise, as a general rule, to adopt one.

The time-honoured formula is that the jury must be satisfied beyond reasonable doubt. As Dixon CJ said in *Dawson* v *The Queen* (1961) 106 CLR 1, 18, attempts to substitute other expressions have never prospered. It is generally sufficient and safe to direct a jury that they must be satisfied beyond reasonable doubt so that they feel sure of the defendant's guilt. Nevertheless, other words will suffice, so long as the message is clear.

Appeal dismissed.

Note

Those instances where a defendant in a criminal case bears a legal burden have already been noted (see (A) *(ii)* above). Where the defendant bears such a burden then it is discharged on a balance of probabilities.

R v Carr-Briant
[1943] KB 607
Court of Criminal Appeal

The defendant who was charged with corruption contrary to the Prevention of Corruption Act 1906, was a director of a firm which entered into a contract for work to be done with the War Department. Payments in respect of work done under the contracts were made on the certificate of an engineer named Baldock, an employee of the War Department, that it had been satisfactorily performed. The appellant gave or lent to Baldock £60 so that Baldock might pay for a car which he had agreed to buy. The trial judge directed the jury that the defendant had not only to discharge the burden of proof and show that he gave the money without a corrupt motive, but had also to do so beyond all reasonable doubt. The defendant was convicted and appealed.

HUMPHREYS J: We agree with and adopt for the purpose of this judgment the language of Lord Hailsham LC, in delivering the judgment of the Privy Council in *Sodeman* v *R* [1936] 2 All ER 1138, [1936] WN 190, 191, where he said:

> The suggestion made by the petitioner was that the jury may have been misled by the judge's language into the impression that the burden of proof resting upon the accused to prove the insanity was as heavy as the burden of proof resting upon the prosecution to prove the facts which they had to establish. In fact there was no doubt that the burden of proof for the defence was not so onerous . . . .. It was certainly plain that the burden in cases in which an accused had to prove insanity might fairly be stated as not being higher than the burden which rested upon a plaintiff or defendant in civil proceedings. That that was the law was not challenged.

What is the burden resting on a plaintiff or defendant in civil proceedings can, we think, best be stated in the words of the classic pronouncement on the subject by Willes J in *Cooper* v *Slade* 6 HL Cas 746. That learned judge referred to an ancient authority in support of what he termed 'the elementary proposition that in civil cases the preponderance of probability may constitute sufficient ground for a verdict.' The authority in question was the judgment of Dyer CJ and a majority of the justices of the Common Pleas in *Newis* v *Lark* (1531) Plowd 403, decided in the reign of Queen Elizabeth. The report contains this passage: 'Where the matter is so far gone that the parties are at issue . . . so that the jury is to give a verdict one way or other, there, if the matter is doubtful, they may found their verdict upon that which appears the most probable and by the same reason that which is most probable shall be good evidence.'

In our judgment, in any case where, either by statute or at common law, some matter is presumed against an accused person 'unless the contrary is proved,' the jury should be directed that it is for them to decide whether the contrary is proved, that the burden of proof required is less than that required at the hands of the prosecution in proving the case beyond a reasonable doubt, and that the burden may be discharged by evidence satisfying the jury of the probability of that which the accused is called upon to establish.

Appeal allowed

(ii)   Civil cases

Hornal v *Neuberger Products Ltd*
[1957] 1 QB 247
Court of Appeal

The plaintiff in an action for damages for breach of warranty or, alternatively, for fraudulent misrepresentation, alleged that the director of the defendant company had in the course of negotiations for the purchase of a used capstan lathe stated that it had been reconditioned by a reputable firm of toolmakers. The defendants denied that the statement had been made. If it had been made, the director must have known it to be untrue.

The county court judge found that the statement had been made, but held on the claim for breach of warranty that it had not been made contractually. On the claim based on fraud he said that he was satisfied on the balance of probability that the statement had been made, and that that was the correct standard to apply; but that he would not have been so satisfied if the criminal standard of proof was to be applied. He gave judgment for the defendants on the ground that the plaintiff had not shown that he had suffered damage by relying on the fraudulent misrepresentation. The plaintiff appealed.

DENNING LJ: I must say that, if I was sitting as a judge alone, and I was satisfied that the statement was made, that would be enough for me, whether the claim was put in warranty or on fraud. I think it would bring the law into contempt if a judge were to say that on the issue of warranty he finds the statement was made, and that on the issue of fraud he finds it was not made.

HODSON LJ: Notwithstanding the existence of some cases where the point appears to have been argued and decided in a contrary sense, I think the true view, and that most strongly supported by authority, is that which the judge took, namely that in a civil case the balance of probability standard is correct . . . .

Students are familiar with Professor Kenny's *Outlines of Criminal Law* (16th ed (1952)), where the following passage appears at p. 416:

A larger minimum of proof is necessary to support an accusation of crime than will suffice when the charge is only of a civil nature. For in the latter it is sufficient that there be a *preponderance* of evidence in favour of the successful party, whereas in criminal cases the burden rests upon the prosecution to prove that the accused is guilty 'beyond reasonable doubt.' When therefore the case for the prosecution is closed after sufficient evidence has been adduced to necessitate an answer from the defence, the defence need do no more than show that there is a *reasonable doubt* as to the guilt of the accused. See *R v Stoddart* (1909) 25 TLR 612. Even in civil proceedings, e.g., in actions of debt, a mere scintilla of evidence would not warrant the jury in finding a verdict for the plaintiff; for there must (as we have seen) be so much evidence that a reasonable man might accept it as establishing the issue. But in criminal cases the presumption of innocence is still stronger, and accordingly a still higher minimum of evidence is required; and the more heinous the crime the higher will be this minimum of necessary proof. The progressive increase in the difficulty of proof, as the gravity of the accusation to be proved increases, is vividly illustrated in an extract from Lord Brougham's speech in defence of Queen Caroline: 'The evidence before us,' he said, 'is inadequate even to prove a debt — impotent to deprive of a civil right — ridiculous for convicting of the pettiest offence — scandalous if brought forward to support a charge of any grave character — monstrous if to ruin the honour of an English Queen.

This passage appears in the earlier editions of this work for which the late Professor Kenny was responsible.

Denning LJ referred both to criminal and civil cases when he expressed the same idea in *Bater* v *Bater* [1951] P 35:

The difference of opinion which has been evoked about the standard of proof in recent cases may well turn out to be more a matter of words than anything else. It is of course true that by our law a higher standard of proof is required in criminal cases than in civil cases. But this is subject to the qualification that there is no absolute standard in either case. In criminal cases the charge must be proved beyond reasonable doubt, but there may be degrees of proof within that standard. As Best CJ, and many other great judges have said, 'in proportion as the crime is enormous, so ought the proof to be clear.' So also in civil cases, the case may be proved by a preponderance of probability, but there may be degrees of probability within that standard. The degree depends on the subject-matter. A civil court, when considering a charge of fraud, will naturally require for itself a higher degree of probability than that which it would require when asking if negligence is established. It does not adopt so high a degree as a criminal court, even when it is considering a charge of a criminal nature; but still it does require a degree of probability which is commensurate with the occasion.

This citation comes from a judgment given on appeal in a divorce case. The House of Lords has now held in *Preston-Jones* v *Preston-Jones* [1951] AC 391 that the words of the Divorce Act [the Matrimonial Causes Act, 1950] produce the same result as the rule in criminal cases although divorce cases are civil actions. Nevertheless, on the general question of the standard of proof in criminal and civil cases, I would like to express my complete concurrence with the words used by Denning LJ in the passage I have cited. Just as in civil cases the balance of probability may be more readily tilted in one case than in another, so in criminal cases proof beyond reasonable doubt may more readily be attained in some cases than in others.

MORRIS LJ: In a criminal case a jury must be directed that the onus is all the time upon the prosecution and that before they convict they must feel sure of the accused's guilt. Authoritative guidance in regard to directing juries in criminal cases is to be found in the judgment of Lord Goddard CJ in *R v Hepworth and Fearnley* [1955] 2 QB 600, and in other cases. It has, however, been emphasised that what is vital is not the mere using of some particular formula of words but the effect of a summing-up in giving true guidance as to the right approach.

It is, I think, clear from the authorities that a difference of approach in civil cases has been recognised. Many judicial utterances show this. The phrase 'balance of probabilities' is often employed as a convenient phrase to express the basis upon which civil issues are decided. It may well be that no clear-cut logical reconciliation can be formulated in regard to the authorities on these topics. But perhaps they illustrate that 'the life of the law is not logic but experience'. In some criminal cases liberty may be involved; in some it may not. In some civil cases the issues may involve questions of reputation which can transcend in importance even questions of personal liberty. Good name in man or woman is 'the immediate jewel of their souls'.

But in truth no real mischief results from an acceptance of the fact that there is some difference of approach in civil actions. Particularly is this so if the words which are used to define that approach are the servants but not the masters of meaning. Though no court and no jury would give less careful attention to issues lacking gravity than to those marked by it, the very elements of gravity become a part of the whole range of circumstances which have to be weighed in the scale when deciding as to the balance of probabilities. This view was denoted by Denning LJ when in his judgment in *Bater* v *Bater* he spoke of a 'degree of probability which is commensurate with the occasion' and of 'a degree of probability which is proportionate to the subject-matter'.

In English law the citizen is regarded as being a free man of good repute. Issues may be raised in a civil action which affect character and reputation, and these will not be forgotten by judges and juries when considering the probabilities in regard to whatever misconduct is alleged. There will be reluctance to rob any man of his good name: there will also be reluctance to make any man pay what is not due or to make any man liable who is not or not liable who is. A court will not be deterred from a conclusion because of regret at its consequences: a court must arrive at such conclusion as is directed by the weight and preponderance of the evidence.

(The court held that, although the judge had applied the correct standard of proof, the plaintiff had suffered damage and was entitled to judgment.)

Appeal allowed.

Note

It was believed that in matrimonial causes, the standard of proof demanded was that of 'beyond reasonable doubt' (see *Bater* v *Bater* [1951] P 35, *Ginesi* v *Ginesi* [1948] P 179). Later authority cast doubt on this proposition (see *Blyth* v *Blyth* [1966] AC 643 and *Bastable* v *Bastable and Saunders* [1968] 1 WLR 1684). Since these decisions, matrimonial law has undergone consider- able reform and it is suggested that the standard of proof in matrimonial causes is the same as in all other areas of the civil law (see further P. Murphy, *A Practical Approach to Evidence*, 4th ed. (London: Blackstone Press, 1992), pp. 113–4).

Miles v Cain
(1989) *The Times*, 15 December 1989
Court of Appeal

SIR JOHN DONALDSON MR: In this action Miss Lorraine Miles successfully claimed damages for indecent assault, rape and buggery by the defendant. Her claim was heard at Chelmsford by Caulfield J without a jury and the hearing lasted for nine days in October-November 1988. The judge reserved judgment for two weeks and then gave his decision and reasons. The defendant now appeals on the issue of liability.

In the light of the public interest in Miss Miles' claim, it may be as well, before turning to the facts and the arguments, to advert to some well settled principles which are applicable to this appeal, although none was in issue between the parties.

The burden and standard of proof

In criminal proceedings it is the prosecution which alleges that the accused is guilty of the offence charged and it therefore the prosecution which must prove that charge. Furthermore it must do so with the degree of certainty required by the criminal standard of proof, namely so that, taking account of all the evidence, the jury is satisfied beyond reasonable doubt, and can say that it is 'sure', that the accused committed the offence. The accused need not prove that he was innocent and rarely does so. Unlike Scotland, we have no verdict of 'not proven' and the accused is entitled to a verdict of 'not guilty' if the jury is left in doubt whether he was guilty of the offence, even if they are far from satisfied that he was innocent of it.

In civil proceedings it is the plaintiff who makes the claim and it is therefore the plaintiff who must prove it. The defendant need never prove that he is not liable, the civil equivalent of being innocent. Again there is no verdict of 'not proven' and the defendant is entitled to judgment if the judge or jury is left in doubt whether the claim has been established with the degree of certainty required by the civil standard of proof.

The civil standard of proof always requires the facts upon which the claim is based to be established at least on the balance of probabilities, but a somewhat higher degree of certainty is required in some cases. In the present case Caulfield J said that:

> the onus is on the plaintiff and the degree of proof necessary to prove a charge as serious as this I take from the case of *Bastable* v *Bastable & Saunders* [1968] 3 All ER 701, [1968] 1 WLR 1684.

No-one has been concerned to argue that that was the wrong standard of proof and I therefore refer to that decision which was that of a Court of Appeal consisting of Willmer, Winn and Edmund Davies LJJ. It was a divorce suit and the issue was one of adultery. Willmer LJ, with the agreement of Winn LJ, approved and applied a dictum of Denning LJ in *Bater* v *Bater* [1951] P 35, 37, [1950] 2 All ER 458, where he said:

> The difference of opinion which has been evoked about the standard of proof in recent cases may well turn out to be more a matter of words than anything else. It is of course true that by our law a higher standard of proof is required in criminal cases than in civil cases. But this is subject to the qualification that there is no absolute standard in either case. In criminal cases the charge must be proved beyond reasonable doubt, but there may be degrees of proof within that standard. As Best, CJ, and many other great judges have said, 'in proportion as the crime is enormous, so ought the proof to be clear,' So also in civil cases, the case may be proved by a preponderance of probability, but there may be degrees of probability within that standard. The degree depends on the subject-matter. A civil court, when considering a charge of fraud, will naturally require for itself a higher degree of probability than that which it would require when asking if negligence is established. It does not adopt so high a degree as a criminal court, even when it is considering

a charge of a criminal nature; but still it does require a degree of probability which is commensurate with the occasion.

Edmund Davies LJ expressed doubt whether 'in proportion as the offence is grave, so ought the proof to be clear' was a distinction which could effectively be made by a jury or indeed by many judges and lawyers, but he did not dissent and indeed purported to apply it.

Questions

1. Do you agree with Donaldson MR that the law relating to standard of proof has 'well settled principles'?
2. Does the standard of proof in a civil case vary according to the nature of the allegation?
3. Would it be more accurate to say that while the standard never varies, the cogency of the evidence needed to reach that standard may well vary and that, in turn, will depend upon the gravity of the allegation?
4. Albert is charged with the murder of his wife, Betty, by shooting her. He claims that the gun went off accidentally as he was cleaning it. He further states that he has experienced a number of blackouts and claims this as an alternative reason for firing the gun. Compose a direction that you, as trial judge, would give to the jury insofar as it affects the burden and standard of proof.
5. Which, if any, of the following directions to a jury accurately represents the law as to the burden and standard of proof?

(a) The accused has alleged that he was insane at the time he committed the assault. If you are to find that he was insane then it is for him to satisfy you of this so that you feel sure of his insanity.

(b) The accused pleaded diminished responsibility in this case. Now, the law says that it is for the accused to satisfy you of that fact. That does not mean that he has to prove it beyond a shadow of a doubt, but it does mean you must feel that it is more likely true than not.

(c) The accused claims he only punched P in order to defend himself. Whether this is true or not is for you to decide. I can tell you, however, that if the prosecution have not demonstrated his story to be false, you must acquit him.

6. Charlie is suing Dredge & Co. on a policy of insurance in respect of a ship which had caught fire and which was insured by Dredge & Co. Dredge's defence is that Charlie committed arson in order to claim the insurance money. Advise the parties as to the burden and standard of proof in this case.

Further Reading

P. Murphy, *A Practical Approach to Evidence*, 4th ed. (1992), Ch. 3
S. Doran, 'Alternative Defences: the "invisible burden" on the trial judge' [1991] Crim LR 878
D. Birch, 'Hunting the Snark: The Elusive Statutory Exception' [1988] Crim LR 221

F. Bennion, 'Statutory Exceptions: A Third Knot in the Golden Thread?' [1988] Crim LR 31
P. Mirfield, 'The Legacy of *Hunt*' [1988] Crim LR 19
A.A.S. Zuckerman, 'The Third Exception to the *Woolmington* Rule' (1976) 92 LQR 402.

3 PRESUMPTIONS

The burden of proof is sometimes allocated or affected by the existence of a presumption. A presumption has been defined by Murphy as 'a rule of law which provides that if a party proves a certain fact (known as the primary fact) then another fact (the presumed fact) will also be taken to be proved, unless evidence is adduced by the opponent to "rebut" the presumption . . .'.

The term 'presumption' is, on occasions, somewhat ineptly used to describe what amounts to no more than a rule of substantive law. For example, it is presumed that every man knows the law. This 'presumption' is an irrebuttable presumption. In other words, it merely states a rule of substantive law. A true presumption is one which admits of evidence in rebuttal.

(A) Terminology

This, as with burdens of proof, is yet another area of the law of evidence which demonstrates how different terms are used to illustrate the same concept. Presumptions have been variously classified by the courts and writers. Some presumptions are termed as 'persuasive' or 'compelling' in that once the primary fact has been proved, the presumed fact can only be rebutted by adducing evidence to the appropriate standard of proof. Other presumptions are classed as 'evidential' or 'provisional' in that they may be rebutted by adducing evidence sufficient to amount to a prima facie case.

A.T. Denning, *Presumptions and Burdens*
(1945) 61 LQR 379

. . . *Provisional Presumptions and Burdens.* In order to discharge a legal burden, the person on whom it lies will often prove relevant facts or rely on presumptions from which he asks the Court to infer the fact in issue which he has to establish in order to succeed. In the instances I have taken he will prove that the prisoner killed a man; or was found in possession of goods recently stolen; or that the thing which caused the accident was under the control of the defendant; or that the ship was lost within a short time of sailing; or that the goods were stolen; or he will rely on the presumption that the testator was of testamentary capacity. Those relevant facts or circumstances are often said to raise a 'presumption' or make a *'prima facie'* case, and so they do in the sense that from them the fact in issue *may* be inferred, but not in the sense that it *must* be inferred unless the contrary is proved. The Court will decline before the end of the case to rule whether the fact in issue should be inferred. It will leave it to the other party to take his own course. He may seek to repel the inference by argument, as by submitting that the facts proved only raise a suspicion as distinct from a legitimate inference; or by contradicting the evidence; or by giving evidence of other facts to explain why the fact in issue should not be inferred; or by raising suspicions which counter-balance the presumptions. As the case proceeds the evidence may first weigh in favour of the inference and then against it, thus producing a burden, sometimes apparent, sometimes real, which may shift from one party to the other as the case proceeds or may remain suspended between them. The party on whom it rests must call evidence or take the consequences, which may not necessarily be adverse: for the place where the burden eventually comes to rest does not necessarily decide the issue: because at the end of the case the Court has to decide as a matter of fact whether the inference should be drawn or not. These presumptions and burdens are therefore *provisional* only. It is a mistake to raise these provisional presumptions into propositions having the force of law. They are recognized by the law but their force depends on ordinary good sense rather than on law. They are only guides to the Court in deciding whether to infer the fact in issue or not. The degree of probability needed to establish an inference varies. When considering the guilt of a person accused of an offence of a criminal nature, the Court requires a high degree of probability. It must be satisfied beyond reasonable doubt. On all other issues, whether in civil or criminal cases, the Court is satisfied with a moderate degree of probability. It is sufficient if there is a greater probability on one side or the other; but if at the end of the case the evidence is so evenly balanced that the Court cannot come to a determinate conclusion, the *legal* burden comes into play and requires the Court to reject the inference.

. . . *Compelling Presumptions*. It often happens that a party proves facts from which the Court *must* in law draw an inference in his favour unless the other side proves the contrary or proves some other fact which the law recognizes as sufficient to rebut the inference. For instance, once money is proved to have been received by a public servant from a person who is seeking a Government contract, it is deemed to have been received corruptly unless the contrary is proved; or, once a child is proved to have been born in wedlock, it is presumed to be legitimate unless the other side prove non-access or incapacity by the husband; or when two people die at about the same time, the younger is presumed to have survived the elder, unless it is proved that the elder survived the younger. These presumptions differ from provisional presumptions in that they have the compelling force of law; and whereas provisional presumptions give rise to provisional burdens within a single issue, a compelling presumption gives rise to a separate issue on which the *legal* burden is on the other side. . . .

. . . *Conclusive Presumptions*. It is a misuse of language to speak of any presumption being conclusive, but the meaning is clear enough. On proof of certain facts the Court must draw a particular inference, whether true or not, and it cannot be rebutted. For instance, once it appears that a deserting husband has been certified as a lunatic for any part, may be only a week, of the three years preceding the petition, the Court must find him not guilty of desertion for that period, however strong the evidence of desertion may be for the remainder of the period for which he was sane.

N. Bridge, *Presumptions and Burdens*
(1949) 12 MLR 273

. . . The word 'presumption' is in no better case; many shades of meaning have been given to it, and although there have been as many attempts to evolve a satisfactory distinguishing terminology, in current judicial usage it is impossible to say of this or that kind of presumption that it has precisely this or that legal effect. It is still true today, as it was fifty years ago, that: 'A change is simply necessary to accurate legal speech and sound legal reasoning; and we may justly expect those who have exact thoughts, and wish to express them with precision, to avail themselves of some discrimination in terminology which will secure their end' (Thayer, *Preliminary Treatise on Evidence*, p. 385). Indeed, the persistence of ambiguity, for another fifty years since these words were written, has intensified the confusion of legal thought. If it appears an almost hopeless task at this late stage to introduce the precise language necessary to clear thought, it is the more urgent that the task be attempted.

. . . The truth is that it is neither an apt use of language, nor is it necessary to any legal distinction, to speak of presumptions at all, when what we mean are those legitimate inferences, which it is in the province of the jury to draw or not to draw, as they think fit.

If the line of distinction between presumptions of law and presumptions of fact were satisfactorily drawn, the latter usage might be tolerable as a harmless anachronism. But it is not. Whereas the different senses of 'burden of proof' can be sufficiently distinguished by qualifying epithets, it seems to me that there is only one kind of rebuttable presumption with any title to be so called. It is not a 'provisional presumption', for it has a distinct and certain legal effect. It is not a 'compelling presumption', because it has nothing to do with the fixed burden of proof. Once the precise function of a presumption is properly understood, it will be seen that the best hope alike for clarity of thought and purity of language will be to reserve for the word 'presumption' in all cases this single and precise meaning.

The true presumption, then, has this effect, that when it arises in favour of one party it entitles that party to have the issue decided in his favour unless and until his opponent introduces *some evidence* to the contrary. In other words a true presumption operates to shift the evidential burden of proof. Besides recognising this positive function of presumptions, it is of equal importance to note that that is the *whole* of their function. Once the party against whom the presumption is operating has introduced the necessary legal minimum of evidence, the presumption is discharged and disappears altogether from the scene; the issue must then be left to be determined by the jury, or the judge of fact, on all the evidence having regard, if need be, to the fixed burden of proof.

A.A.S. Zuckerman, *The Principles of Criminal Evidence*
(1989), pp. 112–5

. . . [T]he technique of presumptions provides an uncomplicated method of distributing the risk of losing the case in respect of different facts which need to be proved in a criminal or civil trial. The nature of individual presumptions is easily described by outlining the basic and the presumed facts, by stating the type of burden in relation to each of them, and by indicating which parties bear the burden. Unfortunately this straightforward method is not always followed and a myriad of terms is employed. Most of these terms are neither generally accepted nor consistently used. A terminological explanation is therefore necessary.

The word 'presumption' is used to describe a number of different things. At times we come across expressions such as the 'presumption of innocence' or the 'presumption of sanity'. The first usually conveys the idea that in criminal cases the probative burden in respect of the accused's guilt rests on the prosecution. The second indicates that the burden of proof in respect of the defence of insanity is on the accused. In neither case is the burden of proof contingent on proof of a basic fact and there is no need to use the word 'presumption' in this context at all.

One sometimes comes across what is known as the classical classification of presumptions, by which presumptions are divided into three groups. First, presumptions of fact. These refer to situations in which, as a matter of common sense and not by force of law, the court may draw a certain factual inference from the existence of a certain set of facts. For example, on a charge of handling stolen goods, if the accused fails to provide a credible explanation for his possession of recently stolen goods there is said to arise a presumption of guilty knowledge. This merely means that the jury may, as a matter of ordinary logic, infer the accused's knowledge that the goods were stolen. 'Presumption of fact' thus refers to circumstances which commonly occur in conjunction. In this sense we may come across the 'presumption of continuance' whereby the trier of fact may infer the existence of a state of affairs from its existence at an earlier point in time. For instance, it may be inferred that a person was alive at a certain time from the fact that he was alive a short time before. In none of these cases is there any formal risk distribution because inferences are left to be drawn in the normal way.

The second classical category consists of 'irrebuttable presumptions of law'. Upon the proof of certain facts the court is duty-bound to find the existence of another set of facts, irrespective of the true state of affairs. For example, it is an irrebuttable common-law presumption that all persons know the law. It is obvious that this is not a rule about the distribution of the risk of judicial mistake in the ascertainment of the true state of affairs. It is simply an awkward way of expressing the substantive rule that ignorance of the law is no defence.

While the two foregoing categories are not presumptions in the central sense mentioned at the outset, the third category in this classification does cover presumptions in this central sense. This category, 'rebuttable presumptions of law', comprises all that is included in our central sense: rules whereby on proof of a basic fact a conclusion as to the presumed fact must be drawn, in the absence of evidence or proof, as the case may be, to the contrary. In order to draw attention to the difference between presumptions which distribute the probative burden and presumptions which distribute the burden of adducing evidence, proposals for more accurate terminology were at one time put forward by Lord Denning and by Professor Glanville Williams.

Professor Williams speaks of presumptions which, upon proof of the basic facts, cast a burden of adducing evidence on the opponent as 'evidential presumption', while to a presumption casting the probative burden he refers as 'persuasive presumption'. Lord Denning, for his part, describes the latter as 'compelling presumption'. However, none of these terms is well established in legal usage and for the sake of clarity it is always advisable to spell out the consequences of any particular presumption.

. . . Traditionally the subject of presumptions has been considered to present enormous difficulties of exposition and analysis. These difficulties are largely due to an unrealistic or misguided belief that the whole subject of presumptions could and should, in principle, be reduced to a comprehensive and coherent system of rules of general application. At the root of this belief lies a resistance to accepting presumptions for what they are: techniques, and no more, for allocating the risk of losing the case.

How the risk of losing on a given issue should be distributed is a question that can only be answered by the substantive law. For instance, the presumption of legitimacy, discussed earlier, arises in that form from the law of persons and has to do with the welfare of children, the obligations of marriage and the like, as well as with the general probabilities concerning legitimacy. It is the policies of the family law that dictate the risk allocation and the technique to be employed for that purpose. The technique itself, the permutations upon the burden of proof, cannot determine when this or that risk allocation is appropriate.

While no one disputes that individual presumptions are the creatures of substantive law it is felt at times that the law of evidence should bring some order into the entire subject of presumptions by devising a system for the grouping of all presumptions. Others believed that much confusion will be avoided by a generally accepted terminology. It is doubtless true that ambiguity of terms can result in ambiguity about the exact effect of individual presumptions but all that is required to secure clarity and certainty is for the lawmaker to state whether it is the probative or the evidential burden that is involved in any individual presumption and the degree of probative force required to discharge the relevant burden. Beyond that it is difficult to see what further contribution the law of evidence can make in this respect.

(B)   Particular presumptions

The following are examples of rebuttable presumptions of law where, once the primary fact is proved, the court will find the presumed fact proved, unless there is evidence to the contrary. In most of these cases, the contentious point revolves around the standard of proof required to rebut the presumption once that presumption becomes operative.

(i)   Presumption of legitimacy

A child is presumed to be legitimate if:

(a)   the child was born to the wife;
(b)   it was born during lawful wedlock or within the normal period of gestation if the marriage has been terminated; and
(c)   the husband was alive at the date of conception.

Two statutes now affect this presumption.

Matrimonial Causes Act 1973

48.   Evidence
(1)   The evidence of a husband or wife shall be admissible in any proceedings to prove that marital intercourse did or did not take place between them during any period.

Family Law Reform Act 1969

26. Rebuttal of presumption as to legitimacy and illegitimacy

Any presumption of law as to the legitimacy or illegitimacy of any person may in any civil proceedings be rebutted by evidence which shows that it is more probable than not that that person is illegitimate or legitimate, as the case may be, and it shall not be necessary to prove that fact beyond reasonable doubt in order to rebut the presumption.

S v *S*

[1972] AC 24

House of Lords

LORD REID: My Lords, these two appeals are concerned with the same question — whether in proceedings regarding the paternity or legitimacy of a child a blood test of the child should be ordered. In rather similar circumstances the Court of Appeal in *S.'s* case decided by a majority (Lord Denning MR and Karminski LJ, Sachs LJ dissenting) that a test should be ordered, but in *W.'s* case decided by a majority (Winn and Cross LJJ, Lord Denning MR dissenting) that a test should not be ordered. I do not think that it is possible to hold that both decisions are right.

In *S.'s* case the spouses were married in 1946. There were three children born in 1947, 1952 and 1954. There is no doubt that they were legitimate. Then on December 15, 1965, the wife bore another child. The husband denied paternity. On March 4, 1966, he petitioned for divorce on the ground of the wife's adultery with a man, M, in and after August 1965. The suit was undefended and obtained a decree nisi on May 17, 1968. Then the commissioner had to be satisfied that proper provision had been made for the children of the marriage and the question arose whether the last child, D, was a 'relevant child,' i.e., a child of the marriage. So the commissioner ordered the trial of an issue as to the legitimacy of this child and ordered a blood test of the husband, wife, M and the child. But M refused to consent. The husband and wife consented to have the test, and in October 1969 a new order was made for a blood test of the husband, wife and child.

The Official Solicitor had been appointed guardian ad litem of the child and he objected to this order and appealed on the ground that it had not been shown that to have a blood test would be for the benefit of the child.

In *W.'s* case the spouses were married in 1957 and they had two children born in 1959 and 1961. Then in 1963 the wife stayed with her mother from time to time when West Indian lodgers were staying in the mother's house. The spouses continued to have sexual relations and apparently the husband did not suspect his wife of misconduct. Then in July 1963 the wife left her husband taking the two children with her and stayed with a man in Bristol acting as housekeeper. While there she gave birth to a child P, on December 6, 1963. On February 8, 1964, she petitioned for divorce on the ground of cruelty. Then in October 1966 the wife sent to the husband at his request a photograph of their three children. This photograph shows a great difference in appearance between the elder children and the youngest child and the husband at once asserted that the youngest child was not his child. He obtained a confession from his wife that she had committed adultery with a West Indian who has now disappeared, and on December 17, 1968, he obtained a decree nisi on the ground of this adultery.

As in *S.'s* case the Official Solicitor was appointed guardian ad litem of the child and an issue was ordered to be tried as to whether P is a child of the husband. The

husband wished to have a blood test but this was refused by Sir Jocelyn Simon P and
an appeal by the husband was dismissed.

I shall not deal further with the facts in these two cases. They will have to be fully
investigated in the trials of the issues as to legitimacy. I will only say that on the
material now available I am unable to forecast what the decisions would be if no blood
tests are made. The law as to the onus of proof is now set out in section 26 of the
Family Law Reform Act 1969 as follows:

> Any presumption of law as to the legitimacy or illegitimacy of any person may in
> any civil proceedings be rebutted by evidence which shows that it is more probable
> than not that that person is illegitimate or legitimate, as the case may be, and it shall
> not be necessary to prove that fact beyond reasonable doubt in order to rebut the
> presumption.

That means that the presumption of legitimacy now merely determines the onus of
proof. Once evidence has been led it must be weighed without using the presumption
as a make-weight in the scale for legitimacy. So even weak evidence against legitimacy
must prevail if there is not other evidence to counterbalance it. The presumption will
only come in at that stage in the very rare case of the evidence being so evenly
balanced that the court is unable to reach a decision on it. I cannot recollect ever
having seen or heard of a case of any kind where the court could not reach a decision
on the evidence before it . . .

LORD MORRIS OF BORTH-Y-GEST: . . . It has to be remembered that the issue
as to legitimacy has to be resolved after a consideration of all the relevant evidence.
If there were no other evidence than that a child was born during wedlock then
legitimacy would not be assailed. But in cases where paternity is repudiated by a
husband there will be much evidence. The spouses themselves may give specific
evidence. Older rules by which they were restricted have been abrogated. On a
weighing of all the evidence a court will have to decide. The presumption of legitimacy
will merely have been at the starting point. Once that is left behind it is the effect and
the weight of all the evidence that will count. It is now laid down by section 26 of the
Family Law Reform Act 1969 that any presumption of law as to the legitimacy or
illegitimacy of any person may in any civil proceedings be rebutted by evidence which
shows that it is more probable than not that that person is illegitimate or legitimate.
Proof beyond reasonable doubt is not necessary to rebut the presumption of legitimacy.

The result is that if a husband repudiates the paternity of a child born during
wedlock and if evidence is given on the trial of an issue as to legitimacy the court will
weigh the evidence and will have to decide on a balance of probabilities whether
illegitimacy is established . . .

Question
In *S* v *S*, Lord Reid states 'So even weak evidence against legitimacy must
prevail . . .' and Lord Morris of Borth-Y-Gest states, 'as to legitimacy the
court will weigh the evidence and will have to decide on a balance of
probabilities whether illegitimacy is established'. Are these two statements
reconcilable?

(ii)   Presumption of marriage

If it is proved that a man and woman either:

(a)   went through a ceremony of marriage; or

(b)   cohabited together;

it will be presumed that they are or were validly married.

Mahadervan v *Mahadervan*
[1964] P 233
Divisional Court

The parties were married in July 1951, in Ceylon. A local statute, namely, the Legislative Enactments of Ceylon, 1938, Marriage General Ordinance, required compliance with certain preliminaries, that the marriage should be solemnised by a registrar in his office, station or other authorised place, and that, in the course of the ceremony, the registrar should address the parties as to the nature of the union. The certificate of marriage purported to show that the marriage had been solemnised by the registrar at his office. The parties cohabited as husband and wife until early in 1952, after which the husband came to England, from whence, until March 1954, he wrote a number of letters to the wife acknowledging her as such.

In August 1958, the husband went through a ceremony of marriage with an English woman with whom he, thereafter, lived in England as husband and wife. In September 1960, the first purported wife came to England and subsequently issued a complaint on the ground of the husband's adultery. At the hearing before the justices her evidence as to the marriage, which was accepted as against that of the husband, was that the ceremony had taken place at the house of her parents; she made no reference to the registrar's address to the parties. The justices rejected the husband's contention that the marriage was invalid for failure to comply with the local formalities and made an order in favour of the wife. From that order the husband appealed:

SIR JOCELYN SIMON P referred to the facts substantially as set out above and to the findings and order of the justices and, after stating that the husband no longer pursued the contentions that the marriage was procured by duress and was potentially polygamous, continued: . . . The real contention before us was that the marriage was void for non-compliance with formalities required by the local law; and this turned principally on two points. It was argued, first, that the marriage was celebrated at a place which was not authorised by the local law for the celebration of a valid marriage; secondly, that it was an essential part of the ceremony that the registrar should address the parties emphasising the monogamous character of the union, and that as he failed to do so the marriage was vitiated. It was also argued, although not very strenuously, that certain preliminaries were not carried out.

. . . Two rules of law expressed in latin maxims therefore come into play: *omnia praesumuntur rite esse acta* as regard the acts of the officials and *omnia praesumuntur pro matrimonio*. Where there is a ceremony followed by cohabitation as husband and wife, a strong presumption arises that the parties are lawfully married. The leading case as to this is *Piers* v *Piers* (1849) 2 HL Cas 331. The validity of the marriage in question depended on the issue of a special licence; but there was no trace of its issue and the bishop of the diocese had no recollection of issuing it. Nevertheless the House of Lords affirmed the marriage. Lord Cottenham cited with approval the words of Lord Lyndhurst in *Morris* v *Davies* (1837) 5 Cl & F 163. 'The presumption of law is not lightly to be repelled. It is not to be broken in upon or shaken by a mere balance of probability. The evidence for the purpose of repelling it must be strong, distinct, satisfactory and conclusive.' Lord Campbell said 'you must show a high degree of probability that there was not a licence. . . . a presumption of this sort, in favour of a marriage, can only be negatived by disproving every reasonable possibility.' The principle has been applied and those passages have been repeatedly cited in cases of the highest authority. A particularly striking and relevant example is *Sastry Velaider Aronegary* v *Sembecutty Vaigalie*. It related to a marriage between Tamils in Ceylon, and it was admitted that not all the necessary ceremonies had been performed owing to disturbances which took place when the marriage was going on. But the Privy Council held the parties to be married, Sir Barnes Peacock saying: 'It does not, therefore, appear to their Lordships that the law of Ceylon is different from that which prevails in this country; namely, that where a man and woman are proved to have lived together as man and wife, the law will presume, unless the contrary be clearly proved, that they were living together in consequence of a valid marriage, and not in a state of concubinage.'

Counsel for the husband argues, however, that today the proper standard of proof is the mere balance of probability, relying on *In re Peete, Peete* v *Crompton* [1952] 2 All ER 599. To my mind it is unnecessary to examine this authority further, because it was expressly limited to the question of capacity to marry and did not go to the formalities of the marriage; and the two cases where it has been cited with approval, *In re Watkins, Watkins* v *Watkins* and *Chard* v *Chard (orse. Northcott)* [1956] P 259, also related to capacity to marry. The general principles stated in *Piers* v *Piers* relied upon by counsel for the wife stand untouched by any later authority so far as the ceremonies of marriage are concerned, although some question had been raised as to the actual terms in which the standard of proof was phrased. Lord Brougham in *Piers* v *Piers* itself had demurred to the use of the word 'conclusive' in the judgment of Lord Cottenham LC: he preferred 'clear, distinct and satisfactory evidence.' Sir Barnes Peacock in *Sastry Velaider Aronegary* v *Sembecutty Vaigalie* used the words 'the clearest and most satisfactory evidence.' Harman LJ in a recent case, *In re Taylor, decd.* [1961] 1 WLR 9, has also criticised the word 'conclusive.' Certainly today 'conclusive' does suggest an irrebuttable presumption, and, as Harman LJ pointed out, it is clear that the presumption can be rebutted, though the evidence in rebuttal must be firm and clear. In *Hill* v *Hill* [1959] 1 WLR 127 the judgment of the Privy Council delivered by Lord Somervell cited *Piers* v *Piers* and went on: 'It is clear that a balance of probabilities is insufficient to rebut the presumption. Various epithets have been used, but their Lordships accept the word in the passage cited by the judge.' That was a passage from Halsbury's Laws of England (2nd ed., vol. 16, p. 599) 'The evidence must be decisive.' 'I would need,' he continued, 'very strong evidence to justify a conclusion that Winter did not conduct the service in accordance with the form in his book . . . there is no sufficiently satisfactory or decisive evidence to establish the invalidity of this ceremony.' If it is not presumptuous to say so, it seems to me that 'decisive' might be said to beg the question: what is the weight of evidence which is required to decide the issue? In my view, where a ceremony of marriage is proved followed by cohabitation as husband and wife, a presumption is raised which cannot be rebutted by evidence which merely goes to show on a balance of probabilities that there was no valid marriage: it must be evidence which satisfies beyond reasonable doubt that there was no valid marriage. In other words, the presumption in favour of marriage in such circumstances is of the same weight as the presumption of innocence in criminal and matrimonial causes. A jury would have to be directed that to displace the presumption, the husband must prove his case in such a way that they can feel sure that there was no marriage.

But counsel for the husband argues that even though that may be the general rule, where it is a necessary averment, or it is the essence of a party's case, or the party assumes the burden of proving that there has been a second marriage which would be rendered bigamous and invalid by the establishment of the first marriage, the presumption in favour of the first marriage is cancelled out by that in favour of the second and the matter falls for determination on a balance of probabilities. A fortiori, he says, where the first marriage is a foreign and the second an English one. It has certainly been accepted, at any rate since Lord Mansfield decided *Morris v Miller* (1767) 4 Burr 2057, that before a conviction for bigamy or a verdict in an action of criminal conversation there must be evidence of a marriage in fact and the inference arising from acknowledgment, cohabitation and reputation is not sufficient. But in my view the extension of such a rule from criminal or quasi-criminal cases to cases like the present is unjustified and is inconsistent with authority. In *Hill v Hibbit*, to which I have already referred, Lord Hatherley LC applied the comparable Scottish doctrine of marriage by habit and repute notwithstanding that the establishment of the marriage invalidated a subsequent marriage. In *In re Thompson, Langham v Thompson*, relied upon on behalf of the wife, it was sought to establish the marriage by evidence of reputation that the parties were married, which might be thought to raise the presumption less strongly than a ceremony followed by cohabitation as husband and wife. It was expressly argued by counsel. 'If it be held that Nathaniel and Patience were married it would follow that Nathaniel committed bigamy.' Kekewich J nevertheless applied the presumption in favour of the marriage having taken place and held that it had.

As for the argument of counsel for the husband that there is no presumption in favour of a marriage where it is a foreign one and its establishment would invalidate a subsequent English one, no ground of principle and no authority could be cited to support it. To accept it would give expression to a legal chauvinism that has no place in any rational system of private international law. Our courts in my view apply exactly the same weight of presumption in favour of a foreign marriage as of an English one, and the nationality of any later marriage brought into question is quite immaterial.

(BAKER J delivered a concurring judgment.)

Note

The case states that the presumption may only be rebutted by adducing evidence beyond reasonable doubt, but it is widely thought that the presumption can be rebutted by adducing evidence to the standard normally associated with matrimonial causes, namely on a balance of probabilities (*Blyth v Blyth* [1966] AC 643).

(iii) Presumption of death

A person will be presumed dead if the following three primary facts are proved:

(a) that no acceptable evidence exists that the person has been alive during a continuous period of seven years or more;

(b)   that persons who are likely to have heard from him during that period have not heard from him; and

(c)   all due inquiries have been made to locate the subject but those inquiries have failed.

Chard v Chard
[1956] P 259
Divisional Court

A wife who was party to a marriage in 1909 was last heard of in 1917 as a normally healthy woman who would, in 1933, have attained the age of 44. She had reasons for not wishing to be heard of by the husband and his family and it was not possible to trace anyone who, since 1917, would naturally have heard of her. No trace of the registration of her death could be found. The husband having remarried in 1933, he and the 1933 wife sought decrees of nullity.

SACHS J: . . . But what, on that footing, is the correct angle from which to approach the question of deciding whether or not she was alive in 1933? Is there a prima facie presumption of continuing life which has not been rebutted? Is there, in this case, a presumption of death after seven years? Or is the matter one in which the court has to draw inferences from the known facts in the same way as a jury charged with deciding the balance of probabilities?

There have been a considerable number of decisions touching these questions of law in each Division of the High Court. Many of these have concerned cases where some statute has laid down the conditions upon which the court shall, prima facie, presume death . . .

In relation to matters such as the present, to which no statute applies, counsel before me have helpfully discussed whether there is applicable any presumption of continuing life or any presumption of death after seven years.

Before going further into dicta which were said to conflict on these points, it is to be observed that in the main presumptions fall, of course, into three categories. There are rebuttable presumptions of fact, which are no more than inferences logically drawn from one fact as to the existence of other facts — as exemplified by the res ipsa loquitur cases: there are rebuttable presumptions of law and there are conclusive presumptions of law (e.g., the innocence of a child under ten). As Phipson remarks, the demarcation lines between classes of presumption are, even when visible, not always regarded in the dicta of judges and textbook writers.

Taking first what is termed the 'presumption of continuance of life' — this is stated in Phipson on Evidence to be one of fact, whilst Taylor on Evidence treats it as a presumption of law. As between these two views I have no hesitation in holding that the former is the correct one. That would tally with the statement by Lush J when he in Rex v Lumley (1869) LR 1 CCR 196 delivered the judgment of the court (Kelly CB Byles J, Lush J and Brett J, and Cleasby B) as follows: 'The existence of the party at an antecedent period may or may not afford a reasonable inference that he was living at the subsequent date . . . Thus the question is entirely for the jury. The law makes no presumption either way.' Similarly it would conform with the statement of Hodson J in MacDarmaid v Attorney-General [1950] P 218 that 'There is no presumption of law as to continuance of life, but each case must be determined on its own facts.'

In view of the misapprehension which it appears to have caused in one or two later cases, I should mention that Lord Denman's statement in *Nepean's* case: 'It is true, the law presumes that a person shown to be alive at a given time remains alive until the contrary be shown . . .' conflicts, on the face of it, with his own statement two years earlier in *Rex v Inhabitants of Harborne*: 'I must take this opportunity of saying, that nothing can be more absurd than the notion, that there is to be any rigid presumption of law on such questions of fact, without reference to accompanying circumstances, such, for instance, as the age or health of the party.' and, later on: '. . . the only questions in such cases are, what evidence is admissible, and what inference may fairly be drawn from it.' It is the latter proposition upon which Hodson J founded his above cited statement 'there is no presumption of law as to continuance of life.'

On the basis, which I have adopted, that any presumption of continuance of life is simply one of fact, the various decisions cited to me and the dicta therein become reconciled. Further, due weight can thus be given in each case to the different circumstances of any given individual, e.g., whether a friendless orphan or a gregarious man in public life, whether in good or in bad health, and whether following a quiet or a dangerous occupation.

Turning next to the question as to presumptions of deaths (whether before or after a lapse of seven years) the same reasoning to my mind generally applies — save in one set of circumstances to which I will refer later. I respectfully agree with Harman J's conclusion in *In re Watkins* that, where no statute applies, there is no 'magic' in the mere fact of a period of seven years elapsing without there being positive evidence of a person being alive. It is, generally speaking, a matter in each case of taking the facts as a whole and of balancing, as a jury would, the respective probabilities of life continuing and having ceased.

That line of approach was adopted by Harman J in the case cited when holding, on the facts, that death was to be presumed in the relevant 26 years. A similar approach was adopted by the Divisional Court (Lord Merriman P and Collingwood J) in their decision in *Bradshaw v Bradshaw*. There the court, upon the facts, declined to accede to the plea of a wife that her first husband be presumed dead by 1940 — where, on the one hand, she had not then heard from him for some 19 years, but, on the other hand, had made no inquiries in that period. Similarly, the decisions of the Divisional Courts in *Ivett v Ivett*, where Hill J and Bateson J were not prepared to assume death after the lapse of some seven years when there were facts which could account for the husband not being heard of, and in *Hogton v Hogton*, where, on the other hand, death within six years was presumed, both appear in the upshot to have turned on the question as to 'what were the proper inferences to be drawn from established facts.' If any dicta in the rather unusual case of *In re Phené's Trusts* (1870) 5 Ch App 139 tend in a contrary direction, then they seem to me to run counter to the general stream of authority. There it was sought to make title to a share in a residuary estate by establishing that Nicholas Phené Hill was alive on January 5, 1861, but on the facts in that case it was held that a United States marine sergeant in good health, who disappeared when on leave from his ship and was then not heard of for more than seven years, was not 'proved affirmatively to have survived' seven months from the time his leave was up, though it was also stated that the court would have inferred that he died whilst on leave during those seven months.

At this point I should mention that the decision in *Bradshaw v Bradshaw* (Mr Campbell helpfully put before me the full terms of the judgment and details of the cases cited) might at first sight appear to conflict with certain passages in the judgment in *Chipchase v Chipchase* [1939] P. 31 if those latter passages were both taken too literally and were intended to apply beyond the particular facts there under consideration. In the *Chipchase* case a lapse of 12 years was being discussed, the wife again being, as in *Bradshaw's* case, the sole witness to the husband not having been heard of, and Sir Boyd Merriman P, when referring to 'the presumption which arises in circumstances of this kind,' stated: 'That presumption — I am taking the statement of it from the judgment of Giffard LJ in *In re Phené's Trusts* — is that the law presumes a person who has not been heard of for over seven years to be dead. . . .' Henn Collins J said: 'As soon as it was established . . . that the former husband . . . had not been heard of for seven years, then undoubtedly there was evidence for their consideration that he was dead, and it was more than evidence because it was a presumption and conclusive evidence until rebutted by evidence which showed, in fact, that he was alive.'

In neither of these passages is there added after the words 'heard of' a phrase such as 'by persons who would naturally have heard of him, if alive,' (*per* Hodson J in *MacDarmaid's* case). *Chipchase's* case was, however, cited in *Bradshaw's* case and not there commented upon, and to my mind there is no conflict between them. The passages above set out related to the facts of the particular case and are to be construed on the footing that the words 'heard of' were used in that particular sense which Lord Blackburn analysed in his speech in *Prudential Assurance Co.* v *Edmonds* where, after referring to the necessity for inquiries and searches, he concluded: 'in order to raise a presumption that a man is dead from his not having been heard of for seven years, you must inquire amongst those who, if he was alive, would be likely to hear of him, and see whether or no there has been *such an absence of hearing of him*' (the italics are mine) 'as would raise the presumption that he was dead.'

Were I, however, to be wrong in my conclusion as to there being no conflict, then I would have elected to follow *Bradshaw's* case, especially as a full range of authorities, including *In re Watkins*, were there laid before the court, whilst in *Chipchase's* case apparently the only authority to which the court was referred was *In re Phené's Trust*: and there the judgment not being concerned with the precise point now under consideration, the reference to the presumption was made in terms of the type which later attracted examination by Lord Blackburn (see also *In re Watkins*).

My view is thus that in matters where no statute lays down an applicable rule, the issue of whether a person is, or is not to be presumed dead, is generally speaking one of fact and not subject to a presumption of law.

To that there is an exception which can be assumed without affecting the present case. By virtue of a long sequence of judicial statements, which either assert or assume such a rule, it appears accepted that there is a convenient presumption of law applicable to certain cases of seven years' absence where no statute applies. That presumption in its modern shape takes effect (without examining its terms too exactly) substantially as follows. Where as regards 'A.B.' there is no acceptable affirmative evidence that he was alive at some time during a continuous period of seven years or more, then if it can be proved first, that there are persons who would be likely to have heard of him over that period, secondly that those persons have not heard of him, and thirdly that all due inquiries have been made appropriate to the circumstances, 'A.B.' will be presumed to have died at some time within that period. (Such a presumption would, of course be one of law, and could not be one of fact, because there can hardly be a logical inference from any particular set of facts that a man had not died within 2,555 days but had died within 2,560.)

Mr Campbell has cogently argued that the greater regimentation and registration of our lives and deaths in 1955 now renders unrealistic any such general presumption, at any rate where a death certificate could be expected to be found but is not; and has suggested that as the dicta really originate from judgments of the first half of last century when the presumption of continuing life was also regarded as one of law, they too are now suspect. Further, it appears on examination that some of the above dicta derive either from some case such as *Nepean's* case, to which some statute applied, and that others, as in *MacDarmaid's* case, were based on earlier judgments in such cases. Against that, however, one can point to yet others, e.g., Lord Ellenborough in *Hopewell* v *de Pinna*, and Lord Blackburn's speech in *Prudential Assurance Co.* v *Edmonds*, where there is no apparent trace of such an origin: and the rule has even been said to have been traced back before the statute of James I, e.g., to *Thorne* v *Rolff*. (See the useful discussion of the rule and its older shapes in the 1890 articles in 34 Solicitors' Journal.) It is, however, not necessary for me to deal further with the questions raised by Mr Campbell because in the present case there is no one who has been shown to have been likely to have heard from the 1909 wife in the years 1917 to 1933 or, indeed, from 1933 to date and so such a rule could not operate.

The present case is thus one where there is no suggestion that in 1917 the 1909 wife was other than a woman of normal health, nor any evidence of any fact by reason of which her expectation of life could be regarded as greatly sub-normal. There are many factors which, as previously mentioned, might have led her not to wish to be heard of by the prisoner or his family, there is no one known who would naturally have heard of her, and there is no registration of a relevant death.

I accordingly approach the matter on the footing (1) that this is a case in which the court is put upon inquiry as to the validity of the 1933 marriage; (2) that once the husband was shown to have contracted the 1909 marriage it is for him (or his present wife) to prove facts from which a cessation before May 18, 1933, of the earlier marriage can be inferred before it can be said that the 1933 marriage is valid (see *MacDarmaid's* case); (3) that there is in the present case no presumption of law either as to the continuance of life or as to death having supervened; (4) that this is thus one of the class of cases which has to be determined on its own facts.

Note

A court will not generally presume that the person died on a particular day within the seven-year period, merely that death occured at some time within it (*Re Phené's Trusts* (1870) 5 Ch App 139). On at least one occasion, this view has not been followed (see *Re Aldersey, Gibson* v *Hall* [1905] 2 Ch 181) although there appears to be no modern English authority on the point.

Law of Property Act 1925

184. Presumption of survivorship in regard to claims to property

In all cases where . . . two or more persons have died in circumstances rendering it uncertain which of them survived the other or others, such deaths shall (subject to any order of the court), for all purposes affecting the title to property, be presumed to have occured in order of seniority, and accordingly the younger shall be deemed to have survived the elder.

Matrimonial Causes Act 1973

19. Presumption of death and dissolution of marriage

(3) In any proceedings under this section the fact that for a period of seven years or more the other party to the marriage has been continually absent from the

petitioner and the petitioner has no reason to believe that the other party has been living within that time shall be evidence that the other party is dead until the contrary is proved.

Offences against the Person Act 1861

57. Bigamy
. . . Provided, that nothing in this section contained shall extend to . . . any person marrying a second time whose husband or wife shall have been continually absent from such person for the space of seven years then last past, and shall not have been known by such person to be living within that time . . . .

(iv) Presumption of regularity

This presumption is often expressed in the maxim *omnia praesumuntur rite et solemniter esse acta* and enables a court (in the absence of evidence in rebuttal) to presume any one of three separate matters:

(a) Where it is proved that an official act has been performed, it is presumed that the act done complied with any necessary formalities and the person so acting was properly appointed for the purpose.

R v Roberts
(CCR) (1878) 14 Cox 101
Crown Cases Reserved

The prisoner was tried before me on the 10th May inst. upon an indictment for perjury.

The indictment alleged the offence to have been committed before 'Joseph Underhill, Esq., then being and sitting as the duly qualified and appointed deputy judge of the County Court of Warwickshire.

A minute of the proceedings of the County Court was put in as evidence on the part of the prosecution, which was intituled as follows:

Minute of judgments, orders, and other proceedings at a court holden at Birmingham, in the county of Warwick, on the 13th Nov. 1877, before Joseph Underhill, Esq., deputy judge of the said court.

A certificate was written on the minute in these words:

We hereby certify that the above is a true copy of an entry in the minute book of judgments, orders, and other proceedings of the County Court of Warwickshire, holden at Birmingham.

Dated this 4th Dec. 1877.

JOHN COLE,   } Registrars
EDWIN PARRY }

The certificate bore the seal of the County Court.

Proof was also given that the alleged perjury took place in the presence of Mr. Underhill, at the County Court.

An objection was taken by the counsel for the prisoner that proof should have been given of the appointment of Mr. Underhill as deputy judge.

LORD COLERIDGE CJ: I am of opinion that the conviction should be affirmed. One of the best recognised principles of law, *Omnia presumuntur esse rite et solemniter acta donec probetur in contrarium*, is applicable to public officers acting in discharge of public duties. The mere acting in a public capacity is sufficient *prima facie* proof of the proper appointment; but it is only a *prima facie* presumption, and it is capable of being rebutted, and in the case of *Rex v Verelst* that presumption was rebutted in fact, and the person who there had acted as surrogate for twenty years was proved to have been improperly appointed. The case of *Rex v Verelst* is exceedingly like this; there the fact of Dr Parson having acted as surrogate was held by Lord Ellenborough CJ, to be sufficient *prima facie* evidence that he was duly appointed, and had competent authority to administer an oath, and for that proposition *Rex v Verelst* was referred to as good law by Lord Campbell CJ, in *Wolton v Gavin*. But it was further shown in *Rex v Verelst* that Dr Parson had never been regularly appointed as surrogate, and Lord Ellenborough then held that the evidence that Dr Parson was not duly appointed a surrogate could not be shut out, however long he might have acted in that capacity, and that the presumption arising from his acting only stood until the contrary was proved. That is an instructive case, as showing the true rule as to the *prima facie* presumption in such cases. It is laid down in all the text books as a recognised principle that a person acting in the capacity of a public officer is *prima facie* to be taken to be so, and that principle was adopted by Patteson J in *Doe dem. Bowley v Barnes*, in 8 QB 1043. In that case there was a demise by the churchwardens and overseers of some parish property, and the fact that they acted as churchwardens and overseers at the time of the demise was held to be sufficient *prima facie* proof for the purpose of an action of ejectment without proving their appointment. His Lordship then referred to the decision of Tindal CJ to the same effect in *Reg. v Newton* (Car & Kir 469), and to *Reg. v Jones* (2 Camp 131). This objection, if it were good, would extend very widely, for, suppose perjury committed on the first time of acting in his office before a judge or a recorder, or a County Court judge, or any person who fills a responsible public position, would it lie on the prosecution to show the appointment of such an officer in the strictest possible way? Mr Jelf has not satisfied me that it would, and no member of the court has any doubt that there is no ground for such a contention . . .

The rest of the Court concurred.

R v Dillon
[1982] AC 484
Privy Council

LORD FRASER OF TULLYBELTON: The appellant defendant is a police constable in Jamaica. He was convicted on indictment before a resident magistrate of having negligently permitted two prisoners lawfully in his custody to escape. There was no evidence from warrants or court orders or other written documents of any authority for holding the prisoners in custody. The issue in the appeal is whether it was necessary for the Crown to prove that the prisoners had been lawfully arrested or were being lawfully detained.

At the close of the case for the prosecution, the attorney who appeared for the defendant submitted to the resident magistrate (Mr A. J. Lambert) that there was no case to answer, on the ground that it was incumbent on the Crown to prove that the prisoners were in lawful custody and that it had omitted to do so. The resident magistrate, without making any specific finding as to the lawfulness of the custody, convicted the defendant on both charges. The defendant appealed to the Court of Appeal of Jamaica which by a majority (Robinson P. and Robotham J.A. (Ag.), Watkins J.A. dissenting) dismissed his appeal.

The facts were found by the resident magistrate and are not now in dispute. On April 25, 1976, the defendant was a member of the Jamaica Constabulary Force, and on that day he was on duty in the downstairs cell block at the central police station lock-up in the parish of Kingston. His duties there included guarding the cells and ensuring that prisoners in custody did not escape. Among the persons in the cells for which the defendant was responsible were Paul Bryan and Robert Blackwood. While the defendant's immediately superior officer was engaged on duties elsewhere, the defendant opened the cells occupied by Bryan and Blackwood and negligently permitted them to escape.

As regards the circumstances in which the prisoners were then being held in the cells, the evidence was to the following effect. Bryan had been arrested on February 28, 1976, and, according to the constable who made the arrest, he had been 'charged for shooting with intent.' That expression was not further explained, and it is not clear whether Bryan had been taken before a magistrate or whether a charge had merely been preferred by the police. In any event he escaped from custody on or about March 2, 1976, but was recaptured on March 24, 1976. There was no evidence to show whether he had been brought before a magistrate at any time between March 24 and his escape on April 25, 1976, or that on the latter date any written authority existed for his detention. But if he had not been brought before a magistrate during that period of a month, his continued detention would by April 25 have become unlawful, as the Crown rightly conceded. The evidence relating to Blackwood was that a detective officer of the constabulary had seen him in the remand section of the General Penitentiary in Kingston on April 16, 1976, and that on April 23, 1976, he had been transferred from the penitentiary to the central lock-up with a view to his being placed on an identification parade in connection with cases of murder which were being investigated. There was no evidence as to any power pursuant to which he had been in the remand section of the General Penitentiary, or had been transferred to the lock-up or held there.

The argument for the Crown, which was accepted by the resident magistrate and by the majority of the Court of Appeal, was that the Crown did not have to prove that the prisoners were in lawful custody as the Crown was entitled to rely on a presumption to that effect in accordance with the maxim *omnia praesumuntur rite et solemniter esse acta donec probetur in contrarium.* Alternatively reliance was placed on the provisions of section 16(2) of the Prisons Act, to be mentioned below.

Their Lordships will consider first the question whether the presumption, quoted above, is applicable to the circumstances of this appeal. In *Hawkin's Pleas of the Crown*, 7th ed. (1795), vol. 3, p. 252, the author considers what shall be judged an escape and states, inter alia, the following rules:

Section 1. First, there must be an actual arrest; . . .

Section 2. Secondly, as there must be an actual arrest, such arrest must also be justifiable; for if it be either for a supposed crime, where no such crime was committed . . . or for such a slight suspicion of an actual crime . . . as will neither justify the arrest nor imprisonment, the officer is not guilty of an escape by suffering the prisoner to go at large: and it seems to be a good general rule, that wherever an imprisonment is so far irregular that it will be no offence in the prisoner to break from it by force, it can be no offence in the officer to suffer him to escape. . . .

Section 4. Fourthly, as the imprisonment must be justifiable, and for some crime, so must its continuance at the time of the escape be grounded on that satisfaction which the public justice demands for such crime; . . .

Accordingly in *Archbold Criminal Pleading Evidence & Practice*, 40th ed. (1979), para. 3428, dealing with the evidence required for proving an indictment against a constable for negligently permitting an escape, we find this:

Prove that AB is a police constable and that he had JN in actual custody *under a lawful warrant*. See 2 Hawk c. 19, ss. 1, 4. And lastly, prove the escape. (Emphasis added).

Their Lordships are of opinion that it was essential for the Crown to establish that the arrest and detention were lawful and that the omission to do so was fatal to the conviction of the defendant (subject to the argument based on section 16(2) below). The lawfulness of the detention was a necessary pre-condition for the offence of permitting escape, and it is well established that the courts will not presume the existence of facts which are central to an offence: see *Reg.* v *Willis* (1872) 12 Cox CC 164; *Scott* v *Baker* [1969] 1 QB 659.

Moreover this particular offence is one which touches the liberty of the subject, and on which there is, for that reason also, no room for presumptions in favour of the Crown. If there were to be a presumption that any person de facto in custody was there lawfully, the scales would be tipped in favour of the fait accompli in a way that might constitute a serious threat to liberty. It has to be remembered that in every case where a police officer commits the offence of negligently permitting a prisoner to escape from lawful custody, the prisoner himself commits an offence by escaping, and it would be contrary to fundamental principles of law that the onus should be upon a prisoner to rebut a presumption that he was being lawfully detained which he could only do by the (notoriously difficult) process of proving a negative.

On the other hand, there is not likely to be any difficulty for the Crown in proving the lawfulness of the detention, when it exists. Production of the warrant for arrest, or of a magistrate's order for detention, or of a suitably certified copy, is normally all that is required, and it should be in the possession of the person in charge of the prison or lock-up. Thus we find that in the case of a person charged with an offence and remanded in custody to any prison or lock-up, section 18 of the Prisons Act provides that the person is to be delivered to the superintendent of the prison or the person in charge of the lock-up 'together with the warrant or commitment.' That is a recognition of the fact that, without some written voucher or authority, the person in charge of a prison or lock-up would not be entitled to receive and detain a prisoner in custody: *Rex* v *Fitzgerald* (1920) 55 Ir LT 60. The only circumstances in which more than comparatively formal evidence would be required and where there is no written authority for the prisoner's detention, for example, in a case where he has been lawfully arrested without a warrant and has escaped before there has been time for him to be brought before a magistrate. But no such circumstances exist in the cases of either of the prisoners Bryan and Blackwood. Bryan had been detained for over a month from the date of his recapture (March 24 to April 25). Blackwood had been detained for nine days from the date when he was first seen in the penitentiary (April 16 to 25) and in any event what is primarily required in his case is authority for his removal from the penitentiary to the lock-up: authority which would apparently be given by an order issued by the minister under section 22 of the Prisons Act. Their Lordships are therefore of opinion that the presumption ought not to have been admitted in this case.

. . . [T]heir Lordships will humbly advise Her Majesty that this appeal should be allowed with costs to the defendant and his convictions quashed.

(b)   If it is proved that some sort of mechanical device is usually in good working order, it will be presumed that it was in good working order on a relevant occasion.

Tingle Jacobs & Co. v *Kennedy*
[1964] 1 WLR 638
Court of Appeal

About 11.40 p.m. on April 4, 1962, a collision occurred on the cross-roads at the junction of Clarence Street and Thames Street, Kingston-upon-Thames, Surrey, between a Vauxhall motor car belonging to the plaintiffs, Tingle Jacobs & Co. (a firm), and driven by their agent, and an Austin car owned and driven by the defendant, James Kennedy. The crossing was controlled in each direction by traffic lights which were phased and staggered. The plaintiffs claimed damages for negligence in respect of the cost of repairs of their Vauxhall and the defendant, denying negligence, counterclaimed for the cost of repairs to the Austin. At the trial the plaintiffs' evidence was that their driver, travelling westwards down Clarence Street, saw that the light was green and was crossing the junction when the defendant's car came across from Thames Street ahead of him and he ran into it. Two witnesses were called in support of that evidence, the driver of a car and a motor cyclist behind, who said that the light was green in Clarence Street when the Vauxhall went over the crossing. Against that evidence, the defendant and his wife, who was with him, gave evidence, the defendant saying that in Thames Street when he first saw the light it was red, but that then it turned to amber, and then to green, and that when it turned to green he went forward in Thames Street, there being a collision in the middle of the crossing. A police sergeant gave evidence of inspection of the lights on January 16 and April 16, 1962, and of their working. The county court judge said that he was unable to hold that the lights were working properly and, having come to the firm conclusion that the court was quite unable to decide where the truth lay as to whether either party had crossed the lights at green, he held that each was negligent towards the other in failing to keep a proper look-out and apportioned liability equally between the parties. The plaintiffs appealed. The case is reported only on the approach of the court to the question whether the traffic lights were in working order.

LORD DENNING MR: . . . In such a case as this it is plain that, whilst not accusing either side of dishonesty, one side or the other must be mistaken: and it is the duty of a judge in such circumstances to come to a decision upon the conflict between them. The judge in this case unfortunately felt himself unable to come to a decision. He said: 'If this court believes that both sets of witnesses were telling the truth, then the only question left is whether the lights were working properly or not.' Then he said: 'I am quite unable to hold that the lights were working properly.' I must say that I do not think that suggestion has any foundation whatsoever. There was a sergeant from the traffic department of New Scotland Yard, who gave evidence of the inspection of these lights. They had been inspected in January and in April and there had been no reports of complaints or any trouble about them at all. It seems to me in the face of that evidence it would not be right to suggest the lights were not working properly. Furthermore, when you have a device of this kind set up for public use in active operation, I should have thought the presumption should be that it is in proper working order unless there is evidence to the contrary; and there was none here. Therefore, I cannot go with the suggestion of the judge that the lights were not working properly. I think the case should be decided on the basis that they were working properly.

[His Lordship considered the judge's conclusions and continued:] I am afraid that in this case the judge did not take the responsibility upon him to come to a decision between these parties. I think he ought to have found which of them crossed on the green; and therefore come to a conclusion as to which was to blame. I think that the only thing this court can do in the circumstances is to remit the case and say there should be a new trial.

PEARSON LJ: agreeing delivered a judgment concurring in ordering a new trial.

SALMON LJ: agreed.

Note
Traffic lights are but one example of the kind of device which will attract this presumption. The list is potentially endless but other examples often encountered in practice would be speedometers of police cars and breath testing equipment.

Question
Dillon (above) suggests that the presumption of regularity cannot be used by the prosecution to establish facts central to the offence. If D is charged with an offence of driving through a red traffic signal, should the prosecution be able to rely on the presumption in order to establish that the traffic signals were working correctly?

(c)   If it is proved that necessary business transactions have been carried out, then if those transactions are required to be in any particular order, it will be presumed that they were effected in that proper order.

Eaglehill Ltd v J. Needham (Builders) Ltd
[1973] AC 992
House of Lords

The appellants were holders for value of a bill of exchange for £7,660 dated 28 August 1970, drawn by the respondent builders and accepted by a furniture company payable at a bank in High Wycombe. The bill was due and payable on 31 December 1970. Shortly after the appellants had discounted the bill the acceptors went into liquidation and the appellants and the respondents knew that the bill would be dishonoured on presentation. The appellants prepared a notice of dishonour dated 1 January 1971. By mistake the notice was posted on 30 December, 1970, and arrived at the acceptors' High Wycombe office by the first post on 31 December 1970. The bill was sent by post to the bank and arrived there also by the first post on 31 December. It was dishonoured on that day.

LORD CROSS OF CHELSEA: My Lords, this is an appeal from an order of the Court of Appeal made on November 30, 1971, whereby by a majority (Sachs and Stamp LJJ, Lord Denning MR dissenting) they allowed an appeal by the respondents, J. Needham Builders, Ltd, from a judgment of Donaldson J given on May 28, 1971, in favour of the appellants, Eaglehill Ltd, for £7,660 on a dishonoured bill of exchange . . .

Not surprisingly there was no evidence to show at what precise moments of time on the morning of December 31 these two pieces of paper were first seen in the offices of the bank and the respondents respectively by persons competent to deal with them. I cannot agree with Sachs LJ that it is more probable that the notice of dishonour was received before than after the bill was dishonoured. It is impossible to say which event happened first. All that one can say is that it is probable that there was only a short interval of time between them. That being so, the respondents say that the appellants have failed to prove that due notice of dishonour was given, while the appellants say that it should be presumed in their favour, in the absence of evidence to the contrary, that the dishonour preceded the notice of dishonour.

The presumption for which the appellants contend may be expressed as follows:

If two acts have been done one of which ought to have been done after the other if it was to be valid and the evidence which could reasonably be expected to be available does not show which was done first they will be presumed to have been done in the proper order.

Such a presumption would not be — as was suggested in argument — an application of the maxim *omnia praesumuntur rite esse acta* for it is abundantly clear that the posting of the notice on December 30 was wholly irregular.

It would be an extension into another field of the maxim that a document which is reasonably capable of two constructions should be construed *ut res magis valeat quam pereat*. Such an extension appears to me to be justified — at all events in the case of commercial documents such as those with which we are here concerned. As it would be rebuttable its existence would not encourage those in whose favour it might operate to be careless whether or not the due time had arrived for the doing of the act in question. In practice it would only operate when as here there had been a mistake and it would have the merit of discouraging those against whom it would operate from seeking to take advantage of a slip by the other side in cases where they could not prove that the slip had led to the acts in question being done in the wrong order. In arguing against the existence of such a presumption counsel for the respondents relied strongly on the case of *Castrique v Bernabo* (1844) 6 QB 498. There after a bill had been dishonoured the plaintiff posted a notice of dishonour to the defendant between 2 and 3 p.m., and issued a writ against him on the same day. The evidence showed that in the ordinary course of post in London in 1844 the letter would have reached the defendant, who lived in Oxford Street, between 4 and 5 p.m., and that the offices of the court were open until 5 p.m., but there was no evidence to show whether the writ was issued before or after the notice reached the defendant. On those facts counsel for the plaintiff asked the court to presume that the receipt of the notice preceded the issue of the writ but Lord Denman, with the approval of Williams, Coleridge and Wightman JJ, refused to do so and held that the plaintiff's action failed because he had failed to discharge the onus which lay on him showing that he had a right of action at the moment at which he issued his writ. It is true that the later case of *Kennedy* v *Thomas* [1894] 2 QB 759 shows that the plaintiff in *Castrique* v *Bernabo* should have failed anyway since, although the dishonour of the bill gives the holder an immediate right of recourse against the indorser, his right of action against him is not complete until after the end of the last day of grace; but the fact that the case could have been decided in the defendant's favour on other grounds may fairly be said to be for present purposes an irrelevant consideration. It is, however, to be observed that in that case there was an obvious gap in the evidence advanced by the plaintiff. He had called no evidence to show at what hour the writ had been issued — a fact which should have been within his knowledge — or given any explanation of his failure to adduce such evidence. Although the judgment as reported does not refer to this circumstance it may well have influenced the decision of the court not to apply the presumption for which the plaintiff was contending. But if the refusal of the court to apply a presumption in favour of the plaintiff cannot be explained in that way then I think that the ratio decidendi of that case was wrong. For these reasons I would allow this appeal.

(v)   The presumption of negligence — res ipsa loquitur

Scott v London and St Katherine Docks Co.
(1865) 3 H & C 596
Court of Exchequer Chamber

ERLE CJ: The majority of the Court have come to the following conclusions: —
There must be reasonable evidence of negligence.
But where the thing is shewn to be under the management of the defendant or his servants, and the accident is such as in the ordinary course of things does not happen if those who have the management use proper care, it affords reasonable evidence, in the absence of explanation by the defendants, that the accident arose from want of care.

Note
It is the effect of the presumption which remains open to debate. If the presumption operates, what standard of evidence is required to rebut it?

Barkway v South Wales Transport Co. Ltd
[1949] 1 KB 54
Court of Appeal

SCOTT LJ: . . . [T]he mounting of the omnibus on the footpath was a fact which raised the presumption expressed in the phrase *res ipsa loquitur*. That phrase, however, represents nothing more than a *prima facie* presumption of fault. It is rebuttable by the same defence as is open to any defendant accused of negligence, against whom the plaintiff's evidence has made out a *prima facie* case. When the plaintiff has done that, the *onus* is said to shift to the defendant. In a case where *res ipsa loquitur* the *onus* starts on the defendant and requires him to prove affirmatively that he has exercised all reasonable care, but that proof is very greatly facilitated if he can show that the event which caused the plaintiff damage happened through some cause for which no blame can attach to him, even though it cannot be specifically identified, and, if it can be so identified, his task is not only facilitated but achieved. If he thus succeeds in demonstrating positively the probable operation of such cause, whether specifically identifiable or not, the *onus* is then discharged, and the presumption of fault on his part ceases and the plaintiff is left in the position of having failed to prove his case. Even if he can point to no specific cause, he still discharges it if he can show that he used all reasonable care . . .

ASQUITH LJ: The position as to *onus* of proof in this case seems to me to be fairly summarised in the following short propositions. (i) If the defendants' omnibus leaves the road and falls down an embankment, and this without more is proved, then *res ipsa loquitur*, there is a presumption that the event is caused by negligence on the part of the defendants, and the plaintiff succeeds unless the defendants can rebut this presumption. (ii) It is no rebuttal for the defendants to show, again without more, that the immediate cause of the omnibus leaving the road is a tyre-burst, since a tyre-burst *per se* is a neutral event consistent, and equally consistent, with negligence or due diligence on the part of the defendants. When a balance has been tilted one way, you cannot redress it by adding an equal weight to each scale. The depressed scale will remain down. This is the effect of the decision in *Laurie* v *Raglan Building Co., Ltd*, where not a tyre-burst but a skid was involved. (iii) To displace the presumption, the defendants must go further and prove (or it must emerge from the evidence as a whole) either (a) that the burst itself was due to a specific cause which does not connote negligence on their part but points to its absence as more probable, or (b), if they can point to no such specific cause, that they used all reasonable care in and about the management of their tyres . . .

Henderson v *Henry E. Jenkins & Sons*
[1970] AC 282
House of Lords

A lorry owned by the first respondents and driven by the second respondent, was descending a hill when the brakes failed and the lorry struck and killed a Post Office driver who had just alighted from his van. The failure was due to the sudden escape of brake fluid from a hole in a pipe in the hydraulic braking system resulting from corrosion of that pipe. The pipe was fixed under the lorry's chassis and only 60 per cent of the pipe could be seen on visual inspection with the pipe *in situ*: only the unseen part of the pipe had been affected by corrosion. The appellant, the widow, claimed damages against the respondents and alleged, *inter alia*, that they had been negligent in failing to keep the braking system in efficient repair. The respondents pleaded that the accident had been caused by a latent defect which had occurred without any fault on their part and the existence of which was not discoverable by the exercise of reasonable care. The evidence showed that the lorry was probably five years old; that weekly maintenance had included washing the lorry and inspection of the pipe *in situ* and that nine months prior to the accident the lorry had been steam cleaned. The Ministry of Transport and the manufacturers did not advocate the removal of the pipes and it was stated that there was a danger of fracturing or kinking them if they were removed for inspection, but there was no evidence as to the lorry's mileage, the loads it had carried and the areas in which it had been used. None of the experts stated an opinion as to the cause of the corrosion, but it was suggested that leakage from a corrosive substance carried by the lorry or salt, either from the lorry travelling near the sea or passing over snow treated with salt, might cause corrosion. Nield J was satisfied that proper care had been taken to maintain the vehicle; that inspection of the pipes *in situ* was all that was required; and that, as the corrosion was at the back of the pipe, the respondents were not to blame for not seeing it; and he found that negligence had not been established. The Court of Appeal, by a majority, upheld his decision.

LORD REID: It may be that they [the defendants] could have proved that so far as they knew or could have discovered by reasonable inquiry nothing unusual ever happened to it which could have led to this corrosion. Or it may be that they did know of something but did not realise the possible danger resulting from it though they ought to have done so. We do not know. They had to prove that in all the circumstances which they knew or ought to have known they took all proper steps to avoid danger. In my opinion they have failed to do that, and I am therefore of opinion that this appeal should be allowed . . .

LORD DONOVAN: It was for the respondents to deal with these matters by evidence. They were asserting, and had to prove, that they exercised all reasonable care; but whether they had or not depended upon what the facts were in the foregoing respects. Yet on these matters they chose to give no evidence at all. The result was that they failed to establish their defence and should have lost the case.

LORD PEARSON: In an action for negligence the plaintiff must allege, and has the burden of proving, that the accident was caused by negligence on the part of the defendants. That is the issue throughout the trial, and in giving judgment at the end of the trial the judge has to decide whether he is satisfied on a balance of probabilities that the accident was caused by negligence on the part of the defendants, and if he is not so satisfied the plaintiff's action fails. The formal burden of proof does not shift. But if in the course of the trial there is proved a set of facts which raises a prima facie inference that the accident was caused by negligence on the part of the defendants, the issue will be decided in the plaintiff's favour unless the defendants by their evidence provide some answer which is adequate to displace the prima facie inference. In this situation there is said to be an evidential burden of proof resting on the defendants. I have some doubts whether it is strictly correct to use the expression 'burden of proof' with this meaning, as there is a risk of it being confused with the formal burden of proof, but it is a familiar and convenient usage . . .

From these facts it seems to me clear, as a prima facie inference, that the accident must have been due to default of the defendants in respect of inspection or maintenance or both. Unless they had a satisfactory answer, sufficient to displace the inference, they should have been held liable.

P.S. Atiyah, '*Res Ipsa Loquitur* in England and Australia' (1972) 35 MLR 337, pp. 340–2

It really is time that English courts made up their minds what the doctrine of *res ipsa loquitur* is all about. Although the maxim has been with us for over

100 years, English courts have still not finally settled (or at least have not consciously settled) the most crucial issue involved in its application. Indeed they frequently appear to be unaware of the nature of this issue, which is all the more surprising since their brethren in the Australian High Court have made their views on this issue abundantly plain in a series of cases extending over the past thirty-five years.

In *Henderson* v *Henry E Jenkins & Sons* . . . the plaintiff's husband was killed when a lorry belonging to the defendants ran down a hill and knocked him over. It was proved that the cause of the accident was a failure of the brakes and this was itself due to the corrosion of a pipe which carried the brake fluid. It was further proved that the pipe was not fully visible or examinable unless removed from the lorry, and that regular and normal maintenance on the lorry had been carried out. The actual cause of the corrosion was not known but it was established that it was due to chemical reaction and that this was probably due to some substance being splashed or spilt onto the pipe and this may have come from a load carried by the lorry. It was also proved that removal of the pipe for detailed examination was not a normally required precaution except on major overhauls after about 300,000 miles had been done, while the lorry in question had only done about 150,000. At this point the evidence stopped and everything was left to inference and even speculation. By a majority the House of Lords held that the plaintiff was entitled to recover.

It is difficult to see how anyone approaching the evidence dispassionately could reasonably take the view that the plaintiff had proved that negligence of the defendants was more probable than not. Even on the view most favourable to the plaintiff it could only be said that it had been proved that probably something unusual had happened to the lorry. There was no evidence *at all* what this 'something unusual' was, whether the defendants knew or ought to have known of it, and what precautions should have been adopted to deal with it. The truth was that the issue of negligence or no-negligence was simply not proved either way; there may or may not have been negligence, and the decision for the plaintiff seems necessarily to involve that the legal burden of disproving negligence was held to be on the defendants. At least two of the majority and also, it would seem, both of the dissenting judges, saw this as the nature of the issue.

Thus Lord Reid says that the accident was probably due to some unusual event affecting the lorry, and points out that the defendants gave no evidence as to any such event or as to any precautions taken to guard against the consequences. He goes on —

It may be that they [the defendants] could have proved that so far as they knew or could have discovered by reasonable inquiry nothing unusual ever happened to it which could have led to this corrosion. Or it may be that they did know of something but did not realise the possible danger resulting from it though they ought to have done so. We do not know. *They had to prove that in all the circumstances which they knew or ought to have known they took all proper steps to avoid danger.* In my opinion they have failed to do that, and I am therefore of opinion that this appeal should be allowed.

Similarly Lord Donovan said —

It was for the respondents [defendants] to deal with these matters by evidence. They were asserting, *and had to prove*, that they exercised all reasonable care; but whether they had or not depended upon what the facts were in the foregoing respects. Yet on these matters they chose to give no evidence at all. The result was that they failed to establish their defence and should have lost the case.

And again —

I differ from Nield J with regret. But the tenor of his judgment suggests that he dealt with this case as though it were the more usual type where the onus of proof lay on the appellant; whereas in fact the burden of proof that they had taken all reasonable care rested on the respondents.

Lord Guest and Viscount Dilhorne, the dissenting judges, both seem to have accepted that the defendants had the burden of disproving negligence but both held that the defendants had in fact discharged the burden. The most difficult judgment to understand on this question is that of the third member of the majority, Lord Pearson. He starts his judgment by saying that the question turns on 'the evidential burden of proof' and specifically distinguishes this from the legal burden. He goes on to say that the legal burden rests throughout on the plaintiff and that 'at the end of the trial the judge has to decide whether he is satisfied on a balance of probabilities that the accident was caused by negligence on the part of the defendants, and if he is not so satisfied the plaintiff's action fails.' He then goes on to make the very puzzling remark that if there is proof of a set of facts which raises a prima facie inference of negligence, 'the issue *will* be decided in the plaintiff's favour unless the defendants by their evidence provide some answer which is adequate to displace the prima facie inference.'

With great respect to Lord Pearson these two passages seem to be inconsistent. If the issue 'will' be decided in the plaintiff's favour should the defendant not displace the inference of negligence it follows that the plaintiff will win though the ultimate factual issue of negligence remains in doubt. And this can only mean that the legal burden is on the defendant. All traditional formulations of the nature of an evidential, as distinguished from a legal, burden of proof stress that failure to discharge an evidential burden 'may' lead to an adverse finding, but that it will not necessarily do so. It is, of course, clear that the distinction between a legal and an evidential burden is much less significant in a trial by judge than in a trial by jury for in the latter case the significance of an evidential burden means that a jury finding that the burden has not been discharged cannot be upset on appeal. However, where trial is by judge alone an appellate court may today be willing to review findings of negligence or no-negligence almost as freely as though it were trying the case itself. Where this is done the distinction between a legal and an evidential burden seems to be reduced to vanishing point. It may be that Lord Pearson was merely reflecting the viewpoint of a modern appellate judge in formulating his definition of an evidential burden. However, on this assumption it is difficult to understand the stress laid by him on the distinction between a legal and an evidential burden.

. . . The upshot of all this seems to be that, while English judges are reluctant openly to acknowledge the fact, the application of *res ipsa loquitur* in English courts has frequently had the effect of casting a legal burden of proof on the defendant, while a contrary view is taken in Australia. A reasonably impartial commentator may be forgiven if he pays tribute to the clarity of the views expressed by Australian judges while deploring the result in policy terms, and at the same time welcomes the results generally arrived at by English judges while deploring their inability to express their views more clearly.

Questions
1.   If the presumption of *res ipsa loquitur* places a legal burden on the defendant, is this likely to result in any injustice?
2.   Is it necessary or desirable that the presumption should always have the same effect?

(C)   Conflicting presumptions

Writers have questioned whether or not it is possible for a case to arise where two presumptions conflict with each other on the same fact and, if so, how should the court resolve this conflict? The following cases provide some insight into the nature of the problem and its possible resolution.

Taylor v *Taylor*
[1965] 1 All ER 872
High Court

The petitioning wife in a matrimonial suit for divorce or for a declaration of nullity of her marriage to the respondent, T, had been married in 1928 to D, with whom she had cohabited for a few months. She had re-married in 1931, and this marriage was dissolved in 1939. She married T on 1 October 1942. Her husband by the marriage of 1928 died on 29 October 1942. After her marriage to T, the petitioner cohabited with him until 1957, when he left her. She had reasonable grounds for believing that her marriage to D had been invalid for the reason that he was married to another woman at the time. This belief was based on hearsay evidence, admitted at the hearing *de bene esse*, and consisting in part of a statement by D to the petitioner that he had been married once before, of a letter to him in 1930 from his solicitors referring to a trust under which there was an allowance for his children, and on a gift in his will leaving property to his wife, naming her, the name not being that of the petitioner. In 1931 the wife had seen a solicitor's letter, subsequently destroyed by bombing during the war, saying that counsel had advised that her marriage to D was void. It was conceded at the hearing that hearsay evidence was not admissible in divorce proceedings in proof or disproof of validity of marriage. The court found there to be doubt whether the petitioner's marriage to D had been valid.

CAIRNS J: Counsel for the Queen's Proctor concedes that evidence of a ceremony of marriage with the respondent and subsequent cohabitation with him raises a presumption that the marriage to him is valid. He says, however, that the next stage is that proof of the ceremony of marriage with Dale-Lace and subsequent cohabitation with him rebuts the original presumption and creates a presumption the other way, which can only be displaced by proof that the marriage with Dale-Lace was void. He cites two cases: *MacDarmaid v A-G* and *F. A. Gatty and P. V. Gatty v A-G* [1951] P 444. In *MacDarmaid v A-G*, Hodson J, had before him a petition for legitimacy, and the facts were that the petitioner in that case had been born in 1894, and that her parents had gone through a ceremony of marriage in 1925. She claimed to have been legitimated by that marriage. At the date when that case was before the court, the petitioner would only be legitimated if her parents were both unmarried in 1894 at the time of her birth. Her father had been married to one R in 1886, and R was last seen in 1891. Hodson J, held that the onus was on the petitioner to prove that the first marriage had ended by 1894, and he refused so to hold because he found, on the facts, that it was probable that R was then still alive.

The second case, *F. A. Gatty and P. V. Gatty v A-G* which was heard by Karminski J, was also a legitimacy suit. The petitioner in that case was born in 1901, of parents who had gone through a ceremony of marriage in Winnipeg in December, 1897. The father had been previously married, but there had been a divorce decree purporting to dissolve that marriage made in the State of North Dakota earlier in the year 1897. There was doubt about the validity of that decree because the father's domicil of origin was English and there was no clear evidence of change of domicil. Karminski J, ruled that the onus was on the petitioner to prove the validity of the 1897 marriage, which meant that he had to prove the validity of the 1897 divorce. A passage in his judgment indicates the reasons why he took that view. He said:

It is, I think, fair, and I hope not irrelevant, to say this: that whatever conclusion I have to come to about the validity of the Winnipeg marriage, I have no doubt at all that the period of cohabitation, to use a neutral term, which lasted almost exactly thirty years between F. A. Gatty and Mrs Frances Gatty was a happy one, and one which both regarded as in every sense of those words a matrimonial cohabitation. But I cannot, in deciding this matter, deal with it on sentimental grounds. It was argued by leading counsel and by junior counsel who followed him, for the petitioners, that when you have a marriage valid on the face of it with the formalities followed by a long period of cohabitation, that is such strong prima facie evidence of a valid marriage as to shift disproof of it to those who contest it. If in this case the matter had rested on the certificate of marriage at Winnipeg, followed by thirty years of open cohabitation as man and wife, no doubt there would be very great substance in that proposition, but in introducing the matter, and indeed in arguing it, counsel for the petitioners with his invariable candour, pointed out that the matter did not rest there because there is no doubt whatsoever in this case that the Quebec marriage of 1885 was a valid one, that the wife to whom F. A. Gatty was married was alive at the time of the second marriage in Winnipeg in 1897, and that the real question for this court to consider is whether or not the North Dakota decree purporting to dissolve the marriage between F. A. Gatty and Mrs Margaret Gatty was one which can be recognised as valid by the courts of this country. So far as the burden of proof is concerned, in my view on the facts of this case the burden of proof is on the petitioner to prove it, and he does not escape by proving the marriage good as to formalities and period of cohabitation if there are other matters which point to its invalidity.

My attention was drawn in the course of the argument to a large number of authorities on this point. I think it is sufficient if I refer to two quite recent cases. In *Russell* v *A-G* [1949] P 391 a question arose as to the validity of a marriage between the petitioner's parents, who had gone through a ceremony of marriage in a Roman Catholic church and lived thereafter together as husband and wife for many years and had issued nine children; but there was some doubt whether the full twenty-one days' notice had been given to the registrar before the ceremony, and there was evidence that the registrar himself had considered the marriage to have been invalid. In the result, the wife was refused a widow's pension by the Minister of Health, although there was no documentary evidence that the twenty-one days had not elapsed; and it was held that in the absence of decisive evidence to the contrary the validity of the marriage should be presumed. In that case, Barnard J, in giving judgment, said this: 'It is clear from the authorities which have been cited to me that where there is evidence of a ceremony of marriage having been performed, followed by a cohabitation of the parties, the validity of the marriage will be presumed, in the absence of decisive evidence to the contrary. It would be both tragic and chaotic if such a ceremony could, on slender evidence, be declared null and void. On the evidence before me I am satisfied that the presumption ought to prevail. There is no decisive evidence before me to the contrary; there is only the evidence that the registrar seemed to think it was an invalid marriage and that he acted accordingly, and that much later on, the Ministry of Health — no doubt with a proper desire to safeguard public money — was not satisfied on the death of the petitioner's father as to the validity of the marriage and refused to grant the widow a pension. But, as I say, I am satisfied that the presumption of law should prevail and that there is no cogent evidence here to rebut it'. Barnard J, made a declaration accordingly.

The other side of the picture was illustrated in *MacDarmaid* v *A-G*. That was a case where a petitioner claimed that her parents had lawfully married in 1925, and that she had become legitimated by the Legitimacy Act, 1926. She was born in 1894, her father having first married another woman in 1886. There was evidence that there were some difficulties between her father and his first wife, who was last seen at a roller-skating rink in 1891, three years before the petitioner's birth, when the first wife would have been twenty-seven years of age. In a considered judgment, Hodson J, said: 'It is argued on behalf of the petitioner that there is no onus cast on her by s. 1(2) of the Legitimacy Act, 1926, to prove that her father's first wife was dead, but that, as the matter is left in doubt by the evidence, she is entitled to succeed. On behalf of the Attorney-General it is argued that sub-s. (1) does not come into operation in the case of a person whose father was married before the date of her birth unless there is evidence on which, despite the marriage, a declaration of legitimacy can be made. In these circumstances, it is contended that the onus is on the petitioner to prove that the death of Rosa occurred on or before Mar. 14, 1894, or to prove circumstances or facts which the court should accept as prima facie evidence that that death occurred. In my judgment, the proposition contended for by the Attorney-General is correct, and, once the fact of the previous marriage is proved, the petitioner must at least prove facts from which the cessation of the first marriage can properly be inferred before she can succeed.

That is the end of the quotation from *MacDarmaid* v *A-G* and Karminski J, continued:

In my view, that is the test to be followed in this case. In other words, was F. A. Gatty free in December, 1897, to contract a valid marriage with Miss Frances Irwin? That question clearly depends for its answer on whether or not the decree of dissolution by the court of North Dakota is a decree which can be recognised as valid in this country, and that in turn depends on this question: was, or was not, F. A. Gatty domiciled in that State of North Dakota at the time of the institution of the proceedings there, namely, in July, 1897?

I have stated in my summary of the facts that it is common ground that F. A. Gatty's domicil of origin was English. It has, therefore, to be shown that in July, 1897, he had acquired a domicil of choice, either in North Dakota or in the Commonwealth of Massachusetts or in the State of New York, or, as his counsel was disposed to argue, in any State of the United States. The burden on him who asserts a change of domicil from a domicil of origin to a domicil of choice is a heavy one.

An important difference between both these cases and the present one is that in those cases there was no question of the validity of the earlier marriage. In each case an unquestionably valid marriage had been celebrated and it followed that the onus was cast on the party who was contending that it had come to an end, in one case by death and in the other by divorce.

On the question of onus, counsel for the petitioner in the present case starts by saying that there is a heavy onus on anybody who asserts that a marriage, valid in form, followed by cohabitation for fifteen years is invalid; and he further prays in aid the marriage to Knox followed by cohabitation for eight years. He contends that any counter-presumption based on the marriage to Dale-Lace and subsequent cohabitation with him is of far less weight since in that case the cohabitation lasted only for a few months. I cannot accept this approach. It is clear from *F. A. Gatty and P. V. Gatty* v *A-G* that if no reason could be shown for doubting the validity of the earlier ceremony and if no question arose as to the ending of the earlier marriage by death or divorce, then evidence of the earlier marriage would displace the original presumption in favour of the later one.

An alternative way in which counsel for the petitioner presents his case is by saying that the two cross-presumptions as to the two ceremonies of marriage cancel each other out and that then the question is to be decided on a balance of probabilities. He cites in favour of that proposition *R* v *Willshire* (1881) 6 QBD 366. That was an appeal by way of Case Stated to the Court for Crown Cases Reserved on a conviction for bigamy. The facts were these. In 1864, Willshire married A. In 1868, he was charged with bigamy in marrying B in 1868, his wife A being then alive. He was convicted on that charge. In 1879, he married C, and in 1880, C being then alive, he married D. Afterwards, on a charge of bigamy in marrying D, C being then alive, Willshire was convicted, it being held by Lord Coleridge CJ, that there was no evidence that A was alive when Willshire married C, or that the marriage with C was invalid by reason of A being then alive. It was held by a court of five judges that the conviction could not be sustained, as the question should have been left to the jury whether on the above facts A was alive or not, when Willshire married C. The passage in the judgment of Lord Coleridge CJ on which counsel for the petitioner principally relied, is a passage to this effect.

It is said, and I think rightly, that there is a presumption in favour of the validity of this latter marriage [that was the marriage in 1879] but the prisoner showed that there was a valid marriage in 1864, and that the woman he then married was alive in 1868. He thus set up the existence of a life in 1868, which, in the absence of any evidence to the contrary will be presumed to have continued to 1879. It is urged, in effect, that the presumption in favour of innocence, a presumption which goes to establish the validity of the marriage of 1879, rebuts the presumption in favour of the duration of life. It is sufficient to raise a question of fact for the jury to determine.

Lindley J, said he was of the same opinion. He set out the facts and said:

It was contended that Charlotte Lavers was not his wife; because another woman, his wife, was living when he married Lavers. Was such other woman then living? There was evidence both ways. This evidence was not left to the jury, consequently the conviction cannot stand.

Hawkins J's reasons for agreeing can be seen by quoting only three sentences from his judgment:

There was proof that Ellen was alive in 1868; there was presumption that her life continued. The only evidence to the contrary was, that the prisoner presented himself as a bachelor to be married in 1879. Whether that would have satisfied the jury that his former wife was then dead was a question for them to decide, but it was not left to them for decision.

Lopes J said:

The conviction cannot be sustained. There was evidence both ways on the question of the life of Ellen Earle on Sept. 7, 1879, which should have been left to the jury.

Bowen J, simply concurred. I observe that of the five judges who took part in that decision only Lord Coleridge CJ dealt with the case as one of cross-presumptions; and what he was saying, in effect, was that if on a single issue of fact in that case (the issue whether a certain person was or was not alive in 1879) there are two presumptions tending in opposite directions and no other evidence, the question of which presumption prevails is a question of fact. In the present case, however, the two presumptions relate to different matters. If there was no evidence other than that from which the presumptions arise, I think that the presumption in favour of the earlier marriage would necessarily prevail because the validity of the 1942 marriage must be tested by inquiring whether the 1928 marriage was valid and was still subsisting.

I have, however, indicated earlier that I am in doubt about the validity of the marriage to Dale-Lace. I have formed the opinion that the existence of a doubtful earlier marriage is not sufficient to displace the presumption in favour of the petitioner's marriage to the respondent. This opinion is based on the principle enunciated by Barnard, J, in *Russell* v *A-G* and founded on many earlier decisions that:

where there is evidence of a ceremony of marriage having been performed, followed by a cohabitation of the parties, the validity of the marriage will be presumed in the absence of decisive evidence to the contrary.

Asking first: 'is there decisive evidence that the 1928 marriage was invalid', the answer must be 'no'. When, however, one goes on to ask: 'is there decisive evidence that the 1942 marriage was invalid?', the answer is again 'no', because Dale-Lace's conflicting statements about his marital status makes the validity of the 1928 ceremony uncertain.

Therefore, the presumption as to the later marriage prevails, because there is no decisive evidence to the contrary. This does not of course mean that Dale-Lace was married to two women at the same time. Once the conclusion is reached that the later marriage was valid, the doubt which existed as to the earlier one must be resolved by holding it to have been void. I am not overlooking the sentence in the judgment of Karminski J, in *F. A. Gatty and P. V. Gatty v A-G*, where he said:

> So far as the burden of proof is concerned, in my view on the facts of this case the burden of proof is on the petitioner to prove it, and he does not escape by proving the marriage good as to formalities and period of cohabitation if there are other matters which point to its invalidity.

The key words in that sentence are the words 'on the facts of this case', and those facts, as Karminski J, indicated only a little earlier, included the fact that there was no doubt whatsoever that the Quebec marriage, the earlier one, was a valid one. Karminski J, did not say — and I am sure had no intention to imply — that wherever there are circumstances which point to the possible invalidity of the later marriage, the onus is thrown back on the petitioner. The presumption of validity of the later marriage would be of little value if that were so. The principle, on which Karminski J, expressly said that he was founding his decision was that derived from *MacDarmaid v A-G*, that once the fact of a previous marriage is proved, the petitioner must then prove facts from which the cessation of the first marriage can be implied. It is one thing to say that when an earlier marriage is proved, as to the validity of which there is no question, the burden is on the party setting up a later marriage to prove that the earlier one has come to an end. It would be quite another thing to say that where an earlier ceremony of marriage is proved, the validity of which is in doubt, the burden is on the party setting up the later marriage to prove affirmatively that the earlier one was invalid . . .

Questions
1. Is the decision in *Taylor v Taylor* consistent with the decision in *Gatty's* case?
2. Is it possible for a case to exist in which two presumptions conflict in relation to the same fact? If so, how would you suggest a court deal with the conflict?
3. W is the wife of H. W has a secret lover, X. H and X are sailors and in January 1985 they spend two days in England. During this two-day period, both H and X have sexual intercourse with W. After their return to sea X confesses to H and writes to W saying that she will never see him again. At the beginning of October 1985, W gives birth to a child, C. In November 1985, X is washed overboard as his ship is entering New York harbour. He is never seen again. In January 1991, H dies. In January 1993, W discovers that X had a large savings account and that his mother is claiming it as his next of kin. She also finds a will made by H in 1984 leaving £5,000 to X 'provided he survives me' and £20,000 to 'any child of mine living at my death'.

W believes C is X's next of kin. W, acting on C's behalf, wishes to claim:

(a) the savings of X;

(b)   the £5,000 left by H to X which now forms part of X's estate;
(c)   the £20,000 left by H.

Consider what presumptions may arise and how, if at all, they would assist W in her claim on C's behalf.

Further Reading
P. Murphy, *A Practical Approach to Evidence*, 4th ed. (1992), Ch. 17.4
G.H. Treitel, 'The Presumption of Death' (1954) 17 MLR 530
T. Ellis Lewis, 'A Ramble with *Res Ipsa Loquitur*' (1953) 11 CLJ 74

4 COMPETENCE AND COMPELLABILITY

If a witness is permitted by law to testify, he is said to be a competent witness. If a witness can be made to give evidence at the instance of the party who calls him, he is said to be a compellable witness. Subject to exceptions, the law has decided that all persons are both competent and compellable as witnesses.

Where an issue as to competence and/or compellability arises, it is for the trial judge, as a matter of law, to rule upon that issue, although any investigation of competence should take place in the presence of the jury in order that they, as trier of the facts, can guage what weight to give to the witness's evidence in the event of the judge ruling that the witness is competent. Generally, the party who calls the witness will have the burden of proving his competence should that be in issue.

(A)   The defendant in criminal cases

The law as it relates to the defendant in criminal cases is about to be reformed courtesy of the Criminal Justice and Public Order Bill 1994 (see A *(ii)* below). The following sections examine the law both before and after the Criminal Justice and Public Order Bill.

(i)   The position before the Criminal Justice and Public Order Bill 1994

Criminal Evidence Act 1898

1.   Competency of witnesses in criminal cases
Every person charged with an offence shall be a competent witness for the defence at every stage of the proceedings, whether the person so charged is charged solely or jointly with any other person. Provided as follows:

(a)   A person so charged shall not be called as a witness in pursuance of this Act except upon his own application;

(b)   The failure of any person charged with an offence to give evidence shall not be made the subject of any comment by the prosecution . . .

R v *Mutch*
[1973] 1 All ER 178
Court of Appeal

The accused was arrested and charged with robbery in a grocer's shop. The accused denied the charge claiming that he was not in the shop at the time of the incident. He was released on bail. No formal identification parade was held by the police as it was alleged by the prosecution that, whilst on bail and for the purpose of confusing anyone attending an identification parade of which he was the suspect member, the accused tried to alter his appearance by tinting his hair and moustache and by reshaping the latter. At his trial, a girl assistant in the shop at the time of the incident identified the accused but he elected not to give evidence. He did however call two witnesses to prove that he had not altered his appearance as alleged. The trial judge, in summing up, told the jury, *inter alia*, that they were entitled to draw inferences unfavourable to the accused where he was not called to establish an innocent explanation of facts proved by the prosecution which, without such an explanation, told for his guilt. The accused was convicted and he appealed.

LAWTON LJ: It was submitted that the judge was wrong to tell the jury that they were entitled to draw inferences unfavourable to the appellant because of his absence from the witness box and that he had made his error worse by repeating what he had said. . . .

Since the first decade of this century, there have been many cases in which this court and its predecessor have had to rule whether comments about an accused's absence from the witness box or a failure to disclose a defence when questioned by the police were permissible, and as Salmon LJ pointed out in *R* v *Sullivan* (1966) 51 Cr App R 102: The line dividing what may be said and what may not be said is a very fine one, and it is perhaps doubtful whether in a case like the present it would be even perceptible to the members of any ordinary jury.' Nevertheless, as long as the law recognises the so called right to silence, judges must keep their comments on the correct side of the line even though the differences between what is permissible and what is not may have little significance for many jurors. In the circumstances of this case there would be no point in reviewing the cases, some of which are not easy to reconcile, as we are firmly of the opinion that the trial judge used a form of words which was inappropriate to the case and the evidence which he was summing up. The words he used might have been permissible if the evidence had established a situation calling for 'confession and avoidance'; they were not proper for one of flat denial as this case was. The court is of the opinion that the trial judge was led into error by the passage in Archbold to which we have already referred. The concept there set out has a limited application and it would be helpful to both judges and practitioners if this was made clear.

Judges who are minded to comment on an accused's absence from the witness box should remember, first, Lord Oaksey's comment in *Waugh* v *R* [1950] AC 203:

It is true that it is a matter for the judge's discretion whether he shall comment on the fact that a prisoner has not given evidence; but the very fact that the prosecution are not permitted to comment on that fact shows how careful a judge should be in making such comment;

and, secondly, that in nearly all cases in which a comment is thought necessary (the R v Corrie and R v Bernard type of cases being rare exceptions) the form of comment should be that which Lord Parker CJ described in R v Bathurst [1968] 2 QB 99, as the accepted form, namely, that:

. . . the accused is not bound to give evidence, that he can sit back and see if the prosecution have proved their case, and that, while the jury have been deprived of the opportunity of hearing his story tested in cross-examination, the one thing that they must not do is to assume that he is guilty because he has not gone into the witness box.

The trial judge in this case went very near to encouraging this assumption.

Appeal allowed. Conviction quashed.

R v Sparrow
[1973] 1 WLR 488
Court of Appeal

A policeman was shot in the course of a car theft by the appellant and his co-accused. At his trial for murder, the defendant did not give evidence to support his plea that the gun used was only intended to frighten anyone attempting to apprehend them. In his summing up the judge, commenting on the appellant's failure to give evidence, said that if he never contemplated that any shooting would take place it was essential that he should give evidence which could be tested in cross-examination. The appellant was convicted of murder.

LAWTON LJ: . . . In the present case, the charge was murder, and the evidence went to establish that when the police officer was shot by the co-defendant the appellant was standing close by and that after the shooting the pair of them drove off together and that one of them within a short time in the presence of the other reloaded the pistol; there has to be added to that the submission of the appellant's counsel that the prosecution's evidence was consistent with the possibility that the joint enterprise between the co-defendant and the appellant was merely to frighten the police officer with a pistol (which the appellant knew was loaded) and that the co-defendant departed from it by pressing the trigger a number of times.

In the judgment of this court, if the trial judge had not commented in strong terms upon the appellant's absence from the witness box he would have been failing in his duty. The object of a summing up is to help the jury and in our experience a jury is not helped by a colourless reading out of the evidence as recorded by the judge in his notebook. The judge is more than a mere referee who takes no part in the trial save to intervene when a rule of procedure or evidence is broken. He and the jury try the case together and it is his duty to give them the benefit of his knowledge of the law and to advise them in the light of his experience as to the significance of the evidence, and when an accused person elects not to give evidence, in most cases but not all the judge should explain to the jury what the consequences of his absence from the witness box are, and if, in his discretion, he thinks that he should do so more than once he may, but he must keep in mind always his duty to be fair. As A T Lawrence J pointed out in *R* v *Voisin* [1918] 1 KB 531, 536:

> Comments on the evidence which are not misdirections do not by being added together constitute a misdirection.

How should this be done? In *R* v *Bathurst* [1968] 2 QB 99 Lord Parker CJ gave judges some guidance, but what he said was, as he appreciated, *obiter*. It was in these terms, at p. 107:

> . . . as is well known, the accepted form of comment is to inform the jury that, of course, he — the defendant — is not bound to give evidence, that he can sit back and see if the prosecution have proved their case, and that while the jury have been deprived of the opportunity of hearing his story tested in cross-examination, the one thing they must not do is to assume that he is guilty because he has not gone into the witness box.

In many cases, a direction in some such terms as these will be all that is required; but we are sure that Lord Parker CJ never intended his words of guidance to be regarded as a judicial directive to be recited to juries in every case in which a defendant elects not to give evidence. What is said must depend upon the facts of each case and in some cases the interests of justice call for a stronger comment. The trial judge, who has the feel of the case, is the person who must exercise his discretion in this matter to ensure that a trial is fair. A discretion is not to be fettered by laying down rules and regulations for its exercise: see *R* v *Selvey* [1970] AC 304, *per* Lord Hodson, at p. 364. What, however, is of the greatest importance in Lord Parker CJ's advice to judges is his reference to the need to avoid telling juries that absence from the witness box is to be equated with guilt. As we have already said, this was implicit in *Waugh* v *The King* [1950] AC 203 and Lord Parker CJ's dictum on this point has been accepted by this court as the law in *R* v *Pratt* [1971] Crim LR 234 and *R* v *Mulch* [1973] Crim LR 111.

How should these principles be applied in this case? In our judgment there is nothing in the complaint about the cumulative effects of the comments, particularly as the trial judge at the beginning of his summing up explained accurately and clearly that the appellant had a right to remain silent and to rest his defence on the presumption that he was innocent until proved guilty. The interests of justice required that the trial judge should get the jury to understand that an exculpatory statement, unverified on oath, such as the appellant had made after arrest, was not evidence save in so far as it contained admissions, and his task was not made easier by the present state of the law which required the Attorney-General to say nothing about the appellant's silence but allowed the co-defendant's counsel to say what he liked and, were he so minded, to put into words what it is almost certain the majority of the jurors were asking themselves, viz., having regard to the strength of the evidence, if the appellant was innocent why had he not gone into the witness box to say so? Our law, however, does not require a defendant to give evidence and a judge must not either by express words or impliedly give jurors to understand that a defence cannot succeed unless the defendant gives evidence. Unfortunately, probably by a slip of the tongue, that is what the trial judge did when he said to the jury:

> Is it not essential that he should go into the witness box and tell you that himself and be subject to cross-examination about it? Well, he did not do so and there it is.

He did overstep the limits of justifiable comment; he should not have said what he did.

How far did these few words in a long summing up affect the jury's verdict? This must always be a matter of speculation, but we are confident on the facts of this case that the jury would have come to the same verdict if the trial judge had not said what he did. There has been no miscarriage of justice.

Appeal dismissed.

Questions
1. How does the decision in *R* v *Sparrow* differ, if at all, from the decision in *R* v *Mutch*?
2. Should a judge ever, in your opinion, be allowed to comment on the failure of an accused to testify?

(ii) The position when the Criminal Justice and Public Order Bill 1994 becomes law

Note
The following clause in the Criminal Justice and Public Order Bill is one of several which impinge upon the defendant's right to silence or, perhaps more accurately, the inferences which may be drawn from the defendant's refusal or failure to testify or answer questions. As we have seen in (A)*(i)* above, the defendant's failure to testify ought not to be adversely commented upon by the trial judge. Indeed, any comment the judge feels compelled to make should include a warning to the jury that they must not draw any adverse inference from the defendant's failure to testify. The following clause specifically addresses how the defendant's silence at trial will be dealt with in the future. This clause, more than any other, has attracted considerable criticism. It is considered particularly objectionable because the jury will observe the judge require the defendant to give evidence. Critics, including the Lord Chief Justice, say this impinges upon the judge's impartiality in a wholly unacceptable way. It is quite possible that this particular clause will receive modification as the Bill makes its passage through Parliament.

(Other clauses relating to silence are dealt with at Chapter 10(B)*(ii)*.)

Criminal Justice and Public Order Bill 1994

28. Effect of accused's silence at trial
(1) At the trial of any person (other than a child) for an offence subsections (2) to (7) below apply unless —
   (a) the accused's guilt is not in issue; or
   (b) it appears to the court that the physical or mental condition of the accused makes it undesirable for him to be called upon to give evidence; but subsection (2) below does not apply if, before any evidence is called for the defence, the accused or his legal representative informs the court that the accused will give evidence.
(2) Before any evidence is called for the defence, the court —
   (a) shall tell the accused that he will be called upon by the court to give evidence in his own defence; and

(b)   shall tell him in ordinary language what the effect of this section will be if —

(i)   when so called upon; he refuses to be sworn;

(ii)   having been sworn, without good cause he refuses to answer any question;
and thereupon the court shall call upon the accused to give evidence.

(3)   If the accused —

(a)   after being called upon by the court to give evidence in pursuance of this
section, or after he or his legal representative has informed the court that he will give
evidence, refuses to be sworn; or

(b)   having been sworn, without good cause refuses to answer any question,
subsection (4) below applies.

(4)   The court or jury, in determining whether the accused is guilty of the offence
charged, may draw such inferences from the refusal as appear proper.

(5)   This section does not render the accused compellable to give evidence on his
own behalf, and he shall accordingly not be guilty of contempt of court by reason of
a refusal to be sworn.

(6)   For the purposes of this section a person who, having been sworn, refuses to
answer any question shall be taken to do so without good cause unless —

(a)   he is entitled to refuse to answer the question by virtue of any enactment,
whenever passed or made, or on the ground of privilege; or

(b)   the court in the exercise of its general discretion excuses him from answering
it.

(7)   Where the age of any person is material for the purposes of subsection (1)
above, his age shall for those purposes be taken to be that which appears to the court
to be his age.

(8)   This section applies —

(a)   in relation to proceedings on indictment for an offence, only if the person
charged with the offence is arraigned on or after the commencement of this section;

(b)   in relation to proceedings in a magistrates' court, only if the time when the
court begins to receive evidence in the proceedings falls after the commencement of
this section.

(9)   Where the accused gives evidence in pursuance of this section, section 3 of the
Criminal Evidence Act 1898 (right of reply) shall have effect as if he had given
evidence in pursuance of that Act.

SCHEDULE 9
CONSEQUENTIAL AMENDMENTS
Evidence of accused in criminal proceedings

(1)   In section 1 of the Criminal Evidence Act 1898 (competency of accused to
give evidence in criminal proceedings) —

(a)   provisos (a) and (b) shall be omitted; and

(b)   in proviso (g), references to that Act shall be construed as including
references to section 28 of this Act.

Questions
1.   How does the Bill affect the common law?
2.   Would the decision in *R* v *Mutch* be different under the proposed new law?
3.   If the defendant refuses, with good cause, to answer certain questions
during cross-examination, would that prevent a trial judge from following the
decision in *R* v *Sparrow?*

4.   Is the change proposed by clause 28 either necessary or desirable?

(iii) The competence and compellability of a co-accused

Note
The preceding sections deal with the competence and compellability of the defendant as a witness on his own behalf. At no time is the defendant in a criminal case competent for the Crown. This prevents the prosecution from calling one co-accused to testify against another co-accused. In other words, if D1 and D2 are being jointly tried for an offence, the prosecution cannot call D1 to give evidence against D2, because D1 is not a competent witness for the prosecution. However, should D1 cease to be a co-accused, he would then become competent and compellable both for the prosecution *and* his former co-accused D2. Persons will be treated as co-accused if they are jointly charged at the moment in time when the question of competence falls to be decided.

R v Rudd
(1948) 32 Cr App R 138
Court of Criminal Appeal

The applicant was convicted of receiving stolen property. It is unnecessary to set out the facts of the case beyond stating that a co-defendant of the applicant named Powell gave evidence implicating the applicant. The applicant applied for leave to appeal.

HUMPHREYS J: Ever since this Court was established it has been the invariable rule to state the law in the same way — that, while a statement made in the absence of the accused person by one of his co-defendants cannot be evidence against him, if a co-defendant goes into the witness box and gives evidence in the course of a joint trial, then what he says becomes evidence for all the purposes of the case including the purpose of being evidence against his co-defendant. That is the law as we have always understood it, and there is ample authority to that effect, and most assuredly *R v Meredith and Others* (1943) 29 Cr App R 40 said nothing to the contrary. In *Meredith and Others (supra)* there were several prisoners, and the Court was dealing with the question whether the summing-up of the learned Recorder of London correctly directed the jury. The learned Recorder said, no doubt accurately, at the end of his summing-up. 'These men all made statements, and it is impossible for you to listen to all those statements and not to realise that they are statements which may implicate some persons other than the men making them. You will do your best, members of the jury, to remember that those statements are only evidence against the persons who make them. I will go further than that. When the individual making a statement of that sort comes into the witness box and gives evidence on oath, it is a different situation. What he says then does become evidence against the other person'. He went on to say this: 'but I endeavour in this class of case where there are a number of prisoners in the dock always to warn juries that so far as possible they should not use any evidence given by a person who is accused, when he is in the witness box, against any one of his co-defendants'. That obviously does not mean: 'I am in the habit of directing juries that what a co-defendant has said is not admissible in evidence against another co-defendant', because the learned Recorder has just said to the jury: 'what he has said does become evidence against the co-defendant'. In our view, it is plain that what the learned Recorder was, in effect, saying to the jury was: 'I always take care to warn juries of the danger of convicting solely upon the evidence of a co-defendant'. That is good sense and, as the Lord Chief Justice (Lord Caldecote) observed in the judgment of the Court, a proper direction. The Lord Chief Justice, therefore, in that case, in giving the judgment of the Court dealing with the question of law, was clearly of the same opinion as all the other Judges in this Court have always been. When it is said that there was in that case, either by the learned Recorder in the first instance or by the Court of Criminal Appeal, a statement in law that a jury would be wrongly directed if they were told that they may take into consideration in considering the case of one defendant what has been said by a co-defendant, that is nonsense. We are satisfied that that was not the meaning of the learned Recorder or of the Lord Chief Justice when he used the expression (at p. 44): 'that was a proper direction, and one that was fair to each of the appellants'. I repeat that, in reading the judgment in *Meredith and Others (supra)* it must be remembered that what the Court was dealing with there was not a statement of law of universal application that evidence by a co-defendant in the witness box is always admissible against another co-defendant. They were merely approving of the practice stated by the learned Recorder in that case as being perfectly fair to the then defendants, and for that reason the Court held that the direction was a perfectly proper one and that the appeal should be dismissed. . . .

R v Turner
(1975) 61 Cr App R 67
Court of Appeal

The nineteen appellants were charged with several robberies. One of the defendants, named Smalls, was offered immunity from prosecution by the Director of Public Prosecutions, in return for giving Queen's evidence against the appellants who included many accomplices. Smalls' evidence was the foundation of the prosecution's case against all the appellants. The appellants were convicted and appealed.

LAWTON LJ: Mr Hutchinson did not suggest that Smalls was not a competent witness. He could not have done so because the courts have ruled time and time again since the seventeenth century that accomplices are competent witnesses (see *Wigmore on Evidence*, 2nd ed, para. 2056). He submitted that for some time past there had been a practice for judges not to admit the evidence of accomplices who could still be influenced by continuing inducements and that this Court in *R v Pipe* (1966) 51 Cr App R 17 had adjudged that this practice had become a rule of law. If this is so, *Pipe (supra)* marks an important change in the law relating to giving Queen's evidence.

Despite Mr Hutchinson's admission that Smalls was a competent witness, Barrett's counsel, Mr Wright, in another appeal, submitted that he was not. It is convenient to deal with that submission now. We inferred that Mr Hutchinson used the word 'competent' in relation to witnesses in the usual way in which it is used in the law of evidence, viz. the capacity which categories of persons have to give evidence. Smalls came into the category of accomplices and, as we have said already, this category can give evidence. If Mr Wright was using the word 'competent' in this sense, his submission was misconceived. He may, however, have used it in a more narrow sense, applying it to a particular witness who for a particular reason should not be allowed to give evidence. If this be so, his submission was really the same as Mr Hutchinson's.

There can be no doubt that at common law an accomplice who gave evidence for the Crown in the expectation of getting a pardon for doing so was a competent witness. The two most persuasive authorities in English law say just that. In *Rudd* (1775) 1 Cowp 331 the Court of King's Bench had to consider an application for bail made by a woman who had given King's evidence and who claimed that in consequence she was entitled to be released on bail pending the grant of the pardon which she submitted she was entitled to as of right. Lord Mansfield CJ adjudged (at p. 334) that hers was not one of the three types of case in which pardons could be claimed as of right (that is, pardons promised by proclamation or given under statute or earned by the ancient procedure of approvement). He continued as follows (at p. 344): There is besides a practice, which indeed does not give a legal right; and that is where accomplices having made a full and fair confession of the whole truth, are in consequence thereof admitted evidence for the Crown and that evidence is afterwards made use of to convict the other offenders. If in that case they act fairly and openly, and discover the whole truth, though they are not entitled as of right to a pardon, yet the usage, lenity and the practice of the Courts is to stop the prosecution against them and they have an equitable title to a recommendation for the King's mercy.

Blackstone wrote to the same effect; see *Commentaries*, 23rd ed (1854), Vol. 4 at p. 440. It is manifest that in the eighteenth century the courts did not consider an accomplice to be incompetent to give evidence because any inducement held out to him to do so was still operating on his mind when he was in the witness box. Blackstone considered that an accomplice could not expect to receive his pardon unless he gave his evidence 'without prevarication or fraud.' The nineteenth century brought about no change in the competence of accomplices to give evidence even though the prospect of immunity from prosecution was before them: see all the editions of S M Phillips' *Treatise on the Law of Evidence* which appeared between 1814 and 1952 — there were ten. . . .

It is against that background that the case of *Pipe (supra)* should be considered. There is nothing in either the arguments or the judgment itself to indicate that the Court thought it was changing a rule of law as to the competency of accomplices to give evidence which had been followed ever since the seventeenth century. The facts of that case must be closely examined. Pipe was being tried on an indictment charging him with housebreaking and larceny. He was alleged to have stolen a safe and its contents. A man named Swan was called to prove that he had helped Pipe to break open the safe. Swan, however, before Pipe's trial had begun had himself been charged with complicity in Pipe's crime in relation to the safe. The form of the charge is not stated in the report. He was not indicted with Pipe. It was intended to try him later. The Court adjudged that Swan should not have been called in these circumstances. 'In the judgment of this Court,' said Lord Parker CJ at p. 21 '. . . it is one thing to call for the prosecution an accomplice, a witness whose evidence is suspect, and about whom the jury must be warned in the recognised way. It is quite another to call a witness who is not only an accomplice but is an accomplice against whom proceedings have been brought which have not been concluded.' The Court expressly approved the practice which was then set out in paragraph 1297 of *Archbold*, 36th ed (now para. 401 of the 38th ed).

In our judgment *Pipe (supra)* is limited to the circumstances set out in *Archbold*. Its *ratio decidendi* is confined to a case in which an accomplice, who has been charged, but not tried, is required to give evidence of his own offence in order to secure the conviction of another accused. *Pipe (supra)* on its facts was clearly a right decision. The same result could have been achieved by adjudging that the trial judge should have exercised his discretion to exclude Swan's evidence on the ground that there was an obvious and powerful inducement for him to ingratiate himself with the prosecution and the Court and that the existence of this inducement made it desirable in the interests of justice to exclude it. See *Noor Mohamed* v *The King* [1949] AC 182 *per* Lord du Parcq at p. 192 and followed in *Harris* v *Director of Public Prosecutions* [1952] AC 694 and 36 Cr App R 39 *per* Viscount Simon at p. 707 and p. 57. To have reached the decision on this basis would, we think, have been more in line with the earlier authorities. Lord Parker CJ in *Pipe (supra)* seems, however, to have viewed the admission of Swan's evidence in the circumstances of that case as more than a wrong exercise of discretion. He described what happened as being 'wholly irregular'. It does not follow, in our judgment, that in all cases calling a witness who can benefit from giving evidence is 'wholly irregular'. To hold so would be absurd. Examples are provided by the prosecution witness who hopes to get a reward which has been offered 'for information leading to a conviction', or even an order for compensation or whose claim for damages may be helped by a conviction.

If the inducement is very powerful, the judge may decide to exercise his discretion; but when doing so he must take into consideration all factors, including those affecting the public. It is in the interests of the public that criminals should be brought to justice; and the more serious the crimes the greater is the need for justice to be done. Employing Queen's evidence to accomplish this end is distasteful and has been distasteful for at least 300 years to judges, lawyers and members of the public. Hale CJ writing about 1650, used strong language of condemnation of the plea of approvement which was the precursor of the modern practice of granting immunity from prosecution, or further prosecution, to accomplices willing to give evidence for the Crown. See Hale, *Pleas of the Crown*, Vol. 2, p. 226. His comments should be remembered by the Director of Public Prosecutions. 'The truth is', he wrote, 'that more mischief hath come to good men, by these kinds of approvements by false accusations, of desperate villains than benefit to the public by the discovery and convicting of real offenders'. The practice has been condemned on ethical grounds. See Professor Sir Leon Radzinowicz, *History of the English Criminal Law* (1956), Vol. 2, p. 53. It is, however, no part of our function to add to the weight of ethical condemnation or to dissipate it. We are concerned to decide what the law is and whether the judge should, as a matter of discretion, have excluded Smalls' evidence, and whether, having admitted it, he gave the jury an adequate warning about acting on it.

When Smalls decided to give the police information about his partners in crime, the prospect of getting himself immunity from further prosecution was a most powerful inducement. It is necessary, however, to consider Smalls' position when he gave evidence. All the charges which had been preferred against him had already been terminated in his favour. By means of the absurd conspiracy charge, the prosecution had tried to give him immunity from prosecution for any offences he had disclosed in his statements. If, after verdicts of 'not guilty' had been entered in his favour, he had refused to give evidence, and the prosecution had tried by relying on the differences between a charge of conspiracy to rob and one of robbing to prosecute him for any substantive offences which he had disclosed, his statements would have been inadmissible because they had been obtained from him by inducements. His statements could not, of course, have been used in any prosecution brought against his wife. When Smalls went into the witness box both before the magistrates and at this trial, there was no real likelihood of his being prosecuted if he refused to give evidence. The only risk he ran was that the police might have withdrawn the protection which he had had and have refused to conduct him in secrecy to where he wanted to go. These facts distinguished this case from *Pipe (supra)* and would have justified the judge in refusing to exercise his discretion to exclude Smalls' evidence had he been asked to do so which he was not.

R v Richardson and Others
(1967) 51 Cr App R 381
Court of Criminal Appeal

H, M and others were originally jointly indicted, but at the beginning of the trial a separate trial had been ordered in the case of M. At a later stage in the trial of H and others, H applied for and obtained a witness summons against M, whom he desired to call as a witness in his defence. The question then arose whether M was in law a compellable witness.

LAWTON J: Mr Platts-Mills has invited my attention to the decision of the Court for Crown Cases Reserved in *Payne* (1872) LR 1 CCR 349. A number of men had been indicted for entering on other people's land, while armed, for the purpose of taking and destroying game. One of the defendants wanted to call another defendant on his behalf. Could he do so? The problem came before a court consisting of Cockburn CJ, Martin and Channell BB, and Keating and Lush JJ. They thought the problem of such importance that they reserved it for consideration by the full Bench. The arguments of counsel before the full Bench have been reported at length together with comments made by the judges in the course of the argument. The judgment itself is very short. The injustice of a situation in not being able to call a man jointly charged as a witness was duly pointed out to the Court, whereupon Cockburn CJ said (at p. 354) 'The remedy for that is to apply to have the prisoners tried separately'. The Chief Justice seems to have thought that, if there were separate trials, the problem of calling one defendant in support of another could be overcome; but that is not this problem. Here the problem is not whether Mottram can be called as a witness for Hall (and it is conceded by counsel that he is a competent witness), but whether he is a compellable one.

In 1883 a similar kind of problem arose at the trial of *R v Bradlaugh* 15 Cox CC 217. At his trial Charles Bradlaugh was indicted with two other men and his defence was that he had not published certain allegedly blasphemous libels. He wanted to call his co-defendants to testify that he had not had any part in the publication. The court was disposed to order a separate trial of Bradlaugh in order to enable him to call his co-defendants. The court, however, heard Mr Avory (later to become Avory J) on behalf of one of the co-defendants whom Bradlaugh wanted to call. Mr Avory's argument is reported as follows (at p. 223): 'Mr Avory, on behalf of Ramsay, objected that this could not be done unless a verdict of acquittal was taken against Ramsay. He cited the observations of Cockburn CJ in *R v Winsor and Harris* (1866) LR 1 QB 289, in which Harris was examined as a witness against Winsor, without being first acquitted, that . . . it was much to be lamented. In all cases where two persons are joined in the same indictment, and it is desired to try them separately, and that the evidence of one should be received against the other, it is better that a verdict of not guilty should be taken against the one called'. Lord Coleridge CJ pointed out that in *Winsor and Harris (supra)* the fellow prisoner had been called for the Crown. Mr Avory continued his argument in this way: 'He urged that this did not matter, as if the co-defendant were called for the defence he would be liable to be cross-examined, and could hardly avoid incriminating himself'. It seems clear that Mr Avory was objecting to his client being called as a witness. Lord Coleridge CJ dealt with the matter at p. 224. He said he should endeavour to avoid that [that is cross-examination which might be incriminating] by not allowing questions to be asked or answered which might have that effect. As to the dictum cited, he observed that Cockburn CJ did not go to the length of saying that the course taken was not legal even when the fellow-prisoner had been called for the prosecution to make out a case against the prisoner being tried. Here, however, the co-defendant was to be called for the defendant under trial. He could not prevent this, nor compel the prosecution to take a verdict of acquittal as to the co-defendant to be called. The co-defendant was to be called simply to disprove publication by the defendant Bradlaugh, and any questions to show publication by anybody else would either not be admissible, or, if they tended to criminate the witness, he would not be compellable to answer'.

That case is authority for the proposition that, if there are separate trials of two men charged in the same indictment, on the trial of one the other can be called as a witness and compelled to answer.

. . . Accordingly, I rule and adjudge that Mottram is a compellable witness at this trial.

Order accordingly.

(B)   The spouse of the defendant

Note
The common law has now been superseded by provisions contained in the Police and Criminal Evidence Act 1984. The first case which follows, *Pitt*, was decided before the Act came into force, but there is no reason to suppose the principle enunciated will differ as a result of the Act.

Police and Criminal Evidence Act 1984

80.   Competence and compellability of accused's spouse
   (1)   In any proceedings the wife or husband of the accused shall be competent to give evidence —
      (a)   subject to subsection (4) below, for the prosecution; and
      (b)   on behalf of the accused or any person jointly charged with the accused.
   (2)   In any proceedings the wife or husband of the accused shall, subject to subsection (4) below, be compellable to give evidence on behalf of the accused.
   (3)   In any proceedings the wife or husband of the accused shall, subject to subsection (4) below, be compellable to give evidence for the prosecution or on behalf of any person jointly charged with the accused if and only if —
      (a)   the offence charged involves an assault on, or injury or a threat of injury to, the wife or husband of the accused or a person who was at the material time under the age of sixteen; or
      (b)   the offence charged is a sexual offence alleged to have been committed in respect of a person who was at the material time under that age; or
      (c)   the offence charged consists of attempting or conspiring to commit, or of aiding, abetting, counselling, procuring or inciting the commission of, an offence falling within paragraph (a) or (b) above.

(4)   Where a husband and wife are jointly charged with an offence neither spouse shall at the trial be competent or compellable by virtue of subsection (1)(a), (2) or (3) above to give evidence in respect of that offence unless that spouse is not, or is no longer, liable to be convicted of that offence at the trial as a result of pleading guilty or for any other reason.

(5)   In any proceedings a person who has been but is no longer married to the accused shall be competent and compellable to give evidence as if that person and the accused had never been married.

(6)   Where in any proceedings the age of any person at any time is material for the purposes of subsection (3) above, his age at the material time shall for the purposes of that provision be deemed to be or to have been that which appears to the court to be or to have been his age at that time.

(7)   In subsection (3)(b) above 'sexual offence' means an offence under the Sexual Offences Act 1956, the Indecency with Children Act 1960, the Sexual Offences Act 1967, section 54 of the Criminal Law Act 1977 or the Protection of Children Act 1978.

(8)   The failure of the wife or husband of the accused to give evidence shall not be made the subject of any comment by the prosecution.

R v *Pitt*
[1983] QB 25
Court of Appeal

The appellant was charged with two offences of assault occasioning actual bodily harm to his eight-month-old baby. His wife made a witness state-ment which was prejudicial to him. She was called as a prosecution witness at his trial, but during her evidence in-chief she gave answers inconsistent with her statement. The judge granted a prosecution application to treat her as hostile, and she was cross-examined on her witness statement. The appellant was convicted.

PETER PAIN J: Up to the point where she goes into the witness box, the wife has a choice: she may refuse to give evidence or waive her right of refusal. The waiver is effective only if made with full knowledge of her right to refuse. If she waives her right of refusal, she becomes an ordinary witness. She is by analogy in the same position as a witness who waives privilege, which would entitle him to refuse to answer questions on a certain topic.

In our view, in these circumstances, once the wife has started upon her evidence, she must complete it. It is not open to her to retreat behind the barrier of non-compellability if she is asked questions that she does not wish to answer. Justice should not allow her to give evidence which might assist, or injure, her husband and then to escape from normal investigation.

It follows that if the nature of her evidence justifies it, an application may be made to treat her as a hostile witness. There is, in our view, no objection in law which will preclude a judge from giving leave to treat as hostile a wife who chooses to give evidence for the prosecution of her husband. We have not been able to find any direct authority upon this point. This makes it particularly important that the wife should understand when she takes the oath that she is waiving her right to refuse to give evidence. It points to the wisdom of the words of Darling J in *R* v *Acaster* (1912) 7 Cr App R 187 when he said, at p. 189:

The only suggestion made for the appellant is founded on a passage which occurred in the argument in *Leach's case* [(1912) 7 Cr App R 187] in the House of Lords, where the Solicitor-General asked whether it was suggested that the prosecution, when a wife came to give evidence, should raise the question whether she knew she could refuse to give evidence, and Lord Atkinson said it was for the witness to take the point and the Lord Chancellor added 'Or for the judge'. Speaking for myself, and I think for the other members of the court, in consequence of these observations I shall, when the wife — in any case where she is not a compellable witness — comes to give evidence against her husband, ask her: 'Do you know you may object to give evidence?' and I shall also do so if she is called on behalf of her husband. That I imagine, is what other judges will do for the present, though there is no decision which binds us to do it, and the point is open to argument on an appeal to this court. So far none of us here remember to have ever done it, nor did it occur to us before that it was necessary.

That decision is now 70 years old and we cannot say that Darling J's counsel of prudence has become a rule of law. Nor do we seek to lay down any rule of practice for the future. This is an unusual case and we are reluctant to make it the basis for any general rule. Nonetheless, this case does illustrate very powerfully why it is necessary for the trial judge to make certain that the wife understands her position before she takes the oath. Had that been done here, there would have been no difficulty.

It seems to us to be desirable that where a wife is called as a witness for the prosecution of her husband, the judge should explain to her in the absence of the jury, that before she takes the oath she has the right to refuse to give evidence, but that if she chooses to give evidence she may be treated like any other witness.

Appeal allowed. Conviction quashed.

Note
If the facts of *R* v *Pitt* were repeated, the spouse would now be compellable on behalf of the Crown by virtue of s. 80(3)(a) (see above).

R v *Khan*
(1987) 84 Cr App R 44
Court of Appeal

The appellant was charged with one A with being knowingly concerned with the importation of a controlled drug, heroin. At their trial a woman gave evidence for the prosecution, during which it transpired that she had gone through a Moslem form of marriage with A whilst his first English wife was still alive. After submissions, the judge ruled that the woman was not A's wife under English law and was therefore a competent witness for the prosecution. The appellant was convicted and appealed on the grounds (1) that a woman with whom a defendant had gone through a religious ceremony of marriage, even though in English law the ceremony might be void, was to be treated as his wife within the common law principle that a wife was not a competent witness for the prosecution either against the defendant or a co-defendant. . . .

GLIDEWELL LJ: . . . [T]he issue with which we are now dealing has already become out of date, because section 80(1) of the Police and Criminal Evidence Act 1984, a section which was brought into force on January 1 1986, has the effect that 'In any proceedings the wife or husband of the accused shall be competent to give evidence (a) subject to subsection (4) below, for the prosecution. . . .' Subsection (4) is not relevant to the facts of the present case. So whether or not Hasina Patel was Mr Allan's wife, if this situation arises in the future, she, or somebody like her, will be a competent witness for the prosecution; not compellable, but competent. The major issue that was raised was whether she was competent.

However, this trial was proceeding under the law as it was before January 1 1986. The rule which then obtained that a wife was not in most cases competent, and was and is not compellable to give evidence against her husband or against his jointly indicted co-accused in a criminal trial, is a common law rule. We were referred to a number of old commentaries. I refer only to one of them: Hawkins Pleas of the Crown, (1824 ed.). Vol. 2 p. 600, Section 67 says:

> As to the Eighth Point, whether a husband and wife may be witnesses for or against one another, it seems agreed, that husband and wife, being as one and the same person in affection and interest, can no more give evidence for one another in any case whatsoever than for themselves; and that regularly the one shall not be admitted to give evidence against the other, nor the examination of the one be made use of against the other, by reason of the implacable dissension which might be caused by it, and the great danger of perjury from taking the oaths of persons under so great a bias, and the extreme hardship of the case.

More recently that principle was referred to in the House of Lords in *Hoskyn* v *Metropolitan Police Commissioner* (1978) 67 Cr App R 88; [1979] AC 474. That was a case in which the husband had been indicted for inflicting personal injury on his wife. That is one of the exceptional cases in which a wife is a competent witness. It seems only common sense that she should be, and happily the law in this case follows common sense. Nevertheless, albeit competent, she is not compellable, so if a wife decides that she does not wish to give evidence against her husband, she cannot be forced to do so.

During the course of the consideration of the matter generally, questions both of competence and compellability were considered. There is a short and typically helpful passage in the speech of Lord Wilberforce at p. 94 and 484C respectively where his Lordship said:

> . . . a wife at common law, was incompetent to give evidence against her husband. Broadly the incompetence according to the authorities can be said to rest upon the doctrine of the unity of husband and wife, coupled with the privilege against self-incrimination. The danger of perjury is also involved — Then there is a reference to the passage from *Hawkins* to which I have referred — and the repugnance likely to be felt by the public seeing one spouse testifying against the other. To the second rule as to competence limited exceptions have been recognised to exist.

I will come to those exceptions in a moment.

We are dealing with the question of whether a wife is competent to give evidence against her husband or his co-accused, and if so whether this lady, Miss Patel, fell within the ambit of that principle. But the common law rule was wider than that because originally at common law a defendant might not give evidence on his own behalf in a criminal trial, and his wife might not give evidence on his behalf either. At the stage when that was still the law, it seems that it may be that the exclusion was somewhat widened to include somebody who was not a wife, but passed as a wife.

In the report of *Campbell* v *Twemlow* (1814) Pri. 81, there is a reference to a trial conducted by that great judge Lord Kenyon in 1782 at Chester Assizes. *Campbell* v *Twemlow* itself does not matter; it was an action for trespass, and the issue was whether a woman with whom the plaintiff had been living for a great number of years, though she was not in fact his wife, was admissible on his behalf. The passages that are of significance are at pp. 83, 84 where, during the course of argument Richards B said:

I remember a prosecution tried at Chester, before my Lord Kenyon, in 1782, at a time when he was perhaps in the zenith of his legal knowledge, wherein his Lordship sanctioned the doctrine of the inadmissibility of the evidence of a person in the situation of this witness. The prisoner in that case was tried on a charge of forgery. Being a man of competent education, he addressed the Court in his defence with considerable effect. In the course of his speech he frequently alluded to a woman who then accompanied him, and whom he spoke of as his wife, and he concluded by offering her evidence in corroboration of some facts which he had stated. When the objection of her being his wife was taken, he said that they were in fact not married. But his Lordship would not permit him to call her, after having spoken of, and represented her as his wife. And he was convicted, and executed.

In the course of his judgment in the *Campbell* v *Twemlow* case, Thomson CB referred briefly to what Lord Kenyon had said and apparently relied upon it. But in the later case to which Mr Shears drew our attention of *Batthews* v *Galindo* (1828) 4 Bing 610, the court having considered the matter, said in effect that Lord Kenyon was not really laying down a principle that a woman who passed as a man's wife albeit she was not married to him was not a competent witness on his behalf, but was deciding on the facts of his particular case that when a man had stoutly claimed that a woman was his wife, he could not suddenly turn round and say that he had not married her and thus that he was able to call her as a witness in his defence after all.

The court in that case held that a mistress, even if treated as a wife and held out as the man's wife, was a competent witness on his behalf. Park J said at p. 612:

I agree in the case cited from Price's Rep. [i.e *Campbell* v *Twemlow*], but I think it has no bearing on the present. Lord Kenyon was right, because the prisoner himself had called the female his wife, through the whole trial, and Lord Kenyon said that, after that, he could not call on the Court to receive her as his mistress. But the mere circumstances of a woman's cohabiting with a man, though it goes to her credit, is no ground for rejecting her testimony.

Best CJ said at p. 614: '. . . but the true principle to follow on such occasions is that which is stated in *Starkie*, that the witness is not to be excluded, unless *de jure* wife of the party.' In other words, unless she is in law the wife of the party.

Exceptions to the rule that a wife was not a competent witness either for or against her husband have been introduced in two ways. First of all in the Criminal Evidence Act 1898, section 1 provides: 'Every person charged with an offence, and the wife or husband, as the case may be, of the person so charged, shall be a competent witness for the defence at every stage of the proceedings, whether the person so charged is charged solely or jointly with any other person . . .' Then there are a number of provisos which must be satisfied if such a person is to be called, but it is clear that a wife may always be called as a witness for her husband during the course of criminal proceedings.

There are now a number of well recognised exceptions to the principle that a wife may not give evidence for the prosecution against her husband. Under section 4 of the same Act she is competent to give evidence in relation to the short list of offences included in the schedule to that Act; and she is competent in certain other sexual cases and in cases of assault upon herself, but with those exceptions she remains not competent.

There is a summary in the present edition of *Archbold's Criminal Pleading Evidence & Practice* (42nd. ed.), in the notes to paragraph 4–280, which in our view accurately sets out the position. It says: 'The present law appears to be as follows: 1. The husband or wife of the prosecutor has always been a competent witness either for the Crown or for the defence.' That is not in issue here. 2. The husband or wife of a defendant is a competent witness for the defence in all criminal cases whether the defendant is charged solely or jointly . . . 3. At common law, as a general rule, the husband or wife of a defendant is not a competent witness for the Crown against the defendant.' Then it goes on to deal with exceptions and says: 'In each of these cases the defendant's spouse is competent but not compellable.' It then says that a divorced spouse remains incompetent to give evidence against her husband or his wife in relation to matters that occurred during the marriage before the decree of divorce was made absolute.

That is therefore the position as it was until January 1, 1986, with regard to wives. But it is accepted by Mr Shears that a woman who is not a wife, but is, to use a term which I suppose is rapidly becoming old-fashioned, a mistress, even one who calls herself a wife in common parlance, may be called by the prosecution. She is a competent witness against the man with whom she is living. If modern authority for that is needed, it is to be found, almost by a sidewind, in the decision of this Court in the case of *Yacoob* (1981) 72 Cr App R 313. That was a case in which one of the prosecution witnesses had gone through a ceremony of marriage with the appellant in 1971, but it was said that that marriage was bigamous because she had already married somebody else in 1968; indeed she was a much married lady. I think altogether she had gone through some four ceremonies of marriage. The question therefore was, first, whether it was established that there was a valid marriage in subsistence at the time of the 1971 marriage; and secondly, whether the burden of proving those facts was on the defence or upon the prosecution. But the decision of the Court makes it clear that it was accepted on all sides, and the Court certainly based its decision upon the proposition, that even though she was living with the man as his wife, if her marriage to him was bigamous and thus invalid, she was a perfectly competent witness against him and could be called on behalf of the prosecution.

If that be the position with somebody who has gone through an invalid ceremony of marriage because it is bigamous, what is the position of a lady who has gone through a ceremony of marriage which under the religious observances of a faith, and under the law of some other countries, is entirely valid, but which, because it is a second polygamous marriage, is of no effect in the law of this country? In our judgment the position so far as her ability and competence to give evidence is concerned is no different from that of a woman who has not been through a ceremony of marriage at all, or one who has been through a ceremony of marriage which is void because it is bigamous. Exactly the same principles in our view apply, and therefore we hold that the learned judge was entirely correct in his reasoning and in deciding that Hasina Patel was a competent witness for the prosecution, both in respect of her husband and in respect of this appellant.

I should say that Mr Shears asked us to consider, and we did consider, a treatise on the effect of marriage in Moslem law to show the position which a wife holds, or should properly hold, in the tenets of that faith, and to emphasise that one of the requirements of a wife in such circumstances is to keep her husband's secrets. But with the greatest of respect to him, that seems to us not material to the question of law which in the end we had to decide. That disposes of the principal point in this appeal.

Note
Although *R v Khan* was decided on the law which existed before the 1984 Act came into force, it will doubtless remain good authority on the meaning of 'spouse'.

(i)   Former spouses

R v Cruttenden
[1991] 2 QB 66
Court of Appeal

GLIDEWELL LJ: . . . On 4 January 1988 the appellant and Brian Carey Thomas were jointly arraigned on an indictment containing 14 counts alleging corruption, contrary to section 1 of the Prevention of Corruption Act 1906. The counts were in pairs, each pair relating to a single transaction. For example, the particulars of offence of the first two counts read as follows:

> Count 1. Brian Carey Thomas being the Chief Planner of Taff Ely Borough Council between 1 June 1983 and 31 August 1983 corruptly accepted for himself the free use of a Rover 3.5 motor car, registration number LJB 298W, as an inducement or reward for showing favour, in relation to his principal's affairs, to Roger Christian Cruttenden in respect of planning applications.
> Count 2. Roger Christian Cruttenden between 1 June 1983 and 31 August 1983 corruptly gave to Brian Carey Thomas, the Chief Planner of Taff Ely Borough Council, the free use of a Rover 3.5 motor car, registration number LJB 298W, as an inducement or reward to Brian Carey Thomas showing favour in relation to his principal's affairs in respect of planning applications.

Thereafter the counts followed the same pattern, the odd numbered counts contained charges against Mr Thomas and the even numbered counts the complementary charges against the appellant.

Both men pleaded not guilty to all counts and the trial commenced before Judge David Smith QC and a jury.

On 21 January 1988, at the conclusion of the evidence for the prosecution, counsel for both defendants submitted that there was no case to answer. The judge did not accede to this submission completely. However he ruled that there was no case to answer, and in due course directed the jury to acquit, in respect of counts 3, 9, 11 and 13 against Mr Thomas, and counts 4, 12 and 14 against the appellant.

Both defendants were convicted on the remaining counts, i.e., Mr Thomas on counts 1, 5 and 7 and the appellant on counts 2, 6, 8 and 10. Mr Thomas was sentenced to nine months' imprisonment on each of the three counts on which he had been convicted concurrently, three months to be served and six months suspended. The appellant was also sentenced to nine months' imprisonment on each of the four counts on which he had been convicted concurrently, six months to be served and three months suspended.

Both appealed against conviction . . .

. . . The first ground of appeal raised an issue of law, namely, whether the judge had been correct in ruling that the former wife of the appellant, Mrs Janet Elizabeth Cruttenden, was a competent and compellable witness to give evidence for the prosecution in respect of matters which occurred during her marriage to the appellant. At our invitation this issue was argued first. At the conclusion of the argument we announced our decision that the judge had been correct in this ruling, and said that we would give our reasons later, which we now do.

. . .

The prosecution case

Broadly the prosecution case was that the appellant over a period of years provided Mr Thomas with cars at preferential low prices through the medium of his company, Dalcastle, and with free petrol, and that in return Mr Thomas sought to influence the borough council in relation to the grant of planning permission for developments in which the appellant's companies were interested, particularly in relation to the application by Silver Knight for planning permission for the Mwyndy site.

The evidence of Mrs Janet Cruttenden

Mrs Janet Cruttenden married the appellant in 1977. During the whole of the period to which the four counts with which we are concerned related, i.e., between January 1981 and March 1985, they were living together. They separated approximately two years before the date of the trial in January 1988, and were subsequently divorced, the decree being made absolute approximately one year before the date of the trial. Thus, in January 1988 Mrs Janet Cruttenden was the former wife of the appellant.

The major part of her evidence related to count 10, the allegation that the appellant had provided Mr Thomas with petrol free of charge. Her evidence was that Mr Thomas had a petrol account at Corner Park Garage. She said that Mr Thomas used to pay his account monthly by cheque. She was however told by the appellant that a cheque received from Mr Thomas would be banked but Mr Thomas would then be given the money back in cash. She said that she asked why this was done, and the answer the appellant gave was that Mr Thomas used to give him favours, so he used to do favours back. The favours were said to be to tell the appellant which properties would be more likely to have planning permission granted than other properties.

The evidence of Mrs Janet Cruttenden was the only evidence to the effect that Mr Thomas had been supplied with petrol free of charge. In other words without her evidence the prosecution had no case on count 10.

Before she came to give her evidence, Mr John Rees for the appellant submitted that she was neither a competent nor a compellable witness for the prosecution and thus that her evidence should not be admitted. He was supported by Mr Pugh for Mr Thomas, albeit the evidence of Mrs Janet Cruttenden about the petrol transaction was hearsay and thus inadmissible as far as Mr Thomas was concerned. As we have said, the judge ruled that Mrs Janet Cruttenden was a competent and compellable witness for the prosecution as against the appellant.

The clear and attractive submissions advanced by Mr John Rees can be summarised as follows.

(i) At common law a wife was generally neither a competent nor a compellable witness for the prosecution against her husband in any criminal prosecution. There was a clear exception to this in cases of personal violence against the wife, and possible exceptions in relation to treason and abduction.

(ii) Various nineteenth century statutes, particularly section 4 of the Criminal Evidence Act 1898, provided that a wife should be a competent witness for the prosecution against her husband in relation to various specified offences, of which corruption was not one.

(iii)   Thus, at the time when the appellant and Mrs Cruttenden had the conversation to which her evidence related about Mr Thomas being in effect provided with free petrol, i.e., before March 1985, Mrs Cruttenden could not have given evidence against her husband in relation to this matter, since she was not competent to do so in law.

(iv)   In *Reg* v *Algar* [1954] 1 QB 279, this court decided that a divorced wife was not competent to give evidence for the prosecution against her husband about matters which had occurred or been said during the course of the marriage, other than matters about which she would have been a competent witness if she had still been married. Thus if the law had remained unaltered, Mrs Janet Cruttenden would not have been a competent witness against the appellant in relation to count 10 of the date of the trial.

(v)   However, the law in this respect was altered when section 80 of the Police and Criminal Evidence Act 1984 came into force on 1 January 1986. The relevant provisions of section 80 are: '(1) In any proceedings the wife or husband of the accused shall be competent to give evidence — (a) subject to subsection (4) below, for the prosecution; . . .' Subsection (2) is not here relevant. Subsection (3) provides in effect that the wife or husband of the accused is not compellable to give evidence for the prosecution in relation to an offence in one of the categories in respect of which he or she would have been a competent witness before the Act of 1984 came into force. Subsection (4) is not here relevant.
Subsection (5) provides:

(5)   In any proceedings a person who has been but is no longer married to the accused shall be competent and compellable to give evidence as if that person and the accused had never been married.

Subsections (6) to (8) are not relevant. Subsection (9) provides: 'Section 1(d) of the Criminal Evidence Act 1898 (communication between husband and wife) . . . shall cease to have effect.'

(vi)   Clearly by virtue of section 80(5) a divorced wife will be competent and compellable to give evidence for the prosecution against her former husband in respect of any matter which occurred or anything said during the course of the marriage, provided that it occurred or was said after 1 January 1986. But the change in the law effected by section 80 cannot have been intended to be retrospective. Thus it can only relate to matters which occurred or which were said after the date on which the section came into force.

(vii)   Since the relevant matters in this case occurred before section 80 of the Act of 1984 was brought into force, Mrs Janet Cruttenden was still neither a competent nor a compellable witness against her former husband at his trial in respect of these matters.

Mr John Rees relies upon the general principle that statutes should not normally be given a retrospective effect, which is set out in *Maxwell on Interpretation of Statutes*, 12th ed. (1969), at pp. 215–216:

Upon the presumption that the legislature does not intend what is unjust rests the leaning against giving certain statutes a retrospective operation. They are construed as operating only in cases or on facts which come into existence after the statutes were passed unless a retrospective effect is clearly intended. It is a fundamental rule of English law that no statute shall be construed to have a retrospective operation unless such a construction appears very clearly in the terms of the Act, or arises by necessary and distinct implication.

The statement of the law contained in the preceding paragraph has been 'so frequently quoted with approval that it now itself enjoys almost judicial authority.' One of the most well known statements of the rule regarding retrospectivity is contained in this passage from the judgment of R. S. Wright J in *In re Athlumney* [1898] 2 QB 547, 551, 552: 'Perhaps no rule of construction is more firmly established than this — that a retrospective operation is not to be given to a statute so as to impair an existing right or obligation, otherwise than as regards matter of procedure, unless that effect cannot be avoided without doing violence to the language of the enactment. If the enactment is expressed in language which is fairly capable of either interpretation, it ought to be construed as prospective only.' The rule has, in fact, two aspects, for it 'involves another and subordinate rule, to the effect that a statute is not to be construed so as to have a greater retrospective operation than its language renders necessary.' If, however, the language or the dominant intention of the enactment so demands, the Act must be construed so as to have a retrospective operation, for 'the rule against the retrospective effect of statutes is not a rigid or inflexible rule but is one to be applied always in the light of the language of the statute and the subject matter with which the statute is dealing.'

Alternatively Mr Rees submits that even if Mrs Janet Cruttenden was a competent witness, the judge should have exercised his discretion under section 78 of the Police and Criminal Evidence Act 1984 not to admit her evidence.

As to this second argument, it is our clear view that if Mrs Janet Cruttenden was a competent witness against her former husband, there was nothing unfair in admitting her evidence. We therefore turn to consider the important point of law which is raised.

In *Yew Bon Tew v Kenderaan Bas Mara* [1983] 1 AC 553, the Privy Council held that on the expiry of a relevant period of limitation, a potential defendant to an action acquired an 'accrued right,' which was not affected by the subsequent repeal of the relevant limitation provisions, unless the contrary intention appeared. The judgment of the Board was delivered by Lord Brightman, who said, at p. 558:

Apart from the provisions of the interpretation statutes, there is at common law a prima facie rule of construction that a statute should not be interpreted retrospectively so as to impair an existing right or obligation unless that result is unavoidable on the language used.

In *Hoskyn v Metropolitan Police Commissioner* [1979] AC 474, the appellant was charged with wounding Janis Scrimshaw with intent, contrary to section 18 of the Offences against the Person Act 1861. At the time of the event which led to the charge the parties were not married to each other, but two days before the trial commenced they were married. Mrs. Hoskyn, as she thus became, was reluctant to give evidence against her husband. It was common ground that she was competent to do so at common law. The question at issue was whether she was also compellable. The judge at the trial ruled that she was, but the House of Lords held that she was not compellable. In his speech Lord Wilberforce said, at p. 484:

a wife, at common law, was incompetent to give evidence against her husband. Broadly the incompetence according to the authorities can be said to rest upon the doctrine of the unity of husband and wife, coupled with the privilege against self-incrimination.

Lord Salmon said, at p. 495:

> At common law, the wife of a defendant charged with a crime however serious was not, as a general rule, a competent witness for the Crown. If a man were charged with murder, for example, much as it would be in the public interest that justice should be done, his wife, whatever vital evidence she might have been able to give was not at common law a competent, let alone a compellable witness at his trial. This rule seems to me to underline the supreme importance attached by the common law to the special status of marriage and to the unity supposed to exist between husband and wife. It also no doubt recognised the natural repugnance of the public at the prospect of a wife giving evidence against her husband in such circumstances. The only relevant exception to the common law rule that a wife was not a competent witness at her husband's trial was when he was charged with a crime of violence against her. There is some doubt as to whether this exception also applies when a husband is charged with treason, but this is not a matter relevant to this appeal. The instant case turns solely upon whether, at common law, the wife of a defendant charged with having committed a crime of violence against her is not only a competent but also a compellable witness against her husband. The main argument on behalf of the Crown is that all persons who are competent witnesses, normally are also compellable witnesses. And therefore, so the argument runs, in cases in which wives are competent witnesses it follows that they also must be compellable witnesses. This seems to me to be a complete non sequitur for it takes no account of the especial importance which the common law attaches to the status of marriage. Clearly, it was for the wife's own protection that the common law made an exception to its general rule by making the wife a competent witness in respect of any charge against her husband for a crime of violence against her. But if she does not want to avail herself of this protection, there is, in my view, no ground for holding that the common law forces it upon her.

Basing himself upon these authorities, Mr John Rees submits that until section 80 of the Act of 1984 came into force a spouse, in this case the husband, had a right or privilege that whatever he did or said in the presence of his wife during the course of the marriage, she was not competent to give evidence in respect of these matters against him in a criminal prosecution, save in the excepted cases referred to above.

It should be noted that in the passage quoted in *Maxwell on Interpretation of Statutes*, 12th ed., pp. 215–216, from *In re Athlumney, Ex parte Wilson* [1898] 2 QB 547, 552, R. S. Wright J said: 'a retrospective operation is not to be given to a statute so as to impair an existing right or obligation, otherwise than as regards matter of procedure . . .'

Mr Kay for the prosecution argues, first, that the wording of section 80(5) of the Act of 1984 provides clearly that an ex-wife or husband is competent and compellable to give evidence at a trial, whether or not the events about which she or he is giving evidence occurred before the subsection came into force. Secondly, he submits that the alteration in the law effected by section 80(5) was a matter of procedure. Thus it came within the exception to the normal rule against statutes having retrospective operation.

Mr Kay relies for this submission on the decision of the Court of Appeal in *Blyth v Blyth and Pugh* [1965] P 411. In that case a husband petitioned for divorce on the ground of his wife's adultery. It was part of the wife's defence that he had condoned the adultery by having sexual intercourse with her long after he knew of her admitted adultery. At the time when the sexual intercourse upon which the wife relied took place, there was an irrebuttable presumption in law that this amounted to condonation. However the law in this respect was altered by section 1 of the Matrimonial Causes Act 1963, which provided that the presumption of condonation 'may be rebutted on the part of a husband . . . by evidence sufficient to negative the necessary intent.' This provision was in force at the time of the trial.

The question was whether the effect of the provision was retrospective, so that evidence as to the husband's intent was relevant and admissible. The judge held that the statute could not be 'construed so as to jeopardise the vested rights which the wife had already acquired when, by engaging in sexual intercourse with her, the husband reinstated her as his wife . . .'

The Court of Appeal reversed his decision. In his judgment Willmer LJ said, at p. 425:

> In the light of these authorities it becomes clear that what section 1 of the Act of 1963 is dealing with is a purely procedural matter, namely, the admissibility of evidence to rebut what had hitherto been held to be conclusive evidence against a husband. The effect of the section is to abolish the procedural anomaly whereby a distinction was drawn between husband and wife with regard to the evidence which they were permitted to give. This being so, I think that the section is to be construed as governing the procedure to be followed in all cases brought to trial after the Act came into force, irrespective of the date of the events to which the evidence may be directed. To say that this involves the section being given retrospective effect is, I think, perhaps misleading. The true view is rather that the section looks forward to the conduct of trials that take place after the coming into force of the Act. In this respect I would respectfully adopt the language used by Scarman J in *Carson* v *Carson* [1964] 1 WLR 511, 517 in the passage from his judgment which I have already read.

Harman LJ said, at p. 430:

> The true view seems to me to be that where an Act is dealing with a matter of the admissibility of evidence, it points quite clearly to the date of the trial, and the date of the happening of the event of which evidence may or may not be given is in truth irrelevant. This is not in my judgment really retrospective legislation at all, but an instruction to the court to be observed at the hearing of suits before it. I would not, therefore, agree with the commissioner on this point.

The issue in *Blyth* v *Blyth and Pugh* [1965] P 411 was whether evidence which would formerly have been inadmissible was at the date of the trial admissible and relevant as a result of the change in the law brought about by statute. The issue in the present case is rather different, namely, whether a witness who stands in a particular relationship to the defendant is a competent witness at the time of trial. In *Hoskyn* v *Metropolitan Police Commissioner* [1974] AC 474 the House of Lords clearly did not take the view that the question whether a wife who was a competent witness was also compellable was purely procedural. Thus we very much doubt whether it can properly be said that the change in the law brought about by section 80(5) of the Act of 1984 was a change of a purely procedural nature.

Nevertheless, we take the view that Mr Kay's first submission is correct. To repeat, the subsection reads:

> (5) In any proceedings a person who has been but is no longer married to the accused shall be competent and compellable to give evidence as if that person and the accused had never been married.

In our view the phrase 'in any proceedings' clearly means any proceedings which take place after this subsection comes into effect. If it were intended to limit the operation of the subsection to evidence only about matters which took place after the subsection came into effect, we think this would have required some additional words in the statute which are not present. For this reason, in agreement with Mr Kay, we conclude that the judge was right in ruling that Mrs Janet Cruttenden was a competent witness against the appellant at his trial.

It is therefore now necessary to turn to the other grounds of appeal advanced on Mr Cruttenden's behalf, which relate to individual counts in the indictment. [His Lordship considered the evidence relating to counts 6 and 8 and continued:] In our view the judge should have ruled in relation to both these counts that there was no case for the appellant to answer, and should have directed the jury to find him not guilty on both these counts. It was for these reasons that we allowed the appeal in relation to both these counts and quashed the convictions upon them.

However, without rehearsing the evidence on count 2, it is our view that there was evidence upon which a jury, properly directed, could have convicted on this count and we therefore take the view that the judge was correct to rule that there was a case to answer on count 2. On count 10, once Mrs Janet Cruttenden's evidence was admitted, there was clearly a case to answer. We therefore turn to consider other issues raised with regard to counts 2 and 10. [His Lordship considered criticisms of irregularities during the course of the prosecution case and of three passages in the summing up and continued:] If there had been only one irregularity during the course of the prosecution case, or only one error of the kind to which we have referred in the summing up, it may well be that we would have thought that the conviction on counts 2 and 10 was nevertheless safe. But we have been driven to the conclusion that the cumulative effect of the matters to which we have referred, both in the conduct of the prosecution case and in the summing up, is such that we cannot say that the conviction on either counts 2 or 10 is safe or satisfactory. We are left with a doubt as to how the jury would have found if these errors had not occurred.

Accordingly, it is for these reasons that we concluded that the convictions on these counts also should be quashed and the appeal against the conviction of the appellant on all four counts allowed.

Note

A spouse is always competent for a co-accused, but only compellable by a co-accused if the charge falls within one of those listed in s. 80(3) of the Police and Criminal Evidence Act 1984.

(ii) Spouses in civil cases

The spouses of the parties in civil cases are both competent and compellable.

Questions
1. Is it justifiable that spouses who have been assaulted by their partners can be compelled to testify for the prosecution even though they do not wish to do so? On what grounds, if any, can this be justified?
2. H is married to W. They have a child, C, who is 15 years old. H is charged with assaulting W and C, occasioning each of them actual bodily harm. H is further charged with assaulting F, W's father, who tried to

intervene when H was assaulting W and C. Consider the competence and compellability of W at H's trial for:

(a) the assault upon herself and C;
(b) H's separate trial for the assault upon F;

assuming that in each case H and W are reconciled and W does not wish to testify.

3. Consider how your answer to 2 above would differ if:

(a) H and W were divorced after the assaults but before the trials took place;
(b) H and W were not married but had cohabited for 17 years;

still assuming W does not wish to testify.

(C) Children

Note

The competency of children as witnesses has had a long and chequered history. In recent years there have been a number of piecemeal statutory reforms, prompted largely by a greater understanding and awareness of the reliability of the evidence of children. Until these reforms, the common law made no real distinction between the evidence of children in criminal cases as opposed to civil cases, the matter essentially falling within the discretion of the trial judge. Now, in criminal cases, the competence of a child witness is to be ascertained in the same way that competency is ascertained for any other witness. In other words, children should not be treated differently from adults when competency is in issue. In civil cases, the test contained in the Children Act 1989 will apply. In this respect, authorities decided on the similar test in the now repealed Children and Young Persons Act 1933 would still seem to have relevance.

Children and Young Persons Act 1933

38. Evidence of child of tender years

(1) Where, in any proceedings against any person for any offence, any child of tender years called as a witness does not in the opinion of the court understand the nature of an oath, his evidence may be received, though not given upon oath, if, in the opinion of the court, he is possessed of sufficient intelligence to justify the reception of the evidence, and understands the duty of speaking the truth . . .

Children Act 1989

96. Evidence given by, or with respect to, children

(1) Subsection (2) applies where a child who is called as a witness in any civil proceedings does not, in the opinion of the court, understand the nature of an oath.

(2)   The child's evidence may be heard by the court if, in its opinion —
   (a)   he understands that it is his duty to speak the truth; and
   (b)   he has sufficient understanding to justify his evidence being heard.

Note

For the purposes of the Children Act 1989, 'child' means a person who has not reached the age of 18 (s. 105 (1)).

R v Z
[1990] 2 QB 355, [1990] 2 ER 971
Court of Appeal

LORD LANE CJ: The question in each case which the court must decide is whether the child is possessed of sufficient intelligence to justify the reception of the evidence, and understands the duty of speaking the truth.

Those criteria will inevitably vary widely from child to child, and may indeed vary according to the circumstances of the case, the nature of the case, and the nature of the evidence which the child is called on to give. Obviously the younger the child the more care the judge must take before he allows the evidence to be received. But the statute lays down no minimum age, and the matter accordingly remains in the discretion of the judge in each case. It may be very rarely that a five-year-old will satisfy the requirements of s. 38(1). But nevertheless the discretion remains to be exercised judicially by the judge according to the well-known criteria for the exercise of judicial discretion.

I put the matter that way in the light of the fact that we have been referred to a decision of this court in *R v Wallwork* (1958) 42 Cr App R 153. That was a case where the appellant was charged with incest with his daughter aged five. Lord Goddard CJ, delivering the judgment of the court, said (at 160–161):

We now come to the point which has given the court considerable difficulty. The child was called as a witness, but said nothing. The court deprecates the calling of a child of this age as a witness. Although the learned judge had the court cleared as far as it can be cleared, it seems to us to be unfortunate that she was called and, with all respect to the learned judge, I am surprised that he allowed her to be called. The jury could not attach any value to the evidence of a child of five; it is ridiculous to suppose that they could. Of course, the child could not be sworn . . . but in any circumstances to call a little child of the age of five seems to us to be most undesirable, and I hope it will not occur again.

So far as *R v Wallwork* is concerned, that decision, some considerable number of years ago in 1958, has really been overtaken by events. First of all, it will be seen from the words of Lord Goddard CJ that part of the concern which he expressed was concern over the position of the child itself in court, when he mentions the fact the court was cleared so far as it was possible to have it cleared. That particular problem has now to a great extent been cured by the system of video links, which of course in Lord Goddard's days were not even imagined . . .

It seems to us that Parliament, by repealing the proviso to s. 38(1), was indicating a change of attitude by Parliament, reflecting in its turn a change of attitude by the public in general to the acceptability of the evidence of young children and of increasing belief that the testimony of young children, when all precautions have been taken, may be just as reliable as that of their elders.

For those reasons we would be reluctant in any way to fetter the discretion of the judge set out in s. 38(1), save to say, which scarcely needs saying, as already expressed the younger the child the more care must be taken before admitting the child's evidence . . .

The next submission was that the judge should have withdrawn the case from the jury, first of all, it was submitted, at the close of the prosecution case . . .

It is suggested by counsel for the applicant that [certain] answers really indicated that the child was either not reliable or did not understand what was going on, and in any event cast such a doubt, goes the submission, on her evidence that the judge should have withdrawn the case from the jury at the close of the prosecution evidence.

The answers to that, in the judgment of this court, is simple. The jury had heard what this little girl had said in chief, . . . The fact that she may have given answers which cast some doubt on that at a later stage was something eminently for the jury to decide. That is what they were there for, to decide whether the little girl was to be relied on as being accurate and truthful or not. It would have been quite improper for the judge to have usurped that function of the jury, and to have taken it on himself to decide at that stage whether the little girl was to be relied upon or not.

Criminal Justice Act 1991

52. Competence of children as witnesses

(1)   After section 33 of the 1988 Act there shall be inserted the following section —

Evidence given by children.

33A. — (1)   A child's evidence in criminal proceedings shall be given unsworn.

(2)   A deposition of a child's unsworn evidence may be taken for the purposes of criminal proceedings as if that evidence had been given on oath.

(3)   In this section 'child' means a person under fourteen years of age.

(2)   Subsection (1) of section 38 of the 1933 Act (evidence of child of tender years to be given on oath or in certain circumstances unsworn) shall cease to have effect: and accordingly the power of the court in any criminal proceedings to determine that a particular person is not competent to give evidence shall apply to children of tender years as it applies to other persons.

D. Birch *'Children's Evidence'*
[1992] Crim LR 262, pp. 266–9

Suppose the following, Amy, aged four, complains to her mother of an indecent assault by an Uncle. Mother is in no doubt that Amy is telling the truth. Horrified, she calls in the police.

. . . Section 52 of the 1991 Act . . . removes the need for any inquiry into Amy's understanding of an oath by providing that children under fourteen shall in all cases give their evidence unsworn. More importantly, the section 38 test is repealed, but with a rather puzzling rider tacked on, thus:

(2)   Subsection (1) of section 38 of the 1933 Act (evidence of child of tender years to be given on oath or in certain circumstances unsworn) shall cease to have effect: *and accordingly the power of the court in any criminal proceedings to determine that a particular person is not competent to give evidence shall apply to children of tender years as it applies to other persons.*

The rider has been criticised by John Spencer because the reference to the power applicable to 'other persons' is potentially misleading. It suggests that when the competence of a young witness is in issue, the court should follow its established practice of dealing with the over-14s. But this is clearly not what it means, because, in the exceptional cases where the issue arises, the dominant consideration with older witnesses concerns their understanding of the oath. (Reported cases are rare, but the best-known modern instance is *Bellamy* where the mentally handicapped adult victim of a rape was examined before being allowed to testify). Given that this inquiry can be of no relevance to a child who is to give unsworn evidence, what does the rider mean?

The answer must be that the competence of an adult at common law depends on more than the ability to take an oath. Witnesses are expected to be able to communicate, to give an understandable account of relevant events, and to understand and respond to questions. This combination of communication skills, together with the appreciation of duty that underlies the oath (the moral element), is well expressed in Stephen's *Digest of the Law of Evidence*, where it is stated:

> A witness is incompetent if, in the opinion of the judge, he is prevented by extreme youth, disease affecting his mind, or any other cause of the same kind, from recollecting the matter on which he is to testify, from understanding the questions put to him, from giving rational answers to those questions, or from knowing that he ought to speak the truth.

Because the moral element merges with the ability to take an oath, if an adult witness's moral competence is questioned the inquiry necessarily tends to precede the oath. This is not necessarily the case with communication skills, which, though they might be tested at a preliminary stage, are generally assumed to be present unless the contrary appears.

The background to the 1991 Act suggests that there was no intention to remove the rational element of competence: on the contrary, it is precisely because Amy may supply a rational account that her testimony ought to be received. It is with regard to the moral element that a change was to be made. Section 52(2) has its roots in the view of the Pigot Committee that courts should not refuse to consider any 'relevant understandable evidence': if a child's account is available it should be heard. The Committee proposed that the section 38 test be entirely dispensed with: the only difficulty foreseen was that once a child had begun to testify she might become incoherent or fail to communicate in a way that makes sense. It was said that this could be dealt with under the judge's existing common law powers to rule incompetent any witness who, because of unsoundness of mind or other defect, proves similarly unsatisfactory. The possible need to invoke this (somewhat obscure) residual common law power explains the rider to section 52(2).

In summary, then, the position under section 52 appears to be this. The court no longer has a duty to inquire into the competence of child witnesses as a class, but it retains the power to declare an individual child incompetent. The ground for the exercise of this power, which it seems applies to all witnesses, is not clear, but the interpretation most consistent with the intention of the legislation is that it should be used only in respect of a person who cannot communicate effectively. This interpretation would leave the prosecutor in Amy's case in a much better position to make decisions. In all probability a video recording of an interview with Amy will have been made to be used as evidence should the case come to trial. The prosecutor (and later the judge) will be able to tell from this if she is coherent, and understands the questions put to her which, coming from trained interviewers, will be appropriate to her age and level of development.

This leaves open the question of what precautions, if any, should be taken to bring to Amy's attention the importance of speaking the truth. If it were thought to be helpful she could, by the use of age-appropriate language, be judicially admonished to tell the truth, as recommended by the Pigot Committee. This does not seem in itself to be inconsistent with the spirit of the legislation. It would, however be inconsistent and inappropriate to reintroduce, as a preliminary to an admonition, some form of judicial duty to test children's understanding of the obligation to speak the truth. Amy will either tell the truth or she will not. If she does not, it is the function of the jury to discern her untruthfulness, aided by cross-examination. This is so (put very bluntly) whether or not she knows that telling lies is wrong.

Child sexual abusers are typically supremely manipulative personalities interested only in their own satisfaction at any cost to others. They have distorted attitudes, blaming their victims and screening out the unlawfulness of their own behaviour. They play victim to try and gain sympathy or advantage. Children, contrary to what was once thought, are not necessarily unreliable at all, and are certainly no less dangerous as witnesses than those who abuse them. Child abuse occurs in part because of the inequalities between child and adult in size, knowledge and power: inequalities which in the past have been institutionalised by one-sided rules of evidence. The new Act must not be interpreted in such a way as to claw back the territory gained.

There remains, of course, the question of how Amy would be likely to stand up to cross-examination, and whether the public interest will be served by bringing the case to trial, particularly if she is unwilling to go to court. Section 52 will not necessarily mean an enormous increase in the number of children appearing as witnesses in criminal trials. But we can certainly expect to see more under-eights and, where appropriate, some under-fives. No-one who has read David Jones' compelling account 'The Evidence of a Three-year old Child.' containing the detailed account by 'Susie' who was abducted, assaulted and left to die in the most distressing circumstances, could doubt that there are some occasions on which even a child of this age could give intelligible and accurate testimony.

(D)   Other cases

(i)   Persons of defective intellect

Note

A witness is not competent if he is unable to give rational evidence because of lunacy, drunkenness or some other similar disability, whether it be temporary or permanent. The question of competence remains one for the trial judge.

R v Bellamy
(1986) 82 Cr App R 222
Court of Appeal

The complainant in a rape trial being mentally handicapped, the trial judge investigated her competence as a witness. He heard evidence from the complainant's social worker and questioned the complainant both about her belief in and knowledge of God and about her understanding of the importance of telling the truth. He decided that she was a competent witness but lacked a sufficient belief in the existence of God to take a binding oath. Accordingly, he required her to affirm. The appellant was convicted of rape and appealed on the ground that the complainant ought to have been required to take the oath.

SIMON BROWN J: The basis of the appeal is that the learned judge was not entitled and had no power in those circumstances to cause the complainant to affirm. And it is said that the fact that the main evidence in the trial (that from the complainant) was given in this unauthorised way goes to the heart of the trial and vitiates the conviction.

As it seems to this Court, the learned judge, although clearly right to investigate whether or not the complainant was a competent witness in so far as having a sufficient understanding of the nature of the proceedings was concerned, ought not to have embarked upon a detailed examination of her theological appreciation.

Applying section 5 of the Oaths Act 1978, given that the judge concluded as he did that the complainant was a competent witness and given that she did not object to being sworn, it is our opinion that he should simply have allowed her to be sworn. Even however, if one took a different view as to that and concluded that the learned judge was entitled also to examine the complainant upon the extent of her belief in God, recent authorities regarding the proper application of section 38(1) of the Children and Young Persons Act 1933 indicate clearly that it is no longer necessary that a witness should have awareness of the divine sanction of the oath in order that that witness may properly be sworn.

This is made abundantly clear by consideration of two decisions of this Court: *Hayes* (1976) 64 Cr App R 194; [1977] 2 All ER 288 and *Campbell* [1983] Crim LR 174. I cite just a short paragraph from each case.

The position in *Hayes* was that two children, respectively aged 12 and 11, had been sworn in a case of gross indecency. They had been examined and had in fact denied having heard of God. The judgment of the Court was given by Bridge LJ (as he then was) in these terms at p. 196 and p. 290 of the respective reports. 'If the series of questions and answers started with the question "Do you think there is a God?" and the answer "Yes" there would really be no substance in Mr Charlesworth's complaints, but the fact that the earlier questions and answers, on their face, reveal the boy declaring that he is wholly ignorant of the existence of God does lend some force to the submission that if the essence of the sanction of the oath is a divine sanction, and if it is an awareness of that divine sanction which the Court is looking for in a child of tender years, then here was a case where, on the face of it, that awareness was absent. The Court is not convinced that that is really the essence of the Court's duty in the difficult situation where the Court has to determine whether a young person can or cannot properly be permitted to take an oath before giving evidence. It is unrealistic not to recognise that, in the present state of society, amongst the adult population the divine sanction of an oath is probably not generally recognised. The important consideration, we think, when a judge has to decide whether a child should properly be sworn, is whether the child has a sufficient appreciation of the solemnity of the occasion, and the added responsibility to tell the truth, which is involved in taking an oath, over and above the duty to tell the truth which is an ordinary duty of normal social conduct.'

Applying that passage in *Campbell*, May LJ, giving the judgment of the Court, said this: 'The two principles to be followed when considering whether a child should properly be sworn set out in *Hayes (supra)* were: that the child had a sufficient appreciation of the seriousness of the occasion and a realisation that taking the oath involved something more than the duty to tell the truth in ordinary day to day life'.

That this complainant had such a realisation is evident and was clearly found by the learned judge, he having noted her evidence that she realised that if she told a lie in the particular circumstances in which she was to give her evidence, then she could 'be put away'.

Those cases of course were concerned with the statute governing the position of children of tender years. *A fortiori* they would apply where, in regard to adult persons such as this complainant, there is no ruling statutory provision.

(ii)   Miscellaneous exceptions to the rule of compellability

Certain persons, whilst being competent, are not compellable. These exceptional (and largely unimportant) situations arise largely from statute. The persons falling within these categories include the Sovereign, foreign heads of state and accredited diplomats of foreign countries.

(E)   Oaths and affirmations

Note

It is a general requirement that the oral evidence of a witness should be sworn evidence. The principal exception is the unsworn evidence of a child under the age of 14 (see (C) above). A witness is required to take an oath or to affirm. If it transpires that the evidence given was unsworn (unless falling within one of the recognised exceptions), any appeal is likely to be successful. The present law is contained in the Oaths Act 1978. The important point to note is that the oath will be valid if it appears to the court to be binding on the witness's conscience and the witness regards himself as being so bound. The fact that other members of the witness's faith would not regard his oath as binding upon his conscience is immaterial.

Oaths Act 1978

1.   Manner of administration of oaths

(1)   Any oath may be administered and taken in England, Wales or Northern Ireland in the following form and manner —

The person taking the oath shall hold the New Testament, or, in the case of a Jew, the Old Testament, in his uplifted hand, and shall say or repeat after the officer administering the oath the words 'I swear by Almighty God that [. . .]', followed by the words of the oath prescribed by law.

(2)   The officer shall (unless the persons about to take the oath voluntarily objects thereto, or is physically incapable of so taking the oath) administer the oath in the form and manner aforesaid without question.

(3)   In the case of a person who is neither a Christian nor a Jew, the oath shall be administered in any lawful manner.

(4)   In this section 'officer' means any person duly authorised to administer oaths.

3.   Swearing with uplifted hand

If any person to whom an oath is administered desires to swear with uplifted hand, in the form and manner in which an oath is usually administered in Scotland, he shall be permitted so to do, and the oath shall be administered to him in such form and manner without further question.

4. Validity of oaths

(1)   In any case in which an oath may lawfully be and has been administered to any person, if it has been administered in a form and manner other than that prescribed by law, he is bound by it if it has been administered in such form and with such ceremonies as he may have declared to be binding.

(2)   Where an oath has been duly administered and taken, the fact that the person to whom it was administered had, at the time of taking it, no religious belief, shall not for any purpose affect the validity of the oath.

5. Making of solemn affirmations

(1)   Any person who objects to being sworn shall be permitted to make his solemn affirmation instead of taking an oath.

(2)   Subsection (1) above shall apply in relation to a person to whom it is not reasonably practicable without inconvenience or delay to administer an oath in the manner appropriate to his religious belief as it applies in relation to a person objecting to be sworn.

(3)   A person who may be permitted under subsection (2) above to make his solemn affirmation may also be required to do so.

(4)   A solemn affirmation shall be of the same force and effect as an oath.

6. Form of affirmation

(1)   Subject to subsection (2) below, every affirmation shall be as follows —
'I,   do solemnly, sincerely and truly declare and affirm,'
and then proceed with the words of the oath prescribed by law, omitting any words of imprecation or calling to witness.

(2)   Every affirmation in writing shall commence —
'I,   of   , do solemnly and sincerely affirm,'
and the form in lieu of jurat shall be 'Affirmed at   this day
of   19   , Before me.'

R v Kemble
[1990] 1 WLR 1111, [1990] 3 All ER 116
Court of Appeal

LORD LANE CJ: On 16 January 1989 at the Central Criminal Court before Judge Machin QC this applicant, Peter Kemble, pleaded guilty to two counts of possessing a firearm without a firearm certificate (counts 3 and 4). On 19 January 1989 before the same court he was convicted by verdict of a jury of having a firearm with intent to commit an indictable offence (count 2) the indictable offence being blackmail. He was sentenced to 12 months' imprisonment to run concurrently on counts 3 and 4 to which he had pleaded guilty, and he was sentenced to 2½ years' imprisonment on count 2, the count to which he had pleaded not guilty but was found guilty, namely, having a firearm with intent to commit an indictable offence. All those sentences were to run concurrently.

This application for leave to appeal against conviction has been referred to the full court by the registrar, and the sole ground of the application is that the main, if not the only relevant, prosecution witness, namely, a man called Tareq Hijab, who is a Muslim by religious conviction, took the oath using the New Testament before he gave evidence. Those are the basic facts of the case.

Mr Banks who has argued the case on behalf of the applicant argues that section 1 of the Oaths Act 1978 has not been complied with, that the chief witness for the prosecution was not properly sworn, that therefore there was a material irregularity and the conviction accordingly was in any event unsafe and unsatisfactory.

Section 1 of the Oaths Act 1978 provides:

(1) Any oath may be administered and taken in England, Wales or Northern Ireland in the following form and manner: — The person taking the oath shall hold the New Testament, or, in the case of a Jew, the Old Testament, in his uplifted hand, and shall say or repeat after the officer administering the oath the words 'I swear by Almighty God that . . .', followed by the words of the oath prescribed by law. (2) The officer shall (unless the person about to take the oath voluntarily objects thereto, or is physically incapable of so taking the oath) administer the oath in the form and manner aforesaid without question. (3) In the case of a person who is neither a Christian nor a Jew, the oath shall be administered in any lawful manner.

The argument of Mr Banks goes as follows. The witness, he says rightly, is a Muslim by faith. Secondly, he says, according to the strict tenets of the Muslim faith which we have had explained to us and explained to us carefully and in detail by an expert in the matter, namely, Professor Yaqub-Zaki, evidence which we of course accept unreservedly — no oath taken by a Muslim is valid unless it is taken upon the Koran, and moreover taken upon a copy of the Koran in Arabic. A translation into English or into any other language will invalidate, so to speak, the book so far as the oath is concerned under these strict religious tenets.

There are also many sub-rules which govern the taking of oaths by persons of the Muslim faith, according to the professor. For instance, a woman who is menstruating, and therefore considered to be unclean, cannot take a valid oath upon the Koran.

What we have to consider however is something else. Whilst respecting, as of course we do, the religious tenets of other faiths, be it Muslim or Jewish or anything else, it is the Act of 1978 which must govern our decision.

Assuming that one cannot simply stop after subsection (2) of section 1, which appears to be the case, we have to ask ourselves this: in the case of a person who is neither a Christian nor a Jew, that is to say, this particular witness, 'the oath shall be administered in any lawful manner.' Accordingly was the oath in the present case administered in a lawful manner?

We had our attention drawn, helpfully by Mr Banks if we may say so, to *Reg. v Chapman* [1980] Crim LR 42. The only passage I need read is a short passage in the part of the report which deals with the decision of the court. The court consisted of Roskill and Ormrod LJJ and Bristow J. The passage runs as follows: 'The efficacy of an oath must depend on it being taken in a way binding, and intended to be binding, upon the conscience of the intended witness.' That case was on cognate facts, although the facts were not by any means precisely the same.

We take the view that the question of whether the administration of an oath is lawful does not depend upon what may be the considerable intricacies of the particular religion which is adhered to by the witness. It concerns two matters and two matters only in our judgment. First of all, is the oath an oath which appears to the court to be binding on the conscience of the witness? And, if so, secondly, and most importantly, is it an oath which the witness himself considers to be binding upon his conscience?

So far as the present case is concerned, quite plainly the first of those matters is satisfied. The court did obviously consider the oath to be one which was binding upon the witness. It was the second matter which was the subject so to speak of dispute before this court. Not only did we have the evidence of the professor, the expert in the Muslim theology but we also had the evidence of the witness himself. He having on this occasion been sworn upon a copy of the Koran in Arabic gave evidence before us that he did consider himself to be bound as to his conscience by the way in which he took the oath at the trial. Indeed he went further. He said, 'Whether I had taken the oath upon the Koran or upon the Bible or upon the Torah, I would have considered that to be binding on my conscience.' He was cross-examined by Mr Banks in an endeavour to show that that was not the truth, but we have no doubt having heard him give his evidence and seen him give his evidence, that that was the truth, and that he did consider all of those to be holy books, and that he did consider that his conscience was bound by the form of oath he took and the way in which he took it. In other words we accept his evidence.

Consequently, applying what we believe to be the principles which we have endeavoured to set out to those facts, we conclude that the witness was properly sworn. We conclude accordingly that there was no irregularity, material of otherwise. There was nothing unsafe or unsatisfactory about the conviction. Accordingly this application is refused.

Question
David is charged with indecent assault on Victoria, a girl of 12. The prosecution wish to call Victoria herself, and two witnesses, Celia and Brian. Celia, a woman of 26, is thought to be mentally retarded. Brian, a man of 37, arrives at court to testify but is drunk. Consider their competence and compellability.

Further Reading
P. Murphy, *A Practical Approach to Evidence*, 4th ed. (1992), Ch. 12

5   THE COURSE OF THE TRIAL

The course of the trial can be conveniently divided into three separate stages, namely: examination-in-chief; cross-examination; and re-examination. At each of these three stages, a witness may be subjected to various questions by the parties in the case. During examination-in-chief, the party who has called the witness will be attempting to elicit from that witness evidence which supports his case. In doing so, the witness may not be asked leading questions (i.e. questions which suggest the required answer or which assume the existence of a disputed fact).

Examination-in chief is followed by cross-examination. Any party who has not called the witness may cross-examine that witness (e.g. a prosecution witness may be cross-examined by the defendant and any co-defendant). The purpose is to elicit facts favourable to the cross-examiner's case and to test the veracity of the witness. Leading questions may be put to the witness during cross-examination.

The party who called the witness may then re-examine that witness. The aim will be to try and restore the witness's credibility which, in all probability, will have been damaged during cross-examination. New matters cannot generally be introduced and questions should be restricted to matters which arose during the cross-examination. Again, leading questions are not permissible.

(A)   Examination-in-chief

The examination-in-chief involves the witness giving his oral evidence to the court for the first time. The witness will be called into the witness box, sworn, and then invited to tell the court his particular 'story'. Counsel for the witness will have a good idea what the witness is going to say, having read the witness's proof of evidence (a signed written statement) in advance of the trial. As mentioned above, counsel is not permitted to lead the witness through his evidence by suggesting the required answer to the witness or by posing questions which assume the existence of a fact which is in dispute.

Three aspects of examination-in-chief are dealt with in the following sections. The first deals with the extent to which a witness is allowed to refresh his memory from some written note or document made prior to the trial. The second deals with the admissibility of a previous consistent statement made by the witness. The third deals with hostile and unfavourable witnesses.

Note
Some witnesses, usually children, are permitted to give their evidence-in-chief from outside the courtroom in certain circumstances and subject to certain conditions. These situations are not dealt with in this work but reference may be made to s. 32 of the Criminal Justice Act 1988 and s. 54 of the Criminal Justice Act 1991.

(i)   Refreshing the memory

R v Richardson
[1971] 2 QB 484
Court of Appeal

Before the trial of the defendant on two charges of burglary and attempted burglary relating to offences which had taken place about 18 months earlier, four prosecution witnesses were shown the statements which they had made to the police a few weeks after the offences. Two of those witnesses had positively identified the defendant, and identification was the sole issue at the trial. The defence submitted that the evidence of all four witnesses was, in the circumstances, inadmissible. The trial judge rejected those submissions. The defendant was convicted and appealed.

SACHS LJ: . . . [i]t is . . . necessary to consider what should be the general approach of the court to there being shown in this way to witnesses their statements — which were not 'contemporaneous' within the meaning of that word as normally applied to documents used to refresh memory.

First, it is to be observed that it is the practice of the courts not to allow a witness to refresh his memory in the witness box by reference to written statements unless made contemporaneously. Secondly, it has been recognised in a circular issued in April 1969 with the approval of the Lord Chief Justice and the judges of the Queen's Bench Division (the repositories of the common law) that witnesses for the prosecution in criminal cases are normally (though not in all circumstances) entitled, if they so request, to copies of any statements taken from them by police officers. Thirdly, it is to be noted that witnesses for the defence are normally, as is known to be the practice, allowed to have copies of their statements and to refresh their memories from them at any time up to the moment when they go into the witness box — indeed, Mr Sedgemore was careful not to submit that there was anything wrong about that. Fourthly, no one has ever suggested that in civil proceedings witnesses may not see their statements up to the time when they go into the witness box. One has only to think for a moment of witnesses going into the box to deal with accidents which took place five or six years previously to conclude that it would be highly unreasonable if they were not allowed to see them.

Is there, then, anything wrong in the witnesses in this case having been offered an opportunity to see that which they were entitled to ask for and to be shown on request? In a case such as the present, is justice more likely to be done if a witness may not see a statement made by him at a time very much closer to that of the incident?

Curiously enough, these questions are very bare of authority. Indeed, the only case which has a direct bearing on this issue is one which was decided not in this country but on appeal in the Supreme Court of Hong Kong in 1966: *Lau Pak Ngam* v *The Queen* [1966] Crim LR 443. In the view of each member of this court this case contains some sage observations, two of which are apt to be quoted. One of them is:

> Testimony in the witness box becomes more a test of memory than of truthfulness if witnesses are deprived of the opportunity of checking their recollection beforehand by reference to statements or notes made at a time closer to the events in question.

The other is:

> Refusal of access to statements would tend to create difficulties for honest witnesses but be likely to do little to hamper dishonest witnesses.

With those views this court agrees. It is true that by the practice of the courts of this country a line is drawn at the moment when a witness enters the witness box; when giving evidence there in chief he cannot refresh his memory except by a document which, to quote the words of *Phipson on Evidence*, 11th ed (1970), p. 634, para 1528: 'must have been written either at the time of the transaction or so shortly afterwards that the facts were fresh in his memory.' (Incidentally, this definition does provide a measure of elasticity and should not be taken to confine witnesses to an over-short period.) This is, moreover, a practice which the courts can enforce: when a witness is in the box the court can see that he complies with it.

The courts, however, must take care not to deprive themselves by new, artificial rules of practice of the best chances of learning the truth. The courts are under no compulsion unnecessarily to follow on a matter of practice the lure of the rules of logic in order to produce unreasonable results which would hinder the course of justice. Obviously it would be wrong if several witnesses were handed statements in circumstances which enabled one to compare with another what each had said. But there can be no general rule (which, incidentally, would be unenforceable, unlike the rule as to what can be done in the witness box) that witnesses may not before trial see the statements which they made at some period reasonably close to the time of the event which is the subject of the trial. Indeed, one can imagine many cases, particularly those of a complex nature, where such a rule would militate very greatly against the interests of justice.

On the basis of this general approach, this court now returns to the facts of the present case. There had been great delay in the matter coming before the court and it appears to this court that nothing unreasonable was done in the particular circumstances.

Appeal dismissed.

R v *Westwell*
[1976] 2 All ER 812
Court of Appeal

The appellant was charged with assault occasioning actual bodily harm. Before the trial, which took place 11 months after the fight which was the subject of the charge, certain prosecution witnesses asked if they could see their written statements and they were allowed to do so. The prosecution did not inform the defence that this had been done, but the fact that it had become known to the defence, who submitted that in consequence the jury ought to be directed to acquit. The judge refused and the appellant was convicted. He appealed.

BRIDGE LJ: There is no general rule that prospective witnesses may not, before giving evidence at a trial, see the statements which they made at or near the time of the events of which they are to testify. They may see them whether they make a request to do so or merely accept an offer to allow them to do so. On the other hand, there is no rule that witnesses must be allowed to see their statements before giving evidence. There may be cases where there is reason to suppose that the witness has some sinister or improper purpose in wanting to see his statement and it is in the interests of justice that he should be denied the opportunity. Examples are suggested in the Home Office circular and in the judgment of this court in *R v Richardson* [1971] 2 QB 484. However, in most cases and particularly where, as often happens, there is a long interval between the alleged offence and the trial, the interests of justice are likely to be best served and witnesses will be more fairly treated if, before giving evidence, they are allowed to refresh their recollection by reference to their own statements made near the time of the events in question. As was said by the Supreme Court of Hong Kong in 1966 [in *Lau Pak Ngam* v *The Queen* [1966] Crim LR 443] in passages quoted with approval by this court in *R v Richardson,* if a witness is deprived of this opportunity his testimony in the witness box becomes more a test of memory than truthfulness; and refusal of access to statements would tend to create difficulties for honest witnesses but would be likely to do little to hamper dishonest witnesses. We have all, from time to time, seen the plight of an apparently honest witness, subjected to captious questioning about minor differences between his evidence in the witness box and the statement he made long ago and has never seen since, although his tormentor has it in his hand and has studied it in detail. Although such cross-examination frequently generates in the jury obvious sympathy with the witness and obvious irritation with the cross-examiner, it must leave a witness who has come to court to do his honest best with a smarting sense of having been treated unfairly.

Neither in the approved statement in the Home Office circular, nor in the judgment of the court in *R v Richardson,* is it laid down that the Crown must inform the defence that a prosecution witness has been allowed to look at his written statement before giving evidence. In *R v Richardson* the defence first discovered the fact for themselves in the course of cross-examination of a prosecution witness. The court made no criticism of the Crown on that account, nor was it invited to do so. Moreover, the decision of the trial judge, refusing to allow previous witnesses to be recalled for cross-examination about their statements, was upheld because in the particular facts of that case no prejudice was thereby caused to the defence.

Since hearing the argument in this appeal, our attention has been called to the decision of the Divisional Court in *Worley* v *Bentley* [1976] 2 All ER 449 in which the same point arose. The court held that it was desirable but not essential that the defence should be informed that witnesses have seen their statements. We agree. In some cases the fact that a witness has read his statement before going into the witness box may be relevant to the weight which can properly be attached to his evidence and injustice might be caused to the defendant if the jury were left in ignorance of that fact.

Accordingly, if the prosecution is aware that statements have been seen by witnesses it will be appropriate to inform the defence. But if, for any reason, this is not done, the omission cannot of itself be a ground for acquittal. If the prosecution tell the defence that the witness has been allowed to see his statement the defence can make such use of the information as it thinks prudent, but in any event the defence, where such a fact may be material, can ask the witness directly when giving evidence whether the witness has recently seen his statement. Where such information is material it does not ultimately matter whether it is volunteered by the prosecution or elicited by the defence. If the mere fact that the prosecution had not volunteered the information were a bar to conviction, this would be an artificial and arbitrary rule more appropriate to a game or a sporting contest than to a judicial process. The question for the court is whether, in the event, the trial can be continued without prejudice or risk of injustice to the defendant.

In the present case the defence knew, before the prosecution case was concluded, that the witnesses had seen their statements. The defence could have applied to recall the witnesses if they thought cross-examination about the statements worthwhile. They could have made whatever points they wished to make with the jury about the weight to be attached to the prosecution evidence.

Appeal dismissed.

Burrough v *Martin*
(1809) 2 Camp 111
King's Bench

In an action on a charter-party, a witness was called to give an account of the voyage, and the logbook was laid before him for the purpose of refreshing his memory. Being asked whether he had written it himself, he said that he had not, but that from time to time he examined the entries in it while the events recorded were fresh in his recollection, and that he always found the entries accurate.

The Attorney-General contended that the witness could make no use of the logbook during his examination, notwithstanding his former inspection of it; and that the only case where a witness could refer to a written paper for the purpose of giving evidence, was where he had actually written it himself and had thus the surest means of knowing the truth of its contents.

LORD ELLENBOROUGH: If the witness looked at the logbook from time to time, while the occurrences mentioned in it were recent and fresh in his recollection, it is as good as if he had written the whole with his own hand. This collation gave him an ample opportunity to ascertain the correctness of the entries; and he may therefore refer to these on the same principles that witnesses are allowed to refresh their memory by reading letters and other documents which they themselves have written.

R v *Cheng*
(1976) 63 Cr App R 20
Court of Appeal

Police officers kept observation on a number of men, including the defendant, who were suspected of peddling heroin. The defendant was later charged with unlawfully supplying a preparation of a dangerous drug, and at his trial one of the officers who had kept observation was called as a prosecution witness. He no longer had the relevant notebook and sought to refresh his memory from a statement he had prepared from his notebook and used at the committal proceedings. The defence objected to the use of the statement because it did not contain the notes about the other men who had been under surveillance and was thus a partial not an exact copy of the notebook. The trial judge ruled that the officer could refer to his statement and the defendant was convicted. He appealed.

LAWTON LJ: The sole question in this case has been whether the judge acted properly and in accordance with law in allowing Constable Moore to refresh his memory from the statement.

Mr Wright, on behalf of the Crown, has reminded the Court that in *Richardson* (1971) 55 Cr App R 244; [1971] 2 QB 484 Sachs LJ, giving the judgment of the Court said this at pp. 251 and 490: 'The Courts, however, must take care not to deprive themselves by new, artificial rules of practice of the best chances of learning the truth. The Courts are under no compulsion unnecessarily to follow the lure of the rules of logic in order to produce results on a matter of practice which are unreasonable and would hinder the course of justice.'

It is because of that approach by this Court as recently as 1971, that we have felt it necessary to find out how the rules about refreshing memory developed. As far as the researches of counsel go (and their researches seem to be supported by textbooks), the first reported case in which the problem of what documents a witness could use to refresh his memory was discussed was *Doe d Church and Phillips* v *Perkins* (1790) 3 Term Rep 749. It is clear from the facts of that case that up to that time there had been no certain rule about what witnesses could look at when giving evidence for the purpose of making a deposition. The witness whose evidence was under consideration in that case had been allowed to refer to a document which had been substantially prepared by her solicitor. Lord Kenyon CJ ruled that this was irregular.

In the 60 years which followed, the problem of what witnesses could look at to refresh their memories came before the Courts in a number of cases. It is manifest that as the years went by the Courts came to the conclusion that too strict a rule was not in the interests of justice. It is not necessary for us to deal with each of the cases which were considered in the 60 odd years after the decision in *Doe d Church and Phillips* v *Perkins (supra)*. It suffices to refer to two.

In *Burton* v *Plummer* (1834) 2 A & E 341, the question before the Court was whether a witness could look at a copy of an original note which he had made. The Court adjudged that he could; but he had to be able to say that the copy was an accurate copy of the original note.

It was almost inevitable after that case that some lawyer would raise the question as to what was an accurate copy. That very problem was considered by the House of Lords in *Horne* v *MacKenzie* (1839) 6 Cl & Fin 628. The point arose in this way: I read from the headnote: 'A, a surveyor, made a survey or report, which he furnished to his employer being afterwards called as a witness, he produced a printed copy of this report, on the margin of which he had, two days before, to assist him in giving his explanations as a witness, made a few jottings. The report had been made up from his original notes, of which it was in substance, though not in words, a transcript . . .' In other words, as appears clear when one looks at the details of the case what he was looking at in the witness box was not strictly a copy at all of his original note. He was allowed to refresh his memory from it and the House of Lords seems to have taken the view, albeit *obiter*, that there was nothing wrong in his doing so.

The judgment of the House was delivered by Lord Cottenham: he said at p. 645: 'If your Lordships think that there should be a new trial on this ground, it will be unnecessary to give any decision on the question of evidence. But I may say that in my opinion the witness was, under the circumstances of this case, entitled to refer to the paper to refresh his memory.'

In our judgment that opinion of the Lord Chancellor resolves this case. What the police constable was doing in this case was what the surveyor had done in that case. He had transcribed that part of his note which he thought was relevant. We can see nothing wrong in that. Indeed if we had felt bound to say that it was wrong for him to refresh his memory from his statement, we would have brought about an absurdity, because it is now established by *Richardson (supra)* to which I have already referred that a witness can see his original statement outside court. If he could read it right up to the court door and learn it off by heart, but was forbidden in the witness box to look at it at all, this would be a triumph of legalism over common sense.

What seems to us to be the position is this. If the statement in this case, or any other transcription of notes in other cases, is substantially what is in the notes and there is evidence to that effect, then the judge should allow the witness to refresh his memory from the statement or transcription as the case may be. But if, after investigation, it turns out that the statement or transcription bears little relation to the original note, then a different situation arises. The judge in the exercise of his discretion would be entitled to refuse to allow a witness to refresh his memory from such an imperfect source of information.

Appeal dismissed.

Note

In criminal cases, it is the oral testimony of the witness which constitutes evidence and not the note which the witness uses to refresh his memory. The cross-examiner may inspect the note and it may also be shown to the jury. This will enable them to judge and assess the credibility of the witness more effectively. If, however, it is alleged that the note has been fabricated, or if cross-examination goes beyond those parts of the note which the witness has used to refresh memory, the note itself may become evidence in the case.

R v Bass
[1953] 1 QB 680
Court of Criminal Appeal

The appellant was convicted of shopbreaking and larceny. The only evidence against him was contained in statements amounting to a confession of guilt which he was alleged to have made, before he was charged, during an interrogation by two police officers at a police station. At the trial the officers gave evidence and read their accounts of the interview from their notebooks. As these accounts appeared to be identical, and the officers denied that they had been prepared in collaboration, the defendant asked that the jury should be allowed to inspect the notebooks, but the application was refused.

BYRNE J: 'With regard to the second ground of appeal, the matter stood in this way. The officers' notes were almost identical. They were not made at the time of the interview. One officer made his notes after the appellant had been charged, and the other officer made his an hour later. Mr Crowder suggested to the officers in cross-examination that they had collaborated. They denied that suggestion. This court has observed that police officers nearly always deny that they have collaborated in the making of notes, and we cannot help wondering why they are the only class of society who do not collaborate in such a matter. It seems to us that nothing could be more natural or proper when two persons have been present at an interview with a third person than that they should afterwards make sure that they have a correct version of what was said. Collaboration would appear to be a better explanation of almost identical notes than the possession of a superhuman memory . . .

The deputy chairman's desire to preserve the confidential nature of the notebooks could probably quite easily have been achieved with the assistance of a pin or a piece of sticking plaster so that only the relevant pages could have been read. Be that as it may, however, the jury should have been permitted to see the notebooks. The credibility and accuracy of the two police officers was a vital mattter, for it was upon their evidence, and their evidence alone, that the whole of the case against the appellant rested, and as they had denied collaboration in the making of their notes, the jury should have been given the opportunity of examining them.

Appeal allowed.

Owen v *Edwards*
(1983) 77 Cr App R 191
Divisional Court

The defendant was charged with an offence against section 5 of the Public Order Act 1936. A policeman, who was a prosecution witness, made notes about the incident and refreshed his memory from his notebook outside court but did not refer to the notebook while giving evidence at the defendant's trial. Counsel for the defence then asked to see the notebook to check whether there were any discrepancies between the notes contained therein and the oral evidence which had been given. The police witness informed the court that he had only looked at part of his notes, but did not formally object to the proposed inspection. The justices ruled that the defence could inspect the notebook but could not cross-examine on matters contained in it which had not been referred to by the witness. Counsel for the defence then closed her cross-examination without inspecting the notebook and, no adjournment being sought, the justices proceeded to hear the whole of the evidence including that of a civilian witness and the police witness as to identity and that of the defendant himself

The defendant was convicted and appealed on the ground that on the basis of the ruling on admissibility the case ought not to be remitted to the justices but the only proper course was to quash the conviction.

McNEIL J: Curiously, the point whether or not an accused's representative may ask to see the notebook of a police officer, or indeed the statement of a witness, from which the witness has refreshed his memory not in the witness box but outside the door of the court, has not been decided in England. There is a passage in *Archbold* (41st ed 1982) para. 4–324, which reads as follows: 'If the witness has not referred to any book in his evidence for the purpose of refreshing his memory, and has merely admitted in cross-examination that he did not make a note, it has been held in

Scotland that he cannot be compelled to produce the book: *Hinshelwood* v *Auld* (1926) SC (J) 4 (police officer's notebook)'. The learned editors continue: 'It is unlikely that this decision would be applied in England or Wales. If, for example, the witness admitted that he had been refreshing his memory from the notebook outside the court door, it would be odd indeed if he could not be required to produce the document after entering the witness box.'

We have been referred to cases on the general proposition as to the production of documents. It is of course clear and hardly needs authority but we were referred to *Senat* v *Senat* [1965] 2 All ER 505 and the words in particular of Sir Jocelyn Simon P on p. 512 that where a document has been used to refresh memory in court then clearly the defendant is entitled to see it. Equally, the right to cross-examine on previous inconsistent statements is well recognised: see, for example, the judgment of this Court in *Worley* v *Bentley* (1976) 62 Cr App R 239: [1976] 2 All ER 449, where Kilner Brown J giving the judgment of this Court, seemed to accept it as axiomatic that a statement would have been shown to the defence if inconsistent with the testimony, and the opinion of the Privy Council in *Baksh* v *R* [1958] AC 167, where Lord Tucker makes observations to the same effect. Those observations are to my mind also in line with the guidelines that were issued by the Attorney-General, to be found in (1982) 74 Cr App R 302 as to the making available to the defence of what is called 'unused material'. Those guidelines, of course, as I read them, apply only to proceedings on committal and have not been applied so far as the Court has been informed to proceedings in the magistrates' court.

The whole tenor of authority appears to indicate that the defence is entitled to see such documents, including notebooks and statements, from which memory has been refreshed subject, of course, only to the well-established rules that a witness can be cross-examined having refreshed his memory upon the material in his notebook from which he has refreshed his memory without the notebook being made evidence in the case, whereas if he is cross-examined beyond those limits into other matters, the cross-examiner takes the risk of the material being evidence and the document being exhibited and therefore available for use by the fact finding tribunal.

As I say, the justices came to the conclusion that counsel was entitled to inspect the notebook but not entitled to cross-examine the witness on matters contained in it and which had not been referred to by the witness. It seems to me that on that aspect of the case I am in total agreement with the learned editors of *Archbold* in saying that the rules which apply to refreshing memory in the witness box should be the same as those which apply if memory has been refreshed outside the door of the court or, in the words of the learned editor, 'It would be odd if it were otherwise'. It is not for this Court on these facts to determine how much earlier than giving evidence the line is to be drawn. That will be for the fact-finding tribunal or some other court to consider, if necessary. On the point of law as posed by the justices, my answer would be that they were wrong in law.

(Nolan J agreed.)

Appeal dismissed.

R v *Virgo*
(1978) 67 Cr App R 323
Court of Appeal

The defendant, the head of the Obscene Publications Squad, was convicted of conspiracy and corruptly accepting bribes. At his trial the judge granted the prosecution permission to allow a leading prosecution witness — a self-confessed dealer in pornography and a very unsavoury character — to use his diaries to refresh his memory while giving evidence, and copies of the diaries were before the jury. The object of the diaries was to assist the witness to give accurate dates. In summing up, the judge directed the jury that the diaries were the most important documents in the case against the defendant, that the entries were powerful evidence, pointing to a corrupt relationship between him and the witness, and that although they did not amount to corroboration in law, they were very important in relation to the witness' evidence.

GEOFFREY LANE LJ: There is always a danger in circumstances such as these when attention has been focussed on a particular document for a long period of time, and when the document has been subjected to a minute and line by line analysis, as these diaries were that the document will achieve an importance which it does not warrant. It was most important in this case that the status of these diaries should be clearly understood throughout the trial and particularly at the end of the trial when the learned judge came to sum up the matter to the jury.

Those diaries were never more, at best, than a means whereby Humphreys might be able to give accurate dates and accurate chapter and verse for the incidents in respect of which he was giving evidence. They were never more than documents prepared by Humphreys and Humphreys was a self-confessed dealer in pornography. He was an accomplice and he was, on any view, a highly unsavoury character in many other ways. His evidence, *par excellence*, required corroboration.

The learned judge made perfectly plain to the jury, in impeccable language at the outset of his direction, the general law relating to corroboration. No one complained about that for a moment, nor could they complain. So far as Humphreys' diaries were concerned, not only did his evidence in general require corroboration, but by the same token, the answers which he gave about his diaries required corroboration. At the very highest, if the jury were convinced that the diaries were genuine, they showed a degree of consistency in Humphreys which otherwise might have been lacking, just as a complaint by the victim of a sexual assault, if made at the first reasonable opportunity thereafter, may show consistency in his or her evidence, though that analogy, one concedes, is not altogether apt. What the diaries could not under any circumstances do, was to support the oral evidence of Humphreys other than in a very limited way which we have already endeavoured to describe. In no way were they evidence of the truth of their contents.

Taking the two steps as set out in the decision in *Turner* (1975) 61 Cr App R 67, to which we have been referred, the diaries might assist the jury to say, in the first instance, that the witness in question was not wholly devoid of credit but what they could in no circumstances do was to contribute to the second stage of *Turner (supra)*, namely the search for corroboration.

Appeal allowed.

R v Da Silva
[1990] 1 WLR 31, [1990] 1 All ER 29
Court of Appeal

In the course of the defendant's trial for robbery the Crown called a witness to give evidence of a conversation which had taken place four days after the offence in which the defendant had admitted his involvement in the crime. The witness had made a statement to that effect about a month later. When he came to give his evidence he could no longer remember the details of the conversation. The trial judge therefore intervened and invited him to withdraw and read his statement. In the absence of the jury, a submission on behalf of the defendant that the procedure was irregular was rejected. The defendant was convicted and sentenced to 11 years' imprisonment.

STUART SMITH LJ: . . . There are two main grounds of appeal. The first relates to the evidence of Collina. He was called by the Crown to give evidence of a conversation with the defendant which had taken place on 21 November 1986, in which the defendant had admitted his involvement in the crime. Collina had made a statement to this effect on 22 December 1986, in which he gave details of the conversation. He had not seen his witness statement before he came into the witness box. When he came to give evidence, he said, to adopt the judge's summary since we do not have a transcript of Collina's evidence: 'I cannot remember now. It is a year ago. I did make a statement at the time.' Thereupon the judge intervened and invited the witness to withdraw and read his statement in the cells, he being a serving prisoner, under the supervision of a prison officer.

It appears that this incident occurred just before the midday break. This having been done, counsel for the defendant submitted, in the absence of the jury, that this procedure was irregular. That submission has been renewed in this court. Mr Bradshaw submits that there is a hard and fast division between contemporaneous statements, that is to say statements made at a time while the events that the witness is recording are fresh in his memory and those that are made at a later time. He submits that in the case of a contemporaneous statement, the witness can be permitted to refresh his memory from it provided he does so in the witness box and the ground for the application for permission is properly laid. In the case of a statement that is not contemporaneous, a witness may refresh his memory by looking at the statement before he goes into the witness box but not thereafter. In this case he submits that the statement, having been made a month after the events related, was not contemporaneous and was not treated as such by the judge. The judge did not make it clear whether he was treating the statement as a contemporaneous one or not.

Mr Kay, on behalf of the Crown, submits that in effect he did so, and that it was only as a matter of convenience, because the incident occurred just before the natural break in the proceedings, that the witness was invited to read the statement in the cells.

Mr Bradshaw has drawn our attention to *Reg.* v *Graham* [1973] Crim LR 628, in which the court said that a judge should hesitate before deciding that a statement made 27 days after the event was contemporaneous. But the court was not there saying that a statement made after that length of time could not be contemporaneous. It is a question of fact and degree in each case, and the matter should be investigated to see that the events were fresh in the witness's mind after the lapse of time. Much will depend on the nature of the evidence to be given. Where, for example, a witness purports to give a verbatim account of a conversation, the note will need to have been made much nearer the time than if he merely purports to give the general effect of a conversation.

We do not think that the judge treated the statement as a contemporaneous one. It does not appear that the proper foundation for so doing was laid, namely to ask the witness whether the events were fresh in his mind when he made the statement.

Moreover, if the statement had been treated as contemporaneous, the witness would have been allowed to refresh his memory in the witness box and refer to it if need be.

In the alternative, Mr Kay submits that there is no rigid rule that even if the statement is not contemporaneous, a witness may in no circumstances look at it once he has started to give evidence. In *Archbold, Criminal Pleading Evidence & Practice*, 43rd ed. (1988), p. 470, the rule is stated in such terms. It is said, at para. 4–294:

> 'A line is drawn at the moment when a witness enters the witness box.' When giving evidence there in chief he cannot refresh his memory 'unless the document he wishes to use falls within the conditions prescribed by the memory refreshing rule.'

The quotations are from the judgment of the court given by Sachs LJ in *Reg.* v *Richardson* [1971] 2 QB 484, 489. The actual decision in that case was that where a long interval had elapsed between statements made fairly soon after events forming the subject matter of the prosecution, but not contemporaneously within the meaning given to that expression, witnesses might be shown their statements before going into the witness box.

The passage cited in *Archbold* was therefore obiter, though it may be said to represent the generally accepted principle. But since in either case, that is to say both with contemporaneous statements and those that do not fall within that class, the witness is refreshing his memory, it may fairly be said that there is no logical reason why in the one case he must do it in the witness box and in the other he must do it before he enters the witness box and not once he has done so. Moreover, if a witness needs to refresh his memory, there is much to be said for it being apparent to the jury that he is doing so and for the jury knowing when the statement was made. What must be avoided is a witness simply reading his statement when he has no real recollection of events; but that can be avoided by removing the statement from him once he has read it to refresh his memory.

In *Reg.* v *Richardson* Sachs LJ continued, at p. 490:

> The courts, however, must take care not to deprive themselves by new, artificial rules of practice of the best chances of learning the truth. The courts are under no compulsion unnecessarily to follow on a matter of practice the lure of the rules of logic in order to produce unreasonable results which would hinder the course of justice. Obviously it would be wrong if several witnesses were handed statements in circumstances which enabled one to compare with another what each had said. But there can be no general rule (which incidentally, would be unenforceable, unlike the rule as to what can be done in the witness box) that witnesses may not before trial see the statements they made at some period reasonably close to the time of the event which is the subject of the trial. Indeed one can imagine many cases, particularly those of a complex nature, where such a rule would militate very greatly against the interests of justice.

The court is concerned to see that the truth emerges so that justice can be done. Two observations of the Supreme Court of Hong Kong in *Lau Pak Ngam* v *The Queen* [1966] Crim LR 443 were approved of by the court in *Reg* v *Richardson*, at p. 489:

> 'Testimony in the witness-box becomes more a test of memory than of truthfulness if witnesses are deprived of the opportunity of checking their recollection beforehand by reference to statements or notes made at a time closer to the events in question.' The other is: 'Refusal of access to statements would tend to create difficulties for honest witnesses, but be likely to do little to hamper dishonest witnesses.'

In our judgment, therefore, it should be open to the judge, in the exercise of his discretion and in the interests of justice, to permit a witness who has begun to give evidence to refresh his memory from a statement made near to the time of events in question, even though it does not come within the definition of contemporaneous, provided he is satisfied: (1) that the witness indicates that he cannot now recall the details of events because of the lapse of time since they took place; (2) that he made a statement much nearer the time of the events and that the contents of the statement represented his recollection at the time he made it; (3) that he had not read the statement before coming into the witness box; (4) that he wished to have an opportunity to read the statement before he continued to give evidence.

We do not think that it matters whether the witness withdraws from the witness box and reads his statement, as he would do if he had had the opportunity before entering the witness box, or whether he reads it in the witness box. What is important is that if the former course is adopted, no communication must be had with the witness, other than to see that he can read the statement in peace. Moreover, if either course is adopted, the statement must be removed from him when he comes to give his evidence and he should not be permitted to refer to it again, unlike a contemporaneous statement which may be used to refresh memory while giving evidence.

In this case the initiative came from the judge, but it is clear that it is no ground of objection if the judge thinks it is in the interests of justice that he intervene: see *Reg.* v *Fotheringham* [1975] Crim LR 710 and *Reg.* v *Tyagi, The Times,* 21 July 1986. In our judgment, it was open to the judge to permit the witness Collina to refresh his memory from the witness statement in the exercise of his discretion, because the conditions set out above were satisfied.

Appeal dismissed.

Note
In civil cases a judge, unlike the jury in a criminal case, may always consider a memory-refreshing document as evidence of the facts which that document contains.

Civil Evidence Act 1968

3. Witness's previous statement, if proved, to be evidence of facts stated
(2) Nothing in this Act shall affect any of the rules of law relating to the circumstances in which, where a person called as a witness in any civil proceedings is cross-examined on a document used by him to refresh his memory, that document may be made evidence in those proceedings; and where a document or any part of a document is received in evidence in any such proceedings by virtue of any such rule of law, any statement made in that document or part by the person using the document to refresh his memory shall by virtue of this subsection be admissible as evidence of any fact stated therein of which direct oral evidence by him would be admissible.

(ii) Previous consistent statements

Note
A witness (W) is not permitted to testify that on some other occasion, he made a statement which is consistent with his present testimony. Nor may a

witness (W1) call another witness (W2) to prove that he (W1) made a statement consistent with his present testimony. The rationale of the rule is that previous consistent statements have no value. They add nothing to the sworn testimony of the witness presently before the court.

There are a number of exceptions to this general rule (see below), but even if the previous consistent statement is admissible, it cannot be treated as evidence of the facts otherwise it would infringe the rule against hearsay (see Chapter 7). It may only be used for the more general purpose of demonstrating that the witness has been consistent.

R v Roberts
[1942] 1 All ER 187
Court of Criminal Appeal

The defendant was convicted of murdering a girl by shooting her. His defence was that the gun went off accidentally while he was trying to make up a quarrel with the girl. Two days after the event he told his father that the defence would be accident. The trial judge would not allow his conversation to be proved.

HUMPHREYS J: In our view the judge was perfectly right in refusing to admit that evidence, because it was in law inadmissible. It might have been, and, perhaps, by some judges would have been, allowed to be given on the ground that it was the evidence which the defence desired to have given, was harmless, and there was no strenuous opposition on the part of the prosecution. Such evidence might have been allowed to be given, but the judge was perfectly entitled to take the view which he did, that in law that evidence was inadmissible. The law upon the matter is well-settled. The rule relating to this is sometimes put in this way, that a party is not permitted to make evidence for himself. That law applies to civil cases as well as to criminal cases. For instance, if A and B enter into an oral contract, and some time afterwards there is a difference of opinion as to what were the actual terms agreed upon and there is litigation about it, one of those persons would not be permitted to call his partner to say: 'My partner a day or two after told me what his view of the contract was and that he had agreed to do' so and so. So, in a criminal case, an accused person is not permitted to call evidence to show that, after he was charged with a criminal offence, he told a number of persons what his defence was going to be, and the reason for the rule appears to us to be that such testimony has no evidential value. It is because it does not assist in the elucidation of the matters in dispute that the evidence is said to be inadmissible on the ground that it is irrelevant. It would not help the jury in this case in the least to be told that the appellant said to a number of persons, whom he saw while he was waiting his trial, or on bail if he was on bail, that his defence was this, that or the other. The evidence asked to be admitted was that the father had been told by his son that it was an accident. We think the evidence was properly refused. Of course, if the statement had been made to the father just at the time of the shooting, that would have been a totally different matter, because it has always been regarded as admissible that a person should be allowed to give in evidence any statement accompanying an act so that it may explain the act. It was put by counsel for the appellant that the statement might be admissible on the ground that the accused had been asked in cross-examination, and it had been suggested to him in cross-examination that this story of accident was one which he had recently concocted. If any such question had been put, undeniably the evidence would have been admissible as showing it was not recently concocted, because the accused had said so on the very day the incident occurred. The answer is that no such question had been put, and no suggestion made, to the accused.

(The defendant's appeal was allowed on other grounds.)

R v Lillyman
[1896] 2 QB 167
Crown Cases Reserved

The defendant was charged with attempted unlawful intercourse with a girl between the ages of 13 and 16; with assault upon her with intent to ravish; and with an indecent assault upon her. The girl gave evidence that the acts complained of had been done without her consent. The prosecution also tendered evidence-in-chief of a complaint made by her to her mistress, in the absence of the defendant, shortly after the commission of the acts, and proposed to ask the details of the complaint as made by the girl. The defence objected to the admission of the evidence, but the trial judge admitted it. The mistress then deposed to all that the girl had said respecting the defendant's conduct towards her. The defendant was convicted.

HAWKINS J: It is necessary, in the first place, to have a clear understanding as to the principles upon which evidence of such a complaint, not on oath, nor made in the presence of the prisoner, nor forming part of the *res gestae*, can be admitted. It clearly is not admissible as evidence of the facts complained of: those facts must therefore be established, if at all, upon oath by the prosecutrix or other credible witness, and, strictly speaking, evidence of them ought to be given before evidence of the complaint is admitted. The complaint can only be used as evidence of the consistency of the conduct of the prosecutrix with the story told by her in the witness box, and as being inconsistent with her consent to that of which she complains.

In every one of the old textbooks proof of complaint is treated as a most material element in the establishment of a charge of rape or other kindred charge . . . .

It is too late, therefore, now to make serious objection to the admissibility of evidence of the fact that a complaint was made, provided it was made as speedily after the acts complained of as could reasonably be expected.

We proceed to consider the second objection, which is, that the evidence of complaint should be limited to the fact that *a complaint* was made without giving any of the particulars of it. No authority binding upon us was cited during the argument, either in support of or against this objection. We must therefore determine the matter upon principle. That the *general usage* has been substantially to limit the evidence of the complaint to proof that the woman made a complaint of something done to her, and that she mentioned in connection with it the name of a particular person, cannot be denied; but it is equally true that judges of great experience have dissented from this limitation, and of those who have adopted the usage none have ever carefully discussed or satisfactorily expressed the grounds upon which their views have been based . . . .

After very careful consideration we have arrived at the conclusion that we are bound by no authority to support the existing usage of limiting evidence of the complaint to the bare fact that a complaint was made, and that reason and good sense are against our doing so. The evidence is admissible only upon the ground that it was a complaint of that which is charged against the prisoner, and can be legitimately used only for the purpose of enabling the jury to judge for themselves whether the conduct of the woman was consistent with her testimony on oath given in the witness box negativing her consent, and affirming that the acts complained of were against her will, and in accordance with the conduct they would expect in a truthful woman under the circumstances detailed by her. The jury, and they only, are the persons to be satisfied whether the woman's conduct was so consistent or not. Without proof of her condition, demeanour, and verbal expressions, all of which are of vital importance in the consideration of that question, how is it possible for them satisfactorily to determine it? Is it to be left to the witness to whom the statement is made to determine and report to the jury whether what the woman said amounted to a real complaint? And are the jury bound to accept the witness's interpretation of her words as binding upon them without having the whole statement before them, and without having the power to require it to be disclosed to them, even though they may feel it essential to enable them to form a reliable opinion? For it must be borne in mind that if such evidence is inadmissible when offered by the prosecution, the jury cannot alter the rule of evidence and make it admissible by asking for it themselves.

In reality, affirmative answers to such stereotyped questions as these, 'Did the prosecutrix make a complaint' (a very leading question, by the way) 'of something done to herself?' 'Did she mention a name?' amount to nothing to which any weight ought to be attached; they tend rather to embarrass than assist a thoughtful jury, for they are consistent either with there having been a complaint or no complaint of the prisoner's conduct. To limit the evidence of the complaint to such questions and answers is to ask the jury to draw important inferences from imperfect materials, perfect materials being at hand and in the cognizance of the witness in the box. In our opinion, nothing ought unnecessarily to be left to speculation or surmise.

It has sometimes been urged that to allow the particulars of the complaint would be calculated to prejudice the interests of the accused, and that the jury would be apt to treat the complaint as evidence of the facts complained of. Of course, if it were so left to the jury they would naturally so treat it. But it never could be legally so left; and we think it is the duty of the judge to impress upon the jury in every case that they are not entitled to make use of the complaint as any evidence whatever of those facts, or for any other purpose than that we have stated. With such a direction, we think the interests of an innocent accused would be more protected than they are under the present usage. For when the whole statement is laid before the jury they are less likely to draw wrong and adverse inferences, and may sometimes come to the conclusion that what the woman said amounted to no real complaint of any offence committed by the accused. Moreover, the present usage and consequent uncertainty in practice (for the usage is not universal) provokes many objections to the evidence on the part of the prisoner's counsel, and these are generally looked upon with disfavour by the jury, and the very object of confining the evidence of the complaint to the few stereotyped questions we have referred to is often defeated by a device, not to be encouraged, by which the name of the accused, though carefully concealed as an inadmissible particular of the complaint, is studiously revealed to the jury by some such question and answer as the following: 'Q In consequence of that complaint did you do anything? A Yes, I went to the house of the prisoner's mother, where he lives, and accused him.' This seems to us to be an objectionable mode of introducing evidence indirectly, which if tendered directly would be inadmissible.

Conviction affirmed.

Questions
1.   Is it necessary or desirable to allow the victim of a sexual offence to narrate the substance of what she said, or should the victim only be allowed to relate the fact of complaint?
2.   Why has the law allowed recent complaints to become an exception to the rule against previous consistent statements?

R v *Osborne*
[1905] 1 KB 551
Crown Cases Reserved

The defendant was convicted of an indecent assault on a girl under the age of 13 years, whose consent to the act was therefore immaterial. At the trial evidence was admitted of the answer given by the girl to a question put by another child, in the absence of the defendant, as to why the girl had not waited for the other child at the defendant's house. The girl's reply was a complaint of the defendant's conduct to her.

RIDLEY J: It was contended for the prisoner that the evidence was inadmissible — first, because the answer made by the girl was not a complaint, but a statement or conversation, having been made in answer to a question; and, secondly, because, as Keziah Parkes was under the age of thirteen, her consent was not material to the charge. As to the first point, the case of *R* v *Merry* 19 Cox CC 442 was quoted. In that case a question had been put to a girl of nine years old by her mother in a case of indecent assault, and the learned judge ruled that, as the proposed evidence was a statement made in answer to a question, it was a conversation and not a complaint, and he declined to allow it to be given in evidence. It does not appear, however, from the report what the question was that was put to the girl. It appears to us that the mere fact that the statement is made in answer to a question in such cases is not of itself sufficient to make it inadmissible as a complaint. Questions of a suggestive or leading character will, indeed, have that effect, and will render it inadmissible; but a question such as this, put by the mother or other person, 'What is the matter?' or 'Why are you crying?' will not do so. These are natural questions which a person in charge will be likely to put; on the other hand, if she were asked, 'Did So-and-so' (naming the prisoner) 'assault you?' 'Did he do this and that to you?' then the result would be different, and the statement ought to be rejected. In each case the decision on the character of the question put, as well as other circumstances, such as the relationship of the questioner to the complainant, must be left to the discretion of the presiding judge. If the circumstances indicate that but for the questioning there probably would have been no voluntary complaint, the answer is inadmissible. If the question merely anticipates a statement which the complainant was about to make, it is not rendered inadmissible by the fact that the questioner happens to speak first. In this particular case, we think that the chairman of quarter sessions acted rightly, and that the putting of this particular question did not render the statement inadmissible.
      Upon the second point it was contended that, although under the decision of *R* v *Lillyman* [1896] 2 QB 167 the particulars of a complaint made may, in some circumstances, be given in evidence on a charge of rape, that ruling does not extend to a charge of criminal knowledge or indecent assault, where, as in the present case, consent is not legally material . . . .

By the judgment in *R* v *Lillyman* it was decided that the complaint was admissible, not as evidence of the facts complained of, nor as being a part of the *res gestae* (which it was not), but as evidence of the consistency of the conduct of the prosecutrix with the story told by her in the witness box, and as being inconsistent with her consent to that of which she complains. Mr Marchant argued upon this that the reasons so given were one only, and that the consistency of the complaint with the story given by the prosecutrix was material only so far as the latter alleged non-consent. If, however, that argument were sound, the words in question might have been omitted from the sentence, and it would have been sufficient to say that the complaint was admissible only and solely because it negatived consent. We think, however, if it were a question of the meaning of words, that the better construction of the judgment is that while the Court dealt with the charge in question as involving in fact, though not in law, the question of consent on the part of the prosecutrix, yet the reasons given for admitting the complaint were two — first, that it was consistent with her story in the witness box; and, secondly, that it was inconsistent with consent. The reasoning proceeded thus: On the second and third counts consent was material in law; on the first it was material in fact; there is, for this purpose, no difference between the two. It is not, therefore, because the charge itself involves proof of the absence of consent that the evidence is admissible; on the contrary, the prosecutrix herself can make it evidence by deposing that she did not consent when that is no part of the charge. In other words, whether non-consent be legally a necessary part of the issue, or whether, on the other hand, it is what may be called a collateral issue of fact, the complaint becomes admissible. But how does non-consent become a collateral issue of fact? The answer must be, in consequence of the story told by the prosecutrix in the witness box. And the judgment treats the two cases on the same footing. If non-consent be a part of the story told by the prosecutrix, or if it be legally a part of the charge, in each case alike the complaint is admissible. But, if that is so, does not the reasoning apply equally to other parts of the story, and not merely to the part in which the prosecutrix has denied consent? If not, it seems illogical to allow, as the Court did allow, that the whole of the story may be given in evidence. The true result is, we think, that, while the decision in *R* v *Lillyman* is not strictly on all-fours with the present case, yet the reasoning which it contains answers the question now raised for decision. But, however that may be, it appears to us that, in accordance with principle, such complaints are admissible, not merely as negativing consent, but because they are consistent with the story of the prosecutrix. In all ordinary cases, indeed, the principle must be observed which rejects statements made by any one in the prisoner's absence. Charges of this kind form an exceptional class, and in them such statements ought, under proper safeguards, to be admitted. Their consistency with the story told is, from the very nature of such cases, of special importance. Did the woman make a complaint at once? If so, that is consistent with her story. Did she not do so? That is inconsistent. And in either case the matter is important for the jury . . . .

We are, at the same time, not insensible of the great importance of carefully observing the proper limits within which such evidence should be given. It is only to cases of this kind that the authorities on which our judgment rests apply; and our judgment also is to them restricted. It applies only where there is a complaint not elicited by questions of a leading and inducing or intimidating character, and only when it is made at the first opportunity after the offence which reasonably offers itself. Within such bounds, we think the evidence should be put before the jury, the judge being careful to inform the jury that the statement is not evidence of the facts complained of, and must not be regarded by them, if believed, as other than corroborative of the complainant's credibility, and, when consent is in issue, of the absence of consent. For these reasons we think the conviction should be affirmed.

Conviction affirmed.

Question
If evidence of recent complaint is only demonstrative of consistency, how can it be permissible to use such evidence as supportive of lack of consent?

R v *Wallwork*
(1958) 42 Cr App R 153
Court of Criminal Appeal

The defendant was convicted of incest with his daughter, aged five. At the trial the child was put in the witness box by the prosecution, but was unable to give any evidence. However, evidence by her grandmother of a complaint made by the child to her, in which she named the defendant as her assailant, was admitted.

LORD GODDARD CJ: . . . [I]n our opinion, in this particular case that evidence was not admissible. In cases of rape or indecent assault it has always been held that evidence of a complaint and the terms of the complaint may be given, but they may be given only for a particular purpose, not as evidence of the fact complained of, because the fact that the woman says not on oath: 'So-and-so assaulted me' cannot be evidence against the prisoner that the assault did take place. The evidence may be and is tendered for the purpose of showing consistency in her conduct and consistency with the evidence she has given in the box. It is material, for instance, where a question of identity is concerned, that she made an immediate complaint or a complaint as soon as she had a reasonable opportunity of making it and made the complaint against the particular man. It is also material, and most material, very often on the point whether the girl or woman was a consenting party. None of these matters arise in this case. The child had given no evidence because when the poor little thing was put into the witness box, she said nothing and could not remember anything. The learned judge had expressly told the jury to disregard her evidence altogether. Therefore, there was no evidence given by her with regard to which it was necessary to say what she had said to her grandmother was consistent; nor could there be any question of the identity of the prisoner or any question of consent. The learned judge, having once admitted that evidence ought — and he omitted to do this — to have told the jury that it was not evidence of the facts complained of by the child.

(The court dismissed the appeal on the ground that no substantial miscarriage of justice was caused by the irregularities.)

R v *Oyesiku*
(1971) 56 Cr App R 240
Court of Appeal

The defendant was convicted of assault occasioning actual bodily harm and assaulting a police officer. At the trial the defendant's wife gave evidence that the police officer was the aggressor. During cross-examination it was put to her that her evidence was a late invention and concocted with a view to helping the defendant. The trial judge refused to admit in evidence an earlier statement made by the wife to a solicitor before she had seen her husband after his arrest. This statement was to the same effect as the evidence she gave in court.

KARMINSKI LJ: It was argued with great force before us by Mr Hazan that this decision to exclude the evidence was wrong in law . . . In *Coll* (1889) 24 LR Ir 522 at p. 541, Holmes J said:

> It is I think clear that the evidence of a witness cannot be corroborated by proving statements to the same effect previously made by him; nor will the fact that his testimony is impeached in cross-examination render such evidence admissible. Even if the impeachment takes the form of showing a contradiction or inconsistency between the evidence given at the trial and something said by the witness on a former occasion it does not follow that the way is open for proof of other statements made by him for the purpose of sustaining his credit. There must be something either in the nature of the inconsistent statement, or in the use made of it by the cross-examiner, to enable such evidence to be given.

We regard that statement of the law as correct, and applicable to the present case.

Our attention has also been drawn to a recent decision in the High Court of Australia, *Nominal Defendant* v *Clement* (1961) 104 CLR 476. I desire to read only one passage from the full judgment of Dixon CJ. He said this (at p. 479):

> The rule of evidence under which it was let in is well recognised and of long standing. If the credit of a witness is impugned as to some material fact to which he deposes upon the ground that his account is a late invention or has been lately devised or reconstructed, even though not with conscious dishonesty, that makes admissible a statement to the same effect as the account he gave as a witness, if it was made by the witness contemporaneously with the event or at a time sufficiently early to be inconsistent with the suggestion that his account is a late invention or reconstruction. But, inasmuch as the rule forms a definite exception to the general principle excluding statements made out of court and admits a possibly self-serving statement made by the witness, great care is called for in applying it. The judge at the trial must determine for himself upon the conduct of the trial before him whether a case for applying the rule of evidence has arisen and, from the nature of the matter, if there be an appeal, great weight should be given to his opinion by the appellate court. It is evidence however that the judge at the trial must exercise care in assuring himself not only that the account given by the witness in his testimony is attacked on the ground of recent invention or reconstruction or that a foundation for such an attack has been laid by the party, but also that the contents of the statement are in fact to the like effect as his account given in his evidence and that having regard to the time and circumstances in which it was made it rationally tends to answer the attack. It is obvious that it may not be easy sometimes to be sure that counsel is laying a foundation for impugning the witness's account of a material incident or fact as a recently invented, devised or reconstructed story. Counsel himself may proceed with a subtlety which is the outcome of caution in pursuing what may prove a dangerous course. That is one reason why the trial judge's opinion has an importance.

Dealing with the last paragraph of that quotation from Dixon CJ, there is no doubt at all that in this case counsel was making an attack, because it was clear from what he said at the trial and indeed what he said to us today. That judgment of the Chief

Justice of Australia, although technically not binding upon us, is a decision of the greatest persuasive power, and one which this Court gratefully accepts as a correct statement of the law applicable to the present appeal.

That is the position in law, and in our view the learned trial judge was wrong to refuse to allow that evidence to be given. The value of it, of course, was a matter for the jury to assess.

Conviction quashed.

R v Tooke
(1990) 90 Cr App R 417
Court of Appeal

LORD LANE CJ: On April 27, 1989, in the Crown Court at Maidstone this appellant was convicted of unlawful wounding and was sentenced to 12 months' detention in a young offender institution. There was a co-accused called Drury. He was similarly convicted and similarly sentenced, except his term was imprisonment and not custody in a young offender institution. His application for leave to appeal against sentence was refused by the single judge and it has not been renewed. This appellant, Mark Adrian Tooke, who is now 21 — he was under 21 at the time when the matter was tried — now appeals both against conviction and sentence by leave of the single judge. The facts of the case were these. It happened on the evening of December 1, 1988, in the lavatory of the Bristol Arms public house in Tunbridge Wells. A man called George Wicker, who was aged 45, had been doing the crossword in the public house over a drink. He eventually decided to go to the lavatory. Whilst he was there, according to him, the appellant and Drury came into the lavatory and jostled him. The appellant then hit him in the face and he fell down with his back to the wall. The two men then, according to him, pulled his jacket over his head and hit him on a number of occasions. He tried to push them away with his clenched fists, but was unable to do so. They ran out. His jacket was covered with blood and when he was taken to the hospital it was found that he had a fractured nose and other less serious injuries to his face. He denied that he had in any way barged into them, or indeed had been responsible for this assault upon himself in any way at all: certainly that he had not provoked them. The bar manager of the public house saw the victim crouching in the lobby outside the lavatory with his jacket over his head. The victim was very distressed. He was crying out that he had been mugged. He was bleeding from the nose.

Very shortly afterwards Drury came out of the lavatory and said to Campion, the bar manager, that 'Mark (the appellant) is in there, get him out.' Thereupon the appellant came out holding a tissue to his nose. There was no doubt that his nose had in some way been broken in this incident. They were asked by Campion what had happened, but no answer was given. Then the appellant came back and Campion heard both the appellant and Mr Wicker, the victim, say the other had hit him first. So each of them was saying, 'He hit me first.'

After the event and some little time later, the appellant went voluntarily down to the police station and at the police station he made a witness statement, on the ordinary witness statement form, setting out his version of events.

A submission was made to the learned judge that the defence should be permitted to cross-examine police Constable Dinnage in order to prove that the appellant had made this statement to him and in order to adduce the statement so that it would become evidence in the case. After argument the learned judge declined to accede to that submission, and that decision is now the subject of this appeal, the appellant submitting that the learned judge was wrong to reject the submission.

There are three principal circumstances in which previous consistent statements, if I may use that expression, are admissible. This is quite apart from the situation of what are called mixed statements, that situation being covered by the decision in this Court in *Duncan* (1981) 73 Cr App R 359 and of the House of Lords in *R v Sharp* (1988) 86 Cr App R 274, [1988] 1 WLR 7. The first situation is where they are part of the events in issue, the res gestae rule; secondly, where they are used to rebut a suggestion that the defendant has recently made up the story — if it can be shown that earlier on he was saying the same thing, of course that would rebut the suggestion — and thirdly (which has nothing to do with this case) the question of recent complaints in cases of sexual allegations.

There is a fourth category, with which we are concerned, and that is a situation which perhaps one can loosely describe as answers of a defendant when taxed with the situation either by the police or by somebody else. That is the area of difficulty which is raised by the facts in this case.

We have been referred helpfully to the decision of this Court in the case of *Pearce* (1979) 69 Cr App R 365. That decision was aimed at clarifying the situation. As appears from the facts of that case, and from the arguments, counsel for the appellant was seeking to persuade the Court that previous consistent statements are generally speaking always admissible subject only to certain exceptions. It is quite plain from the judgment of Lord Widgery CJ, in *Pearce* that the Court was unwilling to take that step as it would entail, it was said, the necessity to rewrite a chapter on the law of evidence. The Court in *Pearce* based their decision upon the earlier decision in *Storey* (1968) 52 Cr App R 334 and another decision in *Donaldson* (1976) 64 Cr App R 59.

The material part of the judgment in *Pearce* at p. 369 reads as follows:

In our view the present case can be disposed of within the principles stated in *Storey and Anwar* (1968) 52 Cr App R 334 and *Donaldson* (1977) 64 Cr App R 59. Those decisions will be found to contain all the guidance that is necessary in practice. We would ourselves summarise the principles as follows:

(1)   A statement which contains an admission is always admissible as a declaration against interest and is evidence of the facts admitted. With this exception a statement made by an accused person is never evidence of the facts in the statement.

(2)(a)   A statement that is not an admission is admissible to show the attitude of the accused at the time when he made it. This however is not to be limited to a statement made on the first encounter with the police. The reference in *Storey* to the reaction of the accused 'when first taxed' should not be read as circumscribing the limits of admissibility. The longer the time that has elapsed after the first encounter the less the weight which will be attached to the denial. The judge is able to direct the jury about the value of such statements . . .

(3)   Although in practice most statements are given in evidence even when they are largely self-serving, there may be a rare occasion when an accused produces a carefully prepared written statement to the police, with a view to it being made part of the prosecution evidence. The trial judge would plainly exclude such a statement as inadmissible.

The result of that is that an area of uncertainty is inevitably left, because it is impossible to define in advance with any precision the line between those statements which should be admitted and those statements which should not be admitted under (2)(a) in *Pearce*.

It seems to us that the test which should be applied is partly that of spontaneity partly that of relevance and partly that of asking whether the statement which is sought to be admitted adds any weight to the other testimony which has been given in the case. Of course it is not an easy task for the judge to decide in his discretion where the dividing line lies.

Perhaps it can be illustrated by two of the cases which Mr Harris has very helpfully cited to us this morning. The first one is *McCarthy* (1980) 71 Cr App R 142. In that case the judge had refused to admit oral and written self-exculpatory statements containing an alibi on the ground that they were all self-serving. The defendant had told the police at the time of making those statements that they were at liberty to check his movements if they so wished.

Lawton LJ giving the judgment of the Court in that case said this at p. 145:

He [counsel for the appellant] pointed out that although the details were not evidence of the facts, the reaction of McCarthy when questioned by the police officer at the beginning of the interview was something which the jury could properly take into account as having some relevance to the genuineness of the defence of alibi. In our judgment Mr Limont was right. One of the best pieces of evidence that an innocent man can produce is his reaction to an accusation to crime. If he has been told, as the appellant was told, that he was suspected of having committed a particular crime at a particular time and place and he says at once, 'that cannot be right, because I was elsewhere,' and gives details of where he was, that is something which the jury can take into account.

So this was plainly a case where the evidence was relevant as bearing closely upon the specific defence which was being raised, namely alibi. It is perhaps in passing helpful to note a passage at p. 146 of that judgment where Lawton, LJ says this:

If it is becoming a practice for counsel in criminal cases, when their clients have made exculpatory statements, not to call them in evidence, they should think very long and hard before they continue with that practice because comment from the Bench is likely to lead the jury to think that there is something very odd about such tactics.

The second case to which counsel referred is really at the other end of the scale. It is the case of *Newsome* (1980) 71 Cr App R 325. I read the headnote:

The appellant was charged with rape. After two interviews with police officers he saw his solicitor and at a third interview refused to answer questions on legal advice. Later still the same day he made a written statement to the police in the presence of his solicitor stating the facts on the basis that the victim had been a consenting party. The prosecution at his trial refused to put that latter statement before the jury. The trial judge, after hearing legal submissions, ruled that statement was inadmissible as self-serving. The trial proceeded and the appellant was convicted. On appeal against the judge's ruling, held, that the trial judge was clearly entitled . . . to take the view that the statement was a self-serving statement; thus the prosecution were right not to put it in evidence, and as they could not be compelled to put it in, the statement could only be got before the jury if counsel for the defence could show that it was admissible — that they had failed to do because the statement was clearly composed on legal advice with the solicitor present and revealed nothing relevant about the attitude of the appellant since it was clearly coloured by the circumstances in which it was made and the circumstances which immediately preceded its making; accordingly, the appeal would be dismissed.

In that case the statement which is was sought to put in was neither spontaneous nor was it relevant. Turning back to the instant case, the facts here are slightly complicated by the fact that this was a statement taken from the appellant before he had been charged. It was a witness statement and not a statement made in answer to a charge. But that, in our judgment, should logically make no difference. The same test should be applied.

What happened here was this. The incident happened shortly after 9 o'clock in the evening. The bar manager, Mr Campion, gave evidence before the jury that immediately afterwards these two men were each blaming the other, the appellant was blaming the victim, the victim was blaming the appellant. Then Police Constable Dinnage appears, no doubt having been summoned by the licensee, because there was a disturbance. He approaches the appellant, and one can imagine the situation: the policeman asked 'What is going on here?' and the answer comes from the appellant saying that he had been the victim of an assault in the toilet of the Bristol Arms. That evidence was admitted and no doubt properly admitted without anyone suggesting otherwise, although it was plainly evidence which was self-exculpatory so far as this appellant was concerned. It was obviously spontaneous. It was very soon after the event and it was to that extent relevant to show what the immediate reaction of the appellant had been at the time or shortly after the incident.

He is then taken down to the police station, or goes down to the police station voluntarily, because he certainly had not been arrested, and at 9.40 makes a witness statement in the usual form, which is the subject of these proceedings, a statement which the judge refused to admit.

Now it is submitted to us by Mr Harris in his attractive argument that first of all this was a spontaneous statement, and there is no doubt that that is true. There is no suggestion that he had time to consult a solicitor or had very much time to think about the matter at all before the witness statement was made.

The next question is whether that statement was relevant. Perhaps put in another way, whether a witness statement added anything to the evidence which was already before the jury about this man's reaction to the suggestion that he had committed an assault.

In our judgment it was not relevant. All that evidence was before the jury in two shapes: first of all in what Mr Campion had said and secondly, from what Police Constable Dinnage had said. Consequently it was not relevant nor did it add anything to the weight of the other testimony. Mr Harris submits that it was only right that the jury should know that this man went to the police station voluntarily and there voluntarily made a statement as a witness. That is perfectly true and there could have been no objection at all to that evidence being extracted from Police Constable Dinnage. Mr Harris seems to have thought that he was in some way being inhibited by the learned judge from adducing that evidence. But as we read the transcript of events that is certainly not the case. The evidence in any event, if it had been admitted, would not have been evidence of the facts contained in the statement. It would only have been relevant to show this man's reaction, and I repeat myself in saying, his reaction was amply proved. It seems to us, in those circumstances, that the necessary foundation for the admission of this evidence was absent and the learned judge was correct in ruling that the evidence should not be admitted.

Before leaving the case there is one other matter to which perhaps it is necessary to draw attention, and that is the judgment in *Barbery* (1976) 62 Cr App R 248. The headnote is all that I need read, which is as follows:

'Where a defendant makes a voluntary statement to the police that he was not involved in an affray and is later charged with that offence, and does not give evidence to that effect, the trial judge is under no duty to remind the jury of that statement as it was not before the Court as evidence as to the truth of its contents.'

In this case, had the situation arisen, that rule would have applied, because the appellant in this case did not go into the witness box. Having said those few matters, it suffices to add that this appeal so far as conviction is concerned is rejected and dismissed.

Appeal against conviction dismissed.

Note
In civil cases, a previous consistent statement may be treated as evidence of the facts and not merely as evidence of consistency (see further Chapter 9).

Civil Evidence Act 1968

2. Admissibility of out-of-court statements as evidence of facts stated
(1)   In any civil proceedings a statement made, whether orally or in a document or otherwise, by any person, whether called as a witness in those proceedings or not, shall be admissible as evidence of any fact stated therein of which direct oral evidence by him would be admissible.

3. Witness's previous statement, if proved, to be evidence of facts stated

(1)   Where in any civil proceedings — . . .
(b)   a previous statement made by a person called [as a witness in those proceedings] is proved for the purpose of rebutting a suggestion that his evidence has been fabricated, that statement shall by virtue of this subsection be admissible as evidence of any fact stated therein of which direct oral evidence by him would be admissible.

Note
Further questions concerning the subject matter of these sections appear at the end of the chapter.

(iii)   Unfavourable and hostile witnesses

Note
A party who calls a witness may be disappointed with the quality of the evidence which that witness gives. Perhaps the witness has become forgetful or confused and, accordingly, does not really advance the case of the party who calls him. Such a witness is often described as 'failing to come up to proof'. In the absence of a suggestion that such witnesses are motivated by malice or ill-will, they are properly described as unfavourable. The party who calls a forgetful witnesses can only call other witnesses hoping they will be better.

It may be, however, that the witness is not being truthful deliberately. Perhaps he has been intimidated or bribed and therefore is no longer desirous of telling the truth. In this situation, the witness is properly described as being a hostile witness. If the judge declares a witness to be hostile, the party who called him will be permitted to cross-examine him and put to him his previous inconsistent statement(s).

Criminal Procedure Act 1865

3.　How far witnesses may be discredited by the party producing

A party producing a witness shall not be allowed to impeach his credit by general evidence of bad character; but he may, in case the witness shall prove adverse, contradict him by other evidence, or, by leave of the judge prove that he has made at other times a statement inconsistent with his present testimony; but before such last-mentioned proof can be given, the circumstances of the supposed statement sufficient to designate the particular occasion, must be mentioned to the witness, and he must be asked whether or not he has made such statement.

Greenough v *Eccles*
(1859) 5 CB (NS) 786
Common Pleas

In an action on a bill of exchange, a witness called by the defendants supported the evidence of the plaintiff. The witness was then asked by the defendant's counsel about a previous statement inconsistent with his present testimony. The defence also proposed to put in evidence the statement. The judge ruled that the witness was not hostile and that therefore he had no power under [s. 3 of the Criminal Procedure Act 1865] to admit such evidence.

WILLIAMS J: The section [s. 3 of the Criminal Procedure Act 1865] lays down three rules as to the power of a party to discredit his own witness, first, he shall not be allowed to impeach his credit by general evidence of his bad character, — secondly, he may contradict him by other evidence, — thirdly, he may prove that he has made at other times a statement inconsistent with his present testimony.

These three rules appear to include the principal questions that have ever arisen on the subject: as may be seen by referring to the chapter in *Phillips on Evidence* which treats 'of the right of a party to disprove or impeach the evidence of his own witness.' And it will there be further seen that the law relating to the first two of these rules was settled before the passing of the act, while, as to the third, the authorities were conflicting: that is to say, the law was clear that you could not discredit your own witness by general evidence of bad character, but you might nevertheless contradict him by other evidence relevant to the issue. Whether you could discredit him by proving that he had made inconsistent statements, was to some extent an unsettled point.

In favour of construing the word 'adverse' to mean merely 'unfavourable', the main arguments are, that, taking the words of the section in their natural and ordinary sense, its object appears to be to declare the whole law on the subject by negativing the right as to the first, and affirming it both on the second and third points; but that it proceeds to fetter the right as to both the latter; for, the right is declared to exist in the former as well as the latter of these two instances, 'in case the witness shall, in the opinion of the judge, prove adverse,' — with the additional qualification, as to the latter, that the leave of the judge must be obtained. The right, it is argued, according to this enactment, is not to exist in either instance, if the judge is not of that opinion. The fetter thus imposed, it is further said, would be harmless in its operation, if 'adverse' be construed 'unfavourable', but most oppressive if it means 'hostile'; because the party producing the witness would be fixed with his evidence, when it proved pernicious, in case the judge did not think the witness 'hostile,' which might often happen; whereas, he could not in such a case fail to think him 'unfavourable' . . . .

But there are two considerations which have influenced my mind to disregard these arguments. The one is, that it is impossible to suppose the legislature could have really intended to impose any fetter whatever on the right of a party to contradict his own witness by other evidence relevant to the issue, — a right not only fully established by authority, but founded on the plainest good sense. The other is, that the section requires the judge to form an opinion that the witness is adverse, before the right to contradict, or prove that he has made inconsistent statements, is to be allowed to operate. This is reasonable, and indeed necessary, if the word 'adverse' means 'hostile', but wholly unreasonable and unnecessary if it means 'unfavourable'.

On these grounds, I think the preferable construction is, that, in case the witness shall, in the opinion of the judge, prove 'hostile', the party producing him may not only contradict him by other witnesses, as he might heretofore have done, and may still do, if the witness is unfavourable, but may also, by leave of the judge, prove that he has made inconsistent statements . . . .

Whatever is the meaning of the word 'adverse', the mere fact of the witness being in that predicament is not to confer the right of discrediting him in this way. The section obviously contemplates that there may be cases where the judge may properly refuse leave to exercise the right, though in his opinion the witness proves 'adverse.' And, as the judge's discretion must be principally, if not wholly, guided by the witness's behaviour and language in the witness box (for, the judge can know nothing, judicially, of his earlier conduct), it is not improbable that the legislature had in view the ordinary case of a judge giving leave to a party producing a witness who proves hostile, to treat him as if he had been produced by the opposite party, so far as to put to him leading and pressing questions; and that the purpose of the section is, to go a step further in this direction, by giving the judge power to allow such a witness to be discredited, by proving his former inconsistent statements, as if he were a witness on the other side.

COCKBURN CJ: The solution by my learned brothers is a solution of a difficulty, otherwise incapable of solution, but I am not satisfied therewith, and without actually dissenting from their judgment, I do not altogether assent to it.

(WILLES J agreed with WILLIAMS J.)

Note
Despite a misleading title, the Criminal Procedure Act 1865 applies to both criminal and civil cases.

R v Thompson
(1976) 64 Cr App R 96
Court of Appeal

The appellant was charged, *inter alia*, with incest with one of his daughters, A. She was called for the prosecution, and after she had been sworn and answered certain preliminary questions, she refused to give evidence. The trial judge said she had to unless she wished to spend some time in prison. He then allowed her to be treated as hostile and be cross-examined about a statement made by her to the police, and the appellant was convicted.

LORD WIDGERY CJ: . . . Thus, one comes from there to Mr Mylne's main point today, his best point as he described it, which is that the girl Anne ought never to have been treated as hostile. He concedes that she was a hostile witness and that the provisions of section 3 of the Criminal Procedure Act 1865 applied to her, but he says, for a reason which I will endeavour to explain in a moment, that that section did not apply to this case . . .

It is to be observed in the text of that section that the party producing a witness is permitted in certain circumstances to contradict, and that he may produce a statement inconsistent with present testimony. The argument of Mr Mylne is that in order to get the benefit of section 3 it is not enough to show, as in this case, that the girl was hostile and stood mute of malice. It is essential, so the argument goes, that there should be a contradiction of a previous statement and an inconsistent current statement, and since in this case there was no such contradiction, the previous statement standing alone and the girl refusing to produce a second statement either consistent or otherwise, it is contended that the section has no application.

We do not find it necessary to express any view upon the section as applied to cases where there is an inconsistent statement. We think this matter must be dealt with by the provisions of the common law in regard to recalcitrant witnesses. Quite apart from what is said in section 3, the common law did recognise that pressure could be brought to bear upon witnesses who refused to cooperate and perform their duties. We have had the advantage of looking at one or two of the earlier cases prior to the Act to which I have already referred and their treatment of this matter.

The first is *Clarke* v *Saffery* (1824) Ry & M 126, and the issue before the Vice-Chancellor does not require to be considered in any detail. But it is to be observed that in the course of the trial the plaintiff's counsel called the defendant, who was also one of the assignees, as a witness, and objection was taken by the defendant's counsel to the mode of examining the defendant. There does not seem to be a second statement contradicting the earlier one there, yet Best CJ said, at p. 126: 'there is no fixed rule which binds the counsel calling a witness to a particular mode of examining him. If a witness, by his conduct in the box, shows himself decidedly adverse, it is always in the discretion of the judge to allow a cross-examination . . .'

I pause there because the rest of Best CJ's judgment is subject to comment in the later cases, but that part which I have read seems to me to stand uncontradicted. That is what we are dealing with here. We are dealing here with a witness who shows himself decidedly adverse, and whereupon, as Best CJ says, it is always in the discretion of the judge to allow cross-examination. After all, we are only talking about the asking of leading questions. If the hostile witness declines to say anything at all that was inconsistent with his or her duty as making a second and inconsistent statement about the facts, Best CJ is recognising as a feature of the common law the right in the discretion of the judge always to allow cross-examination in those circumstances.

Then in the case of *Bastin* v *Carew* (1824) Ry & M 127 Lord Abbott CJ said, at p 127: 'I mean to decide this, and no further. But in each particular case there must be some discretion in the presiding judge as to the mode in which the examination should be conducted, in order best to answer the purposes of justice.'

The statement, which is consistently supported in later authorities, again seems to us to cover this case admirably. The short question after all is: was the judge right in allowing counsel to cross-examine in the sense of asking leading questions? On the authority of *Clarke* v *Saffrey* and *Bastin* v *Carew* it seems to us that he was right and there is no reason to suppose that the subsequent statutory intervention into this subject has in any way destroyed or removed the basic common law right of the judge in his discretion to allow cross-examination when a witness proves to be hostile.

Appeal dismissed.

R v *Golder, Jones and Porritt*
[1960] 1 WLR 1169
Court of Criminal Appeal

The defendants were charged with burglary and larceny. A witness, whose evidence on deposition at the committal proceedings incriminated the defendants, repudiated her statement at the trial and, although treated as hostile by the prosecution, refused to admit that her deposition was true. The trial judge, in effect, directed that it was open to the jury to act upon the evidence contained in the deposition and the jury convicted.

LORD PARKER CJ: A long line of authority has laid down the principle that while previous statements may be put to an adverse witness to destroy his credit and thus to render his evidence given at the trial negligible, they are not admissible evidence of the truth of the facts stated therein. It is unnecessary to refer to the cases in detail; the following extract from the judgment of this court in *R* v *Harris* (1927) 20 Cr App R 144, 147 is a sufficient statement of the principle:

It was permissible to cross-examine this girl upon the assertions she had previously made, not for the purpose of substituting those unsworn assertions for her sworn testimony, but for the purpose of showing that her sworn testimony, in the light of those unsworn assertions, could not be regarded as being of importance. It is upon that matter that confusion has sometimes arisen. It has undoubtedly sometimes been thought that where a witness is cross-examined upon a previous unsworn statement and admits that the statement was made, but says that the statement was untrue, that unsworn statement may sometimes be treated as if it could be accepted by the jury in preference to the sworn statement in the witness box . . . That of course is all wrong, as has been pointed out on various occasions by this court, and not least in the case of *White* (1922) 17 Cr App R 60.

In both *Harris* and *White* the previous statement was unsworn and not made in the presence of the accused. It could not, therefore, on any view be evidence against him. The principle, however, is equally applicable to earlier statements made on oath as it is to unsworn statements: cf *R* v *Birch* (1924) 18 Cr App R 26 . . . .

In the judgment of this court, when a witness is shown to have made previous statements inconsistent with the evidence given by that witness at the trial, the jury should not merely be directed that the evidence given at the trial should be regarded as unreliable; they should also be directed that the previous statements, whether sworn or unsworn, do not constitute evidence upon which they can act.

Appeals allowed.

Civil Evidence Act 1968

3. Witness's previous statement, if proved, to be evidence of facts stated

(1)   Where in any civil proceedings —

(a)   a previous inconsistent or contradictory statement made by a person called as a witness in those proceedings is proved by virtue of section 3 of the Criminal Procedure Act 1865 . . . that statement shall by virtue of this subsection be admissible as evidence of any fact stated therein of which direct oral evidence by him would be admissible.

Note

In *R* v *Nelson* [1992] Crim LR 653, the Crown successfully applied to have W treated as a hostile witness and put to her previous inconsistent statements. The Court of Appeal stated that *in most cases* a hostile witness who was shown to have made inconsistent statements was discredited. If, however, the witness was not wholly discredited, then the evidence upon which the jury could act was the witness's evidence at trial and not any earlier inconsistent statement.

Questions

1.   A proved previous inconsistent statement may be used by the defendant in a civil action as evidence of the facts which the statement contains. Does it make sense that the defendant in a criminal trial can only use a proved previous inconsistent statement as evidence which discredits the witness who made it?

2.   Would you advocate that the distinction which exists in this area be abolished? If so, which rule is preferrable?

(B)   Cross-examination

When a witness has concluded giving his evidence-in-chief, he may then be cross-examined by the other party or parties in the case. So, where there are two co-accused, D1 and D2, and D1 has testified on his own behalf, he may be cross-examined by counsel for the prosecution and counsel for D2. When conducting cross-examination, counsel will be seeking to test the truthfulness of the evidence given by the witness and to elicit any facts which are favourable to his own client's case. There is no relaxation of the rules governing admissibility of evidence merely because a cross-examination is taking place, so, for example, if the defendant is seeking to introduce hearsay evidence whilst being cross-examined about his defence, the evidence will still be excluded if it does not fall within one of the recognised exceptions to the rule (see further Chapters 7, 8 and 9). It should be noted, however, that when the defendant in a criminal case is being cross-examined, certain restrictions are placed upon the type of questions which the prosecution may ask (see further Chapter 11).

The following sections deal with four important aspects of cross-examination. First, the nature and conduct of cross-examination. Secondly, previous inconsistent statements made by witnesses. Thirdly, cross-examination and its relationship with collateral issues and lastly, special problems associated with the cross-examination of victims of rape offences.

(i)   Nature and conduct of cross-examination

R v Thomson
[1912] 3 KB 19
Court of Criminal Appeal

At the trial of the appellant upon a charge of having used an instrument upon a woman in order to procure a miscarriage, his defence was that he had done nothing to her, but that she had performed such an operation upon herself. His counsel, in cross-examination, sought to ask questions of a witness for the prosecution as to statements made by the woman (who was dead) sometime before her miscarriage that she intended to operate upon herself, and shortly after her miscarriage that she had operated upon herself; but the judge refused to permit these questions.

LORD ALVERSTONE CJ: . . . This point is one of importance and at first appeared to be difficult. Counsel for the appellant was not allowed in cross-examination to put questions to a witness for the prosecution as to what the deceased woman had told her some time before the miscarriage as to her intentions and also a few days before her death as to what she had done. If put in a popular way, the argument for the appellant, that what the woman had said she had done to herself ought to be admissible evidence for the defence, might be attractive; but upon consideration it is seen to be a dangerous argument, and, in the opinion of the Court, the rejection of evidence of that kind is much more in favour of the accused than of the prosecution. If such evidence is admissible for one side it must also be admissible for the other.

In our opinion there is no principle upon which this evidence is admissible any more than any other hearsay evidence. If it were admissible, then all those decisions in which it was considered whether statements were admissible in evidence as dying declarations, or as part of the *res gestae,* or as admissions against pecuniary or proprietary interest, would have been unnecessary. The only ground upon which it has been suggested in argument that such evidence ought to be admitted is that since the Criminal Evidence Act 1898, and the Criminal Appeal Act 1907, a new rule of evidence has been introduced under which anything must be admitted in evidence which will help the accused to prove his defence. There is a decision of a great authority, Charles J, against that contention. In *R v Gloster* 16 Cox CC 471 the prisoner was charged with having caused the death of a woman by an illegal operation, and it was sought to give in evidence statements made by the woman a few days after the operation as to who had caused the injuries from which she died. Charles J refused to admit the evidence and said: 'Mr Poland proposes to ask the witness what the deceased said as to her bodily condition and what had been done to her. My judgment is this: that the statements must be confined to contemporaneous symptoms and nothing in the nature of a narrative is admissible as to who caused them or how they were caused'. In this case it cannot be argued that the statements were admissible as part of the *res gestae;* the statements sought to be proved were not made at the time when anything was being done to the woman.

Appeal dismissed.

R v Fenlon, Neal and Neal
(1980) 71 Cr App R 307
Court of Appeal

The appellant F and the applicants N were convicted of rape. The victim they were said to have raped had been picked up by them at a public house after which they and four other men had gone with her to the flat of the parents of one of the men. F appealed on the ground, *inter alia,* that the judge wrongly ruled, after F had finished his examination-in-chief, that it was the duty of counsel for the co-defendants to cross-examine him by putting to him their client's case whenever it might differ from F's evidence and thus perform Crown counsel's task.

LORD LANE CJ: We are told (and there is no reason to doubt it) that there seems to have been in the past a difference of approach between judges to this particular matter. We have been referred to a decision of the House of Lords, albeit in a civil case, *Browne* v *Dunn* (1894) 6 R 67, the material parts of the headnote in which read: 'If in the course of a case it is intended to suggest that a witness is not speaking the truth upon a particular point, his attention must be directed to the fact by cross-examination showing that that imputation is intended to be made, so that he may have an opportunity of making any explanation which is open to him, unless it is otherwise perfectly clear that he has had full notice beforehand that there is an intention to impeach the credibility of his story or (*per* Lord Morris) the story is of an incredible and romancing character'. The passage in the speeches to which we were referred is at p. 70, the speech of Lord Herschell LC, and reads:

> These witnesses all of them depose to having suffered from such annoyances; they further depose to having consulted the defendant on the subject, and to have given him instructions which resulted in their signing this document; and when they were called there was no suggestion made to them in cross-examination that that was not the case. Their evidence was taken; to some of them it was said, 'I have no questions to ask'; in the case of others their cross-examination was on a point quite beside the evidence to which I have just called attention. Now, my Lords, I cannot help saying that it seems to me to be absolutely essential to the proper conduct of a case, where it is intended to suggest that a witness is not speaking the truth on a particular point, to direct his attention to the fact by some questions put in cross-examination showing that that imputation is intended to be made, and not to take his evidence and pass it by as a matter altogether unchallenged, and then, when it is impossible for him to explain, as perhaps he might have been able to do if such questions had been put to him, the circumstances which it is suggested indicate that the story he tells ought not to be believed, to argue that he is a witness unworthy of credit.

Mr Goldberg submits that that is a rule which applies to counsel prosecuting on behalf of the Crown. It is his clear duty, he concedes, to put to witnesses the version of events for which he contends, so that they can answer it. But he further submits that it is not the duty of one defendant to put to another defendant his version of events where it differs from the version given by that other defendant.

We can see no distinction in principle between the one situation and the other. The basis of the rule, as Lord Herschell pointed out, is to give a witness of whom it is going to be said or suggested that he was not telling the truth an opportunity of explaining and if necessary of advancing further facts in confirmation of the evidence which he has given. There seems to be no reason why there should be any different rule relating to defendants between themselves from that applying to the prosecution *vis-à-vis* the defendant or the defence *vis-à-vis* the prosecution. It is the duty of counsel who intends to suggest that a witness is not telling the truth to make it clear to the witness in cross-examination that he challenges his veracity and to give the witness an opportunity of replying. It need not be done in minute detail, but it is the duty of counsel to make it plain to the witness, albeit he may be a co-defendant, that his evidence is not accepted and in what respects it is not accepted.

Appeal dismissed.

(ii)   Previous inconsistent statements

Criminal Procedure Act 1865

4.   As to proof of contradictory statements of adverse witness
If a witness upon cross-examination as to a former statement made by him relative to the subject-matter of the indictment or proceeding, and inconsistent with his present testimony, does not distinctly admit that he has made such statement, proof may be given that he did in fact make it; but before such proof can be given the circumstances of the supposed statement, sufficient to designate the particular occasion, must be mentioned to the witness, and he must be asked whether or not he has made such statement.

5.   Cross-examinations as to previous statements in writing
A witness may be cross-examined as to previous statements made by him in writing, or reduced into writing, relative to the subject-matter of the indictment or proceeding, without such writing being shown to him; but if it is intended to contradict such witness by the writing, his attention must, before such contradictory proof can be given, be called to those parts of the writing which are to be used for the purpose of so contradicting him: Provided always, that it shall be competent for the judge, at any time during the trial, to require the production of the writing for his inspection, and he may thereupon make such use of it for the purposes of the trial as he may think fit.

Civil Evidence Act 1968

3.   Witness's previous statement, if proved, to be evidence of facts stated
    (1)   Where in any civil proceedings —
    (a)   a previous inconsistent or contradictory statement made by a person called as a witness in those proceedings is proved by virtue of section 3, 4 or 5 of the Criminal Procedure Act, 1865 . . . that statement shall by virtue of this subsection be admissible as evidence of any fact stated therein of which direct oral evidence by him would be admissible.

(iii)   Cross-examination and collateral issues

Note
When cross-examination deviates from the issues in the case to collateral issues, special rules exist to prevent time being wasted. The most important collateral issue is the credibility of the witness. The general rule is that a

witness's answers to questions relating to credit are final (i.e. they may not be contradicted or rebutted by the calling of other evidence). As with most general rules, however, there are a number of exceptions.

(a)   What is a collateral issue?

Attorney-General v *Hitchcock*
(1847) 1 Exch 91
Exchequer

The defendant, a maltster, was charged with using a cistern in breach of certain statutory requirements. A prosecution witness was asked in cross-examination whether he had not previously said that he had been offered £20 by officers of the Crown, if he would state in evidence that the cistern had been so used. The witness denied the allegation, whereupon the defence proposed to call a witness of their own to state that the prosecution witness had said this. The judge held that the question tended to raise a collateral issue and ruled that it could not be put. The defence obtained a rule for a new trial on the ground that this evidence was improperly rejected.

POLLOCK CB: . . . the test, whether the matter is collateral or not, is this: if the answer of a witness is a matter which you would be allowed on your part to prove in evidence — if it have such a connection with the issue, that you would be allowed to give it in evidence — then it is a matter on which you may contradict him. Or it may be as well put, or perhaps better, in the language of my Brother Alderson this morning, that, if you ask a witness whether he has not said so and so, and the matter he is supposed to have said would, if he had said it, contradict any other part of his testimony, then you may call another witness to prove that he had said so, in order that the jury may believe the account of the transaction which he gave to that other witness to be the truth, and that the statement he makes on oath in the witness box is not true.

ALDERSON B: The reason why a party is obliged to take the answer of a witness is, that if he were permitted to go into it, it is only justice to allow the witness to call other evidence in support of the testimony he has given, and as those witnesses might be cross-examined as to their conduct, such a course would be productive of endless collateral issues. Suppose, for instance, witness A is accused of having committed some offence; witness B is called to prove it, when, on witness B's cross-examination, he is asked whether he has not made some statement, to prove which witness C is called, so that it would be necessary to try all those issues, before one step could be obtained towards the adjudication of the particular case before the Court. On the contrary, if the answer be taken as given, if the witness speaks falsely he may be indicted for perjury. That is the proper remedy. Then in the next place, in my opinion, when the question is not relevant, strictly speaking, to the issue, but tending to contradict the witness, his answer must be taken, although it tends to shew that he, in that particular instance, speaks falsely, and although it is not altogether immaterial to the matter in issue, for the sake of the general public convenience; for great inconvenience would follow from a continual course of those sorts of cross-examinations which would be let in in the case of a witness being called for the purposes of contradiction. I think those are the rules by which these cases have always been governed, and the application of which is easy and short. In this case the party is asked, A have you not said B offered you £20 to make a certain statement, which I agree is material in the cause. He says, no, I have not said any such thing. Is that material to the issue, or does it qualify or contradict anything that he had said before? What he had said before was, that the cistern was used; the offer of a bribe to make a statement to the contrary, if he had not accepted it, would not have had a different tendency. If he had said, that he had been offered a bribe, if he had answered in the affirmative, it would not in the slightest degree have disproved the matter. If it would not, it does not qualify or contradict that which he had before stated; and I think that it is not allowable to call a witness to contradict him in that, which, if answered by him in the affirmative, would not have qualified or contradicted his statement.

ROLFE B: If we lived for a thousand years instead of about sixty or seventy, and every case were of sufficient importance, it might be possible, and perhaps proper, to throw a light on matters in which every possible question might be suggested, for the purpose of seeing by such means whether the whole was unfounded, or what portion of it was not, and to raise every possible inquiry as to the truth of the statements made. But I do not see how that could be; in fact, mankind find it to be impossible.

Rule discharged.

Note
See further *R* v *Funderburk* [1990] 1 WLR 587 (5(B)(iv) below) which adds confusion to the difference between an 'issue' and a 'collateral matter'.

(b) *Criminal convictions*

Criminal Procedure Act 1865

6. Proof of conviction of witness . . .
A witness may be questioned as to whether he has been convicted of any misdemeanour, and upon being so questioned, if he either denies or does not admit the fact, or refuses to answer, it shall be lawful for the cross-examining party to prove such conviction . . . .

(c) *Bias or partiality*

R v *Mendy*
(1976) 64 Cr App R 4
Court of Appeal

The appellant was charged with assault. At her trial all the witnesses were kept out of court in accordance with normal practice. While a detective was giving evidence about the assault, a constable in court noticed a man in the public gallery taking notes. This man was then seen to leave court and the same constable and a court officer saw him discussing the case with the appellant's husband, apparently describing the detective's evidence to him. The husband then gave evidence and in cross-examination denied that the incident with the man had occurred and the prosecution was given leave to call evidence by the constable and the court officer in rebuttal. The appellant was convicted and appealed on the ground that this evidence in rebuttal had been wrongly admitted, as the husband's answers in cross-examination were answers as to credit and the prosecution was not entitled to call evidence to contradict them.

GEOFFREY LANE LJ: . . . Was the evidence admissible? A party may not, in general, impeach the credit of his opponent's witnesses by calling witnesses to contradict him on collateral matters, and his answers thereon will be conclusive — see *Harris* v *Tippett* (1811) 2 Camp 637, and *Phipson on Evidence,* 11th ed, paragraph 1553. The rule is of great practical use. It serves to prevent the indefinite prolongation of trials which would result from a minute examination of the character and credit of witnesses. It seems to have caused very little trouble in operation, judging by the paucity of authority on the subject. Difficulties may sometimes arise in determining what matters are merely collateral, see *Phillips* (1936) 26 Cr App R 17, but no one seriously suggests that the issue in the present case was other than collateral. On the other hand, it seems strange, if it be the case, that the Court and jury have to be kept in ignorance of behaviour by a witness such as that in the present case. The suggestion which lay behind the evidence in question was that Mr Mendy was prepared to lend himself to a scheme designed to defeat the purpose of keeping prospective witnesses out of Court; that he allowed the messenger to give him details of what Detective Constable Price had been saying in the witness box about the assault which the appellant was alleged to have committed. If the evidence of the Court officer and Constable Thatcher was to be believed, the jury could be in little doubt that the witness's object in receiving such instruction must have been to enable him the more convincingly to describe how he and not the appellant had caused the injuries to the policeman.

The truth of the matter is, as one would expect, that the rule is not all-embracing. It has always been permissible to call evidence to contradict a witness's denial of bias or partiality towards one of the parties and to show that he is prejudiced so far as the case being tried is concerned.

Pollock CB in *Attorney-General* v *Hitchcock* (1847) 1 Exch 91 puts the matter thus at p. 101:

> It is no disparagement to a man that a bribe is offered to him; it may be a disparagement to the man who makes the offer. If therefore the witness is asked about the fact and denies it or if he is asked whether he said so and so and he denies it he cannot be contradicted as to what he has said. *Lord Stafford's Case* [(1680) 7 How St Tr 1400) was totally different. There the witness himself had been implicated in offering a bribe to some other person. That immediately affected him as proving that he had acted the part of a suborner for the purpose of preventing the truth. In that case the evidence was to show that the witness was offered a bribe in a particular case, and the object was to show that he was so far affected towards the party accused as to be willing to adopt any corrupt course in order to carry out his purposes.

In *Lord Staffords Case, (supra)* the evidence was admitted.

Those words apply almost precisely to the facts in the present case. The witness was prepared to cheat in order to deceive the jury and help the defendant. The jury were entitled to be apprised of that fact.

Appeal dismissed.

R v Busby
(1981) 75 Cr App R 79
Court of Appeal

The appellant was charged with offences of burglary and handling stolen goods. He was alleged to have made certain remarks to the police when interviewed about the alleged offences which were not specific admissions but were very damaging. At his trial he did not give evidence, and on his behalf two police officers were cross-examined to establish, *inter alia,* that the appellant had made the remarks aforesaid and also that one officer, in the presence of the other, had threatened a potential witness for the defence to stop him giving evidence. Both officers denied that they had threatened that witness. The witness was then called. Thereupon the Crown objected to his giving evidence about the officers' visit to him. The trial judge upheld the objection on the ground that that evidence was merely an attack upon credit and did not go to the facts in issue. The trial proceeded and the appellant was convicted. He appealed.

EVELEIGH LJ: It is not always easy to determine when a question relates to facts which are collateral only, and therefore to be treated as final, and when it is relevant to the issue which has to be tried. In *Attorney-General v Hitchcock* (1847) 1 Exch 91, a witness was asked in cross-examination whether he had not told one Cook that excise officers had offered him a bribe to give his evidence. He denied saying this to Cook and it was held that Cook was not to be called on the matter. The fact that he had been offered a bribe would cast no light on his attitude to giving evidence in the case. If it had been suggested that he had actually received a bribe the position would have been different.

We are of the opinion that the learned judge was wrong to refuse to admit the evidence. If true, it would have shown that the police were prepared to go to improper lengths in order to secure the accused's conviction. It was the accused's case that the statement attributed to him had been fabricated, a suggestion which could not be accepted by the jury unless they thought that the officers concerned were prepared to go to improper lengths to secure a conviction.

In *Phillips* (1936) 26 Cr App R 17, the Court of Criminal Appeal held that the accused should have been allowed to call evidence to rebut his daughters' denial that they had been schooled by their mother to give evidence against him. Again, in *Mendy* (1976) 64 Cr App R 4, it was held that evidence in rebuttal could be called after a denial by the witness that he had been spoken to by someone who left the court after hearing evidence. As Professor Sir Rupert Cross summarised the matter in *Cross on Evidence* (5th ed) p. 267: 'It was held that evidence in rebuttal might be called because the episode indicated that the husband was a prejudiced witness, prepared to cheat in furtherance of his wife's case'. In the present case, the evidence, if true, would have indicated that the officers were prepared to cheat in furtherance of the prosecution.

Appeal allowed. Convictions quashed.

R v Edwards
[1991] 1 WLR 207
Court of Appeal

LORD LANE CJ: On 8 December 1988 in the Crown Court at Birmingham before Judge Cole and a jury, the appellant was convicted of robbery and possession of a firearm at the time of committing the robbery. He was sentenced to 14 years' imprisonment on each count to run concurrently. He now appeals against conviction by leave of the single judge. There is no criticism of the summing up or the conduct of the trial, both of which were impeccable. The main thrust of the appeal is that, if evidence which is now available had been adduced at the trial, the course of the trial would have been radically different and would or might have resulted in the acquittal of the appellant.

The facts of the robbery are not in dispute. The only relevant dispute is whether the appellant was proved to be one of the robbers. On 3 November 1987 a Post Office in Birmingham was attacked by three armed men who had earlier concealed them-selves in the false ceiling of the premises. They handcuffed or tied up the staff and made off with £45,000. One of the men was McDonald, the second was a man called Barlow and the third was alleged to be this appellant.

The evidence against the appellant was in essence twofold: first, Barlow gave evidence at the trial that the appellant was the third man, secondly, police officers gave evidence that he had on more than one occasion stated to them that he was indeed the third man, although he had declined to sign the notes of interview which contained those admissions. Barlow being an accomplice, the judge was required to give the usual warning about corroboration, which he did, again impeccably. The potential corroborative evidence were the alleged admissions to the police made on the following occasions:

1. After 11.10 p.m. on Tuesday 10 November en route to Stetchford police station in a police car in the presence of Detective Sergeant Owen and Detective Constable Woodley.

2. Between two minutes after midnight and 2.07 a.m. on 11 November, namely, the same night, at Stetchford police station in the presence of the same two officers.

3. Between 10.50 a.m. and 12.05 p.m. on Wednesday 11 November at the police station and in a police car (Detective Sergeant Bowen and Detective Constable Quin). The background to this incident was as follows. According to the police officers the appellant had told them that he would show them the hotel where the three men stayed before the robbery. There followed a journey in the police car during the course of which, according to the police but denied by him, he pointed out the Anglo-Maltese, a bed-breakfast house, and the Westbourne Lodge Hotel, both of which he said had been used by the robbers. The evidence showed that the robbers did in fact use those hotels. The appellant's case is that the police must have obtained the information from Barlow, despite his and their denials. The robbers had booked into the Westbourne Lodge Hotel with false names, and one had given his address as 26, Fenny Street, Salford, a street in which it so happens the appellant had once lived, albeit not at No. 26.

4. Between 12.20 p.m. and 1.04 p.m. the same day at the police station (again Detective Sergeant Bowen and Detective Constable Quin).

The last three of these interviews were said to have been recorded contempor-aneously. The second interview was recorded on an interview form countersigned by Detective Inspector Goodchild. The fourth interview was on such a form countersig-ned both by Detective Inspector Goodchild and by Detective Superintendent Brown.

We turn now to the grounds of appeal as advanced by Mr Marti-Sperry at the original hearing before us.

. . .

The behaviour in other cases of police officers concerned in this case
At the original hearing before us Mr Martin-Sperry indicated that he wished to

develop further the arguments which he had adduced under paragraph 10 of his perfected grounds. With the agreement of all parties we therefore adjourned the hearing in order that further inquiries might be made. We enlarged the legal aid certificate to include leading counsel and at the resumed hearing we heard Mr Anthony Hacking on behalf of the appellant. We have had the advantage of a considerable body of information from the Police Complaints Authority as will appear. We acknowledge the great assistance which this information has provided.

Mr Hacking's submissions concerned the behaviour in other cases of police officers involved in the instant case and the extent to which the court is entitled or obliged to enquire into such behaviour as possibly throwing light on the reliability of those officers at the trial of the appellant.

His argument runs as follows.

(1)　It would have been permissible to cross-examine each of the police officers at trial, had the appellant's then advisers known then what is known now, to allege a course of conduct or system. Such cross-examination would go not merely to credit or the lack of it, but would be probative of the appellant's assertion at trial that he was 'fitted up' with false evidence.

(2)　The evidence of the behaviour of these police officers in other cases, together with the behaviour of other police officers in the West Midlands Serious Crime Squad (the Squad) in such cases and in further cases, establishes a consistent course of conduct or system of a strikingly similar pattern in 1986, 1987 and 1988, following the introduction of the Police and Criminal Evidence Act 1984 in January 1986. This, it is suggested, involved police officers in the squad tampering with and fabricating evidence to the detriment of persons arrested by the Squad. This evidence is credible and admissible on the issue of whether evidence was fabricated in the appellant's case.

(3)　The appellant, if he had known of the said course of conduct, would have been entitled to call evidence in his defence to establish that there was such a course of conduct in the squad towards persons arrested and this would have been credible and admissible on the issue of fabrication. Such evidence was relevant and goes to the heart of the defence put forward at trial and provides, adopting the words of Neill LJ in *Reg.* v *Shore* (1988) 89 Cr App R 32, 43, 'an underlying unity of probative value in relation to' the defence at trial.

(4)　Mr Hacking points out correctly that it is now known that the police officers involved in the appellant's case are the subject of a large number of allegations by members of the public which are being investigated by the Police Complaints Authority.

(5)　It is known that one of the officers involved has been charged with the offence of perjury in respect of which proceedings are likely to start very soon.

(6)　It is known that other trials involving members of the West Midlands Serious Crime Squad have resulted in acquittals or in some cases the quashing of convictions by this court.

We turn now to consider whether those submissions are well founded.

If the defence had had this information at the trial, to what extent could they have made use of it? The test is primarily one of relevance, and this is so whether one is considering evidence in chief or questions in cross-examination. To be admissible questions must be relevant to the issue before the court.

Issues are of varying degrees of relevance or importance. A distinction has to be drawn between, on the one hand, the issue in the case upon which the jury will be pronouncing their verdict and, on the other hand, collateral issues of which the credibility of the witnesses may be one. Generally speaking, questions may be put to a witness as to any improper conduct of which he may have been guilty, for the purpose of testing his credit.

The limits to such questioning were defined by Sankey LJ in *Hobbs* v *Tinling & Co.* [1929] 2 KB 1, 50–51:

> The court can always exercise its discretion to decide whether a question as to credit is one which the witness should be compelled to answer . . . in the exercise of its discretion the court should have regard to the following considerations: '(1) Such questions are proper if they are of such a nature that the truth of the imputation conveyed by them would seriously affect the opinion of the court as to the credibility of the witness on the matter to which he testifies. (2) Such questions are improper if the imputation which they convey relates to matters so remote in time, or of such a character, that the truth of the imputation would not affect, or would affect in a slight degree, the opinion of the court as to the credibility of the witness on the matter to which he testifies. (3) Such questions are improper if there is a great disproportion between the importance of the imputation made against the witness's character and the importance of his evidence.'

The distinction between the issue in the case and matters collateral to the issue is often difficult to draw, but it is of considerable importance. Where cross-examination is directed at collateral issues such as the credibility of the witness, as a rule the answers of the witness are final and evidence to contradict them will not be permitted: see Lawrence J in *Harris* v *Tippett* (1811) 2 Camp 637, 638. The rule is necessary to confine the ambit of a trial within proper limits and to prevent the true issue from becoming submerged in a welter of detail.

There are however exceptions to that rule, of which one of the most important is to show bias on the part of the witness: *Reg.* v *Shaw* (1888) 16 Cox CC 503. Facts showing that the witness is biased or partial in relation to the parties or the cause may be elicited on cross-examination: or, if denied, independently proved:' *Phipson on Evidence*, 14th ed. (1990) p. 265, para. 12–34.

[After referring to earlier authorities His Lordship continued . . .] The result of those two decisions seems to be this. The acquittal of a defendant in case A, where the prosecution case depended largely or entirely upon the evidence of a police officer, does not normally render that officer liable to cross-examination as to credit in case B. But where a police officer who has allegedly fabricated an admission in case B, has also given evidence of an admission in case A, where there was an acquittal by virtue of which his evidence is demonstrated to have been disbelieved, it is proper that the jury in case B should be made aware of that fact. However, where the acquittal in case A does not necessarily indicate that the jury disbelieved the officer, such cross-examination should not be allowed. In such a case the verdict of not guilty may mean no more than that the jury entertained some doubt about the prosecution case, not necessarily that they believed any witness was lying.

. . .

That leaves the second question, namely, whether it would have been proper to allow the defence to call evidence to contradict any answers given by the police officers in cross-examination, in the unlikely event of those officers giving answers unfavourable to the defence? In our judgment this questioning would have been as to credit alone, that is to say, on a collateral issue. It would not have fallen within any exception to the general rule.

. . .

Appeal allowed. Conviction quashed.

Questions
1. Is the decision in *R* v *Busby* an illustration of the bias exception to the rule of finality or does it create a new exception?
2. How, if at all, does *R* v *Edwards* differ from *R* v *Busby?*

(d)   Medical evidence impugning reliability

Toohey v Commissioner of Police of the Metropolis
[1965] AC 595
House of Lords

The appellant was tried, with two other men, on an indictment which included a count of assault with intent to rob M a boy aged 16. The jury having disagreed, a second trial took place. At both trials the prosecution's case was substantially the same, being based mainly on the evidence of M as to the alleged assault and also the evidence of two police officers who stated that they had come upon the accused and M in an alleyway, M being in a dishevelled and hysterical state and asking for police help, while the defendants were denying the assault. The defendants stated that they had come on M in a bad state and apparently the worse for drink and had decided to help him home, that he had become hysterical and that the charge was ridiculous.

The case for the defence at both trials was also substantially the same, being a denial of the assault, save that, at the first trial, evidence for the defence was given by a police surgeon, who had examined M shortly after he had been taken to the police station and who stated that M had been in a state of hysteria at the time. In his evidence in chief he had been asked his opinion as to the part played by alcohol in the condition described as hysteria, and replied that it was hard to say, but that alcohol would exacerbate it. In re-examination he was asked what, from his examination of M, he would consider his normal behaviour to be, and gave his opinion that he might well be more prone to hysteria than the normal person. At the first trial neither the judge nor the prosecution objected to this opinion being elicited, but at the second trial, before the doctor was called, the judge intimated that he would not allow questions designed to elicit the opinions given by the doctor at the first trial, on the ground that they were evidence of the kind held to be inadmissible in *R* v *Gunewardene* [1951] 2 KB 600; namely evidence by a doctor that a witness was suffering from such a mental disease that the doctor would regard his testimony as unreliable.

At the second trial all the accused were convicted on the count of assault with intent to rob. The appellant appealed against conviction on the ground that *R* v *Gunewardene* was distinguishable.

LORD PEARCE: It is common knowledge that hysteria can be produced by fear. The hysteria of the victim of an alleged assault may, if he is a person of normal stability, confirm a jury in the belief that he has been assaulted. When, however, the victim is unstable and hysterical by nature, the hysteria can raise a doubt whether in truth an assault ever occurred or whether it was the figment of an hysterical imagination. Here the real question to be determined was whether, as the prosecution alleged, the episode created the hysteria, or whether, on the other hand, as the defence alleged, the hysteria created the episode. To that issue medical evidence as to the hysterical and unstable nature of the alleged victim was relevant. It might be that, on a careful examination of the medical evidence, the predisposition to hysteria and instability was not enough to create an episode of this kind without some assault to provoke it. But, equally, that evidence might have created a real doubt whether there was any assault at all and might have inclined the jury to believe the account given by the accused. On that ground the defence was entitled to have the evidence considered by the jury.

The second question, whether it was permissible to impeach the credibility of Madden, *qua* witness, by medical evidence of his hysterical and unstable nature, raises a wider and more important problem which applies to evidence in criminal and civil cases alike.

The Court of Criminal Appeal held that such evidence was not admissible since they were bound by the case of *Gunewardene*. Undoubtedly they were right in thinking that on this point the present case is not distinguishable from it. In *Gunewardene's* case the appellant (to quote the words of Lord Goddard CJ) 'wished to call [Doctor Leigh] to say that he . . . had examined the witness and had come to the conclusion that the man was suffering from a disease of the mind and that therefore he regarded his testimony as unreliable. In our opinion that is exactly what the cases show cannot be done'. It was there held that the most that the doctor could have been asked on oath was: 'From your knowledge of the witness, would you believe him on his oath?' And although it was open to the other side in cross-examination to probe the particular reasons for the belief, the doctor could not give them in examination-in-chief. Thus, the only evidence which a doctor could give in chief would seem mysterious or meaningless to the jury; and if it was not amplified by questions in cross-examination (from which opposing counsel might well refrain) it would be liable to be robbed of its proper effect. Moreover, the principle in *Gunewardene's* case would exclude altogether the evidence of a doctor who cannot go so far as to say that he would not believe the witness on oath. It would not allow a doctor to testify (as is desired in the present case) to the abnormality and unreliability of the witness, or (as may happen in some other case), to the fact that the witness, by reason of some delusion, would on some matters not be credible, whereas on others he might be quite reliable.

Throughout *Gunewardene's* case the court dealt with the problem created by the mental disease and mental abnormality of the witness as if it were identical with the problem of moral discredit and unveracity. They referred to many cases dealing with bad character and reputation, but to none which dealt with mental disturbance.

From olden times it has been the practice to allow evidence of bad reputation to discredit a witness's testimony. It is perhaps not very logical and not very useful to allow such evidence founded on hearsay. None of your Lordships and none of the counsel before you could remember being concerned in a case where such evidence was called. But the rule has been sanctified through the centuries in legal examinations and textbooks and in some rare cases, and it does not create injustice. Its scope is conveniently summarised by Professor Cross *(Evidence,* 2nd ed (1963), p. 225):

In *Mawson* v *Hartsink* (1802) 4 Esp 102; it was held that the witness must be asked whether he is aware of the impugned witness's reputation for veracity and whether, from such knowledge, he would believe the impugned witness on oath. In *R* v *Watson* (1817) 2 Stark 116, however, it was held that the witness might simply state whether he would believe the oath of the person about whom he was asked, and although *R* v *Rowton* (1865) Le & Ca 520 decides that, when asked about a prisoner's character, the witness must speak to the accused's general reputation and not give his personal opinion of the accused's disposition, *R* v *Brown and Hedley* (1867) 10 Cox CC 453 sanctions the form of question approved in *R* v *Watson*.

Where a witness's general reputation, so far as concerns veracity, has been thus demolished, it seems that it may be reinstated by other witnesses who give evidence that he is worthy of credit or who discredit the discrediting witness *(Taylor on Evidence,* 12th ed, Vol. II, para. 1473; *Stephen on Evidence,* 12th ed, art. 146). Thus far, and no further, it appears, may the process of recrimination go (Taylor, para. 1473, citing *R* v *Lord Stafford* (1680) 7 How St Tr 1400). How far the evidence is confined to veracity alone or may extend to moral turpitude generally seems a matter of some doubt (see Taylor, para. 1471).

There seems little point, however, for present purposes in exploring these archaic niceties. The old cases are concerned with lying as an aspect of bad character and are of little help in establishing any principle that will deal with modern scientific knowledge of mental disease and its effect on the reliability of a witness. I accept all of the judgment in *Gunewardene's* case in so far as it deals with the older cases and the topic with which they were concerned. But, in my opinion, the court erred in using it as a guide to the admissibility of medical evidence concerning illness or abnormality affecting the mind of a witness and reducing his capacity to give reliable evidence. This unreliability may have two aspects either separate from one another or acting jointly to create confusion. The witness may, through his mental trouble, derive a fanciful or untrue picture from events while they are actually occurring, or he may have a fanciful or untrue recollection of them which distorts his evidence at the time when he is giving it.

The only general principles which can be derived from the older cases are these. On the one hand, the courts have sought to prevent juries from being beguiled by the evidence of witnesses who could be shown to be, through defect of character, wholly unworthy of belief. On the other hand, however, they have sought to prevent the trial of a case becoming clogged with a number of side issues, such as might arise if there could be an investigation of matters which had no relevance to the issue save in so far as they tended to show the veracity or falsity of the witness who was giving evidence which *was* relevant to the issue. Many controversies which might thus obliquely throw some light on the issues must in practice be discarded because there is not an infinity of time, money and mental comprehension available to make use of them.

There is one older case (*R* v *Hill* (1851) 20 LJMC 222) in which the Court for Crown Cases Reserved considered how it should deal with the evidence of a lunatic who was rational on some points. Evidence was given by doctors as to his credibility. Alderson B in argument made the sensible observation: 'It seems to me almost approaching to an absurdity to say that a jury may, by hearing the statement of doctors, be able to say whether a man was insane when he made his will, and yet that they should not be competent to say whether a man be in a state of mind to enable him to give credible evidence when they see him before them'. Lord Campbell CJ in giving judgment said: 'The true rule seems to me to be that it was for the judge to see whether the witness understands the nature of an oath and, if he does, to admit his testimony. No doubt, before he is sworn, the lunatic may be cross-examined, and evidence may be called to show that he labours under such a diseased mind as to be inadmissible; but, in the absence of such evidence he is *prima facie* admissible, and the jury may give such credit as they please to his testimony'. The point was not quite the same as that which is before your Lordships, since the question was whether the lunatic should be allowed to give evidence at all. But there is inherent, I think, in the judgments an intention that the jury should have the best opportunity of arriving at the truth and that the medical evidence with regard to the witness's credibility should be before them.

Human evidence shares the frailties of those who give it. It is subject to many cross-currents such as partiality, prejudice, self-interest and, above all, imagination and inaccuracy. Those are matters with which the jury, helped by cross-examination and common sense, must do their best. But when a witness through physical (in which I include mental) disease or abnormality is not capable of giving a true or reliable account to the jury, it must surely be allowable for medical science to reveal this vital hidden fact to them. If a witness purported to give evidence of something which he believed that he had seen at a distance of 50 yards, it must surely be possible to call the evidence of an oculist to the effect that the witness could not possibly see anything at a greater distance than 20 yards, or the evidence of a surgeon who had removed a cataract from which the witness was suffering at the material time and which would have prevented him from seeing what he thought he saw. So, too, must it be allowable to call medical evidence of mental illness which makes a witness incapable of giving reliable evidence, whether through the existence of delusions or otherwise.

It is obviously in the interest of justice that such evidence should be available. The only argument that I can see against its admission is that there might be a conflict between the doctors and that there would then be a trial within a trial. But such cases would be rare and, if they arose, they would not create any insuperable difficulty, since there are many cases in practice where a trial within a trial is achieved without difficulty. And in such a case (unlike the issues relating to confessions) there would not be the inconvenience of having to exclude the jury since the dispute would be for their use and their instruction.

Mr Buzzard very fairly expressed himself as unable to support the judgment in the case of *Gunewardene* since, in the Crown's view, the important thing was that the jury should be enabled to arrive at the truth and do justice.

In *R v Pedrini, The Times*, 28 July, 1967 before the Court of Criminal Appeal no reliance was placed on *Gunewardene's* case. Without opposition from the Crown, since justice seemed to demand it, the court considered the evidence of three doctors as to the mental condition at the relevant time of a witness who had subsequently become insane. Lord Parker CJ said of that evidence: 'That it is fresh evidence this court is prepared to accept: that it is relevant evidence there is no doubt; that it is credible evidence in the sense that it is capable of belief and of carrying some weight is also clear'. In my view, the court was right in not excluding the medical evidence in that case.

Gunewardene's case was, in my opinion, wrongly decided. Medical evidence is admissible to show that a witness suffers from some disease or defect or abnormality of mind that affects the reliability of his evidence. Such evidence is not confined to a general opinion of the unreliability of the witness but may give all the matters necessary to show, not only the foundation of and reasons for the diagnosis, but also the extent to which the credibility of the witness is affected.

(LORDS REID, MORRIS of BORTH-Y-GEST, HODSON and DONOVAN concurred.)

Appeal allowed.

(e)   Reputation for untruthfulness

R v *Richardson;* R v *Longman*
[1969] 1 QB 299
Court of Appeal

The defendants were tried on indictment with conspiring together to pervert the course of justice by trying to influence a jury and by suborning witnesses at a trial at which the brother of one of the defendants was among those tried. At the trial the chief prosecution witness gave evidence, and in order to discredit her the defence called a witness (a doctor) who was asked whether he would believe the prosecution witness on her oath and he replied that in certain particulars she could be believed on oath. The judge refused to allow the witness to be asked the further question whether from his personal knowledge of her he would believe the prosecution witness on her oath nor was the witness permitted to qualify his previous answer. The defendants were convicted and appealed.

EDMUND DAVIES LJ: . . . The legal position may be thus summarised:
1   A witness may be asked whether he has knowledge of the impugned witness's general reputation for veracity and whether (from such knowledge) he would believe the impugned witness's sworn testimony.
2   The witness called to impeach the credibility of a previous witness may also express his individual opinion (based upon his personal knowledge) as to whether the latter is to be believed upon his oath and is *not* confined to giving evidence merely of general reputation.
3   But whether his opinion as to the impugned witness's credibility be based simply upon the latter's general reputation for veracity or upon his personal knowledge, the witness cannot be permitted to indicate during his examination-in-chief the particular facts, circumstances or incidents which formed the basis of his opinion, although he may be cross-examined as to them . . . [I]t is said that, while Mr Lassman was permitted to ask Dr Hitchens whether, in the light of Mrs Clemence's general reputation for veracity, he would be prepared to believe her on her oath, the question was never allowed to be answered in its entirety. It is submitted that the form of such answer as Dr Hitchens gave showed that he desired to qualify it in some way and was prevented by the judge from uttering more than the single qualifying word, 'But — —'

It is clear from the transcript that Mr Lassman also desired to ask another question of Dr Hitchens, and we were told (and we accept) that it would have been in this form: 'From your personal knowledge of Mrs Clemence would you believe her on her oath?' That question, in our judgment, he should have been permitted to put, but we have some sympathy with the trial judge suddenly confronted as he was with a situation which so rarely arises that not one of the learned Lords who decided *Toohey's* case [1965] AC 595 had throughout their extensive careers ever experienced it. Nevertheless, we are obliged to hold that the trial judge was technically wrong in ruling out that further question. As to whether he was also wrong in cutting short Dr Hitchens's attempt to qualify his earlier answer is far less clear: for it looks very much as though the witness was proceeding to adduce his reasons for qualifying it, and we know of no authority which permits that to be done.

Appeal dismissed.

(iv)   Cross-examination in rape cases

Sexual Offences (Amendment) Act 1976

2.   Restrictions on evidence at trials for rape etc.

(1)   If at a trial any person is for the time being charged with a rape offence to which he pleads not guilty, then, except with the leave of the judge, no evidence and no question in cross-examination shall be adduced or asked at the trial, by or on behalf of any defendant at the trial, about any sexual experience of a complainant with a person other than that defendant.

(2)   The judge shall not give leave in pursuance of the preceding subsection for any evidence or question except on an application made to him in the absence of the jury by or on behalf of a defendant; and on such an application the judge shall give leave if and only if he is satisfied that it would be unfair to that defendant to refuse to allow the evidence to be adduced or the question to be asked.

R v Viola
[1982] 1 WLR 1138
Court of Appeal

At the appellant's trial on a charge of rape, the issue was whether or not the complainant, who had given evidence in-chief, had consented to the sexual intercourse. The appellant sought leave under s. 2 of the Sexual Offences (Amendment) Act 1976 to cross-examine her about her sexual experiences with other men, the proposed questions being based on statements made by eye witnesses concerning incidents with different men some hours before and some hours after the alleged rape. The judge refused leave and the appellant was convicted. He appealed.

LORD LANE CJ: . . . It is, we think apparent from those words [s. 2 of the Sexual Offences (Amendment) Act 1976], without more, that the first question which the judge must ask himself is this: are the questions proposed to be put relevant according to the ordinary common law rules of evidence and relevant to the case as it is being put? If they are not so relevant, that is the end of the matter . . . .

The second matter which the judge must consider is this. If the questions are relevant, then whether they should be allowed or not will of course depend upon the terms of section 2, which limits the admissibility of relevant evidence. That section has been the subject of judicial consideration first of all by May J in *R v Lawrence* [1977] Crim LR 492; a passage, which is taken verbatim from the transcript of the ruling, reads, at p. 493:

> The important part of the statute which I think needs construction are the words 'if and only if [the judge] is satisfied that it would be unfair to that defendant to refuse to allow the evidence to be adduced or the question to be asked.' And, in my judgment, before a judge is satisfied or may be said to be satisfied that to refuse to allow a particular question or a series of questions in cross-examination would be unfair to a defendant he must take the view that it is more likely than not that the particular question or line of cross-examination, if allowed, might reasonably lead the jury, properly directed in the summing up, to take a different view of the complainant's evidence from that which they might take if the question or series of questions was or were not allowed.

That statement was approved by this court in *R v Mills (Leroy)* (1978) 68 Cr App R 327. Roskill LJ, giving the judgment of the court said, at p. 329:

> The second ground of appeal is different in character. It was alleged that the complainant had had a good deal of earlier sexual experience. As is well known, in former times cross-examination in rape cases was permitted with a view to attacking the character of the complainant on the ground that she had had such previous sexual experience. That practice was the subject of widespread public condemnation and ultimately the Sexual Offences (Amendment) Act 1976 was passed.

Then Roskill LJ reads the contents of section 2 and continues:

> Application was made during cross-examination of this complainant by Mr Hunt that he should be allowed to cross-examine her as to her antecedent sexual experience. On the face of it such cross-examination would be contrary to section 2(1). Accordingly the learned judge was only empowered by subsection (2) to give leave 'if and only if he is satisfied that it would be unfair to that defendant to refuse to allow the evidence to be adduced or the question to be asked'. That was therefore the question to which the learned judge had to direct his attention.
>   This section has not yet, as far as this court is aware, been considered by this court. It was however considered by May J a few months before the present trial in *R v Lawrence* [1977] Crim LR 492, which that learned judge heard at Nottingham Crown Court . . .

Then Roskill LJ reads out the part of the judgment of May J which we have already read, and continues, on p. 330: 'This is, as we pointed out to Mr Hunt in the course of argument, essentially a matter for the exercise of discretion by the trial judge within the framework of the Act, bearing in mind that that statutory provision is designed to secure protection for complainants. The learned judge here exercised his discretion after having had that decision of May J quoted to him. Mr Hunt found himself unable to say that this was not a matter for the exercise of the learned judge's discretion, but argued that this court should substitute its own discretion for that of the learned judge. With respect, it would be entirely wrong for us to do so . . .'. Then Roskill LJ said that the court over which he presided felt that the ruling of May J, which they approved, was entirely right, and said, 'It would be impossible, and it would be quite wrong, for this court in any way to seek to disturb that exercise of discretion which seems to us to be wholly in accordance with section 2(1) and (2) of the statute'. The application was refused.

That approval by this court of the decision in *R v Lawrence* [1977] Crim LR 492 means that we are bound by the words of May J to which we have referred. In the end the judge will have to ask himself the question whether he is satisfied in the terms expounded by May J. It will be a problem for him to apply that *dictum* to the particular facts of the case. In those circumstances it seems to us it would be both improper and, perhaps more important, very unwise for us to try to say in advance what may or may not be unfair in any particular case.

We would further like to say this about the judgment in *R v Mills (Leroy)*, 68 Cr App R 327, and say it with the greatest possible deference to that court. It has been agreed on all hands, not only by the appellant and by the Crown but also by Mr Green who has assisted us as *amicus curiae*, that it is wrong to speak of a judge's 'discretion' in this context. The judge has to make a judgment as to whether he is satisfied or not in the terms of section 2. But once having reached his judgment on the particular facts, he has no discretion. If he comes to the conclusion that he is satisfied it would be unfair to exclude the evidence, then the evidence has to be admitted and the questions have to be allowed.

Having said that, when one considers the purposes which lay behind the passing of this Act as expounded by Roskill LJ it is clear that it was aimed primarily at protecting complainants from cross-examination as to credit, from questions which went merely to credit and no more. The result is that generally speaking — I use these words advisedly, of course there will always be exceptions — if the proposed questions merely seek to establish that the complainant has had sexual experience with other men to whom she was not married, so as to suggest that for that reason she ought not to be believed under oath, the judge will exclude the evidence. In the present climate of opinion a jury is unlikely to be influenced by such considerations, nor should it be influenced. In other words questions of this sort going simply to credit will seldom be allowed. That is borne out by the cases to which we have been referred: not only those which I have cited, but other unreported cases which have been before this court, to which perhaps it is not necessary to make reference.

On the other hand if the questions are relevant to an issue in the trial in the light of the way the case is being run, for instance relevant to the issue of consent, as opposed merely to credit, they are likely to be admitted, because to exclude a relevant question on an issue in the trial as the trial is being run will usually mean that the jury are being prevented from hearing something which, if they did hear it, might cause them to change their minds about the evidence given by the complainant. But, I repeat, we are very far from laying down any hard and fast rule.

Inevitably in this situation, as in so many similar situations in the law, there is a grey area which exists between the two types of relevance, namely, relevance to credit and relevance to an issue in the case. On one hand evidence of sexual promiscuity may be so strong or so closely contemporaneous in time to the event in issue as to come near to, or indeed to reach the border between mere credit and an issue in the case. Conversely, the relevance of the evidence to an issue in the case may be so slight as to lead the judge to the conclusion that he is far from satisfied that the exclusion of the evidence or the question from the consideration of the jury would be unfair to the defendant.

We have had drawn to our attention some of the difficulties which face a judge. It is perfectly true to say that normally he has to make this decision at an early stage of the trial. It will be, generally speaking, when the complainant's evidence in chief is concluded that counsel in the absence of the jury will make the necessary application under section 2. At this stage it may not be easy for the judge to reach a conclusion, but this is a problem which is continually being faced by judges, sometimes in even more trying circumstances, for example, when he is asked to determine whether a count should be tried separately or whether defendants should be tried separately and so on, before the trial has got under way at all. He has to reach the best conclusion that he can.

The second matter is: is this court entitled to differ from the conclusions of the judge? As already pointed out, this is the exercise of judgment by the judge not an exercise of his discretion. This court is in many respects in as good a position as the judge to reach a conclusion. The judge has certainly heard the complainant give evidence, but only in chief. So far as the proposed questions are concerned, the statements upon which the questions were to be asked or the way in which the matter was going to be put to the jury are presented in exactly the same way to this court as they were to the judge at first instance. We have been told what it was that counsel sought in the course of his submission to the judge and indeed we have been given the statements which were to be the basis of the questions which he was going to ask.

So what we have to decide is whether the judge was right or wrong in the conclusion which he reached, applying the test of May J in *R v Lawrence* [1977] Crim LR 492, 493. Like so many decisions in the grey area, it is not an easy decision to make.

Appeal allowed. Conviction quashed.

R v Cox
(1987) 84 Cr App R 132
Court of Appeal

LORD LANE CJ: On January 13, 1986 at the Crown Court at Dudley, this appellant, David Cox, was convicted of rape and was sentenced to 21 months' imprisonment.

He now appeals against that conviction by leave of the single judge.

The complainant was a young woman of 20. She lived in a flat with her boy friend Graham and their two young children. The appellant and his brother called Mark were friends of Graham.

On July 4, 1985 unfortunately Graham was arrested by the police for being drunk and disorderly. He was foolish enough to decline to give his address to the police and consequently he remained in police custody. That was known to the appellant, it was known to the complainant and it was also known to the appellant's brother Mark.

The three of them and one other man found themselves in the complainant's flat. All the others left, but the appellant stayed behind. Then, according to the complainant, the appellant made advances to her and raped her on the sofa twice. She cried and tried to push him away. She said she made it clear she did not consent. That was on the night of July 4.

. . .

The only ground of appeal put forward by Mr Stanley on the appellant's behalf is that the judge came to a wrong conclusion as to the admissibility of certain evidence under the provisions of section 2 of the Sexual Offences (Amendment) Act 1976, the material parts of which read as follows:

[His Lordship cited s. 2 of the Act and continued . . .]

The defence wished to cross-examine the complainant, and possibly also to seek to call evidence, about an earlier occasion affecting the complainant. The earlier occasion, it was said, involved the following facts, that she, when Graham was away, had had sexual intercourse with another man called Steven. Having had sexual intercourse with her, Steven, somewhat ungallantly, went and told Graham what had happened. Graham was enraged and had tackled the complainant about it, whereupon she had said that she had been raped by Steven, that the sexual intercourse with him, albeit it had happened, had been without her consent.

There was a proof of evidence from Steven available to the defence and we have a copy of it ourselves. Steven asserts that that was the case, that he had had sexual intercourse with her consent. He asserted in his proof that he had told Graham about it. He said that he had heard that he was being accused of rape by the complainant. He had gone round to see Graham and the complainant together, and in the presence of Graham the complainant had admitted that she had accused him of rape and had admitted that that accusation was false. That was the evidence which the defence wished to broach by way of cross-examination of the complainant.

The judge ruled against the defence, and it is desirable that I should read the passage in his ruling which is relevant:

Perhaps she [the complainant] would say, 'Yes,' to the suggestion, but it seems to me that whatever be the fact of that, the question for me is the same, is that matter relevant to the question whether she consented or not on the occasion the subject of the indictment, to sexual intercourse with the defendant? Speaking strictly, in my judgment, it is not relevant to that question. I apply what I understand to be the ordinary tests of relevance so far as I understand them and I do not think that that matter is relevant to the question whether or not she consented to intercourse with this defendant, but I acknowledge that such cross-examination could affect her credit. Whether it affected it substantially or not might well depend on how the case developed, and so it seems to me that as it is of relevance in that sense, possible relevance to her credit, that I have to consider whether in fairness I should allow cross-examination, applying the test of whether or not it would be unfair to prevent the cross-examination. I have thought carefully about that and I acknowledge that the situation might change if the case went in a way that justified a further application and reconsideration of the matter, but at the moment, in my judgment, it is not unfair for the defendant to refuse leave to cross-examine because the girl may quite properly be asked questions without any leave from me to establish that she did not want Graham to know about what had happened and to establish that she was sure in the sense that she powerfully believed that he would leave her, or might leave her, if he did know that she had willingly had intercourse with the defendant, if that were the case, and it could be put to her that she knew that Graham perhaps, being a fair man, would not leave her if he believed that she had been raped. I suppose it could even be put to her that he had told her so, but that is not for me to decide how the questions should be put, they are in safe hands . . . I rule that you cannot adduce that evidence. You can adduce evidence of her saying it should not have happened, but you must not, please, if you can possibly avoid it, ask a question which encourages your client to say that she made any reference to, 'Last time.'

[His Lordship then cited from *R* v *Viola* and continued . . .]
The result of that and the effect of the proposed questions and evidence is to indicate that it was not so much the sexual intercourse with Steven in the earlier event which was of importance, but what she said about it afterwards, and it was really that which was the subject of the application. It is true that the learned judge indicated that there was a line of questioning which was open to the defendant falling short of the question which he had ruled should not be put. But if the defence was to be prevented from putting to the complainant the real nub of the Steven incident, namely that she had accused him of rape and had then admitted later that that accusation was false, the effect of the cross-examination would be largely lost.

We have come to the conclusion that to stop the questioning short of that point was unfair to the defendant. The chances are that, if that cross-examination had been allowed, the jury might very well have come to a conclusion, against the background of the case as I have illustrated, which would not have been the same as the conclusion at which they actually arrived.

For those reasons, whilst once again acknowledging the difficulties this section presents to judges who are faced with a submission based upon it, we have come to the conclusion that this conviction was unsafe and unsatisfactory, and accordingly the appeal is allowed and the conviction is quashed.

R v *Brown*
(1989) 89 Cr App R 97
Court of Appeal

MAY LJ: On July 17, 1987, in the Crown Court at Sheffield, the appellant was convicted of one offence of abduction and one of rape and was sentenced to seven years' imprisonment on each count concurrent. He now appeals against his conviction by leave of the single judge.

In brief the Crown case was that on the night of September 26, 1986, the complainant, Sylvia Martin, went out to a night-club in Sheffield with some friends. At about 1.30 or 2 a.m. she met the appellant there. She had had some trouble with him the previous week at a public house, when he had slapped her and threatened a friend of hers with a glass. She therefore did not want anything to do with him, but he kept on asking her to dance. He continued to press his attentions on her, saying that he was feeling sexy and that she had to go with him that night. She refused and attempted to get away from him, but as she was leaving he came up to her again and pulled her into a passage way. He again told her that she was coming with him, but she refused and tried to fight him off. Two girl friends of hers tried to intervene, but the appellant threw stones at them and was abusive. In the end he forced her to go with him to a nearby house and upstairs to the bedroom. In the course of doing so he pulled her along and hit her on the head. She was shaking and frightened. He then told her to take her clothes off, and shouted and screamed when she refused. As she was terrified she agreed to undress. The appellant then pushed her on to the bed. She was crying her eyes out. Between then and the following morning the appellant had intercourse with her on three occasions against her consent. At 8.30 a.m. the complainant asked if she could leave, not for the first time. After they had both dressed and when she said she wanted a taxi the appellant showed her where she could telephone, and stayed with her until the taxi arrived.

Once back at home the appellant went straight to bed. Earlier, when her friends had been unable to find her, they had telephoned the police and an officer had come to her house at about 3.50 a.m. On her return home her friends told her that the police had been and that she was to telephone them. However, she refused to do so because she was afraid that she might be beaten up. Ultimately she was seen by police at 10 a.m., and their evidence was that she had been crying and appeared to be dishevelled and upset.

The appellant was arrested and interviewed that afternoon, when he maintained that the complainant had consented. His defence in answer to the police and at trial was that he had seen the complainant in the club quite frequently on Friday nights. He said that they had first had intercourse about eight weeks before the alleged offence on the first occasion they had met. She had asked him not to tell her friends. On the night of the alleged offence they had danced and talked and he had left by himself. He had met the complainant outside the club, and she said that she would come home with him, having already said when they were dancing that she might do so. They went home, and after talking for about half an hour they went upstairs.

There they had intercourse together with her complete consent on two occasions. In the morning he woke her up and at her request walked her to a telephone box to call a taxi.

The police surgeon who examined the complainant on the day following the alleged offences said that there were no marks of violence or injuries to any part of the complainant. The doctor's report also contained material, not given in evidence before the jury, from which the clear inference was that in her opinion the complainant was suffering from some venereal disease. The appellant in cross-examination said that as a result of the intercourse that he had had with the complainant he had himself also contracted that disease.

After the complainant had given evidence-in-chief, counsel for the appellant applied to the learned judge for leave to cross-examine her about her sexual relations with other men. He relied on the decisions in *Lawrence* [1977] Crim LR 492, and *Viola*

(1982) 75 Cr App R 125. He indicated that he wished to put to the complainant, first, the evidence of the police surgeon that she had found signs of venereal disease; secondly, that part of the complainant's own deposition where she described her relationship with her then boy-friend as a 'casual sex relationship,' and which he (the boy-friend) had said had been going on for only some 10 days; thirdly, that the complainant had had a child six months earlier by yet another man. Counsel submitted that this was evidence of promiscuity and that it went to the issue of consent.

Counsel for the Crown resisted the application on the basis that, even if these matters did show promiscuity on the part of the complainant, this was not relevant to the defence that she consented, although it might have had some relevance if the defence had been a genuine belief in her consent. . . .

What counsel for the appellant wished to do at the trial in this case, as he told us and as appears from the transcript, was to seek to show that the complainant was promiscuous, that is to say, that not only had she had sexual experience with men to whom she was not married but that she had done so casually and with little discrimination. It was, of course, in any event fundamental to such a submission that there was a factual basis for suggesting sexual promiscuity in this case.

Nevertheless, if the purpose of such questions was merely to show that for that reason the complainant ought not to be believed under oath, then the judge properly excluded the evidence. On the other hand, if the proposed questions were relevant to the issue of consent, as opposed merely to credit, then they would be likely to be admitted. As was said in the judgment of the Court in *Viola* at p. 130, this is because:

> To exclude a relevant question on an issue in the trial as the trial is being run will usually mean that the jury are being prevented from hearing something which, if they did hear it, might cause them to change their minds about the evidence given by the complainant.

This is in many cases not an easy concept, because in one sense questions even going only to credit can be said to be relevant to the issue of consent. If a complainant who gives evidence of a defendant having sexual intercourse with her without consent is not to be believed in the witness-box, then the absence of that consent will not be proved. However, again as was pointed out in *Viola's* case, in the present climate of opinion a jury would be unlikely to be influenced, nor should it be influenced, when considering veracity by the mere fact that the complainant may have been promiscuous in the sense indicated.

This was realised by the Court in *Viola* in this passage at p. 130:

> Inevitably in this situation, as in so many similar situations in the law, there is a grey area which exists between the two types of relevance, namely relevance to credit and relevance to an issue in the case. On one hand evidence of sexual promiscuity may be so strong or so closely contemporaneous in time to the event in issue as to come near to, or indeed to reach, the border between mere credit and an issue in the case. Conversely, the relevance of the evidence to an issue in the case may be so slight as to lead the Judge to the conclusion that he is far from satisfied that the exclusion of the evidence or the question from the consideration of the jury would be unfair to the defendant.

The real inquiry is whether on the facts of the particular case the complainant's attitude to sexual relations could be material upon which in these days a jury could reasonably rely to conclude that the complainant may indeed have consented to the sexual intercourse on the material occasion, despite her evidence to the contrary. It is in every case a question of degree.

Further, the question whether it is unfair to exclude such cross-examination in a case on or near the borderline referred to may be affected by the consideration whether there are other features relevant to consent which could tip the balance between fairness and unfairness. In the present case the complainant did not seek help from her boyfriend when the appellant, on her evidence, was forcing her away from the club. She did not shout out to her friends who were there at the time and who saw what was happening. She did not complain to the taxi-driver the following morning when she was picked up at the appellant's home. May these features have been due to her attitude towards casual sexual relations, and in combination with that attitude sufficiently material to the question whether she consented or not so as to make it unfair to exclude the questions sought to be asked?

In our opinion, this was a case near the borderline. Clearly the complainant was prepared to have intercourse with a number of different men, but we do not think that the mere fact that she was suffering from some venereal disease is necessarily evidence of substantial promiscuity. Before it could be so considered there would have to be cross-examination, largely on a 'fishing basis,' to discover the circumstances in which she came to be infected. There are also the other features to which we have referred.

Nevertheless, although we have not found it easy to reach a decision on this appeal, in the end we do not think that the 'evidence of sexual promiscuity' of the complainant was 'so strong or so closely contemporaneous in time to the event in issue as to . . . reach the border between mere credit and an issue in the case.'

For these reasons we dismiss this appeal.

Questions

1.   Is the decision in *R* v *Brown* consistent with *R* v *Cox* and *R* v *Viola*?

2.   Does the Sexual Offences (Amendment) Act 1976, s. 2, as interpreted in the cases, strike the correct balance between the interests of the complainant and the interests of the accused?

3.   Is it possible to make a clear distinction between relevance to an issue and relevance to credibility?

R v *Funderburk*
[1990] 1 WLR 587
Court of Appeal

HENRY J: On 28 September 1988 in the Crown Court at Reading, before McNeill J, the appellant was convicted on three counts of sexual intercourse with a girl of 13 years — in law, a child — and was sentenced to consecutive terms of 18, 15 and 12 months' imprisonment. The three counts were specimen counts covering 10 or 11 alleged acts of intercourse.

The first count covered the month of November 1987, the second, December 1987 and the third, February 1988. He now appeals against conviction and sentence by leave of the single judge.

The facts are that the appellant was a master sergeant in the United States Air Force who lived with Joanne Potts in Berkshire. Until about Christmas 1987 a friend of his had lived with a lady who was the mother of the child, the complainant, who was then aged 13. The mother herself was only 31.

At Christmas the child, who had been living with the grandparents, began to live with her mother and step-brothers. They moved in with the appellant and Miss Potts as lodgers. They left at the beginning of March after arguments concerning money. It was after that parting that these events came to the notice of the authorities.

The complainant gave evidence that she began to have a crush on the appellant when in November 1987 he took her to a nightclub as a reward for babysitting for him. She described in some detail in the witness box the acts of intercourse which had occurred, as I say, on 10 or 11 occasions.

The transcript of her evidence shows that it came out in a way which strongly suggested that on the occasion of the first act of intercourse, which she said was a week or so after the nightclub visit, she was a virgin. She had been asked in the introductory questions during her evidence-in-chief about her previous boyfriends and the innocence of her association with them. She said that the appellant had said to her: 'You've got to do it one day; why not now?' Then followed her description of the penetration, the pain caused by it and the bleeding which she later discovered.

It being made clear at the same time that she was not then menstruating, it seems to us that it must have been perfectly clear to the jury that in giving that description of the first occasion she was describing the loss of her virginity.

The appellant's defence was that the child was lying from beginning to end. Her motive in this was to support her mother who — as the child agreed in the witness box — had it in for the appellant as a result of the disputes which had arisen between them.

One difficulty which the defence had to meet was that if she was lying, how could so young a girl have given so detailed and varied accounts as the accounts that she in fact gave of the acts of intercourse? The answer which the defence suggested as to this was that despite her age she was both experienced and sexually interested, and that she had either transposed experiences which she had had with others to this appellant and/or fantasised about experience with the appellant on whom she freely admitted having had this crush. In support of that, defence counsel wished, and it is this matter which gives rise to the appeal against conviction, first to put to her that she had told Miss Potts, a potential defence witness, that before the first incident complained of she had had sexual intercourse with two named men and consequently she had wanted to undergo a pregnancy test.

As will be seen, counsel was not permitted to put those questions in cross-examination. For convenience we refer to them as 'the disputed questions.' Having laid the basis in cross-examination, counsel wished subsequently to call Miss Potts to give evidence of that conversation. As will be seen, he was not able to do that either, and we call this 'the disputed evidence.'

Counsel made the application on the basis not only that it went to her credibility but also on the basis that it went to an issue in the case. Somewhat surprisingly when that application was originally made there was no mention of the Criminal Procedure Act 1865 ('Lord Denman's Act') until the judge brought it up himself after the overnight adjournment. This was one of the difficulties with which the judge had to cope.

The case was heard on circuit. Library facilities are often scant there, as they seemed to have been in this case. None of the authorities which have been cited to us were cited to the trial judge. He had a difficult task.

The ruling which is challenged in this appeal is the judge's ruling that whether or not the child was a virgin at the time of the first incident was not an issue material to the charge of unlawful sexual intercourse. He commented that the prosecution had rightly avoided any inquiry as to her virginity.

It is right to say that the prosecution had never asked her directly the question, 'Were you a virgin at the time?' although it was clearly implicit from her evidence that that was what she was saying she was. The judge went on to rule that if the child had, as the defence contended, implicitly averred her previous virginity her previous inconsistent statement, namely, that she had had sexual intercourse with two other men before this date, could not be put to her as a challenge to her credibility, as her virginity was, in the judge's words, 'immaterial to establishing or refuting the charge that this defendant had sexual intercourse with the girl.'

For our part we are quite satisfied that both the prosecution and the child herself were putting her forward as a virgin before the first incident and that the jury cannot have doubted she was telling them of the loss of her virginity.

Before we come to answering the questions posed we think it necessary to go back to first principles. One starts with the obvious proposition that in a trial relevant evidence should be admitted and irrelevant evidence excluded. 'Relevant' means relevant according to the ordinary common law rules of evidence and relevant to the case as it is being put, as Lord Lane CJ put it in *Reg.* v *Viola* [1982] 1 WLR 1138, 1141c.

But as relevance is a matter of degree in each case, the question in reality is whether or not the evidence is or is not sufficiently relevant. For in order to keep criminal trials within bounds and to assist the jury in concentrating on what matters and not being distracted by doubts as to marginal events, it is necessary in the interests of justice to avoid multiplicity of issues where possible. In every case this is a matter for the trial judge on the evidence and on the way the case is put before him.

When one comes to cross-examination, questions in cross-examination equally have to be relevant to the issues before the court, and those issues of course include the credibility of the witness giving evidence as to those issues. But a practical distinction must be drawn between questions going to an issue before the court and questions merely going either to the credibility of the witness or to facts that are merely collateral. Where questions go solely to the credibility of the witness or to collateral facts the general rule is that answers given to such questions are final and cannot be contradicted by rebutting evidence. This is because of the requirement to avoid multiplicity of issues in the overall interests of justice.

The authorities show that the defence may call evidence contradicting that of the prosecution witnesses where their evidence: (a) goes to an issue in the case (that is obvious); (b) shows that the witness made a previous inconsistent statement relating to an issue in the case (Denman's Act, which we deal with below); (c) shows bias in the witness: *Rex.* v *Phillips* (1936) 26 Cr App R 17; (d) shows that the police are prepared to go to improper lengths to secure a conviction; *Reg.* v *Busby* (1981) 75 Cr App R 79; (e) in certain circumstances proves the witness's previous convictions; (f) shows that the witness has a general reputation for untruthfulness; (g) shows that medical causes would have affected the reliability of his testimony.

All those categories listed, other than category (a), might be considered exceptions to the general rule as to the finality requirement of questions put on issues of credibility and collateral matters. They demonstrate the obvious proposition that a general rule designed to serve the interests of justice should not be used where so far from serving those interests it might defeat them. On that basic summary of the law two questions arise in this case. First, should the disputed questions have been permitted as questions either going to an issue or going to the credibility of the child? Second, if so, were her answers to such questions final or could evidence be given of previous inconsistent statements relating to previous sexual activities?

We deal first with admission of the questions as going to credit. Originally counsel for the prosecution conceded that the disputed questions could be asked as going to credit, subject to the answers being final, but in the course of submissions he withdrew this concession. The question of roaming cross-examinations as to the credit of complainants in rape cases rightly exercised Parliament and such cross-examination was statutorily restricted by section 2 of the Sexual Offences (Amendment) Act 1976 . . . . Counsel for the defendant on making his application to the judge accurately submitted that the offence here charged was not a rape offence within the meaning of the section and so the cross-examination here would not be governed by those restrictions. However, not surprisingly, the trial judge was naturally concerned as to the extent of any cross-examination of a 13-year-old child on sexual matters. Even though in under age cases the question of consent is not the issue, some of the considerations which concerned Parliament in rape cases apply.

We have found it useful in considering the limits of cross-examination in this case to remind ourselves of the Lord Chief Justice's analysis of section 2 in the well-known case of *Reg.* v *Viola* [1982] 1 WLR 1138 to which I have already referred. First, Lord Lane CJ, at p. 1141, made it clear that the court must ask itself whether the questions are relevant under 'the ordinary common law rules of evidence and relevant to the case as it is being put.' Only then did section 2 come into play. . . .

So though the limits on cross-examination as to credit imposed by that Act do not apply to this case, the court will not wish to see the mischief sought to be prevented by that Act perpetuated in this context and therefore will be astute to see that such cross-examination is not abused or extended unnecessarily. McNeill J was rightly concerned as to the ordeal of this child.

So far as concerns the general test as to the limits of cross-examination as to credit, the locus classicus of that is to be found in the judgment of Lawton J in *Reg.* v *Sweet-Escott* (1971) 55 Cr App R 316, 320. There the witness was cross-examined as to his credit in relation to convictions 20 years ago. As a general test Lawton J, having found that the question should not have been allowed, said:

> What, then, is the principle upon which the judge should draw the line? It seems to me that it is this. Since the purpose of cross-examination as to credit is to show that the witness ought not to be believed on oath, the matters about which he is questioned must relate to his likely standing after cross-examination with the tribunal which is trying him or listening to his evidence.

The echoes of that passage in Lord Lane CJ's judgment will be noted.

As is clear from our summary of the judge's refusal of the application in this case, that is not the test that the trial judge here applied. He applied the test set out in section 4 of Denman's Act as to the admissibility of proof of previous inconsistent statements. I should read that section to show the test he applied. Section 4 of that Act deals with oral statements and provides:

> If a witness, upon cross-examination as to a former statement made by him — and these are the important words — relative to the subject matter of the indictment or proceeding, and inconsistent with his present testimony, does not distinctly admit that he has made such statement, proof may be given that he did in fact make it; but before such proof can be given the circumstances of the supposed statement, sufficient to designate the particular occasion, must be mentioned to the witness, and he must be asked whether or not he has made such a statement.

It was on the basis of that section that the application as to Joanne Potts' evidence could, it seems to us, have most strongly been made. The trial judge, having found that the virginity or non-virginity of the child on the occasion of the first alleged act of intercourse was not a material issue, disallowed both the disputed questions and the calling of the witness to make good what would have been put in the disputed questions.

Was the trial judge right to apply the test set out in section 4 of that Act (dealing with the calling of evidence relating to the cross-examination) instead of the ordinary test set out in *Reg.* v *Sweet-Escott* relating to allowing questions going to the credibility of a witness? We see nothing in section 4 which would prevent a witness's previous statement inconsistent with his testimony before the judge being put to him to challenge his credibility even where the section did not allow the evidence of the making of the inconsistent statement to be given. So this court assumed in *Reg.* v *Hart* (1957) 42 Cr App R 47. There the appellant was convicted of wounding with intent to do grievous bodily harm, the wound being a severe knife wound concerning one Humphreys. The defence case was that the wound was caused accidentally when Humphreys came at him with a bottle. The prosecution case was that Humphreys had no bottle. It was put to him in cross-examination that he, the prosecution witness, had told a defence witness the opposite. However, the judge did not allow the defence witness to give evidence on this matter on the erroneous basis that the Act only applied to sworn statements. The court held that the judge was wrong in excluding the evidence but in that case applied the proviso. In giving the judgment of the court Devlin J made the distinction between questions going to the issue and questions going merely to credit, at p. 50:

> The provision under which that evidence was sought to be made admissible — and this is the inconsistent statement — is now contained in section 4 of the Criminal Law Procedure Act 1865, which re-enacted the Common Law Procedure Act 1854. Before that it had probably been the common law that, quite apart from any statute, questions were admissible — certainly in the ordinary common law courts — whereby if a witness gave evidence of a fact that was relevant to the issue (*and that is important, because if the question merely goes to credit, he cannot be contradicted*) — I stress that parenthesis — it could be put to him that on some earlier occasion he had made a contrary statement to somebody else and, if he denied it, that somebody else could be called.

There the distinction is clearly made between questions going to the issue and questions going to credit. Examination of the judgment suggests that the court proceeded on the basis that the question went to the issue 'accident or not,' because the jury might have thought the point as to whether Humphreys had a bottle important.

Accordingly we can see no basis either on the authorities or as a matter of principle for applying the Denman's Act test, relating to the calling of contradictory evidence, to the question of allowing cross-examination as to credit. To that problem it seems to us that the test suggested by Lawton J in *Reg.* v *Sweet-Escott*, 55 Cr App R 316, is appropriate: how might the matters put to him affect his standing with the jury after cross-examination?

. . .

We are disposed to agree with the editors of *Cross on Evidence*, 6th ed. (1985), p. 295 that where the disputed issue is a sexual one between two persons in private the difference between questions going to credit and questions going to the issue is reduced to vanishing point. I read from that work:

> It has also been remarked that sexual intercourse, whether or not consensual, most often takes place in private, and leaves few visible traces of having occurred.

Evidence is often effectively limited to that of the parties, and much is likely to depend on the balance of credibility between them. This has important effects for the law of evidence since it is capable of reducing the difference between questions going to credit and questions going to the issue to vanishing point.

Similar problems arise when considering what facts are collateral. Again, we cite from *Cross*, at p. 283:

> As relevance is a matter of degree, it is impossible to devise an exhaustive means of determining when a question is collateral for the purpose of the rule under consideration; Pollock CB said in the leading case of *Attorney-General v Hitchcock* (1847) 1 Exch 91 99: 'The test whether the matter is collateral or not is this: if the answer of a witness is a matter which you would be allowed on your own part to prove in evidence — if it have such a connection with the issues, that you would be allowed to give it in evidence — then it is a matter on which you may contradict him.'

The difficulty we have in applying that celebrated test is that it seems to us to be circular. If a fact is not collateral then clearly you can call evidence to contradict it, but the so-called test is silent on how you decide whether that fact is collateral. The utility of the test may lie in the fact that the answer is an instinctive one based on the prosecutor's and the court's sense of fair play rather than any philosophic or analytic process. Applying the test in argument, Morland J put to Mr Hillman for the Crown the hypothetical question, 'If the defence had medical evidence that this child was not a virgin before the date on which she gave her account of losing her virginity, would the defence be allowed to call such evidence?' On reflection, Mr Hillman accepted that they would be allowed to call such evidence, and we think that answer to the question not only right but inevitable. Otherwise there would be the danger that the jury would make their decision as to credit on an account of the original incident in which the most emotive, memorable and potentially persuasive fact was, to the knowledge of all in the case save the jury, false.

If that is right, then a fortiori conflicting statements must be 'relative to the subject matter of the indictment' within the meaning of Lord Denman's Act. It seems to us that on the way the prosecution presented the evidence the challenge to the loss of virginity was a challenge that not only did the jury deserve to know about on the basis that it might have affected their view on the central question of credit, but was sufficiently closely related to the subject matter of the indictment for justice to require investigation for the basis of such a challenge.

. . .

Accordingly it seems to us that the defence should have been allowed to put the disputed questions and, if met with a denial, to call the disputed evidence. Against this background we consider the proviso, namely, whether we are satisfied that no miscarriage of justice has occurred. With the disputed questions asked and the disputed evidence called would the jury inevitably have come to the same conclusion? Mr Hillman for the Crown submitted that the child's evidence was entirely convincing and the jury had clearly shown that they preferred it to the appellant's.

Reading that evidence we can see the force of that submission, but the effect of the cross-examination which was denied and the evidence which was not called is simply incalculable, and we cannot apply the proviso on the basis that it would have made no difference to the jury's view of the child's credit. But even putting the girl's evidence aside, so far as concerns the third specimen count relating to an offence in February, the appellant made a clear admission of one such offence in his statement to the police, a statement signed and initialled by him, a master sergeant in the United States Air Force, whose glowing military reports describe him as 'one of our bright young non-commissioned officers.'

His attempts to explain away this confession are quite unconvincing. We are satisfied that there was no miscarriage of justice in respect of count 3 to which he confessed, nor is there any basis for an appeal against sentence on that count. Accordingly we allow this appeal against conviction on counts 1 and 2 and apply the proviso in respect of count 3 for which he was sentenced to 12 months' imprisonment.

J. Temkin, 'Sexual History Evidence — the Ravishment of Section 2' [1993] Crim LR 3, pp. 4–7

Matters got off to a bad start with the reporting in the *Criminal Law Review* of the ruling of May J at Nottingham Crown Court in *Lawrence* that questions about the complainant's sexual relationships with other men should be allowed only where they 'might reasonably lead the jury, properly directed in the summing up, to take a different view of the complainant's evidence from that which they might take if the question or series of questions was or were not allowed.' But that, of course, is the whole nub of the problem. If a jury is told about a woman's sexual past, it may be prejudiced against her and may well take a different view of her evidence. This problem cannot simply be resolved by the use of the word 'reasonably.' The Heilbron Committee put it this way: 'Questioning of this sort may result in the jury feeling that she is the type of person who should either not be believed, or else deserves no protection from the law, or was likely to have consented anyway.'

Within the enclosed and cut-off realm of the court-room, a jury may accept an account of the world as set out by the defence which in no way corresponds to the actual sexual mores of today's society but exemplifies the double standard of sexual morality in its most virulent form. In the case of defendants, the jury is prevented from learning of past misconduct precisely because of the prejudicial impact of such information. To base a test for the inclusion of sexual history evidence on the reaction of the jury could not have been less helpful. May J went on to say that 'Cross-examination designed to form a basis for the unspoken comment, "Well, there you are, members of the jury, that is the sort of girl she is" was not permissible.' This, however, has proved insufficient to redeem the situation.

In the later decision of the Court of the Appeal in *Viola*, the *Lawrence* test was approved and the court went on to say that 'if the questions are relevant to an issue in the trial in the light of the way the case is being run, for instance relevant to the issue of consent, as opposed merely to credit, they are likely to be admitted.' This took us from bad to worse. It left the door open for rulings that evidence of past sexual experience was in any particular case relevant to the issue of consent and therefore admissible. At common law, as mentioned above, only two categories of case were regarded as relevant to consent, *viz.* evidence of prostitution or notorious reputation for lack of chastity and evidence of a past sexual relationship with the defendant. As section 2(4) makes clear, the limitations imposed by the Sexual Offences (Amendment) Act were intended to be in addition to and not in place of the common law restrictions, but there appears to be insufficient recognition of this in *Viola* or the subsequent case law. The question of what is thought to be relevant to consent on the facts of the case and in the light of the way the case is being run has now become the dominant consideration.

Is a woman's sexual past ever relevant to whether she consented to this particular man on the occasion in question? Heilbron considered that such evidence was scarcely ever relevant but it is clear that the Court of Appeal today does not share this view and neither do some academic writers. The problem is that relevance is an insufficiently objective criterion. As L'Heureux-Dubé J stated in the Supreme Court of Canada's decision in *Seaboyer*:

> Regardless of the definition used, the content of any relevancy decision will be filled by the particular judge's experience, common sense and/or logic . . . There are certain areas of enquiry where experience, common sense and logic are informed by stereotype and myth . . . This area of the law [i.e. sexual history evidence] has been particularly prone to the utilization of stereotype in determinations of relevance.

Notably lacking from the discourse in *Viola* and later cases is any discussion of what might be described as the degree of relevance needed to qualify for admissibility in this context. It has been pointed out that evidence 'must not merely be remotely relevant, but proximately so. Again it must not unnecessarily complicate the case, or too much tend to confuse, mislead or tire . . . the jury, or withdraw their attention too much from the real issues of the case.' Relevance is, as Hoffmann has explained, 'a variable standard, the probative value of the evidence being balanced against the disadvantages of receiving it such as taking up a lot of time or causing confusion' or, it might be added, causing undue prejudice which is likely to impede rather than assist the search for truth. These issues, so very pertinent where sexual history is concerned, might be thought to have merited some judicial consideration.

Since *Viola*, a number of sexual history cases have come before the Court of Appeal. Some have been concerned with promiscuity, some with virginity and some have involved situations in which the defendant has sought to counter the complainant's assertions in support of her case with evidence which highlights her sexual past.

Evidence of promiscuity
The issue of promiscuity was directly raised in *Brown*. Brown's appeal was based on the trial judge's exclusion of evidence of the complainant's alleged promiscuity as witnessed by the fact that she was a single parent with a six-month-old baby, had at the time a 'casual sex relationship' with a boyfriend (not the child's father) and, after the rape, was found to have some trace of venereal disease. The Court of Appeal was sympathetic to the appeal. In *Viola*, it had been suggested that where the evidence of promiscuity was so strong or so closely contemporaneous to the events in question, this might place it near or on the border between mere credit and an issue in the case which might then justify its admission. Following *Viola*, the court concluded that this case approached the borderline because, excluding the venereal disease which was not in itself necessarily evidence of substantial promiscuity, 'the complainant was prepared to have intercourse with a number of different men.' Thus the Court of Appeal classified her as promiscuous on the strength of evidence that she had had sexual intercourse with two men, notably the father of her child and her current boyfriend. It concluded, however, that the evidence of promiscuity was neither sufficiently strong nor sufficiently contemporaneous to reach close enough to the border to justify its inclusion.

The court went on to add that the decision whether or not to admit sexual history evidence in cases on or near the borderline may be affected by consideration of other features of the case relevant to consent. In other words, where there are features of the case which raise doubts, it may help to know if the woman is promiscuous since that may explain what really happened. In this case, it was said, the complainant's failure to shout for help when Brown dragged her off and her further failure to tell the taxi driver who brought her home after the alleged rape what had happened to her were features which might have been explained by her attitude to sexual relations such as to justify admission of her promiscuous past had the evidence of promiscuity been strong enough.

Although the appeal was dismissed in this case, the implications of the judgment are worrying. First, the court's interpretation of female promiscuity is so broad that there will hardly be a woman in the land who could not be characterised in this way. That extra something required to render the evidence of promiscuity strong enough to classify it as a borderline or close to the borderline case was not made clear. Secondly, the Court of Appeal has provided us with an insight into its view of how genuine rape victims should behave. Genuine rape victims shout for help and reveal all that has happened to them to the first person they encounter afterwards. But this rigid stereotype has little basis in reality, as numerous studies now show. Confused or frightened women frequently do not scream or shout. Raped women frequently do not wish to tell all to the first stranger they meet. What is alarming about this judgment is that cases where the victim's behaviour does not conform to the stereotype may be regarded as those with doubtful features relevant to consent such as to justify the inclusion of evidence of promiscuity where this is deemed sufficiently strong or contemporaneous.

. . .

Conclusion

The Court of Appeal is currently under attack for the rigidity of its attitude to appeals and its unwillingness to quash decisions of trial courts. This criticism could not be less apt in cases where trial judges have excluded sexual history evidence. Here the chances of a successful appeal have never been better. Despite the Heilbron Report and all that is known about current sexual mores, the Court of Appeal continues to attribute undue significance to the sexual past of complainants in rape trials. In its manifesto for a safer environment for women, the Labour Party proposed to restrict the use of sexual history evidence. It is to be hoped that the present Government will also see the need to look once again at this issue.

(C)   Re-examination and related matters

When cross-examination of the witness has finished, the party who called the witness will have the opportunity to re-examine him. Invariably, the credibility of the witness will have been shaken during the cross-examination. Re-examination provides the opportunity to restore damaged credibility by giving the witness an opportunity to explain any inconsistencies, contradictions, etc. which arose whilst he was being cross-examined. New matters cannot generally be introduced at this stage, counsel having to confine himself to matters which arose during cross-examination (*Prince v Samo* (1838) 7 LJQB 123).

At this stage, it is convenient to consider two matters which, although not directly concerned with re-examination, are closely related to it. The first concerns matters which arise *ex improviso*, i.e. matters which could not be introduced before the close of the party's case because human ingenuity could not have forseen the need to do so. The second considers what power, if any, the trial judge has to call a witness to give evidence in the case.

(i)   Matters arising ex improviso

R v Pilcher
(1974) 60 Cr App R 1
Court of Appeal

The appellant was convicted of perjury and sentenced to four years' imprisonment. After the close of the prosecution case and after the case for the defence had proceeded some way, the prosecution applied for leave to call additional witness. The trial judge granted leave, holding that he had a discretion to allow the witness then to be called, if he felt that the interests of justice in a broad sense required that the jury should hear the evidence.

LORD WIDGERY CJ: . . . [A]fter the prosecution had completed their case and after Lilley had finished the presentation of his case, the prosecution on October 16, applied to call an additional witness, a Mrs Oddy. Mrs Oddy was the occupier of the house 120 Tolworth Rise; she had, according to a statement which she made, been present for part of the time on this morning of January 19 when Cockerell, Hansford and Lilley were at her house; indeed, she said she had taken her child to school which she normally did at nine o'clock, and when she got back from having taken her child to school, to her consternation there were three large men in the house; they were the three men to whom I have referred. She gave evidence at the trial to the effect that when she came back at twenty to half past nine Lilley was still there. It was of course an extremely important piece of evidence on the vital question as to whether the parcel had gone in at 0908 or 0809. The prosecution asked leave to call Mrs Oddy on October 16; this was about a month after the trial had begun and about a month before it was to finish, just about midway. Additionally to that, it was considerably after the prosecution had closed its case and indeed when the defence cases were well advanced. In applying for leave to call Mrs Oddy late, that is to say, later than she would normally have been called in accordance with the rules, the Crown accepted that they had had some possibility of appreciating the importance of her evidence at earlier stages in the preparation of the case, but perhaps understandably enough, in what Mr Leary calls the welter of evidence, the fact that Mrs Oddy might be a helpful witness had gone unnoticed even when Mr Cockerell referred to a lady coming back from taking her child to school in his evidence. It was not realised what a potentially important witness she was. It was not until October 12 that a senior police officer went to see Mrs Oddy to find if she had any evidence to give, and he found she had this extremely important evidence to give and which she would give; hence the application of the prosecution to call her late whilst the cases for the respective defendants were in the course of being presented.

The principles about the sequence in which witnesses should be called are perhaps not altogether clear, but there is a helpful passage in the current edition of *Archbold* (38th ed., 1973), para. 586, headed 'Evidence in Rebuttal' which sets out the rules, the general application of which seems to this Court to be proper. The first rule is 'Evidence available to the prosecution *ab initio* the relevance of which does not arise *ex improviso* and which remedies the defect in the prosecution case (is) inadmissible.' For authority for that is cited the case of *Day* (1931) 23 Cr App R 175.

That that is the universal view and has been the universal view for all time is by no means clear. We have been referred by Mr Leary to the case of *Crippen* (1911) 5 Cr App R 260; [1911] 1 KB 149 where a very much more relaxed rule seems to be laid down for the introduction at the judge's discretion of evidence in favour of the prosecution and sought to be called by them after the completion of the prosecution's case. It is clearly established that there are exceptions to the general rule which I have read, and the most important exception is evidence which arises *ex improviso*, evidence which becomes relevant in circumstances which the prosecution could not have foreseen at the time when they presented their case. But in this case it was conceded below that Mrs Oddy's evidence did not arise *ex improviso*, and although Mr Leary has sought to challenge that conclusion in part before us, we are satisfied that the conclusion below that it was not *ex improviso* was right. In deference to Mr Leary's argument I should say Mrs Oddy's statement when eventually obtained was in two parts; the first part concerned what she saw on January 19, the second part related to an incident in which she was invited to identify Mr Lilley, the second part of the statement was unrelated to anything that had gone on in the trial and can be said to be *ex improviso*, but the first part which was the only relevant part was evidence which could have been obtained from her at an earlier stage and which the prosecution, being wise after the event, might have been well advised to obtain at an earlier stage.

The submission before us today is that the learned judge wrongly admitted evidence of Mrs Oddy and consequently the convictions in respect of those two counts 7 and 8 should be set aside. At the hearing of submissions on this point in the Court below the learned judge was apprised of all the authorities and he took the view that, if the interests of justice in a broad sense required that the jury should hear Mrs Oddy's evidence, that that would suffice to enable him to give leave for that evidence to be called. We think with all deference to the learned trial judge that that was putting the test on much too wide a basis. Almost any additional relevant evidence will be of value to a jury, and if the only question one had to ask oneself was: was justice more likely to be done if the jury heard this evidence, the results might well be almost any fact arising late in a trial would be let in by an ever-widening door. It is clear that is not the practice in our Courts. The rule that the prosecution must finish their case once and for all before the defence starts is a very important and salutary rule. It means that the defence does not have to meet the case until it has seen the whole case, and, if the rule were as wide as the learned judge stated in this case, the conclusion would be very far-reaching and very undesirable. We do not say that in cases like the present where the matter has not arisen *ex improviso* the judge had no kind of discretion at all, but we are firmly of opinion that in cases where the matter does not arise *ex improviso* the judge's discretion should not be exercised to allow the late introduction of an additional witness called for the prosecution whose evidence was available before the case for the prosecution closed. One must have sympathy with overworked prosecution solicitors in long cases of this kind, but it seems to me in the interests of finality and in the interests of fairness to the defence one must take a strict line not to let in prosecution evidence coming in late in the proceedings if it is outside the *ex improviso* rule. It certainly cannot be admitted merely on the broad basis applied by the trial judge in the present instance, and we have therefore come to the conclusion that he admitted the evidence of Mrs Oddy wrongly.

What is the consequence? In the Criminal Appeal Act 1968, section 2, the Court is enjoined to allow an appeal if they think that there has been a material irregularity in the course of the trial. From what I have already said it must be obvious we think there was a material irregularity in the course of the trial. The quashing of the conviction would therefore follow subject to the proviso to the same section which is very well known, but I must read it: 'Provided that the Court may, notwithstanding that they are of opinion that the point raised in the appeal might be decided in favour of the appellant, dismiss the appeal if they consider that no miscarriage of justice has actually occurred,' in other words we have to ask ourselves whether to operate that proviso on the footing that despite the irregularity below, no actual miscarriage of justice has occurred. There is no lack of authority on how we are supposed to exercise that jurisdiction either, and it probably suffices if I refer to the case of *Brown* (1971) 55 Cr App R 478, which is accepted by Mr Leary as correctly stating the law, and is I think acceptable to the argument put forward on behalf of these applicants.

In a judgment of Cairns LJ he sums up the question of the application of the proviso by saying at p. 484: 'We approach the question whether or not it is our duty to apply the proviso here by considering whether the evidence was overwhelming and whether a jury properly directed in this case could have come to any other verdict than that of Guilty.'

The same point has been made in different language over and over again. It simply means that the Court must not apply the proviso unless it is quite clear that in the absence of the irregularity the consequence of the case would have been the same, and the final question for us is whether this is such a case.

We have come to the conclusion that we ought to apply the proviso here, because when one has regard to the meticulous evidence of Cockerell and Hansford, the care which they obviously exercised in the compilation of that evidence and the notes which Cockerell took at the same time, we find it quite impossible to believe that any jury would have any doubt that the time when the parcel went into No. 120 Tolworth Rise was eight minutes past nine and not nine minutes past eight. It seems to us quite incredible, if Mr Cockerell was accepted as an honest witness, that, as he obviously was, he should have made an error of that kind and stuck to it throughout the proceedings. We think therefore, if one had disregarded Mrs Oddy and her late evidence, the conclusion must have been the same that there was a conviction on counts 7 and 8. It follows from that that on all the counts giving rise to convictions the applications for leave to appeal against convictions must fail.

R v Day
[1940] 1 All ER 402
Court of Criminal Appeal

HILBERY J: In this case, the appellant was convicted on two counts of an indictment which charged him with forging a banker's cheque and causing £5, the proceeds of that cheque, to be paid over. He was sentenced to 18 months' imprisonment with hard labour, and he now appeals on certificate against conviction.

. . . When the case for the defence was closed on the Saturday of the trial, the judge adjourned the case, and, in adjourning it, said this:

> I shall adjourn the case at this point until 11 o'clock on Monday morning. In the meantime the prosecution can consider whether they will or will not make an application to me for leave to tender further evidence, always remembering that, before such an application can be made, notice of any proposed additional evidence must be served upon the defence.

Then, turning to the jury, the judge said:

> I think it is better that we should have this case properly investigated.

On the Monday morning, the prosecution asked permission of the court to call additional evidence, that is to say, the evidence of a handwriting expert to say that there were similarities between the known genuine handwriting of the appellant and the handwriting of the signature on the cheque in question. Counsel for the defence took this objection to that course:

> In my submission, this is a case in which both the prosecution and the defence have closed their case, and nothing has arisen *ex improviso* which could justify the calling of fresh evidence.

It is true to say that he added the words 'by your Lordship,' who, in the discussion which took place, made it clear that the principle applied whether the fresh evidence was to be called by the court or by the prosecution. The judge overruled that objection and admitted the evidence. In the result, the accused was convicted.

We think that the law is now well decided. It is true to say that, if a question as to the time at which evidence is to be received arises in the course of the trial, it may be that the judge may be called upon to decide the appropriate time, and, in so doing, exercise a judicial discretion. However, this was not such a case. This was a case where all that was being done was to seek to remedy an obvious deficiency in the evidence in support of the case for the prosecution, not only after the case for the prosecution had been closed, but also after the evidence for the defence had been heard, and it was an endeavour to call that supplementary evidence, although the material upon which that evidence was to be given had been in the hands of the prosecution from the beginning. It was evidence upon one branch of the prosecution's case, upon which it must have been realised that they must give positive evidence.

The law has been laid down and expounded in *R v Harris* where it is said, at p. 594:

> But it is obvious that injustice may be done to an accused person unless some limitation is put upon the exercise of that right, and for the purpose of this case we adopt the rule laid down by Tindal, CJ, in *R v Frost* (1839) 4 St Tr NS 85 where Tindal, CJ, said: 'There is no doubt that the general rule is that where the Crown begins its case like a plaintiff in a civil suit, they cannot afterwards support their case by calling fresh witnesses, because they are met by certain evidence that contradicts it. They stand or fall by the evidence they have given. They must close their case before the defence begins; but if any matter arises *ex improviso*, which no human ingenuity can foresee, on the part of a defendant in a civil suit, or a prisoner in a criminal case, there seems to me no reason why that matter which so arose *ex improviso* may not be answered by contrary evidence on the part of the Crown.' That rule applies only to a witness called by the Crown and on behalf of the Crown, but we think that the rule should also apply to a case where a witness is called in a criminal trial by the judge after the case for the defence is closed,

Counsel for the prosecution sought to say that the rule relied upon for the appellant was confined to cases in which the fresh evidence was being called by the judge, but that passage answers that contention and makes the rule apply to evidence called on behalf of the Crown and by the judge. The judge continued, at p. 595:

> and that the practice should be limited to a case where a matter arises *ex improviso*, which no human ingenuity can foresee, on the part of a prisoner, otherwise injustice would ensue.

In other words, the principle is to be applied whether the witness is called by the court or by the Crown. Now that case has been followed and that principle applied twice in this court. It was applied in the case of *R v McMahon*, and that passage to which I have referred was there again quoted by Lord Hewart, LCJ, who gave the judgment in that case, and after quoting that passage, and immediately after the words

. . . but in order that injustice should not be done to an accused person, a Judge should not call a witness in a criminal trial after the case for the defence is closed except 'in a case where a matter arises *ex improviso*, which no human ingenuity can foresee, on the part of the prisoner, otherwise injustice would ensue,'

added these words at p. 97:

Now in our opinion those conditions were not fulfilled with regard to these witnesses and it follows that the evidence of these six witnesses was, in our view, wrongly admitted.

If those words are applied to the case which we have now under consideration, it becomes manifest, I think, that those conditions were not fulfilled in this case. First, the matter whether this handwriting was the handwriting of the appellant — that is, whether his was the hand which wrote the forgery with which he was charged — was a question about which from the outset the burden had been upon the prosecution to show that the handwriting was that of the appellant. It was, therefore, evidence concerning material which had been in the hands of the prosecution before the case was heard, and it was evidence the necessity of which was obvious from the start. Indeed, the judge had no hesitation in saying that, without it, it was impossible to ask the jury to act as handwriting experts and to pass a verdict which might be a conviction. It cannot be said, in the circumstances, that this evidence was evidence upon any matter which arose *ex improviso*, if those Latin words are given the meaning which was originally attributed to them. Nor can it be said that it was evidence the necessity of which no human ingenuity could foresee. It was evidence the necessity of which was obvious. In addition, in this case, the unfortunate thing is that, in the view of the judge at the trial, unless that evidence was given, there was no corroboration of the evidence of the accomplice whose evidence had been given for the prosecution. It was obvious from the course of the trial that the evidence of the accomplice was not such as the jury could reasonably be expected to accept if it stood alone, and, in our view, without the evidence, which was wrongly admitted, it seems probable that the jury must have acquitted.

That is sufficient to dispose of the matter, but how unfortunate it would be if such a practice as this were allowed to grow up is well instanced and explained by Lord Hewart, LCJ, in another case in which this principle was being applied, *R v Liddle*, at p. 13:

Nothing had suddenly emerged which required the calling of witnesses, and the circumstances in which the witnesses were called were such as gravely to imperil the defence and put the defence to an unfair disadvantage. [I have pointed out that in the circumstances the wrongful admission of the evidence destroyed a defence which otherwise probably would have succeeded.] If the same reasoning were to apply, it would have been perfectly open for the defendant, on the second of these adjourned hearings, to require a further adjournment in order that he might call, in his turn, rebutting evidence, and so the inquiry might wander on indefinitely.

In this case, it would have been open to counsel for the prisoner to ask for a further adjournment on his side, so that he might have an opportunity of consulting a handwriting expert and, perhaps, of calling that handwriting expert on another occasion. The eventuality of experts differing is not unheard of, and so the inquiry might have wandered on. In our view, the necessary conditions which had to be fulfilled before this evidence could be admitted were not fulfilled, and it is impossible to say that, if they had been fulfilled, the verdict of the jury would have been the same. The appeal is allowed and the conviction quashed.

Question

If the aim of the courts is to dispense justice, why should a party who has closed his case ever be prevented from calling another witness whose evidence might be vital?

(ii)   The judge's power to call a witness

R v Tregear
[1967] 2 QB 574
Court of Appeal

The appellant had been convicted of riot and wounding with intent for which he was sentenced to a total of four years' imprisonment. He appealed, *inter alia*, on the ground that the trial judge had erred in calling a further witness at the conclusion of the defence case.

DAVIES LJ: . . . What is submitted is that there is an inflexible rule that in no circumstances whatever may a judge call a witness after the close of the case for the defence. That proposition is supported by a citation of a number of authorities which at first sight do lend support to the existence of such a general rule. I would only refer to two of them. In the first, *Rex v Harris*, Avory J said:

> The two questions for this court are, was the course taken of calling Benton at the stage at which he was called in accordance with the recognised rules, and assuming that it was, was there a proper direction on the corroboration of accomplices? It is clear from the cases that only in a criminal case may the judge call a witness at all, but in no case is there a definite rule at what stage he may do so. But it is obvious that injustice may be done to a defendant unless some limitation is put on the power, and for this case we adopt the words of Tindal CJ (cited *Sullivan* (above) from *Frost*): 'Where the Crown begins its case like a plaintiff in a civil suit, they cannot afterwards support their case by calling fresh witnesses because they are met by certain evidence that contradicts it. They stand or fall by the evidence they have given. They must close their case before the defence begins; but if any matter arises ex improviso, which no human ingenuity can foresee, on the part of a defendant in a civil suit, or a prisoner in a criminal case, there seems to me no reason why that matter which so arose ex improviso may not be answered by contrary evidence on the part of the Crown.' That passage only applies to the Crown, but it should also apply to the judge who calls a witness, i.e., after the close of the case for the defence fresh evidence is limited to something arising ex improviso. Bramwell B acted on this principle in *Reg. v Haynes*. A further objection in this case (and this seems to me to be a most important point in the decision in *Harris*) is that Benton was present in the dock throughout, and no doubt understood that he was asked to supplement the case against this appellant; moreover, he was then unsentenced, and therefore had everything to expect from the judge. In these circumstances (and mark these words) and without laying it down that in no circumstances may an additional witness be called by the judge after the close of the defence, we think that in this case it was irregular, and calculated to do an injustice to this appellant.

That, as indicated by the judgment, was an odd case. The man Benton had pleaded guilty, but for some reason had not been sent down to the cells and had remained sitting in the dock listening to all the evidence. Then, after the defence was closed, the recorder himself called him as a witness for the prosecution; and, being unsentenced, the witness probably thought that the better the evidence he gave for the prosecution, the lighter the sentence he would get from the court.

While appreciating the weight of the observations there and in other cases, that case is not one (indeed the last words of the judgment which I have read indicate this) which says that in all circumstances and in all cases a judge may not call a witness.

The second case to which I would refer is *Rex v McMahon*, from which I will quote a passage which refers back to another authority. Lord Hewart CJ said:

As was said by this court in *Rex v Liddle*: 'A judge at a criminal trial has the right to call a witness not called by either the prosecution or the defence, without the consent of either the prosecution or the defence, if in his opinion that course is necessary in the interests of justice, but in order that injustice should not be done to an accused person, a judge should not call a witness in a criminal trial after the case for the defence is closed, except in a case where a matter arises ex improviso, which no human ingenuity can foresee, on the part of the prisoner, otherwise injustice would ensue.' Now in our opinion those conditions were not fulfilled with regard to these witnesses and it follows that the evidence of these six witnesses was, in our view, wrongly admitted.

That is applying a general approach to the matter without any reference to any particular circumstances of any particular case.

In our view the present case does not fall within the ambit of the general rule. Here the defence, who had been insisting on the calling of these two witnesses, had called the witness Chown but chose not to call Jarman. The judge, I suppose, if he wanted to avoid calling Jarman at the close of the defence, could have taken one of two courses. He could have interrupted the evidence of the appellant, and then, or else immediately the last question had been put to Chown and before the defence had closed its case, he could have called Jarman. But he did not. In our view this case falls outside the application of the general rule owing to the fact that here, as is, I think, apparent, the judge was not seeking to supplement the prosecution by calling this witness Jarman. Chown had been called by the defence, who had submitted that both should be called as witnesses for the prosecution. The judge considered it right, not in order to supplement the evidence for the prosecution, but to ascertain the truth and put all the evidence before the jury, that this witness should be called by him and subjected to cross-examination by counsel for the prosecution and for the defence. In the event cross-examination by counsel for the defence was more in the nature of re-examination, since this witness was wholly favourable to the defence. Thus Chown and Jarman were both called, and the jury rejected their evidence.

It is difficult, I think, in the circumstances of this case to accept the submission of Mr Worsley that this was a matter ex improviso, the surprise being that Jarman was not called by the defence. But we accept his contention that in the circumstances of this case there was no objection to the calling of Jarman by the judge. Therefore, in our judgment the second contention on the part of the appellant with regard to his conviction fails like the first.

Fenton Atkinson J reminds me that I might add to what I have already said, in expressing the view of the court about this appeal against conviction, that even if we had come to another conclusion on these technical points — and I use the word technical not in any offensive sense — which have been raised in support of the appeal, this, in our view, is a case which would clearly fall within the proviso, that is to say, a case in which there was no miscarriage of justice.

[His Lordship then considered the appeal against sentence, which was dismissed.]

R v Cleghorn
[1967] 2 QB 584
Court of Appeal

LORD PARKER CJ: At the Central Criminal Court in July, 1966, the defendant was convicted of rape, and sentenced to six years' imprisonment. He now appeals to this court against his conviction. Having regard to the point raised in the case, it is unnecessary to go through the facts in any detail. The prosecution case was that a young French au pair girl of 19 called Martine had been raped by the defendant on the evening of March 4 of last year.

The case against him rested on the evidence of Martine and a friend of hers, another girl called Therese. According to them, they had been to a club called The Europa Club in Finchley Road, they met the defendant and a man called Geoff Thompson, and that after some time there they had gone away in a car and had finally ended up at the defendant's flat. As to what took place there, Martine and the other girl maintained that the defendant's manner changed, that he started making obscene jokes, that he ordered Thompson and Therese into another room, producing a gun which later proved to be a toy gun, that he then made Martine undress and raped her twice.

At an early stage in the case the judge was clearly concerned whether any of the parties were going to call Geoff Thompson, and before the prosecution case had ended he said:

I shall wait with interest to see what evidence the defence call and whether Geoff is called, but if, at the end of the case for the prosecution and the defence, Geoff is not called by either side, I shall have to consider whether I, as the judge presiding over this court, shall not exercise my undoubted right to have Geoff in the witness box.

In due course the defence opened and closed their case, the defendant alone being called. The judge meanwhile had issued a subpoena to Geoff Thompson. Finally the judge said:

In the circumstances, as neither the prosecution nor the defence have seen fit to call Thompson, I think in the interests of justice it is only right that the witness Thompson should be called to give evidence, so the jury can form some conclusion as to his reliability.

Thereupon Thompson was called and examined by the court, and was cross-examined by both the prosecution and the defence. His evidence, if believed, strongly supported the prosecution's case.

The first and main ground of appeal here, and the only one with which the court finds it necessary to deal, is the submission that the judge should not have called this witness, as he did, at the end of the defendant's case.

It is abundantly clear that a judge in a criminal case where the liberty of the subject is at stake and where the sole object of the proceedings is to make certain that justice should be done as between the subject and the state should have a right to call a witness who has not been called by either party. It is clear, of course, that the discretion to call such a witness should be carefully exercised, and indeed, as was said in *Reg. v Edwards* by Erle J:

There are, no doubt, cases in which a judge might think it a matter of justice so to interfere; but, generally speaking, we ought to be careful not to overrule the discretion of counsel, who are, of course, more fully aware of the facts of the case than we can be.

There clearly are, however, cases in which the judge is justified in calling a witness. In *Reg.* v. *Oliva*, dealing with the failure of the prosecution to call or to tender for cross-examination a witness whose name was on the back of the indictment, the court said:

> If the prosecution appear to be exercising that discretion improperly, it is open to the judge of trial to interfere and in his discretion in turn to invite the prosecution to call a particular witness, and if they refuse there is the ultimate sanction in the judge himself calling that witness.

However, when dealing with a case such as this in which the witness is only called at the end of the defendant's case, the court has sought to ensure that that should only be done in cases where no injustice or prejudice could be caused to a defendant, and for that purpose laid down a rule of practice that in general it should only be done where some matter arises ex improviso. The first case dealing with this matter is *Rex* v *Harris*. Giving the judgment of the court Avory J said:

> It is true that in none of the cases has any rule been laid down limiting the point in the proceedings at which the judge may exercise that right. But it is obvious that injustice may be done to an accused person unless some limitation is put on the exercise of that right, and for the purpose of this case we adopt the rule laid down by Tindal CJ in *Reg.* v *Frost*.

The passage that Avory J then read was dealing with the right of a plaintiff to call evidence at the end of the defendant's case, which, of course, is permissible only where a matter does arise ex improviso which no human ingenuity could foresee. Avory J continued:

> That rule applies only to a witness called by the Crown and on behalf of the Crown, but we think that the rule should also apply to a case where a witness is called in a criminal trial by the judge after the case for the defence is closed, and that the practice

I emphasise 'practice'

> should be limited to a case where a matter arises ex improviso, which no human ingenuity can foresee, on the part of a prisoner, otherwise injustice would ensue.

That rule of practice has been adopted and approved first in *Rex* v *Liddle* and finally in *Rex* v *McMahon*. It is to be observed that Avory J in *Rex* v *Harris* said:

> In the circumstances, without laying down that in no case can an additional witness be called by the judge at the close of the trial after the case for the defence has been closed, we are of opinion that in this particular case the course that was adopted was irregular, and was calculated to do injustice to the appellant Harris.

There may, as Avory J said, be cases where it would not be right to be bound by the general practice to which he had referred, and in a recent case before another court of the Criminal Division of the Court of Appeal, as recently as February 17, 1967, *Reg.* v *Tregear* [1967] 2 QB 574, the court held that in the particular circumstances of that case, they ought not to treat themselves as bound by that general rule of practice. The special circumstances of that case were that the defence had been urging that the prosecution should call two witnesses; the prosecution did not call those two witnesses and the defence in fact called one and only one of them. It was in those circumstances that the judge, who incidentally was the same judge as in the present case, felt that it was right that he should call the other witness as a witness of the court. The Court of Appeal in *Reg.* v *Tregear* upheld his conduct in calling that witness, but upheld it on the basis, as this court understands it, that it was really at the request of the defence that the witness was to be called. It is to be noted in that connection that in those circumstances there was no question whatever of the trial having been continued by the calling of or recalling of witnesses.

The court, however, in the present case, can find no sufficient ground for departing from the general rule of practice laid down in the cases to which I have referred. In particular, it is to be observed that once the judge in this case had called Geoff Thompson, it became necessary for much more to be done; the defendant himself had to be recalled, counsel had to take further instructions, in fact two further defence witnesses were called who otherwise would not have been called, and the trial took on a completely different aspect.

While recognising that this rule of practice is only a general rule, and that there may be occasions to depart from it, this court can see no ground in the present case for so departing. Accordingly, the court has come to the conclusion, though it confesses with some reluctance, that this is a case in which the conviction must be quashed. So far therefore as this case is concerned at any rate, the prisoner is discharged.

Questions

1. Why should the judge's power to call a witness be used sparingly and only where it is necessary in the interests of justice?

2. You are acting for Albert, a plaintiff who is claiming damages for injuries sustained in a road accident. The evidence in your possession is as follows: Albert was riding a bicycle along a country road near Barton; he knew nothing of the accident and was unconscious for several days afterwards. Bernard, accompanied by his wife, Celia, was driving his car on the same road: after overtaking Albert, he saw in his mirror a blue car driving rapidly behind him; it knocked Albert off his bicycle; the blue car overtook Bernard. Bernard stopped his car, told Celia to take the number of the blue car, and went to look after Albert. Sergeant Douglas accompanied by Edward, a police cadet, arrived about ten minutes later: Celia, in the presence of Bernard, told the police that the blue car's number was ABC 123V, and Douglas wrote this in his notebook. Douglas and Edward ascertained that the car was owned by a partnership, Fred and George, and they visited the premises later that day: Fred was in the office: he said that he had been in the office all day, but that George had been to visit a client in Barton: later George arrived, and said that he had been out, but in the firm's other car, XYZ 789W, and had not been to Barton: he also said that there was another car in the neighbourhood, ACB 122W, which was sometimes mistaken for theirs; the officers examined ABC 123V which was old and battered. Douglas took a note of the interview: after returning to the police station, Edward copied out Douglas' note. Douglas later decided that there was insufficient evidence to prosecute George and destroyed his note.

Albert is suing George, whose insurers maintain that he was not driving near Barton that day, and that the accident was probably caused by Bernard. You are aware that Bernard was convicted on a charge of fraud some years ago, but do not know if the insurers are aware of this. Albert's medical consultant says that Albert's condition is unusually complex, and that he would have difficulty in explaining this to the court without reference to medical textbooks and statistical tables. Discuss.

3.   You are acting for Harry, a young man of previous good character, who is charged with raping Irene on the night of the 1/2 August.

The prosecution are proposing to call the following witnesses:

(a)   Irene, who will say that she spent the evening of 1 August drinking with Harry and Jack in the Jolly Sailor; Harry was pestering her all evening and after Jack left at about 10 p.m. Harry enticed her outside and raped her.

(b)   Jack, who will say that he and Irene and Harry were drinking together and that Harry was chatting Irene up; he was anxious about leaving Irene and Harry together, but he had to leave at 10 p.m. because his mother got worried if he was late.

(c)   Mrs Knowles, Irene's mother, who will say that Irene arrived home at 2 a.m. on the 2 August in a state of distress and said that Harry had raped her.

(d)   Dr Lambert, who will say that he examined Irene on the 2 August and found evidence of recent intercourse.

(e)   Detective Constable Michael who will say that he interviewed Harry briefly on the 2 August, and that Harry made a statement admitting having intercourse with Irene, but saying that it was with her consent.

Harry has told you that he had been having intercourse with Irene on a regular basis and always with her consent; he says that she has been with all the lads in town. He admits making a statement to DC Michael, but says that the interview lasted an hour and that DC Michael was scribbling in his notebook the whole time. You have taken a statement from Jack, who has told you that while they were in the Jolly Sailor, Irene was egging Harry on; he left at 10 p.m. because he thought they wanted to be left alone together; when asked why he had given the police a different story, he told you that his father was in trouble, and he didn't want to make things worse. You also have on file a statement from Norman whom you previously represented on a charge of unlawful intercourse with Olive, a 15-year-old friend of Irene: Norman pleaded guilty but he told you that he had regularly been having intercourse with Irene, and had only had intercourse with Olive because Irene had told him 'It was time Olive learnt how to do it'. Your clerk has seen Mrs Knowles and, although he cannot be sure, he thinks he has recognised her as a woman who previously lived with a scrap-metal dealer called Peters under the name of Mrs Peters and had a series of convictions for handling stolen metal.

How will you conduct Harry's defence?

Further Reading
P. Murphy, *A Practical Approach to Evidence*, 4th ed. (1992), Chs 13 and 14
Z. Adler, 'Rape — the intention of parliament and the practice of the courts' (1982) 45 MLR 664
D.W. Elliott, 'Rape complainants' sexual experience with third parties' [1984] Crim LR 4
J. Temkin, 'Regulating sexual evidence history: the limits of discretionary legislation' (1984) 47 MLR 625
A.A.S. Zuckerman, *Principles of Criminal Evidence* (1989), Ch. 7

6 CORROBORATION

Corroboration is evidence which tends to confirm or support some fact of which other evidence is also given. If W1 testifies as to fact X and W2 also testifies as to fact X then, assuming the evidence of both is accepted, corroboration is present. As a general proposition, it is true to say that the law does not require corroboration to found a conviction or to enter a judgment. There are, however, a number of situations where corroboration may be required either as a matter of law or as a matter of practice.

At the time of writing, the law is about to undergo substantial change. The Criminal Justice and Public Order Bill 1994 contains clauses which will abrogate the present need for a trial judge to warn the jury of the dangers of acting on the uncorroborated evidence of certain classes of witness (see (B) (*i*) and (*ii*) below). This reform is also expected, at least by the Law Commission, to have the additional effect of abrogating the technical meaning ascribed to the nature of corroboration and what may constitute corroborative evidence. The Bill also contains clauses abolishing the need for corroboration as a matter of law for those offences committed under certain sections of the Sexual Offences Act 1956 (see (A) below).

Essentially, these reforms will free judges from the present obligation they have to warn juries of the danger of acting on the uncorroborated evidence of certain types of witness. Similarly, they will be freed from the consequential obligation to identify for the jury what kinds of evidence may, as a matter of law, amount to corroboration. The judge will therefore be left with a discretion to warn the jury of any particular weaknesses in the prosecution case as befits the particular facts, and this might well include warning the jury of any inherent dangers the judge perceives to be present in the evidence of a particular class of witness (see *R* v *Beck* and *R* v *Spencer* at B (*iii*) below).

The net result of these reforms will be to render much of the existing law on corroboration redundant. Until the new law comes into force, however, the existing rules will still apply. In other words, judges will, for the time being, be obliged to warn juries in certain cases of the dangers of acting on the uncorroborated evidence of particular witnesses, as well as having to go on to identify for their benefit any items of evidence present in the case which the law allows to be considered as corroborative evidence. Consequently, this chapter addresses both the existing law and the law as it will be should the relevant clauses of the Bill, as seems highly likely, reach the statute book unamended. However, in anticipation of the proposed reforms becoming law during 1994, the treatment given to the existing law will be kept to a minimum.

(A)   Corroboration required as a matter of law

Perjury Act 1911

13.   Corroboration
A person shall not be liable to be convicted of any offence against this Act, or of any offence declared by any other Act to be perjury or subornation of perjury, or to be punishable as perjury or subornation of perjury, solely upon the evidence of one witness as to the falsity of any statement alleged to be false.

R v Rider
(1986) 83 Cr App R 207
Court of Appeal

MUSTILL LJ: After a trial at the Central Criminal Court Theresa Ann Rider was convicted on a single count of perjury and received a sentence of six months' imprisonment. Against this conviction she now appeals by leave of the single judge.

The facts may be stated briefly. During 1979 the appellant married Neil Rider. The marriage encountered difficulties. The appellant twice left her husband to live with Alan Dean but returned on each occasion to her husband. Latterly the couple visited Dean's parents and an agreement was reached whereby Dean would for the time being cease to see the appellant: that the couple would see a marriage guidance counsellor, and that, if after six months matters had not worked out, a divorce would be considered. The couple did in fact go to see a marriage counsellor on occasions between January 20 and April 3, 1983 and continued to live together until October, 1983.

Meanwhile on some unknown date probably during March, 1983 the appellant had brought into existence a petition for divorce. There was also brought into existence a document headed, 'Acknowledgment of Service — Respondent Spouse.' The first four questions in the form received handwritten answers as follows:

1.   Have you received the petition for divorce delivered with this form? Yes.
2.   On what date and at what address did you receive it? On the 24 day of February (*sic*) 1983 at 63 Chadwell Ave, Cheshunt.
3.   Are you the person named as the Respondent in the Petition? Yes.
4.   Do you intend to defend the case? No.

In the space for a signature were written the words, 'Neil Rider', followed by the same address in Cheshunt as was given in the fourth answer.

The appellant lodged this document with Edmonton County Court together with an affidavit verifying the petition and giving some particulars of the husband's behaviour to which she took exception. The document read:

I Theresa Ann Rider . . . make oath and say as follows: 1. I am the petitioner in this cause. 2 . . . . 3. I identify the signature Neil Rider appearing on the copy acknowledgment of service now produced to me and marked 'A' as the signature of my husband, the respondent in the cause.

The document concluded with a jurat in common form.

On May 20, 1983 the matter came before the County Court judge at Edmonton and a decree nisi was pronounced, there being no appearance by the husband. In due course the decree was made absolute on October 5, 1983. A copy of the decree absolute was then sent to the husband.

According to the husband, this came as a complete surprise. He had had no idea that his wife had filed divorce proceedings against him whilst they were living in the same house. He had not received the petition nor had he signed nor even seen the acknowledgment of service. This discovery led to an investigation by the police and ultimately to the indictment of the appellant on a single count under section 1(1) of the Perjury Act 1911, which provides: 'If any person lawfully sworn as a witness . . . in a judicial proceeding wilfully makes a statement material in the proceeding which he knows to be false or does not believe to be true, he shall be guilty of perjury . . .' Subsection (3) of section 1 prescribes that a statement made on oath for the purposes of a judicial proceeding before a person authorised by law to administer an oath and to record or authenticate the statement shall be treated as having been made in a judicial proceeding. The affidavit of the appellant verifying the purported signature of the husband was thus to be treated as a statement in her divorce proceedings.

The particulars of the offence as laid in the indictment read:

Theresa Ann Rider on the 21st day of March 1983 being the petitioner in divorce proceedings instituted in the Edmonton County Court wilfully made a statement material in the said proceeding which she knew to be false or did not believe to be true, namely that the signature on the copy acknowledgment of service was that of her husband Neil Rider.

At the trial the husband gave evidence on the lines already summarised. No other direct evidence, such as from a handwriting expert, was called to show that the signature of the acknowledgment of service was not that of the husband. There were, however, a number of witnesses who testified that (a) the appellant had used words tantamount to an admission of obtaining a divorce behind her husband's back and (b) the couple had been on holiday together only four days before the decree was made absolute and had been on cordial terms inconsistent with an immediately impending dissolution of their marriage.

In his direction the trial judge laid the evidence before the jury in a way to which no exception could be taken. It is, however, urged that the direction was fatally flawed because the learned judge did not refer the jury to section 13 to the Perjury Act, which is in the following terms: 'A person shall not be liable to be convicted of any offence under this Act . . . solely upon the evidence of one witness as to the falsity of any statement alleged to be false.' By analogy with the cases where the law requires corroboration of a complainant's evidence it is maintained that a failure to draw the attention of the jury to this requirement amounts to a material misdirection, even though evidence in support of that given by the husband was in fact led by the prosecution.

Stated in this bald way, the proposition is, in our view, unsound. As Mr Heslop pointed out on behalf of the prosecution, section 13 is concerned with the evidence which must be called to establish that the statement alleged by the prosecution to be false is in fact false. The subsection says nothing about the manner of establishing the defendant's knowledge or belief, and no amount of evidence on this aspect of the offence can save the conviction if the evidence that the statement was untrue does not meet the demands of the statute. Conversely, if section 13 is complied with the presence or absence of corroborative evidence as to the defendant's state of mind is immaterial.

. . . The problem is to apply these principles to the present case. Although the indictment, which followed the wording of the Act, was wide enough to embrace an allegation that the appellant was guilty whether her affidavit was true or not, there is no doubt that the prosecution set out to prove that it was untrue. Thus there was a need for more than one witness to prove the untruth and a corresponding need for a direction on the subject, unless it can fairly be said no longer to have been in issue when the time came for the judge to direct the jury.

Unfortunately, it is impossible now to reconstruct with certainty what happened at the trial. It is known that the husband was not cross-examined with specific reference to his evidence that the signature on the acknowledgment of service was not his; but the veracity of the whole of his story was, of course, put in issue as the central point of the case. In addition, there was a discussion between the learned judge and counsel for the defence, not transcribed for this Court, to the effect that it was not part of the defendant's case to assert affirmatively that the signature was that of the husband. In these circumstances it is not, in our view, possible to hold that the truthfulness of the statement had ceased to be an issue in the case.

We are thus constrained to hold that there should have been a direction on section 13. Such a direction could have been brief and could legitimately have drawn attention to the other evidence adduced by the prosecution (the truthfulness of which the jury would in any event have had to assess in relation to the case as a whole) and to the absence of any positive evidence directed to show that the signature was that of the husband. Nevertheless, brief though it could properly have been, the absence of any direction at all amounted to a material irregularity.

We therefore turn to consider whether the Court should apply the proviso to section 2(1) of the Criminal Appeal Act 1968. In this context careful note must be taken of the observations in *Hamid* (1979) 69 Cr App R 324, regarding the application of the proviso in a perjury case where there was a failure to give a direction concerning section 13. There must, however, be cases where the proviso can properly be applied, and we have no doubt that this is such a case. The prosecution alleged that the appellant had engineered the divorce behind the husband's back, and that the obtaining of a false signature was part of an unbroken course of conduct which concealed from him that his marriage was in the course of being dissolved. The appellant maintained that he knew all about it but was pretending to relatives that no proceedings were afoot. The case on each side and the evidence in support of it was all of a piece and stood or fell together. The jury accepted the case for the prosecution. We think it inconceivable that if the jury had been given a short direction on section 13 they would not have found in the other evidence led by the prosecution sufficient material to corroborate the evidence of the husband on a matter which was only technically in issue.

Accordingly this appeal must be dismissed.

Road Traffic Regulation Act 1984

89. Speeding offences generally

(1) A person who drives a motor vehicle on a road at a speed exceeding a limit imposed by or under any enactment to which this section applies shall be guilty of an offence.

(2) A person prosecuted for such an offence shall not be liable to be convicted solely on the evidence of one witness to the effect that, in the opinion of the witness, the person prosecuted was driving the vehicle at a speed exceeding a specified limit.

Sexual Offences Act 1956

2. Procurement of woman by threats

(1) It is an offence for a person to procure a woman, by threats or intimidation, to have unlawful sexual intercourse in any part of the world.

(2) A person shall not be convicted of an offence under this section on the evidence of one witness only, unless the witness is corroborated in some material particular by evidence implicating the accused.

3. Procurement of woman by false pretences

(1) It is an offence for a person to procure a woman, by false pretences or false representations, to have unlawful sexual intercourse in any part of the world.

(2) A person shall not be convicted of an offence under this section on the evidence of one witness only, unless the witness is corroborated in some material particular by evidence implicating the accused.

4. Administering drugs to obtain or facilitate intercourse

(1) It is an offence for a person to apply or administer to, or cause to be taken by, a woman any drug, matter or thing with intent to stupefy or overpower her so as thereby to enable any man to have unlawful sexual intercourse with her.

(2) A person shall not be convicted of an offence under this section on the evidence of one witness only, unless the witness is corroborated in some material particular by evidence implicating the accused.

22. Causing prostitution of women

(1) It is an offence for a person —

(a) to procure a woman to become, in any part of the world, a common prostitute; or

(b) to procure a woman to leave the United Kingdom, intending her to become an inmate of or frequent a brothel elsewhere; or

(c) to procure a woman to leave her usual place of abode in the United Kingdom, intending her to become an inmate of or frequent a brothel in any part of the world for the purposes of prostitution.

(2) A person shall not be convicted of an offence under this section on the evidence of one witness only, unless the witness is corroborated in some material particular by evidence implicating the accused.

23. Procuration of girl under twenty-one

(1) It is an offence for a person to procure a girl under the age of twenty-one to have unlawful sexual intercourse in any part of the world with a third person.

(2) A person shall not be convicted of an offence under this section on the evidence of one witness only, unless the witness is corroborated in some material particular by evidence implicating the accused.

Criminal Justice and Public Order Bill 1994

26. Abolition of corroboration requirements under Sexual Offences Act 1956
    (1) The following provisions of the Sexual Offences Act 1956 (which provide that a person shall not be convicted of the offence concerned on the evidence of one witness only unless the witness is corroborated) are hereby repealed —
    (a)   section 2(2) (procurement of woman by threats),
    (b)   section 3(2) (procurement of woman by false pretences),
    (c)   section 4(2) (administering drugs to obtain or facilitate intercourse),
    (d)   section 22(2) (causing prostitution of women), and
    (e)   section 23(2) (procuration of girl under twenty-one).
    (2)   Nothing in this section applies in relation to —
    (a)   any trial, or
    (b)   any proceedings before a magistrates' court as examining justices,
which began before the commencement of this section.

Note
The number of cases which require corroboration before a conviction or judgment can be obtained has decreased significantly in modern times. Notably, corroboration requirements in respect of the evidence of children, affiliation proceedings and in certain offences of electoral malpractice have all disappeared in recent years. The new Bill continues this erosion by removing the requirement of corroboration for those offences indicated under the Sexual Offences Act 1956.

Questions
1. Why do (or did) the offences contained in ss. 2, 3, 4, 22 and 23 of the Sexual Offences Act 1956 require corroboration before a conviction can (or could) be obtained?
2. Is it appropriate that the requirement for corroboration is (or has been) removed?

(B) Corroboration required as a matter of practice

In these cases, the court can act on the testimony of one witness without corroboration. What the law actually requires is that the judge warn the jury (or himself) of the desirability of corroboration. The fact that no corroboration exists will not, as a matter of law, prevent the court from finding a defendant guilty. So properly put, what the law actually demands is that in certain cases a warning be given to the jury of the dangers of acting on the uncorroborated evidence in question but, once the warning has been properly given, the jury may convict on that uncorroborated evidence. The categories which attract the mandatory warning follow below, but it is as well to note that there are certain cases falling outside the established categories which also seem to call for some type of corroboration warning.

(i) Accomplices

Davies v Director of Public Prosecutions
[1954] AC 378
House of Lords

The defendant, together with other youths, attacked with their fists another group, one of whom subsequently died from stab wounds inflicted by a knife. Six youths, including the defendant and one Lawson, were charged with murder but finally the defendant alone was convicted. Lawson having been among four against whom no evidence was offered and who were found not guilty of murder but convicted of common assault. At the defendant's trial Lawson gave evidence for the prosecution as to an admission by the defendant of the use of a knife by him but the judge did not warn the jury of the danger of accepting his evidence without corroboration. The defendant's conviction was affirmed by the Court of Criminal Appeal, and he appealed to the House of Lords.

LORD SIMONDS LC: The true rule has been, in my view, accurately formulated by the appellant's counsel in his first three propositions, more particularly in the third. These propositions as amended read as follows:

(1)   In a criminal trial where a person who is an accomplice gives evidence on behalf of the prosecution, it is the duty of the judge to warn the jury that, although they may convict upon his evidence, it is dangerous to do so unless it is corroborated.

(2)   This rule, although a rule of practice, now has the force of a rule of law.

(3)   Where the judge fails to warn the jury in accordance with this rule, the conviction will be quashed, even if in fact there be ample corroboration of the evidence of the accomplice, unless the appellate court can apply the proviso . . .

The rule, it will be observed, applies only to witnesses for the prosecution. The remaining questions, therefore, on the main issue are [w]hat is an 'accomplice' within the rule? And has the rule, on the proper construction of the word 'accomplice' contained in it, any application to Lawson in the present case?

There is in the authorities no formal definition of the term 'accomplice', and your Lordships are forced to deduce a meaning for the word from the cases in which X, Y and Z have been held to be, or held liable to be treated as, accomplices. On the cases it would appear that the following persons, if called as witnesses for the prosecution, have been treated as falling within the category: —

(1)   On any view, persons who are *participes criminis* in respect of the actual crime charged, whether as principals or accessories before or after the fact (in felonies) or persons committing, procuring or aiding and abetting (in the case of misdemeanors). This is surely the natural and primary meaning of the term 'accomplice'. But in two cases, persons falling strictly outside the ambit of this category have, in particular decisions, been held to be accomplices for the purpose of the rule: viz.:

(2)   Receivers have been held to be accomplices of the thieves from whom they receive goods on a trial of the latter for [theft] (*R* v *Jennings* (1912) 7 Cr App R 242: *R* v *Dixon* (1925) 19 Cr App R 36):

(3)   When X has been charged with a specific offence on a particular occasion, and evidence is admissible, and has been admitted, of his having committed crimes of this identical type on other occasions, as proving system and intent and negativing accident; in such cases the court has held that in relation to such other similar offences, if evidence of them were given by parties to them, the evidence of such other parties should not be left to the jury without a warning that it is dangerous to accept it without corroboration. (*R* v *Farid* (1945) 30 Cr App R 168.)

In both of these cases (2) and (3) a person not a party or not necessarily a party to the substantive crime charged was treated as an accomplice for the purpose of the requirement of warning. (I say 'not necessarily' to cover the case of receivers. A receiver may on the facts of a particular case have procured the theft, or aided and abetted it, or may have helped to shield the thief from justice. But he can be a receiver without doing any of these things.) The primary meaning of the term 'accomplice', then, has been extended to embrace these two anomalous cases. In each case there are special circumstances to justify or at least excuse the extension. A receiver is not only committing a crime intimately allied in character with that of theft: he could not commit the crime of receiving at all without the crime of theft having preceded it. The two crimes are in a relationship of 'one-side dependence'. In the case of 'system', the requirement of warning within the special field of similar crimes committed is a logical application within that collateral field of the general principle, though it involves a warning as to the evidence of persons not accomplices to the substantive crime charged.

My Lords, these extensions of the term are imbedded in our case law and it would be inconvenient for any authority other than the legislature to disturb them. Neither of them affects this case. Lawson was not a receiver, nor was there any question of 'system'; Lawson, if he was to be an accomplice at all had to be an accomplice to the crime of murder. I can see no reason for any further extension of the term 'accomplice'. In particular, I can see no reason why, if half a dozen boys fight another crowd, and one of them produces a knife and stabs one of the opponents to death, all the rest of his group should be treated as accomplices in the use of a knife and the infliction of mortal injury by that means, unless there is evidence that the rest intended or concerted or at least contemplated an attack with a knife by one of their number, as opposed to a common assault. If all that was designed or envisaged was in fact a common assault, and there was no evidence that Lawson, a party to that common assault, knew that any of his companions had a knife, then Lawson was not an accomplice in the crime consisting in its felonious use. It should be borne in mind in this connexion that all suggestion of a concerted *felonious* onslaught had, by consent at the instance of counsel for the defence himself, been expunged from the Crown's case and from the issues put to the jury. Your Lordships would, I feel, be slow to permit counsel for the defence, having got that suggestion buried, to disinter it for the purpose of suggesting that Lawson was constructively an accomplice to the crime of murder and for that reason attracted the rule as to warning.

My Lords, I have tried to define the term 'accomplice'. The branch of the definition relevant to this case is that which covers *participes criminis* in respect of the actual crime charged, 'whether as principals or accessories before or after the fact'. But, it may reasonably be asked, who is to decide, or how is it to be decided, whether a particular witness was a *particeps criminis* in the case in hand? In many or most cases this question answers itself, or, to be more exact, is answered by the witness in question himself, by confessing to participation, by pleading guilty to it, or by being convicted of it. But it is indisputable that there are witnesses outside these straightforward categories, in respect of whom the answer has to be sought elsewhere. The witnesses concerned may never have confessed, or may never have been arraigned or put on trial, in respect of the crime involved. Such cases fall into two classes. In the first, the judge can properly rule that there is no evidence that the witness was, what I will, for short, call a participant. The present case, in my view, happens to fall within this class, and can be decided on the narrow ground. But there are other cases within this field in which there is evidence on which a reasonable jury could find that a witness was a 'participant'. In such a case the issue of *accomplice vel non* is for the jury's decision; and a judge should direct them that if they consider on the evidence that the witness was an accomplice, it is dangerous for them to act on his evidence unless corroborated: though it is competent for them to do so if, after that warning, they still think fit to do so.'

(LORDS PORTER, OAKSEY, TUCKER and ASQUITH OF BISHOPSTONE concurred.)

Appeal dismissed.

Questions
1.   What are the justifications for treating the evidence of an accomplice with caution?
2.   Is the definition of 'accomplice' in *Davies* v *DPP* too narrow?
3.   Why does the requirement for a warning apply only to accomplices called to testify for the prosecution? Why should it not apply to an accomplice who gives evidence on his own behalf against a co-accused?

(ii)   Evidence of complainants in sexual cases

R v Trigg
(1963) 47 Cr App R 94
Court of Appeal

ASHWORTH J: On July 23, 1962, at Lewes Assizes the appellant was convicted of rape and sentenced to five years' imprisonment, and he now appeals to this court by the leave of the single judge.

It is perhaps worth mentioning at this stage that leave to appeal was given on one particular issue, namely, the question whether in the course of his summing-up the learned judge fell into error by describing the tattoo marks on the appellant's arms as being on his wrists, whereas the appellant claims that one of them, at least, is on his left hand. Having listened to Mr Charles, and having ourselves seen the marks on the appellant's arms, it is sufficient to say that, if this appeal depended for its result solely upon that point, it would be dismissed. Further reference need not be made to it.

Other grounds of appeal are put forward on his behalf. In particular, after the hearing of the appeal had been started, the question was raised whether there was any reference to the topic of corroboration in the summing-up, and, with the leave of the court, Mr Charles, for the appellant, amended his grounds of appeal by submitting further grounds, in which the first is that the learned judge misdirected the jury in that he failed to give them any direction upon corroboration. In passing, it may be said that it is quite plain that in fact there was no such direction.

. . . There was no direction whatever in regard to corroboration, and counsel is unable to recollect whether in fact the topic was referred to at all during the trial. That there should have been such a direction is now well established. In the case in this court of *Sawyer* (1959) 43 Cr App R 187 the headnote reads: 'On a charge of a sexual offence it is essential that the summing-up should contain a warning on corroboration . . .'

. . . The matter again came before this court in the following year in the case of *Clynes* (1960) 44 Cr App R 158, and at the top of p. 161 these words appear:

> It was submitted by Mr Montgomery that, in a case where the issue is one of identity and where there is no dispute as to the actual assault, it is not necessary for the court to give a direction on corroboration at all. That is not the view of this court, nor was it the view of this court in *Sawyer* (*supra*), where the charge was one of a different sexual offence, and the only issue was identity, and the court stressed the necessity for a warning on corroboration.

In those circumstances it is quite impossible to give effect to an argument but faintly put forward by Mr Parker that this issue was still open. In the view of this court these decisions establish quite plainly that in a sexual case of this sort the jury must be warned of the danger of acting on the complainant's evidence unless there is corroboration.

Criminal Justice and Public Order Bill 1994

25. Abolition of corroboration rules

(1) Any requirement whereby at a trial on indictment it is obligatory for the court to give the jury a warning about convicting the accused on the uncorroborated evidence of a person merely because that person is —

(a) an alleged accomplice of the accused, or

(b) where the offence charged is a sexual offence, the person in respect of whom it is alleged to have been committed, is hereby abrogated.

(2) In section 34(2) of the Criminal Justice Act 1988 (abolition of requirement of corroboration warning in respect of evidence of a child) the words from 'in relation to' to the end shall be omitted.

(3) Any requirement that —

(a) is applicable at the summary trial of a person for an offence, and

(b) corresponds to the requirement mentioned in subsection (1) above or that mentioned in section 34(2) of the Criminal Justice Act 1988, is hereby abrogated.

(4) Nothing in this section applies in relation to —

(a) any trial, or

(b) any proceedings before a magistrates' court as examining justices, which began before the commencement of this section.

Question

Are the reforms contained in clause 25 of the Bill desirable?

(iii) Cases falling outside the established categories

The Criminal Justice and Public Order Bill 1994 does not propose to remove any discretion that a trial judge might have to warn a jury of any particular weaknesses or 'dangers' which might be present in a case, irrespective of whether or not it relates to the evidence of an accomplice or the victim of a sexual offence. Before the emergence of the Bill, a series of cases decided that even where the evidence of a witness fell outside one of the established categories which called for a corroboration warning, the trial judge might still, in the exercise of his discretion, comment upon that evidence. Essentially, they fall into two broad categories — witnesses who might have some 'purpose of their own to serve' by giving false or tainted evidence, and witnesses who, for some other reason, may not be thought of as reliable. These cases, which appear below, will be unaffected by the provisions contained in clause 25 of the Bill. They were, however, decided on a parallel track with the corroboration rules and the judgments draw analogies with these rules. When clause 25 is enacted, the principles enunciated in these cases will remain intact, despite the fact that the corroboration rules will be rendered largely redundant.

R v Beck
[1982] 1 WLR 461
Court of Appeal

The appellant, who effectively controlled a business, was tried on a charge of conspiracy to defraud a company financing the business. A co-defendant, who pleaded guilty, gave evidence for the prosecution, and prosecution evidence was given also by three witnesses of the finance company in respect of whom there was no suggestion that they were the appellant's accomplices, but they had an alleged purpose of their own to serve in covering up false representations made, or acceded to, by them in an insurance claim unconnected with the charge against the appellant. The judge directed the jury about the need for corroboration of the evidence of the co-defendant as an accomplice, and the appellant was convicted. He appealed on the grounds that the judge should have directed the jury, in relation to the evidence of the three witnesses, as though each were an accomplice since he had a substantial interest of his own to serve in giving evidence, and evidence was capable of amounting to corroboration only if and in so far as it directly corroborated a piece of evidence given by an accomplice.

ACKNER LJ: . . . Mr Lloyd-Eley bases his contention that such a warning should have been given essentially upon *R v Prater* [1960] 2 QB 464. In that case a co-prisoner, who could have been considered an accomplice, gave evidence. The Common Serjeant did not give warning in regard to his testimony and the danger of acting upon it unless corroborated. Edmund Davies J, in the course of the judgment of the court, said, at p. 466:

> For the purposes of this present appeal, this court is content to accept that whether the label to be attached to Welham in this case was strictly that of an accomplice or not, in practice it is desirable that a warning should be given that the witness, whether he comes from the dock, as in this case, or whether he be a Crown witness, may be a witness with some purpose of his own to serve . . . . In the circumstances of the present appeal it is sufficient for this court to express the view that it is

desirable that, in cases where a person may be regarded as having some purpose of his own to serve, the warning against uncorroborated evidence should be given. But every case must be looked at in the light of its own facts . . .

The court also considered the position of a witness called for the prosecution in regard to whom questions were put in cross-examination suggesting that he was an accomplice. Edmund Davies J said, at p. 466:

This court has looked in vain at the transcript of the summing-up, and has listened in vain, with respect to Mr Fitch, for any satisfactory indication that there was material upon which the Common Serjeant would have been justified in presenting Truman to the jury as being an accomplice. As my brother Hilbery said, it is easy to make suggestions to a witness. That is one thing. But more than that is required to clothe a witness for the Crown or any other witness with the garment of an accomplice. This court is unable, on the material before it, to hold that it is shown that any warning was in strict law or in prudence called for, for it is by no means satisfied that there was any material upon which Truman could properly be described as an accomplice . . .

In the course of his judgment, Edmund Davies J had referred to the *locus classicus* on accomplices and the requirement of corroboration, namely *Davies* v *Director of Public Prosecutions* [1954] AC 378. Lord Simonds LC, giving the decision of the House, said, at p. 401.

My Lords, I have tried to define the term 'accomplice'. The branch of the definition relevant to this case is that which covers *participes criminis* in respect of the actual crime charged, 'whether as principals or accessories before or after the fact'. But, it may reasonably be asked, who is to decide, or how is it to be decided, whether a particular witness was a *participes criminis* in the case in hand? In many or most cases this question answers itself, or, to be more exact, is answered by the witness in question himself, by confessing to participation, by pleading guilty to it or by being convicted of it. But it is indisputable that there are witnesses outside these straightforward categories, in respect of whom the answer has to be sought elsewhere. The witnesses concerned may never have confessed, or may never have been arraigned or put on trial, in respect of the crime involved. Such cases fall into two classes. In the first, the judge can properly rule that there is no evidence that the witness was, what I will, for short, call a participant. The present case, in my view, happens to fall within this class, and can be decided on that narrow ground. But there are other cases within this field in which there is evidence on which a reasonable jury could find that a witness was a 'participant'. In such a case the issue of '*accomplice vel non*' is for the jury's decision: and a judge should direct them that if they consider on the evidence that the witness was an accomplice, it is dangerous for them to act on his evidence unless corroborated: though it is competent for them to do so if, after that warning, they still think fit to do so.

Prater's case [1960] 2 QB 464 has been the subject of strong comment in the Court of Criminal Appeal in *R* v *Stannard* [1965] 2 QB 1, where Winn J said, at p. 14:

The rule, if it be a rule, enunciated in *R* v *Prater* [1960] 2 QB 464 is no more than a rule of practice. I say deliberately 'if it be a rule' because, reading the passage of the judgment as I have just read it, it really seems to amount to no more than an expression of what is desirable and what, it is to be hoped, will more usually than not be adopted, at any rate, where it seems to be appropriate to the judge. It certainly is not a rule of law . . .

It was looked upon as 'a qualified decision' in *R v Whitaker* (1976) 63 Cr App R 193.

Mr Lloyd-Eley accepts that an accomplice direction cannot be required whenever a witness may be regarded as having some purpose of his own to serve. Merely because there is some material to justify the suggestion that a witness is giving unfavourable evidence, for example, out of spite, ill-will, to level some old score, to obtain some financial advantage, cannot Mr Lloyd-Eley concedes, in every case necessitate the accomplice warning, if there is no material to suggest that the witness may be an accomplice. But, submits Mr Lloyd-Eley, even though there is no material to suggest any involvement by the witness in the crime, if he has a 'substantial interest' of his own for giving false evidence, then the accomplice direction must be given. Where one draws the line, he submits is a question of degree, but once the boundary is crossed the obligation to give the accomplice warning is not a matter of discretion. We cannot accept this contention. In many trials today, the burden upon the trial judge of the summing-up is a heavy one. It would be a totally unjustifiable addition to require him, not only fairly to put before the jury the defence's contention that a witness was suspect, because he had an axe to grind, but also to evaluate the weight of that axe and oblige him, where the weight is 'substantial', to give an accomplice warning with the appropriate direction as to the meaning of corroboration together with the identification of the potential corroborative material.

We take the view that if and in so far as *R v Prater* [1960] 2 QB 464 was not a decision on its particular facts, it in no way extended the law as laid down in *Davies's* case [1954] AC 378. There was material upon which a reasonable jury could have concluded that Welham was an accomplice. Equally, there was no such material in regard to Truman. In short, the phrase in *R v Prater* [1960] 2 QB 464, 466; 'it is desirable that, in cases where a person may be regarded as having some purpose of his own to serve, the warning against uncorroborated evidence should be given,' is related to cases where witnesses may be participants or involved in the crime charged.

This view is borne out by *R v Daniels* (unreported), 13 April 1967. In that case the appellant was convicted of receiving just over 9 cwt. of copper wire knowing it to have been stolen. Copper wire was discovered in a lorry and in the driving cab was the appellant, a man called Fisher, and the owner of the lorry. The owner gave evidence to the effect that he had lent the lorry to the appellant as he wanted to collect some scrap. It was an odd story, since no time was specified for the loan and nothing was paid for the hire of the lorry. The appellant's defence was that he was given £3 to collect a fully-loaded lorry and had driven it away unsuspectingly. The court concluded that theoretically there were three possibilities; one was that the owner of the lorry was telling the truth, the second was that the appellant was wholly innocent and that the owner of the lorry had received the copper wire knowing it to have been stolen and had hired the innocent appellant to drive the lorry away. The third possibility was that both the appellant and the owner of the lorry were liars and in the crime together. Clearly in that situation the owner who was cross-examined to show that he was a liar, had a purpose of his own, if he was lying, which was to hide his own involvement in the offence charged. He was potentially a participant in the crime. Salmon LJ, giving the judgment of the court, referred to *R v Prater* [1960] 2 QB 464 and to that part which we have quoted. He was clearly treating that case as being an accomplice or potential accomplice case. He said, in regard to the judge's summing up:

He should then have reviewed the evidence to see what corroboration there was and he should have told them that bearing in mind the lorry owner's strong motives for putting the blame on the appellant and the danger of convicting him on his uncorroborated evidence alone, if nevertheless they felt quite certain that what the lorry owner was saying was true they were still entitled to convict without corroboration.

Mr Lloyd-Eley drew our attention to *Archbold, Criminal Pleading Evidence & Practice*, 40th ed (1979), para. 1425a which reads:

> . . . a general rule seems to be developing that when a witness in a criminal case, whether he be a fellow accused or called for the Crown, may reasonably be regarded as having some purpose of his own to serve which may lead him to give false evidence against an accused, the judge should warn the jury of the danger of convicting that accused on that witness's evidence unless it is corroborated: . . .

And then a reference is made to *Prater* and to *R v Kilbourne* [1973] AC 729, *per* Lord Hailsham of St Marylebone LC. Significantly in the instant case, where potential corroborative material was discussed in relation to Mayze, who was a self-confessed accomplice, neither counsel for the prosecution, then Mr Farquharson QC, nor Mr Lloyd-Eley suggested in relation to the three directors of Coach House that any special direction was required, let alone the accomplice warning.

While we in no way wish to detract from the obligation upon a judge to advise a jury to proceed with caution where there is material to suggest that a witness's evidence may be tainted by an improper motive, and the strength of that advice must vary according to the facts of the case, we cannot accept that there is any obligation to give the accomplice warning with all that that entails, when it is common ground that there is no basis for suggesting that the witness is a participant or in any way involved in the crime the subject matter of the trial.

Mr Lloyd-Eley accepts that if the single judge who gave leave to appeal did so having regard to the decision of the Court of Appeal (Criminal Division) a few months earlier, it was not a proper foundation for the grant of leave in this case. That case was *R v Riley* (1980) 70 Cr App R 1 in which a witness was called for the prosecution in regard to whom there was material to suggest that he might be an accomplice of the defendant.

It is alleged in the notice of appeal:

> . . . on the evidence of Jorg (the chief auditor of the American company which owned First Fortune), the witnesses Noble, Knight and Hochenberg had all lied to him in the period June to September 1975 when they told him that they had no knowledge of the use of personal loan documents by Coach House Finance prior to Jorg raising the question with them. This statement by the three witnesses was vital to an insurance claim of approximately £600,000 which relied in part upon Mayze having introduced and used the personal loan documents over a period from June 1974 to June 1975 without the knowledge or approval of Noble, Knight or Hochenberg.

Thus, it is made palpably clear that the alleged purpose of Noble, Knight and Hochenberg in giving evidence was, we quote again: 'to cover up false representations made or acceded to by them in the insurance claim.' It was accepted that this insurance claim was not connected with the offence charged against the appellant. It provided no material in support of the proposition nor indeed was it ever suggested that Noble, Knight and Hochenberg were possible accomplices of the appellant. Mr Lloyd-Eley made it clear that he was not seeking to make that contention before us.

We have set out the general ground of our decision in order to assist trial judges by dispelling belief in the 'general rule' to which the editors of *Archbold* were referring in paragraph 1425a. We accept of course that there is a far narrower ground which could justify the rejection of the appellant's first contention, namely, the authority of *Whitaker's* case (1976) 63 Cr App R 193, where Lord Widgery CJ, having referred to *Prater's* case said, at p. 197:

> Furthermore, since any question of referring to corroborative evidence in this context is a matter primarily for the trial judge, it is no ground of criticism in this case that the trial judge did not deal with the matter. Indeed, as I have already said, it was not raised in argument for his specific consideration in the case. It seems to us therefore that as a matter of law Mr Temple cannot sustain his argument that there was here a failure to warn of the kind referred to in *Prater's* case.

We prefer, however, to base our decision on the general principles to which we have referred above.

Appeal dismissed.

R v *Spencer; R* v *Smails*
[1987] 1 AC 128
House of Lords

The appellants, who were nursing staff at a special hospital, were charged with ill-treating patients, contrary to s. 126 of the Mental Health Act 1959. In two separate trials before the same judge, the prosecution relied wholly on the uncorroborated evidence of patients who had criminal convictions or were suffering from mental disorders.

At both trials Judge Hopkin directed the jury to approach the evidence of the patients with great caution but did not warn them that it would be dangerous to convict on the patients' uncorroborated evidence. The appellants were all convicted. They appealed to the Court of Appeal which dismissed the appeals, holding that the evidence of patients at a secure hospital did not fall into the category of evidence of witnesses where a full warning of the danger of conviction on their uncorroborated evidence was necessary. The appellants appealed to the House of Lords.

LORD ACKNER: . . . To my mind the question raised by these appeals is both simple to define and simple to answer. Given that it is common ground that a warning was required as to the way in which the jury should treat the evidence of the complainants, the question is: was that warning sufficient? Did it in clear terms bring home to the jury the danger of basing a conviction on the unconfirmed evidence of the complainants?

In the three established categories where the 'full warning' is obligatory, the inherent unreliability of the witness may well not be apparent to the jury. Hence the phrase often used in a summing up — it is the experience of the courts accumulated over many years etc. etc. Complainants of sexual assaults do on occasions give false evidence for a variety of reasons, some of which may not have occurred to a jury. Accomplices may have hidden reasons for lying, and this possibility may again not be apparent to a jury . . . All this needs properly to be spelt out to the jury. Hence the well established rule of practice.

In other cases the potential unreliability of the sole or principal witness for the prosecution is obvious for all to see. These were such cases. The complainants were men of bad character. They had been sent to Rampton rather than to an ordinary prison, because they were mentally unbalanced. That they were anti-authoritarian, prone to lie or exaggerate, and could well have old scores which they were seeking to pay off, was not disputed. Notwithstanding that the possibility of their evidence being unreliable was patent, that it was clearly dangerous to prefer their evidence to that of the defendants, all men of good character on whose behalf witnesses had spoken in glowing terms, the judge nevertheless told the jury in the clearest possible terms and repeated himself, that they must approach the evidence of the complainants with great caution. It is common ground that having given that warning, he then identified the very dangers which justified the exercise of great caution. He gave three reasons. First, they were all persons of bad character; secondly, they were all persons suffering from some form of mental disorder, and thirdly, they may have all conspired together to make false allegations. Thus the judge warned the jury of the dangers of relying on the complainants' testimony because, for the reasons which he gave, such testimony could well be unreliable. The judge, however, did not leave the matter there. As previously stated he pointed out, when dealing with each count, the details of the background of the complainant, his past criminal record, the nature of his mental disturbance and his history in the hospital, and perhaps most important of all, the hospital psychiatrist's view of the personality defects from which the patient suffered and of which I have already given a typical example. I agree with the Court of Appeal that he gave the emphatic warning which was required to meet the justice of the case. Indeed had this been one of the category of cases which required the 'full warning' then the judge's direction would have been fully adequate.

The certified point of law is in these terms:

> In a case where the evidence for the Crown is solely that of a witness who is not in one of the accepted categories of suspect witnesses, but who, by reason of his particular mental condition and criminal connection, fulfilled the same criteria, must the judge warn the jury that it is dangerous to convict on his uncorroborated evidence.

I would amend the question by substituting for the words 'the same criteria' 'analogous criteria.' I would then answer the question in the affirmative, adding, for the sake of clarity, that while it may often be convenient to use the words 'danger' or 'dangerous,' the use of such words is not essential to an adequate warning, so long as the jury are made fully aware of the dangers of convicting on such evidence. Again, for the sake of clarity I would further add that *Reg v Beck* [1982] 1 WLR 461 was rightly decided and that in a case which does not fall into the three established categories and where there exists potential corroborative material, the extent to which the trial judge should make reference to that material depends upon the facts of each case. The overriding rule is that he must put the defence fairly and adequately.

LORD HAILSHAM LC: . . . [T]he modern cases, quite correctly in my view, are reluctant to insist on any magic formula or incantation, and stress instead the need that each summing up should be tailor-made to suit the requirements of the individual case; cf *DPP v Hester* [1972] 3 All ER 1056 at 1060, 1069, 1073, 1076, [1973] AC 296 at 309, 321, 325, 328 per Lord Morris, Lord Pearson and Lord Diplock. In particular, when, as here, it is agreed that no corroboration exists, a disquisition on what can or could amount to such if corroboration were needed is emphatically not required and greatly to be discouraged (see [1972] 3 All ER 1056 at 1076, [1973] AC 296 at 328 per Lord Diplock). Speaking for myself, I even dislike the expression 'categories' as applied to the cases. They are simply classes of cases where the experience of the courts has gradually hardened into rules of practice, owing, as my noble and learned friend points out, partly to the inherent dangers involved, and partly to the fact that the danger is not necessarily obvious to a lay mind. The less juries are confused by superfluous learning and the more their minds are directed to the particular issues relevant to the case before them, the more likely they are, in my view, to arrive at a just verdict.

(LORDS BRIDGE OF HARWICH, BRANDON OF OAKBROOK and MACKAY OF CLASHFERN agreed.)

Questions
1. According to *Beck* and *Spencer*, what is the duty of a trial judge when evidence is given against the accused by a 'suspect' witness, but the witness does not fall within one of the established categories which compel (or compelled) the judge to give a corroboration warning? How should this duty be discharged?
2. If the trial judge decides not to comment upon the evidence of a 'suspect' witness, is his decision likely to lead to a successful appeal?

(iv)   The evidence of children

Note
The sworn evidence of a child used to require a full corroboration warning. It used to be the case that the unsworn and uncorroborated evidence of a child was incapable of founding a conviction. We have already seen how the competence of a child as a witness has been affected by s. 52 of the Criminal Justice Act 1991 (see Chapter 4(C) above). Statute has also addressed the issue of a child's evidence and corroboration.

Criminal Justice Act 1988

34. Abolition of requirement of corroboration for unsworn evidence of children
(2)   Any requirement whereby at a trial on indictment it is obligatory for the court to give the jury a warning about convicting the accused on the uncorroborated evidence of a child is abrogated *in relation to cases where such a warning is required by reason only that the evidence is the evidence of a child.*
(3)   Unsworn evidence admitted by virtue of section 52 of the Criminal Justice Act 1991 may corroborate evidence (sworn or unsworn) given by any other person.

Note
The Criminal Justice and Public Order Bill 1994 proposes to amend s. 34 (2) by removing the words shown in italics as they will be superfluous when the other clauses in the Bill take effect. It should also be noted that until the Bill becomes law, should a child witness fall within one of the established categories which attract a mandatory corroboration warning (e.g. the child is the victim of a sexual offence) then a corroboration warning must still be given.

Question
P, a child of 9 years, testifies that D indecently assaulted her. S, a child of 8 years, testifies that she saw D indecently assault P. How will the judge direct the jury if:

(a) the Criminal Justice and Public Order Bill has not been enacted?
(b) the Criminal justice and Public Order Bill has been enacted?

Which direction is to be preferred?

(C) The nature and qualities of corroborative evidence

If corroboration is required as a matter of law, or if the judge is obliged to warn the jury of the dangers of acting upon the uncorroborated evidence of a particular witness, the judge must also identify for the jury's benefit those items of evidence (if any) which, as a matter of law, are capable of amounting to corroboration. The essential features which permit evidence to be classed as corroborative are:

(a) its independence from the person whose evidence requires corroborating; and
(b) its tendency to show not only that the offence has been committed but that it was committed by the defendant.

The rules which have developed at common law are often intricate and complex and are open to as much criticism as the categories of witness which attract them. The Criminal Justice and Public Order Bill does not contain a clause which deals specifically with the rules as formulated in the following cases. The potential consequences of this are dealt with towards the end of this section.

R v Baskerville
[1916] 2 KB 658
Court of Criminal Appeal

The defendant was convicted of having committed acts of gross indecency with two boys. The only direct evidence of the commission of the acts charged was that of the boys themselves, who on their own statement were accomplices in the offences. However, a letter was proved to have been sent to one of the boys by the defendant in his handwriting signed by him with his initial B, enclosing a 10s note for both boys, and making an appointment for them to meet the defendant 'as arranged'. The judge told the jury that the letter afforded evidence which they would be entitled to find was sufficient corroboration of the boys' evidence.

LORD READING LC: . . . [W]e have come to the conclusion that the better opinion of the law upon this point is that stated in *R v Stubbs* (1855) Dears 555 by Parke B, namely, that the evidence of an accomplice must be confirmed not only as to the circumstances of the crime, but also as to the identity of the prisoner. The learned Baron does not mean that there must be confirmation of all the circumstances of the crime; as we have already stated, that is unnecessary. It is sufficient if there is confirmation as to a material circumstance of the crime and of the identity of the accused in relation to the crime. . . .

We hold that evidence in corroboration must be independent testimony which affects the accused by connecting or tending to connect him with the crime. In other words, it must be evidence which implicates him, that is, which confirms in some material particular not only the evidence that the crime has been committed, but also that the prisoner committed it. The test applicable to determine the nature and extent of the corroboration is thus the same whether the case falls within the rule of practice at common law or within that class of offences for which corroboration is required by statute. The language of the statute, 'implicates the accused', compendiously incorporates the test applicable at common law in the rule of practice. The nature of the corroboration will necessarily vary according to the particular circumstances of the offence charged. It would be in high degree dangerous to attempt to formulate the kind of evidence which would be regarded as corroboration, except to say that corroborative evidence is evidence which shows or tends to show that the story of the accomplice that the accused committed the crime is true, not merely that the crime has been committed, but that it was committed by the accused.

James v *R*
(1970) 55 Cr App R 299
Privy Council

The appellant was convicted of rape. The complainant alleged that a man whom she subsequently identified as the appellant had raped her at knife point. There was medical evidence showing that the complainant had had sexual intercourse at about a time consistent with her allegation. The trial judge directed that this evidence might corroborate that of the complainant.

VISCOUNT DILHORNE: . . . Where the charge is of rape, the corroborative evidence must confirm in some material particular that intercourse has taken place and that it has taken place without the woman's consent, and also that the accused was the man who committed the crime. In sexual cases, in view of the possibility of error in identification by the complainant, corroborative evidence confirming in a material particular her evidence that the accused was the guilty man is just as important as such evidence confirming that intercourse took place without her consent . . .

True it is that the medical evidence and the evidence of what was found on Miss Hall's clothing and on the articles taken from her bed confirmed her testimony that intercourse with her had taken place on her bed, but there was no medical evidence that the intercourse had taken place without her consent; and the judge directed the jury that, if they accepted that evidence, it could amount to corroboration in the sense in which he had already explained to them that the word was to be understood.

In their Lordship's view, this direction was entirely wrong. Independent evidence that intercourse had taken place is not evidence confirming in some material particular either that the crime of rape had been committed or, if it had been, that it had been committed by the accused. It does not show that the intercourse took place without consent or that the accused was a party to it. There was in this case no evidence capable of amounting to corroboration of Miss Hall's evidence that she had been raped, and raped by the accused. The judge should have told the jury that. His failure to do so was a serious misdirection, so serious as to make it inevitable that the conviction should be quashed.

R v Chauhan
(1981) 73 Cr App R 232
Court of Appeal

The appellant accompanied his sister to premises where she had applied for employment, and while she was being interviewed he waited in another room where a female employee was working alone. They entered into conversation, whereupon it was alleged by the victim that the appellant touched her breast and tried to kiss her. She extricated herself and ran upstairs to the ladies' lavatory crying. A fellow employee heard her cries and followed her. The victim explained to her fellow employee what had happened. The police later interviewed the appellant who admitted being alone with the victim but denied any incident took place in which he had touched her. He maintained that when she left the room she had been behaving normally. The appellant was charged with indecent assault. At the end of the prosecution case counsel for the appellant submitted that there was insufficient corroboration for the issue to be left to the jury. The recorder ruled that the jury were entitled to regard the victim's distressed condition described by the fellow employee as corroboration if they thought it right to do so. The appellant was convicted. He appealed on the ground, *inter alia,* that the evidence of distress could not amount to corroboration.

LORD LANE CJ: We have been referred to a number of authorities on the matter. It is right that at least brief reference should be made to them. The first one in point of time is the case of *Redpath* (1962) 46 Cr App R 319. The headnote encapsulates adequately the effect of that case. It reads as follows: 'In a sexual offence the distressed condition of the complainant is capable of amounting to corroboration of the complainant's evidence, but the weight of such evidence as corroboration will vary according to the circumstances of the case'.

At p. 321, Lord Parker CJ said this:

So far as any question of indecent assault is concerned, the learned judge told the jury that her distressed condition observed by Mr Hall and spoken to by Mr Hall was capable of being corroboration. The point in this appeal is whether that is so. Mr Harper has argued that the distressed condition of the complainant is no more corroborative than the complaint, if any, that the complainant makes, and that while the latter merely shows that the story is consistent and is not corroborative, so the distressed condition is not corroborative. This Court is quite unable to accept that argument. It seems to this Court that the distressed condition of a complainant is quite clearly capable of amounting to corroboration. Of course, the circumstances will vary enormously, and in some circumstances quite clearly no weight, or little weight, could be attached to such evidence as corroboration. Thus, if a girl goes in a distressed condition to her mother and makes a complaint, while the mother's evidence as to the girl's condition may in law be capable of amounting to corroboration, quite clearly the jury should be told that they should attach little, if any, weight to that evidence, because it is all part and parcel of the complaint. The girl making the complaint might well put on an act and simulate distress. But in the present case the circumstances are entirely different.

In respect of that, the circumstances there were that the distressed condition of the little girl who had been the subject of the assault was observed by someone whom the little girl did not know to be there.

The next case to which we were referred was *Okoye* [1964] Crim LR 416. That was a judgment of the Court of Criminal Appeal. It is a very brief, sparse report. The second half of the holding reads as follows: '2 The judge did not emphasise sufficiently that a distressed condition at the time of making a complaint can only amount at the most to the very slightest evidence of corroboration . . .'

That was a case, as was the next one, *Luisi* [1964] Crim LR 605, where the only issue was consent and where undoubtedly there had been some form of sexual activity between the parties. It seems to this Court that in those circumstances what was said in that type of case is of very little value in considering this type of case, where, on the appellant's evidence, no form of contact, or sexual contact, or indecent sexual contact took place at all. But I read a very short passage from the judgment in *Luisi (supra)*, as reported, in skeleton form, in the same volume of the *Criminal Law Review*. It reads as follows: 'The significance of the girl's distress was over-emphasised. There may be cases (e.g., *Redpath* (1962) 46 Cr App R 319) where there can be no suggestion that the distress was feigned. In normal cases, however, the weight to be given to distress varies infinitely, and juries should be warned that, although it may amount to corroboration they must be fully satisfied that there is no question of it having been feigned'.

For purposes of completeness, there are two other cases. The first is *Knight* (1966) 50 Cr App R 122; [1966] 1 WLR 230. I read a passage from p. 125 and p. 233 respectively, from the judgment of the Court given by Lord Parker CJ: 'Despite what was said in that judgment', (he is referring there to *Redpath (supra)*), 'there has been a tendency since then for judges to leave to the jury almost every case where a complainant is seen to be in a distressed condition, and in several cases since *Redpath (supra)*, and in particular two cases to which we have been referred, *Okoye (supra)*, and *Luisi (supra)*, I endeavoured to stress that the distress shown by a complainant must not be over-emphasised in the sense that juries should be warned that except in special circumstances little weight ought to be given to that evidence.'

Finally, the case of *Wilson* (1973) 58 Cr App R 304. I read a passage from the judgment of Edmund-Davies LJ at the foot of page 309: 'In granting leave to appeal, the Court drew attention with understandable brevity to the fact that, while the appearance and emotional state of a complainant may in very special circumstances be regarded as capable of constituting corroboration, it is an approach which has to be very guarded, and whether the matter was sufficiently elaborated by the learned judge in the present instance was something which the court thought called for further examination'.

One other short passage, at p. 312: 'We regard it' (said Edmund-Davies LJ) 'as of considerable importance that the type of warning adverted to by Lord Parker CJ in *Knight (supra)* is constantly borne in mind when such cases as the present are before the courts and that a trial judge cannot be too zealous in heeding that warning. For these reasons we allow the appeal' . . .

It seems to us that in this case the circumstances, as we have already indicated, were very different from those in many of the cases which appear in the reports. Here there were only two people in the room. Here there was a total denial by the appellant that anything of an indecent nature, or anything to which exception could be taken ever took place in the room at all. In those circumstances, it seems to us that it was essential for the jury to have before them the evidence of what happened when this lady left the room; evidence coming from Mrs Hindle. If they had not had that evidence before them, they could have legitimately complained that they were being deprived of a valuable aid to them in deciding the case properly according to the directions given to them by the recorder.

Appeal dismissed.

Questions
1.   Was the evidence of the distress of the complainant in *R v Chauhan* truly independent in terms of the *Baskerville* test?
2.   Considering that the main justification for the corroboration rule in such cases is the possibility of fabrication, why is the decision in *R v Chauhan* open to criticism?

R v Lucas
[1981] QB 720
Court of Appeal

The appellant was tried on a count charging her with being knowingly concerned in the fraudulent evasion of the prohibition on importation of a controlled drug. Evidence implicating her was given by an accomplice. The appellant gave evidence which was challenged as being partly lies. The jury were warned of the dangers of convicting on the accomplice's uncorroborated evidence and were directed in terms which suggested that lies told by the appellant in court could be considered as corroborative of the accomplice's evidence. The appellant was convicted and appealed.

LORD LANE CJ: . . . The fact that the jury may feel sure that the accomplice's evidence is to be preferred to that of the defendant and that the defendant accordingly must have been lying in the witness box is not of itself something which can be treated by the jury as corroboration of the accomplice's evidence. It is only if the accomplice's evidence is believed that there is any necessity to look for corroboration of it. If the belief that the accomplice is truthful means that the defendant was untruthful and if that untruthfulness can be used as corroboration, the practical effect would be to dispense with the need of corroboration altogether.

The matter was put in this way by Lord MacDermott in *Tumahole Bereng v The King* [1949] AC 253, 270:

Nor does an accused corroborate an accomplice merely by giving evidence which is not accepted and must therefore be regarded as false. Corroboration may well be found in the evidence of an accused person; but that is a different matter, for there confirmation comes, if at all, from what is said, and not from the falsity of what is said.

There is, without doubt, some confusion in the authorities as to the extent to which lies may in some circumstances provide corroboration and it was this confusion which probably and understandably led the judge astray in the present case. In our judgment the position is as follows. Statements made out of court, for example, statements to the police, which are proved or admitted to be false may in certain circumstances amount to corroboration. There is no shortage of authority for this proposition: see, for example, *R* v *Knight* [1966] 1 WLR 230, *Credland* v *Knowler* (1951) 35 Cr App R 48. It accords with good sense that a lie told by a defendant about a material issue may show that the liar knew if he told the truth he would be sealing his fate. In the words of Lord Dunedin in *Dawson* v *M'kenzie,* 1908 SC 648, 649, cited with approval by Lord Goddard CJ in *Credland* v *Knowler,* 35 Cr App R 48, 55:

> . . . the opportunity may have a complexion put upon it by statements made by the defender which are proved to be false. It is not that a false statement made by the defender proves that the pursuer's statements are true, but it may give to a proved opportunity a different complexion from what it would have borne had no such false statement been made.

To be capable of amounting to corroboration the lie told out of court must first of all be deliberate. Secondly it must relate to a material issue. Thirdly the motive for the lie must be a realisation of guilt and a fear of the truth. The jury should in appropriate cases be reminded that people sometimes lie, for example, in an attempt to bolster up a just cause, or out of shame or out of a wish to conceal disgraceful behaviour from their family. Fourthly the statement must be clearly shown to be a lie by evidence other than that of the accomplice who is to be corroborated, that is to say by admission or by evidence from an independent witness.

As a matter of good sense it is difficult to see why, subject to the same safeguards, lies proved to have been told in court by a defendant should not equally be capable of providing corroboration. In other common law jurisdictions they are so treated; see the cases collated by Professor J D Heydon in 'Can Lies Corroborate?' (1973) 89 LQR 552, 561, and cited with apparent approval in *Cross on Evidence,* 5th ed (1979), p. 210 (footnote).

It has been suggested that there are dicta in *R* v *Chapman* [1973] QB 774, to the effect that lies so told in court can never be capable of providing corroboration of other evidence given against a defendant. We agree with the comment upon this case in *Cross on Evidence,* 5th ed pp. 210-211, that the court there may only have been intending to go no further than to apply the passage from the speech of Lord MacDermott in *Tumahole Bereng* v *The King* [1949] AC 253, 270 which we have already cited.

In our view the decision in *R* v *Chapman* [1973] QB 774 on the point there in issue was correct. The decision should not, however, be regarded as going any further than we have already stated. Properly understood, it is not authority for the proposition that in no circumstances can lies told by a defendant in court provide material corroboration of an accomplice. We find ourselves in agreement with the comment upon this decision made by this court in *R* v *Boardman* [1975] AC 421, 428-429. That point was not subsequently discussed when that case was before the House of Lords.

The main evidence against Chapman and Baldwin was a man called Thatcher, who was undoubtedly an accomplice in the alleged theft and dishonest handling of large quantities of clothing. The defence was that Thatcher was lying when he implicated the defendants and that he must himself have stolen the goods. The judge gave the jury the necessary warning about accomplice evidence and the requirement of corroboration, and then went on to say, at p. 779:

If you think that Chapman's story about the disappearance of the van and its contents is so obviously untrue that you do not attach any weight to it at all — in other words, you think Chapman is lying to you — then I direct you that that is capable of corroborating Thatcher, because, members of the jury, if Chapman is lying about the van, can there be any explanation except that Thatcher is telling the truth about how it came to disappear? . . . My direction is that it is capable in law of corroborating Thatcher. Similarly in the case of Baldwin, if you think that Baldwin's story about going up to London and buying these . . . is untrue — in other words he has told you lies about that — then . . . that I direct you, so far as he is concerned, is capable of amounting to corroboration of Thatcher.

That being the direction which this court was then considering, the decision is plainly correct, because the jury were being invited to prefer the evidence of the accomplice to that of the defendant and then without more to use their disbelief of the defendant as corroboration of the accomplice.

Providing that the lies told in court fulfil the four criteria which we have set out above, we are unable to see why they should not be available for the jury to consider in just the same way as lies told out of court. So far as the instant case is concerned, the judge, we feel, fell into the same error as the judge did in *R v Chapman* [1973] QB 774. The lie told by the appellant was clearly not shown to be a lie by evidence other than that of the accomplice who was to be corroborated and consequently the apparent direction that a lie was capable of providing corroboration was erroneous.

Appeal allowed.

R v Reeves
(1979) 68 Cr App R 331
Court of Appeal

The appellant pleaded not guilty to handling stolen goods and his co-accused, M, pleaded guilty to theft of the same goods. M then proceeded to give evidence against the appellant who was convicted. The main ground of appeal was that the trial judge had failed to indicate to the jury what evidence was capable of corroborating M's evidence.

LORD WIDGERY CJ: The criticism of the learned judge's treatment of the whole question of corroboration is that, whereas on that page that I have just read the general direction is given certainly in adequate terms, what the judge fails to do is to indicate to the jury whether there was in the evidence in this case any matter which could be regarded as corroborative. It is becoming progressively more clearly recognised that this is a very important feature of the summing-up where the judge has to deal with such questions. The reason for that is that an identification of evidence which is capable of corroboration is not always easy. Even lawyers find it difficult sometimes, and it is, therefore, quite vital that the trial judge should not dispose of the matter as this judge did merely by describing the dangers of acting on uncorroborated evidence unless he produces the back-up direction which tells the jury what evidence can be regarded as corroborative for this purpose. I have said that the tendency of modern authority is to be more stringent in this regard, and that, I think, can be made out by one or two of the authorities which have been shown to us. First, there is the case of *Rance* (1975) 62 Cr App R 118. That was a decision of this Court, and it deals, amongst other things, with the argument in that case on the very subject with which

I am seeking now to deal. The matters which were held in *Rance (supra)* were, first of all, whether the summing-up was at fault through not identifying the evidence capable of corroboration, and, secondly, in dealing with whether one accomplice could corroborate another. The report, in fairness to the prosecution in this case, does not indicate that in *Rance's* case *(supra)* the conviction was upset solely on the ground that the evidence capable of corroboration was not identified. That was taken as a point though it does not seem by itself to have been regarded as fatal to the success of the prosecution.

However, in a later decision in the case of *Charles and Others* [(1976) 68 Cr App R 334] where the presiding judge was Lawton LJ and where the date of the hearing was 29 June 1976, in that case this Court came out strongly with the proposition that items capable of corroborating should be identified.

I turn particularly to that part of the judgment in *Charles* where Lawton LJ said this, [at] p. 340: 'There was a time some 20 years ago when the old Court of Criminal Appeal ruled that it was unnecessary for a judge to direct the jury as to what evidence was capable of being corroboration. Since that time the general practice has changed and it is now generally accepted, certainly in cases of any complication, that the judge should indicate to the jury what evidence is and what evidence is not capable of being corroboration'.

That principle, reasserted by Lawton LJ at that point, is supported and confirmed by us sitting in this Court today.

Appeal allowed. Conviction quashed.

Note

As mentioned at B *(iii)* above, nothing in the Bill prevents the judge from exercising his discretion to comment upon the evidence of a witness as befits the particular case. Indeed, the Law Commission, on whose initial draft Bill clause 25 was modelled, fully expect trial judges, as a matter of discretion, to comment on the evidence of certain witnesses as is appropriate to the particular facts.

One further issue, mentioned briefly under (C) above, relates to the absence from the Bill of a clause dealing specifically with the rules concerning the nature and qualities of corroborative evidence as laid down in *Baskerville* and subsequent cases. After the Bill is enacted, what will happen if a trial judge, either by design or accident, warns the jury of the desirability of seeking corroboration? Because he has introduced the matter of corroboration (even though he not obliged to do so), will this mean he is then bound by the 'old' rules as formulated in *Baskerville* and the other cases? As will be seen from the following extract, the Law Commission is confident that when the obligation to warn the jury dies, so does *Baskerville*.

Corroboration of Evidence in Criminal Trials
(Law Commission Report No. 202, Cmnd 1620)

4.10   These rules as to what evidence can constitute 'corroboration' are thus not part of the general law, but apply only to determine the content of the corroboration warning required by the present corroboration rules. It might therefore seem self-evident that with the abolition of the requirement to give the corroboration warning by clause 1(1) of the draft Bill annexed to this Report the rules as to what is 'corroboration' will cease to have effect. We are indeed confident that that is the effect of this Bill, as it was of the similar formulation in section 34(2) of the Criminal Justice Act 1988 that abolished the requirement of a corroboration warning in the case of children's evidence; but the issue demands a little more discussion since this point, or something cognate to it, did cause some initial difficulty after legislation in respect of corroboration warnings had been introduced in the Australian State of Victoria.

4.11   The issue can only arise if, after the abolition of the *requirement* to give a corroboration warning, the judge, in the exercise of his discretion as to how to direct the jury, gave them what was intended to be, or could be interpreted as being, a corroboration warning in the old sense; or, even, simply spoke of 'corroboration' in the technical sense of the word. Then, it might be said, the judge would have attracted all the old rules as to 'corroboration', and thus, for instance, irrespective of the circumstances of the particular case, it would automatically be a misdirection for him to suggest that the evidence of one accomplice is capable of corroborating that of another accomplice. Even on this view however, those rules would bind him only if, in the exercise of his discretion, he chose to direct the jury in a particular way; and it might be difficult to know, in any particular case, whether his direction did in fact address 'corroboration' in the technical sense.

4.12   The true position, however, is that, even if the judge invoked corroboration, that would not result, in any case, in his continuing to be bound by the rules as to what is corroboration. With the abolition of the obligation to give a corroboration warning, the rules as to what is capable of being corroboration in law will simply have no standing, no grounding and no purpose, because those rules have been developed for the precise and only purpose of, and solely and only in the context of, deciding what counts as 'corroboration' in order to fulfil the requirements of that warning, and the obligations that the form of that warning places on the jury. With the abolition of the obligation to give the corroboration warning, the rules as to the content of that warning simply fall away. The principal such rule is the rule as to what constitutes 'corroboration'.

4.13   Following abolition of the requirement to give the *corroboration* warning the judge would be free, in the exercise of his general discretion, not only to warn in the strongest terms, but also to make use of any of the concepts and distinctions now embodied in the rules as to what is corroborative. He will, however, have to be careful that the use of such concepts and their application to the particular evidence in the case does not give the jury a distorted or misleading account of the evidence. For that reason, he may wish to be cautious about talking about the 'corroboration' of one piece of evidence by another, rather than about the way in which the evidence generally does or does not fit together, since it would (for instance) be a misdirection if the jury were given the impression, prejudicial to the interests of the accused, that evidence that was 'corroborative' in the former strict sense continued to have some special legal effect, or should be treated by the jury in some special way.

4.14   These considerations can be demonstrated by the way in which the effects of the abolition of a requirement to give a corroboration warning in one particular class of case have been worked out in jurisdictions in Australia.

4.15   In Victoria, legislation enacted in 1980 abolished the requirement to give the corroboration warning in respect of the evidence of complainants in sexual cases, but left untouched the obligation to give the corroboration warning in accomplice cases. The provision was tested in *Kehagias*, a case in which three defendants were convicted of the rape and attempted rape of two girls. The judge gave a warning containing some features of the old corroboration warning, and then went on to tell the jury that the evidence of the two girls could constitute mutual corroboration. By a majority of 2–1, the Court of Criminal Appeal held that the convictions could not stand because, having chosen to give what could be analysed as a corroboration warning, the judge had not complied with the rules, at least as they applied in that jurisdiction, governing what evidence might and might not be treated by the jury as corroborative. In particular, he had erred in directing the jury that the evidence of the two complainants could be mutually corroborative.

4.16   Insofar as the majority in *Kehagias* determined that the trial judge had been *bound* by a rule that complainants could not corroborate each other, they were in our respectful view mistaken, for the reasons indicated above. In subsequent decisions in Victoria the Court of Criminal Appeal and the Supreme Court, while not refusing to follow the majority in *Kehagias*, have emphasised both the freedom of the trial judge from any rules and his obligation not (as may have occurred in *Kehagias*) to use concepts such as that of corroboration in a way that may confuse the jury. As we have suggested in paragraph 4.13 above, this latter consideration is likely to be in the minds of English judges when directing juries after the obligation to talk about corroboration has been abolished.

4.17   Another Australian jurisdiction, South Australia, has taken a fresh look at the question, again in the context of legislation that abolished the obligation to give the corroboration warning in sexual offence cases. but not otherwise. The majority view in *Kehagias* has been consciously departed from, although Victorian precedent is usually highly persuasive in South Australia. In *Pahuja* the Court of Criminal Appeal held that abolition of the *requirement* to give the corroboration warning had resulted in the falling of the associated rules in sexual cases. Following that abolition, a judge who cautioned or warned the jury as to their approach to the evidence of a complainant in a sexual case would do so as part of his general duty to provide guidance to the jury as to the evidence and the facts. He was therefore now free to frame the caution or warning in such terms as he saw fit, but must not convey the impression that the warning was given as a matter of law, nor that the jury was not free to reject his approach to the evidence.

4.18   It is to be noted that the provisions under construction in *Kehagias* and the other Australian cases merely withdrew one category of case, that of sexual complainants, from a continuing system of mandatory warnings. The background therefore differed from that which will obtain under our Bill, when the whole of the system of mandatory warnings will have been destroyed. Murphy J and the Court of Criminal Appeal of South Australia were however quite clear that even when the requirement to give the warning had been removed in only some cases, in respect of those cases where the requirement had been removed the associated rules fell with it. That approach, and in particular the analysis of the Court of Criminal Appeal in South Australia in the latest case, fortifies us in our conclusion that clause 1 of the Bill in Appendix A to this Report, abolishing as it does the requirement to warn in both the remaining cases under the common law corroboration rules, will have the result of also abrogating in both of those cases the rules as to what constitutes 'corroboration'.

Questions
1.   Do you find the Law Commission's argument convincing?
2.   Can you see any possible way in which the Court of Appeal might reach a different conclusion to that reached by the Law Commission?

(D)   Identification evidence

A number of modern and well-publicised cases have highlighted the dangers of acting solely upon identification evidence. Acting upon the evidence of a witness who testifies that he saw defendant commit the crime in question, especially in the absence of any other evidence, may indeed be particularly dangerous. The dangers were highlighted by the Criminal Law Revision Committee in its 11th Report (Cmnd 4991, 1972) where, *inter alia*, the Committee referred to the wealth of psychological research which illustrates how a witness may be entirely honest in testifying that he saw D commit the offence and yet, for a number of reasons, be quite mistaken. Strangely perhaps, an acute danger presents itself because the witness is honest. Because he is honest, he will appear to be credible in the eyes of the jury. Indeed, he is much more likely to be unshakeable under cross-examination and, therefore, the jury are more likely to believe him. There is not, nor has there ever been, any formal requirement that identification evidence needs to be corroborated but, as Murphy puts it, there is 'an indication that a quasi-corroborative rule has developed . . .'

R v *Turnbull*
[1977] QB 224
Court of Appeal

The Court of Appeal considered four separate appeals against conviction, all on the ground that the identification of the defendant was unsatisfactory.

LORD WIDGERY CJ: . . . Each of these appeals raises problems relating to evidence of visual identification in criminal cases. Such evidence can bring about miscarriages of justice and has done so in a few cases in recent years. The number of such cases, although small compared with the number in which evidence of visual identification is known to be satisfactory, necessitates steps being taken by the courts, including this court, to reduce that number as far as is possible. In our judgment the danger of miscarriages of justice occurring can be much reduced if trial judges sum up to juries in the way indicated in this judgment.

First, whenever the case against an accused depends wholly or substantially on the correctness of one or more identifications of the accused which the defence alleges to be mistaken, the judge should warn the jury of the special need for caution before convicting the accused in reliance on the correctness of the identification or identifications. In addition he should instruct them as to the reason for the need for such a warning and should make some reference to the possibility that a mistaken witness can be a convincing one and that a number of such witnesses can all be mistaken. Provided this is done in clear terms the judge need not use any particular form of words.

Secondly, the judge should direct the jury to examine closely the circumstances in which the identification by each witness came to be made. How long did the witness have the accused under observation? At what distance? In what light? Was the observation impeded in any way, as for example by passing traffic or a press of people?

Had the witness ever seen the accused before? How often? If only occasionally, had he any special reason for remembering the accused? How long elapsed between the original observation and the subsequent identification to the police? Was there any material discrepancy between the description of the accused given to the police by the witness when first seen by them and his actual appearance? If in any case, whether it is being dealt with summarily or on indictment, the prosecution have reason to believe that there is such a material discrepancy they should supply the accused or his legal advisers with particulars of the description the police were first given. In all cases if the accused asks to be given particulars of such descriptions, the prosecution should supply them. Finally, he should remind the jury of any specific weaknesses which had appeared in the identification evidence.

Recognition may be more reliable than identification of a stranger; but even when the witness is purporting to recognise someone whom he knows, the jury should be reminded that mistakes in recognition of close relatives and friends are sometimes made.

All these matters go to the quality of the identification evidence. If the quality is good and remains good at the close of the accused's case, the danger of a mistaken identification is lessened; but the poorer the quality, the greater the danger.

In our judgment when the quality is good, as for example when the identification is made after a long period of observation, or in satisfactory conditions by a relative, neighbour, a close friend, a workmate and the like, the jury can safely be left to assess the value of the identifying evidence even though there is no other evidence to support it: provided always, however, that an adequate warning has been given about the special need for caution. Were the courts to adjudge otherwise, affronts to justice would frequently occur. A few examples taken over the whole spectrum of criminal activity, will illustrate what the effects upon the maintenance of law and order would be if any law were enacted that no person could be convicted on evidence of visual identification alone.

Here are the examples. A had been kidnapped and held to ransom over many days. His captor stayed with him all the time. At last he was released but he did not know the identity of his kidnapper nor where he had been kept. Months later the police arrested X for robbery and as a result of what they had been told by an informer they suspected him of the kidnapping. They had no other evidence. They arranged for A to attend an identity parade. He picked out X without hesitation. At X's trial, is the trial judge to rule at the end of the prosecution's case that X must be acquitted?

This is another example. Over a period of a week two police officers, B and C, kept observation in turn on a house which was suspected of being a distribution centre for drugs. A suspected supplier, Y, visited it from time to time. On the last day of the observation B saw Y enter the house. He at once signalled to other waiting police officers, who had a search warrant to enter. They did so; but by the time they got in, Y had escaped by a back window. Six months later C saw Y in the street and arrested him. Y at once alleged that C had mistaken him for someone else. At an identity parade he was picked out by B. Would it really be right and in the interests of justice for a judge to direct Y's acquittal at the end of the prosecution's case?

A rule such as the one under consideration would gravely impede the police in their work and would make the conviction of street offenders such as pickpockets, car thieves and the disorderly very difficult. But it would not only be the police who might be aggrieved by such a rule. Take the case of a factory worker, D, who during the course of his work went to the locker room to get something from his jacket which he had forgotten. As he went in he saw a workmate, Z, whom he had known for years and who worked nearby him in the same shop, standing by D's open locker with his hand inside. He hailed the thief by name. Z turned round and faced D; he dropped D's wallet on the floor and ran out of the locker room by another door. D reported what he had seen to his chargehand. When the chargehand went to find Z, he saw him walking towards his machine. Z alleged that D had been mistaken. A directed acquittal might well be greatly resented not only by D but by many others in the same shop.

When, in the judgment of the trial judge, the quality of the identifying evidence is poor, as for example when it depends solely on a fleeting glance or on a longer observation made in difficult conditions, the situation is very different. The judge should then withdraw the case from the jury and direct an acquittal unless there is other evidence which goes to support the correctness of the identification. This may be corroboration in the sense lawyers use that word; but it need not be so if its effect is to make the jury sure that there has been no mistaken identification: for example, X sees the accused snatch a woman's handbag; he gets only a fleeting glance of the thief s face as he runs off but he does see him entering a nearby house. Later he picks out the accused on an identity parade. If there was no more evidence than this, the poor quality of the identification would require the judge to withdraw the case from the jury; but this would not be so if there was evidence that the house into which the accused was alleged by X to have run was his father's. Another example of supporting evidence not amounting to corroboration in a technical sense is to be found in *R v Long* (1973) 57 Cr App R 871. The accused, who was charged with robbery, had been identified by three witnesses in different places on different occasions but each had only a momentary opportunity for observation. Immediately after the robbery the accused had left his home and could not be found by the police. When later he was seen by them he claimed to know who had done the robbery and offered to help to find the robbers. At his trial he put forward an alibi which the jury rejected. It was an odd coincidence that the witnesses should have identified a man who had behaved in this way. In our judgment odd coincidences can, if unexplained, be supporting evidence.

The trial judge should identify to the jury the evidence which he adjudges is capable of supporting the evidence of identification. If there is any evidence or circumstances which the jury might think was supporting when it did not have this quality, the judge should say so. A jury, for example, might think that support for identification evidence could be found in the fact that the accused had not given evidence before them. An accused's absence from the witness box cannot provide evidence of anything and the judge should tell the jury so. But he would be entitled to tell them that when assessing the quality of the identification evidence they could take into consideration the fact it was uncontradicted by any evidence coming from the accused himself.

Care should be taken by the judge when directing the jury about the support for an identification which may be derived from the fact that they have rejected an alibi. False alibis may be put forward for many reasons: an accused, for example, who has only his own truthful evidence to rely on may stupidly fabricate an alibi and get lying witnesses to support it out of fear that his own evidence will not be enough. Further, alibi witnesses can make genuine mistakes about dates and occasions like any other witnesses can. It is only when the jury is satisfied that the sole reason for the fabrication was to deceive them and there is no other explanation for its being put forward can fabrication provide any support for identification evidence. The jury should be reminded that proving the accused has told lies about where he was at the material time does not by itself prove that he was where the identifying witness says he was.

In setting out these guidelines for trial judges, which involve only changes of practice, not law, we have tried to follow the recommendations set out in the Report which Lord Devlin's Committee made to the Secretary of State for the Home Department in April 1976. We have not followed that report in using the phrase 'exceptional circumstances' to describe situations in which the risk of mistaken identification is reduced. In our judgment the use of such a phrase is likely to result in the build up of case law as to what circumstances can properly be described as exceptional and what cannot. Case law of this kind is likely to be a fetter on the administration of justice when so much depends upon the quality of the evidence in each case. Quality is what matters in the end. In many cases the exceptional circumstances to which the report refers will provide evidence of good quality, but they may not: the converse is also true.

A failure to follow these guidelines is likely to result in a conviction being quashed and will do so if in the judgment of this court on all the evidence the verdict is either unsatisfactory or unsafe.

R v *Weeder*
(1980) 71 Cr App R 228
Court of Appeal

The appellant was charged with wounding with intent contrary to s. 18 of the Offences Against the Person Act 1861, following a street attack at night on T. T was struck on the back of the head from behind and fell to the ground underneath a lamp-post. The street lamp provided a bright light and he had a good look at the appellant. M looked out of a window during the attack and saw the appellant's face. She was acquainted with him. T identified the appellant in a street identification. The judge in summing-up told the jury that one identification could constitute support for the identification by another. The appellant was convicted and appealed.

LORD LANE CJ: . . . Mr Locke suggested that the learned judge might have been wrong in law in suggesting that one identification can act as supporting evidence for another. The learned judge disagreed and after reference to *Turnbull's* case [[1977] QB 224] said that he accepted that Mr Locke was right to this extent, that the judge should warn the jury that because the identification is supported by another one it does not mean that the possibility of a mistake has disappeared. This satisfied Mr Locke and this point was then made by the learned judge when he resumed his summing-up.

Mr Locke, however, now returns to the charge and the main ground of his appeal is that the learned judge was wrong to direct the jury that an identification by one witness can constitute support for the identification by another. He submits that because a number of identifying witnesses can all be mistaken, the jury should be instructed to look at the evidence of each such witness separately in, so to speak, a hermetically sealed compartment and that they should be warned not to allow themselves to be affected by the accumulation of such evidence.

If this Court were to accept Mr Locke's submission, we would be imposing upon trial judges the obligation to pronounce a wholly useless incantation in the course of their summing-up. No jury, urged to use their common sense, could realistically be expected to follow, let alone understand, the reasoning of such direction. Take the simple case of violence at a football match. If a dozen witnesses, all of whom had in satisfactory conditions a good opportunity of observing who was committing the particular act of violence complained of, all identified the accused, is their evidence not to be viewed as capable of supporting each other?

In our judgment the position is a simple one and the guidance provided by this Court in *Turnbull (supra)* fully covers the position:

(1)   When the quality of the identifying evidence is poor the judge should withdraw the case from the jury and direct an acquittal unless there is other evidence which goes to support the correctness of the identification. The identification evidence can be poor, even though it is given by a number of witnesses. They may all have had only the opportunity of a fleeting glance or a longer observation made in difficult conditions, e.g., the occupants of a bus who observed the incident at night as they drove past.

(2)   Where the quality of the identification evidence is such that the jury can be safely left to assess its value, even though there is no other evidence to support it, then the trial judge is fully entitled, if so minded, to direct the jury that an identification by one witness can constitute support for the identification by another, *provided* that he warns them in clear terms that even a number of honest witnesses can all be mistaken.

Appeal dismissed.

R v Oakwell
[1978] 1 WLR 32
Court of Appeal

The defendant was one of a group of young people seen fighting by a police officer. The officer intervened and told the defendant that he was arresting him for breach of the peace. The police officer was then assaulted and he alleged that his assailant was the defendant. The defendant was charged with using threatening behaviour and assaulting a constable. He was convicted and appealed.

LORD WIDGERY CJ: It is alleged that the directions given in the recent case of *R v Turnbull* [1977] QB 224, were not applied to the identification problem which it is said arose in this case.

To start with, it was something of a surprise to the court to realise that any identification problem arose in this case at all. But further investigation shows that it amounts to this. There was a period when PC Tapson was on the ground when he had not got the defendant in his sight, and the suggestion is that there may have been confusion in PC Tapson's mind between the man who knocked him down and the defendant, who was standing up beside him when he got up again. This is not the sort of identity problem which *R v Turnbull* is really intended to cope with. *Turnbull* is intended primarily to deal with the ghastly risk run in cases of fleeting encounters. This certainly was not that kind of case.

Prompted by counsel doing their duty, the judge gave the jury a special passage in the summing-up on identification at the end, and we think it was perfectly adequate for the relatively minor identification problem which is eventually disclosed in this case, it being possible to say there might have been a mistake made.

Appeal dismissed.

R v Penman
(1986) 82 Cr App R 44
Court of Appeal

The appellant was charged with burglary. The principal evidence on which the prosecution relied was scientific evidence which was not and could not sensibly have been challenged. The appellant's defence was an alibi. The judge's summing-up contained no suggestion that the jury should, if they concluded that the alibi was untrue, regard that as supporting or corroborating the forensic evidence, and he dealt in the most neutral terms with the discrepancies between what the appellant said to the police and what he said in evidence. The appellant was convicted and appealed.

HUTCHISON J: . . . Mr Salmon relied on a passage in the judgment of this Court in the case of *Turnbull and Others* (1976) 63 Cr App R 132. That case, as is well known, is concerned with the way in which juries should be directed in cases where the evidence against the defendants depends wholly or substantially on the correctness of visual identification alleged by the defence to be mistaken. The passage on which Mr Salmon relies, at p. 139, is in the following terms:

> Care should be taken by the judge when directing the jury about the support for an identification which may be derived from the fact that they have rejected an alibi. False alibis may be put forward for many reasons: an accused, for example, who has only his own truthful evidence to rely on may stupidly fabricate an alibi and get lying witnesses to support it out of fear that his own evidence will not be enough. Further, alibi witnesses can make genuine mistakes about dates and occasions like any other witnesses can. It is only when the jury is satisfied that the sole reason for the fabrication was to deceive them and there is no other explanation for its being put forward, that fabrication can provide any support for identification evidence. The jury should be reminded that proving the accused has told lies about where he was at the material time does not by itself prove that he was where the identifying witness says he was.

Basing himself upon this passage, Mr Salmon argued that it was incumbent upon the learned judge in the present case to warn the jury that a lying alibi was not necessarily indicative of guilt. As he originally developed it, his argument involved the contention that the present was in truth a case where identity was in issue. However, his argument finally came to this: that wherever an alibi was relied upon and there was a possibility that in rejecting the alibi evidence the jury might conclude that the defendant was lying, the judge was obliged to give a warning of the sort mentioned in *Turnbull* (*supra*). While it was unnecessary for Mr Salmon in the present case to contend for any wider proposition, it is difficult to see why, if his argument in relation to cases where an alibi is relied on be correct, the judge should not be obliged to give a similar warning in any case where the jury are invited to conclude that the defendant had lied either to the police or in evidence.

Counsel were unable to refer us to any case which supported so wide a proposition and we know of none. There are, of course, many authorities dealing with the question whether lies by the defendant can constitute corroboration, in those cases where corroboration is either necessary or desirable. It appears to us that in the passage in *Turnbull* (*supra*) upon which Mr Salmon relies, this Court was dealing with an analogous situation. We draw attention, in particular, to the first and last sentences of the quoted passage. As we understand it, the court was not there purporting to lay down any general proposition of the sort contended for by Mr Salmon. Still less do we think that the passage supports the wider proposition to which we have suggested his argument would logically lead.

It is, of course, true that the observations of this Court as to the reasons which may cause a defendant to put forward a false alibi must be of general application. It would be absurd to suggest that those reasons exist only in cases where the evidence against the defendant consists wholly or mainly of evidence of visual identification. However, as the first and last sentences of the quoted passage show, the particular question to which the Court, in making those observations was addressing itself was whether and in what circumstances a lying alibi could be regarded as providing support for a visual identification which was challenged. In such a case, it is the duty of the trial judge to identify evidence capable of supporting the evidence of identification and, in some such cases, the supporting evidence may take the form of a false alibi which has been fabricated by the defendant in order to deceive the jury. When the judge refers, in such a case, to lies by the defendant as being capable of constituting supporting evidence, he should remind the jury that the mere fact that the defendant has told lies about his whereabouts does not of itself prove that he was at the place where the identifying witness said he was. Similarly, in other cases in which a judge refers to lies by the defendant as being capable of constituting corroboration, his direction to the jury will indicate that the defendant's motive for lying must have been realisation of his guilt and fear of the truth.

It appears to us that the present case is wholly different. The principle evidence on which the prosecution relied was scientific evidence which was not and could not sensibly have been challenged. It was for the jury to decide whether they were prepared to infer from that evidence that the appellant was one of the burglars. In deciding whether to draw that inference they, of course, had to take into account what he had said to the police and what he had said in evidence as to his movements that night. Plainly, as their verdict shows, they did not believe his account, and they must have been prepared to draw the inference from the forensic evidence that he was one of the men involved. The learned judge's summing-up contains no suggestion that the jury should, if they concluded that the alibi was untrue, regard that as supporting or corroborating the forensic evidence. Indeed, as the passages we have cited from his summing up show, the learned judge dealt in the most neutral possible terms with the discrepancies between what the defendant said to the police and what he said in evidence. The present case was, as we have said, in no way comparable with those cases which have to do with lies as corroboration, or with the case of *Turnbull* (*supra*).

In our judgment, there is no rule which, in a case such as the present, requires a warning in the terms contemplated by Mr Salmon's third ground of appeal. Of course, the circumstances of individual cases vary infinitely, and very often when a question arises as to whether a defendant has been lying, either to the police or in evidence, a judge will consider it appropriate to advise the jury that the mere fact that he has told lies does not prove guilt because there may be many reasons why a person will lie. However, as we have indicated, there is in our judgment no rule which requires that such a warning should invariably be given whenever the veracity of the defendant or the truth of an alibi defence is challenged, and we can well understand why the learned judge felt it unnecessary to give any such warning in the present case.

Appeal dismissed.

Questions
1.   Do you agree with Lord Widgery's statement in *R* v *Oakwell* that *R* v *Turnbull* is intended primarily to deal with the risk run in cases of fleeting encounters?
2.   Donald, a man in his twenties, is charged with raping Ethel, a 13-year-old schoolgirl, in a field at about 5 p.m. on the 1 June. The case has gone to trial and the following evidence has been given:

(a)   Ethel has said that Donald, who was a neighbour, met her at school, started to walk home with her, enticed her off the road, and pushed her over and had intercourse with her;

(b)   Freda, Ethel's schoolfriend, has said that she saw Donald hanging around the school gates at about 4 p.m. on the 1 June, and that he and Ethel started to walk home together. Freda's sister, Molly, used to be Donald's girlfriend, but he ended their relationship two weeks before the alleged offence. Freda was very upset at seeing Molly rejected;

(c)   Gillian, Ethel's mother, has said that Ethel came home late on 1 June: her clothes were dirty and dishevelled and Ethel told her that Donald had been wicked;

(d)   The police doctor who examined Ethel on 1 June has said that Ethel appeared to have had sexual intercourse recently;

(e)   PC Harry has said that he interviewed Donald who told him that he was waiting outside the school to meet his niece, Jane, that he did speak to Ethel, but he did not start to walk home with her.

Donald has testified that Ethel has fabricated the entire story. He has not called any witnesses.

Consider what directions the judge must or may give the jury.

Further Reading
P. Murphy, *A Practical Approach to Evidence*, 4th ed. (1992), Ch. 15
P. Mirfield, 'An Alternative Future for Corroboration Warnings' (1991) 107 LQR 450
S. Bronitt, '*Baskerville* Revisited' [1991] Crim LR 30

7 THE RULE AGAINST HEARSAY — I NATURE AND SCOPE OF THE RULE

The rule against hearsay evidence remains one of the most important exclusionary rules of the law of evidence. It has been variously defined by many eminent authors. It is defined in *Cross on Evidence* as 'an assertion other than one made by a person while giving oral evidence in the proceedings is inadmissible *as evidence of any fact asserted*' (7th ed., p. 42). In this and the following chapters, the rule and many of its exceptions will be considered. This chapter will specifically consider the nature of the hearsay rule as well as its scope.

(A) Nature of the hearsay rule

The rule against hearsay has been described by Cross as 'one of the oldest, most complex and most confusing of the exclusionary rules of evidence'. The most obvious form of hearsay arises during the course of oral testimony. Imagine that D is being tried for murder, it being alleged that D stabbed P with a knife. Witness W wishes to testify that X said to him 'I saw D stab P'. The testimony of W would amount to hearsay evidence as it seeks to rely upon the assertion of X as evidence of the fact that D stabbed P. Similarly, if X had written in a document that he saw D stab P, the document would amount to hearsay evidence. The rule even extends to cover conduct as well as written or spoken words. If X was deaf and dumb and used sign language or gestures to demonstrate to W that D stabbed P, W could not repeat those signs or gestures without infringing the hearsay rule. As the following cases illustrate, however, the rule extends only to those assertions which are relied upon testimonially, i.e. where it is sought to rely upon the assertion as being *evidence of the fact asserted*. If the statement is admitted for some other purpose, then the hearsay rule is not infringed.

Subramaniam v Public Prosecutor
[1956] 1 WLR 965
Privy Council

The appellant was charged with unlawful possession of ammunition. It would have been a defence that the appellant had a lawful excuse for his possession, and he sought to give evidence that he had been captured by terrorists and was acting under duress. The trial judge ruled that he could not state in evidence what the terrorists had said to him. The appellant was convicted and appealed.

MR L M D DE SILVA: . . . Evidence of a statement made to a witness by a person who is not himself called as a witness may or may not be hearsay. It is hearsay and inadmissible when the object of the evidence is to establish the truth of what is contained in the statement. It is not hearsay and is admissible when it is proposed to establish by the evidence, not the truth of the statement, but the fact that it was made. The fact that the statement was made, quite apart from its truth, is frequently relevant in considering the mental state and conduct thereafter of the witness or of some other person in whose presence the statement was made. In the case before their Lordships statements could have been made to the appellant by the terrorists, which, whether true or not, if they had been believed by the appellant, might reasonably have induced in him an apprehension of instant death if he failed to conform to their wishes.

Appeal allowed.

Myers v Department of Public Prosecutions
[1965] AC 1001
House of Lords

The appellant was convicted of offences of dishonesty in relation to motor vehicles. His practice was to buy up wrecked cars with their log-books, to disguise stolen cars so that they corresponded as nearly as possible with the wrecks and their log-books, and to sell the stolen cars as if they were the wrecks, repaired by him. In order to prove their case, the prosecution adduced evidence from a witness in charge of records which were kept on microfilm, containing details of every car made at the works of a certain manufacturer. The microfilm was prepared from records compiled by workmen on cards, which were destroyed after being filmed, and which recorded the cylinder-block number of each car. Since the cylinder-block number was stamped indelibly on the engine of each vehicle, the evidence was of some value to the prosecution in proving the true identity of the cars in question. The trial judge admitted this evidence and the Court of Criminal Appeal upheld this.

LORD REID: The reason why this evidence is maintained to have been inadmissible is that its cogency depends on hearsay. The witness could only say that a record made by someone else showed that, if the record was correctly made, a car had left the works bearing three particular numbers. He could not prove that the record was correct or that the numbers which it contained were in fact the numbers on the car when it was made. This is a highly technical point, but the law regarding hearsay evidence is technical, and I would say absurdly technical. . . .

At the trial counsel for the prosecution sought to support the existing practice of admitting such records, if produced by the persons in charge of them, by arguing that they were not adduced to prove the truth of the recorded particulars but only to prove that they were records kept in the normal course of business. Counsel for the accused then asked the very pertinent question - if they were not intended to prove the truth of the entries what were they intended to prove? I ask what the jury would infer from them: obviously that they were probably true records. If they were not capable of supporting an inference that they were probably true records, then I do not see what probative value they could have, and their admission was bound to mislead the jury . . . .

In argument the Solicitor-General maintained that, although the general rule may be against the admission of private records to prove the truth of entries in them, the trial judge has a discretion to admit a record in a particular case if satisfied that it is trustworthy and that justice requires its admission. That appears to me to be contrary to the whole framework of the existing law. It is true that a judge has a discretion to exclude legally admissible evidence if justice so requires, but it is a very different thing to say that he has a discretion to admit legally inadmissible evidence. The whole development of the exceptions to the hearsay rule is based on the determination of certain classes of evidence as admissible or inadmissible and not on the apparent credibility of particular evidence tendered. No matter how cogent particular evidence may seem to be, unless it comes within a class which is admissible, it is excluded. Half a dozen witnesses may offer to prove that they heard two men of high character who cannot now be found discuss in detail the fact now in issue and agree on a credible account of it, but that evidence would not be admitted although it might be by far the best evidence available.

(LORDS MORRIS OF BORTH-Y-GEST and HODSON delivered concurring judgments holding that the evidence should not be received. LORDS DONOVAN and PEARCE dissented on the question of admissibility. Their Lordships were unanimous in applying the proviso to s. [2(1) of the Criminal Appeal Act 1968].)

Appeal dismissed.

Questions
1.   One of the main objections to hearsay evidence is its unreliability due to the possibility of distortion or its inaccuracy following repetition. Was that danger present in *Myers* v *DPP*?
2.   If the House of Lords in *Myers* v *DPP* had ruled the evidence admissible, would this have been unjust to the defendant? Why?

Note
The effect of *Myers* v *DPP* was quickly reversed by legislation. The current legislation concerning documentary hearsay evidence is dealt with in Chapter 9.

Patel v *Comptroller of Customs*
[1966] AC 356
Privy Council

The appellant imported from Singapore into Fiji a quantity of corriander seed, which was shipped in bags. He correctly engrossed the Customs

Import Entry Form A in accordance with the particulars contained in the invoice referable to the purchase of the seed. On investigation at arrival, however, five bags were found each to be contained in an outer bag marked with the appellant's trade name, but the inner bags had written on them: 'Alberdan/AD/4152/Corriander Favourite Singapore' and at the base of them the legend 'Produce of Morocco'. In the import entry form the country of origin was stated to be India. The appellant was charged and convicted with making a false declaration in a customs import entry produced to an officer of customs in that in respect of the five bags instead of declaring the origin of the seed to be Morocco he declared it to be India. He appealed against conviction.

LORD HODSON: . . . The next question was whether there was any evidence upon which the appellant could be convicted of making a false declaration as charged.

The only entry as to which the allegation of falsity is made is the word 'India' in the column headed 'country of origin,' which is part of the import entry form signed by the appellant. The only evidence purporting to show that this entry was false is the legend 'Produce of Morocco' written upon the bags. Their Lordships are asked by the respondent to say that the inference can be drawn that the goods contained in the bags were produced in Morocco. This they are unable to do. From an evidentiary point of view the words are hearsay and cannot assist the prosecution. This matter need not be elaborated in view of the decision of the House of Lords in *Myers* v *Director of Public Prosecutions* [1965] AC 1001, given after the Fiji courts had considered the case. The decision of the House, however, makes clear beyond doubt that the list of exceptions to the hearsay rule cannot be extended judicially to include such things as labels or markings. Nothing is to be gained by comparing the legend in this case with the records considered in *Myers* v *Director of Public Prosecutions*. Nothing here is known of when and by whom the markings on the bags were affixed and no evidence was called to prove any fact which tended to show that the goods in question in fact came from Morocco.

Some reliance was placed by the respondent on *R* v *Rice* [1963] 1 QB 857, where a used airline ticket was admitted as an exhibit in a criminal prosecution. It is sufficient to say that the Court of Criminal Appeal in admitting the document said that it must not be treated as speaking its contents, for what it might say could only be hearsay.

Appeal allowed.

Jones v *Metcalfe*
[1967] 1 WLR 1286
Divisional Court

A collision took place between two cars, caused by the action of a lorry. An eye witness reported the registration number of the lorry to the police. The appellant was charged with driving without due care and attention. The eye witness gave evidence that he had reported the number to the police, but was unable to quote the number to the court. The other evidence was that of a police officer who said that as a result of information, he interviewed the appellant, put to him what was alleged to have taken place, stated that his information was that the motor lorry concerned was EWH 820 and that the appellant admitted that he was the driver of a lorry bearing that number at the time and date in question, but denied that any accident occurred due to his driving. The appellant was convicted.

LORD PARKER: . . . It was no wonder really that in those circumstances a submission was made that no evidence had been adduced to show that the lorry EWH 820 was the lorry concerned in the incident, or put another way, that the appellant was the driver of the lorry involved in the incident. This court is getting a number of cases of this kind; in most it is true the independent witness, who after a lapse of time has forgotten the number which he took, can produce other matters of identification; for instance Mr Dickinson might or might not have been able to say that the lorry concerned was not merely a lorry but was a brewer's lorry, or he might have been able to identify the driver as a man with red hair or with spectacles, and have in this way produced some identification of the lorry which the appellant admitted to be driving. There is no such additional evidence in the present case. This is simply a case where the evidence was that the independent witness gave a number to a policeman, and that a policeman, not necessarily the same policeman, on information obtained, whether from Mr Dickinson or somebody else we do not know, then proceeded to interview the appellant.

The justices, and I have very much sympathy with them, accepted the common sense approach that they were entitled to come to the conclusion that the police officer acted on the information given by Mr Dickinson and that Mr Dickinson must have identified the lorry as EWH 820. In my judgment, however, they were not entitled to do it. To do so is really to make inroads into the principle under which we still act, that hearsay evidence is inadmissible. I also think that if they had been referred at an earlier stage — because I gather they did not hear the case until after they had convicted the appellant — to *Grew* v *Cubitt* [1951] 2 TLR 305, DC, they would have been forced to come to a different conclusion. There the independent witness had not given a number to the police, but he gave evidence that he had got his wife to write it down. Again as the result of information received the police officer went and interviewed the appellant. In that case it is to be observed that the prosecution case could have been proved in one of two ways: they could have called the wife who wrote the number down; equally they could have asked the independent witness whether he had seen the wife write the number down and, if so, on production of the note he could have refreshed his memory and stated what the number was.

As the court there held, although there was a strong probability that the police officer acted on information obtained from the wife or from the wife's note, there was in fact, under our rules of evidence, no connecting link, and the prosecution had not proved their case.

In my judgment the same really applies here. If Mr Dickinson had been able to say that he gave a number to the police officer, that he saw the police officer write it down in his note book and had then been asked to refresh his memory from the production of that note book then albeit it was not in his own handwriting, it was in effect his note and the prosecution could have proved their case.

DIPLOCK LJ: I reluctantly agree. Like my Lord I have every sympathy with the justices because the inference of fact that the appellant was the driver of the lorry at the time of the accident is irresistible as a matter of common sense. But this is a branch of the law which has little to do with common sense. The inference that the appellant was the driver of the lorry was really an inference of what the independent witness had said to the police when he gave them the number of the lorry, and since what he had said to the police would have been inadmissible as hearsay, to infer what he said to the police is inadmissible also.

Appeal allowed.

Question
Diplock LJ in *Jones* v *Metcalfe* states that 'this is a branch of law which has little to do with common sense'. Do you agree?

R v *Lydon*
(1987) 85 Cr App R 221
Court of Appeal

WOOLF LJ: After a trial lasting three days at the Crown Court in Oxford, the appellant was found guilty of one offence of taking a conveyance without authority, in respect of which he was sentenced to 12 months' imprisonment, and one offence of robbery, in respect of which he was sentenced to seven years' imprisonment concurrent. In addition the appellant, having admitted being in breach of a conditional discharge, was sentenced to six months' imprisonment consecutive to the previous sentences, making the total sentence one of seven and a half years' imprisonment.

He now appeals against conviction by leave of the single judge.

The robbery took place on July 31, 1985, and was of a post office at Crowmarsh Gifford in Oxfordshire. The sum taken was £1,700. The robbery was carried out by two men, one of whom was the appellant's co-accused Fernandez who pleaded guilty.

The only issue at the trial was whether or not the appellant was the second man.

The other count related to the car used for the robbery, which was taken from the Neasden area of London on the same morning as the robbery.

. . .

The principal ground of appeal relates to the evidence which was put before the jury notwithstanding an objection made by Mr Grunwald on behalf of the appellant, that the evidence was hearsay and in any event more prejudicial than it was probative.

The evidence was as to the discovery of a gun on the grass verge, 12 inches from the edge of the road which would have been used by the getaway car when travelling towards Nettlebed and about a mile from where the robbery took place. The gun was in four pieces. Immediately in the vicinity of it was found two pieces of rolled up paper which had written upon them 'Sean rules' and 'Sean rules 85.' The gun had broken into four pieces. On the surface of the broken gun barrel there was a heavy smear of blue ink on the inside which, according to the forensic evidence, was similar in appearance and dye composition to that on the pieces of paper, so that the ink could have originated from the same pen. However, the gun was black and silver, whereas Mr Ham, who only saw part of the barrel of the gun and who was the only witness at the scene to give a description, said that it was dark brown in colour and had a makeshift look about it.

The appellant gave evidence on his own behalf, and it was his case, supported by witnesses, that at the time of the offence he was in Neasden.

Mr Grunwald on behalf of the appellant contended that, apart from the writing on the paper referring to 'Sean,' there was nothing to connect the accused with the gun and he submitted that the references to 'Sean' were hearsay and in any event, bearing in mind that there are a great many people who are called Sean, the evidence was highly prejudicial. He accepted that the decision of this Court in *Rice* (1963) 47 Cr App R 79, [1963] 1 QB 857 was some support for the ruling of the learned recorder, since in that case this Court upheld the use of an air ticket to establish that Rice flew from London to Manchester on a particular day. However, he submitted that that decision had been overruled by implication by the House of Lords in *Myers v Director of Public Prosecutions* (1964) 48 Cr App R 348, [1965] AC 1001.

He drew the Court's attention to a decision of the Supreme Court of Australia, *Romeo* (1982) 30 SASR 243, in which Cox J examined in detail the English and Australian decisions, and expressed the view that the decision of this Court was inconsistent with the reasoning of the majority of the House of Lords in *Myers v DPP* (*supra*).

In *Rice* Winn J, in giving the judgment of this Court at p. 90 and p. 872 respectively, drew a distinction between the relevance and probative significance of the ticket as distinct from its contents, since 'what it might say could only be hearsay,' and Cox J recognised this distinction in his judgment (at p. 262). He said:

'Sometimes it is possible to avoid the hearsay rule by showing that a statement made in a document is being used as an original and independent fact — for instance, that a person who made use of the document had certain information in his possession at a relevant time — and not as evidence of the facts stated. It is always important, therefore, whenever an objection is taken on hearsay grounds, to ascertain for precisely what purpose the evidence is being tendered. It may be hearsay for one purpose and not, and therefore admissible, for another.'

However he went on to say (at p. 263) with some justification,

'It is clear that the airline ticket in *Rice*, in the absence of any other evidence, was being put forward as proof of the truth of the statement implicit in it, namely, that a man named Rice flew from London to Manchester on the flight mentioned in the ticket.'

However, whether or not the case of *Rice* is still good law, the decision of the learned recorder in this case can be supported on the approach adopted by Cox J. The reference to Sean could be regarded as no more than a statement of fact involving no assertion as to the truth of the contents of the document.

. . .

In dealing with the distinction between writing which is admissible and which is not admissible in these circumstances, *Cross on Evidence* (6th ed. at p. 464) states:

In these cases it seems that the writing when properly admissible at all, is relevant not as an assertion of the state of facts but as itself a fact which affords circumstantial evidence upon the basis of which the jury may draw an inference as it may from any other relevant circumstance of the case.

The inference that the jury could draw from the words written on the piece of paper is that the paper had been in the possession of someone who wished to write 'Sean rules,' and that person would presumably either be named Sean himself or at least be associated with such a person, and thus it creates an inferential link with the appellant. By itself it could not possibly satisfy the jury that the appellant was the other robber, but it could be circumstantial evidence which could help to satisfy the jury that the Crown's case was correct.

This approach to the probative value and relevance of the evidence can be readily illustrated by examples where it could not be suggested that the evidence was inadmissible as being hearsay. If instead of the word 'Sean' appearing on the paper the paper had blood upon it and could be linked to the gun by other evidence, or the gun also had blood upon it, and both samples were of the same blood group as that of the appellant, or again if the gun was proved to have been used in the robbery, the samples could provide evidence which the jury could perfectly properly be asked to take into account, albeit that the appellant's blood group was one which was extremely common. The rarity of the blood group would only go to the weight of the evidence and not its admissibility.

Similarly, if the gun had been wrapped in a local paper normally only circulating in Neasden, that again, having regard to the fact that the appellant admittedly came from Neasden, would have been relevant circumstantial evidence. If there had been written on the pieces of paper the appellant's full name, then clearly that would have been much stronger circumstantial evidence, but, although the name 'Sean' may be fairly common, it is still material to which the jury could have regard.

. . .

Appeal dismissed.

R v Turner (Bryan James)
(1975) 61 Cr App R 67
Court of Appeal

The defendant was charged with robbery. The trial judge refused to admit evidence to the effect that a person not called as a witness had admitted having committed the offence charged. The defendant was convicted and appealed.

MILMO J: . . . Assuming for the present purpose that it was relevant to prove that Saunders had been one of the robbers at Ilford, the defence would have been entitled to call witnesses to prove the fact of their own knowledge, such as people who had actually seen him at the bank. They could have called Saunders himself. No such evidence was called and evidence of what Saunders said to a third party was not probative of anything. It would have been hearsay evidence which did not come within any of the well settled exceptions to the general rule that hearsay evidence is not admissible. That the categories of these exceptions is now closed and cannot be added to without legislation was made clear by Lord Reid in his speech in *Myers v Director of Public Prosecutions* [1965] AC 1001, 48 Cr App R 348, a case in which it had been sought to extend the exceptions to the ban on the reception of hearsay in evidence. At p. 1021E and p. 362 Lord Reid said: 'The common law must be developed to meet the changing economic conditions and habits of thought, and I would not be deterred by expressions of opinion in this House in old cases. But there are limits to what we can or should do. If we are to extend the law it must be by the development and application of fundamental principles. We cannot introduce arbitrary conditions or limitations: that must be left to legislation.'

Mr Wright cited a number of authorities which he contended supported his argument that evidence of what Saunders was alleged to have said to the police was admissible. These included *Greenberg* (1923) 17 Cr App R 107; *Phillips* (1936) 26 Cr App R 17; and *Cooper (Sean)* [1969] 1 QB 267, 53 Cr App R 82.

The case of *Greenberg (supra)* was one of rape in which the trial had been conducted on the footing that the complainant who had given evidence for the Crown was a modest woman. On appeal leave was given to cross-examine her on her character and to call two witnesses to give evidence of her companionship with men on the basis of their own observations and of statements made by her that she had brought the charge against the accused in order to get money. The Court held that the new evidence was such that the jury might not have convicted had it been before them.

Phillips' case (*supra*) was one of incest. The defence was that the case was fabricated and that the two girls concerned had been schooled by their mother to give false evidence against their father. It was put to each of the girls in cross-examination that they had admitted to another person that their evidence was false and each of them denied it. The defence then sought to call evidence of the making of these admissions, but the trial judge ruled that such evidence went to credit only and declined to admit it. From the report it seems to this Court that the evidence was clearly admissible under s. 4 of the Criminal Procedure Act 1865 and it is stated that the Crown on the hearing of the appeal conceded that it was admissible. The Court of Criminal Appeal held that the evidence which it was sought to call went beyond the credibility of the girls and went to the very foundation of the prisoner's answer to the charge, namely, that the witnesses called for the Crown were biased and were parties to a plot to frame the accused.

Cooper's case (*supra*) was somewhat curious. In the re-examination of a defence witness, hearsay evidence was given without objection by the Crown, that a third person who had not been called as a witness had admitted that he was the person who had committed the offence with which the accused was charged. The Court of Criminal Appeal allowed the appeal upon the ground that the conviction was unsafe or unsatisfactory. It is significant that throughout the report the word 'hearsay' does not appear and it would seem that the point was never taken that the admission in question was hearsay and as such inadmissible.

The Court does not find in any of these cases any authority for the proposition advanced in this case that hearsay evidence is admissible in a criminal case to show that a third party who has not been called as a witness in the case has admitted committing the offence charged. The idea, which may be gaining prevalence in some quarters, that in a criminal trial the defence is entitled to adduce hearsay evidence to establish facts, which if proved would be relevant and would assist the defence, is wholly erroneous.

Appeal dismissed.

Question
Consider which, if any, of the following pieces of testimony amount to hearsay evidence:

(a) David pleads insanity in defence to a charge of murder. Eric testifies that on several occasions he overheard David say 'I am Adolf Hitler reincarnate';

(b) Fred is suing his employer for damages following an incident at work which he alleges rendered him permanently impotent. Greta wishes to testify that three months after the incident she overheard Fred say to Harry 'I made it in bed with Susan last night';

(c) Jack is charged with the murder of Ken. Lisa wishes to testify that two days before the alleged murder she overheard Jack say to an unknown person 'I'm going to kill Ken for what he's done'.

(d)   Michelle wishes to testify that four days after the alleged murder she overheard Nigel say to an unknown person 'I told you that I would get even with Ken. I fixed him good and proper'.

R v Osbourne; R v Virtue
[1973] QB 678
Court of Appeal

The defendants were convicted of robbery. Both defendants had been picked out at an identification parade, Osbourne by Mrs B and Virtue by Mrs H. At the trial, some seven months after the parade, Mrs B said that she could not remember having picked out anyone at a parade; and Mrs H first said that she thought one of the defendants to be a man she had picked out at a parade, and then said that she did not think that that man was in court. The police inspector in charge of the parade was then called and gave evidence that the women had identified the defendants.

LAWTON LJ: Now I turn to the point which was taken on behalf of the defendant Osbourne about the admissibility of Chief Inspector Stevenson's evidence. It is right that I should stress that the point was that such evidence was inadmissible. Its weight was another matter altogether and, as I have pointed out already, the trial judge advised the jury to attach little, if any, weight to Mrs Head's evidence of identification. He reminded the jury of Mrs Brookes' lapse of memory. It was strenuously argued before the trial judge and equally strenuously argued before us, that such evidence was not admissible at all and that its wrongful admission made the conviction unsafe. An analogy was drawn between the situation which arose in this case with those two ladies and the situation which can arise in the witness box when a witness for the prosecution gives evidence which the Crown does not like. Our attention was drawn to the Criminal Law Procedure Act 1865. The situation envisaged by section 3 of the Act of 1865 did not arise in this case at all because nobody suggested that those two ladies were acting in the way envisaged by that Act, namely, adversely, or, to use the modern term, hostilely, but it was said that the trial judge allowed the prosecution to call evidence to contradict them, which is not admissible.

We do not agree that Chief Inspector Stevenson's evidence contradicted their evidence. All that Mrs Brookes had said was that she did not remember, and, as I have already indicated, that is very understandable after a delay of seven and a half months. She had, however, done something. Within four days of the robbery she had attended an identification parade. She had been told in the presence and hearing of the defendant Osbourne, as is the usual practice, what she was to do, namely, point out anybody whom she had seen at the time of the raid. She did point somebody out and it was the defendant Osbourne. One asks oneself as a matter of commonsense why, when a witness has forgotten what she did, evidence should not be given by another witness with a better memory to establish what, in fact, she did when the events were fresh in her mind. Much the same situation arises with regard to Mrs Head. She said in the witness box that she had picked somebody out. She did not think that the man she had picked out was in court, but that again is understandable because appearances can change after seven and a half months, and if the experience of this court is anything to go by, accused persons often look much smarter in the dock than they do when they are first arrested. This court can see no reason at all in principle why evidence of that kind should not be admitted.

It was submitted that the admission of that evidence was contrary to a decision of the House of Lords in *R v Christie* [1914] AC 545. That case has long been regarded as a difficult one to understand because the speeches of their Lordships were not directed to the same points, but this can be got from the speeches: that evidence of identification other than identification in the witness box is admissible. All that the prosecution were seeking to do was to establish the fact of identification at the identification parades held on November 20. This court can see no reason why that evidence should not have been admitted. The court is fortified in that view by a passage in the judgment of Sachs LJ which appears in *R v Richardson* [1971] 2 QB 484, which was a very different case from the present case, but the principle enunciated by Sachs LJ is applicable. Sachs LJ said, at p. 490:

> The courts, however, must take care not to deprive themselves by new, artificial rules of practice of the best chances of learning the truth. The courts are under no compulsion unnecessarily to follow on a matter of practice the lure of the rules of logic in order to produce unreasonable results which would hinder the course of justice.

It is pertinent to point out that in 1914 when the House of Lords came to consider *R v Christie* [1914] AC 545 the modern practice of identity parades did not exist. The whole object of identification parades is for the protection of the suspect, and what happens at those parades is highly relevant to the establishment of the truth. It would be wrong, in the judgment of this court, to set up artificial rules of evidence, which hinder the administration of justice. The evidence was admissible.

Appeal dismissed.

Note

In *R v McCay* [1991] 1 All ER 232, the witness attended an identification parade and, in the presence of a police inspector and the defendant's solicitor, said 'It's number 8'. The defendant was standing in position number 8. At trial, the witness could not remember in which position the defendant had been standing. The prosecution called the police inspector and he was asked to repeat the words of the witness, namely that the witness had said 'It's number 8'. The trial judge rejected a defence submission that this evidence was inadmissible hearsay. The Court of Appeal upheld the trial judge's ruling finding that even if the words were hearsay, they were admissible as part of the *res gestae* (see 8(c)(*i*)) or, alternatively, by authority of the Codes of Practice. The case of *R v Osbourne* (above) was cited to the court in argument, but was not referred to in the judgment.

Question

In *Sparks v R* [1964] AC 964, Lord Morris of Borth-y-Gest said, 'There is no rule which permits the giving of hearsay evidence merely because it relates to identity'. Are the decisions in *R v Osbourne* and *R v McCay* consistent with this statement?

(B) Scope of the hearsay rule

One difficult question is whether or not statements which impliedly assert a fact are caught by the hearsay rule. It is not doubted that statements (oral or by conduct) which expressly assert a fact are caught by the rule. If, however, the statement or conduct is not intended to assert a fact but nevertheless rests on some assumption of fact which the maker of the statement believes to be true, can the court admit the statement in order to infer the existence of that fact? A frequently cited example is a statement by W, 'Hello X'. Clearly the statement 'Hello X' is not intended by its maker to be assertive of any particular fact, yet from it may be inferred several things. For example, it implies that the second person was X; that X was present at the time; that X is not deaf; that X can speak English; etc. Would such a statement be caught by the hearsay rule? In civil cases, this problem has now been rendered redundant by s. 2 of the Civil Evidence Act 1968 (see Chapter 9). In criminal cases, the problem continues to be the subject of some debate although the balance of authority is in favour of excluding implied assertions as being caught by the hearsay rule.

Wright v *Doe d Tatham*
(1837) 7 A & E 313
Court of Exchequer Chamber

This was an action concerning land owned by John Marsden, deceased. The defendant, Wright, claimed as devisee under Marsden's will. The plaintiff, Tatham, claimed as heir at law, alleging that the will was void on the ground that the testator had insufficient mental capacity to make a valid will. He introduced the following evidence without objection: that Marsden was treated as a child by his own servants; that in his youth he was called, in the village where he lived, 'Silly Jack', and 'Silly Marsden'; that a witness had seen boys shouting after him, 'There goes crazy Marsden' and throwing dirt at him, and had persuaded a person passing by to see him home. As evidence of competency, Wright sought to produce letters which had been written to Marsden by persons who knew him well to show that they treated him as sane. The trial judge excluded these letters and the jury found for Tatham. Wright filed a bill of exceptions in the Court of Exchequer Chamber.

BOSANQUET J: It is obvious that the contents of letters may be dictated by various motives, according to the dispositions and circumstances of the writers. Language of affection, of respect, of rational or amusing information, may be addressed from the best of motives to persons in a state of considerable imbecility, or labouring under the strangest delusions. The habitual treatment of deranged persons as rational is one mode of promoting their recovery. A tone of insult or derision may be employed in a moment of irritation in writing to a person in full possession of his reason; what judgment can be formed of the intention of the writers, without an endless examination into the circumstances which may have influenced them? And what opinion can be collected of the capacity of the receiver without ascertaining how he acted when he read the language addressed to him? To me it appears that the admission in proof of capacity of letters unaccompanied by other circumstances than such as are stated in this record would establish an entirely new precedent in a Court of Common Law, from which very great inconvenience might result upon trials of sanity, as well of the living as of the dead.

PARKE B: It is admitted, and most properly, that you have no right to use in evidence the fact of writing and sending a letter to a third person containing a statement of competence, on the ground that it affords an inference that such an act would not have been done unless the statement was true, or believed to be true, although such an inference no doubt would be raised in the conduct of the ordinary affairs of life, if the statement were made by a man of veracity. But it cannot be raised in a judicial inquiry; and, if such an argument were admissible, it would lead to the indiscriminate admission of hearsay evidence of all manner of facts.

Further, it is clear that an acting to a much greater extent and degree upon such statements to a third person would not make the statements admissible. For example, if a wager to a large amount had been made as to the matter in issue by two third persons, the payment of that wager, however large the sum, would not be admissible to prove the truth of the matter in issue. You would not have had any right to present it to the jury as raising an inference of the truth of the fact, on the ground that otherwise the bet would not have been paid. It is, after all, nothing but the mere statement of that fact, with strong evidence of the belief of it by the party making it. Could it make any difference that the wager was between the third person and one of the parties to the suit? Certainly not. The payment by other underwriters on the same policy to the plaintiff could not be given in evidence to prove that the subject insured had been lost. Yet there is an act done, a payment strongly attesting the truth of the statement, which it implies, that there had been a loss. To illustrate this point still further, let us suppose a third person had betted a wager with Mr Marsden that he could not solve some mathematical problem, the solution of which required a high degree of capacity; would payment of that wager to Mr Marsden's banker be admissible evidence that he possessed that capacity? The answer is certain; it would not. It would be evidence of the fact of competence given by a third party not upon oath.

Let us suppose the parties who wrote these letters to have stated the matter therein contained, that is, their knowledge of his personal qualities and capacity for business, on oath before a magistrate, or in some judicial proceeding to which the plaintiff and defendant were not parties. No one could contend that such statement would be admissible on this issue; and yet there would have been an act done on the faith of the statement being true, and a very solemn one, which would raise in the ordinary conduct of affairs a strong belief in the truth of the statement, if the writers were faith-worthy. The acting in this case is of much less importance, and certainly is not equal to the sanction of an extra-judicial oath.

Many other instances of a similar nature, by way of illustration, were suggested by the learned counsel for the defendant in error, which, on the most cursory consideration, any one would at once declare to be inadmissible in evidence. Others were supposed on the part of the plaintiff in error, which, at first sight, have the appearance of being mere facts, and therefore admissible, though on further consideration they are open to precisely the same objection. Of the first description are the supposed cases of a letter by a third person to any one demanding a debt, which may be said to be a treatment of him as a debtor, being offered as proof that the debt was really due; a note, congratulating him on his high state of bodily vigour, being proposed as evidence of his being in good health; both of which are manifestly at first sight objectionable. To the latter class belong the supposed conduct of the family or relations of a testator, taking the same precautions in his absence as if he were a lunatic; his election, in his absence, to some high and responsible office; the conduct of a physician who permitted a will to be executed by a sick testator; the conduct of a deceased captain on a question of seaworthiness, who, after examining every part of the vessel, embarked in it with his family; all these, when deliberately considered, are, with reference to the matter in issue in each case, mere instances of hearsay evidence, mere statements, not on oath, but implied in or vouched by the actual conduct of persons by whose acts the litigant parties are not to be bound.

(TINDALL CJ, GURNEY B, and COLTMAN and PARK JJ delivered concurring judgments.)

Trial verdict confirmed. Subsequently the House of Lords also affirmed the verdict in favour of the plaintiff (see (1838) 4 Bing NC 489).

Woodhouse v *Hall*
(1981) 72 Cr App R 39
Divisional Court

The defendant was charged with managing a brothel at certain premises, described as a sauna and massage parlour. In order to prove that the premises were being used as a brothel, the prosecution sought to adduce evidence of conversations between police officers and women employed as masseuses at the premises, in which details of the availability and cost of sexual services were discussed. The magistrates rejected this evidence as hearsay and dismissed the charge. The prosecution appealed.

DONALDSON LJ: We have been referred to *Ratten* v *R* (1971) 56 Cr App R 18, [1972] AC 378, a Privy Council decision, but one which reflects English law. For my part I think it is sufficient to refer to a short passage in the opinion of the Board which was delivered by Lord Wilberforce and appears at p. 23 and p. 387 of the respective reports:

The mere fact that evidence of a witness includes evidence as to words spoken by another person who is not called, is no objection to its admissibility. Words spoken are facts just as much as any other action by a human being. If the speaking of the words is a relevant fact, a witness may give evidence that they were spoken. A question of hearsay only arises when the words spoken are relied on 'testimonially,' i.e., as establishing some fact narrated by the words. Authority is hardly needed for this proposition, but their Lordships will restate what was said in the judgment of the Board in *Subramaniam* v *Public Prosecutor* [1956] 1 WLR 965, 970: 'Evidence of a statement made to a witness by a person who is not himself called as a witness may or may not be hearsay. It is hearsay and inadmissible when the object of the evidence is to establish the truth of what is contained in the statement. It is not hearsay and is admissible when it is proposed to establish by the evidence, not the truth of the statement, but the fact that it was made.'

I suspect that the justices were misled by *Subramaniam's* case (*supra*) and thought that this was a hearsay case, because they may have thought that they had to be satisfied as to the truth of what the ladies said or were alleged to have said in the sense they had to satisfy themselves that the words were not a joke but were meant seriously and something of that sort. But this is not a matter of truth or falsity. It is a matter of what was really said — the quality of the words, the message being transmitted.

That arises in every case where the words themselves are a relevant fact. The quality of the words has to be assessed, but that is quite different from the situation where the words are evidence of some other matter. Then their truth and accuracy has to be assessed and they are hearsay.

There is no question here of the hearsay rule arising at all. The relevant issue was did these ladies make these offers? The offers were oral and the police officers were entitled to give evidence of them. The evidence, in my judgment, was wrongly excluded and should have been admitted. What the result would have been is of course another matter.

Appeal allowed.

R v Blastland
[1986] AC 41
House of Lords

The appellant was charged on indictment with buggery and murder, the case for the prosecution being that he had forcibly buggered a 12-year-old boy and then strangled him with a scarf. He pleaded not guilty. He gave evidence that he had attempted to bugger the boy but had desisted when the boy had complained of pain. Shortly afterwards, he had seen M nearby and, afraid that he had been seen committing a serious offence, had run off and returned to his home. His case was that it had been M, not he, who had committed the offences with which he was charged. He sought to call a number of witnesses to give evidence that M had said, before the boy's body had been discovered, that a young boy had been murdered. The judge ruled that that evidence was hearsay and inadmissible. He also refused an application to call M and treat him as a hostile witness. The appellant was convicted on both counts, and his appeal against conviction, on the ground that the judge had been wrong to exclude the evidence in question, was dismissed by the Court of Appeal. The appellant further appealed to the House of Lords.

LORD BRIDGE Of HARWICH: Hearsay evidence is not excluded because it has no logically probative value. Given that the subject matter of the hearsay is relevant to some issue in the trial, it may clearly be potentially probative. The rationale of excluding it as inadmissible, rooted as it is in the system of trial by jury, is a recognition of the great difficulty, even more acute for a juror than for a trained judicial mind, of assessing what, if any, weight can properly be given to a statement by a person whom the jury have not seen or heard and which has not been subject to any test of reliability by cross-examination. As Lord Normand put it, delivering the judgment of the Privy Council in *Teper v The Queen* [1952] AC 480, 486:

> The rule against the admission of hearsay evidence is fundamental. It is not the best evidence and it is not delivered on oath. The truthfulness and accuracy of the person whose words are spoken to by another witness cannot be tested by cross-examination, and the light which his demeanour would throw on his testimony is lost.

The danger against which this fundamental rule provides a safeguard is that untested hearsay evidence will be treated as having a probative force which it does not deserve.

It is, of course, elementary that statements made to a witness by a third party are not excluded by the hearsay rule when they are put in evidence solely to prove the state of mind either of the maker of the statement or of the person to whom it was made. What a person said or heard said may well be the best and most direct evidence of that person's state of mind. This principle can only apply, however, when the state of mind evidenced by the statement is either itself directly in issue at the trial or of direct and immediate relevance to an issue which arises at the trial. It is at this point, as it seems to me, that the argument for the appellant breaks down. The issue at the trial of the appellant was whether it was proved that the appellant had buggered and murdered Karl Fletcher. Mark's knowledge that Karl had been murdered was neither itself in issue, nor was it, *per se,* of any relevance to the issue. What was relevant was not the fact of Mark's knowledge but how he had come by that knowledge. He might have done so in a number of ways, but the two most obvious possibilities were either that he had witnessed the commission of the murder by the appellant or that he had committed it himself. The statements which it was sought to prove that Mark made, indicating his knowledge of the murder, provided no rational basis whatever on which the jury could be invited to draw an inference as to the source of that knowledge. To do so would have been mere speculation. Thus, to allow this evidence of what Mark said to be put before the jury as supporting the conclusion that he, rather than the appellant, may have been the murderer seems to me, in the light of the principles on which the exclusion of hearsay depends, to be open to still graver objection than allowing evidence that he had directly admitted the crime. If the latter is excluded as evidence to which no probative value can safely be attributed, the same objection applies *a fortiori* to the admission of the former.

The basic rule that, when a person's state of mind is directly in issue, it may be proved by what was said by or to that person is well illustrated by two very straightforward cases. In *Thomas* v *Connell* (1838) 4 M & W 266, the plaintiff sought to recover money paid to the defendant by one Cheetham on the ground of fraudulent preference. To make good his case, he needed to prove that at or before the time of the disputed payment, Cheetham both was insolvent in fact and knew that he was insolvent. A statement made by Cheetham indicating knowledge of his insolvency was admitted in evidence. Discharging a rule *nisi* for a new trial on the ground of misreception of evidence, the judgments of Lord Abinger CB, Parke B, and Gurney B, make clear that, provided the fact of Cheetham's insolvency could be, as it was, proved *aliunde,* his knowledge of it could be proved by evidence of his statement. There could be no plainer case where the knowledge of the maker of the statement was the very fact in issue.

The classic illustration of a statement admissible to prove the state of mind, again directly in issue, of the person to whom the statement was made is *Subramaniam* v *Public Prosecutor* [1956] 1 WLR 965. The appellant had been captured in the Federation of Malaya by security forces operating against terrorists. He was tried and convicted of unlawful possession of ammunition, which was at that time a capital offence in the Federation of Malaya. His defence was that he acted under duress. At his trial he sought to give evidence of threats made to him by terrorists, but this was ruled inadmissible as hearsay. His appeal against conviction to the Privy Council was allowed on the ground that, if the threats were made to him and he believed them, the excluded evidence went directly to support his defence of duress. As it was put by Mr L M D de Silva, delivering the judgment of the Board, at p. 970:

In the case before their Lordships statements could have been made to the appellant by the terrorists, which, whether true or not, if they had been believed by the appellant, might reasonably have induced in him an apprehension of instant death if he failed to conform to their wishes.

The same principle was applied by the Court of Criminal Appeal in *R v Willis* [1960] 1 WLR 55. I do not find it necessary to analyse the somewhat complex facts of that case, but content myself with citing a single sentence from the judgment of Lord Parker CJ, delivering the judgment of the court. He said with reference to *Subramaniam,* at p. 59:

> It is true that the Board were there considering the state of mind and conduct of the defendant at the time of the commission of the offence, but *provided the evidence as to his state of mind and conduct is relevant,* it matters not whether it was in regard to the conduct at the time of the commission of the offence or, as here, at a subsequent time, to explain his answers to the police and his conduct when charged. (Emphasis added.)

The decision of your Lordships' House in *Lloyd v Powell Duffryn Steam Coal Co. Ltd* [1914] AC 733 requires examination in a little detail. It concerned a claim for compensation under the Workmen's Compensation Act 1906, by a posthumous illegitimate child as a dependant of its putative father, who was killed by accident arising out of and in the course of his employment with the respondents. At the hearing the mother gave evidence that the deceased was the father of her child and that, shortly before his death, he had told her he intended to marry her in plenty of time before the birth of the child. The deceased man's landlady said that he had told her that he was troubled by what he had heard from the mother, 'but that it did not matter because he would marry her soon enough' (p. 734). A room-mate spoke of a conversation in which the deceased said the mother was in trouble and it was a case of getting married. He wanted to provide a home for himself and the mother. The county court judge admitted these statements as declarations by a deceased person against interest. The Court of Appeal, allowing the respondents's appeal, held that this ground of admissibility of the statements was not sustainable. In your Lordships' House the admissibility of the statements was argued and affirmed on entirely different grounds, the House concurring in the view taken by the Court of Appeal of the only point that had been argued before them. Their Lordships discussed the relevance and admissibility of the disputed evidence with reference to the issues of both paternity and dependency. This seems strange since counsel for the respondents is reported as saying, at p. 736: 'The respondents do not contest the paternity of the child, but they submit that the evidence of the statement of the deceased that he intended to marry the girl is inadmissible and irrelevant: . . .' Admissibility on the issue of dependency was very clearly disputed. The speeches of their Lordships are, if I may say so with all respect, somewhat diffuse, and I do not find it possible to distil from them any single clear-cut *ratio decidendi.* If I found passages in the speeches which appeared to afford support for Mr Judge's argument, I would certainly refer to them. But I do not. I content myself with citing a single passage from the judgment of Lord Moulton, which seems to me to explain the ground of the decision in a way which is clear, convincing, and entirely consistent with the principles which I have discussed earlier in this opinion, which underlie the other authorities already referred to. After expressing his agreement with the reasoning of the Court of Appeal, Lord Moulton continued, at p. 751:

> . . . the argument before your Lordships was based on a wholly different ground,
> namely, that the state of mind of the deceased, so far as it bore on his acceptance
> of his position as the father of the child and his intention to fulfil his duties as such,
> was *relevant to the issue* of dependency, and that the evidence in question was
> admissible as being proper to determine his state of mind. I am of opinion, my

Lords, that on this ground the evidence was admissible. It can scarcely be contested that the state of mind of the putative father and his intentions with regard to the child are matters *relevant to the issue,* whether there was a reasonable anticipation that he would support the child when born. It may be that an intention on his part so to do might be implied from the fact of his paternity and his recognition of it. But whether this be so or not, the attitude of mind of the putative father is that from which alone one can draw conclusions as to the greater or less probability of his supporting the child when born, and therefore evidence to prove that attitude of mind must be admissible if it be the proper evidence to establish such a fact. Now, it is well established in English jurisprudence, in accordance with the dictates of common sense, that the words and acts of a person are admissible as evidence of his state of mind. (Emphasis added.)

I need only make passing reference to *Mawaz Khan* v *The Queen* [1967] 1 AC 454. This was a case where defendants, jointly charged with murder, against whom the primary evidence was circumstantial, had both made statements to the police setting up the same alibi story. The Crown called direct evidence to demonstrate the falsity of the alibi. The direction to the jury of which the defendants complained on appeal against conviction is set out in the headnote as follows, at p. 455:

A statement which is made by an accused person in the absence of the other is not evidence against the other; it is evidence against the maker of the statement but against him only . . . . The Crown's case here is not that these statements are true and that what one says ought to be considered as evidence of what actually happened. What the Crown say is that these statements have been shown to be a tissue of lies and that they disclose an attempt to fabricate a joint story . . . . If you come to that conclusion then the fabrication of a joint story would be evidence against both. It would be evidence that they had cooperated after the alleged crime.

The Privy Council dismissed the appeal. All that this case demonstrates, which seems elementary common sense, is that, if two men have put their heads together to concoct a false alibi, this is *prima facie* evidence against both of a guilty state of mind. This is far removed from the issue arising in the present appeal and I derive no assistance from it.

The authority on which Mr Judge places greatest reliance is the decision of the Privy Council in *Ratten* v *The Queen* [1972] AC 378, dismissing an appeal from the Supreme Court of Victoria against the appellant's conviction of murder. The appellant's wife had been killed by a cartridge discharged from a shotgun held in the hands of the appellant. The evidence established the time of the shooting as between 1.12 and 1.20 pm. The appellant's defence was that the shooting occurred accidentally while he was in course of cleaning the gun. The evidence of the appellant was that after the shooting he immediately telephoned for an ambulance and that shortly afterwards the police telephoned him upon which he asked them to come immediately. He denied that any telephone call had been made by his wife, and also denied that he had telephoned for the police. To rebut the appellant's account, the prosecution called the evidence of a telephonist at the telephone exchange of a call from the appellant's number received at about 1.15 pm from a woman saying: 'Get me the police please.' According to the telephonist, the woman was hysterical and sobbing. The Board, in a judgment delivered by Lord Wilberforce, held this evidence admissible on the grounds both that it was directly relevant to the issue and that it was part of the *res gestae.* We need not consider the second ground, which is not raised in the present appeal. On the first ground the reasoning of the Board appears in the following critical passage from the judgment, at pp. 387-388:

The evidence relating to the act of telephoning by the deceased was, in their Lordships' view, factual and relevant. It can be analysed into the following elements:

(1) At about 1.15 pm the number Echuca 1494 rang. I plugged into that number.
(2) I opened the speak key and said 'Number please'.
(3) A female voice answered.
(4) The voice was hysterical and sobbed.
(5) The voice said 'Get me the police please.'

The factual items numbered (1)-(3) were relevant in order to show that, contrary to the evidence of the appellant, a call was made, only some three to five minutes before the fatal shooting, by a woman. It not being suggested that there was anybody in the house other than the appellant, his wife and small children, this woman, the caller, could only have been the deceased. Items (4) and (5) were relevant as possibly showing (if the jury thought fit to draw the inference) that the deceased woman was at this time in a state of emotion or fear (cf. *Aveson* v *Lord Kinnaird* (1805) 6 East 188, 193, *per* Lord Ellenborough CJ). They were relevant and necessary, evidence in order to explain and complete the fact of the call being made. A telephone call is a composite act, made up of manual operations together with the utterance of words (cf. *McGregor* v *Stokes* [1952] VLR 347 and remarks of Salmond J therein quoted). To confine the evidence to the first would be to deprive the act of most of its significance. The act had content when it was known that the call was made in a state of emotion. The knowledge that the caller desired the police to be called helped to indicate the nature of the emotion — anxiety or fear at an existing or impending emergency. It was a matter for the jury to decide what light (if any) this evidence, in the absence of any explanation from the appellant, who was in the house, threw upon what situation was occurring, or developing at the time.

Mr Judge emphasises particularly the concluding sentence in this passage. It establishes, he submits, the proposition that evidence of A's state of mind (the wife's fear in *Ratten's* case — Mark's knowledge in the instant case) should be left to the jury to decide what inference they draw from it with respect to B's action (whether the appellant in *Ratten's* case fired deliberately or accidentally — whether or not, in the instant case, the appellant murdered Karl Fletcher).

Ratten's case is not technically binding on your Lordships' House, but considering the constitution of the Board (Lord Reid, Lord Hodson, Lord Wilberforce, Lord Diplock and Lord Cross of Chelsea) is of the highest persuasive authority and, for my part, I should certainly feel constrained to follow it, if persuaded that it established a principle applicable in the appellant's favour in the circumstances of the present appeal. I am not so persuaded and consider *Ratten's* case clearly distinguishable. First, the telephone call in *Ratten's* case was, although it could be analysed into component elements, nevertheless, as Lord Wilberforce said, 'a composite act, made up of manual operations together with the utterance of words.' The implication is that its admissibility had to be considered as a whole. The very fact that the call had been made contradicted a critically important part of the appellant's evidence. Secondly, the appellant's denial that the call had been made precluded him from either offering any explanation of it or suggesting that it was made in some other room out of his hearing. This led to a powerful inference that what the wife said on the telephone was said in his presence. Thirdly, in these circumstances, both the making of the call and the wife's state of fear manifested by it were directly relevant to the critical issue in the trial as rebutting the appellant's defence of an accidental shooting. There are no analogous considerations applicable in the present case.

R v Moghal (1977) 65 Cr App R 56 was a case presenting exceptional, indeed one may hope unique, features. A man named Rashid had been murdered by stabbing. Only two persons, a woman named Sadiga and her current lover, Moghal, were present when the murder was committed. Rashid had been Sadiga's lover for some years previously. Sadiga and Moghal were jointly indicted for Rashid's murder, which had clearly been committed by one or other or both of them. For reasons which I need not examine, an application by Sadiga for separate trials was successful. Sadiga was tried first and acquitted. When Moghal's trial followed, it was accepted by the Crown, as had indeed been the Crown's case throughout, that it was Sadiga by whose hand Rashid died. The case against Moghal was that he was a willing accomplice in the killing. Moghal's defence was that Sadiga was the dominant character and that he was no more than a cowed and terrified spectator of the murder. Moghal was convicted and appealed. The only relevance of the case for present purposes lies in the discussion in the judgment of the Court of Appeal (Criminal Division) (Scarman and Shaw LJJ and Thompson J), delivered by Scarman LJ, of the possible relevance and admissibility of a tape recording of a family conference some six months before Rashid's murder, in which Sadiga's voice could be heard expressing in virulent terms her hatred of Rashid and her determination to kill him. Deprived of the opportunity to cross-examine Sadiga in a joint trial, counsel for Moghal canvassed with the judge, *inter alia*, the possibility of introducing this tape recording in evidence, though he never made any formal application that it be admitted. In the Court of Appeal, therefore, the issue was discussed, not on the basis of any irregularity in the trial, but in relation to the question whether the verdict of guilty against Moghal was safe and satisfactory. The prosecution, who were clearly much concerned to mitigate, as far as they properly could, the difficulties which the separate trial and acquittal of Sadiga presented for the defence of Moghal, had formally admitted, that, at the family conference, Sadiga had uttered threats against the life of Rashid. Against this background it is difficult to see how the court could have reached any other conclusion than that the verdict of guilty was safe and satisfactory. The passage in the judgment on which Mr Judge particularly relies is in the following terms, at p. 63:

> The tape-recording of the family conference is, however, a very different matter. It records what she said at the family conference of her then state of mind and feeling. Being contemporaneous, these statements are admissible: for we accept — and the Crown by making its formal admission, [that at the family conference Sadiga offered threats against the life of Rashid], has really conceded — that her state of mind at that time was relevant to the appellant's defence.

The opinion here expressed that Sadiga's statements at the family conference were admissible was both *obiter* and plainly influenced by the concession implicit in a formal admission made by the Crown. With all respect, I venture to doubt whether it was correct, precisely because I cannot see how a threat by Sadiga against Rashid's life, made six months before the murder, however virulently the threat was expressed, was of any relevance to the issue whether Moghal was a willing accomplice or an unwilling spectator when the murder was committed. I well understand the Court of Appeal's, and indeed the prosecution's sympathetic approach to the difficulties which the wholly exceptional course of ordering separate trials of a joint indictment created for Moghal's defence following Sadiga's acquittal. But I am certainly not prepared to treat this *obiter dictum* as expressing any principle of general application which assists the appellant in the instant case.

Perhaps a still more remarkable case is the recent decision of the Court of Appeal (Criminal Division) in *R v Roberts (John Marcus)* (1985) 80 Cr App R 89. A man was shot in the head in October 1980. His body was buried and was not discovered until March 1982. Roberts and another man named Evans were in due course tried and both convicted of the murder. Roberts alone appealed against his conviction. The appeal was dismissed. The only ground of the appeal which is of any relevance for present purposes was that the trial judge wrongly refused to allow the appellant to call in his defence two witnesses named Passey and Tong who could have testified that Paul Evans, the brother of the appellant's co-accused, made statements to them, at a time before the discovery of the victim's body, which revealed a detailed knowledge of the circumstances in which the murder had been committed. At risk of excessively lengthening this already lengthy opinion, I think I can only do justice to the judgment of the Court of Appeal (May LJ, Boreham and Nolan JJ), delivered by May LJ, by quoting the whole passage in which the admissibility of the evidence of Passey and Tong is examined. The passage reads as follows, at pp. 94-95:

After considering the point overnight, the learned judge ruled that such evidence could not be called. He accepted that if it were relevant, such evidence would be admissible. If the only purpose of tendering the evidence was to seek to show the state of Paul's knowledge at the material time, but not the correctness or accuracy of the details of that knowledge, then it could not be assailed as being hearsay. However, he disagreed that the evidence, if called, did implicate Paul in the murder as counsel for the appellant contended. As we have said, he accepted that it might indeed show knowledge on the part of Paul of relevant details of the murder, but he pointed out that that knowledge could have been obtained either from his brother, the defendant Richard Evans, despite the fact that the latter denied discussing the matter with Paul; or Paul could have obtained the information from the present appellant; or he could have done so from some other party who had himself obtained the information from either of the two defendants; or he could have acquired the relevant knowledge from someone who had in his turn obtained the information first, second or third hand, but originating from the two defendants; or Paul Evans could himself have visited the farm on either of the two days following the actual killing whilst the burial of Sands' body was still going on. Further, the learned judge felt that as no one then knew what Paul himself would say were he called to give evidence, if counsel were allowed to call Passey and Tong for this purpose, this would open a series of new issues involving the investigation of all people to whom Paul Evans had given other statements revealing the source of his knowledge. Further, given that the real purpose of calling the evidence was to suggest that Paul had taken part in the murder, it would also become relevant to hear evidence where Paul was at the material times. Finally, even if Paul had been present at the time of the killing, this would not have meant that the appellant could not have been there also. The learned judge therefore ruled that the evidence sought to be called was inadmissible. Although the learned judge did not put his ruling in precisely these terms we think that it is clear that his view was that the evidence was admissible to show Paul's knowledge, if that were relevant; for that limited purpose it could not properly be described as hearsay. But nevertheless, even if it were proved that Paul did have that knowledge, it could only be speculation how he acquired it, and it tended neither to prove nor disprove the Crown's contention that the appellant had been a party to the murder, nor any link in the evidentiary chain which it was said led to that conclusion. In those circumstances the evidence was not relevant to the issues before the jury and was thus inadmissible.

Mr Judge relies in particular on the words 'it is clear that his view was that the evidence was admissible to show Paul's knowledge, if that were relevant; for that limited purpose it could not properly be described as hearsay.' The implication, he submits, is that the Court of Appeal approved the trial judge's view that the disputed evidence was not hearsay.

However, the more carefully I have sought to analyse the whole passage I have cited from the judgment, the more forcibly am I impelled to the conclusion that the basic reasoning refutes, rather than supports, the submission made for the appellant in the instant case. In summary what the judgment is saying seems to me to be:

(1)   If Paul Evans' statements were put in evidence solely to prove his knowledge, they would not be excluded as hearsay;
(2)   The statements could not, however, be put in evidence as the basis for an inference as to the source of his knowledge for which there was no rational foundation;
(3)   Paul Evans' knowledge, *per se,* was of no relevance to the issue whether or not the appellant was guilty of the murder.

If this is a correct distillation of the essence of the decision that the evidence of Paul Evans' statements was rightly ruled inadmissible, I fully agree with it. Indeed, it seems to me to come very near to the reasoning which commends itself to me as applicable in the instant case. If there is to be extracted from the passage some *obiter dictum* which points in the contrary direction, I cannot agree with it.

At the conclusion of the examination of the relevant authorities I have found nothing to displace the opinion I expressed earlier as a matter of principle that the evidence here in question was rightly excluded. On the contrary, with the exception of a single *obiter dictum* in *R v Moghal*, 65 Cr App R 56, the authorities, if they are considered, as they should be, with due regard to the nature of the issues to which the evidence examined in each case was directed, seem to me consistently to support that opinion.

(LORDS FRASER OF TULLYBELTON, EDMUND-DAVIES, BRIGHTMAN and TEMPLEMAN agreed.)

Appeal dismissed.

Question
Does the decision in *R v Blastland* accord with the notion that justice must not only be done but be seen to be done?

A. Ashworth and R. Pattenden,
'Reliability, Hearsay Evidence and the English Criminal Trial'
(1986) 102 LQR 292

Another difficult issue in the borderlands of the hearsay rule is whether implied verbal assertions, that is, assertions inferred from statements which though intended to be assertive are not intended to communicate the fact for which they are introduced as evidence, ought to be treated as hearsay. Clearly the characterisation depends on the issue in the case and on the purpose for which the words are relied upon. One approach would be to enquire whether the dangers against which the hearsay rule guards — such as insincerity and inaccuracy — are materially less in the particular type of case. Another would be the purely definitional approach taken in *Ratten*: are the words being relied upon testimonially, *i.e.* as establishing some fact narrated by the words, or for some other relevant purpose? The boundary between inadmissible hearsay and admissible implied assertions has been the subject of considerable debate, and three appellate decisions since *Myers* shed light on the approach of the courts.

In *Ratten v R* the accused was convicted of murdering his wife by shooting her between 1.12 and 1.20 p.m. His defence had been that the shooting was accidental. The telephonist at the local exchange received a call at about 1.15 p.m. from the accused's house. A female voice, hysterical and sobbing, said 'Get me the police, please.' Lord Wilberforce, delivering the judgment of the Privy Council, held that the words were admissible

> as possibly showing (if the jury thought fit to draw the inference) that the deceased woman was at the time in a state of emotion or fear . . . They were relevant and necessary evidence in order to explain and complete the fact of the call being made . . . The act had content when it was known that the call was made in a state of emotion. The knowledge that the caller desired the police . . . helped to indicate the nature of the emotion, anxiety or fear at an existing or impending emergency.

The last sentence of this passage shows that the words spoken to the telephonist were being treated as an implied assertion that there was some crisis at the caller's house. This was relevant because of the accused's defence of accident. Lord Wilberforce emphasised that the words were to be used as the basis for a possible inference, which suggests that the words should be regarded as circumstantial evidence rather than hearsay. The words showed the caller's state of emotion and the existence of an emergency at the house; from this the jury might infer that the shooting was not an accident but intentional.

The second case is *Woodhouse v Hall*. The accused was charged with managing a brothel contrary to section 33 of the Sexual Offences Act 1956. At the trial the prosecution was not allowed to call police officers to testify that whilst being massaged by female employees of the accused (but out of her presence and hearing) they had been offered 'hand relief'. The justices ruled that the evidence was hearsay, and inadmissible unless the women alleged to have spoken the words gave evidence. The Divisional Court did not agree: 'The relevant issue was, did these ladies make these offers? The offers were oral and the police officers were entitled to give evidence of them.' The case may appear to be a simple one, once it is appreciated that the making of the offers was relevant as the basis for a possible inference that the premises were being run as a brothel. An earlier Scottish case took a similar approach. The difficulty lies in the reason given by the Court of Appeal for admitting the evidence, namely that the prosecution was not relying on the truth of the offers. An offer cannot be true or untrue, but it can be sincerely meant or made flippantly, in jest or as a pretence. Now it might be argued that the offer of immoral services in *Woodhouse v Hall* should be treated as an example of operative words, that 'the substantive law has an objective test of the speaker's intention, as with words of gift or contractual offer,' and therefore it is enough to prove that the words were uttered without establishing that they were sincerely meant. Even if this is a correct interpretation of the substantive law applied in *Woodhouse v Hall*, it is questionable whether this rule of civil law should be transplanted into the criminal law without consideration of the consequences. The hearsay rule calls for a check on sincerity by means of cross-examination of the speaker of the words. To borrow the 'operative words' approach is to run the risk of convicting defendants on the basis of words spoken insincerely, even if one is satisfied entirely about the reliability of the evidence in *Woodhouse*.

A firm reminder of the dangers of admitting evidence of words spoken by another (who does not testify) as a basis for an inference crucial to the case is provided by the House of Lords' decision in *Blastland*. In this case a known homosexual, M, had made a number of statements that a boy had been murdered before others discovered the body of the 12 year old boy of whose murder and buggery the accused was convicted. The defence applied to bring witnesses to testify to the making of these statements, in order to show the state of M's mind. The trial judge ruled that since the real purpose of adducing the statements was to establish an implied admission by M that he was the murderer this evidence was hearsay. The House of Lords held that the statements were not admissible to show M's state of mind because that was not in issue at the trial of this defendant, and did not dissent from the trial judge's characterisation of the evidence as hearsay.

It is often argued that the absence of an intention to assert the relevant fact means that the sincerity of the person making the assertion is not in doubt: this probably underlies the view of Cross and Tapper that 'the presence of an intention to assert provides the most defensible watershed between hearsay and non-hearsay both as a matter of logical coherence and of practical commonsense.' For the same reason the United States Federal Rules do not treat implied assertions as hearsay. However, *Blastland* and *Woodhouse v Hall* show that there are issues of meaning and of sincerity which should not be overlooked. In *Blastland* the meaning of M's statements was uncertain. What did they imply?

> What was relevant was not the fact of M's knowledge but how he had come by that knowledge. He might have done so in a number of ways, but the two most obvious possibilities were either that he had witnessed the commission of the murder by the appellant or that he had committed it himself. The statements which it was sought to prove that M made, indicating his knowledge of the murder, provided no rational basis whatever on which the jury could be invited to draw an inference as to the source of that knowledge. To do so would have been mere speculation. Thus, to allow this evidence of what M said to be put before the jury as supporting the conclusion that he, rather than the appellant, may have been the murderer seems to me, in the light of the principles on which the exclusion of hearsay depends, to be open to still graver objection than allowing evidence that he had directly admitted the crime. If the latter is excluded as evidence to which no probative value can safely be attributed, the same objection applies a fortiori to the admission of the former.

The last sentence effectively holds that if a statement has no probative value it should be excluded, either as hearsay or on an analogy with the hearsay rule. This corresponds to the functional approach towards exceptions to the hearsay rule which has been noticed earlier in this article, and which has led courts to extend the exceptions where evidence is manifestly reliable. It might also be possible to justify the result in *Blastland*, if not the reasoning, on a strict definitional approach. That approach, as adopted in *Ratten*, holds that evidence of words spoken by another is not hearsay when tendered to show the speaker's state of mind. The words in *Blastland* might then be excluded from the category of implied assertions because it was so very uncertain what the statements did imply: the category of implied assertions could be limited to cases in which the implication is clear. There are some who would go further and link this to the functional approach, arguing that the uncertainty of the inferences to be drawn from implied assertions is sufficient justification for bringing them all within the ban of the hearsay rule.

R v Kearley
[1992] 2 WLR 656
House of Lords

Police officers arrested the defendant who was suspected of supplying drugs from certain premises. A number of telephone calls were received by the officers at the defendant's premises from unknown callers who were interested in buying drugs. The defendant was not present when the calls were received. The prosecution sought to adduce the evidence of the calls in order to prove that K was a dealer and that his premises were being used for the supply of drugs. The Court of Appeal held that the evidence of the calls were non-hearsay and admissible to prove the premises were being used for the supply of drugs and the identity of the supplier. The defendant appealed to the House of Lords. The majority of their Lordships held that evidence of the callers' beliefs was irrelevant but, even if relevant, should have been excluded as hearsay.

LORD OLIVER OF AYLMERTON: My Lords, this appeal raises an important and difficult question regarding the admissibility in a criminal trial of statements made in the absence of the accused by persons who are not called as witnesses. In general and subject to certain statutory or defined common law exceptions an assertion other than one made by a person while giving oral evidence in the proceedings and tendered as evidence of the facts asserted is inadmissible as hearsay evidence. Its rejection enshrines an important principle of justice more particularly in cases where the liberty of the subject may depend upon whether or not such evidence is permitted to be put before a jury. In delivering the opinion of the Board in *Lejzor Teper* v *The Queen* [1952] AC 480, Lord Normand observed, at p. 486:

> The rule against the admission of hearsay evidence is fundamental. It is not the best evidence and it is not delivered on oath. The truthfulness and accuracy of the person whose words are spoken to by another witness cannot be tested by cross-examination, and the light which his demeanour would throw on his testimony is lost.

That is a rationale which most clearly applies when what is sought to be adduced as evidence of A's action or state of mind is a statement made about it to or in the hearing of B by a third person, C, who is not called as a witness to testify to the accuracy of the statement. The present appeal, however, concerns a more subtle variation, where evidence is tendered of words uttered by a person not called as a witness, not for the purpose of establishing the accuracy of any statement made by that person, but in order that there may be drawn, from the combination of the words used by the speaker and the circumstances in which they were uttered, an inference as to the actions and intentions of another person not present at the time. The question raised by the appeal is one upon which there appears to be a divergence of view between our own jurisprudence and that of at least some other common law jurisdictions and it may be conveniently expressed as follows: does the rule regarding the exclusion as hearsay in criminal trials of express assertions of persons not called as witnesses apply also to implied assertions?

. . .

The circumstances giving rise to this appeal are these. After raiding the premises and after the appellant had been arrested, police officers remained on the premises for several hours. During that period some 15 telephone calls from a variety of callers were made to the premises and were intercepted by police officers either in the absence of the appellant or at any rate without his hearing their content. In 10 of these the caller asked for 'Chippie,' a nickname by which the appellant was known, and asked for drugs. During the same period nine visitors, some at least being apparently persons who had earlier telephoned, came to the door of the premises seeking 'Chippie.' Seven of these callers indicated that they wanted to purchase drugs and some at least were carrying cash in their hands. None of these persons, with the exception of a Mr Fry, who was named specifically in connection with count 5 upon which the appellant was convicted and who gave evidence in connection with that count, was called as a witness. The prosecution, however, proposed to call the police officers who had intercepted the telephone calls or had received the callers at the house to give evidence of the facts of the telephone calls or personal calls and of the contents of the conversations which they then had with those persons. That evidence was objected to on the ground that it was inadmissible as hearsay, since it was to be adduced not simply as evidence of the fact that calls were made but for the purpose of showing (a) that drugs were being supplied at the premises on a commercial scale and (b) that it was the appellant who was supplying them. After considerable argument in the absence of the jury, the objection was overruled and the officers' testimony was received, although it is fair to say that the judge gave a most careful warning to the jury as to the circumspection with which such evidence should be received. On the footing that, contrary to the appellant's contention, this evidence was admissible at all, the judge's direction was a model of fairness and cannot, I think, be faulted in any particular. The central — indeed the only — question on this appeal is whether the evidence ought to have been admitted at all.

The appellant appealed to the Court of Appeal (Criminal Division), 93 Cr App R 222 against his conviction on count 6. On 29 November 1990 that court dismissed the appeal but gave leave to appeal to this House and certified the following question as one of general public importance:

Whether evidence may be adduced at a trial of words spoken (namely a request for drugs to be supplied by the defendant), not spoken in the presence or hearing of the defendant, by a person not called as a witness, for the purpose not of establishing the truth of any fact narrated by the words, but of inviting the jury to draw an inference from the fact that the words were spoken (namely that the defendant was a supplier of drugs).

My Lords, granted that, to use Lord Normand's words in *Lejzor Teper* v *The Queen* [1952] AC 480, 486, the rule against the admission of hearsay evidence is 'fundamental' (for the reasons which he gave), it is necessary in every case where evidence is tendered of words spoken by a person who is not called as a witness to have clearly in mind the purpose for which such evidence is sought to be adduced. Such evidence does not fall foul of the hearsay rule if its purpose is to prove not the correctness of what was said (or, more accurately, of what is said to have been said) but the fact that it was said. That fact, as was observed in the opinion of the Board of the Privy Council in *Subramaniam* v *Public Prosecutor* [1956] 1 WLR 965, 970, may, apart altogether from the truth of the statement, quite frequently be relevant in considering the mental state and conduct of the witness or of some other person in whose presence the statement was made, not excluding the maker of the statement himself. The distinction between utterance as relevant fact and utterance as evidence of the accuracy of what is uttered is neatly expressed in the opinion of the Board of the Privy Council delivered by Lord Wilberforce in *Ratten* v *The Queen* [1972] AC 378, 387:

> The mere fact that evidence of a witness includes evidence as to words spoken by another person who is not called, is no objection to its admissibility. Words spoken are facts just as much as any other action by a human being. If the speaking of the words is a relevant fact, a witness may give evidence that they were spoken. A question of hearsay only arises when the words spoken are relied on 'testimonially,' i.e., as establishing some fact narrated by the words.

Thus, in that case, a telephone call from the wife of the accused, who had been shot dead by him, as he claimed accidentally, and in which she asked for the police, was held to be rightly admitted as evidence simply of a telephone call made by a lady in a distressed state made at a time when the accused denied that any call was made and in the context of his contention that the shooting was accidental. It is to be noted, however, that in so far as it was admissible as evidence from which the jury could be invited to infer that the caller was being attacked by her husband, the Board found it admissible only as part of the res gestae, i.e. as an exception to the hearsay rule.

Thus the question which presents itself in the instant appeal can be expressed thus: was the evidence of the police officers being tendered simply as evidence of the fact of the conversation or was it introduced 'testimonially' in order to demonstrate the truth either of something that was said or of something that was implicit in or to be inferred from something that was said?

Miss Goddard, for the Crown, has submitted that the evidence admitted by the judge of what was said by the callers did not fall foul of the hearsay rule at all. It was not tendered as hearsay evidence but simply as probative of the fact that calls were made on the day in question either at or to the house and that the callers were seeking to purchase drugs from 'Chippie.' There was independent evidence of the presence of drugs at the premises and the fact that there were calls at or to the house by persons seeking drugs was relevant, simply as a fact, as tending to show that the accused had an intent to supply, the contents of the conversations being admissible as material explaining the making of the calls. Mr de Navarro, for the appellant, contends that this submission simply fails to analyse both the true purpose and the effect of the evidence tendered. The fact that callers asked for drugs in the absence of the appellant, there being no evidence of any reaction by him to the requests, cannot possibly, it is said, go any distance at all towards showing what had to be proved, that is to say, that the appellant had an intention to supply drugs. It proved no more than that the callers made the calls in the belief, which the jury were invited to infer from the words spoken, that the appellant had drugs and was willing to supply them. That belief, no grounds being stated or capable of being investigated, was being tendered as evidence that the fact believed was true and in the form in which it was tendered could not have been admitted even if the callers had themselves given evidence. So, it is said, the jury were being invited to draw a double inference, that is to say, first, an inference that what the callers were saying was, in effect, 'Chippie has drugs and intends to supply them,' and, secondly, an inference that because the caller believed this to be the case, it was therefore true. Thus this was evidence which, standing alone and without supplementary information indicating the grounds of the caller's belief, could not have been admitted even if given directly by the caller; and, tendered as it was through the mouth of the police officer who heard the statement, it was in any event hearsay and thus inadmissible.

My Lords, to any ordinary layman asked to consider the matter, one might think that the resort of a large number of persons to 11, Perth Close all asking for 'Chippie,' all carrying sums of cash and all asking to be supplied with drugs, would be as clear an indication as he could reasonably expect to have that 11, Perth Close, was a place at which drugs were available; and if he were to be asked whether or not this showed also that 'Chippie' was dealing in drugs, I cannot help feeling that his answer would be 'Of course it does.' But so simple — perhaps, one might say, so attractively common sense — a layman's approach is not necessarily a reliable guide in a criminal trial. I have in mind Parke B's observation in *Wright* v *Doe d. Tatham*, 7 Ad & E 313, 386, that although an inference from a statement that an act would not have been done unless the statement were true, or at least believed to be true,

> no doubt would be raised in the conduct of the ordinary affairs of life, if the statement were made by a man of veracity . . . it cannot be raised in a judicial inquiry . . .

Indeed, even accepting the layman's immediate impression, if one goes on to ask 'Why do you say, "Of course?"' the matter becomes a little more complex. The answer to that question has to be 'because, of course, they would not go and ask for drugs unless they expected to get them.' But then if one asks, 'Well, why did they expect to get them?' even the layman is compelled into an area of speculation. They expected to get them either because they had got them before or because they had been told, rightly or wrongly, or had heard or thought or guessed that there was somebody called 'Chippie' at 11, Perth Close who supplied drugs. So, straight away, even the layman is, on analysis, compelled to accept that his instinctive 'of course' rests upon a process of deductive reasoning which starts from an assumption about the state of mind or belief of a number of previously unknown individuals of whom the only known facts are that they telephoned or called at 11, Perth Close and made offers to purchase drugs.

Now if we translate that inquiry into the context of a criminal trial in which the accused, by pleading not guilty, is saying to the prosecution, as he is entitled to do: 'I challenge you to prove, by relevant and admissible evidence, that I was in possession of the drugs found at 11, Perth Close with intent to supply them,' we have to start with the terms of the charge and ask ourselves whether and to what extent the evidence of a police officer that he heard a number of callers to or at the premises asking for drugs goes any way at all towards establishing that the accused, one of the three residents at the premises, was intending to supply drugs.

. . . And here, as it seems to me, we are directly up against the hearsay rule which forms one of the major established exceptions to the admissibility of relevant evidence. Clearly if, at the trial, the prosecution had sought to adduce evidence from a witness to the effect that the appellant had, in the past, supplied him with quantities of drugs, that evidence would have been both relevant and admissible; but equally clearly, if it had been sought to introduce the evidence of a police constable to the effect that a person not called as a witness had told him, in a conversation in a public house, that the appellant had supplied drugs, that would have been inadmissible hearsay evidence and so objectionable. It cannot, it is cogently argued, make any difference that exactly the same evidence is introduced in an indirect way by way of evidence from a witness that he has overheard a request by some other person for 'the usual,' from which the jury is to be asked to infer that which cannot be proved by evidence of that other person's direct assertion. Equally if, at the trial, the prosecution had sought to adduce evidence from a witness not that drugs had been supplied but that it was his opinion or belief that drugs had been or would be supplied, that evidence would be inadmissible as amounting to no more than a statement of belief or opinion unsupported by facts upon which the belief is grounded. A fortiori, it is argued, that same inadmissible belief or opinion cannot be introduced by inference from the reported statement of someone who is not even called as a witness. Thus, it is said, in seeking to introduce the evidence of the police officers of what callers said, the Crown faces the difficulty that it has to contend that by combining two inadmissible items of evidence — that is to say, the evidence of the calls (which are, standing alone, inadmissible because irrelevant) and the evidence of what was said by the callers (which might be relevant but is inadmissible because hearsay) — it can produce a single item of admissible evidence.

The impermissibility of such a course rests upon a well established principle expounded in the context of civil proceedings some 150 years ago in *Wright* v *Doe d. Tatham*, 7 Ad & E 313. That was an action of ejectment the outcome of which depended upon the validity of the will of a testator who had died in 1826 and whose mental capacity was alleged to be such that he was incapable of making a valid will. The particular question with which the court was concerned was the admissibility in evidence of three letters written to the testator during his lifetime by persons deceased at the date of the trial and therefore incapable of being called to give evidence. These letters were sought to be adduced as evidence supporting the testator's mental capacity, their significance being that, in them, the writers treat him as a person capable of understanding ordinary business affairs. The court was split upon the factual question of whether there was anything in the circumstances from which there could be inferred any act of the testator suggesting that he adopted them or understood their contents, but the principles upon which the unsworn opinions of the writers as to the matters in issue were excluded are clearly stated in the judgments of Coltman J, Bosanquet J and Parke B. We see in the judgment of Coltman J the reflection of an argument very similar to that advanced by Miss Goddard in the instant case, viz. that evidence of the acts of persons (the callers) was admissible as direct evidence of the fact and that what was said by them is admissible as a declaration accompanying and explaining the act. He said, at p. 361,

> But it is contended that the writing of a letter is an act done, and that the contents of the letter are a declaration accompanying an act, and that an opinion (though not evidence per se) is yet evidence when embodied in an act. Now it appears to me that, if the letter is admissible on this ground, it must be either because the act is evidence by itself, or because the opinion is evidence. Where an act done is evidence per se, a declaration accompanying that act may well be evidence if it reflects light upon or qualifies the act. But I am not aware of any case, where the act done is, in its own nature, irrelevant to the issue, and where the declaration per se is inadmissible, in which it has been held that the union of the two has rendered them admissible.

Similarly, Bosanquet J, at pp. 372–373:

> the letters cannot be admissible unless they are relevant to the matter in issue, which matter is the capacity of the testator. The contents of the letters have no direct relation to the testator's state of mind, but may be taken to show the opinion of the writers that the person addressed was of competent understanding. If the writers of these letters were produced as witnesses and examined upon oath, their opinion would be receivable in evidence, because the grounds of their knowledge and the credibility of their testimony might be ascertained by cross-examination; but I know

of no rule by which the opinion, however clearly expressed, of a person, however well informed, is receivable in evidence, unless it be given in the course of legal examination. . . . In all cases where the judgment of third persons upon any matter in issue is receivable, personal examination upon oath is required.

But perhaps the strongest opinion in the Exchequer Chamber and the one most apposite to the facts of the instant case is that of Parke B, at p. 384:

One great principle in this law is, that all facts which are relevant to the issue may be proved; another is, that all such facts as have not been admitted by the party against whom they are offered, or some one under whom he claims, ought to be proved under the sanction of an oath . . . either on the trial of the issue or some other issue involving the same question between the same parties or those to whom they are privy.

. . .

Now certainly the rigour with which hearsay evidence is excluded has been considerably modified by statute, but the general soundness of the views expressed by the Court of Exchequer Chamber in *Wright* v *Doe d. Tatham*, 7 Ad & E 313, outwith the statutory and common law exceptions, has not, so far as I am aware, been challenged in or affected by subsequent authority during the past 150 years. Indeed, in *Myers* v *Director of Public Prosecutions* [1965] AC 1001 — a case which exemplifies the operation of the rule in a manner which might seem absurd to a layman and which has since been rectified by statute — the majority in this House reaffirmed the strictness of the rule and resisted the temptation to reform the law by what Lord Hodson described, at p. 1034, as 'judicial legislation with a vengeance.'

I do not, moreover, think that the admission of the evidence of the police officers in the present case can be justified by seeking to equiparate it with the evidence of the telephone call which was held to have been rightly admitted in *Ratten* v *The Queen* [1972] AC 378, for there, as already mentioned, the evidence had a double relevance. The fact that a call was made from the premises at all at that time was directly in issue and the circumstance in which it was made, that is to say, that it was made by a woman who was both frightened and hysterical, was clearly material to the jury's determination of the likelihood or unlikelihood of the accused's claim that the shooting took place accidentally while he was engaged in the innocuous process of cleaning his gun. That is a long way from the instant case where the conversation is relied upon not as a circumstance surrounding an act of the accused but as indicative of the speaker's view of the accused's intentions. In so far as it was considered permissible in *Ratten* to draw from the contents of the call the inference that the deceased was saying that she was under attack from her husband and that that was true, that could be justified only by treating the contents as part of the res gestae. It has not been contended that the calls in the present case, made after the arrest of the appellant, can come into that category.

A more modern example of the impermissibility of drawing inferences from hearsay assertions is provided by *Reg.* v *Blastland* [1986] AC 41, where the accused, who was charged with murder, attempted to call witnesses to testify that a third person, not called as a witness, had stated, before the body was found, that a young boy had been murdered. That evidence was tendered for the purpose of enabling an inference to be drawn, from the knowledge of the maker of the statement of the boy's death, that he had been responsible for it, although it was accepted that evidence of a confession of guilt by the same persons was rightly excluded as inadmissible hearsay. In the course of his speech, my noble and learned friend, Lord Bridge of Harwich quoted and approved the following words of the trial judge (Bush J), at p. 53:

The real purpose and relevance of calling the evidence as to the state of mind is to say that in effect that was an implied admission of the knowledge of the crime, which is an implied admission of the crime itself and that too I regard as hearsay evidence and inadmissible.

Lord Bridge went on to observe, at pp. 53–54:

Hearsay evidence is not excluded because it has no logically probative value. Given that the subject matter of the hearsay is relevant to some issue in the trial, it may clearly be potentially probative. The rationale of excluding it as inadmissible, rooted as it is in the system of trial by jury, is a recognition of the great difficulty, even more acute for a juror than for a trained judicial mind, of assessing what, if any, weight can properly be given to a statement by a person whom the jury have not seen or heard and which has not been subject to any test of reliability by cross-examination. . . . It is, of course, elementary that statements made to a witness by a third party are not excluded by the hearsay rule when they are put in evidence solely to prove the state of mind either of the maker of the statement or the person to whom it was made. What a person said or heard said may well be the best and most direct evidence of that person's state of mind. This principle can only apply, however, when the state of mind evidenced by the statement is either itself directly in issue at the trial or of direct and immediate relevance to an issue which arises at the trial. It is at this point, as it seems to me, that the argument for the appellant breaks down.

If we now apply that to the facts of the instant case, what is in issue is the state of mind of the appellant: did he or did he not have an intent to deal in drugs? Is the existence of that state of mind in the appellant proved or rendered more probable by the fact that a third person, not even proved to have been known to him, has called at the premises where he and two other persons live and has asked a police officer to supply drugs? I find it very difficult to see how it can be except by treating it as an assertion by the caller to the police officer that the appellant is a supplier of drugs, an assertion clearly inadmissible as hearsay because tendered as evidence of fact. To put it another way, the circumstance of the call and the request in combination becomes relevant only by virtue of the latter's very inadmissibility. So one is faced with a circular and self-defeating process. The requests of the callers cannot establish or, without more, render probable the existence of that state of mind in the appellant. They establish only what was the state of mind or belief of the callers, which was never in issue and which can be relevant to the issue only if there exists and can be proved the state of mind of the appellant, which is the very thing that they are tendered to establish.

A somewhat similar question to that raised in this appeal arose in *Reg. v Harry*, 86 Cr App R 105 where the appellant, as here, was charged with possessing and supplying a controlled drug. Here again, police officers had intercepted calls from premises occupied by the appellant and by another person, P, who was also charged. The Crown did not there seek to introduce the calls in evidence but the appellant's counsel sought to cross-examine the officers with a view to establishing that the calls were made to P and thus, inferentially, to establish that it was he, and not the appellant, who was dealing. Both P's counsel and the prosecution having objected on the ground that evidence of what was said, introduced for this purpose, was inadmissible as hearsay, the objection was upheld by the trial judge. The appellant was convicted and subsequently appealed to the Court of Appeal (Criminal Division). That court, presided over by Lawton LJ, than whom no judge of his generation had greater experience of criminal trials, upheld the judge's decision and dismissed the appeal.

In the Court of Appeal (Criminal Division) in the instant case, 93 Cr App R 222 Lloyd LJ, who delivered the judgment of the court, was clearly offended — as I confess I myself was initially — at the notion that there might be withdrawn from the consideration of the jury evidence which plainly pointed to a reputation of the premises as a place at which drugs could be obtained and a reputation in the appellant as a person willing and able to supply them. Members of the public do not normally telephone or turn up on the doorstep with offers to purchase drugs unless they have, or at least think that they have, good reason to suppose that their offers are likely to be accepted. 'What better evidence,' he asked, at p. 224, 'could there be of the commercial supply of drugs from the appellant's home than the number of those resorting to his home in search of drugs?' An acceptable and attractively simple answer to this question was found by the court by equiparating the acts of persons outside the premises offering to purchase with acts of persons on the premises offering to sell. The inference to be drawn from offers from outside was that it followed that there were persons inside who were ready to supply and the inference to be drawn from inquiries made for the appellant was that the appellant was the supplier. *Reg.* v *Harry* was relied upon by the appellant but was distinguished on the ground that the use of the premises in that case for the supplying of drugs was not in issue and that the evidence was sought to be adduced solely on the issue of the identity of the supplier. Reliance was placed by the Crown upon the earlier decision of *Woodhouse* v *Hall*, 72 Cr App R 39, which the court found to be indistinguishable from the instant case. I confess that I have found it difficult to follow the court's reasoning here. That case involved no question whatever of the admission of hearsay evidence. The defendant was charged with managing a brothel which had been visited by police officers who gave evidence that two women, who were employed there under the management of the defendant, had made direct offers to them of sexual services. That evidence was tendered as direct evidence and solely for the purpose of establishing that the premises were being used as a brothel. It was direct evidence of disorderly conduct by persons employed at the premises and was no more hearsay than would have been, for instance, evidence of a written notice on the premises advertising the services available, or evidence tendered by police officers of witnessing a lewd exhibition. The case is, as it seems to me, not remotely parallel to the instant case. To obtain a parallel one would have to envisage evidence by police officers of conversations with an inquirer on the doorstep as to whether sexual services were available. (An actual example is cited by Gibson J in the course of his judgment in *Marshall* v *Watt* [1953] Tas SR 1 of a set of barristers' chambers established at premises previously occupied by ladies engaged in a different profession.) Such testimony plainly could not, I should have thought, have been any evidence at all of what activity was carried on inside the premises. At highest it could constitute no more than evidence that the inquirer thought that such services might be available. Such belief could be relevant and admissible only if accompanied by admissible evidence of the grounds for the belief, as, for instance, by the reaction of the accused to the inquiries. Suppose, for instance, a case in which the issue is whether premises are being used for the retailing of goods in breach of a covenant in a lease. Quite clearly evidence by a witness of a conversation in a public house with another person not called to give evidence, who told him that he either believed goods to be sold on the premises or that he had himself purchased goods there, would be inadmissible as evidence of the fact in issue. Such a conversation becomes no more admissible as evidence of the fact if the witness narrates that it took place, not in a public house, but in the street outside the premises where the maker of the statement was standing carrying a shopping bag. I cannot, for my part, follow why it should be said to become any more admissible by evidence that the maker of the statement evinced his belief by knocking at the door and asking to purchase goods. On the other hand, evidence that persons employed on the premises were offering goods for sale would obviously fall into quite a different category.

In the Court of Appeal (Criminal Division), 93 Cr App R 222 the problem was approached by treating the evidence tendered as raising two separate, though possibly interrelated, questions. First, it was asked, was it admissible solely for the purpose of proving that amphetamines either had been or were being supplied from the premises where the appellant lived? That was answered in the affirmative simply by reference to *Woodhouse* v *Hall*, 72 Cr App R 39. Lloyd LJ, in the course of his judgment, 93 Cr App R 222, 224, postulated the question, 'What difference could there be between offers to sell sexual services and offers to buy drugs?' and observed, at pp. 224–225:

> If the police officers could give original evidence, without infringing the hearsay rule, that offers were made in the one case in order to establish that the premises were a brothel, then they could give original evidence to the like effect in the other case to establish that the premises were being used for the supply of drugs.

Such analogical reasoning, however, does not, with respect, stand up to analysis. There is a world of difference between evidence by a witness of his own observation of disorderly conduct by persons employed at the premises tendered to prove their use as a disorderly house and evidence of what a witness has heard from an unconnected caller regarding his belief as to what goes on at the premises. Whilst it is no doubt true that the mere supplying of drugs from premises necessarily implies the existence of customers anxious to acquire them, that is not a proposition which can legitimately be used to demonstrate the converse, i.e. that the existence of such customers implies the supply of drugs. That can be demonstrated only by establishing the truth of the customer's belief that they will be supplied. That belief cannot by itself be prayed in aid to substantiate its own veracity.

As regards the second and separate question of whether the evidence of the police officers was admissible for the purpose of showing that the appellant was the supplier, the court regarded that as part and parcel of the purpose of showing that the premises were being used for the supply of drugs and concluded that if it were admissible for the latter purpose it was also admissible for the former. For the reasons which I have endeavoured to explain, I do not consider that it was admissible for the latter purpose, but it seems to me that it was plainly inadmissible for the former. One can, perhaps, test it by asking whether, if the caller had been produced as a witness and his only evidence had been 'I went to 11, Perth Close and offered to buy drugs from Chippie,' that could have been admitted as evidence that Chippie was a supplier. The answer must, as it seems to me, be that it would have had to have been excluded quite simply as being irrelevant. It cannot be right that that which would be irrelevant and objectionable if tendered directly nevertheless becomes relevant and admissible if tendered as hearsay. Ex nihilo, nihil fit.

It cannot, I think, be right in any event to regard the evidence as serving a dual purpose and to test its admissibility for one purpose by reference to its admissibility for another. Indeed, Lloyd LJ himself recognised this. He observed, 93 Cr App R 222, 226:

> We have been assuming that the words had a dual purpose, first to show the commercial supply of drugs from the premises, and, secondly, to show that the appellant was the supplier. But in truth there is no distinction. It was all part and

parcel of the same purpose. If the evidence was admissible to prove the first purpose, it was admissible to prove the second. Any attempt to draw a line between the two would, we think, be indefensible.

With this last sentence I agree. There is no logically defensible distinction. Looking once again at the terms of the charge, what was in issue was not the user of the premises for supplying drugs commercially. It was whether the appellant was in possession of drugs with intent to supply. So far as the evidence was directed to furnishing a ground for an inference as to the user of the premises, that user was relevant to the charge only so far as it was permissible to infer from it that it was the appellant who was using them for that purpose. That in turn could be inferred only from the words used. There was in fact only one purpose, namely that of establishing the appellant's intention.

I have had the advantage of reading in draft the speeches prepared by my noble and learned friends, Lord Griffiths and Lord Browne-Wilkinson. Whilst I share their unease at the rejection of what any layman would regard as a tolerably plain indication that the appellant had been engaged in trading in drugs, I have not felt able to accept their analysis of the relevance and admissibility of the evidence tendered. The pith of the argument — and I hope that I do not misstate it — is that the acts of callers in going or telephoning to the premises, explained by their states of mind as revealed by their contemporaneous words, is some evidence which a jury could properly take into account in deciding whether the appellant had an intention to supply because it demonstrates that there was an established potential market, i.e. a pool of willing purchasers, which the accused had the opportunity of supplying. It is the relevance of this in relation to the only issue in the case — the intention of the accused to supply that market — that I have not felt able to accept. 'Some evidence which a jury could take into account' means no more than that the evidence is probative. But then, one asks, of what is it probative? What is it about the existence of a potential customer or of a body of customers, whether substantial or not, that tends to render it more or less likely that a given individual intends to supply their requirements? Can one, for instance, legitimately infer an intention to make a gift to charity from evidence of calls made by collectors seeking donations?

Clearly the existence of a body of potential customers provides the *opportunity* to the accused (and, indeed, to anyone else who knows of their existence) to supply their requirements if he has the wish or intention to do so. But in what way does it establish that intention? The fact that potential customers make statements indicative of their existence as potential customers demonstrates no more than their desire to be supplied by anyone minded to supply them, which would, on this analysis, include also the police officers who intercepted the calls. The general proposition that any statement indicating that the maker of the statement is a potential customer of an accused person for the purpose of purchasing drugs is admissible as evidence of the accused's intent to supply is manifestly insupportable.

. . . I confess that I find difficulty in seeing a logically defensible distinction between a inference to be drawn from an express assertion (viz. that that which is asserted is true) (impermissible) and an inference to be drawn from precisely the same assertion made by implication (permissible). That calls are made to premises is, by itself, irrelevant, for it is probative of nothing but the fact that the calls have been made.

. . . I cannot, for my part, see any logical difference between evidence of a positive assertion and evidence of an assertion expressed as a question from which the positive assertion is to be inferred. In both cases the opinion or belief of the maker is unsworn and untested by cross-examination and is equally prejudicial. To admit such statements as evidence of the fact would, in my opinion, not only entail a radical departure from the underlying reasoning in *Reg.* v *Blastland* [1986] AC 41 and *Myers* v *Director of Public Prosecutions* [1965] AC 1001 and the overruling of a case of high authority which has stood unchallenged for a century and a half but would involve embarking upon a process of judicial legislation. The possibility of such a course was referred to by Lord Reid in the course of his speech in *Myers* when he said, at pp. 1021–1022:

> I have never taken a narrow view of the functions of this House as an appellate tribunal. The common law must be developed to meet changing economic conditions and habits of thought, and I would not be deterred by expressions of opinion in this House in old cases. But there are limits to what we can or should do. If we are to extend the law it must be by the development and application of fundamental principles. We cannot introduce arbitrary conditions or limitations: that must be left to legislation. And if we do in effect change the law, we ought in my opinion only to do that in cases where our decision will produce some finality or certainty. If we disregard technicalities in this case and seek to apply principle and common sense, there are a number of other parts of the existing law of hearsay susceptible of similar treatment, and we shall probably have a series of appeals in cases where the existing technical limitations produce an unjust result. If we are to give a wide interpretation to our judicial functions questions of policy cannot be wholly excluded, and it seems to me to be against public policy to produce uncertainty. The only satisfactory solution is by legislation following on a wide survey of the whole field, and I think that such a survey is overdue. A policy of make do and mend is no longer adequate.

That remains, in my opinion, as valid today as it was in 1964 and the limits to which the legislature has considered it right to go since appear from the provisions of the Civil Evidence Act 1968, the Police and Criminal Evidence Act 1984 and the Criminal Justice Act 1988. I am very conscious of the difficulty of obtaining direct evidence from witnesses in the prosecution of drug offences and there may well be a good case for relaxing the rule which excludes hearsay either generally or in cases such as the present so long as the jury receives an appropriate direction as to the circumspection with which hearsay evidence should be received. But the rule has been evolved and applied over many years in the interest of fairness to persons accused of crime and if it is now to be modified that should, in my opinion, be done only by the legislature. I would accordingly allow the appeal.

LORD BROWNE-WILKINSON: My Lords. I have the misfortune to disagree with the majority of your Lordships and must state as shortly as I can my reasons for so doing.

The relevant facts are fully stated in the speech of my noble and learned friend, Lord Oliver of Aylmerton. In essence, the appellant was arrested at 11, Perth Close, Christchurch, where drugs were discovered. In the hours following the arrest, police officers (in the absence of the accused) answered 15 telephone calls. Ten of those calls asked for 'Chippie' (a name by which other evidence proved the appellant to be known) and asked for drugs. There were also nine persons who called in person at the premises and asked for 'Chippie:' seven of them indicated that they wished to purchase drugs. At the trial of the accused on a charge, inter alia, of being in possession of drugs with intent to supply, the police officers were allowed to give evidence of those calls including evidence of what was said by the callers. With one irrelevant exception, the callers themselves did not give evidence. The accused was convicted. The question is whether the evidence given by the police officers as to the calls was admissible.

The certified question before this House is as follows:

Whether evidence may be adduced at a trial of words spoken (namely a request for drugs to be supplied by the defendant), not spoken in the presence or hearing of the defendant, by a person not called as a witness, for the purpose not of establishing the truth of any fact narrated by the words, but of inviting the jury to draw an inference from the fact that the words were spoken (namely that the defendant was a supplier of drugs).

I regard that question as being unfortunately framed for two reasons. First, it raises the question of the admissibility of the evidence in relation to only one caller, whereas in fact there were numerous callers. Second, the question suggests that the issue is whether the jury can draw an inference from the words spoken by the caller, rather than from the making of the call itself as explained by the words used by the caller. For those reasons, I will first address the problem in the light of the actual facts of the case and at the end revert to the certified question.

There are two questions in this case: first, whether the making of these calls by persons seeking drugs is relevant at all to the charge that the accused had an intent to supply. Second, if relevant, could those facts be proved by the police officers' evidence of the calls or did such evidence breach the hearsay rule? In my view it is critical to keep those questions separate so far as possible although the position is much complicated by the fact that the purpose of the calls cannot be ascertained except by reference to the words spoken by the callers.

. . . [His Lordship went on to consider whether or not the evidence of the telephone calls was relevant and after deciding such evidence was relevant continued. . . .]

In considering relevance, I have so far assumed that it can be proved (a) that calls were made and (b) that the purpose of the calls was to acquire drugs from Chippie. Unless both (a) and (b) are proved, the calls do not satisfy the requirements of relevance. Telephone or personal calls, in the absence of proof of the purpose of the calls, are evidence of nothing. The only evidence of the purposes of the calls was the police officers' account of what the callers said. Is such evidence inadmissible on the grounds that it breaches the hearsay rule?

It is important to bear in mind that not all evidence of what a third party said is hearsay. In *Subramaniam* v *Public Prosecutor* [1956] 1 WLR 965, 970 the Privy Council said:

Evidence of a statement made to a witness by a person who is not himself called as a witness may or may not be hearsay. It is hearsay and inadmissible when the object of the evidence is to establish the truth of what is contained in the statement. It is not hearsay and is admissible when it is proposed to establish by the evidence, not the truth of the statement, but the fact that it was made.

One of the classic examples of evidence which does not fall within the hearsay rule is a statement by a third party accompanying and explaining his acts, sometimes called verbal acts. Such evidence is admitted not to prove the truth of what the third party said but to explain the acts of the third party.

This approach has been adopted so as to permit a recipient of a telephone call to give evidence of what was said to him by the caller. The most important authority on this is the decision of the Privy Council in *Ratten* v *The Queen* [1972] AC 378, but before considering that case I must first revert to the New Zealand and Australian authorities, since they are referred to with approval in *Ratten*.

In *Davidson* v *Quirke* [1923] NZLR 552 Salmond J, in the course of dealing with the admissibility of evidence from police officers of what had been said by the telephone callers, said, at p. 556:

If the testimony of the police officers was limited to the mere fact that on the day in question a large number of persons rang up the appellant's house within the space of an hour and twenty five minutes, all evidence as to the contents of the communications being excluded, such testimony would prove merely that the premises were being used for a business of some kind, but would fall far short of proving that they were used for the business of betting. I am of opinion that, notwithstanding the general rule which excludes evidence of statements, the contents of those telephone messages as received and testified to by the police officers are legally admissible in evidence. This is an illustration of the principle that, notwithstanding the rule against hearsay, where the purpose or meaning of an act done is relevant, evidence of contemparaneous declarations accompanying and explaining the act is admissible in proof of such purpose or meaning. . . . since the act of numerous strangers in using the appellant's telephone for the purpose of betting is relevant to the issue, the statements made by them at the same time are admissible as explaining their actions and showing the purpose of them.

In *McGregor* v *Stokes* [1952] VLR 347 Herring CJ in the Supreme Court of Victoria had to consider the same point. In holding that the evidence of the police officers as to the words used by the callers was admissible, he applied the passage from the judgment of Salmond J which I have just quoted. He also said, at pp. 350–351:

What the caller had to say in each case was an utterance that accompanied his act of calling, and also explained his purpose in calling. Without the words his act taken as a whole was incomplete. The fact that he has called on the telephone by itself tells you no more than that he has made the call and the making of the call unexplained is an equivocal act. Until you know what he has had to say, you cannot tell whether he has rung up to ask the occupant about a dog or to invite him to dinner or what his purpose was. And so it is in the case of so many things we do that our acts are partly conduct and partly utterance. A man walks into a shop for example, but the significance of his visit cannot be ascertained until he states his business. The learned author of *Wigmore on Evidence* 3rd ed., vol. 6 (1940), para. 1772, at pp. 190–191, has this to say about utterances that form a verbal part of an act: 'A second kind of situation in which utterances are not offered testimonially arises when the utterance accompanies conduct to which it is desired to attach some legal effect. The conduct or act has intrinsically no definite significance, or only an ambiguous one, and its whole purport or tenor is to be more precisely ascertained by considering the words accompanying it. The utterance thus enters merely as a verbal part of the act, or, in common phrase, a "verbal act".'

These, therefore, are two clear authorities that in cases such as the present there is no contravention of the hearsay rule if a witness gives evidence of what the callers said provided the evidence is not being used testimonially (i.e to prove the truth of what they said) but only to explain the callers' purpose in making the calls. In *McGregor* v *Stokes* that is put on two grounds, which may in fact be the same. The first is that the telephone call is, in itself, an act, the words used by the caller being admissible to explain that act. The second is that the telephone call and the words used by the caller together constitute one act and the words used are admitted as part of that act.

It is particularly to be noticed that in neither of the two cases did the telephone calls by themselves (without reference to what was said) have any relevance or probative value.

In *Ratten* v *The Queen* [1972] AC 378 the accused was charged with murdering his wife by shooting her at their home. His defence was that the gun had gone off by accident. He denied that any telephone call had been made by his wife around the time of the killing. The prosecution called a telephonist the gist of whose evidence was analysed by Lord Wilberforce as follows, at p. 387:

> (1) At about 1.15 p.m. the number Echuca 1494 rang. I plugged into that number. (2) I opened the speak key and said 'Number please.' (3) A female voice answered. (4) The voice was hysterical and sobbed. (5) The voice said 'Get me the police please.'

The Privy Council held that all the evidence given by the telephonist was relevant and admissible as being evidence of fact. Lord Wilberforce, after making the analysis of the contents of the call, continued, at pp. 387–388:

> The factual items numbered (1)—(3) were relevant in order to show that contrary to the evidence of the appellant, a call was made, only some 3–5 minutes before the fatal shooting, by a woman. It not being suggested that there was anybody in the house other than the appellant, his wife and small children, this woman, the caller, could only have been the deceased. Items (4) and (5) were relevant as possibly showing (if the jury thought fit to draw the inference) that the deceased woman was at this time in a state of emotion or fear . . . They were relevant and necessary evidence in order to explain and complete the fact of the call being made. A telephone call is a composite act, made up of manual operations together with the utterance of words (cf. *McGregor* v *Stokes* [1952] VLR 347 and remarks of Salmond J therein quoted). To confine the evidence to the first would be to deprive the act of most of its significance. The act had content when it was known that the call was made in a state of emotion. The knowledge that the caller desired the police to be called helped to indicate the nature of the emotion — anxiety or fear at an existing or impending emergency. It was a matter for the jury to decide what light (if any) this evidence, in the absence of any explanation from the appellant, who was in the house, threw upon what situation was occurring, or developing at the time. If then, this evidence had been presented in this way, as evidence purely of relevant facts, its admissibility could hardly have been plausibly challenged.

It is true that in *Ratten* the telephone call (divorced from the words used by the caller) was per se relevant to rebut the accused's evidence that no such call had been made. But that factor would not have required any evidence of the words used by the caller and would not have rendered admissible items (4) and (5). Those items were only admissible because the whole call was one composite act 'made up of manual operations together with the [words used].'

I am unable to accept the view that the evidence on items (4) and (5) was only admissible as being part of the res gestae. Lord Wilberforce makes it clear that the whole call was admissible as being relevant and factual. The Board only went on, obiter, to consider the question of res gestae because, it was said, the call had been treated in the summing up as evidence of an assertion by the deceased that she was being attacked by the deceased, i.e. testimonially.

Ratten is also important since it cited and applied the principles cited by Salmond J and Herring CJ which I have quoted. As was said by my noble and learned friend, Lord Bridge of Harwich in *Reg* v *Blastland* [1986] AC 41, 58, although

> *Ratten*'s case is not technically binding on your Lordships' House . . . the constitution of the Board (Lord Reid, Lord Hodson, Lord Wilberforce, Lord Diplock and Lord Cross of Chelsea) is of the highest persuasive authority. . . .

For myself the acceptance by the Board in *Ratten* of the decisions in *Davidson* v *Quirke* [1923] NZLR 552 and *McGregor* v *Stokes* [1952] VLR 347 is a powerful reason for not treating those cases as having been wrongly decided. Moreover, those cases have been frequently (though not invariably) followed in the courts of New Zealand and Australia in the decisions referred to by my noble and learned friend, Lord Oliver of Aylmerton.

I turn to consider the cases which in the view of the majority of your Lordships lead to the opposite conclusion. It will be found that in each case the crucial question is 'for what purpose is the evidence tendered'. As I have stated, the evidence if tendered as evidence of the existence of a market willing to purchase drugs from Chippie at the premises is factual and relevant. The majority of your Lordships apparently either do not accept that the availability of such a market is relevant or regard the evidence of the calls as being evidence *only* of the beliefs or opinions of the callers. In the present case, there is no doubt that evidence of the beliefs or opinions of the callers is not admissible. But in some cases such evidence is admissible. Such a case was *Wright* v *Doe d. Tatham*, 7 Ad & E 313; (1838) 5 Cl & F 670.

In that case, the issue was whether a testator had the capacity to make a will. It was common ground that witnesses could have been called to give evidence of their own opinions or beliefs as to his competence. However, it was sought to put in evidence letters written to the testator by persons who had died on the grounds that the contents of those letters inferentially showed the beliefs of the writers that the testator had capacity. The very large number of judges who considered the case were all of the view that the letters were not admissible unless the testator was shown to have adopted or understood them. On that latter point the judges were sharply divided. The grounds of the decision were that the letters were inadmissible as being hearsay in that they constituted an attempt to prove from the contents of the letters an implied assertion as to the writers' view of the capacity of the testator, i.e. the letters were being introduced testimonially as evidence of the truth of the inference to be drawn from their contents. If, as your Lordships consider, the evidence of the callers in the present case is evidence only of the callers' beliefs, *Wright v Doe d. Tatham* is unnecessary to bolster that view because, in any event in the present case, evidence of the callers' belief is irrelevant. If, on the other hand, I am correct in thinking that the calls show an admissible fact, i.e. the existence of a potential market, the case is not in point. The letters in *Wright v Doe d. Tatham* were being tendered testimonially to prove the belief of the writers: the calls in this case are being tendered to prove a relevant fact and not the belief of the callers. Accordingly the hearsay rule does not apply.

That this is a valid distinction is shown by the words of Parke B, at p. 385:

> That the three letters were each of them written by the persons whose names they bear, and sent, at some time before they were found, to the testator's house, no doubt are *facts*, and those facts are proved on oath; and the letters are without doubt admissible on an issue in which the fact of sending such letters by those persons, and within that limit of time, is relevant to the matter in dispute . . . Verbal declarations of the same parties are also *facts*, and in like manner admissible under the same circumstances; and so would letters or declarations to third persons upon the like supposition. But the question is, whether the contents of these letters are evidence of the *fact to be proved upon this issue*, — that is, the actual existence of the qualities which the testator is, in those letters, by implication, stated to possess: and those letters may be considered in this respect to be on the same footing as if they contained a direct and positive statement that he was competent. *For this purpose* they are mere hearsay evidence . . .

In my judgment the opening words of that passage show that Parke B would have adopted the same view as the Privy Council in *Ratten v The Queen* [1972] AC 378 if the sending of a letter and its contents had itself been a circumstantial fact from which an inference (other than an inference as to the writer's opinion) could be drawn.

In *Reg.* v *Blastland* [1986] AC 41 the accused was charged with the murder of a boy. He sought to show that it was not he, but M, who had killed the boy. For that purpose the accused sought to call witnesses to prove that M had said that a boy's body had been found at a time before the body had been generally discovered. Such evidence was held to have been rightly excluded as hearsay. The appellant's argument was that the evidence was admissible to prove M's state of mind, i.e. his knowledge of the murder before the body was found, a fact which should have been left to the jury and from which the jury could draw the inference that it was M, not the accused, who had killed the boy. My noble and learned friend Lord Bridge of Harwich, at p. 54D-F, held that the fact sought to be proved (M's knowledge) was not per se relevant: what was relevant was how M had come by that knowledge which might have been either through having committed the murder himself or by having witnessed someone else committing it. Therefore M's knowledge as such was not relevant to the issue and evidence as to it was inadmissible. In my judgment that decision does not touch on this case if, as I believe, the making of the calls in the present case is direct evidence of a relevant fact, i.e. the existence of the potential customers willing and anxious to purchase drugs at the premises from Chippie.

Finally, in *Reg.* v *Harry*, 86 Cr App R 105, Harry and P were charged with possession of drugs with intent to supply. As in the present case, telephone calls were intercepted by the police asking for drugs. All the callers asked for P, not for Harry. The prosecution did not introduce evidence of those calls, but counsel for Harry wished to cross-examine the police on the calls with a view to showing it was P, not Harry, from whom supply was sought. The Court of Appeal (Criminal Division) upheld the judge's decision to exclude such evidence as being hearsay on the grounds that the callers' words were being used testimonially. It may be that the case can be supported on the basis that it was common ground that the premises were being used for the supply of drugs and that accordingly the only issue was whether it was P or Harry or both who were supplying. But in my view *Reg.* v *Harry* (which Lawton LJ recognised was on the borderline and which has been widely criticised) was wrongly decided because it was a relevant fact that P had customers asking for supply. There is no indication in the report that the New Zealand and Australian cases were cited to the court.

I must now revert to the certified question before this House and consider the case on the basis that there was only one caller. Would evidence of his call alone be admissible? In my judgment the reasoning which has led me to the view that evidence of multiple calls is both relevant and admissible applies also to one call alone: the caller is a potential customer. But a single call would have little probative value in showing the existence of a market. The possible prejudice to the accused by the jury drawing the wrong inference would be so great that I would expect a judge in his discretion to exclude it. I would also modify the question so as to make it clear that the inference to be drawn by the jury is to be drawn not from the words used by the callers but from the fact that there were callers who (from the words used) were shown to be seeking to acquire drugs.

For these reasons, my Lords, I can find no reason why the evidence of multiple calls should not have been admitted. For myself I would have dismissed the appeal and answered the certified question (as amended) in the affirmative. In the event, I can only express the view that there may well be a good case for the legislature to review the hearsay rule in criminal law. In cases such as the present it hampers effective prosecution by excluding evidence which your Lordships all agree is highly probative and, since it comes from the unprompted actions of the callers, is very creditworthy. The hearsay rule can also operate to the detriment of the accused, as the decisions in *Reg.* v *Harry*, 86 Cr App R 105 and *Reg.* v *Blastland* [1986] AC 41 both show. A review of the operation of the hearsay rule in criminal cases is long overdue.

[Lord Bridge of Harwich and Lord Ackner delivered speeches which concurred with Lord Oliver of Aylmerton. Lord Griffiths delivered a speech which concurred with Lord Browne-Wilkinson.]

Appeal allowed.

Questions

1.   Do you prefer the reasoning of Lord Oliver or that of Lord Browne-Wilkinson? Why?

2.   How does Lord Oliver distinguish *Woodhouse* v *Hall* from the instant case? Is this a valid distinction?

3.   Do you agree with the majority that the words spoken in *Ratten* v *R* were not hearsay because they were not relied on 'testimonially'?

4.   Does the decision in *R* v *Kearley* accord with common sense?

5.   A patient sues a doctor alleging negligence in administering drug X instead of drug Y. The patient wishes to call a nurse to testify that she saw the doctor take a jar marked 'drug X' and give pills from the jar to the patient. Is this hearsay or not?

6.   A nephew brings an action to set aside his uncle's will on the ground that the uncle lacked testamentary capacity. The nephew wishes to call evidence that the uncle frequently told friends that 'he was Adolf Hitler reincarnate'. Is this hearsay or not?

7.   The issue arises whether the uncle intended to omit the nephew from his will. The aunt is prepared to testify that at about the time he executed his will, the uncle said to her, 'my nephew is the most deserving of my relatives'. Is this hearsay or not?

8.   Baldrick and Cato are charged with conspiracy to cause explosions. When Cato is arrested, the police find a letter in his possession, written to him some days earlier by Baldrick, in which Baldrick sets out arrangements for planting explosives. The prosecution wish to adduce the letter at trial. Is this hearsay or not?

Further Reading

P. Murphy, *A Practical Approach to Evidence*, 4th ed. (1992), Ch. 6

R. Pattenden, 'Conceptual Versus Pragmatic Approaches to Hearsay' (1993) 56 MLR 138

S. Guest, 'The Scope of the Hearsay Rule' (1985) 101 LQR 385

8 THE RULE AGAINST HEARSAY—II COMMON LAW EXCEPTIONS

Merely because a piece of evidence is caught by the hearsay rule does not mean it is automatically inadmissible. Many exceptions have developed, both common law and statutory, which admit hearsay evidence. A great many of the exceptions which developed at common law have now been superseded by statutory exceptions (see Chapters 9 and 10). It has become unnecessary, therefore, to discuss at any length many of the common law exceptions which still exist but which, in practice, are of little value in the modern law. The categories which remain of some significance are:

(a) declarations made by persons since deceased;
(b) statements contained in public documents; and
(c) the *res gestae* principle.

It is the *res gestae* principle which remains the single most important exception at common law. It is important to remember that where an exception to the hearsay rule operates, the evidence admitted by virtue of the exception remains hearsay but is nevertheless evidence of the truth of the facts contained in the statement.

(A) Declarations by persons since deceased

Where the maker of a statement dies before the trial, his statement could not normally be admitted because of the rule against hearsay. The common law therefore developed a number of exceptions to the hearsay rule which allow the statement of a person since deceased to be admitted into evidence. These exceptions apply to statements which were made either orally or in writing. It should be noted that where the statement was made in writing, there may be some overlap with the provisions of the Criminal Justice Act 1988, and in civil cases, oral or written hearsay statements are made generally admissible by virtue of the Civil Evidence Act 1968 (see Chapter 9). The net result is that the following exceptions have a practical impact only in criminal cases.

There are three principal categories which retain some significance, namely: (i) declarations against interest, (ii) declarations made in the course of a duty, and (iii) dying declarations in homicide cases. Some works refer to a fourth category which concerns matters of custom, pedigree and public rights. These are no longer of any real significance in criminal cases and, so far as they arise in civil cases, they are dealt with by the Civil Evidence Act 1968 (see Chapter 9).

(i) Declarations against interest

In criminal cases the oral or written declaration by a person since deceased of a fact which he knew to be against his pecuniary or proprietary interest at the time the declaration was made is admissible as evidence of the facts stated so long as the declarant had personal knowledge of such facts. If it cannot be shown that the deceased person was aware the statement was against his interest, the evidence remains inadmissible.

Tucker v *Oldbury Urban Council*
[1912] 2 KB 317
Court of Appeal

FLETCHER MOULTON LJ: This is an employers' appeal against the decision of his Honour Judge Howard Smith in an application for compensation under the Workmen's Compensation Act to the dependants of WH Tucker, a deceased workman.

The point raised is that the learned judge was wrong in law in rejecting evidence of certain alleged statements of the deceased workman under the circumstances hereinafter appearing.

The evidence for the applicants was to the effect that in the course of his work a foreign body (such as a piece of steel or the like) was driven under his thumb-nail and caused septic poisoning leading to septicaemia. The accident was alleged to have been on June 6, and the workman continued working until June 19, and death occurred on June 27.

The respondents called their general manager, who deposed that he saw Tucker on June 19, the day he left off work, and that he then had his thumb wrapped up. He then said that he asked him what was the matter. Counsel for the respondents proceeded to ask him what reply the deceased man had given. Objection was taken to this question being answered on the ground that the statements of the deceased workman were not admissible in evidence. The judge upheld the objection, and it is against this decision that the present appeal is brought.

Counsel for the appellants sought to support the appeal on two grounds, i.e., (1) that the statements of the deceased workman were admissible as admissions, and (2) that they were admissible as declarations against interest.

With regard to the first of these grounds, I am of opinion that it is untenable. The applicants in the present case have as dependants a direct statutory right against the employer under Sched. I (1)(a); the deceased workman is not a party to the litigation, nor do they derive their title to compensation by derivation from him. No admission therefore made by him can be evidence against the present applicants.

The second objection gives rise to more difficulty. To decide whether it applies one must of course know the nature of the declaration in order to judge whether or not it was a declaration against interest on the part of the deceased. We were informed that the statements were to the effect that he had a whitlow on his thumb, and that on the witness further asking him whether he had been hammering his thumb the deceased said 'No.'

This ground of admissibility has nothing whatever to do with the fact that the deceased was the workman himself. It would apply equally to a declaration against interest on the part of any witness. Such declarations are admitted as evidence in our jurisprudence on the ground that declarations made by persons against their own interests are extremely unlikely to be false. It follows therefore that to support the admissibility it must be shewn that the statement was to the knowledge of the deceased contrary to his interest. And it is now settled that the declaration must be against pecuniary interests (or against proprietary interests, which is much the same thing): see *Sussex Peerage Case* (1844) 11 Cl & F 85 and the judgment of Blackburn J, in *Smith* v *Blakey* (1867) LR 2 QB 326.

In my opinion the proposed statements fail to satisfy the requirements of the law and the evidence was rightly rejected. At the date when they were made no claim had been made, and there is no reason to believe that the workman knew that he ever would be able to make a claim. Up to that moment there had been no incapacity. He had continued working as usual and he undoubtedly was unable at that time to foresee the rapid and fatal development of the mischief. It must be remembered that if the incapacity lasts less than two weeks no compensation is payable in respect of the first week.

But apart from this I am of opinion that the statements themselves were not necessarily against the interest of the decease[d]. The description of the trouble in his thumb as a whitlow was in the mouth of an ordinary workman a natural description which does not seem to me to be, when properly understood, contrary to the facts of the case or inimical to a claim on his part, if he had lived to make one. A whitlow is a septic condition resembling very much the early stages of such an affection as that of which the workman died. Nor does the statement that he had not been hammering his thumb appear to me to militate against the success of any such claim. It certainly does not amount to a statement that he had not while working run a piece of iron or steel under his nail.

But although I have examined these statements from the point of view whether they are statements which would have been against the interests of his claim had he made a claim, I base my decision on the fact that he had not made a claim nor could be shewn to have known that he could make a claim, and that therefore they were not declarations against his pecuniary interests. It is not sufficient that they should be such as it turns out were against his interests. For instance, the record by a deceased man of a contract will not become admissible because it turns out that the contract would have been a very disastrous one: see *Massey* v *Allen* (1879) 13 Ch D 558. It is therefore immaterial to consider whether these statements would assist the employers in resisting the present claim or not. The claim had not been made or the grounds formulated, and therefore there was nothing in the statements which at the time entitled them to be viewed as against the pecuniary interest of the person making them.

I am therefore of opinion that this appeal should be dismissed with costs.

Question
Do you agree that a declaration made by a person since deceased, which he knew to be against his interest, is extremely unlikely to be false?

Note
Whilst recognising that a declaration made against pecuniary or proprietary interest is admissible as an exception to the hearsay rule, the English courts have seemingly decided that a declaration against penal interest is not admissible. By a declaration against penal interest is meant a declaration which exposes the maker to a criminal prosecution. For example, D is being tried for the murder of P. Before the trial, X confesses to W that he (X) killed P. X has since died. Would X's confession be admissible at D's trial as a declaration against interest?

The only direct English authority is the *Sussex Peerage Case* (1884) 11 Cl & F 85, which held that a declaration made by a clergyman which would have made him liable to criminal prosecution was not admissible in evidence. The Canadian courts have reached a different conclusion, holding that a declaration against penal interest is admissible in evidence. In *R v O'Brien* (1977) 76 DLR (3d) 513, D was charged with drug offences and convicted. Under the protection of a certain statute, X made a statement to the effect that he alone had committed the offence, absolving D of any responsibility. The statute prevented the statement being used against X in any subsequent proceedings. Before D's appeal could be heard X died. The court recognised the existence of the doctrine of declarations against penal interest but concluded that as X knew his statement could not be used against him in any proceedings, it was not against his interest when he made it.

Question
Could D's declaration against penal interest also expose him to the risk of an action for damages? If so, would his statement then be admissible as a declaration against pecuniary interest?

(ii)   Declarations made in the course of a duty

An oral or written statement made by a person since deceased is admissible if it was made in pursuance of a duty to record or report his acts and it was made contemporaneously with the act. As is usual, whether contemporaneity exists has to be answered in the light of all the circumstances of the case (see Chapter 5(A)(*i*)). As this exception overlaps considerably with s. 24 of the Criminal Justice Act 1988 (see Chapter 9), no detailed consideration of the cases need be made here. The exception may, however, still be of some use in modern times (see *R v McGuire* [1985] Crim LR 663).

(iii)   Dying declarations in homicide cases

Oral or written statements made by a person since deceased are admissible evidence of the cause of his death at a trial for his murder or manslaughter.

At present, the exception has not been applied to other kinds of criminal offence which, whilst not being murder or manslaughter, have resulted in another's death. If the exception were not extended to other such offences, potential anomalies would result. For example, consider the offence of causing death by dangerous driving, contrary to s. 1 of the Road Traffic Act 1988. A person who causes the death of another by the manner in which he drives a vehicle might face any one of a number of charges. The aforementioned statutory offence is one possibility, but so is the common law offence of manslaughter provided the requisite *mens rea* of recklessness is present. The substance of both these offences is that the accused caused the victim's death. Can it be right that a crucial piece of evidence may or may not be admissible depending upon which offence is charged? As yet, no authority has dealt with the point.

What is certain is that the statement must be made whilst the declarant is under a 'settled and hopeless expectation of death' (*R* v *Jenkins* (1869) LR CCR 1 CCR 187) and the deceased, had he survived, must have made a competent witness (*R* v *Pike* (1829) 3 C & P 598).

R v *Perry*
[1909] 2 KB 697
Court of Criminal Appeal

LORD ALVERSTONE CJ: This appeal raises a very important question. The trial was one for murder arising out of the death of the girl Agnes Margaret Summersby through an illegal operation performed upon her. The evidence was not in all probability sufficient to secure the conviction of the prisoner apart from a dying declaration made by the deceased girl. At the trial Lawrance J admitted the declaration, but expressed the opinion that the case was one fit for appeal in order that a definite ruling might be given by this Court, if possible, as to the admissibility of the statement made by the deceased girl to her sister. Before dealing with the actual terms of the statement we desire to point out that the principle has been recognized for many years and can be expressed clearly and definitely. In our opinion that principle cannot be expressed in better terms than those used by Eyre CB in *Rex* v *Woodcock* (1789) 1 Leach 500. He said:

> Now the general principle on which this species of evidence is admitted is, that they are declarations made in extremity, when the party is at the point of death, and when every hope of this world is gone: when every motive to falsehood is silenced, and the mind is induced by the most powerful considerations to speak the truth; a situation so solemn and so awful is considered by the law as creating an obligation equal to that which is imposed by a positive oath administered in a Court of justice.

The expression 'at the point of death' which is there used has given rise to some misapprehension, and in *Reg.* v *Osman* (1881) 15 Cox CC 1 Lush LJ said that there must be a settled hopeless expectation of 'immediate death.' We are of opinion that the presence or absence of expectation on the part of the declarant of immediate death is not the true test as to whether a statement as to the cause of death is admissible or not. Death must be imminent, but the material point is that the statement must be made when every hope of life has gone from the person making the statement. We think that that principle has been recognized in the later cases, to one or two of which we desire to call attention. In *Reg.* v *Peel* (1860) 2 F & F 21 Willes J said: 'It must be proved that the man was dying, and there must be a settled hopeless expectation of death in the declarant.' That sentence expresses in very clear and crisp language the rule which I have been trying to explain. In *Reg.* v *Gloster* (1888) 16 Cox CC 471 Charles J, after examining the cases and citing *Rex* v *Woodcock*, *Reg.* v *Peel*, and *Reg.* v *Osman* (where Lush LJ used the expression 'immediate death'), and after expressing his view that the word 'immediate' might be misunderstood, said: 'The whole of the facts must be looked at from first to last; and I may say before I refer to the evidence in detail that it goes no further than this: that the woman thought that she was dying, thought that she would not recover, but in my judgment — and it is a most difficult thing to form a judgment of what was passing through the mind of this unfortunate woman — she did not entirely give up hope. And unless I can come to the conclusion that every hope was extinguished and gone I cannot admit the statement.' It is also desirable to read a passage in the earlier part of the judgment in which Charles J referred to the reasons why he differed from Lush LJ. He said:

> In the latest case of all (*Reg.* v *Osman*) Lush LJ lays down the principle in these terms: 'A dying declaration is admitted in evidence because it is presumed that no person who is immediately going into the presence of his Maker, will do so with a lie on his lips. But the person making the declaration must entertain a settled hopeless expectation of immediate death. If he thinks he will die to-morrow it will not do.' That is the judgment of Willes J with this addition, that Lush LJ inserts the word 'immediate' before death, and goes on to say: 'If he thinks he will die to-morrow it will not do.' With the greatest deference to the latter very learned judge I would rather prefer to adopt the language of Willes J and say that the declarant must be under a 'settled hopeless expectation of death.' 'Immediate death' must be construed in the sense of death impending, not on the instant, but within a very very short distance indeed. These are the principles that have been laid down and are to guide me in the exercise of my judgment.

In other words the test is whether all hope of life has been abandoned so that the person making the statement thinks that death must follow. In our opinion that is the true principle.

I now propose to apply that principle to the present case. It is for the judge at a trial for murder to admit as evidence a statement made by a deceased person for whose murder the prisoner is being tried if he thinks the statement was a declaration made in circumstances which render it admissible. In the present case it was contended on behalf of the prisoner that the language used by Lawrance J at the trial at the time he admitted evidence of the declaration shewed that he would have come to the conclusion, had it not been for the existence of the Court of Criminal Appeal, that the statement was not made by the deceased girl with all hope of life gone, and that he would therefore not have admitted the evidence.

We have communicated with Lawrance J, and he informs us that what he intended to express at the trial was that he thought it was a case in which this Court should have the opportunity of laying down the principle upon which the admissibility of evidence of such statements ought to be determined. He informs us that he has no doubt that the deceased girl had abandoned all hope of life at the time she made the statement. We are of opinion that the right view is that in determining whether a declaration is admissible in evidence the judge at the trial ought to consider whether the death of the deceased was imminent at the time the declaration was made and to determine from the language used by the deceased whether the statement was made at a time when the deceased had 'a settled hopeless expectation of death.' In the present case, if the expression 'I shall go' is taken alone, it might mean I shall die some day; but, taking into consideration the whole sentence, we concur with the opinion of Lawrance J that the statement was made by the deceased with the hopeless expectation of death. By the expression 'hopeless expectation of death' I mean that the deceased had abandoned all hope of living. The statement is therefore admissible as a dying declaration made by her. On these grounds we are of the opinion that the appeal must be dismissed.

Question
Is there more or less risk of unreliability when a person makes a dying declaration?

(B) Statements in public documents

Statements contained in public documents may be admitted at common law as evidence of the facts contained in them although those facts are capable of rebuttal by other evidence. Examples of such documents would include records of births, deaths and marriages. The practical use of this exception has, in most cases, been overtaken by statutory provisions (see Chapter 9). In view of its reduced importance only two cases need be considered here.

Lilley v *Pettit*
[1946] KB 401
Court of Appeal

LORD GODDARD CJ: This is a special case stated by the recorder of Cambridge who allowed an appeal, and quashed the conviction of the respondent by the court of summary jurisdiction sitting at Cambridge, for having on May 15, 1944, made a false statement relating to a birth contrary to the Perjury Act, 1911, s. 4.

Quite shortly the facts were that the respondent in registering the birth of a child gave her husband's name as the father, and it was alleged by the prosecution that her husband had been called up for service at the beginning of the war and they tried to prove that when the child was conceived he was overseas. The child was born on May 1, 1944, and in order to prove the date when the husband went overseas a civilian staff officer at the War Office, who stated that he had charge of the records relating to the respondent's husband, was called as a witness. He stated that these records were official records and documents kept by a government department and preserved at the regimental records office; that they were not documents to which the public have access, nor were they kept for the use or information of the public. The recorder held that the records were not admissible under the common law. It was conceded, at least before this court, that the documents were not admissible under s. 163 of the Army Act as the charge was not one under that Act. Nor could the Evidence Act of 1938 make the documents admissible as that Act has no application to a criminal charge. Another document which the prosecution sought to prove was rejected by the recorder and it was not contended before us that it was admissible. There was no other evidence from which any conclusion could be drawn as to where and when the respondent's husband was serving during any relevant time and there being no evidence, therefore, to show impossibility of access, the recorder found that the case was not proved and allowed the appeal.

The only question now before this court is whether the recorder was right in refusing to admit the regimental records.

The next case to which reference may be made on this subject is *Sturla* v *Freccia* (1880) 5 App Cas 623, in which Lord Blackburn considered *The Irish Society* v *The Bishop of Derry* (1846) 12 Cl & F 641 and dealt in some detail with what can be described as a public document. The case was concerned with a report of a committee appointed by a public department in a foreign state and acted on by the government of that state, but the House held it was not admissible as a public document. Lord Blackburn, after quoting Parke B's judgment, went on to say:

> Now, my Lords, taking that decision, the principle upon which it goes is, that it should be a public inquiry, a public document, and made by a public officer. I do not think that 'public' there is to be taken in the sense of meaning the whole world. . . . But it must be a public document, and it must be made by a public officer. I understand a public document there to mean a document that is made *for the purpose of the public making use of it, and being able to refer to it.* It is meant to be where there is a judicial, or quasi-judicial, duty to inquire, as might be said to be the case with the bishop acting under the writs issued by the Crown. That may be said to be quasi-judicial. He is acting for the public when that is done; but I think the very object of it must be that it should be made *for the purpose of being kept public, so that the persons concerned with it may have access to it afterwards.*

(The italics are mine.) Later, in the judgment, he referred to the case of *Arnold* v *The Bishop of Bath and Wells*, and said:

> Supposing . . . . the entry had been made by the bishop on his visitation that such and such a man was the clergyman of the parish, and had been admitted some twenty years before, secundum consuetudinem, and suppose it was wrong to admit him, that falls completely within the principle which I think the case of *The Irish Society* v *The Bishop of Derry* establishes. It seems to me that it is clearly within that principle. The bishop made his visitation, and recorded it *with the wish and intent that it should be kept publicly as a register, to be seen by everybody in his diocese.* If the bishop had not the right to make such an inquiry, so as to make it evidence in future, that is another affair; but if he had, then he was a public officer performing what he thought a public duty, *with the view and intent that it should be public.*

(Again, the italics are mine.) It seems to me clear from the noble and learned lord's speech that to be a public document it must be one made for the purpose of the public making use of it. Its object must be that all persons concerned in it may have access to it.

Here it appears to be beyond controversy, and indeed, it was found as a fact, that the public has no right of access to these records. They are records which, in my opinion, an officer of the Crown could refuse to produce on a subpoena if it was considered contrary to the public interest so to do. If a document is a public document it must be so equally in time of war as in time of peace and it is obvious that it might be most detrimental to the public interest to allow, in time of war, persons to have access to these records as they would show the movement of troops. The very fact that no defence regulation was passed prohibiting access to these records tends to show that they are not public, otherwise it is impossible to suppose that precautions would not have been taken to prevent or restrict access to them. And again, the fact that by s. 163, of the Army Act, 1881, special provision is made which would in my opinion, include these records or some of them in proceedings under the Act whether before a civil court or a court martial, also indicates that these are not public documents, for if they were there would have been no necessity to provide specially that they should be admissible. The only case in which it seems any part of a soldier's record has ever been accepted by a court is that of *Gleen* v *Gleen*, where Sir Francis Jeune P, appears to have admitted the medical sheet of a soldier to prove that he was suffering from a disease so as to establish adultery. That was an undefended case so the question was not argued and the report is very meagre, but in my opinion that case ought not to be followed if the learned President admitted the sheet as a public document. The provisions which have since been made by the Evidence Act, 1938, and the divorce rules, may have the effect of admitting these documents in matrimonial causes but these rules have no application to the present case, and I express no opinion regarding them in the present case which is of a criminal nature.

In my opinion these records are not within the class that can be described as public documents. They are not kept for the information of the public but for the information of the Crown and the executive, and accordingly, in my opinion, the recorder was right in refusing to admit them as evidence. It follows that this appeal must be dismissed with costs.

Question
Is there any reason to suppose that regimental records are less reliable than other similar documents which are open to public inspection?

R v *Halpin*
[1975] QB 907
Court of Appeal

GEOFFREY LANE LJ: On July 18, 1974, at the Central Criminal Court, after a trial lasting some 32 working days, the defendant was convicted of conspiracy to cheat and defraud and was sentenced to three years' imprisonment. He now appeals against that conviction by leave of the single judge.

The prosecution alleged that between March 1969 and October 1972 the defendant who, at the lowest, was one of the leading lights of a company known as Pavings and Pipelines Ltd (referred to hereafter as 'P & P') conspired with a man called Joseph Halvey, who was an employee of P & P, and also with a man called Jackson, who was employed by the Brent London Borough Council, to cheat the council by means of putting in bogus claims for paving work allegedly done in the borough by P & P.

Halvey was convicted on the conspiracy count and was sentenced to 18 months' imprisonment suspended for two years. Jackson pleaded guilty to that count on the fifth day of the trial and was sentenced to 18 months' imprisonment. There was another defendant by the name of Fowlie. He was Jackson's superior in the council and was also charged with that conspiracy. He was acquitted.

The Crown adduced in evidence an extract from the annual returns kept in the Companies Register, the annual returns made by P & P. The admission of that evidence was the subject of an objection at the trial and forms part of the grounds of appeal in the present case and will have to be dealt with more fully at a later stage of this judgment. According to that extract, on March 31, 1968, the defendant and his wife, Mrs Halpin (not to be confused with the defendant's sister-in-law, who acted as secretary for P & P) became the sole directors of P & P. On July 8, 1968, shares were transferred, so that the defendant owned 348 of the 350 shares, and his wife, Mrs Halpin, owned the other two shares.

However, according to that return, Mrs Halpin resigned on November 7, 1971, and a man called Cagney was appointed. On November 27, 1971, there was an allotment of shares to Cagney and a man called Hall and to the defendant. Whether or not the defendant was in fact a director of P & P there is no doubt that he was closely connected with the council paving contracts. [His Lordship considered the facts and the other grounds of the appeal which he rejected, and continued:] There remains the strongest point made on behalf of the defendant, which was most energetically argued by Mr Anns. The prosecution, as part of their case, sought to prove that the defendant and his wife were in effect the sole shareholders and directors of P & P during the period October 1968 to 1971 and in order to prove the position of the defendant and his wife in the company they sought to produce the file from the Companies Register containing the statutory annual returns made by the company under the Companies Act 1948. The relevant contents of that file were collated in a document which was agreed between the parties as providing an accurate précis of the contents.

The admissibility of that file, however, was disputed, and the judge rejected a submission by the defence that the file was inadmissible as being hearsay. Mr Anns renews his submission before this court. The situation is this. The Companies Act 1948 does not itself make these documents admissible to prove their contents. There are certain matters which the Act of 1948 does make admissible, despite the fact that without such provision they would undoubtedly be hearsay.

Section 15 deals with the conclusiveness of a certificate of incorporation. Section 118 deals with the register of members and reads as follows: 'The register of members shall be prima facie evidence of any matters by this Act directed or authorised to be inserted therein.' Section 145 deals with minutes of proceedings of meetings of company and of directors and management. Section 145 (2) reads:

> Any such minute if purporting to be signed by the chairman of the meeting at which the proceedings were had, or by the chairman of the next succeeding meeting, shall be evidence of the proceedings.

Nowhere in the Act is there a corresponding provision making the contents of the annual returns evidence in a similar way. Therefore, if these documents are to be admissible, it can only be by virtue of the common law rules. If they are inapplicable, the document remains hearsay and does not form an exception to the hearsay rule and would, accordingly, be inadmissible.

Mr Anns contends that there are four conditions which must be satisfied before a document of this sort can be admitted in evidence. First, the document must be brought into existence and preserved for public use on a public matter. Secondly, it must be open to public inspection. Thirdly, the entry must be made promptly after the events which it purports to record. Fourthly, the entry must be made by a person having a duty to inquire and satisfy himself as to the truth of the recorded facts.

In the present case the first two conditions are clearly satisfied. There has been no dispute on either side as to that. As to the third, that is the matter of promptness, this court is of the view that that may affect the weight of the evidence but it does not affect its admissibility. It is as to the fourth point that the real dispute exists, namely, that the entry must be made, it is submitted, by a person having a duty to inquire and satisfy himself of the truth of the recorded facts.

[After reviewing the authorities His Lordship continued. . . .]

It seems to be inescapable from those authorities that it was a condition of admissibility that the official making the record should either have had personal knowledge of the matters which he was recording or should have inquired into the accuracy of the facts.

There is no doubt that in a case such as the present the official in the Companies Registry has no personal knowledge of the matters which he is putting on the file or recording. There is equally no doubt that it would be most convenient if the identity of directors and so on could be established simply by production of the file from the company's register containing the returns made by the company. We do not, however, feel that convenience on its own is an adequate substitute for precedent, tempting though such a solution might be. The common law, as expressed in the earlier cases which have been cited, was plainly designed to apply to an uncomplicated community when those charged with keeping registers would, more often than not, be personally acquainted with the people whose affairs they were recording and the vicar, as already indicated, would probably himself have officiated at the baptism, marriage or burial which he later recorded in the presence of the churchwardens on the register before putting it back in the coffers. But the common law should move with the times and should recognise the fact that the official charged with recording matters of public import can no longer in this highly complicated world, as like as not, have personal knowledge of their accuracy.

What has happened now is that the function originally performed by one man has had to be shared between two: the first having the knowledge and the statutory duty to record that knowledge and forward it to the Registrar of Companies, the second having the duty to preserve that document and to show it to members of the public under proper conditions as required.

Where a duty is cast upon a limited company by statute to make accurate returns of company matters to the Registrar of Companies, so that those returns can be filed and inspected by members of the public, the necessary conditions, in the judgment of this court, have been fulfilled for that document to have been admissible. All statements on the return are admissible as prima facie proof of the truth of their contents.

Appeal dismissed.

(C) The *res gestae* principle

The term '*res gestae*' has been adopted as a convenient term to cover a number of situations which form an exception to the hearsay rule. As Murphy puts it, 'It connotes simply that there are of necessity many facts and events, of which accompanying, contemporaneous statements are an integral part; so that the fact or event, if narrated without reference to the statement, would be ambiguous, meaningless or misleading'. The common thread which runs through the *res gestae* principle is contemporaneity.

(i) Statements which accompany and explain an act

A statement which is made by a person at the time of his performing an act and which explains that act is admissible as evidence of the truth of the facts contained in the statement. The reception of such evidence is said to be justified on the ground that the actor is the best person to explain his actions. The statement must be contemporaneous with the act and it must relate to the act being performed.

R v Bliss
(1837) 7 A & E 550
Court of Appeal

The issue was whether or not a certain road was public or private. The prosecution sought to adduce evidence that a person who was planting a tree was heard to say that he was doing so on the boundary of his property.

LORD DENMAN CJ: The question in this case was, whether the road obstructed was or was not a public highway. To prove that it was so, a witness was called whose statement was calculated to make a great impression on the jury. He stated that Ramplin, a former occupier of the meadow over which the road ran, had planted a willow, and, in doing so, said that he planted it to shew where the boundary of the road was when Ramplin was a boy. And it is inferred, from the circumstances, that he meant to speak of the road as having been public. I think the evidence was not admissible. It is not every declaration accompanying an act that is receivable in evidence: if it were so, persons would be enabled to dispose of the rights of others in the most unjust manner. The facts that Ramplin planted a willow on the spot, and that persons kept within the line pointed out by it, would have been evidence; but a declaration to shew that the party planted it with a particular motive is not so.

PATTESON J: . . . Then it was said that the declaration might be proved as accompanying an act; but whether it accompanied the act, as explanatory of it, is equivocal; and, at any rate, the declaration signified nothing in this case, the question being not of boundary, but as to the character of the road, whether public or private. The mere fact of the tree being placed there could not, I think, be relevant, unless as introductory to other matters.

WILLIAMS J: Declarations accompanying acts are a wide field of evidence and to be carefully watched. The declaration here had no connection with the act done; and the doing of the act cannot make such a declaration evidence.

R v McCay
[1990] 1 WLR 645
Court of Appeal

RUSSELL LJ: This appeal raises a short point concerning new procedures for the conduct of identification parades which are being adopted up and down the country.

The facts are not in dispute. On 4 April 1988 in a public house in Grove Park, south-east London, a man was attacked and a beer glass thrust in his face, causing him serious injuries. The attack was witnessed by the licensee, Mr Paul Beach. The assailant left the premises. Some 12 weeks later on 27 June 1988 Mr Beach was invited to attend an identification parade. The appellant was alleged to have been the attacker and he agreed to attend the parade, which was held at the Brixton police station. What is called the identification suite at Brixton police station consists of two parallel rooms divided by a two-way mirror. The suspect and volunteers, each numbered, are in one room, whilst the witness, a police inspector and a solicitor representing the suspect are in the other. The witness can see those on the parade, but those on the parade cannot see anyone in the viewing room. The system is also soundproofed so that those on the parade cannot hear what is said in the viewing room.

The appellant occupied position number 8. There being no physical contact between anyone on the parade and the witness, Mr Beach was invited to make his identification by indicating verbally the number of the person whom he identified. This he did by saying, 'It is number 8.' No complaint as to the conduct of the parade was made either by the appellant or by his solicitor.

The trial of the appellant, who was charged with wounding with intent to cause grievous bodily harm, took place in the Crown Court at Inner London Sessions before Judge Fabyan Evans and a jury on 12 September 1988. On the second day of the proceedings Mr Beach was called to give evidence, nearly three months after the identification parade. The witness was asked if he attended the parade and there made an identification. He answered affirmatively. When asked if he could recall the number of the person whom he had identified, he told the court that he could not remember the number. So far as we are aware, the witness was not shown his witness statement before going into the witness box. That statement is dated 27 June 1988, the same day as the identification parade, and refers in terms to the identification as being of a man bearing a number 8 at the parade. Had Mr Beach been shown that statement before he went into the witness box perhaps the problem that ensued would not have arisen.

Inspector Murfin, who had conducted the parade, was the next witness. He told the court that the appellant occupied position number 8 and was then asked what the identifying witness told him as he made his identification. Objection was taken to the question by counsel for the appellant on the ground that, if the inspector told the jury that the witness had said, 'It is number 8', such testimony would be hearsay and inadmissible. The trial judge overruled the objection and the evidence was admitted. In due course the jury convicted the appellant. There was no other evidence of identification and the sole ground of appeal is that inadmissible evidence was adduced, that amounting to a material irregularity in the trial.

We say at once that in our judgment the evidence was properly admitted. As is pointed out in *Cross on Evidence* (6th edn, 1985) p 453:

The rule against hearsay is one of the oldest, most complex and most confusing of the exclusionary rules of evidence. Lord Reid has said [in *Myers* v *DPP* [1964] 2 All ER 881 at 884, [1965] AC 1001 at 1019] that 'it is difficult to make any general statement about the law of hearsay which is entirely accurate.' One of the reasons is that its definition, and the ambit of exceptions to it are both unclear.

We are satisfied, however, that the admissibility of the words 'It is number 8' can be fully justified, albeit spoken by the witness in the absence of the appellant, because the contemporary statement accompanied a relevant act and was necessary to explain that relevant act. The statement was not relevant as to the identity of the assailant, but it was relevant as to the identification of the suspect by the witness. Whether that identification assisted the jury was a matter for them. In asserting that the man whom the witness thought was the assailant was numbered 8 on the parade, Mr Beach was doing no more and no less than explaining his physical and intellectual activity in making the identification at the material time.

Counsel for the appellant was constrained to acknowledge that if the words 'It is number 8' had been accompanied by some physical touching of the appellant by Mr Beach (the normal procedure adopted in the old style identification parades) he could not have objected to Insp Murfin giving evidence of what he heard from the witness. The reason for this concession was that the words would then accompany a physical act, whereas no such physical act was part of the identification process employed in the instant case. We consider this to be a distinction without a difference. In our judgment the procedure of looking at the suspect through the mirror, employing the physical activity of seeing coupled with the intellectual activity of recognising are together sufficient to amount to a relevant act in respect of which accompanying words are admissible. As Grove J said long ago in *Howe* v *Malkin* (1878) 40 LT 196:

> . . . though you cannot give in evidence a declaration *per se*, yet when there is an act accompanied by a statement which is so mixed up with it as to become part of the *res gestae*, evidence of such statement may be given [in evidence].

In our view, whether the true analysis of the statement is that it was original evidence or whether it was admissible as an exception to the hearsay rule, the judge came to a proper decision.

. . .

Whilst in future it may be desirable for witnesses attending identification parades to be invited to make a contemporaneous note of their identification which may be used at a later stage to refresh memory, we are satisfied that the absence of any such aide-mémoire is not fatal. For all these reasons we take the view that this appeal must be dismissed.

Questions

1. In *R* v *McCay*, Russell LJ states, 'whether the true analysis of the statement is that it was original evidence or . . . admissible as an exception to the hearsay rule, the judge came to a proper decision'. Is there any question of the relevant evidence in this case being anything other than hearsay?
2. Do you agree that words which accompany an intellectual process (such as identification) where there is no physical act should be admitted as an exception to the hearsay rule?
3. Is there any distinction between *R* v *McCay* and *R* v *Osbourne* (see Chapter 7(A))?

(ii)   Spontaneous statements relating to events in issue

A spontaneous statement made by a participant in an event in issue, be that person a victim, an observer or the defendant, may be admitted as evidence of the facts contained therein. The rationale behind this particular exception is that because the mind of the person is so wrapped up in the event that is happening, there is no opportunity for any reflection on the event before the statement is made, thus the chance of fabrication is minimal. In deciding whether or not to admit the statement into evidence for the jury's consideration, the judge will ask himself, *inter alia*, whether or not the possibility of concoction can be disregarded. The answer will depend on all the surrounding circumstances which were present at the time the statement was made.

R v *Andrews*
[1987] AC 281
House of Lords

Two men entered M's flat and attacked him with knives; property was stolen. Shortly afterwards M, grievously wounded, made his way to the flat below his own to obtain assistance. Two police officers arrived within minutes and M informed them that O and the defendant had been the assailants. Two months later M died as a result of his injuries. The defendant was jointly charged with O with aggravated burglary and the murder of M. At the trial the Crown sought to have the deceased's statement admitted, not as a dying declaration, but as evidence of the truth of the facts that he had asserted, namely, that he had been attacked by O and the defendant, and therefore it was admissible in the circumstances as evidence coming within the *res gestae* exception to the hearsay rule. The judge ruled in favour of its admissibility. The defendant was convicted of aggravated burglary and manslaughter. On appeal by the defendant, the Court of Appeal dismissed the appeal. The defendant further appealed.

LORD ACKNER: Mr Worsley sought to have the statement of the deceased admitted as evidence of the truth of the facts that he had asserted, namely that he had been attacked by both O'Neill and the appellant. Since evidence of this statement could only be given by a witness who had merely heard it, such evidence was clearly hearsay evidence. It was not being tendered as evidence limited to the fact that an assertion had been made, without reference to the truth of anything alleged in the assertion. The evidence merely of the fact that such an assertion was made would not have related to any issue in the trial and therefore would not have been admissible. Had, for example, the deceased's state of mind been in issue and had his exclamation been relevant to his state of mind, then evidence of *the fact* that such an assertion was made, would not have been hearsay evidence since it would have been tendered without reference to the truth of anything alleged in the assertion. Such evidence is often classified as 'original' evidence.

Mr Worsley based his submission that this hearsay evidence was admissible upon the so-called doctrine of *res gestae*. He could not submit that the statement was a 'dying declaration' since there was no evidence to suggest that at the time when the deceased made the statement (two months before his ultimate death), he was aware that he had been mortally injured. Mr Worsley in support of his submission, both before the Common Serjeant, the Court of Appeal and in your Lordships' House relied essentially on a decision of the Privy Council, *Ratten v The Queen* [1972] AC 378, an appeal from a conviction for murder by the Supreme Court of the State of Victoria in which the opinion of the Board was given by Lord Wilberforce. Mr Worsley, for whose researches into this field of law I readily express my gratitude, invited your Lordships' attention to American, Canadian and Australian authorities in order to demonstrate their consistency with that decision and to support his contention, which is the real issue in this appeal *viz.* that your Lordships should accept the analysis, reasoning and advice tended by the Privy Council as being good English law.

I do not think it is necessary to burden this speech by travelling again over all the ground, which, if I may say so respectfully, was so admirably covered by Lord Wilberforce in his judgment. Before turning to the decision in *Ratten's* case, it is convenient at this stage to quote from *Cross on Evidence*, 6th ed (1985), p. 585:

Before Lord Wilberforce's important review of the authorities in *Ratten v The Queen*, the law concerning the admissibility of statements under this exception to the hearsay rule [the *res gestae* doctrine] was in danger of becoming enmeshed in conceptualism of the worst type. Great stress was placed on the need for contemporaneity of the statement with the event, but, what was far more serious, much attention was devoted to the question whether the words could be said to form part of the transaction or event with all the attendant insoluble problems of when the transaction or event began and ended.

The appellant was charged with the murder of his wife by shooting her with a shotgun. He accepted that he had shot her, but his defence was that the gun had gone off accidentally, whilst he was cleaning it. There was evidence that the deceased was alive and behaving normally at 1.12 pm and less than 10 minutes later she had been shot. To rebut that defence, the prosecution called evidence from a telephone operator as to a telephone call which she had received at 1.15 pm from the deceased's home. She said the call came from a female who sounded hysterical and who said 'get me the police, please —,' gave her address, but before a connection could be made to the police station, the caller hung up. The appellant objected to that evidence on the ground that it was hearsay and did not come within any of the recognised exceptions to the rule against the admission of such evidence. The Judicial Committee held that the telephone operator's evidence had been rightly received. They concluded that the evidence was not hearsay, but was admissible as evidence of facts relevant to the following issues. First, as rebutting the defendant's statement that his call for the ambulance after he had shot his wife was the only call that went out of the house between 1.12 and 1.20, by which time his wife was dead. Secondly, that the telephonist's evidence that the caller was a woman speaking in a hysterical voice was capable of relating to the state of mind of the deceased and was material from which the jury were entitled to infer that Mrs Ratten was suffering from anxiety or fear of an existing or impending emergency. Lord Wilberforce said, at p. 387:

> The mere fact that evidence of a witness includes evidence as to words spoken by another person who is not called, is no objection to its admissibility. Words spoken are facts just as much as any other action by a human being. If the speaking of the words is a relevant fact, a witness may give evidence that they were spoken. A question of hearsay only arises when the words spoken are relied on 'testimonially', i.e., as establishing some fact narrated by the words. Authority is hardly needed for this proposition, but their Lordships will restate what was said in the judgment of the Board in *Subramaniam v Public Prosecutor* [1956] 1 WLR 965, 970: 'Evidence of a statement made to a witness by a person who is not himself called as a witness may or may not be hearsay. It is hearsay and inadmissible when the object of the evidence is to establish the truth of what is contained in the statement. It is not hearsay and is admissible when it is proposed to establish by the evidence, not the truth of the statement, but the fact that it was made.

Lord Wilberforce then proceeded to deal with the appellant's submission, on the assumption that the words were hearsay in that they involved an assertion of the truth of some facts stated in them and that they may have been so understood by the jury. He said, at pp. 388-390:

> The expression *res gestae*, like many Latin phrases, is often used to cover situations insufficiently analysed in clear English terms. In the context of the law of evidence it may be used in at least three different ways:
>
> (1) When a situation of fact (e.g., a killing) is being considered, the question may arise when does the situation begin and when does it end. It may be arbitrary and artificial to confine the evidence to the firing of the gun or the insertion of the knife, without knowing in a broader sense what was happening. Thus in *O'Leary v*

The King (1946) 73 CLR 566 evidence was admitted of assaults, prior to a killing, committed by the accused during what was said to be a continuous orgy. As Dixon J said at p. 577: 'Without evidence of what, during that time, was done by those men who took any significant part in the matter and especially evidence of the behaviour of the prisoner, the transaction of which the alleged murder formed an integral part could not be truly understood and, isolated from it, could only be presented as an unreal and not very intelligible event.'

(2)   The evidence may be concerned with spoken words as such (apart from the truth of what they convey). The words are then themselves the *res gestae* or part of the *res gestae*, i.e., are the relevant facts or part of them.

(3)   A hearsay statement is made either by the victim of an attack or by a bystander — indicating directly or indirectly the identity of the attacker. The admissibility of the statement is then said to depend on whether it was made as part of the *res gestae*. A classical instance of this is the much debated case of *R v Bedingfield* (1879) 14 Cox CC 341, and there are other instances of its application in reported cases. These tend to apply different standards, and some of them carry less than conviction. The reason, why this is so, is that concentration tends to be focused upon the opaque or at least imprecise Latin phrase rather than upon the basic reason for excluding the type of evidence which this group of cases is concerned with. There is no doubt what this reason is: it is twofold. The first is that there may be uncertainty as to the exact words used and because of their transmission through the evidence of another person than the speaker. The second is because of the risk of concoction of false evidence by persons who have been victims of assault or accident. The first matter goes to weight. The person testifying to the words used is liable to cross-examination: the accused person (as he could not at the time when earlier reported cases were decided) can give his own account if different. There is no such difference in kind or substance between evidence of what was said and evidence of what was done (for example between evidence of what the victim said as to an attack and evidence that he (or she) was seen in a terrified state or was heard to shriek) as to require a total rejection of one and admission of the other.

The possibility of concoction, or fabrication, where it exists, is on the other hand an entirely valid reason for exclusion, and is probably the real test which judges in fact apply. In their Lordships' opinion this should be recognised and applied directly as the relevant test: the test should be not the uncertain one whether the making of the statement was in some sense part of the event or transaction. This may often be difficult to establish: such external matters as the time which elapses between the events and the speaking of the words (or *vice versa),* and the differences in location being relevant factors but not, taken by themselves, decisive criteria. As regards statements made after the event it must be for the judge, by preliminary ruling, to satisfy himself that the statement was so clearly made in circumstances of spontaneity or involvement in the event that the possibility of concoction can be disregarded. Conversely, if he considers that the statement was made by way of narrative of a detached prior event so that the speaker was so disengaged from it as to be able to construct or adapt his account, he should exclude it. And the same must in principle be true of statements made before the event. The test should be not the uncertain one, whether the making of the statement should be regarded as part of the event or transaction. This may often be difficult to show. But if the drama, leading up to the climax, has commenced and assumed such intensity and pressure that the utterance can safely be regarded as a true reflection of what was unrolling or actually happening, it ought to be received. The expression *res gestae* may conveniently sum up these criteria, but the reality of them must always be kept in mind: it is this that lies behind the best reasoned of the judges' rulings.

Lord Wilberforce then reviewed a number of cases, in England, in Scotland, in Australia and America and concluded, at p. 391, that those authorities: 'show that there is ample support for the principle that hearsay evidence may be admitted if the statement providing it is made in such conditions (always being those of approximate but not exact contemporaneity) of involvement or pressure as to exclude the possibility of concoction or distortion to the advantage of the maker or the disadvantage of the accused.' Applying that principle to the facts of the *Ratten* appeal [1972] AC 378, there was in their Lordships' judgment ample evidence of the close and intimate connection between the statement ascribed to the deceased and the shooting which occurred very shortly afterwards. Lord Wilberforce commented, at p. 391: 'The way in which the statement came to be made (in a call for the police) and the tone of voice used, showed intrinsically that the statement was being forced from the deceased by an overwhelming pressure of contemporary event. It carried its own stamp of spontaneity and this was endorsed by the proved time sequence and the proved proximity of the deceased to the accused with his gun.' Thus, on the assumption that there was an element of hearsay in the words used, the Privy Council concluded that they had been properly admitted.

In *R v Blastland* [1986] AC 41, 58, my noble and learned friend Lord Bridge of Harwich, regarded the authority of the *Ratten* case [1972] AC 378 as being of the highest persuasive authority. It was followed and applied in the instant case by the Common Serjeant and by the Court of Appeal (Criminal Division) and accordingly the appellant's appeal against his conviction for manslaughter was dismissed. It had previously been applied in *R v Nye* (1978) 66 Cr App R 252, by the Court of Appeal where a victim of a criminal assault, which had occurred within a few yards of a police station, in a statement to police officers made within minutes of the assault, identified the defendant as the man who had hit him in the face. Lawton LJ in giving the judgment of the court put, as he described it, a gloss upon Lord Wilberforce's test by adding as an additional factor to be taken into consideration 'was there any real possibility of error?' I will return to this particular point later. In *R v Turnbull* (1985) 80 Cr App R 104 the Court of Appeal again applied the *Ratten* approach, where a man who had been mortally wounded staggered into the bar of a public house and in answer to questions put to him in the bar and in the ambulance on the way to hospital he was understood to say that 'Ronnie Tommo' had done it. He died half-an-hour later in hospital. The victim had a Scottish accent and had consumed a great quantity of alcohol and the name 'Ronnie Tommo' was said to constitute his attempt to name the appellant. There have been two further decisions of the Court of Appeal this year which have followed *Ratten's* case. *R v Boyle* (unreported) decided on 6 March 1986, involved the theft of a grandfather clock from an old lady to whose home the appellant had obtained access by a false representation. When he took away the clock she came out of the house with a piece of paper in her hand and when asked by a neighbour, 'what is happening?' she said 'I am coming for his address.' This statement was admitted to support the victim's account that the removal of the clock was against her will and to negative the defence that it was being taken away by the defendant with her consent, to have it repaired. I, for myself, would doubt whether this evidence was hearsay evidence. A clear issue in the case was the state of mind of the victim in relation to the removal of her clock. Her statement in the circumstances, as the car drove off, was evidence from which the jury could infer that she was not consenting to the clock being taken away. *R v O'Shea* (unreported) decided on 24 July 1986, is a clearer case. The appellant was charged with burglary and manslaughter. The prosecution case against the appellant was that he went to a second floor flat and while he was battering down the door, the occupier of the flat who was 79 years of age, attempted to escape through the window, slipped and fell some 20 feet and sustained bruising to his heart, which resulted in his death a week later. The statement made by the deceased to two passers-by an hour or so later, when they found him lying where he had fallen, that he had tried to get out of his flat because he was frightened that two robbers who were trying to break down his door would kill him and that he had therefore jumped from the window to escape, was admitted, as was a similar statement which he made to two police officers less than 20 minutes later.

Mr Sedley for the appellant submitted, first that there is no such exception to the rule against the admission of hearsay evidence as that said to be covered by the *res gestae* doctrine. Having regard to the authorities there is no substance in this proposition. Secondly, he submitted that a hearsay statement cannot be admitted under the doctrine if made after the criminal act or acts charged have ceased. He contended that the hearsay statement must form part of the criminal act for which the accused is being tried. He relied strongly upon *R* v *Bedingfield*, 14 Cox CC 341. In that case the accused was charged with murder. The defence was suicide. The accused was seen to enter a house and a minute or two later the victim rushed out of the house with her throat cut and said to her aunt 'See what Harry has done.' This exclamation was not admitted by Cockburn CJ at pp. 342-343 because 'it was something stated by her after it was all over, whatever it was, and after the act was completed.' Mr Sedley submits that the decision in *Ratten's* case involved an extension of the existing hearsay rule and so was in conflict with the ruling of the majority in your Lordships' House in *Myers* v *Director of Public Prosecutions* [1965] AC 1001 that it is now too late to add a further exception to the rule against hearsay otherwise than by legislation. This submission is not assisted by the fact that both Lord Reid and Lord Hodson, who were party to the majority decision in the *Myers* case, were also members of the Board in the *Ratten* case [1972] AC 378.

I do not accept that the principles identified by Lord Wilberforce involved any extension to the exception to the hearsay rule. Lord Wilberforce clarified the basis of the *res gestae* exception and isolated the matters of which the trial judge, by preliminary ruling, must satisfy himself before admitting the statement. I respectfully accept the accuracy and the value of this clarification. Thus it must, of course, follow that *R* v *Bedingfield*, 14 Cox CC 341 would not be so decided today. Indeed, there could, as Lord Wilberforce observed, hardly be a case where the words uttered carried more clearly the mark of spontaneity and intense involvement.

My Lords, may I therefore summarise the position which confronts the trial judge when faced in a criminal case with an application under the *res gestae* doctrine to admit evidence of statements, with a view to establishing the truth of some fact thus narrated, such evidence being truly categorised as 'hearsay evidence?'

(1) The primary question which the judge must ask himself is — can the possibility of concoction or distortion be disregarded?

(2) To answer that question the judge must first consider the circumstances in which the particular statement was made, in order to satisfy himself that the event was so unusual or startling or dramatic as to dominate the thoughts of the victim, so that his utterance was an instinctive reaction to that event, thus giving no real opportunity for reasoned reflection. In such a situation the judge would be entitled to conclude that the involvement or the pressure of the event would exclude the possibility of concoction or distortion, providing that the statement was made in conditions of approximate but not exact contemporaneity.

(3)   In order for the statement to be sufficiently 'spontaneous' it must be so closely associated with the event which has excited the statement, that it can be fairly stated that the mind of the declarant was still dominated by the event. Thus the judge must be satisfied that the event, which provided the trigger mechanism for the statement, was still operative. The fact that the statement was made in answer to a question is but one factor to consider under this heading.

(4)   Quite apart from the time factor, there may be special features in the case, which relate to the possibility of concoction or distortion. In the instant appeal the defence relied upon evidence to support the contention that the deceased had a motive of his own to fabricate or concoct, namely, a malice which resided in him against O'Neill and the appellant because, so he believed, O'Neill had attacked and damaged his house and was accompanied by the appellant, who ran away on a previous occasion. The judge must be satisfied that the circumstances were such that having regard to the special feature of malice, there was no possibility of any concoction or distortion to the advantage of the maker or the disadvantage of the accused.

(5)   As to the possibility of error in the facts narrated in the statement, if only the ordinary fallibility of human recollection is relied upon, this goes to the weight to be attached to and not to the admissibility of the statement and is therefore a matter for the jury. However, here again there may be special features that may give rise to the possibility of error. In the instant case there was evidence that the deceased had drunk to excess, well over double the permitted limit for driving a motor car. Another example would be where the identification was made in circumstances of particular difficulty or where the declarant suffered from defective eyesight. In such circumstances the trial judge must consider whether he can exclude the possibility of error.

My Lords, the doctrine of *res gestae* applies to civil as well as criminal proceedings. There is, however, special legislation as to the admissibility of hearsay evidence in civil proceedings. I wholly accept that the doctrine admits the hearsay statements, not only where the declarant is dead or otherwise not available but when he is called as a witness. Whatever may be the position in civil proceedings, I would, however, strongly deprecate any attempt in criminal prosecutions to use the doctrine as a device to avoid calling, when he is available, the maker of the statement. Thus to deprive the defence of the opportunity to cross-examine him, would not be consistent with the fundamental duty of the prosecution to place all the relevant material facts before the court, so as to ensure that justice is done.

Appeal dismissed.

Questions
1.   Is the test approved in R v *Andrews* preferable to the previous approach?
2.   Would R v *Bedingfield* be decided in the same way today?
3.   Does the decision in R v *Andrews* support or cast doubt upon the correctness of the Court of Appeal's decision in R v *Nye*?

(iii)   Contemporaneous declarations concerning the physical or mental state of the speaker

Such statements may be admitted for the purpose of demonstrating the maker's state of mind and/or physical sensations at the time they were made. The rationale for admitting such statements is simply that the person best able to state what he or she is feeling is the person who actually feels it. If X feels pain in his stomach then X is the person best able to say so. Indeed, X may be the only person capable of saying so. Where the statement concerns the maker's state of mind, then that state of mind must be a relevant issue at the trial otherwise it will be inadmissible as irrelevant (see *R v Blastland*, Chapter 7). Note that while the statement may be admitted for the purpose of demonstrating the maker's feelings, nothing which indicates the cause of those feelings is admissible under this exception.

R v Nicholas
(1846) 2 Car & K 246
Court of Appeal

POLLOCK CB: If a man says to his surgeon, 'I have a pain in the head,' or a pain in such a part of the body, that is evidence; but, if he says to his surgeon, 'I have a wound'; and was to add, 'I met John Thomas, who had a sword, and ran me through the body with it,' that would be no evidence against John Thomas . . .

Note
Although this category of *res gestae* is well established, the authorities are old and often vague. Examples of cases include *R v Conde* (1868) 10 Cox CC 547, where evidence of a child's complaint of feeling hungry was held to be admissible in support of a charge of neglect, and *R v Black* (1922) 16 Cr App R 118, where witnesses were allowed to testify that the defendant's wife had complained to them of vomiting and pain after taking medicine.

Questions
1.   Sandra is charged with the murder of Thomas. Victor is prepared to testify that Thomas telephoned him and said, 'Please come quickly; Sandra is threatening to stab me . . .', the phone then going dead. Victor rushed to Thomas's house and found him lying in a pool of blood. Thomas said, 'You're too late Victor. She's done me in. I have great pain in the stomach where she stabbed me'.
    Discuss the proposed testimony of Victor.
2.   Hector is charged with the murder of Ian by strangling him with a rope. Is evidence admissible:

    (a)   that Rupert, who was walking past Ian's business premises at about the relevant time, heard a voice shouting, 'What are you doing with that rope Hector'?
    (b)   that Steven, when dying of leukemia two months after the killing, confessed that he was the person who killed Ian?
    (c)   that Trevor, a stocktaker, made a written report of the contents of Ian's premises, the report showing that six yards of rope was in stock? (Trevor has since died.)
    (d)   that Viv told her friend William that a man had been strangled before the police had discovered Ian's body and his death had become generally known?

Further Reading
D. Birch, 'Hearsay logic and hearsay-fiddles: *Blastland* revisited', in *Criminal Law: Essays in Honour of JC Smith* (ed. P Smith) (1987)

9 THE RULE AGAINST HEARSAY — III STATUTORY EXCEPTIONS

This chapter is concerned with statutory exceptions to the rule against hearsay. All the major statutory exceptions are dealt with but it would not be possible, or practicable, to mention every statute which might contain a section which deals with hearsay evidence. Instead, this chapter focuses on those statutes which contain provisions which have a major impact on the application of the hearsay rule. As far as civil cases are concerned, the principal statute is the Civil Evidence Act 1968 which governs the admissibility of hearsay evidence in almost all forms of civil litigation. In criminal cases, the single most important statute is the Criminal Justice Act 1988.

(A) Civil cases

As mentioned above, the principal statute as far as civil cases are concerned is the Civil Evidence Act 1968. The Act provides an almost global framework for the admissibility of hearsay evidence in civil cases. Unusually, the Act provides for hearsay statements to be admitted even where the maker of the statement is available to give oral testimony. One point of particular importance is that the Act cures only the defect of hearsay. If the evidence is defective for some other reason, it remains inadmissible notwithstanding the provisions of the Act. For this reason the Civil Evidence Act 1972, provides that hearsay statements which contain matters of opinion will, subject to certain conditions, be admissible in civil cases. The 1972 Act is also dealt with in this section (see (A) (*ii*) below). As yet these statutory provisions apply only to civil proceedings in the County Court and High Court. They have not been extended to cover civil proceedings in the magistrates' courts.

Civil proceedings in magistrates' courts continue to attract the common law rules and the provisions of the Evidence Act 1938. This section also deals with a particular statutory provision contained in the Children Act 1989.

(i) Civil Evidence Act 1968

Civil Evidence Act 1968

1. Hearsay evidence to be admissible only by virtue of this Act and other statutory provisions, or by agreement

(1) In any civil proceedings a statement other than one made by a person while giving oral evidence in those proceedings shall be admissible as evidence of any fact stated therein to the extent that it is so admissible by virtue of any provision of this Part of this Act or by virtue of any other statutory provision or by agreement of the parties, but not otherwise.

(2) In this section 'statutory provision' means any provision contained in, or in an instrument made under, this or any other Act, including any Act passed after this Act.

2. Admissibility of out-of-court statements as evidence of facts stated

(1) In any civil proceedings a statement made, whether orally or in a document or otherwise, by any person, whether called as a witness in those proceedings or not, shall, subject to this section and to rules of court, be admissible as evidence of any fact stated therein of which direct oral evidence by him would be admissible.

(2) Where in any civil proceedings a party desiring to give a statement in evidence by virtue of this section has called or intends to call as a witness in the proceedings the person by whom the statement was made, the statement —

(a) shall not be given in evidence by virtue of this section on behalf of the party without the leave of the court; and

(b) without prejudice to paragraph (a) above, shall not be given in evidence by virtue of this section on behalf of that party before the conclusion of the examination-in-chief of the person by whom it was made, except —

(i) where before that person is called the court allows evidence of the making of the statement to be given on behalf of that party by some other person; or

(ii) in so far as the court allows the person by whom the statement was made to narrate it in the course of his examination-in-chief on the ground that to prevent him from doing so would adversely affect the intelligibility of his evidence.

(3) Where in any civil proceedings a statement which was made otherwise than in a document is admissible by virtue of this section, no evidence other than direct oral evidence by the person who made the statement or any person who heard or otherwise perceived it being made shall be admissible for the purpose of proving it:

Provided that if the statement in question was made by a person while giving oral evidence in some other legal proceedings (whether civil or criminal), it may be proved in any manner authorized by the court.

3. Witness's previous statement, if proved, to be evidence of facts stated

(1) Where in any civil proceedings —

(a) a previous inconsistent or contradictory statement made by a person called as a witness in those proceedings is proved by virtue of section 3, 4 or 5 of the Criminal Procedure Act, 1865; or

(b) a previous statement made by a person called as aforesaid is proved for the purpose of rebutting a suggestion that his evidence has been fabricated, that statement shall by virtue of this subsection be admissible as evidence of any fact stated therein of which direct oral evidence by him would be admissible.

(2)　Nothing in this Act shall affect any of the rules of law relating to the circumstances in which, where a person called as a witness in any civil proceedings is cross-examined on a document used by him to refresh his memory, that document may be made evidence in those proceedings: and where a document or any part of a document is received in evidence in any such proceedings by virtue of any such rule of law, any statement made in that document or part by the person using the document to refresh his memory shall by virtue of this subsection be admissible as evidence of any fact stated therein of which direct oral evidence by him would be admissible.

4.　Admissibility of certain records as evidence of facts stated

(1)　Without prejudice to section 5 of this Act, in any civil proceedings a statement contained in a document shall, subject to this section and to rules of court, be admissible as evidence of any fact stated therein of which direct oral evidence would be admissible, if the document is, or forms part of, a record compiled by a person acting under a duty from information which was supplied by a person (whether acting under a duty or not) who had, or may reasonably be supposed to have had, personal knowledge of the matters dealt with in that information and which, if not supplied by that person to the compiler of the record directly, was supplied by him to the compiler of the record indirectly through one or more intermediaries each acting under a duty.

(2)　Where in any civil proceedings a party desiring to give a statement in evidence by virtue of this section has called or intends to call as a witness in the proceedings the person who originally supplied the information from which the record containing the statement was compiled, the statement —

(a)　shall not be given in evidence by virtue of this section on behalf of that party without the leave of the court; and

(b)　without prejudice to paragraph (a) above, shall not without the leave of the court be given in evidence by virtue of this section on behalf of that party before the conclusion of the examination in chief of the person who originally supplied the said information.

(3)　Any reference in this section to a person acting under a duty includes a reference to a person acting in the course of any trade, business, profession or other occupation in which he is engaged or employed or for the purposes of any paid or unpaid office held by him.

5.　Admissibility of statements produced by computers

(1)　In any civil proceedings a statement contained in a document produced by a computer shall, subject to rules of court, be admissible as evidence of any fact stated therein of which direct oral evidence would be admissible, if it is shown that the conditions mentioned in subsection (2) below are satisfied in relation to the statement and computer in question.

(2)　The said conditions are —

(a)　that the document containing the statement was produced by the computer during a period over which the computer was used regularly to store or process information for the purposes of any activities regularly carried on over that period, whether for profit or not, by any body, whether corporate or not, or by any individual;

(b)　that over that period there was regularly supplied to the computer in the ordinary course of those activities information of the kind contained in the statement or of the kind from which the information so contained is derived;

(c)   that throughout the material part of that period the computer was operating properly or, if not, that any respect in which it was not operating properly or was out of operation during that part of that period was not such as to affect the production of the document or the accuracy of its contents; and

(d)   that the information contained in the statement reproduces or is derived from information supplied to the computer in the ordinary course of those activities.

(3)   Where over a period the function of storing or processing information for the purposes of any activities regularly carried on over that period as mentioned in subsection (2)(a) above was regularly performed by computers, whether —

(a)   by a combination of computers operating over that period; or

(b)   by different computers operating in succession over that period; or

(c)   by different combinations of computers operating in succession over that period; or

(d)   in any other manner involving the successive operation over that period, in whatever order, of one or more computers and one or more combinations of computers, all the computers used for that purpose during that period shall be treated for the purposes of this Part of this Act as constituting a single computer; and references in this Part of this Act to a computer shall be construed accordingly.

(4)   In any civil proceedings where it is desired to give a statement in evidence by virtue of this section, a certificate doing any of the following things, that is to say —

(a)   identifying the document containing the statement and describing the manner in which it was produced;

(b)   giving such particulars of any device involved in the production of that document as may be appropriate for the purpose of showing that the document was produced by a computer;

(c)   dealing with any of the matters to which the conditions mentioned in subsection (2) above relate,
and purporting to be signed by a person occupying a responsible position in relation to the operation of the relevant device or the management of the relevant activities (whichever is appropriate) shall be evidence of any matter stated in the certificate; and for the purposes of this subsection it shall be sufficient for a matter to be stated to the best of the knowledge and belief of the person stating it.

(5)   For the purposes of this Part of this Act —

(a)   information shall be taken to be supplied to a computer if it is supplied thereto in any appropriate form and whether it is so supplied directly or (with or without human intervention) by means of any appropriate equipment;

(b)   where, in the course of activities carried on by any individual or body, information is supplied with a view to its being stored or processed for the purposes of those activities by a computer operated otherwise than in the course of those activities, that information, if duly supplied to that computer, shall be taken to be supplied to it in the course of those activities;

(c)   a document shall be taken to have been produced by a computer whether it was produced by it directly or (with or without human intervention) by means of any appropriate equipment.

(6)   Subject to subsection (3) above, in this Part of this Act 'computer' means any device for storing and processing information, and any reference to information being derived from other information is a reference to its being derived therefrom by calculation, comparison or any other process.

6.   Provisions supplementary to ss. 2 to 5

(1)   Where in any civil proceedings a statement contained in a document is proposed to be given in evidence by virtue of section 2, 4 or 5 of this Act it may,

subject to any rules of court, be proved by the production of that document or (whether or not that document is still in existence) by the production of a copy of that document, or of the material part thereof, authenticated in such manner as the court may approve.

(2) For the purpose of deciding whether or not a statement is admissible in evidence by virtue of section 2, 4 or 5 of this Act, the court may draw any reasonable inference from the circumstances in which the statement was made or otherwise came into being or from any other circumstances, including, in the case of a statement contained in a document, the form and contents of that document.

(3) In estimating the weight, if any, to be attached to a statement admissible in evidence by virtue of section 2, 3, 4 or 5 of this Act regard shall be had to all the circumstances from which any inference can reasonably be drawn as to the accuracy or otherwise of the statement and, in particular —

(a) in the case of a statement falling within section 2(1) or 3(1) or (2) of this Act, to the question whether or not the statement was made contemporaneously with the occurrence or existence of the facts stated, and to the question whether or not the maker of the statement had any incentive to conceal or misrepresent the facts;

(b) in the case of a statement falling within section 4(1) of this Act, to the question whether or not the person who originally supplied the information from which the record containing the statement was compiled did so contemporaneously with the occurrence or existence of the facts dealt with in that information, and to the question whether or not that person, or any person concerned with compiling or keeping the record containing the statement, had any incentive to conceal or misrepresent the facts; and

(c) in the case of a statement falling within section 5(1) of this Act, to the question whether or not the information which the information contained in the statement reproduces or is derived from was supplied to the relevant computer, or recorded for the purpose of being supplied thereto, contemporaneously with the occurrence or existence of the facts dealt with in that information, and to the question whether or not any person concerned with the supply of information to that computer or with the operation of that computer or any equipment by means of which the document containing the statement was produced by it, had any incentive to conceal or misrepresent the facts.

(4) For the purpose of any enactment or rule of law or practice requiring evidence to be corroborated or regulating the manner in which uncorroborated evidence is to be treated —

(a) a statement which is admissible in evidence by virtue of section 2 or 3 of this Act shall not be capable of corroborating evidence given by the maker of the statement; and

(b) a statement which is admissible in evidence by virtue of section 4 of this Act shall not be capable of corroborating evidence given by the person who originally supplied the information from which the record containing the statement was compiled.

(5) If any person in a certificate tendered in evidence in civil proceedings by virtue of section 5(4) of this Act wilfully makes a statement material in those proceedings which he knows to be false or does not believe to be true, he shall be liable on conviction on indictment to imprisonment for a term not exceeding two years or a fine or both.

7. Admissibility of evidence as to credibility of maker etc. of statement admitted under s. 2 or 4

(1) Subject to rules of court, where in any civil proceedings a statement made by a person who is not called as a witness in those proceedings is given in evidence by virtue of section 2 of this Act —

(a)   any evidence which, if that person had been so called would be admissible for the purpose of destroying or supporting his credibility as a witness shall be admissible for that purpose in those proceedings; and

(b)   evidence tending to prove that, whether before or after he made that statement, that person made (whether orally or in a document or otherwise) another statement inconsistent therewith shall be admissible for the purpose of showing that that person has contradicted himself.

Provided that nothing in this subsection shall enable evidence to be given of any matter of which, if the person in question had been called as a witness and had denied that matter in cross-examination, evidence could not have been adduced by the cross-examining party.

(2)   Subsection (1) above shall apply in relation to a statement given in evidence by virtue of section 4 of this Act as it applies in relation to a statement given in evidence by virtue of section 2 of this Act, except that references to the person who made the statement and to his making the statement shall be construed respectively as references to the person who originally supplied the information from which the record containing the statement was compiled and to his supplying that information.

(3)   Section 3(1) of this Act shall apply to any statement proved by virtue of subsection (1)(b) above as it applies to a previous inconsistent or contradictory statement made by a person called as a witness which is proved as mentioned in paragraph (a) of the said section 3(1).

8.   Rules of court

(1)   Provision shall be made by rules of court as to the procedure which, subject to any exceptions provided for in the rules, must be followed and the other conditions which, subject as aforesaid, must be fulfilled before a statement can be given in evidence in civil proceedings by virtue of section 2, 4 or 5 of this Act.

(2)   Rules of court made in pursuance of subsection (1) above shall in particular, subject to such exceptions (if any) as may be provided for in the rules —

(a)   require a party to any civil proceedings who desires to give in evidence any such statement as is mentioned in that subsection to give to every other party to the proceeding such notice of his desire to do so and such particulars of or relating to the statement as may be specified in the rules, including particulars of such one or more of the persons connected with the making or recording of the statement or, in the case of a statement falling within section 5(1) of this Act, such one or more of the persons concerned as mentioned in section 6(3)(c) of this Act as the rules may in any case require; and

(b)   enable any party who receives such notice as aforesaid by counter-notice to require any person of whom particulars were given with the notice to be called as a witness in the proceedings unless that person is dead, or beyond the seas, or unfit by reason of his bodily or mental condition to attend as a witness, or cannot with reasonable diligence be identified or found, or cannot reasonably be expected (having regard to the time which has elapsed since he was connected or concerned as aforesaid and to all the circumstances) to have any recollection of matters relevant to the accuracy or otherwise of the statement.

(3)   Rules of court made in pursuance of subsection (1) above-

(a)   may confer on the court in any civil proceedings a discretion to allow a statement falling within section 2(1), 4(1) or 5(1) of this Act to be given in evidence notwithstanding that any requirement of the rules affecting the admissibility of that statement has not been complied with, but except in pursuance of paragraph (b) below shall not confer on the court a discretion to exclude such a statement where the requirements of the rules affecting its admissibility have been complied with;

(b)   may confer on the court power, where a party to any civil proceedings has given notice that he desires to give in evidence —

(i)   a statement falling within section 2(1) of this Act which was made by a person, whether orally or in a document, in the course of giving evidence in some other legal proceedings (whether civil or criminal); or

(ii)   a statement falling within section 4(1) of this Act which is contained in a record of any direct oral evidence given in some other legal proceedings (whether civil or criminal),

to give directions on the application of any party to the proceedings as to whether, and if so on what conditions, the party desiring to give the statement in evidence will be permitted to do so and (where applicable) as to the manner in which that statement and any other evidence given in those other proceedings is to be proved; and

(c)   may make different provision for different circumstances, and in particular may make different provision with respect to statements falling within section 2(1), 4(1) and 5(1) of this Act respectively;

and any discretion conferred on the court by rules of court made as aforesaid may be either a general discretion or a discretion exercisable only in such circumstances as may be specified in the rules.

(4)   Rules of court may make provision for preventing a party to any civil proceedings (subject to any exceptions provided for in the rules) from adducing in relation to a person who is not called as a witness in those proceedings any evidence which could otherwise be adduced by him by virtue of section 7 of this Act unless that party has in pursuance of the rules given in respect of that person such a counter-notice as is mentioned in subsection (2)(b) above.

(5)   In deciding for the purpose of any rules of court made in pursuance of this section whether or not a person is fit to attend as a witness, a court may act on a certificate purporting to be a certificate of a fully registered medical practitioner.

9.   Admissibility of certain hearsay evidence formerly admissible at common law

(1)   In any civil proceedings a statement which, if this Part of this Act had not been passed, would by virtue of any rule of law mentioned in subsection (2) below have been admissible as evidence of any fact stated therein shall be admissible as evidence of that fact by virtue of this subsection.

(2)   The rules of law referred to in subsection (1) above are the following, that is to say any rule of law —

(a)   whereby in any civil proceedings an admission adverse to a party to the proceedings, whether made by that party or by another person, may be given in evidence against that party for the purpose of proving any fact stated in the admission;

(b)   whereby in any civil proceedings published works dealing with matters of a public nature (for example, histories, scientific works, dictionaries and maps) are admissible as evidence of facts of a public nature stated therein;

(c)   whereby in any civil proceedings public documents (for example, public registers, and returns made under public authority with respect to matters of public interest) are admissible as evidence of facts stated therein; or

(d)   whereby in any civil proceedings records (for example, the records of certain courts, treaties, Crown grants, pardons and commissions) are admissible as evidence of facts stated therein.

In this subsection 'admission' includes any representation of fact, whether made in words or otherwise.

(3)   In any civil proceedings a statement which tends to establish reputation or family tradition with respect to any matter and which, if this Act had not been passed,

would have been admissible in evidence by virtue of any rule of law mentioned in subsection (4) below —

(a)   shall be admissible in evidence by virtue of this paragraph in so far as it is not capable of being rendered admissible under section 2 or 4 of this Act; and

(b)   if given in evidence under this Part of this Act (whether by virtue of paragraph (a) above or otherwise) shall by virtue of this paragraph be admissible as evidence of the matter reputed or handed down;

and, without prejudice to paragraph (b) above, reputation shall for the purposes of this Part of this Act be treated as a fact and not as a statement or multiplicity of statements dealing with the matter reputed.

(4)   The rules of law referred to in subsection (3) above are the following, that is to say any rule of law —

(a)   whereby in any civil proceedings evidence of a person's reputation is admissible for the purpose of establishing his good or bad character;

(b)   whereby in any civil proceedings involving a question of pedigree or in which the existence of a marriage is in issue evidence of reputation or family tradition is admissible for the purpose of proving or disproving pedigree or the existence of the marriage, as the case may be; or

(c)   whereby in any civil proceedings evidence of reputation or family tradition is admissible for the purpose of proving or disproving the existence of any public or general right or of identifying any person or thing.

(5)   It is hereby declared that in so far as any statement is admissible in any civil proceedings by virtue of subsection (1) or (3)(a) above, it may be given in evidence in those proceedings notwithstanding anything in sections 2 to 7 of this Act or in any rules of court made in pursuance of section 8 of this Act.

(6)   The words in which any rule of law mentioned in subsection (2) or (4) above is there described are intended only to identify the rule in question and shall not be construed as altering that rule in any way.

10.   Interpretation of Part I, and application to arbitrations, etc.

(1)   In this Part of this Act —

'computer' has the meaning assigned by section 5 of this Act;

'document' includes, in addition to a document in writing —

(a)   any map, plan, graph or drawing;

(b)   any photograph;

(c)   any disc, tape, sound track or other device in which sounds or other data (not being visual images) are embodied so as to be capable (with or without the aid of some other equipment) of being reproduced therefrom; and

(d)   any film, negative, tape or other device in which one or more visual images are embodied so as to be capable (as aforesaid) of being reproduced therefrom;

'film' includes a microfilm;

'statement' includes any representation of fact, whether made in words or otherwise.

(2)   In this Part of this Act any reference to a copy of a document includes —

(a)   in the case of a document falling within paragraph (c) but not (d) of the definition of 'document' in the foregoing subsection, a transcript of the sounds or other data embodied therein;

(b)   in the case of a document falling within paragraph (d) but not (c) of that definition, a reproduction or still reproduction of the image or images embodied therein, whether enlarged or not;

(c)   in the case of a document falling within both those paragraphs, such a transcript together with such a still reproduction; and

(d)   in the case of a document not falling within the said paragraph (d) of which a visual image is embodied in a document falling within that paragraph, a reproduction of that image, whether enlarged or not.
and any reference to a copy of the material part of a document shall be construed accordingly.

. . .

Note

The Civil Evidence Act 1968 deals only with hearsay statements of fact. For hearsay statements of opinion see (*ii*) below.

Questions

1.   How does the Act deal with implied assertions?
2.   Do ss. 2 and 4 overlap? If so, in what way? Is there any particular benefit to be gained by using one section rather than the other?

Knight and others v David and others
[1971] 1 WLR 1671
Chancery Division

A claim by the plaintiffs to certain land depended upon events which occurred in 1886, and for the purpose of establishing that claim, the plaintiffs sought to put in evidence a tithe map and tithe apportionment survey, made under the provisions of the Tithe Act 1836.

GOULDING J: . . . the plaintiffs rely on section 4 of the Civil Evidence Act 1968, the material part of which is contained in subsection (1) . . .

Mr Francis argued that the tithe document is not within that subsection on either or both of two grounds: First, he says that the statements therein are statements relating to title, and direct oral evidence of title would not be admissible. I find this perhaps the most difficult point in the question I am considering, but, on the whole, I conclude that Mr Francis's argument must fail if a living person could state in evidence that the machinery of the Act was carried out, and that a certain person was, and another was not, entered as proprietor of certain land. In my judgment, such a statement would be admissible.

Mr Francis's second point was that it was not established that the record compiled by the officers under the Act of 1836 was compiled from information supplied by persons who had, or might be supposed to have had, personal knowledge of the matters dealt with. In my judgment, having regard to the nature of the document and the lapse of time, it is right for the court to infer that this condition is satisfied. Therefore . . . I should also be prepared to admit this evidence under section 4 of the Act of 1968.

H v Schering Chemicals Ltd
[1983] 1 WLR 143
Queen's Bench Division

The plaintiffs claimed damages for personal injuries alleged to have been caused by the effect of a drug marketed and manufactured by the defendant pharmaceutical company. They wished to introduce copies of certain specified documents, which they claimed were records for the purposes of s. 4 of the Civil Evidence Act 1968. The documents included summaries of the results of research, articles and letters published in medical journals concerning the drug.

BINGHAM J: The first question in this case is whether these documents are records. Mr Weitzman submits that the tendency which the Act was intended to advance is towards admitting hearsay evidence, subject always to the questions of weight which are left for the determination of the trial court. He further points out that the word 'record' is given a wide meaning, and he is certainly right in submitting that in *R v Jones (Benjamin)* [1978] 1 WLR 195, a very wide meaning is given to that expression, significantly wider than was indicated in *R v Tirado* (1974) 59 Cr App R 80, 90.

Mr Beldam submits that, be that as it may, these documents, in issue in this case, are simply not records. They are, he says, an analysis of records or a digest of records but not themselves a record. He further says that there is a danger in admitting material, sometimes said in the course of the material itself to be tentative, and that there is too much unknown about the research underlying these documents to make it safe to admit them as evidence.

Having considered the matter as best I can in the light of the arguments and the authorities, I have come to the conclusion that the documents which form part of the large bundle before me are not records within the meaning of section 4 of the Act. The intention of that section was, I believe, to admit in evidence records which a historian would regard as original or primary sources, that is, documents which either give effect to a transaction itself or which contain a contemporaneous register of information supplied by those with direct knowledge of the facts.

Judged by this standard, the commercial documents in *R v Jones (Benjamin)* [1978] 1 WLR 195; the tithe map in *Knight v David* [1971] 1 WLR 1671; the record in *Edmonds v Edmonds* [1947] P 67 and the transcript in *Taylor (J) v Taylor (IL)* [1970] 1 WLR 1148, would rank as records, as in those cases they were held to be. On the other hand, the documents in *Ioannou v Demetriou* [1952] AC 84; the file of letters in *R v Tirado*, 59 Cr App R 80, and the summary of cases in *In re Koscot Interplanetary (UK) Ltd* [1972] 3 All ER 829, would fail to be admitted as records, as in the first two cases they did.

Judged by the same standard the documents in the present case, I think, are not records and are not primary or original sources. They are a digest or analysis of records which must exist or have existed, but they are not themselves those records. If the plaintiffs' submission were right it would, I think, mean that anyone who wrote a letter to *The Times,* having done research and summarising the result of that research in his letter, would find his letter admissible as evidence of the facts under section 4. That is not, I think, the intent of the section, and accordingly, whatever counter-notice was served in response to the plaintiffs' notice the effect would not, in my judgment, be to make the evidence admissible under section 4.

Application dismissed.

Rasool v West Midlands Passenger Transport Executive
[1974] 3 All ER 638
Queen's Bench Division

The plaintiff commenced an action against the defendants for damages in respect of personal injuries sustained by him as a result of the negligence of a bus driver employed by the defendants. The defendants served notice on the plaintiff under RSC, Ord 38, r. 21(1), of their intention to give in evidence at the trial a statement made by C who had been an eye-witness to the plaintiff's accident. C's statement was to the effect that the bus driver was in no way to blame for the accident. The defendant's notice asserted that C could not be called as a witness since 'she has left her former address in Birmingham and cannot at present be found. It is understood that she is now beyond the seas and is probably resident in Jamaica'. On the available evidence, this account appeared to be accurate, although the defendants had made no effort to trace C there. It was contended for the plaintiff that C's statement was inadmissible since, although C was beyond the seas, it was still necessary under s. 8(2)(b) of the Civil Evidence Act 1968 for the defendants to prove that despite the exercise of reasonable diligence she could not be found.

FINER J: In amending the law regarding the admissibility of hearsay evidence in civil proceedings, the Civil Evidence Act 1968, as appears from ss. 1 and 8, left much of the detail to be worked out by rules of court which are now to be found in Part III of RSC, Ord 38. Many of the questions which arise thus entail a reading of the 1968 Act and of the rules in close conjunction with each other. The scheme of things, so far as material in the present circumstances, may be summarised as follows. Section 2(1) of the 1968 Act provides:

> In any civil proceedings a statement made, whether orally or in a document or otherwise, by any person, whether called as a witness in those proceedings or not, shall, subject to this section and to rules of court, be admissible as evidence of any fact stated therein of which direct oral evidence by him would be admissible . . ..

Section 8 of the 1968 Act enacts further that provision shall be made by rules of court as to the procedure which must be followed and the other conditions which must be fulfilled before a statement can be given in evidence by virtue of s. 2. Section 8(2) sets out requirements to which the rules must conform. Subject to such exceptions, if any, which may be provided for in the rules themselves they must, in the first instance, require the party desiring to put in the statement to give to every other party to the proceedings notice of such desire, with such particulars, as may be specified in the rules. Secondly, by s. 8(2)(b) the rules must —

> . . . enable any party who receives such notice . . . by counter-notice to require any person of whom particulars were given with the notice to be called as a witness in the proceedings unless that person is dead, or beyond the seas, or unfit by reason of his bodily or mental condition to attend as a witness, or cannot with reasonable diligence be identified or found, or cannot reasonably be expected . . . to have any recollection of matters relevant to the accuracy or otherwise of the statement.

Thirdly, it is provided by s. 8(3)(a) that although the rules may confer on the court a discretion to allow a statement to be given in evidence notwithstanding that the requirements of the rules have not been complied with, they cannot, subject to immaterial exceptions, 'confer on the court a discretion to exclude such a statement where the requirements of the rules . . . have been complied with'.

Turning now to the rules, RSC Ord 38, rr. 21 and 22(2) provide for the notice to be given in the case of a statement admissible by virtue of s. 2 of the 1968 Act and made in a document. Rule 22(3) provides:

If the party giving the notice alleges that any person, particulars of whom are contained in the notice, cannot or should not be called as a witness at the trial or hearing for any of the reasons specified in rule 25, the notice must contain a statement to that effect specifying the reason relied on.

The reasons specified in r. 25 are the same as those mentioned in s. 8(2)(b) to which I have already referred, as disentitling the recipient of a notice to require the witness to be called in the proceedings. Rule 26(2) then provides:

Where any notice under rule 21 contains a statement that any person particulars of whom are contained in the notice cannot or should not be called as a witness for the reason specified therein, a party shall not be entitled to serve a counter-notice under this rule requiring that person to be called as a witness at the trial or hearing of the cause or matter unless he contends that that person can or, as the case may be, should be called, and in that case he must include in his counter-notice a statement to that effect.

Finally, r. 27(1) provides:

Where . . . a question arises whether any of the reasons specified in rule 25 applies in relation to a person particulars of whom are contained in a notice under rule 21, the Court may, on the application of any party . . . determine that question before the trial or hearing of the cause or matter or give directions for it to be determined before the trial or hearing and for the manner in which it is to be so determined.

Now the short effect of all these complicated provisions seems to be as follows: that the system for adducing a written statement in evidence without calling the maker involves the service by the party wishing to take that course on the other parties of a notice in a prescribed form. A party receiving such a notice who objects to the proposal to put in the statement can, by an appropriate counter-notice, require the witness to be called, failing which the statement (subject to an overriding discretion which the court has to admit it under r. 29) will be excluded. This right of objection, however, is modified in the case where the stated reason for desiring to put the statement in evidence without calling the witness is one or other of the five reasons mentioned in s. 8(2)(b) of the 1968 Act and r. 25. In such a case the objecting party must, despite the assertion in the notice that the witness cannot or should not be called because he is dead, or beyond the seas, or as the case may be, state in his counter-notice that the witness can or should be called. This raises the issue as to the truth or validity of the reason relied on, and that issue will be determined, as it is being now, under the procedure laid down by r. 27.

In the instant case, the defendants' notice to the plaintiff asserted that Mrs Collum could not be called as a witness at the hearing because —

she has left her former address number 325 Charles Road, Small Heath, Birmingham and cannot at present be found. It is understood that she is now beyond the seas and is probably resident in Jamaica.

Strictly speaking, this probably invokes only one of the five specified reasons, namely that despite the exercise of reasonable diligence it was not possible to find the witness. By common consent however, the notice at the hearing before myself was treated as invoking both that reason and the further reason that Mrs Collum was beyond the seas . . ..

[As] I read s. 8(2)(b) of the 1968 Act and the rules which reflect it, the five reasons that may be relied on for not calling a witness are disjunctive reasons. If the maker of the statement is beyond the seas it does not have to be proved also that he cannot by reasonable diligence be found. His whereabouts abroad may be precisely known, yet if it be established that he is indeed abroad that is in itself a sufficient reason for admitting the statement. It would follow that the application in this case (the terms of which were followed in the order) should not have been based on the ground that Mrs Collum had left her former address and could not be found. The real ground was that she was beyond the seas.

In fending, however, that the absence of the maker beyond the seas is a sufficient reason in itself for admitting the statement, even if no effort is made to trace the precise whereabouts of the proposed witness, or even if those whereabouts are known, I have deliberately elided the question whether the court nevertheless has any discretion to exclude it. At first sight it seems peculiar that there should be no such discretion. Take the case of a witness who has been party to a conversation in which it is common ground that the plaintiff and defendant made a contract, but they dispute the terms they agreed. The witness lives at a known address in Paris, despite which the plaintiff seeks to adduce his evidence in the form of a statement, relying on the fact the witness is beyond the seas. Or in the present case, one may imagine that it was Mrs Collum, a professed eye-witness to a serious accident whose statement may damn the plaintiff, who lived at a known address in Paris. Nevertheless, I find it a clear conclusion from the provisions of the statute and the rules which I have earlier mentioned that if the court is satisfied on any of the five specified reasons the statement becomes admissible, and there is no residuary discretion to exclude it by reference to other circumstances. The relevant provisions leave no room for such a discretion. The scheme of the law is that the counter-notice is ineffectual unless it raises an issue regarding the reason alleged in the notice which is ultimately determined in favour of the giver of the counter-notice. If the counter-notice is ineffectual, the notice takes effect. I consider that this would be the result even apart from s. 8(3)(a), but that provision clinches the point by providing in terms that the rules cannot — with the exceptions provided for in s. 8(3)(b), which has no application to the present case — confer on the court a discretion to exclude a statement where the requirements of the rules affecting its admissibility have been complied with.

The weight to be attached to the statement admitted in evidence remains a matter for the court. In the circumstances postulated in the examples I gave, where the whereabouts abroad of an important witness in a substantial case are known or can be easily ascertained, but the party relying on his evidence nevertheless adopts a method of adducing it which does not permit of cross-examination, no doubt the court would pay little attention to it. It may be that this is a risk which the defendants run if they make no efforts to find Mrs Collum in Jamaica, so as to permit at least the possibility of evidence being taken on commission. But all that will be a matter for the trial judge.

I should add that in deciding as I have on the matter of discretion I have not overlooked s. 18(5) of the 1968 Act which provides that nothing in the Act —

shall prejudice . . . any power of a court, in any legal proceedings, to exclude evidence (whether by preventing questions from being put or otherwise) at its discretion . . .

The exact meaning of this provision would be an interesting field for enquiry in appropriate circumstances, but it has no relevance that I can detect for the present case.

As I have already explained, the defendants' notice was out of order in that it specified a reason which I doubt whether they made out, and did not specify the good reason on which they have succeeded. This matter has been argued, however, on the footing that the defect is waived. I shall vary the registrar's order by substituting for the words 'because she has left her former address number 325 Charles Road, Small Heath, Birmingham and cannot at present be found', the words 'because she is beyond the seas'. The order will otherwise be affirmed.

Appeal dismissed.

Ford v Lewis
[1971] 1 WLR 623
Court of Appeal

The infant plaintiff, who was attempting to cross a road, was struck by a van driven by the defendant. The plaintiff was at the material time in the charge of her parents. By the time of the trial (ten years later) the defendant had become a patient in a mental hospital and it was agreed that he was unfit to be called as a witness. At the trial his counsel sought to put in evidence, under s. 2(1) of the Civil Evidence Act 1968, a photostat copy of a written statement, proved by the guardian *ad litem* to be in the defendant's handwriting, giving his version of the accident, and also, under s. 4(1) of the Act, hospital records relating to the plaintiff's father which stated that he had been in a state of intoxication when admitted to hospital after the accident. No notice of intention to put those documents in evidence had been served on the plaintiff's advisers as required by RSC, Ord 38, rr. 21(1), 22 and 23, and the reason for non-compliance was not disclosed to the judge. Plaintiff's counsel refused an adjournment offered by the judge who thereupon, in the exercise of his discretion under RSC, Ord 38, r. 29(1), admitted the documents. He found that the statement attributed to the defendant rang true, acquitted him of negligence and dismissed the claim.

The plaintiff appealed on the ground that the judge had wrongly exercised his discretion in permitting the admission of the defendant's statement and the hospital notes.

EDMUND DAVIES LJ: [T]he point of substance involved in this appeal relates to the application of the Civil Evidence Act 1968 and RSC, Ord 38, to the circumstances of this case . . . .

Section 8(1) provides for the making of rules of court 'as to the procedure which, subject to any exceptions provided for in the rules, must be followed before a statement can be given in evidence in civil proceedings by virtue of section 2 . . . of this Act.'. . .

Rule 21 thereof makes it obligatory on the party desiring to adduce hearsay evidence by virtue of section 2 of the Act to serve notice on the other party of his intention to do so. If he does not, he will, subject to the court's discretion under rule 29, be precluded from giving the statement in evidence. Rule 22 provides that 'the notice must contain particulars of — (a) the time, place and circumstances at or in which the statement was made; (b) the person by whom, and the person to whom, the statement was made; . . .' Furthermore, 'If the statement . . . was made in a document, a copy or transcript of the document, or of the relevant part thereof, must be annexed to the notice'. Finally,

> If the party giving the notice alleges that any person, particulars of whom are contained in the notice, cannot or should not be called as a witness at the trial or hearing for any of the reasons specified . . ., the notice must contain a statement to that effect specifying the reason relied on.

Rule 26 enables the party receiving such a notice to serve a counter-notice, requiring the other side to call as a witness at the trial any person to whom the original notice related. If that counter-notice is served, rule 27 provides the machinery whereby the necessity for the absent maker of the statement being actually called as a witness can be decided before the trial.

It is well known that the statutory provisions which led to the formulation of these rules were the subject matter of considerable controversy. On the one hand, there were the die-hards who would have no further relaxation of the prohibition against hearsay than that already provided by the Evidence Act 1938. On the other hand, there were those who clamoured under modern conditions for a far more relaxed approach to the problem. A compromise was finally reached within the terms of section 8 of the Act of 1968 and its offspring RSC, Ord 38. The object of the latter is expressed with admirable clarity in the notes thereto which appear in the *Supreme Court Practice* (1970), and I cannot do better than to quote them. I am quoting from the thin supplement, para. 38/20/6:

> The machinery of Part III of this Order is designed to achieve two main objectives, namely, (a) that all questions concerning the giving of hearsay evidence at the trial should, so far as practicable, be dealt with and disposed of before the trial, so that the trial itself should proceed smoothly without unnecessary objections relating to such hearsay evidence, and (b) that in relation to any hearsay evidence which any party desires to adduce, there should be no surprises at the trial. In this latter respect, it is to be noted that the machinery of Part III of this Order makes a departure from the general rule of practice that a party is not required to disclose the evidence which he intends to adduce at the trial, for these rules do require such disclosure of the proposed hearsay evidence to be made. The principle is that if a party wishes to obtain the advantage of adducing secondary evidence at the trial, he should pay the price of disclosing such evidence before the trial, and affording the other party the opportunity to resist its admission in that form.

That being the object of Order 38, it is common ground that the defendant never did comply with it. For a substantial period his advisers had been in possession of a statement attributed to him which they had it in mind to place before the court in lieu of calling him as a witness. Despite their non-compliance, Veale J allowed them to adduce it in evidence. It clearly played an effective part in leading him to dismiss the plaintiff's claim, for he made express reference to its contents in his judgment, saying: 'It is not necessary for me to read it; it is only necessary for me to say that I think it rings true'.

In proper circumstances, a trial judge is undoubtedly entitled to admit evidence of an out-of-court statement notwithstanding non-compliance with the initially mandatory requirement. Section 8(3)(a) of the Act of 1968 made express provision for this and was the foundation of rule 29 of Order 38. This provides that: '(1) . . . the court may, if it thinks it just to do so, allow a statement falling within section 2(1), . . . of the Act to be given in evidence . . . notwithstanding — (a) that the statement is one in relation to which rule 21(1) applies and that the party desiring to give the statement in evidence has failed to comply with that rule, . . .' It was by virtue of this provision that Veale J admitted the absentee defendant's out-of-court statement.

I think it is imperative to consider briefly the circumstances in which he was led to do so. He had himself addressed some sharp questions to the defence as to why they had not given the statutory notice, and he received no adequate answer — if, indeed, any real answer at all was forthcoming. But, his offer to adjourn the proceedings until the following assizes having been declined by plaintiff's counsel, the judge admitted the statement.

In these circumstances, it is urged on behalf of the defendant that this exercise of his discretion under rule 29 ought not now to be disturbed. For my part, I cannot accept this. Rule 29(1) empowers the court to admit such a statement as is here in question, notwithstanding failing to comply with the preceding rules, 'if it thinks it just to do so.' In order that the court may adjudicate upon the justice of relaxing the rules in favour of a defaulting party, it must surely be placed in possession of all the relevant facts. In the present case Veale J was left ignorant of the vital fact that non-compliance by the defendant with the statutory requirement was due to no inability, inadvertence, or slackness on the part of his advisers, but resulted from a deliberate decision not to comply. This emerged from the completely candid statement of leading counsel for the defendant, who, in response to a direct inquiry from the Bench, took sole responsibility for the failure to give any notice of the kind required by rule 22. He was equally candid about his reason for advising this course of action, namely, that he suspected that, were the existence, nature and contents of the defendant's written statement made known to the plaintiff and her parents before the trial, it might have led to their evidence being in some way adjusted in order to meet and destroy it in advance. Put in plain words, this means that the tactics adopted were precisely those which the statutory provisions as to notice and counter-notice were designed to prevent, namely, the taking of a party by surprise by suddenly and without warning producing at the trial an out-of-court statement of someone not proposed to be called as a witness.

In these most unfortunate circumstances, it seems to me impossible that the defendant should be permitted to rely upon the judge's purported exercise of his discretion under rule 29. I hold that there can be no valid exercise of such discretion if there has (for any reason) been a deliberate withholding from the court of the reason for non-compliance. Had Veale J known that this was the result of a deliberate decision based upon the tactical value of surprise, I regard it as inconceivable that he would have ruled in favour of admitting the statement . . . .

[E]ven if he had, such an attitude ought not to be countenanced, by this court. A suitor who deliberately flouts the rules has no right to ask the court to exercise in his favour a discretionary indulgence created by those very same rules. Furthermore, a judge who, to his knowledge, finds himself confronted by such a situation would not, as I think, be acting judicially if he nevertheless exercised his discretion in favour of the recalcitrant suitor. The rules are there to be respected, and those who defy them should not be indulged or excused. Slackness is one thing; deliberate disobedience another. The former may be overlooked; the latter never, even though, as here, it derives from mistaken zeal on the client's behalf. To tolerate it would be dangerous to justice.

(DAVIES LJ also delivered a judgment. Whilst condemning the course adopted on behalf of the defendant, his lordship was against the granting of a new trial on the ground of the already considerable delay and because it seemed to him that the ultimate result must be the same. KARMINSKI LJ agreed with EDMUND DAVIES LJ.)

Appeal allowed. New trial ordered.

Morris v Stratford-on-Avon RDC
[1973] 1 WLR 1059
Court of Appeal

The plaintiff was struck by a lorry driven by an employee of the defendants. At the trial, which took place five years after the event, the driver gave evidence for the defendants. His evidence was inconsistent and confused, and at the end of his examination-in-chief counsel for the defendants applied for leave to put in evidence, under s. 2 of the Civil Evidence Act 1968, a proof of evidence given by the driver to the defendants' insurers some nine months after the accident. Although prior notice had not been given to the other side as required by RSC, Ord 38, r. 21(1) and despite objections made by the plaintiff's counsel, the judge exercised his discretion and admitted the statement. He found on the evidence that the plaintiff had failed to establish that the defendants had been in any way negligent and dismissed the claim. The plaintiff appealed.

MEGAW LJ: Counsel for the plaintiff submits that the court, under the Civil Evidence Act 1968 and the Rules of Court made thereunder, has, in a case like this, not one but two discretions to exercise. The first discretion is that which is given to it by section 2 of the Act. That section, which provides for the admissibility of out-of-court statements as evidence of the facts stated, does say, in subsection (2)(a), that the statement 'shall not be given in evidence by virtue of this section on behalf of that party without the leave of the court': hence there is discretion coming in at *that* stage. Then in RSC, Ord 38, r. 29, it is provided that 'without prejudice to', *inter alia,* section 2(2)(a) of the Act, 'the court may, if it thinks it just to do so, allow a statement falling within section 2(1) . . . of the Act to be given in evidence at the trial or hearing . . .' — and then (departing from the words of the rule), notwithstanding that the advance notices, which are required by the rules to be given where it is intended to seek to take advantage of the Act, have not been given.

I do not think it matters whether one regards these as being two separate discretions or as being one discretion with the matters which are relevant under Ord 38, r. 29 being taken into account when the judge is dealing with the exercise of his discretion under section 2 of the Act or *vice versa*. There is no doubt that the judge has to consider all the relevant matters in exercising his discretion; and if the proper notices for which the Act and the rules provide have not been given, then the judge must consider that matter with care and must given the opposite party every opportunity to make submissions before he can properly decide whether or not the non-compliance with the rules is such that justice requires that the statement should be admitted.

Nothing that I say must be taken in any way as suggesting that non-compliance with the rules as to notices is a matter that can be lightly overlooked. On the other hand, there must be cases in which there is, sensibly and reasonably, no ground for supposing that a statement which is in existence is going to be used by a party. It would perhaps be unfortunate if the matter were to be so interpreted that, in every case, those who are advising a party felt it necessary to advise him that, if there is any possibility, however remote, that, as a result of something which may happen hereafter, an application might be sought to be made, then notice should be given in advance. But, quite clearly, if there is reason to suppose, on proper consideration of the evidence, that such an application may be made, then care must be taken that the proper notices should be given.

As I say, it is important that the notices should be given. We were told by counsel for the defendants, and I have no doubt whatever but that it is correct, that in the present case it had not crossed his mind that this statement would be one which there would be occasion to put in in evidence, and that it was only when the evidence of Mr Pattison came to be taken that it occurred to him that it would be desirable that application should be made. In my judgment, no blame whatever attaches to counsel for making the application at that stage.

Let me say that the present case is, in my judgment, totally different from the case in this court of *Ford* v *Lewis* [1971] 1 WLR 623, ...

It is perfectly apparent that this case bears no conceivable relationship to the matters which motivated the court to take the course that it did in that case. However, it is right that careful consideration should always be given, on an application of this sort, to matters such as those that were stressed before us by counsel for the plaintiff: for example, that the statement was taken as a proof of evidence and that it was not closely contemporary with the time of the accident but was taken some nine months later. Those are matters which of course go to weight; but they can also be relevant on the question of a decision as to the exercise of discretion. Another matter which in my judgment must always be carefully watched, when an application of this sort is made under the Civil Evidence Act 1968 without proper notices having been given, is for the judge to make sure, so far as he can, that no injustice will be done to the other party by reason of the statement being allowed to be put in evidence. If there is ground to suppose that there will be any injustice caused, or that the other party will be materially prejudiced or embarrassed, then the judge should either refuse to allow the document to be admitted or, in his discretion, allow it on terms, such as an adjournment at the cost of the party seeking to put in the statement.

If I thought that in the present case there was any possibility that the plaintiff was prejudiced or that injustice might have been done by reason of the admitting of this statement when it was admitted, I should have had no hesitation in saying that the judge would have been wrong in admitting it. But, having regard to all the circumstances of which we have heard in this case, I am satisfied that there has been no such prejudice and that no injustice resulted. Accordingly, I take the view that Stirling J was not wrong in the manner in which he exercised his discretion.

(DAVIES LJ and WALTON J agreed.)

Appeal dismissed.

Question
Why is this case 'totally different' from *Ford* v *Lewis*?

(ii)   Civil Evidence Act 1972

Civil Evidence Act 1972

1.   Application of Part I of the Civil Evidence Act 1968 to statements of opinion
(1)   Subject to the provisions of this section, Part I (hearsay evidence) of the Civil Evidence Act 1968, except section 5 (statements produced by computers), shall apply in relation to statements of opinion as it applies in relation to statements of fact, subject to the necessary modifications and in particular the modification that any

reference to a fact stated in a statement shall be construed as a reference to a matter dealt with therein.

(2)   Section 4 (admissibility of certain records) of the Civil Evidence Act 1968, as applied by subsection (1) above, shall not render admissible in any civil proceedings a statement of opinion contained in a record unless that statement would be admissible in those proceedings if made in the course of giving oral evidence by the person who originally supplied the information from which the record was compiled; but where a statement of opinion contained in a record deals with a matter on which the person who originally supplied the information from which the record was compiled is (or would if living be) qualified to give oral expert evidence, the said section 4, as applied by subsection (1) above, shall have effect in relation to that statement as if so much of subsection (1) of that section as requires personal knowledge on the part of that person was omitted.

(iii)   *Children*

Children Act 1989

96.   Evidence given by, or with respect to, children

(1)   Subsection (2) applies to any civil proceedings where a child who is called as a witness in any civil proceedings does not, in the opinion of the court, understand the nature of an oath.

(2)   The child's evidence may be heard by the court if, in its opinion —

    (a)   he understands that it is his duty to speak the truth; and

    (b)   he has sufficient understanding to justify his evidence being heard.

(3)   The Lord Chancellor may by order make provision for the admissibility of evidence which would otherwise be inadmissible under any rule of law relating to hearsay.

(4)   An order under subsection (3) may only be made with respect to —

    (a)   civil proceedings in general or such civil proceedings, or class of civil proceedings, as may be prescribed; and

    (b)   evidence in connection with the upbringing, maintenance or welfare of a child.

(5)   An order under subsection (3) —

    (a)   may, in particular, provide for the admissibility of statements which are made orally or in a prescribed form or which are recorded by any prescribed method of recording;

    (b)   may make different provision for different purposes and in relation to different descriptions of court; and

    (c)   may make such amendments and repeals in any enactment relating to evidence (other than in this Act) as the Lord Chancellor considers necessary or expedient in consequence of the provision made by the order.

(6)   Subsection (5)(b) is without prejudice to section 104(4):

(7)   In this section —

'civil proceedings' and 'court' have the same meaning as they have in the Civil Evidence Act 1968 by virtue of section 18 of that Act; and 'prescribed' means prescribed by an order under subsection (3).

Note

The Children (Admissibility of Hearsay Evidence) Order 1990, (SI 1990 No. 143) provides in art. 2(1), that in civil proceedings before the High Court or county court, evidence given in connection with the upbringing, maintenance or welfare of a child shall be admissible notwithstanding any rule of law relating to hearsay.

Question
Martin was knocked off his bicycle when he was crossing a road junction controlled by traffic lights. It is alleged that he was knocked off his bicycle by Harold who crossed the junction in his car against a red traffic light. PC John arrived at the scene some five minutes after the incident and found Charles, a witness, comforting Martin. Charles told PC John that Martin had been knocked off his bike by a blue Metro, and he later signed a written statement to that effect.

David, who had been standing about 50 yards away, said he had been taking down car numbers with his eight-year-old son, Nigel. David called out the numbers and Nigel wrote them down in an exercise book. PC John copied down the last two numbers in the book and it was discovered that one of the numbers belonged to a blue Metro owned by Harold.

Martin sues Harold for negligence. Consider the issues raised should Martin seek to introduce PC John's notebook into evidence.

(B) Criminal cases

The decision in *Myers* v *DPP* (see Chapter 7(A)), lead to the passing of the Criminal Evidence Act 1965, which provided for the admissibility of certain documentary evidence in criminal proceedings. For reasons which we need not pursue here, the 1965 Act was repealed and replaced by certain provisions in the Police and Criminal Evidence Act 1984. The provisions dealing with hearsay evidence in the 1984 Act have now been replaced by provisions contained in the Criminal Justice Act 1988. The present law is contained in ss. 23 to 28 of the Criminal Justice Act 1988, supplemented by the provisions contained in sch. 2. The Act provides only for the admissibilty of hearsay statements contained in documents, reflecting the assumption that documents compiled in certain situations are likely to be reliable, or at least more reliable than oral hearsay statements. As with the Civil Evidence Act 1968, the Criminal Justice Act 1988 cures only the defect of hearsay. Evidence which is inadmissible because it suffers from some defect other than hearsay remains inadmissible.

(i) Documentary evidence

Criminal Justice Act 1988

23. First-hand hearsay
(1) Subject —
    (a) to subsection (4) below;
    (b) to paragraph 1A of Schedule 2 to the Criminal Appeal Act 1968 (evidence given orally at original trial to be given orally at retrial); and

(c)   to section 69 of the Police and Criminal Evidence Act 1984 (evidence from computer records),

a statement made by a person in a document shall be admissible in criminal proceedings as evidence of any fact of which direct oral evidence by him would be admissible if —

(i)   the requirements of one of the paragraphs of subsection (2) below are satisfied; or

(ii)   the requirements of subsection (3) below are satisfied.

(2)   The requirements mentioned in subsection (1)(i) above are —

(a)   that the person who made the statement is dead or by reason of his bodily or mental condition unfit to attend as a witness;

(b)   that —

(i)   the person who made the statement is outside the United Kingdom; and

(ii)   it is not reasonably practicable to secure his attendance; or

(c)   that all reasonable steps have been taken to find the person who made the statement, but that he cannot be found.

(3)   The requirements mentioned in subsection (1)(ii) above are —

(a)   that the statement was made to a police officer or some other person charged with the duty of investigating offences or charging offenders; and

(b)   that the person who made it does not give oral evidence through fear or because he is kept out of the way.

(4)   Subsection (1) above does not render admissible a confession made by an accused person that would not be admissible under section 76 of the Police and Criminal Evidence Act 1984.

24. Business etc. documents

(1)   Subject —

(a)   to subsections (3) and (4) below;

(b)   to paragraph 1A of Schedule 2 to the Criminal Appeal Act 1968; and

(c)   to section 69 of the Police and Criminal Evidence Act 1984,

a statement in a document shall be admissible in criminal proceedings as evidence of any fact of which direct oral evidence would be admissible, if the following conditions are satisfied —

(i)   the document was created or received by a person in the course of a trade, business, profession or other occupation, or as the holder of a paid or unpaid office; and

(ii)   the information contained in the document was supplied by a person (whether or not the maker of the statement) who had, or may reasonably be supposed to have had, personal knowledge of the matters dealt with.

(2)   Subsection (1) above applies whether the information contained in the document was supplied directly or indirectly but if it was supplied indirectly, only if each person through whom it was supplied received it —

(a)   in the course of a trade, business, profession or other occupation; or

(b)   as the holder of a paid or unpaid office.

(3)   Subsection (1) above does not render admissible a confession made by an accused person that would not be admissible under section 76 of the Police and Criminal Evidence Act 1984.

(4)   A statement prepared otherwise than in accordance with section 3 of the Criminal Justice (International Co-operation) Act 1990 below or an order under paragraph 6 of Schedule 13 to this Act or under section 30 or 31 below for the purposes —

(a)   of pending or contemplated criminal proceedings; or

(b)   of a criminal investigation,

shall not be admissible by virtue of subsection (1) above unless —

(i)   the requirements of one of the paragraphs of subsection (2) of section 23 above are satisfied; or

(ii)   the requirements of subsection (3) of that section are satisfied; or

(iii)   the person who made the statement cannot reasonably be expected (having regard to the time which has elapsed since he made the statement and to all the circumstances) to have any recollection of the matters dealt with in the statement.

25.   Principles to be followed by court

(1)   If, having regard to all the circumstances —

(a)   the Crown Court —

(i)   on a trial on indictment;

(ii)   on an appeal from a magistrates' court; or

(iii)   on the hearing of an application under section 6 of the Criminal Justice Act 1987 (applications for dismissal or charges of fraud transferred from magistrates' court or Crown Court); or

(b)   the criminal division of the Court of Appeal; or

(c)   a magistrates' court on a trial of an information,

is of the opinion that in the interests of justice a statement which is admissible by virtue of section 23 or 24 above nevertheless ought not to be admitted, it may direct that the statement shall not be admitted.

(2)   Without prejudice to the generality of subsection (1) above, it shall be the duty of the court to have regard —

(a)   to the nature and source of the document containing the statement and to whether or not, having regard to its nature and source and to any other circumstances that appear to the court to be relevant, it is likely that the document is authentic;

(b)   to the extent to which the statement appears to supply evidence which would otherwise not be readily available;

(c)   to the relevance of the evidence that it appears to supply to any issue which is likely to have to be determined in the proceedings; and

(d)   to any risk, having regard in particular to whether it is likely to be possible to controvert the statement if the person making it does not attend to give oral evidence in the proceedings, that its admission or exclusion will result in unfairness to the accused or, if there is more than one, to any of them.

26.   Statements in documents that appear to have been prepared for purposes of criminal proceedings or investigations

Where a statement which is admissible in criminal proceedings by virtue of section 23 or 24 above appears to the court to have been prepared, otherwise than in accordance with section 3 of the Criminal Justice (International Co-operation) Act 1990 below or an order under paragraph 6 of Schedule 13 to this Act or under section 30 or 31 below, for the purposes —

(a)   of pending or contemplated criminal proceedings; or

(b)   of a criminal investigation,

the statement shall not be given in evidence in any criminal proceedings without the leave of the court, and the court shall not give leave unless it is of the opinion that the statement ought to be admitted in the interests of justice; and in considering whether its admission would be in the interests of justice, it shall be the duty of the court to have regard —

(i)   to the contents of the statement;

(ii)   to any risk, having regard in particular to whether it is likely to be possible to controvert the statement if the person making it does not attend to give oral evidence in the proceedings, that its admission or exclusion will result in unfairness to the accused or, if there is more than one, to any of them; and

(iii)   to any other circumstances that appear to the court to be relevant.

27.   Proof of statements contained in documents

Where a statement contained in a document is admissible as evidence in criminal proceedings, it may be proved —

(a)   by the production of that document; or

(b)   (whether or not that document is still in existence) by the production of a copy of that document, or of the material part of it,

authenticated in such manner as the court may approve; and it is immaterial for the purposes of this subsection how many removes there are between a copy and the original.

28.   Documentary evidence — supplementary

(1)   Nothing in this Part of this Act shall prejudice —

(a)   the admissibility of a statement not made by a person while giving oral evidence in court which is admissible otherwise than by virtue of this Part of this Act; or

(b)   any power of a court to exclude at its discretion a statement admissible by virtue of this Part of this Act.

(2)   Schedule 2 to this Act shall have effect for the purpose of supplementing this Part of this Act.

SCHEDULE 2
DOCUMENTARY EVIDENCE — SUPPLEMENTARY

1.   Where a statement is admitted as evidence in criminal proceedings by virtue of Part II of this Act —

(a)   any evidence which, if the person making the statement had been called as a witness, would have been admissible as relevant to his credibility as a witness shall be admissible for that purpose in those proceedings;

(b)   evidence may, with the leave of the court, be given of any matter which, if that person had been called as a witness, could have been put to him in cross-examination as relevant to his credibility as a witness but of which evidence could not have been adduced by the cross-examining party; and

(c)   evidence tending to prove that that person, whether before or after making the statement, made (whether orally or not) some other statement which is inconsistent with it shall be admissible for the purpose of showing that he has contradicted himself.

2.   A statement which is given in evidence by virtue of Part II of this Act shall not be capable of corroborating evidence given by the person making it.

3.   In estimating the weight, if any, to be attached to such a statement regard shall be had to all the circumstances from which any inference can reasonably be drawn as to its accuracy or otherwise.

4.   Without prejudice to the generality of any enactment conferring power to make them —

(a)   Crown Court Rules;

(b) Criminal Appeal Rules; and
(c) rules under section 144 of the Magistrates' Courts Act 1980,

may make such provision as appears to the authority making any of them to be necessary or expedient for the purposes of Part II of this Act.

5. Expressions used in Part II of this Act and in Part II of the Civil Evidence Act 1968 are to be construed in Part II of this Act in accordance with section 10 of that Act.

6. In Part II of this Act 'confession' has the meaning assigned to it by section 82 of the Police and Criminal Evidence Act 1984.

Questions

1. Do ss. 23 and 24 overlap at all? If so, is there any particular benefit to be gained by using one rather than the other?

2. Does s. 26 enable the court to achieve anything that could not have been achieved by using s. 25?

3. Does s. 24 guarantee the accuracy of the document(s) admitted under its provisions?

R* v *Cole
[1990] 1 WLR 866
Court of Appeal

RALPH GIBSON LJ: On 25 July 1989 in the Crown Court at Kingston before Judge Hamilton the defendant was convicted of assault occasioning actual bodily harm and was sentenced to 12 months' imprisonment. He appeals against conviction by leave of the single judge. He has not renewed his application for leave to appeal against sentence.

The case for the prosecution at the trial was as follows. Ronald Barham, aged 58, was struck and injured by the defendant. Barham was employed at Wimbledon Stadium as a part-time admission and security officer. On Sunday 27 November 1988 at about 9.20 p.m., when a stockcar meeting was being held, some 12 children, including the defendant's 12-year old daughter Michelle, were larking about, throwing chairs and knocking tables about. Barham caught hold of the hand of an 8-year old boy and told him to stop. Michelle, who was the sister of that boy, punched and kicked Barham and told him to let her brother alone. Michelle ran away but returned about 15 minutes later with the defendant, her father, who walked up to Barham and said 'Leave my daughter alone.' He punched Barham once on the chin and once in the eye. Barham fell and was taken to hospital. He had sustained a bruised eye, a laceration to the chin, a hairline fracture of the jaw, and a fracture to the wrist caused by the fall.

Thomas Phillips, a security guard, was also on duty. He saw Michelle with the defendant and she pointed out first Mr Luff, another security guard. The defendant moved towards Mr Luff but Michelle said, 'No, not him, him,' meaning Barham. Phillips did not see the blows struck because Mr Luff was in the way. He would have intervened but there were three men in the way who told him not to interfere.

On the application of the prosecution the statement of Mr Luff was read out to the jury. The judge permitted the statement to be read because Mr Luff had died in 1989. The statement was a formal witness statement made in the usual way and was part of the evidence upon which the defendant had been committed for trial. It therefore contained the usual caption to the effect that Mr Luff made the statement:

knowing that, if it is tendered in evidence, I shall be liable to prosecution if I have wilfully stated anything which I know to be false or do not believe to be true.

He gave his occupation and address. He had worked as a security guard at the stadium for six months. The statement continued:

> . . . I . . . was . . . stationed at the grandstand entrance. At approximately 9.30 p.m. I was sitting at the entrance when a group of . . . eight to nine males entered the grandstand followed by a group of teenagers. These teenagers were asked by Mr Bannister, Head of Security on Sundays, and the police earlier in the evening to leave the premises, which is why I was stationed at the grandstand entrance. A male in the group said to one of the female teenagers, 'which one touched you?' She pointed towards me. The male stepped forward towards me, when the female said 'No, not him, him' pointing towards Ron, who is another employee at the grandstand. The male came round the gate, spoke to Ron saying 'Did you touch my daughter?' Before Ron could answer, the male hit Ron at least twice in the face, then he fell to the floor. The male and the rest of the party left the stadium.

The statement ended with a description of the defendant. It is common ground that the reference to 'Ron' was to Mr Ronald Barham.

The defendant was arrested at the White Lion public house shortly after the incident. He was interviewed at the police station. The interview was recorded. He agreed that he had assaulted a security guard at the stadium. He described his daughter coming to the public house with a complaint that she had been grabbed round the throat. He went round to Wimbledon Stadium. He continued:

> I asked a few people, the guards, if they had attacked my daughter. Eventually the guy came through from the back and raised his hands. I didn't know if he was going to grab me so I raised my hands to protect myself. We had a sort of struggle and then he went down on the floor. It was as simple as that. I did tug him. I did ask him if he had strangled my daughter.

He was asked if he had punched the guard in the face and said, 'not intentionally.' He was told that witnesses had claimed that he had punched the guard twice and his reply was that that could not be the case. There had not been, according to him, two deliberate punches. He had just pushed him away.

At the trial the defendant gave evidence and called witnesses. He said that Barham was coming towards him with his fists clenched at chest height. The defendant hit Barham because he thought that he was going to be hit by Barham. His daughter Michelle gave evidence and supported the account given by the defendant. Charles Mason gave evidence to the same effect. Mason had seen Barham coming forward with his hands raised and he thought that the defendant was going to be hit by Barham. He saw one blow at least which the defendant had struck.

The defendant was convicted by a unanimous verdict of the jury.

The sole ground of appeal was based upon the alleged wrongful admission in evidence of the statement of Mr Luff. It was rightly acknowledged by Mr Blaxland on behalf of the defendant that if the statement was properly admitted the judge's direction with reference to it was correct and fair. The judge said:

> As far as Mr Luff's statement is concerned, you have heard it read out. It has these obvious limitations; when someone's statement is read out you do not have the opportunity of seeing that person in the witness box and sometimes when you see someone in the witness box you get a very much clearer opinion of whether or not

that person is sincere and honest and accurate. Furthermore, when that evidence is tested under cross-examination you may get an even clearer view. Sometimes cross-examination takes away very much from a witness's reliability, sometimes it adds to it so you can say, 'despite the testing I am absolutely certain he is right,' but that process cannot happen in the present case because Mr Luff is dead so I would suggest to you that you cannot possibly pay as much attention to Mr Luff's evidence as anybody else but for what it is worth let me summarise it.

The judge then referred to the substance of the statement.

So far as we are aware, this is the first occasion upon which this court has had to consider the meaning and effect of the sections contained in Part II of the Criminal Justice Act 1988 under which the issue in this appeal is to be decided. The particular provision under which the judge ruled that Mr Luff's statement should be admitted was section 26 of the Act of 1988, of which the heading and provisions are as follows:

[His Lordship cited s. 26 and continued . . .]

The contention for the defendant has been that the judge misdirected himself in his approach to the question whether the statement should be admitted, because the judge took into consideration the fact that the defendant might, if he chose, by his own evidence or that of other witnesses, controvert the statement of Mr Luff. Further it has been said that no judge, properly exercising his discretion in the circumstances of this case, could have allowed this statement to be read to the jury.

The application for leave to put the statement in was apparently made at the commencement of the trial.

There will be cases in which the prosecution will need to know whether or not a statement will be admitted before a decision is made as to what other witnesses should be called, or upon the order of calling those witnesses. Notice of the intention to make the application should of course be given to the accused. It will, we think, in many cases be convenient for the application to be made and decided in the course of the hearing at the point at which it is desired to put the statement before the jury. The court will then often have a better understanding of the evidential issues and of the likely course of the hearing; but the defence may in some cases wish the question as to the admission of the document to be decided at the commencement of the hearing so that decisions can be taken by the defence as to the necessary course of cross-examination of the witnesses who are to be called.

. . .

The first ground of appeal advanced by Mr Blaxland was that the judge took into account an irrelevant consideration, namely the availability of other witnesses to controvert the statement of Mr Luff, including witnesses for the defence. The availability of possible defence evidence was irrelevant and any question as to its existence tended to place pressure upon the defence to call evidence which pressure was improper: reference was made to *Reg.* v *Keenan* [1989] 3 WLR 1193.

Mr Blaxland submitted that with reference to the availability of witnesses, the only relevant consideration on the matter of 'any risk, having regard in particular to whether it is likely to be possible to controvert the statement . . . that its admission . . . will result in unfairness to the accused . . .', was whether any witness would be called for the prosecution to whom questions could be put in cross-examination. Mr Blaxland conceded that there were such witnesses, namely Mr Barham and Mr Phillips, but if the judge had considered only that possibility, he must have concluded that it would not be in the interests of justice to admit the statement. It was, it was submitted, unfair to the defendant to admit the statement because it gave support to Barham's account while depriving the defendant of any effective opportunity to challenge the accuracy of the statement.

On this part of his submissions Mr Blaxland relied upon *Reg.* v *Blithing*, 77 Cr App R 86. He acknowledged that that decision was dealing with what is technically a different discretion but he submitted that the view of the court of the essential unfairness of permitting important evidence to be admitted when the defendant is deprived of the opportunity to cross-examine should be followed and applied by this court in this case.

Our attention was drawn to the decision of the Privy Council in *Scott* v *The Queen* [1989] AC 1242, a case concerned with the discretion of the court in Jamaica to exclude a statement made admissible by a statutory provision similar to the unamended provisions of section 13(3) of the Act of 1925. In giving the judgment of the Board, Lord Griffiths made reference to a number of decisions in which, in this court, a deposition had been excluded. After reference to *Reg.* v *Linley* [1959] Crim LR 123 and to *Reg.* v *O'Loughlin* [1988] 3 All ER 431, Lord Griffiths continued, at pp. 1257–1258:

> In *Reg.* v *Blithing* [1984] RTR 18 the Court of Appeal allowed an appeal on the ground that the trial judge should have exercised his discretion to exclude a statement tendered in committal proceedings . . . The Court of Appeal held that the discretion should be exercised to ensure that the defendant received a fair trial . . . Their Lordships are very doubtful whether they would have exercised the discretion in the same way as the Court of Appeal on the facts of that case but do not dissent from the proposition that the discretion should be exercised to ensure a fair trial for the accused.'

In a further passage, Lord Griffiths continued, at pp. 1258–1259:

> In the light of these authorities their Lordships are satisfied that the discretion of a judge to ensure a fair trial includes a power to exclude the admission of a deposition. It is, however, a power that should be exercised with great restraint. The mere fact that the deponent will not be available for cross-examination is obviously an insufficient ground for excluding the deposition for that is a feature common to the admission of all depositions which must have been contemplated and accepted by the legislature when it gave statutory sanction to their admission in evidence . . . It will of course be necessary in every case to warn the jury that they have not had the benefit of hearing the evidence of the deponent tested in cross-examination and to take that into consideration when considering how far they can safely rely on the evidence in the deposition. No doubt in many cases it will be appropriate for a judge to develop this warning by pointing out the particular features of the evidence in the deposition which conflict with other evidence and which could have been explored in cross-examination: but no rules can usefully be laid down to control the detail to which a judge should descend in the individual case.

The reference to exercising with great restraint the discretion to exclude a deposition in the case of the statutory discretion under consideration in *Scott's* case, is clearly, we think, not applicable to the discretion of the court under section 26. Mr Blaxland invited this court to follow and apply the view expressed in *Reg.* v *Blithing*, 77 Cr App R 86 as to the necessity to exclude a statement of which the contents were 'heavily prejudicial' to the defendant and with reference to which he was deprived of the opportunity to cross-examine.

Next Mr Blaxland submitted that by directing himself by reference to the test 'will the defendant have a fair trial,' the judge had failed to apply the right test. He should, in particular, have had regard to the question whether there was 'any risk' (see section

26(ii)) having regard to the loss of the opportunity for the defendant to cross-examine Mr Luff, that the admission of the statement would result in unfairness. Having regard to the importance of the statement in the proceedings there was, it was said, plainly such a risk of resulting unfairness that the judge, properly directing himself, must have excluded it.

We do not accept the conclusion to which Mr Blaxland's submissions were directed. The nature of the discretion to be exercised by the court under sections 25 and 26 of the Act of 1988, and the matters to which in exercising that discretion the court is required to have regard, have been laid down by Parliament and, in the view of this court, are clearly expressed. There will be difficulty in applying those provisions to the facts of particular cases.

The overall purpose of the provisions was to widen the power of the court to admit documentary hearsay evidence while ensuring that the accused receives a fair trial. In judging how to achieve the fairness of the trial a balance must on occasions be struck between the interests of the public in enabling the prosecution case to be properly presented and the interest of a particular defendant in not being put in a disadvantageous position, for example by the death or illness of a witness. The public of course also has a direct interest in the proper protection of the individual accused. The point of balance, as directed by Parliament, is set out in the sections.

It is not of course the case that these provisions are available only to enable the prosecution to put evidence before the court. A defendant also may wish to make use of the provisions, in order to get before the jury documentary evidence which would not otherwise be admissible.

Next, some comment on the structure of these sections is necessary. By section 25, if, having regard to all the circumstances, the court is of the opinion that a statement, admissible by virtue of section 23 or section 24, 'in the interests of justice ought not to be admitted,' it may direct that it be not admitted. The court is then, in considering that question, directed to have regard to the list of matters set out in section 25(2). They include 'any risk' of unfairness caused by admission or exclusion of the statement 'having regard in particular to whether it is likely to be possible to controvert the statement if the person making it does not attend.' In short the court must be made to hold the opinion that the statement ought not to be admitted.

By contrast under section 26, which deals with documents prepared for purpose of criminal proceedings or investigations, when a statement is admissible in criminal proceedings by virtue of section 23 or section 24, and was prepared for the purposes of criminal proceedings, the statement shall not be given in evidence unless the court is of opinion that the statement *ought to be admitted in the interests of justice.* The matters to which the court must have regard have been set out above and they include, again, 'any risk' of unfairness caused by admission or exclusion having regard to the possibility of controverting the statement. Again, in short, the court is not to admit the statement unless made to hold the opinion that in the interests of justice it *ought to be admitted.* The emphasis is the other way round.

The first submission of Mr Blaxland was that the words 'whether it is likely to be possible to controvert the statement if the person making it does not attend' contemplate only, and should be restricted to, the possibility of controverting the statement by cross-examination directed to witnesses to be called for the prosecution.

We reject that submission. We see no reason to imply any such restriction upon the plain meaning of the words. The meaning of 'controvert' includes that of 'dispute' or 'contradict.' The court is entitled, in our judgment, to have regard to such information as it has at the time that the application is made which shows 'whether it is likely to be possible to controvert the statement' in the absence of the ability to cross-examine the maker. The court cannot require to be told whether the accused intends to give evidence or to call witnesses, but the court is not required, in our judgment, to assess the possibility of controverting the statement upon the basis that the accused will not give evidence or call witnesses known to be available to him. The decision by an accused whether or not to give evidence or to call witnesses is to be made by him by reference to the admissible evidence put before the court; and the accused has no right, as we think, for the purposes of this provision, to be treated as having no possibility of controverting the statement because of his right not to give evidence or to call witnesses. If Parliament had intended the question to be considered on that basis, express words would, we think, have been used to make the intention clear.

This question however is only one part of a complex balancing exercise which the court must perform. For example the fact that the court concludes that it is likely to be possible for the accused to controvert the statement if the person making it cannot be cross-examined does not mean that the court will therefore necessarily be of opinion that admission of the statement will not result in unfairness to the accused or that the statement ought not to be admitted in the interests of justice.

The court must consider the contents of the statement, as explained in *Reg.* v *Blithing*, 77 Cr App R 86, where the court was concerned with section 13(3) of the Act of 1925; the statement may leave relevant questions unanswered and appear to provide evidence of greater certainty than is warranted having regard to the absence of those answers. As Lord Griffiths observed in *Scott* v *The Queen* [1989] AC 1242, 1259, after reference to a need for proper warnings when a statement is admitted:

> It is the quality of the evidence in the deposition that is the crucial factor that should determine the exercise of the discretion. By way of example if the deposition contains evidence of identification that is so weak that a judge in the absence of corroborative evidence would withdraw the case from the jury; then, if there is no corroborative evidence the judge should exercise his discretion to refuse to admit the deposition for it would be unsafe to allow the jury to convict upon it.

Thus the weight to be attached to the inability to cross-examine and the magnitude of any consequential risk that admission of the statement will result in unfairness to the accused, will depend in part upon the court's assessment of the quality of the evidence shown by the contents of the statement. Each case, as is obvious, must turn upon its own facts. The court should, we accept, consider whether, as was the court's view in *Reg.* v *Blithing*, the inability to probe a statement by cross-examination of the maker of it must be regarded as having such consequences, having regard to the terms and substance of the statement in the light of the issues in the case, that for that reason the statement should be excluded.

In considering a submission to that effect the court is entitled, and in our view required, to consider how far any potential unfairness, arising from the inability to cross-examine on the particular statement, may be effectively counter-balanced by the sort of warning and explanation in the summing up described by Lord Griffiths and in fact given by the judge in this case. The court will also, for example, consider whether, having regard to other evidence available to the prosecution, the interests of justice will be properly served by excluding the statement.

We do not think that the decision in *Reg.* v *Keenan* [1989] 3 WLR 1193 cited above requires us to reach any different conclusion. That case was concerned with evidence obtained in circumstances where there had been breaches of the provisions of the Code of Practice for the Detention Treatment and Questioning of Persons by Police Officers and the relationship between section 78(1) of the Police and Criminal

Evidence Act 1984 and the provisions of that Code of Practice. For the reasons we have given it is our view that in exercising its discretion under section 26 the court is not required to disregard the likelihood of the possibility of controverting the statement by the evidence of the accused or of witnesses called on his behalf.

We conclude that the judge did not err in law by having regard to the likelihood of it being possible for the defendant to controvert the statement of Mr Luff by himself giving evidence and by calling the evidence of other witnesses.

As to the submission that the judge misdirected himself by failing to direct himself exclusively by reference to the provisions of section 26, the judge's attention was directed to the section, and we have no doubt that he intended to apply the principles there stated. For the reasons which we have given, those were the primary principles by which the judge was required to direct himself in this case and that has been Mr Blaxland's submission before this court. The judge considered the 'fair trial' point because the matter had been put forward before him in those terms on behalf of the accused.

It would have been better, we think, if he had referred expressly to the terms of section 26, but we are satisfied that there was here no irregularity and that the conviction is not in any way unsafe. The judge asked himself whether it had been shown that it was in the interests of justice that the statement be admitted. He clearly thought that the risk of unfairness, having regard to the availability of other witnesses for cross-examination and of other evidence, was minimal. It was, in the view of the judge, in the interests of justice for the jury to be given the fuller picture provided by the statement, subject of course to the necessary warning. That was a conclusion which, in our judgment, the judge was fully entitled to reach.

For these reasons this appeal is dismissed.

Question
Does s. 25 create a presumption that the document will be admissible?

Note
In the earlier case of *R v O'Loughlin* [1988] 3 All ER 431, Kenneth Jones J sitting at first instance, was called upon to consider the operation of s. 13(3) of the Criminal Justice Act 1925. This section provides that, subject to certain conditions, the deposition of a witness taken before examining justices may be read as evidence at the subsequent trial. One of the conditions which may lead to the deposition being admissible is if the prosecution are able to prove that the witness who made the deposition is 'kept out of the way'. The Criminal Justice Act 1988 contains a similar condition in s. 23(3)(b), namely that the statement in the document shall be admissible if 'the person who made it does not give oral evidence through *fear* or because he is *kept out of the way*' (emphasis added).

In construing this phrase in the context of the 1925 Act, the learned judge held that in order to establish that a witness has been 'kept out of the way', the prosecution must adduce admissible evidence from a credible witness. Accordingly, police officers were not allowed to testify about threats which the absent witnesses had told others they had received in order to prove they had been kept out of the way. This would have been permitting the police officers to give hearsay evidence. There is no reason to suppose that the same reasoning will not be adopted by the courts when considering s. 23(3)(b).

Questions
1. If the note above correctly states the law, how will the prosecution ever be able to establish that a witness does not give oral evidence through *fear* or because he is *kept out of the way?*
2. If PC John visits W's home and W tells him, 'I'm not coming to court to give evidence because D has threatened to beat me up', will the prosecution be able to establish that either of the requirements of s. 23(3) is satisfied?

(See also *Neill* v *Northern Antrim Magistrates' Court* [1993] Crim LR 945, HL.)

(ii)   Documentary evidence produced by computer

Police and Criminal Evidence Act 1984

69.   Evidence from computer records
(1)   In any proceedings, a statement in a document produced by a computer shall not be admissible as evidence of any fact stated therein unless it is shown —
(a)   that there are no reasonable grounds for believing that the statement is inaccurate because of improper use of the computer;
(b)   that at all material times the computer was operating properly, or if not, that any respect in which it was not operating properly or was out of operation was not such as to affect the production of the document or the accuracy of its contents; and
(c)   that any relevant conditions specified in rules of court under subsection (2) below are satisfied.
(2)   Provision may be made by rules of court requiring that in any proceedings where it is desired to give a statement in evidence by virtue of this section such information concerning the statement as may be required by the rules shall be provided in such form and at such time as may be so required.

SCHEDULE 3
PROVISIONS SUPPLEMENTARY TO SECTION 69

8.   In any proceedings where it is desired to give a statement in evidence in accordance with section 69 above, a certificate —
(a)   identifying the document containing the statement and describing the manner in which it was produced;
(b)   giving such particulars of any device involved in the production of that document as may be appropriate for the purpose of showing that the document was produced by a computer;
(c)   dealing with any of the matters mentioned in subsection (1) of section 69 above; and
(d)   purporting to be signed by a person occupying a responsible position in relation to the operation of the computer,
shall be evidence of anything stated in it; and for the purposes of this paragraph it shall be sufficient for a matter to be stated to the best of the knowledge and belief of the person stating it.
9.   Notwithstanding paragraph 8 above, a court may require oral evidence to be given of anything of which evidence could be given by a certificate under that paragraph. . . .

11. In estimating the weight, if any, to be attached to a statement regard shall be had to all the circumstances from which any inference can reasonably be drawn as to the accuracy or otherwise of the statement and, in particular —

(a) to the question whether or not the information which the information contained in the statement reproduces or is derived from was supplied to the relevant computer, or recorded for the purpose of being supplied to it, contemporaneously with the occurrence or existence of the facts dealt with in that information; and

(b) to the question whether or not any person concerned with the supply of information to that computer, or with the operation of that computer or any equipment by means of which the document containing the statement was produced by it, had any incentive to conceal or misrepresent the facts.

12. For the purposes of paragraph 11 above information shall be taken to be supplied to a computer whether it is supplied directly or (with or without human intervention) by means of any appropriate equipment.

13. Where in any proceedings a statement contained in a document is admissible in evidence . . . in accordance with section 69 above it may be proved —

(a) by the production of that document; or

(b) (whether or not that document is still in existence) by the production of a copy of that document, or of the material part of it,

authenticated in such manner as the court may approve.

14. For the purpose of deciding whether or not a statement is so admissible the court may draw any reasonable inference —

(a) from the circumstances in which the statement was made or otherwise came into being; or

(b) from any other circumstances, including the form and contents of the document in which the statement is contained.

15. Provision may be made by rules of court for supplementing the provisions of section . . . 69 above or this Schedule.

Note

A statement contained in a document which has been produced by a computer may or may not be hearsay. Some cases have demonstrated confusion on the part of the courts as to the hearsay issues (*R v Pettigrew* (1980) 70 Cr App R 39, *R v Spiby* (1990) 91 Cr App R 186). If the computer is doing no more than collecting, recording and processing information automatically, without any input of facts from a human mind, it is not hearsay. The document produced must, however, comply with the requirements of s. 69 irrespective of whether or not it is hearsay. An example of such a document would be that produced by the computer of an hotel which records guests' telephone calls. If the document produced by a computer relies for its contents on the input of facts supplied by a human mind and it is sought to rely on the facts contained in the document as evidence of their truth, then the document must comply with the relevant provision of the Criminal Justice Act 1988 *and* s. 69 of the Police and Criminal Evidence Act 1984.

R v Shepherd
[1993] 1 All ER 225
House of Lords

LORD GRIFFITHS: My Lords, the Court of Appeal has certified the following point of law of general public importance:

Whether a party seeking to rely on computer evidence can discharge the burden under section 69(1)(b) of the Police and Criminal Evidence Act 1984 without calling a computer expert, and if so how?

The point of law falls to be considered against the following background of fact. The appellant was arrested at her home at Maple Cross, Rickmansworth at about 5.30 p.m. on 17 March 1989. In her car were goods from Marks & Spencers worth £78.36. The goods consisted of various items of food, including a joint of beef priced at £12.57 and five items of clothing. The appellant had no receipt. In an initial interview on 17 March 1989 she declined to answer questions. She was interviewed again on 29 April 1989 when she said that she had bought the goods at Marks & Spencers at St Alban's. When she returned to her car the bags had split so she transferred the shopping to a bag of her own. She said she never kept receipts and denied stealing the goods.

The principal evidence for the prosecution was given by a store detective employed by Marks & Spencers at their St Alban's branch. She said that at 10 a.m. on the morning of 18 March she removed all the till rolls from the tills and recovered a further two till rolls from a cupboard which bore the date 17 March. She explained that the tills were connected to a central computer which fed in the date, time, customer number and till number on each of the till rolls.

She further explained that each item of clothing has upon it a seven-figure numbered label known as a unique product code or UPC. The UPC numbers are unique to clothing of a particular type, size and colour. The till operator punches in the UPC number on the till, which then registers the appropriate price.

In the case of food each item of food has a price upon it and the operator punches in the price of each item on the till. She said they had had no trouble with the operation of the central computer.

She carried out an examination of all the till rolls which she had recovered from the tills which would have been those in use on 17 March and stamped as such by the central computer and she also examined the two till rolls also stamped and dated 17 March which had been placed in the cupboard where all used till rolls were kept. She thus examined all the tills rolls in use on 17 March.

She said that there was no trace on the till rolls of the UPCs for the clothing found in the appellant's car. She said there was no record on any of the till rolls of an item of food costing £12.57, the price of the beef. Nor was there any group of prices matching the items of food found in the car.

It was quite apparent from the store detective's evidence that she was thoroughly familiar with the operation of these tills and of the computer, albeit she did not pretend to any technical understanding of the operation of the computer.

The appellant did not herself give evidence and no evidence was called on her behalf. The jury convicted her. If the till rolls were properly admitted in evidence this is hardly surprising for they provided the most powerful evidence of guilt.

It is however submitted that the till rolls should not have been admitted in evidence because the store detective's evidence did not satisfy the provisions of s. 69 of the Criminal Evidence Act 1984. . . .

The object of s. 69 of the Act is clear enough. It requires anyone who wishes to introduce computer evidence to produce evidence that will establish that it is safe to rely on the documents produced by the computer. This is an affirmative duty emphatically stated (sub-s. (1)):

> . . . a statement in a document produced by a computer shall not be admissible as evidence of any fact stated therein *unless it is shown* . . .

Such a duty cannot be discharged without evidence by the application of the presumption that the computer is working correctly expressed in the maxim *omnia praesumuntur rite esse acta* as appears to be suggested in some of the cases. Nor does it make any difference whether the computer document has been produced with or without the input of information provided by the human mind and thus may or may not be hearsay. If the document produced by the computer is hearsay it will be necessary to comply with the provisions of s. 24 of the Criminal Justice Act 1988, the successor to s. 68 of the Police and Criminal Evidence Act 1984, before the document can be admitted as evidence and it will also be necessary to comply with the provisions of s. 69 of the 1984 Act. I see no warrant for an interpretation of the 1984 Act which limits the operation of s. 69 to cases that fall within s. 68 of that Act or s. 24 of the Criminal Justice Act 1988. This however was the construction of the 1984 Act adopted by the Court of Appeal in *R v Minors, R v Harper* [1989] 2 All ER 208, [1989] 1 WLR 441 and which has been followed in a number of subsequent cases most notably *R v Spiby* (1990) 91 Cr App R 186 and *R v Neville* [1991] Crim LR 288.

In *R v Minors* [1989] 2 All ER 208 at 212, [1989] 1 WLR 441 at 446 it is stated in the judgment:

> . . . to the extent to which a computer is merely used to perform functions of calculation, no question of hearsay is involved and the requirements of ss 68 and 69 do not apply: see *R v Wood* (1982) 76 Cr App R 23 and *Sophocleous v Ringer* [1988] RTR 52.

I do not think that these authorities give any support to the proposition that s. 69 does not apply. *R v Wood* deals with the circumstances in which the contents of a computer print-out are to be regarded as real rather than hearsay evidence. It naturally does not touch upon the requirements of s. 69 as the 1984 Act had not yet been enacted. In *Sophocleous v Ringer* the accused was charged with driving after consuming so much alcohol that the proportion of it in his breath exceeded the prescribed limit. Evidence was given against him by an analyst who had analysed a specimen of his blood through a technology known as gas chromatography for which a computer is used. She was permitted to refresh her memory by looking at the graph produced by the computer during the course of her work. The graph was not put in evidence by the prosecution nor did the defence require it to be exhibited. As the graph had not been put in evidence the court rightly pointed out that s. 69 had no application on the facts of that case. I would add that if the graph had been made an exhibit in that case, the analyst would have been well-qualified to give the necessary evidence under s. 69 (as will appear from later passages in my speech).

In a later passage of the judgment the court said ([1989] 2 All ER 208 at 212, [1989] 1 WLR 441 at 446):

> In the courts below it was assumed by all concerned that s. 69 constitutes a self-contained code governing the admissibility of computer records in criminal proceedings. Undoubtedly, that is a legislative technique which Parliament could have adopted. The question is whether Parliament *did* adopt it. (The court's emphasis.)

The court then gave as its reason for confining the operation of s. 69 to cases falling within s. 68 the fact that in *R v Ewing* [1983] 2 All ER 645, [1983] QB 1039 a computer print-out of an appellant's bank account was held admissible under s. 1 of the Criminal Evidence Act 1965 which was the forerunner of s. 68 of the 1984 Act from which the court drew the inference that Parliament must therefore have intended

s. 69 to apply only to computer documents falling within the meaning of s. 68. I cannot accept this reasoning. When *R* v *Ewing* was decided the safeguards later introduced by s. 69 had not yet been enacted and I see no reason to suppose that because of the decision in *R* v *Ewing* Parliament intended the language of s. 69 which is in general terms to be read in a restricted sense. It is surely every bit as important that a document produced by a computer and tendered as proof of guilt should be reliable whether or not it contains hearsay. In *R* v *Spiby* (1990) 91 Cr App R 186 the accused was charged with smuggling drugs into this country. As a part of the proof of his guilt the prosecution wished to show he was in touch with an accomplice in France. They invited the jury to draw this inference from a computer print-out that recorded a number of telephone calls made from a hotel in Cherbourg at which the accomplice was staying to the accused's home in England. The computer did not record the contents of the conversations but it did show the date, the time, the number of the hotel room from which the call was made, the number to which the call was made in England; not, the duration and the cost. It seems to me as important to have an assurance that the computer was recording this information accurately as it would if the computer had also recorded the conversation. The important link in the chain of evidence was not what these men said to each other but the fact that they were in constant touch with one another and for this the prosecution was relying solely on the reliability of the computer record. In such circumstances evidence to satisfy s. 69 is required and in so far as *R* v *Spiby* holds to the contrary it should not be followed; furthermore affirmative evidence is required and it is not sufficient to rely on the presumption expressed in the Latin phrase *omnia praesumuntur rite esse acta*. In fact there was satisfactory evidence given by the sub-manager of the hotel who was familiar with the operation of the computer and could speak to its reliability.

I therefore approach this question upon the basis that if the prosecution wish to rely upon a document produced by a computer they must comply with s. 69 in all cases.

The principal argument for the appellant starts with the proposition that the store detective was not 'a person occupying a responsible position in relation to the operation of the computer' within the meaning of para. 8(d) of Sch. 3 and therefore was not qualified to sign a certificate for the purpose of providing proof of the matters contained in s. 69(1). This I accept. Although the store detective understood the operation of the computer and could speak of its reliability she had no responsibility for its operation.

I cannot however accept the next step in the appellant's argument, which is that oral evidence is only acceptable if given by a person who is qualified to sign the certificate. The appellant does not go so far as to submit that evidence must be given by a computer expert but insists that it must be someone who has responsibility for the operation of the computer, either the operator or someone with managerial responsibility for the operation of the computer.

Proof that the computer is reliable can be provided in two ways: either by calling oral evidence or by tendering a written certificate in accordance with the terms of para. 8 of Sch. 3, subject to the power of the judge to require oral evidence. It is understandable that if a certificate is to be relied upon it should show on its face that it is signed by a person who from his job description can confidently be expected to be in a position to give reliable evidence about the operation of the computer. This enables the defendant to decide whether to accept the certificate at its face value or to ask the judge to require oral evidence which can be challenged in cross-examination. A defendant seeing a certificate signed by a store detective would not necessarily assume that such a person was familiar with the operation of the computer or had any responsibility for it and might well challenge the certificate. It does not however follow that the store detective cannot in fact give evidence that shows she is fully familiar with the operation of the store's computer and can speak to its reliability.

The appellant's argument requires one to read into s. 69(1) after the words 'unless it is shown' the following words lifted from para. 8 of Sch. 3: 'by [the oral evidence of] a person occupying a responsible position in relation to the operation of the computer'.

These words do not appear in the section. They are, for the reasons I have given, contained in Sch. 3 as a necessary qualification to sign a certificate but I can see no reason to read them into s. 69(1) when oral evidence will be open to challenge by cross-examination.

Documents produced by computers are an increasingly common feature of all business and more and more people are becoming familiar with their uses and operation. Computers vary immensely in their complexity and in the operations they perform. The nature of the evidence to discharge the burden of showing that there has been no improper use of the computer and that it was operating properly will inevitably vary from case to case. The evidence must be tailored to suit the needs of the case. I suspect that it will very rarely be necessary to call an expert and that in the vast majority of cases it will be possible to discharge the burden by calling a witness who is familiar with the operation of the computer in the sense of knowing what the computer is required to do and who can say that it is doing it properly.

The computer in this case was of the simplest kind printing limited basic information on each till roll. The store detective was able to describe how the tills operated, what the computer did, that there had been no trouble with the computer and how she had also examined all the till rolls, which showed no evidence of malfunction either by the tills or the central computer.

In these circumstances I agree with the Court of Appeal that she was fully qualified to give the evidence required by s. 69 and that in the light of her evidence the till rolls were properly admitted as part of the prosecution case.

I therefore answer the certified question by saying that s. 69(1) of the Police and Criminal Evidence Act 1984 can be satisfied by the oral evidence of a person familiar with the operation of the computer who can give evidence of its reliability and such a person need not be a computer expert.

For these reasons I would dismiss this appeal.

LORD EMSLIE: My Lords, I have had the advantage of reading in draft the speech of my noble and learned friend Lord Griffiths. I entirely agree with him and for the reasons which he gives I, too, would dismiss this appeal.

LORD ROSKILL: My Lords, I have had the advantage of reading in draft the speech of my noble and learned friend Lord Griffiths. I agree with him and for the reasons which he gives I, too, would dismiss this appeal.

LORD ACKNER: My Lords, I have had the advantage of reading in draft the speech of my noble and learned friend Lord Griffiths. I agree with it and, for the reasons given by my noble and learned friend, I, too, would answer the certified question in the way that he has done and would dismiss the appeal.

LORD LOWRY: My Lords, I have had the advantage of reading in draft the speech of my noble and learned friend Lord Griffiths. I agree with it and, for the reasons given by my noble and learned friend, I, too, would answer the certified question in the way that he has done and would dismiss the appeal.

Questions
1. Peter attends a football match at Greenside United's stadium. As each spectator enters the ground through the turnstiles, a signal is automatically

sent to a computer database and the number of spectators entering the ground is recorded. Peter receives severe crush injuries caused by the large crowd pushing forward when Greenside score a goal. The local Health and Safety Executive have previously certified that the maximum safe crowd capacity at the ground is 30,000. The computer printout shows that on the relevant day, 37,000 people had passed through the turnstiles.

(a)   If Peter sues the football club for negligence, will the computer printout be admissible in evidence, and if so, admissible evidence of what?

(b)   If the Health and Safety Executive prosecute the football club for exceeding the ground's safe capacity, will the computer printout be admissible in evidence, and if so, admissible evidence of what?

(c)   Would your answer to (a) or (b) above differ if turnstile operators each pressed a button whenever a spectator entered the ground, in order to signal that fact to the computer?

2.   Harold is a delivery driver employed by Sparks plc. While out making his deliveries, he sees a collision occur between two cars, one of which drives away from the scene. Harold is certain that the car which drives away is a white Sierra. A witness, Ian, says to Harold, 'I got the number of that car that drove off, it's L123 ABC'. Harold writes the number down on a spare page in his delivery record book. The number is traced and found to belong to a white Sierra car owned by David. David is prosecuted for several motoring offences but denies he was involved in the incident. Would the delivery book be admissible, and if so, admissible evidence of what?

Further reading
P. Murphy, *A Practical Approach to Evidence*, 4th ed. (1992), Ch. 8
D. Birch, 'The Criminal Justice Act 1988' [1989] Crim LR 15
M. Ockleton, 'Documentary Hearsay in Criminal Cases' [1992] Crim LR 15

10 CONFESSIONS

A confession may be admitted into evidence as an exception to the rule against hearsay. The principles of admissibility used to belong to the common law but are now contained in the Police and Criminal Evidence Act 1984. Many of the cases decided under the common law may continue to have some relevance to issues which arise under the Act, but space precludes any detailed treatment of those cases here. In particular, readers may wish to refer to *Ibrahim* v *R* [1914] AC 599 (PC); *Commissioners of Customs & Excise* v *Harz and Power* [1967] 1 AC 760 (HL); *DPP* v *Ping Lin* [1976] AC 574 (HL); *R* v *Rennie* [1982] 1 WLR 64 (CA); *R* v *Miller* [1986] 1 WLR 1191.

(A)   Admissibility of confessions

The law which governs the admissibility of a confession is now contained in s. 76 of the Police and Criminal Evidence Act 1984. In essence, s. 76 introduces two 'hurdles' which must be overcome as a precursor to admissibility. The prosecution must prove beyond reasonable doubt that the confession was not obtained by 'oppression' or as a consequence of 'anything said or done which was likely . . . to render unreliable any confession'. The latter hurdle is frequently referred to as 'the reliability ground'. Section 76 must also be read in conjunction with the definition of 'confession' in s. 82, and consideration must also be given to the Codes of Practice issued under the authority of s. 66.

A further and somewhat unexpected development in this area has concerned s. 78(1) of the Act. This section provides the court with a discretion to exclude any evidence on which the prosecution propose to rely if the court considers its admission will have an adverse effect on the fairness of the proceedings (see also Chapter 1(B)). The courts now frequently consider both s. 76 and s. 78 together when ruling upon the admissibility of a confession.

Police and Criminal Evidence Act 1984

76. Confessions

(1) In any proceedings a confession made by an accused person may be given in evidence against him in so far as it is relevant to any matter in issue in the proceedings and is not excluded by the court in pursuance of this section.

(2) If, in any proceedings where the prosecution proposes to give in evidence a confession made by an accused person, it is represented to the court that the confession was or may have been obtained —

(a) by oppression of the person who made it; or

(b) in consequence of anything said or done which was likely, in the circumstances existing at the time, to render unreliable any confession which might be made by him in consequence thereof,

the court shall not allow the confession to be given in evidence against him except in so far as the prosecution proves to the court beyond reasonable doubt that the confession (notwithstanding that it may be true) was not obtained as aforesaid.

(3) In any proceedings where the prosecution proposes to give in evidence a confession made by an accused person, the court may of its own motion require the prosecution, as a condition of allowing it to do so, to prove that the confession was not obtained as mentioned in subsection (2) above.

(4) The fact that a confession is wholly or partly excluded in pursuance of this section shall not affect the admissibility in evidence —

(a) of any facts discovered as a result of the confession; or

(b) where the confession is relevant as showing that the accused speaks, writes or expresses himself in a particular way, of so much of the confession as is necessary to show that he does so.

(5) Evidence that a fact to which this subsection applies was discovered as a result of a statement made by an accused person shall not be admissible unless evidence of how it was discovered is given by him or on his behalf.

(6) Subsection (5) above applies —

(a) to any fact discovered as a result of a confession which is wholly excluded in pursuance of this section; and

(b) to any fact discovered as a result of a confession which is partly so excluded, if the fact is discovered as a result of the excluded part of the confession.

(7) Nothing in Part VII of this Act shall prejudice the admissibility of a confession made by an accused person.

(8) In this section 'oppression' includes torture, inhuman or degrading treatment, and the use or threat of violence (whether or not amounting to torture).

77. Confessions by mentally handicapped persons

(1) Without prejudice to the general duty of the court at a trial on indictment to direct the jury on any matter on which it appears to the court appropriate to do so, where at such a trial —

(a) the case against the accused depends wholly or substantially on a confession by him; and

(b) the court is satisfied —

(i) that he is mentally handicapped; and

(ii) that the confession was not made in the presence of an independent person, the court shall warn the jury that there is special need for caution before convicting the accused in reliance on the confession, and shall explain that the need arises because of the circumstances mentioned in paragraphs (a) and (b) above.

(2)   In any case where at the summary trial of a person for an offence it appears to the court that a warning under subsection (1) above would be required if the trial were on indictment, the court shall treat the case as one in which there is a special need for caution before convicting the accused on his confession.

(3)   In this section —
'independent person' does not include a police officer or a person employed for, or engaged on, police purposes;
'mentally handicapped', in relation to a person, means that he is in a state of arrested or incomplete development of mind which includes significant impairment of intelligence and social functioning; and
'police purposes' has the meaning assigned to it by section 64 of the Police Act 1964.

78.   Exclusion of unfair evidence

(1)   In any proceedings the court may refuse to allow evidence on which the prosecution proposes to rely to be given if it appears to the court that, having regard to all the circumstances, including the circumstances in which the evidence was obtained, the admission of the evidence would have such an adverse effect on the fairness of the proceedings that the court ought not to admit it.

(2)   Nothing in this section shall prejudice any rule of law requiring a court to exclude evidence.

82.   Part VIII — Interpretation

(1)   In this Part of this Act —
'confession', includes any statement wholly or partly adverse to the person who made it, whether made to a person in authority or not and whether made in words or otherwise; . . .

(3)   Nothing in this Part of this Act shall prejudice any power of a court to exclude evidence (whether by preventing questions being put or otherwise) at its discretion.

Questions
1.   Would a confession excluded under s. 76(2)(a) always fall to be excluded under s. 76(2)(b)?
2.   In s. 76(2)(b), the words 'anything said or done which was likely' were substituted for 'any threat or inducement of a sort likely' which appeared in a draft Bill. What difference does this make?
3.   Are the tests contained in s. 76(2) objective or subjective?

(i)   Oppression

R v Fulling
[1987] 2 WLR 923
Court of Appeal

At the appellant's trial the prosecution proposed to give evidence of a confession made by her after persistent questioning in police custody. She submitted that the confession should be ruled inadmissible under s. 76(2)(a) of the Police and Criminal Evidence Act 1984 in that the confession was or might have been obtained by oppression of her and the prosecution had not proved beyond reasonable doubt that the confession was not so obtained. The judge ruled that oppression meant something above and beyond what was inherently oppressive in police custody and imported some oppression actively applied in an improper manner by the police and that, even accepting the appellant's version of events as accurate, oppression could not be made out on the evidence. The submission was rejected and the appellant was convicted. She appealed.

LORD LANE CJ: . . . Mr Davey has drawn our attention to a number of authorities on the meaning of 'oppression.' Sachs LJ in *R v Priestley (Note)* (1966) 51 Cr App R 1 said, at pp. 1, 2-3:

> . . . to my mind [oppression] in the context of the principles under consideration imports something which tends to sap, and has sapped, that free will which must exist before a confession is voluntary. . . . the courts are not concerned with ascertaining the precise motive of a particular statement. The question before them is whether the prosecution have shown the statement to be voluntary, whatever the motive may be, and that is always the point to which all arguments must return. To solve it, the court has to look to the questions which I have already mentioned. First, was there in fact something which could properly be styled or might well be oppression? Secondly, did whatever happened in the way of oppression or likely oppression induce the statement in question?

R v Prager [1972] 1 WLR 260, was another decision on note (e) to the Judges' Rules 1964, which required that a statement by the defendant before being admitted in evidence must be proved to be 'voluntary' in the sense that it has not been obtained by fear of prejudice or hope of advantage or by oppression. Edmund Davies LJ, who delivered the judgment of the court, said, at p. 266:

> As we have already indicated, the criticism directed in the present case against the police is that their interrogation constituted 'oppression.' This word appeared for the first time in the Judges' Rules 1964, and it closely followed the observation of Lord Parker CJ in *Callis v Gunn* [1964] 1 QB 495, 501, condemning confessions 'obtained in an oppressive manner'.

Edmund Davies LJ, having cited the relevant passage from *R v Priestley (Note)*, 51 Cr App R 1 continued:

> In an address to the Bentham Club in 1968, Lord MacDermott described 'oppressive questioning' as 'questioning which by its nature, duration, or other attendant circumstances (including the fact of custody) excites hopes (such as the hope of release) or fears, or so affects the mind of the subject that his will crumbles and he speaks when otherwise he would have stayed silent.' We adopt these definitions or descriptions. . .

Director of Public Prosecutions v *Ping Lin* [1976] AC 574, was again a case in which the question was whether a statement by the defendant was shown to be voluntary. It was held that a trial judge faced by the problem should approach the task in a common sense way and should ask himself whether the prosecution had proved that the contested statement was voluntary in the sense that it was not obtained by fear of prejudice or hope of advantage excited or held out by a person in authority. Lord Wilberforce, Lord Morris of Borth-y-Gest and Lord Hailsham of St Marylebone expressed the opinion that:

> . . . it is not necessary, before a statement is held to be inadmissible because not shown to have been voluntary, that it should be thought or held that there was impropriety in the conduct of the person to whom the statement was made; . . .

What has to be considered is whether a statement is shown to have been voluntary rather than one brought about in one of the ways referred to.

Finally Mr Davey referred us to a judgment of this court in *R v Rennie* [1982] 1 WLR 64.

Mr Davey submits to us that on the strength of those decisions the basis of the judge's ruling was wrong; in particular when he held that the word 'oppression' means something above and beyond that which is inherently oppressive in police custody and must import some impropriety, some oppression actively applied in an improper manner by the police. It is submitted that that flies in the face of the opinions of their Lordships in *Director of Public Prosecutions v Ping Lin* [1976] AC 574.

The point is one of statutory construction. The wording of the Act of 1984 does not follow the wording of earlier rules or decisions, nor is it expressed to be a consolidating Act, nor yet to be declaratory of the common law. The preamble runs:

> An Act to make further provision in relation to the powers and duties of the police, persons in police detention, criminal evidence, police discipline and complaints against the police; to provide for arrangements for obtaining the views of the community on policing and for a rank of deputy chief constable; to amend the law relating to the Police Federations and Police Forces and Police Cadets in Scotland; and for connected purposes.

It is a codifying Act, and therefore the principles set out in *Bank of England v Vagliano Brothers* [1891] AC 107, 144 apply. Lord Herschell, having pointed out that the Bills of Exchange Act 1882 which was under consideration was intended to be a codifying Act, said, at pp. 144-145:

> I think the proper course is in the first instance to examine the language of the statute and to ask what is its natural meaning, uninfluenced by any considerations derived from the previous state of the law, and not to start with inquiring how the law previously stood, and then, assuming that it was probably intended to leave it unaltered, to see if the words of the enactment will bear an interpretation in conformity with this view. If a statute, intended to embody in a code a particular branch of the law, is to be treated in this fashion, it appears to me that its utility will be almost entirely destroyed, and the very object with which it was enacted will be frustrated. The purpose of such a statute surely was that on any point specifically dealt with by it, the law should be ascertained by interpreting the language used instead of, as before, by roaming over a vast number of authorities in order to discover what the law was, extracting it by a minute critical examination of the prior decisions, dependent upon a knowledge of the exact effect even of an obsolete proceeding such as a demurrer to evidence.

Similar observations are to be found in *Bristol Tramways & Carriage Co. Ltd v Fiat Motors Ltd* [1910] 2 KB 831, 836 *per* Cozens-Hardy MR.

Section 76(2) of the Act of 1984 distinguishes between two different ways in which a confession may be rendered inadmissible: (a) where it has been obtained by oppression; (b) where it has been made in consequence of anything said or done which was likely in the circumstances to render unreliable any confession which might be made by the defendant in consequence thereof. Paragraph (b) is wider than the old formulation, namely that the confession must be shown to be voluntary in the sense that it was not obtained by fear of prejudice or hope of advantage, excited or held out by a person in authority. It is wide enough to cover some of the circumstances which under the earlier rule were embraced by what seems to us to be the artificially wide definition of oppression approved in *R v Prager* [1972] 1 WLR 260.

This in turn leads us to believe that 'oppression' in section 76(2)(a) should be given its ordinary dictionary meaning. The *Oxford English Dictionary* as its third definition of the word runs as follows: 'Exercise of authority or power in a burdensome, harsh, or wrongful manner; unjust or cruel treatment of subjects, inferiors, etc.; the imposition of unreasonable or unjust burdens.' One of the quotations given under that paragraph runs as follows. 'There is not a word in our language which expresses more detestable wickedness than oppression.'

We find it hard to envisage any circumstances in which such oppression would not entail some impropriety on the part of the interrogator. We do not think that the judge was wrong in using that test. What however is abundantly clear is that a confession may be invalidated under section 76(2)(b) where there is no suspicion of impropriety. No reliance was placed on the words of section 76(2)(b) either before the judge at trial or before this court. Even if there had been such reliance, we do not consider that the policeman's remark was likely to make unreliable any confession of the appellant's own criminal activities, and she expressly exonerated — or tried to exonerate — her unfaithful lover.

In those circumstances, in the judgment of this court, the judge was correct to reject the submission made to him under section 76 of the Act of 1984.

Appeal dismissed.

Questions
1.   Why did the court in *Fulling* not refer to s. 76(8)?
2.   In order for a confession to be excluded under s. 76(2)(a), need there be any impropriety on the part of the police?

Note
There have been relatively few reported cases dealing with the concept of oppression as a primary issue. In *R v Emmerson* (1991) 92 Cr App R 284, the Court of Appeal rejected an argument that a police officer who had raised his voice and sworn at the defendant was guilty of oppressive conduct. It is clear that much will depend on the particular facts of the case. What may be oppressive to one defendant may not be oppressive to another. Further examples are provided by *R v Davison* [1988] Crim LR 442 and *R v Seelig* [1992] 1 WLR 148.

(ii)   Unreliable confessions

R v Goldenberg
(1989) 88 Cr App R 285
Court of Appeal

NEILL LJ: On September 8, 1987, at the Crown Court at Snaresbrook, the appellant, Meir Goldenberg, was convicted following a trial lasting eight days on an indictment charging him together with two other men with conspiracy to supply diamorphine. The other men were found not guilty. The appellant was convicted by a majority of ten to two.

On September 9, the appellant was sentenced to a term of six years' imprisonment and a confiscation order was made in the sum of £7,810, with a term of nine months' imprisonment to be served consecutively in default of payment.

The appellant now appeals against conviction by leave of the full Court, given on February 29, 1988 following refusal by the single judge.

On June 11, 1987, police officers, including Detective Sergeant McElwee, entered the appellant's first floor flat in North London. There they found the appellant. As the police officers entered the flat, he was seen by another officer, who was stationed at the rear of the premises, to come out on to a balcony and throw a small plastic bag and two pieces of silver foil on to the ground. The plastic bag was subsequently found to contain a small quantity of heroin in powder form. Inside the flat the police officers found a small brown block of heroin on a table. The appellant was arrested.

Meanwhile other police officers, including Detective Inspector Atkins and Detective Sergeant Leader, went to a house owned by the appellant in another part of North London and there arrested the other two men who were subsequently tried with him, Bishop and Butterworth. In the house the officers found a burnt spoon, a syringe and two pieces of paper on which were calculations which appeared to relate to drugs. In a drawer the officers found £1,600 in money. After being questioned Bishop and Butterworth were arrested and taken to Dalston police station.

Detective Inspector Atkins and Detective Sergeant Leader then drove to the appellant's flat and from there they took the appellant together with Detective Sergeant McElwee to Hackney police station. During the journey some conversation took place which was subsequently relied on by the Crown at the trial. Later that day the appellant was interviewed at Hackney police station by Detective Sergeant Leader in the presence of Detective Sergeant McElwee. A record of this interview was prepared but the appellant declined to read or to sign it.

Five days later, on June 16, 1987, the appellant was interviewed again. This interview took place at Boreham Wood police station at the request of the appellant. According to the record of this interview, Detective Sergeant Leader, who on this occasion was accompanied by Detective Sergeant Blackwell, started the interview with these words: 'We are here because I understand from your solicitor that you want to speak to us. This is a colleague, D.S. Blackwell. He will write down everything that is said. I must tell you that we cannot discuss the matter with which you have been charged. Do you understand?'

At the conclusion of the interview, in the course of which the appellant allegedly gave some information about a man who he said had supplied him with heroin, the appellant declined to read or sign the record prepared by Detective Sergeant Blackwell.

In support of the appeal counsel for the appellant advanced two grounds. We shall consider these grounds separately.

[The court then considered and dismissed the first ground of appeal and continued . . .]

The second ground of appeal concerned the interview which took place at Boreham Wood police station on June 16, 1987. At the trial counsel for the appellant sought to exclude evidence about this interview on the basis that it was unreliable. It was also argued at one stage that this evidence was not relevant and that its prejudicial effect outweighed its probative value.

The judge rejected these arguments in the following ruling:

Mr Pownall relies in substance on the basis that the evidence may be unreliable under section 76 of the Police and Criminal Evidence Act. He submitted initially that such evidence was not relevant and that its prejudicial value in any event outweighed its probative value. He did not pursue that ultimately, and rightly so, as the evidence in my view is obviously relevant and highly probative. Its only prejudicial value is that all that follows is admissions. I have to decide therefore the sole issue as to its reliability. Mr Pownall says that it may be unreliable because, on the face of it, the admissions in the interview are an attempt to get bail and, secondly, that as Mr Goldenberg was a heroin addict and as he had been in custody for some weeks, it might be expected that he would do or say anything, however false, to get bail, presumably thus to be able to feed his addiction. The earlier admissions by Mr Goldenberg seem to me highly relevant. He accepted in those earlier admissions following shortly after his arrest that in substance he had acquired heroin in order to sell that on through his co-defendants but at that early stage was not prepared to go into any further details. In these admissions he does go into some further detail but seems to limit those details, suggesting that he can only provide the fullness of them if and when granted bail. It seems to me, therefore, that this confession is perfectly consistent and follows on from his previous confessions. Bail may well have been in his mind, as indeed other motives may well have been, but there is nothing that I can see which suggests in any way that this confession is in any way unreliable. There is no evidence before me that he was suffering from heroin addiction at the time or shortly before June 16 but even if he had been, my view of the admissibility of this interview remains the same. I can see nothing, even in those circumstances, which would in any way render the admissions or the interview in any way unreliable. Of course, it is for the prosecution to satisfy me that the admissions in the interview are not unreliable and for the reasons that I have given they have done so. In my view, therefore, this interview (and the admissions contained in it) is admissible.

In this Court, though counsel did not abandon his submission that the evidence was more prejudicial than probative, the argument against the admissibility of evidence about the June 16 interview was put in two principal ways: (a) that the judge should have ruled against the admissibility of the evidence in accordance with section 76(2)(b) of the Police and Criminal Evidence Act 1984 (the 1984 Act) and (b) that, in the alternative, the Judge should have excluded the evidence in accordance with section 78 of the 1984 Act.

. . . The submission based on section 78 of the 1984 Act can be dealt with quite shortly. It will be seen that by this section the court is given a discretion to exclude evidence in certain circumstances. It does not appear however that in the present case any submission was made to the judge at the trial to the effect that the evidence should be excluded in accordance with section 78. In these circumstances it does not appear to us that it would be right for this Court to give effect to a submission which depends on the failure of a judge to exclude evidence by a discretion which at the trial he was not asked to exercise.

We turn therefore to the argument based on section 76 of the 1984 Act. Here, if the argument is well founded, the exclusion of the evidence is mandatory and in any event it is clear that the point was fully canvassed before the judge.

It was submitted on behalf of the appellant that the words 'said or done' in the phrase 'in consequence of anything said or done' could include what was said or done by the appellant himself.

He had requested the interview and his motive, it was said, was to obtain bail or alternatively, as one of the police officers said in the course of the trial, to obtain credit for helping the police. It was also submitted, though without great force, that the confession was unreliable because of the words used by Detective Sergeant Leader at the outset of the interview which might have led the appellant to think that anything he said would be 'off the record,' or at any rate would not be used against him in the present proceedings. It is to be noted that this alternative submission was not advanced at the trial.

It is important to remember that in the present case there was an application on behalf of the appellant that the evidence should not be admitted. The case therefore fell within section 76(2) of the 1984 Act rather than within section 76(3), under which the court may, of its own motion, require the prosecution to prove the reliability of a confession.

It follows therefore that if criticism is now to be made of the judge's ruling, it is necessary to bear in mind the arguments addressed to him at the trial. Thus the obligation on the Court under section 76(2) arises where 'it is represented to the court that the confession was or may have been obtained in consequence of anything said or done which was likely, in the circumstances existing at the time, to render unreliable any confession which might be made by him in consequence thereof.'

In the present case it is clear that no reliance was placed at the trial on anything said or done by Detective Sergeant Leader at the start of the interview. The argument was based on what was said or done by the appellant himself and on his state of mind. It is in that context that the judge's ruling has to be considered. It is also to be noted that on the *voire dire* the appellant himself did not give evidence.

It was submitted on behalf of the appellant that in a case to which section 76(2)(b) of the 1984 Act applied, the Court was concerned with the objective reliability of the confession and not merely with the conduct of any police officer or other person to whom the confession was made. Accordingly the Court might have to look at what was said or done by the person making the confession, because the confession might have been made 'in consequence' of what he himself had said or done and his words or actions might indicate that this confession was or might be unreliable.

In our judgment the words 'said or done' in section 76(2)(b) of the 1984 Act do not extend so as to include anything said or done by the person making the confession. It is clear from the wording of the section and the use of the words 'in consequence' that a causal link must be shown between what was said or done and the subsequent confession.

In our view it necessarily follows that 'anything said or done' is limited to something external to the person making the confession and to something which is likely to have some influence on him.

In the circumstances of the present case we are satisfied that on the proper construction of section 76(2)(b) the judge's ruling as to the admissibility of evidence relating to the June 16 interview was correct. We are also satisfied that the judge was right to rule against the submission that the prejudicial effect of this evidence outweighed its probative value. We therefore reject the second ground of appeal. Accordingly for these reasons the appeal against conviction must be dismissed.

Questions

1. Consider whether or not D's confession may be excluded under s. 76(2)(b) in each of the following separate circumstances:

(a)   D suffers from claustrophobia. The police are unaware of this fact and, as is normal practice, place him in a cell to await questioning. After two hours, D is taken from the cell to an interview room where, terrified of being returned to the cell, he confesses in the hope that he will be bailed;

(b)   As (a) above, but the police are at all times aware of D's condition;

(c)   D is placed in a cell awaiting interview and complains of a pain in his chest. The police doctor is called and he examines D. The doctor tells D that the pain is caused by the effects of stress and not to worry. D asks the doctor what he should do. The doctor tells him that it would be better if he admitted his offence as this would lead to an early release from the police station and a lighter sentence in court. When the police interview D he makes a full confession.

2.   D is arrested for the robbery of a bank. The robber handed a note to the bank clerk which read 'hand over a thowsand pounds in used notes or you die'. D makes a confession which he writes himself. He states, 'I went to the bank and got the money. I put the money which was a thowsand pounds in a box and buried it in the garden next to an apple tree'. The police discover the box and money in the place that D indicated.

If D's confession is excluded from evidence under s. 76 what use, if any, can be made of:

(a)   the confession itself?
(b)   the finding of the box and the money?

(iii)   Discretionary exclusion of confessions

Note

The Codes of Practice issued pursuant to s. 66 of the Police and Criminal Evidence Act 1984, deal with the relationship between suspect and investigator and cover such things as treatment in police stations, cautions, etc. The Codes are complimentary to substantive provisions in the Act which deal with matters such as the right to legal advice. It has frequently been argued that where the police breach the Codes of Practice and have obtained a confession, this should be excluded from evidence. Certainly, if a causal link can be shown between the breach and the confession, thus bringing it within s. 76(2)(b), there can be little doubt the confession should be excluded. The more difficult question is what should happen where a Code has been breached and this appears to have had no effect on the reliability of D's confession? Should the courts adopt a disciplinary approach and exclude the confession as a means of demonstrating their disapproval of improper police conduct? What effect should be given to s. 78(1) of the Act dealing with the exclusion of prosecution evidence where, having regard to all the circumstances, including those in which the evidence was obtained, the court feels its admission would have such an adverse effect on the fairness of the proceedings it ought not to be admitted?

Few areas of law have, in such a short period of time, generated as many cases as this one. Rational and coherent principles are often difficult to discern and the following cases represent only a small sample of those decided.

Police and Criminal Evidence Act 1984

56.   Right to have someone informed when arrested
    (1)   Where a person has been arrested and is being held in custody in a police station or other premises, he shall be entitled, if he so requests, to have one friend or relative or other person who is known to him or who is likely to take an interest in his

welfare told, as soon as is practicable except to the extent that delay is permitted by this section, that he has been arrested and is being detained there.

(2)   Delay is only permitted —

(a)   in the case of a person who is in police detention for a serious arrestable offence; and

(b)   if an officer of at least the rank of superintendent authorises it.

(3)   In any case the person in custody must be permitted to exercise the right conferred by subsection (1) above within 36 hours from the relevant time, as defined in section 41(2) above.

(4)   An officer may give an authorisation under subsection (2) above orally or in writing but, if he gives it orally, he shall confirm it in writing as soon as is practicable.

(5)   An officer may only authorise delay where he has reasonable grounds for believing that telling the named person of the arrest —

(a)   will lead to interference with or harm to evidence connected with a serious arrestable offence or interference with or physical injury to other persons; or

(b)   will lead to the alerting of other persons suspected of having committed such an offence but not yet arrested for it; or

(c)   will hinder the recovery of any property obtained as a result of such an offence.

(6)   If a delay is authorised —

(a)   the detained person shall be told the reason for it; and

(b)   the reason shall be noted on his custody record.

(7)   The duties imposed by subsection (6) above shall be performed as soon as is practicable.

(8)   The rights conferred by this section on a person detained at a police station or other premises are exercisable whenever he is transferred from one place to another; and this section applies to each subsequent occasion on which they are exercisable as it applies to the first such occasion.

(9)   There may be no further delay in permitting the exercise of the right conferred by subsection (1) above once the reason for authorising delay ceases to subsist.

(10)   In the foregoing provisions of this section references to a person who has been arrested include references to a person who has been detained under the terrorism provisions and 'arrest' includes detention under those provisions.

(11)   In its application to a person who has been arrested or detained under the terrorism provisions —

(a)   subsection (2)(a) above shall have effect as if for the words 'for a serious arrestable offence' there were substituted the words 'under the terrorism provisions';

(b)   subsection (3) above shall have effect as if for the words from 'within' onwards there were substituted the words 'before the end of the period beyond which he may no longer be detained without the authority of the Secretary of State'; and

(c)   subsection (5) above shall have effect as if at the end there were added 'or

(d)   will lead to interference with the gathering of information about the commission, preparation or instigation of acts of terrorism; or

(e)   by alerting any person, will make it more difficult —

(i)   to prevent an act of terrorism; or

(ii)   to secure the apprehension, prosecution or conviction of any person in connection with the commission, preparation or instigation of an act of terrorism.'

58.   Access to legal advice

(1)   A person arrested and held in custody in a police station or other premises shall be entitled, if he so requests, to consult a solicitor privately at any time . . . .

(2) Subject to subsection (3) below, a request under subsection (1) above and the time at which it was made shall be recorded in the custody record.

(3) Such a request need not be recorded in the custody record of a person who makes it at a time while he is at a court after being charged with an offence.

(4) If a person makes such a request, he must be permitted to consult a solicitor as soon as is practicable except to the extent that delay is permitted by this section.

(5) In any case he must be permitted to consult a solicitor within 36 hours from the relevant time, as defined in section 41(2) above.

(6) Delay in compliance with a request is only permitted —

(a) in the case of a person who is in police detention for a serious arrestable offence; and

(b) if an officer of at least the rank of superintendent authorises it.

(7) An officer may give an authorisation under subsection (6) above orally or in writing but, if he gives it orally, he shall confirm it in writing as soon as is practicable.

(8) An officer may only authorise delay where he has reasonable grounds for believing that the exercise of the right conferred by subsection (1) above at the time when the person detained desires to exercise it —

(a) will lead to interference with or harm to evidence connected with a serious arrestable offence or interference with or physical injury to other persons; or

(b) will lead to the alerting of other persons suspected of having committed such an offence but not yet arrested for it; or

(c) will hinder the recovery of any property obtained as a result of such an offence.

(9) If delay is authorised —

(a) the detained person shall be told the reason for it; and

(b) the reason shall be noted on his custody record.

(10) The duties imposed by subsection (9) above shall be performed as soon as is practicable.

(11) There may be no further delay in permitting the exercise of the right conferred by subsection (1) above once the reason for authorising delay ceases to subsist.

(12) The reference in subsection (1) above to a person arrested includes a reference to a person who has been detained under the terrorism provisions.

(13) In the application of this section to a person who has been arrested or detained under the terrorism provisions —

(a) subsection (5) above shall have effect as if for the words from 'within' onwards there were substituted the words 'before the end of the period beyond which he may no longer be detained without the authority of the Secretary of State';

(b) subsection (6)(a) above shall have effect as if for the words 'for a serious arrestable offence' there were substituted the words 'under the terrorism provisions'; and

(c) subsection (8) above shall have effect as if at the end there were added 'or

(d) will lead to interference with the gathering of information about the commission, preparation or instigation of acts of terrorism; or

(e) by alerting any person, will make it more difficult —

(i) to prevent an act of terrorism; or

(ii) to secure the apprehension, prosecution or conviction of any person in connection with the commission, preparation or instigation of an act of terrorism.'

(14) If an officer of appropriate rank has reasonable grounds for believing that, unless he gives a direction under subsection (15) below, the exercise by a person arrested or detained under the terrorism provisions of the right conferred by

subsection (1) above will have any of the consequences specified in subsection (8) above (as it has effect by virtue of subsection (13) above), he may give a direction under that subsection.

(15) A direction under this subsection is a direction that a person desiring to exercise the right conferred by subsection (1) above may only consult a solicitor in the sight and hearing of a qualified officer of the uniformed branch of the force of which the officer giving the direction is a member.

(16) An officer is qualified for the purpose of subsection (15) above if —

(a) he is of at least the rank of inspector; and

(b) in the opinion of the officer giving the direction he has no connection with the case.

(17) An officer is of appropriate rank to give a direction under subsection (15) above if he is of at least the rank of Commander or Assistant Chief Constable.

(18) A direction under subsection (15) above shall cease to have effect once the reason for giving it ceases to subsist.

66. Codes of practice
The Secretary of State shall issue codes of practice in connection with — . . .

(b) the detention, treatment, questioning and identification of persons by police officers;

67. Codes of practice — supplementary
(9) Persons other than police officers who are charged with the duty of investigating offences or charging offenders shall in the discharge of that duty have regard to any relevant provision of such a code . . .

(11) In all criminal and civil proceedings any such code shall be admissible in evidence; and if any provision of such a code appears to the court or tribunal conducting the proceedings to be relevant to any question arising in the proceedings it shall be taken into account in determining that question.

CODE OF PRACTICE FOR THE DETENTION, TREATMENT AND QUESTIONING OF PERSONS BY POLICE OFFICERS (CODE C)

1. General
1.1 All persons in custody must be dealt with expeditiously, and released as soon as the need for detention has ceased to apply.

1.2 This code of practice must be readily available at all police stations for consultation by police officers, detained persons and members of the public.

1.3 The notes for guidance included are not provisions of this code, but are guidance to police officers and others about its application and interpretation. Provisions in the annexes to this code are provisions of this code.

1.4 If an officer has any suspicion, or is told in good faith, that a person of any age may be mentally disordered or mentally handicapped, or mentally incapable of understanding the significance of questions put to him or his replies, then that person shall be treated as a mentally disordered or mentally handicapped person for the purposes of this code.

1.5 If anyone appears to be under the age of 17 then he shall be treated as a juvenile for the purposes of this code in the absence of clear evidence to show that he is older.

1.6 If a person appears to be blind or seriously visually handicapped, deaf, unable to read, unable to speak or has difficulty orally because of a speech impediment, he should be treated as such for the purposes of this code in the absence of clear evidence to the contrary.

1.7   In this code 'the appropriate adult' means:
   (a)   in the case of a juvenile:
      (i)   his parent or guardian (or, if he is in care, the care authority or voluntary organisation);
      (ii)   a social worker; or
      (iii)   failing either of the above, another responsible adult aged 18 or over who is not a police officer or employed by the police.
   (b)   in the case of a person who is mentally disordered or mentally handicapped:
      (i)   a relative, guardian or other person responsible for his care or custody;
      (ii)   someone who has experience of dealing with mentally disordered or mentally handicapped persons but is not a police officer or employed by the police (such as an approved social worker as defined by the Mental Health Act 1983 or a specialist social worker); or
      (iii)   failing either of the above, some other responsible adult aged 18 or over who is not a police officer or employed by the police.
1.8   Whenever this code requires a person to be given certain information he does not have to be given it if he is incapable at the time of understanding what is said to him or is violent or likely to become violent or is in urgent need of medical attention, but he must be given it as soon as practicable.
1.9   Any reference to a custody officer in this code includes an officer who is performing the functions of a custody officer.
1.10   This code applies to persons who are in custody at police stations whether or not they have been arrested for an offence and to those who have been removed to a police station as a place of safety under sections 135 and 136 of the Mental Health Act 1983. Section 15, however, applies solely to persons in police detention.
1.11   Persons in police detention include persons taken to a police station after being arrested under section 14 of the Prevention of Terrorism (Temporary Provisions) Act 1989 or under paragraph 6 of schedule 5 to that Act by an examining officer who is a constable.

2.   Custody records

2.1   A separate custody record must be opened as soon as practicable for each person who is brought to a police station under arrest or is arrested at the police station having attended there voluntarily. All information which has to be recorded under this code must be recorded as soon as practicable, in the custody record unless otherwise specified.
2.2   In the case of any action requiring the authority of an officer of a specified rank, his name and rank must be noted in the custody record. The recording of names does not apply to officers dealing with persons detained under the Prevention of Terrorism (Temporary Provisions) Act 1989. Instead the record shall state the warrant number and duty station of such officers.
2.3   The custody officer is responsible for the accuracy and completeness of the custody record and for ensuring that the record or a copy of the record accompanies a detained person if he is transferred to another police station. The record shall show the time of and reason for transfer and the time a person is released from detention.
2.4   When a person leaves police detention or is taken before a court he or his legal representative or his appropriate adult shall be supplied on request with a copy of the custody record as soon as practicable. This entitlement lasts for 12 months after his release.
2.5   The person who has been detained, the appropriate adult, or legal representative who gives reasonable notice of a request to inspect the original custody record after

the person has left police detention should be allowed to do so. A note of any such inspection should be made in the custody record.

2.6 All entries in custody records must be timed and signed by the maker. In the case of a record entered on a computer this should be timed and contain the operator's identification. Warrant numbers should be used rather than names in the case of detention under the Prevention of Terrorism (Temporary Provisions) Act 1989.

2.7 The fact and time of any refusal by a person to sign a custody record when asked to do so in accordance with the provisions of this code must itself be recorded.

5. Right not to be held incommunicado
(a) Action
5.1 Any person arrested and held in custody at a police station or other premises may on request have one person known to him or who is likely to take an interest in his welfare informed at public expense as soon as practicable of his whereabouts. If the person cannot be contacted the person who has made the request may choose up to two alternatives. If they too cannot be contacted the person in charge of detention or of the investigation has discretion to allow further attempts until the information has been conveyed.

5.2 The exercise of the above right in respect of each of the persons nominated may be delayed only in accordance with Annex B to this code.

5.3 The above right may be exercised on each occasion that a person is taken to another police station.

5.4 The person may receive visits at the custody officer's discretion.

5.5 Where an enquiry as to the whereabouts of the person is made by a friend, relative or person with an interest in his welfare, this information shall be given, if he agrees and if Annex B does not apply.

5.6 Subject to the following condition, the person should be supplied with writing materials on request and allowed to speak on the telephone for a reasonable time to one person. Where an officer of the rank of Inspector or above considers that the sending of a letter or the making of a telephone call may result in:

(a) any of the consequences set out in the first and second paragraph of Annex B and the person is detained in connection with an arrestable or a serious arrestable offence; or

(b) either of the consequences set out in paragraph 8 of Annex B and the person is detained under the Prevention of Terrorism (Temporary Provisions) Act 1989, that officer can deny or delay the exercise of either or both these privileges. However, nothing in this section permits the restriction or denial of the rights set out in sections 5.1 and 6.1.

5.7 Before any letter or message is sent, or telephone call made, the person shall be informed that what he says in any letter, call or message (other than in the case of a communication to a solicitor) may be read or listened to as appropriate and may be given in evidence. A telephone call may be terminated if it is being abused. The costs can be at public expense at the discretion of the custody officer.

(b) Documentation
5.8 A record must be kept of:

(a) any request made under this section and the action taken on it;

(b) any letters, messages or telephone calls made or received or visits received; and

(c) any refusal on the part of the person to have information about himself or his whereabouts given to an outside enquirer. The person must be asked to countersign the record accordingly and any refusal to sign should be recorded.

6. Right to legal advice

(a)   Action

6.1   Subject to paragraph 6.2, any person may at any time consult and communicate privately, whether in person, in writing or on the telephone with a solicitor.

6.2   The exercise of the above right may be delayed only in accordance with Annex B to this code. Whenever legal advice is requested (and unless Annex B applies) the custody officer must act without delay to secure the provision of such advice to the person concerned.

6.3   A poster advertising the right to have legal advice must be prominently displayed in the charging area of every police station.

6.4   No attempt should be made to dissuade the suspect from obtaining legal advice.

6.5   Reminders of the right to free legal advice must be given in accordance with paragraphs 11.2, 15.3 and paragraphs 2.15(ii) and 5.2 of code of practice D.

6.6   A person who wants legal advice may not be interviewed or continue to be interviewed until he has received it unless:

   (a)   Annex B applies; or

   (b)   An officer of the rank of superintendent or above has reasonable grounds for believing that:

      (i)   delay will involve an immediate risk of harm to persons or serious loss of, or damage to, property; or

      (ii)   where a solicitor, including a duty solicitor, has been contacted and has agreed to attend, awaiting his arrival would cause unreasonable delay to the process of investigation; or

   (c)   the solicitor nominated by the person, or selected by him from a list:

      (i)   cannot be contacted; or

      (ii)   has previously indicated that he does not wish to be contacted; or

      (iii) having been contacted, has declined to attend;

and the person has been advised of the Duty Solicitor Scheme (where one is in operation) but has declined to ask for the duty solicitor, or the duty solicitor is unavailable. (In these circumstances the interview may be started or continued without further delay provided that an officer of the rank of Inspector or above has given agreement for the interview to proceed in those circumstances).

   (d)   The person who wanted legal advice changes his mind. In these circumstances the interview may be started or continued without further delay provided that the person has given his agreement in writing or on tape to being interviewed without receiving legal advice and that an officer of the rank of Inspector or above has given agreement for the interview to proceed in those circumstances.

6.7   Where 6.6(b)(i) applies, once sufficient information to avert the risk has been obtained, questioning must cease until the person has received legal advice or 6.6(a), (b)(ii), (c) or (d) apply.

6.8   Where a person has been permitted to consult a solicitor and the solicitor is available (i.e., present at the station or on his way to the station or easily contactable by telephone) at the time the interview begins or is in progress, he must be allowed to have his solicitor present while he is interviewed.

6.9   The solicitor may only be required to leave the interview if his conduct is such that the investigating officer is unable properly to put questions to the suspect.

6.10   If the investigating officer considers that a solicitor is acting in such a way, he will stop the interview and consult an officer not below the rank of superintendent, if one is readily available, and otherwise an officer not below the rank of inspector who is not connected with the investigation. After speaking to the solicitor, the officer who has been consulted will decide whether or not the interview should continue in the presence of that solicitor. If he decides that it should not, the suspect will be given the opportunity to consult another solicitor before the interview continues and that solicitor will be given an opportunity to be present at the interview.

6.11 The removal of a solicitor from an interview is a serious step and, if it occurs, the officer of superintendent rank or above who took the decision will consider whether the incident should be reported to the Law Society. If the decision to remove the solicitor has been taken by an officer below the rank of superintendent, the facts must be reported to an officer of superintendent rank or above who will similarly consider whether a report to the Law Society would be appropriate. Where the solicitor concerned is a duty solicitor, the report should be both to the Law Society and to the Legal Aid Board.

6.12 In this code 'solicitor' means a solicitor qualified to practise in accordance with the Solicitors Act 1974. If a solicitor wishes to send a clerk or legal executive to provide advice on his behalf, then the clerk or legal executive shall be admitted to the police station for this purpose unless an officer of the rank of inspector or above considers that such a visit will hinder the investigation of crime and directs otherwise. Once admitted to the police station, the provisions of paragraphs 6.6 to 6.10 apply.

6.13 In exercising his discretion under paragraph 6.12, the officer should take into account in particular whether the identity and status of the clerk or legal executive have been satisfactorily established; whether he is of suitable character to provide legal advice (a person with a criminal record is unlikely to be suitable unless the conviction was for a minor offence and is not of recent date); and any other matters in any written letter of authorisation provided by the solicitor on whose behalf the clerk or legal executive is attending the police station.

6.14 If the inspector refuses access to a clerk or legal executive or a decision is taken that such a person should not be permitted to remain at an interview, he must forthwith notify a solicitor on whose behalf the clerk or legal executive was to have acted or was acting, and give him an opportunity of making alternative arrangements. The detained person must also be informed and the custody record noted.

6.15 If a solicitor arrives at the station to see a particular person, that person must (unless Annex B applies) be informed of the solicitor's arrival and asked whether he would like to see him. This applies even if the person concerned has already declined legal advice. The solicitor's attendance and the detained person's decision must be noted in the custody record.

(b) Documentation

6.16 Any request for legal advice and the action taken on it shall be recorded.

6.17 If a person has asked for legal advice and an interview is begun in the absence of a solicitor or his representative (or the solicitor or his representative has been required to leave an interview), a record shall be made in the interview record.

10. Cautions

(a) When a caution must be given

10.1 A person whom there are grounds to suspect of an offence must be cautioned before any questions about it (or further questions if it is his answers to previous questions that provide grounds for suspicion) are put to him for the purpose of obtaining evidence which may be given to a court in a prosecution. He therefore need not be cautioned if questions are put for other purposes, for example, to establish his identity or his ownership of any vehicle or the need to search him in the exercise of powers of stop and search.

10.2 Whenever a person who is not under arrest is initially cautioned before or during an interview he must at the same time be told that he is not under arrest and is not obliged to remain with the officer (see paragraph 3.15).

10.3   A person must be cautioned upon arrest for an offence unless:
    (a)   it is impracticable to do so by reason of his condition or behaviour at the time; or
    (b)   he has already been cautioned immediately prior to arrest in accordance with paragraph 10.1 above.
(b)   Action: general
10.4   The caution shall be in the following terms:

> You do not have to say anything unless you wish to do so, but what you say may be given in evidence.

Minor deviations do not constitute a breach of this requirement provided that the sense of the caution is preserved.
10.5   When there is a break in questioning under caution the interviewing officer must ensure that the person being questioned is aware that he remains under caution. If there is any doubt the caution should be given again in full when the interview resumes.
(c)   Juveniles, the mentally disordered and the mentally handicapped
10.6   If a juvenile or a person who is mentally disordered or mentally handicapped is cautioned in the absence of the appropriate adult, the caution must be repeated in the adult's presence.
(d)   Documentation
10.7   A record shall be made when a caution is given under this section, either in the officer's pocket book or in the inteview record as appropriate.

Note
Should clauses 27 to 30 of the Criminal Justice and Public Order Bill 1994 be enacted (see further 10B*(ii)* below), it will be necessary to introduce a new caution which incorporates a reference to the consequences which may flow from a defendant choosing not to answer questions. The power of the Secretary of State to issue revised Codes is contained in ss. 66 and 67 of the Police and Criminal Evidence Act 1984. It has been suggested that a new caution might read: 'I am going to put some questions to you. You are not obliged to answer them. But if you do not mention something now which you later use in your defence, the court may decide that your failure to mention it now strengthens the case against you.'

11.   Interviews: general
(a)   Action
11.1   Following a decision to arrest a suspect he must not be interviewed about the relevant offence except at a police station (or other authorised place of detention) unless the consequent delay would be likely:
    (a)   to lead to interference with or harm to evidence connected with an offence or interference with or physical harm to other persons; or
    (b)   to lead to the alerting of other persons suspected of having committed an offence but not yet arrested for it; or
    (c)   to hinder the recovery of property obtained in consequence of the commission of an offence.
Interviewing in any of these circumstances should cease once the relevant risk has been averted or the necessary questions have been put in order to attempt to avert that risk.

11.2   Immediately prior to the commencement or re-commencement of any interview at a police station or other authorised place of detention, the interviewing officer should remind the suspect of his entitlement to free legal advice. It is the responsibility of the interviewing officer to ensure that all such reminders are noted in the record of interview.

11.3   No police officer may try to obtain answers to questions or to elicit a statement by the use of oppression or shall indicate, except in answer to a direct question, what action will be taken on the part of the police if the person being interviewed answers questions, makes a statement or refuses to do either. If the person asks the officer directly what action will be taken in the event of his answering questions, making a statement or refusing to do either, then the officer may inform the person what action the police propose to take in that event provided that that action is itself proper and warranted.

11.4   As soon as a police officer who is making enquiries of any person about an offence believes that a prosecution should be brought against him and that there is sufficient evidence for it to succeed, he should ask the person if he has anything further to say. If the person indicates that he has nothing more to say the officer shall without delay cease to question him about that offence. This should not, however, be taken to prevent officers in revenue cases or acting under the confiscation provisions of the Criminal Justice Act 1988 or the Drug Trafficking Offences Act 1986 from inviting suspects to complete a formal question and answer record after the interview is concluded.

(b)   Interview records

11.5(a)   An accurate record must be made of each interview with a person suspected of an offence, whether or not the interview takes place at a police station.

(b)   The record must state the place of the interview, the time it begins and ends, the time the record is made (if different), any breaks in the interview and the names of all those present; and must be made on the forms provided for this purpose or in the officer's pocket-book or in accordance with the code of practice for the tape-recording of police interviews with suspects.

(c)   The record must be made during the course of the interview, unless in the investigating officer's view this would not be practicable or would interfere with the conduct of the interview, and must constitute either a verbatim record of what has been said or, failing this, an account of the interview which adequately and accurately summarises it.

11.6   The requirement to record the names of all those present at an interview does not apply to police officers interviewing persons detained under the Prevention of Terrorism (Temporary Provisions) Act 1989. Instead the record shall state the warrant number and duty station of such officers.

11.7   If an interview record is not made during the course of the interview it must be made as soon as practicable after its completion.

11.8   Written interview records must be timed and signed by the maker.

11.9   If an interview record is not completed in the course of the interview the reason must be recorded in the officer's pocket book.

11.10   Unless it is impracticable the person interviewed shall be given the opportunity to read the interview record and to sign it as correct or to indicate the respects in which he considers it inaccurate. If the interview is tape-recorded the arrangements set out in the relevant code of practice apply. If the person concerned cannot read or refuses to read the record or to sign it, the senior police officer present shall read it over to him and ask him whether he would like to sign it as correct (or make his mark) or to indicate the respects in which he considers it inaccurate. The police officer shall then certify on the interview record itself what has occurred.

11.11 If the appropriate adult or the person's solicitor is present during the interview, he should also be given an opportunity to read and sign the interview record (or any written statement taken down by a police officer).

11.12 Any refusal by a person to sign an interview record when asked to do so in accordance with the provisions of this code must itself be recorded.

11.13 A written record should also be made of any comments made by a suspected person, including unsolicited comments, which are outside the context of an interview but which might be relevant to the offence. Any such record must be timed and signed by the maker. Where practicable the person shall be given the opportunity to read that record and to sign it as correct or to indicate the respects in which he considers it inaccurate. Any refusal to sign should be recorded.

(c) Juveniles, the mentally disordered and the mentally handicapped

11.14 A juvenile or a person who is mentally disordered or mentally handicapped, whether suspected or not, must not be interviewed or asked to provide or sign a written statement in the absence of the appropriate adult unless Annex C applies.

11.15 Juveniles may only be interviewed at their places of education in exceptional circumstances and then only where the principal or his nominee agrees. Every effort should be made to notify both the parent(s) or other person responsible for the juvenile's welfare and the appropriate adult (if this is a different person) that the police want to interview the juvenile and reasonable time should be allowed to enable the appropriate adult to be present at the interview. Where awaiting the appropriate adult would cause unreasonable delay and unless the interviewee is suspected of an offence against the educational establishment, the principal or his nominee can act as the appropriate adult for the purposes of the interview.

11.16 Where the appropriate adult is present at an interview, he should be informed that he is not expected to act simply as an observer; and also that the purposes of his presence are, first, to advise the person being questioned and to observe whether or not the interview is being conducted properly and fairly, and, secondly, to facilitate communication with the person being interviewed.

12. Interviews in police stations

(a) Action

12.1 If a police officer wishes to interview, or conduct enquiries which require the presence of a detained person the custody officer is responsible for deciding whether to deliver him into his custody.

12.2 In any period of 24 hours a detained person must be allowed a continuous period of at least 8 hours for rest, free from questioning, travel or any interruption arising out of the investigation concerned. This period should normally be at night. The period of rest may not be interrupted or delayed unless there are reasonable grounds for believing that it would:

(i) involve a risk of harm to persons or serious loss of, or damage to, property;

(ii) delay unnecessarily the person's release from custody; or

(iii) otherwise prejudice the outcome of the investigation.

If a person is arrested at a police station after going there voluntarily, the period of 24 hours runs from the time of his arrest and not the time of arrival at the police station.

12.3 A detained person may not be supplied with intoxicating liquor except on medical directions. No person who is unfit through drink or drugs to the extent that he is unable to appreciate the significance of questions put to him and his answers may be questioned about an alleged offence in that condition except in accordance with Annex C.

12.4 As far as practicable interviews shall take place in interview rooms which must be adequately heated, lit and ventilated.

12.5 Persons being questioned or making statements shall not be required to stand.

12.6 Before the commencement of an interview each interviewing officer shall identify himself and any other officers present by name and rank to the person being interviewed, except in the case of persons detained under the Prevention of Terrorism (Temporary Provisions) Act 1989 when each officer shall identify himself by his warrant number and rank rather than his name.

12.7 Breaks from interviewing shall be made at recognised meal times. Short breaks for refreshment shall also be provided at intervals of approximately two hours, subject to the interviewing officer's discretion to delay a break if there are reasonable grounds for believing that it would:

    (i) involve a risk of harm to persons or serious loss of, or damage to, property;

    (ii) delay unnecessarily the person's release from custody; or

    (iii) otherwise prejudice the outcome of the investigation.

12.8 If in the course of the interview a complaint is made by the person being questioned or on his behalf concerning the provisions of this code then the interviewing officer shall:

    (i) record it in the interview record; and

    (ii) inform the custody officer, who is then responsible for dealing with it in accordance with section 9 of this code.

(b) Documentation

12.9 A record must be made of the times at which a detained person is not in the custody of the custody officer, and why; and of the reason for any refusal to deliver him out of that custody.

12.10 A record must be made of any intoxicating liquor supplied to a detained person, in accordance with paragraph 12.3 above.

12.11 Any decision to delay a break in an interview must be recorded, with grounds, in the interview record.

12.12 All written statements made at police stations under caution shall be written on the forms provided for the purpose.

12.13 All written statements made under caution shall be taken in accordance with Annex D to this code.

ANNEX B
DELAY IN NOTIFYING ARREST OR ALLOWING ACCESS TO LEGAL ADVICE

A. Persons detained under the Police and Criminal Evidence Act 1984

(a) Action

1. The rights set out in sections 5 or 6 of the code or both may be delayed if the person is in police detention in connection with a serious arrestable offence, has not yet been charged with an offence and an officer of the rank of superintendent or above has reasonable grounds for believing that the exercise of either right:

    (i) will lead to interference with or harm to evidence connected with a serious arrestable offence or interference with or physical injury to other persons; or

    (ii) will lead to the alerting of other persons suspected of having committed such an offence but not yet arrested for it; or

    (iii) will hinder the recovery of property obtained as a result of such an offence.

2.   These rights may also be delayed where the serious arrestable offence is either:

(i)   a drug trafficking offence and the officer has reasonable grounds for believing that the detained person has benefited from drug trafficking, and that the recovery of the value of that person's proceeds of drug trafficking will be hindered by the exercise of either right; or

(ii)   an offence to which Part VI of the Criminal Justice Act 1988 (covering confiscation orders) applies and the officer has reasonable grounds for believing that the detained person has benefited from the offence, and that the recovery of the value of the property obtained by that person from or in connection with the offence or if the pecuniary advantage derived by him from or in connection with it will be hindered by the exercise of either right.

3.   Access to a solicitor may not be delayed on the grounds that he might advise the person not to answer any questions or that the solicitor was initially asked to attend the police station by someone else, provided that the person himself then wishes to see the solicitor. In the latter case the detained person must be told that the solicitor has come to the police station at another person's request, and must be asked to sign the custody record to signify whether or not he wishes to see the solicitor.

4.   These rights may be delayed only for as long as is necessary and, subject to paragraph 9 below, in no case beyond 36 hours after the relevant time as defined in section 41 of the Police and Criminal Evidence Act 1984. If the above grounds cease to apply within this time, the person must as soon as practicable be asked if he wishes to exercise either right, the custody record must be noted accordingly, and action must be taken in accordance with the relevant section of the code.

5.   A detained person must be permitted to consult a solicitor for a reasonable time before any court hearing.

(b)   Documentation

6.   The grounds for action under this Annex shall be recorded and the person informed of them as soon as practicable.

7.   Any reply given by a person under paragraphs 4 or 9 must be recorded and the person asked to endorse the record in relation to whether he wishes to receive legal advice at this point.

B.   Persons detained under the Prevention of Terrorism (Temporary Provisions) Act 1989

(a)   Action

8.   The rights set out in sections 5 or 6 of this code or both may be delayed if paragraph 1 above applies or if an officer of the rank of superintendent or above has reasonable grounds for believing that the exercise of either right:

(a)   will lead to interference with the gathering of information about the commission, preparation or instigation of acts of terrorism; or

(b)   by alerting any person, will make it more difficult to prevent an act of terrorism or to secure the apprehension, prosecution or conviction of any person in connection with the commission, preparation or instigation of an act of terrorism.

9.   These rights may be delayed only for as long as is necessary and in no case beyond 48 hours from the time of arrest. If the above grounds cease to apply within this time, the person must as soon as practicable be asked if he wishes to exercise either right, the custody record must be noted accordingly, and action must be taken in accordance with the relevant section of this code.

10.   Paragraphs 3 and 5 above apply.

ANNEX C
URGENT INTERVIEWS

1. If, and only if, an officer of the rank of superintendent or above considers that delay will involve an immediate risk of harm to persons or serious loss of or serious damage to property:

    (a) a person heavily under the influence of drink or drugs may be interviewed in that state; or

    (b) an arrested juvenile or a person who is mentally disordered or mentally handicapped may be interviewed in the absence of the appropriate adult; or

    (c) a person who has difficulty in understanding English or who has a hearing disability may be interviewed in the absence of an interpreter.

2. Questioning in these circumstances may not continue once sufficient information to avert the immediate risk has been obtained.

3. A record shall be made of the grounds for any decision to interview a person under paragraph 1 above.

Note for Guidance

C1 The special groups referred to in Annex C are all particularly vulnerable. The provisions of the annex, which override safeguards designed to protect them and to minimise the risk of interviews producing unreliable evidence, should be applied only in exceptional cases of need.

ANNEX D
WRITTEN STATEMENTS UNDER CAUTION (see paragraph 12.13)

(*a*) *Written by a person under caution*

1. A person shall always be invited to write down himself what he wants to say.

2. Where the person wishes to write it himself, he shall be asked to write out and sign before writing what he wants to say, the following:

> I make this statement of my own free will. I understand that I need not say anything unless I wish to do so and that what I say may be given in evidence.

3. Any person writing his own statement shall be allowed to do so without any prompting except that a police officer may indicate to him which matters are material or question any ambiguity in the statement.

(*b*) *Written by a police officer*

4. If a person says that he would like someone to write it for him, a police officer shall write the statement, but, before starting, he must ask him to sign, or make his mark, to the following:

> I, ... , wish to make a statement. I want someone to write down what I say. I understand that I need not say anything unless I wish to do so and that what I say may be given in evidence.

5. Where a police officer writes the statement, he must take down the exact words spoken by the person making it and he must not edit or paraphrase it. Any questions that are necessary (e.g., to make it more intelligible) and the answers given must be recorded contemporaneously on the statement form.

6. When the writing of a statement by a police officer is finished the person making it shall be asked to read it and to make any corrections, alterations or additions he wishes. When he has finished reading it he shall be asked to write and sign or make his mark on the following certificate at the end of the statement:

> I have read the above statement, and I have been able to correct, alter or add anything I wish. This statement is true. I have made it of my own free will.

7. If the person making the statement cannot read, or refuses to read it, or to write the above mentioned certificate at the end of it or to sign it, the senior police officer present shall read it over to him whether he would like to correct, alter or add anything and to put his signature or make his mark at the end. The police officer shall then certify on the statement itself what has occurred.

R v Mason
[1988] 1 WLR 139
Court of Appeal

WATKINS LJ: On 26 February 1987 in the Crown Court at Newcastle upon Tyne before Judge Percy the appellant was convicted of arson and on 20 March sentenced for that to two years' youth custody. He appeals against conviction by way of a certificate from the trial judge. The point of law certified by him is thus stated:

A point of law arose concerning the admissibility of evidence which it was submitted ought to have been excluded under the Police and Criminal Evidence Act 1984, sections 76 and 78.

It is as well we think to preface the remainder of this judgment by observing that upon the evidence this is an appeal without merit, but the point of law raised is one of real substance.

The facts are that on 1 July 1986 a motor car belonging to a Mr Askew was set on fire. It was very badly damaged. The cost of repairing the damage was something in the region of £1,000. It was obvious to those who later went on to inspect the damage that the fire had been caused by an inflammable liquid thrown against the car and ignited. Before that incident there had been bad feeling between the appellant, who is 20 years of age, and Mr Askew. Mr Askew has a daughter who is 18 years of age. The appellant and this young lady had been going out together. She became pregnant by him. She was not willing to bear his child. She decided to have an abortion and she did. She also broke off her relationship with the appellant. He did not take that at all well. His erstwhile girlfriend's father and mother did not look upon what had happened with any great favour either; nor did they feel any pleasure in seeing the appellant any more. They began to receive midnight telephone calls. Upon each occasion they answered the telephone, whoever was at the other end put the receiver down. They suspected the appellant of making those calls. It may be that their suspicions were well-founded.

At two o'clock in the morning of 1 July 1986 Mr Askew while in bed was woken up by a screech of tyres on the road outside his house. He thought no more of it then and went back to sleep, but a few minutes later he was again woken up, this time it was by a telephone call from a neighbour. As a result of that he ran to a window and saw that his motor car, which was parked outside, was on fire. There was nobody near the car. He had a foam fire extinguisher handy and with that he succeeded in putting out the fire. There were other parked cars nearby. If Mr Askew had not succeeded in putting out the fire, it may well have been that the petrol in the car would have ignited and the fire spread to the other cars.

When the police came to the scene there was a lot of broken glass, as they discovered, about the place near the car. It was soon found that an inflammable liquid had been used, probably a combination of petrol and paint thinners. About 12 hours or so later the police paid a visit to the appellant. He denied having been involved in setting fire to the car. On 10 July he was arrested. Be it noted that upon arrest the police had in their possession no evidence at all to associate him with the cause of the fire. Before arrest one or more police officers decided to invent evidence and to acquaint the appellant of that so-called evidence as though it was genuinely possessed. What they decided to do was to tell the appellant that a fingerprint of his had been found in a very telling place. As to that Detective Constable Gunton said:

> Detective Constable Walton and I set out deliberately to make the defendant believe we had a fingerprint on some of the glass fragments from the bottle that was used to perpetrate this crime. I agreed with the detective constable to this play-acting and it was a trick. The bottle, or the fragments of it, had not even been sent for fingerprint testing at that stage. We set about 'conning' the defendant. We had a suspicion, but only suspicion against him and we realised that we needed more proof . . . I felt the only way to get the truth from him was to do this.

Having been told by these police officers, falsely, that a fingerprint of his had been found on a fragment of glass from the bottle, the appellant saw his solicitor and told him his version of what had happened. The solicitor asked DC Gunton to confirm the fact, as the police were asserting, that they had found a fingerprint upon a fragment of glass at the scene of the crime. He confirmed to the solicitor that that was so. That was a deliberate falsehood. When giving evidence DC Gunton said:

> My motive . . . was because if the defendant had had nothing to do with this glass bottle there was no way he would produce a confession. If he . . . knew very well he had handled . . . the bottle and been active in the preparation, of course, he would begin to doubt himself and whether or not he was going to be discovered.

The solicitor, influenced by what he had been told by the police as to the fingerprint, advised the appellant to answer their questions and to give his explanation of any involvement he had had in the incident. What he told the police as a consequence of that was that he was not present when the car was set alight. He had asked a friend, whom he refused to name, if he would do it. This was because Mr Askew had been threatening him, and setting fire to his car would frighten Mr Askew away from repeating conduct of that kind. The only involvement which he (the appellant) had in the incident was to fill the bottles which were used, one with petrol and the other with paint thinners. That was done at his home. The bottles were then taken away by the friend and the fire started.

The appellant did not give evidence at the trial. Before the end of the prosecution case and when the confession — because that is what it amounted to — was sought to be put in evidence by counsel for the prosecution, objection to its admissibility was made by counsel for the appellant. The judge heard argument in the absence of the jury and heard some evidence from the police as to how the confession had been obtained. He decided that the confession was, in his discretion, admissible. He was referred in the course of argument to sections 76 and 78 of the Police and Criminal Evidence Act 1984. He gave a ruling at the conclusion of argument and then said he would allow the prosecution to adduce that evidence. He dealt with what he believed to be the effects of sections 76 and 78, and went on to say, with the provisions of section 78 in mind:

> I have no doubt that this defendant was well aware of his right to remain silent and could have remained silent, with his solicitor being present, had he so chosen that alternative. But he did not choose that alternative; he chose to give the interview, listen to the questions and decide individually which questions he was going to answer. In fact he answered all of them. I see nothing in his doing that which adversely affects the fairness of the proceedings.

It is contended here by Mr Knox for the appellant that the judge exercised his discretion wrongly. Mr Lowden, who also appeared in the court below for the prosecution, has argued that the judge undoubtedly had a discretion and that in exercising it he took account of all the matters which it was necessary for him to take into account and did not give thought to any impermissible matter in coming to his conclusion. Mr Lowden has also submitted that there is no authority for the proposition that section 78 of the Act refers to confessions and admissions, seeing that they are specially dealt with in section 76 . . .

It is submitted that when a comparison is made between the provisions of those two sections and reference made to *Reg.* v *Sang* [1980] AC 402, it was not the intention of Parliament that section 78 be understood as though the word 'evidence' includes evidence of confessions and admissions. We see no reason whatsoever to put that in our view extremely strained construction upon the plain words used in this section. In our judgment on a proper construction of it the word 'evidence' includes all the evidence which may be introduced by the prosecution into a trial. Thus it is that regardless of whether the admissibility of a confession falls to be considered under section 76(2), a trial judge has a discretion to deal with the admissibility of a confession under section 78 which, in our opinion, does no more than to re-state the power which judges had at common law before the Act of 1984 was passed. That power gave a trial judge a discretion whether solely in the interests of the fairness of a trial he would permit the prosecution to introduce admissible evidence sought to be relied upon, especially that of a confession or an admission. That being so, we now return to the circumstances of the present case.

It is obvious from the undisputed evidence that the police practised a deceit not only upon the appellant, which is bad enough, but also upon the solicitor whose duty it was to advise him. In effect, they hoodwinked both solicitor and client. That was a most reprehensible thing to do. It is not however because we regard as misbehaviour of a serious kind conduct of that nature that we have come to the decision soon to be made plain. This is not the place to discipline the police. That has been made clear here on a number of previous occasions. We are concerned with the application of the proper law. The law is, as I have already said, that a trial judge has a discretion to be exercised of course upon right principles to reject admissible evidence in the interests of a defendant having a fair trial. The judge in the present case appreciated that, as the quotation from his ruling shows. So the only question to be answered by this court is whether, having regard to the way the police behaved, the judge exercised that discretion correctly. In our judgment he did not. He omitted a vital factor from his consideration, namely, the deceit practised upon the appellant's solicitor. If he had included that in his consideration of the matter we have not the slightest doubt that he would have been driven to an opposite conclusion, namely, that the confession be ruled out and the jury not permitted therefore to hear of it. If that had been done, an acquittal would have followed for there was no other evidence in the possession of the prosecution.

For those reasons we have no alternative but to quash this conviction.

Before parting with this case, despite what I have said about the role of the court in relation to disciplining the police, we think we ought to say that we hope never again to hear of deceit such as this being practised upon an accused person, and more particularly possibly on a solicitor whose duty it is to advise him unfettered by false information from the police.

Appeal allowed. Conviction quashed.

R v *Alladice*
(1988) 87 Cr App R 380
Court of Appeal

LORD LANE CJ: On April 2, 1987, in the Crown Court at Birmingham the appellant was convicted of robbery and was sentenced to eight years' youth custody.

He now appeals against conviction by leave of the single judge.

Four others were charged with the same offence. Two pleaded guilty. Two were convicted by the jury, one of whom has since had his conviction quashed by this Court on grounds which were unrelated to the present appeal.

The scene of the robbery was a post office at Balsall Heath, Birmingham, on July 4, 1986. Five men, one of them armed with a gun, terrorised the staff and stole some £29,000 in cash.

The appellant was eventually interviewed and, according to the police, admitted that he was one of the robbers. There was further evidence that immediately after the robbery the appellant, who was aged 18 and unemployed, had spent almost £3,000 on buying and insuring a BMW motor car and paying off debts. The alleged admissions were however the foundation of the prosecution case against him.

The appellant now contends that the judge was wrong to admit the evidence of those admissions. The basis of that contention is that the appellant was denied the access to a solicitor which he had requested; that that denial was contrary to the provisions of the Police and Criminal Evidence Act 1984 (referred to hereafter as the Act) and the code of practice issued thereunder for two reasons: (1) the officer who denied access was under the terms of the Act not qualified to make the decision; and (2) on a true construction of the Act and the code of practice there was no proper basis in fact for his decision to refuse access.

[After holding that there was a breach of s. 58 and the code of practice the court continued . . .]

The breach of section 58 and of paragraph [C6.6] of the Code is however not the end of the matter. There is no express sanction contained in section 58 or elsewhere for any such breach. Such a breach is no doubt one of the matters which the court has to consider under sections 76 and 78 of the Act.

. . .

It is not suggested that there was any oppression in the present case.

There remains the question under sub-paragraph (b) [of s. 76(2)] whether the confession may have been obtained in consequence of the breach of section 58, and if so whether that was likely in all the circumstances to render the confession unreliable.

We very much doubt whether it can be said that the confession may have been obtained as a result of the refusal of access to a solicitor. Even assuming that that may have been the case, there is no reason to believe that that fact was likely in all the circumstances to render a confession unreliable. We do not consider that the judge was obliged to rule the evidence inadmissible under section 76.

. . .

If the police have acted in bad faith, the court will have little difficulty in ruling any confession inadmissible under section 78, if not under section 76. If the police, albeit in good faith, have nevertheless fallen foul of section 58, it is still necessary for the Court to decide whether to admit the evidence would adversely affect the fairness of the proceedings, and would do so to such an extent that the confession ought to be excluded. No doubt in many cases it will, and it behoves the police to use their powers of delaying access to a solicitor only with great circumspection. It is not possible to say in advance what would or would not be fair.

In *Samuel* [1988] QB 615 for instance, the solicitor in question gave evidence. He said it was not his policy always to advise a client not to answer questions put to him by the police. He took the view that it was in many cases of advantage to a detainee to answer proper questions put to him. In that particular case, however, he knew that his client had already been interviewed on four occasions on all of which he had strenuously denied being involved in the crime and had already been charged with two serious offences. He took the view that in those circumstances he would probably have advised his client to refuse to answer any further questions. The Court came to the conclusion that the judge, had he arrived at a correct conclusion on the two points argued before him, might well have decided that the refusal of access to a solicitor compelled him to find that the admission of the evidence would have had 'such an adverse effect on the fairness of the proceedings' that he ought not to have admitted it.

The judge in the instant case decided that the authorisation of delay was properly given, and consequently did not have to consider the question whether section 78 was applicable in the light of a breach of section 58.

What the appellant himself said in evidence was that he was well able to cope with the interviews; that he had been given the appropriate caution before each of them; that he had understood the caution and was aware of his rights. Indeed he asserted that he had said nothing at all after the first four (innocuous) questions, and what had been written down by the interviewing officer was nothing that he said but had been invented by the writer. His reason for wanting a solicitor was to have some sort of check on the conduct of the police during the interview.

The judge rejected the allegations that the police had invented the admissions. He found as a fact that the interviews had been conducted properly. He concluded that the only difference the presence of a solicitor would have made would have been to provide additional advice as to the appellant's right to say nothing, a right which he knew and understood and indeed at times during the interview exercised.

It may seldom happen that a defendant is so forthcoming about his attitude towards the presence of a legal adviser. That candour does however simplify the task of deciding whether the admission of the evidence 'would have such an adverse effect on the fairness of the proceedings' that it should not have been admitted. Had the solicitor been present, his advice would have added nothing to the knowledge of his rights which the appellant already had. The police, as the judge found, had acted with propriety at the interviews and therefore the solicitor's presence would not have improved the appellant's case in that respect.

This is therefore a case where a clear breach of section 58 nevertheless does not require the Court to rule inadmissible subsequent statements made by the defendant.

This appeal is accordingly dismissed.

[The Court then went on to consider the appeal against sentence. His Lordship stated that the appellant's sentence was marginally too long and would be reduced to seven years' youth custody.]

R v Delaney
(1989) 88 Cr App R 338
Court of Appeal

LORD LANE CJ: On April 14, 1987, in the Crown Court at Lewes, Joseph Patrick Delaney was, upon conviction, sentenced to five years' youth custody for an offence of indecent assault upon a little girl of three years of age. He now appeals against conviction by leave of the Full Court. He appeals against sentence by leave of the single judge.

There is no need to spend very much time on describing the offence itself. There is no doubt but that someone indecently assaulted the little girl. It was indeed a horrifying case. The assailant, whoever he was, took the little girl from where she had been playing with some friends to some woods nearby. He there stripped her completely of her clothes, and with his fingers penetrated both her vagina and her anus. He then made off, leaving the child to make her way home as best she could. She was found in the road crying and naked, by a kindly woman who took steps to restore her to her family.

It is not difficult to imagine the sort of feelings which this type of offence would be likely to engender in the minds of any jury trying the case.

The assault took place on October 17, 1986, in Hastings. It was some twelve days later, on October 29, that this appellant was interviewed by the police, first of all, at the place where he was living and then later at the police station. He was questioned about his movements on October 17. He was then 17 years of age. The evidence before the court from an educational psychologist was that he, the appellant, was educationally subnormal, with an intelligence quotient of about 80. His personality, according to the psychologist, was such that when being interviewed as a suspect he would be subject to quick emotional arousal which might lead him to wish to rid himself of the interview by bringing it to an end as rapidly as possible.

These were circumstances in which, par excellence, any interrogation should have been conducted with meticulous care and with meticulous observance of the rules of fairness, whether those rules were by virtue of common law or by statute or otherwise. Unhappily, that is not what happened. After a lengthy interview at the police station lasting for about an hour and a half, the appellant eventually said that it was he who had assaulted the little girl. He followed up that admission with further admissions at further interviews which took place. That initial admission and what followed was in effect the whole basis of the prosecution case. Without it and without the further admissions, the case against the appellant was non-existent. There is no dispute about that.

The learned judge was called upon to rule whether the confession should be admitted in evidence. It was submitted that by virtue of section 76 of the Police and Criminal Evidence Act 1984 it was his duty to reject it and that by virtue of section 78 of the Police and Criminal Evidence Act 1984 in his discretion he ought to have rejected it.

In a ruling which is as clear and succinct as one comes to expect from Judge Gower, he ruled that the confessions should be admitted. It is the appellant's contention, advanced before this Court by Mr Hunt, that that ruling should have been otherwise.

. . .

The officers' assertion that it was not practicable to make a verbatim record was described by the judge as being the sheerest nonsense, a comment with which this court entirely agrees. That flagrant breach of the Code, as the judge correctly described it, was the starting point of the submission made to the judge by counsel for the appellant that the confessions should be rejected. But the mere fact that there has been a breach of the Codes of Practice does not of itself mean that evidence has to be rejected. It is no part of the duty of the court to rule a statement inadmissible simply in order to punish the police for failure to observe the Codes of Practice.

. . .

By failing to make a contemporaneous note, or indeed any note, as soon as practicable, the officers deprived the court of what was, in all likelihood, the most cogent evidence as to what did indeed happen during these interviews and what did induce the appellant to confess. To use the words of Mr Hunt to the court this morning, the judge and the prosecution were *pro tanto* disabled by the omission of the officers to act in accordance with the Codes of Practice, disabled from having the full knowledge upon which the judge could base his decision. The judge of course is entitled to ask himself why the officers broke the rules. Was it mere laziness or was it something more devious? Was it perhaps a desire to conceal from the court the full truth of the suggestions they had held out to the defendant? These are matters which may well tip the scales in favour of the defendant in these circumstances and make it impossible for the judge to say that he is satisfied beyond reasonable doubt, and so require him to reject the evidence.

In this case, even on their own account, the officers, as the judge found, said things which could well be regarded as improper persuasion to the defendant to admit guilt; for example, the references to the need for psychiatric help and the assertion that if such an offender admitted what he had done people would go out of their way to help him. Detective Constable Kitchen agreed that he had deliberately sought to play down the seriousness of the assault because he had the feeling that the defendant was the man responsible and he, Detective Constable Kitchen, did not want to frighten the appellant away from confessing his guilt. He seems to have overlooked the possibility that he might, by the same token, be encouraging a false confession.

Mr Hunt seeks to derive assistance from what was said in *Fulling* (1987) 85 Cr App R 136, 140, 141, where in the judgment there are set out a number of examples of what, prior to the 1984 Act, were properly described as oppression, but since the 1984 Act may well fall within the terms not of oppression but of section 76(2)(b) of the Act, the part of the Act which we are now considering.

The judge considered these matters, but he came to the conclusion that the defendant, when he made his admissions, did not think that the effect of the admissions would be to enable him to go home. He thought, rightly, that the probability was that it would lead him to being kept in custody and not granted bail. It was for those reasons that the judge came to the conclusion, despite the flagrant and serious breaches of the code, that the confession was not obtained in the consequence of anything said or done likely to render unreliable any confession made by the defendant.

We hesitate to criticise that conclusion, coming as it does from this particular judge, a judge who had, moreover, seen and heard both the appellant and the police officers, which of course we have not. However, it seems to us that Mr Hunt's submission is correct, namely, that it was not so much the question of immediate release which was exercising the mind of the appellant at interview. The evidence from the psychologist was that this man was poorly equipped to cope with sustained interrogation and the longer the pressure was imposed upon him the more confused he was likely to be in his own mind. He would experience what we have already described, the heightened sense of arousal from which he would want to escape. As the judge said, the appellant was under no illusions about the possibility of immediate release were he to confess, but what the officers, even on their own account of the interview, had been stressing, was that it was in the long run that treatment was required rather than punishment. We think that it was this long term prospect, as Mr Hunt has rightly described it, to which the judge paid insufficient attention. The appellant may have felt it was easier to get away from the unpleasant state of arousal by making these confessions, particularly in the light of the suggestion that what was required was treatment rather than prison.

Much the same considerations apply to the discretionary power under section 78(1) of the Act, which it is not necessary for this court to read. Likewise, the further power under section 82(3) which reads as follows: 'Nothing in this Part of this Act shall prejudice any power of a court to exclude evidence (whether by preventing questions from being put or otherwise) at its discretion.'

Had the learned judge paid the attention which we think he should have paid to the long term expectations of the appellant rather than to the prospects of immediate release, and had he paid attention to the fact that the breaches of the code deprived the court of the knowledge which should have been available to it, namely of precisely what was said by these officers in the vital interview, the judge would, and we think should, have ruled against the admission of these confessions, particularly so against the background of the appellant's age, his subnormal mentality and the behaviour of the police and what they had admittedly said to him.

Finally, we add this. The learned judge was troubled by this case. We are likewise troubled. It is a case, in our judgment, where the conviction can properly be described as unsafe or unsatisfactory. Consequently, this appeal is allowed and the conviction will be quashed.

Questions

1. In *Alladice*, the Lord Chief Justice states, 'If the police have acted in bad faith, the court will have little difficulty in ruling any confession inadmissible under section 78'. In *Delaney*, the Lord Chief Justice describes the police officer's breach of the code as flagrant and then states, 'It is no part of the duty of the court to rule a statement inadmissible simply in order to punish the police for failure to observe the codes of practice'.

Are these statements reconcilable?

2. The court in *Mason* expressly denied that the confession was being excluded as a means of disciplining the police. Do you agree?

R v Walsh
(1990) 89 Cr App R 161
Court of Appeal

SAVILLE J: On July 6, 1988, in the Central Criminal Court, the appellant was convicted after a trial of robbery (count 1) and of having a firearm with intent to commit an indictable offence (count 2). He was sentenced to nine years' imprisonment for the robbery and three years concurrent for the firearms offence. He was also sentenced to 12 months' concurrent for the possession of a firearm in a public place and to three years for possessing a firearm when prohibited from doing so. He appeals with the leave of the single judge against his conviction on counts 1 and 2, having pleaded guilty to the other two counts.

It is common ground that on January 15, 1988, in the City of London a man robbed a security guard of a deposit box containing some £4,000. As the man ran away the security system in the box went off, emitting an alarm signal and also orange smoke. The robber, who had a pistol with him, then dropped the box and ran off. It was the Crown's case that a witness then followed the man until he got into a taxi, alerted the police who shortly afterwards found the appellant, with a pistol in his possession, in the taxi.

The appellant's case was that he had nothing to do with the robbery but was merely — if that is the right word — in the vicinity to collect a pistol from somebody else at a cafe.

The basis of this appeal against conviction on counts 1 and 2 is that the trial judge should have exercised his powers under section 78(1) of the Police and Criminal Evidence Act, 1984 to exclude evidence of admissions allegedly made by the appellant in the course of an interview with two police officers at Bishopsgate Police Station. It is submitted that there had not only been a breach of section 58 of this Act, but also a failure to comply with certain provisions contained in Code C of the Codes of Practice which where issued by the Secretary of State under section 66 of the Act; and that these circumstances meant that the admission of the evidence would have such an adverse effect on the fairness of the proceedings that the judge was wrong to admit it.

It is common ground that there was a breach of section 58 of the Act. The appellant had therefore been arrested and was being held in custody at the police station. He requested a solicitor, but was denied access to one on grounds that the Crown do not seek to suggest fell within the exceptions set out in that section. It is also common ground that in breach of Code C the police conducted the interview with a person who had asked for but not received legal advice . . . , that they failed to make contemporaneous notes . . . that they failed to record in the officers' pocket books the reasons for not keeping a record in the course of the interview . . . , that they failed to give the appellant a chance to read and sign an interview record . . . It was also suggested that since the interview was conducted in a cell there had therefore been a failure to conduct it in an interview room . . . , but this the Crown do not necessarily accept, on the grounds which the Code of course allows, that it was not practicable in the circumstances.

In his ruling after the *voire dire* in which he had heard evidence from the senior police officers involved, the trial judge concluded that none of the officers had acted in bad faith. The trial judge further expressed the view that he did not feel, as he put it, that the provision of a solicitor would have made any difference to what was said during the interview. Overall, the trial judge in effect concluded that it did not appear to him that (using the words of s. 78) the admission of the evidence of the interviews would have such an adverse effect on the fairness of the proceedings that the court ought not to admit that evidence.

The main object of section 58 of the Act and indeed of the Codes of Practice is to achieve fairness — to an accused or suspected person so as, among other things, to preserve and protect his legal rights; but also fairness for the Crown and its officers so that again, among other things, there might be reduced the incidence or effectiveness of unfounded allegations of malpractice.

To our minds it follows that if there are significant and substantial breaches of section 58 or the provisions of the Code, then prima facie at least the standards of fairness set by Parliament have not been met. So far as a defendant is concerned, it seems to us also to follow that to admit evidence against him which has been obtained in circumstances where these standards have not been met, cannot but have an adverse effect on the fairness of the proceedings. This does not mean, of course, that in every case of a significant or substantial breach of section 58 or the Code of Practice the evidence concerned will automatically be excluded. Section 78 does not so provide. The task of the court is not merely to consider whether there would be an adverse effect on the fairness of the proceedings, but such an adverse effect that justice requires the evidence to be excluded.

In the present case, we have no material which would lead us to suppose that the judge erred in concluding that the police officers were acting in good faith. However, although bad faith may make substantial or significant that which might not otherwise be so, the contrary does not follow. Breaches which are in themselves significant and substantial are not rendered otherwise by the good faith of the officers concerned.

In our judgment, leaving aside the possible breach in respect of where the interview was conducted, it seems to us that the breaches in this case were both significant and substantial. For no good reason the officers concerned failed to follow the proper proceedings, denying the appellant legal advice and neither protecting or preserving his right in the way laid down in the Code.

The trial judge expressed the view that even if a solicitor had been present he did not feel that this would have made any difference. However, Mr Kamlish pointed out that the trial judge had not heard the appellant and, what is more, it is the fact that after the appellant had eventually seen a solicitor he exercised his right to not answer questions. It may be that the judge was influenced by the fact that the appellant had been cautioned before the interview under attack, but this seems to ignore the fact that the appellant was not only entitled to be cautioned, but also entitled to the benefit of legal advice from a solicitor.

Having considered the matter, we can see nothing in this case which could properly lead the court to the conclusion that the breach of section 58 made no difference; or in other words that it was likely that the appellant would have made the admissions in any event. The very highest it could be put, to our minds, was that it was perhaps uncertain whether or not the presence of a solicitor would have made any difference. Added to this, of course, is the fact that it appeared through the cross-examination of the officers during the *voire dire* that the appellant was challenging root and branch that he had made any admissions at all. Accordingly, it seems to us that a major, if not the major, premise on which the learned judge exercised his discretion was a false premise. This distinguishes the present case from such decisions as *Smith and Campbell*, which was cited to us. We should observe at this point that a number of other authorities have been brought to our attention on the Act, but since we consider that the judge proceeded on a false basis, it seems to us that they are only of general assistance in the circumstances of this particular case.

In these circumstances, coupled with the failure of the police officers to comply with the Code in the respects that we have categorised as significant and substantial, we consider that to admit the evidence would have such an adverse effect on the proceedings that the judge should have excluded it.

To our minds, in the present case and in the present circumstances, the presence or absence of other evidence against the appellant makes little or any difference to this conclusion. Proceedings are not rendered fair by the fact that other evidence is available, while the absence of any other such evidence merely reinforces the unfairness that already exists. Where the strength or otherwise of the other evidence is relevant is in considering the proviso, for if this court concludes that notwithstanding the unfairness of the trial the appellant would have been convicted anyway had the trial been wholly fair, then at the end there may have been no real miscarriage of justice at all.

We do not reach that conclusion in this case. The other evidence, whilst substantial, was not overwhelming. There were discrepencies between the description of the robber and that of the appellant. No one identified the appellant as the robber and there was expert evidence to the effect that the robber's clothing would have been impregnated with smoke and dye from the deposit box security system. None was found on the appellant's clothing. Furthermore, the person who followed the robber agreed that he had lost sight of him on more than one occasion and was to a degree at least picking him up again because he, unlike most other City workers, was wearing casual clothing.

In those circumstances, we have concluded that we should allow the appeal and quash the convictions on counts 1 and 2. The convictions and sentences on the other counts will, of course, stand.

Question

Compare the cases of *Alladice* and *Walsh*. Is there any material difference between them which is capable of explaining the different outcomes?

D. Birch, '*The Pace Hots Up*'
[1989] Crim LR 95, pp. 110–4

If, as appears likely, section 78 provides a general discretion to exclude unreliable evidence, this power must apply to confessions equally with other evidence. Here also, problems of overlap arise. How will section 78 ever get a chance to operate in this way in relation to confessions given the comprehensive coverage of section 76? Or, to try a slightly different tack, if an unreliable confession will have such an adverse effect on the fairness of the proceedings that it ought not to be given in evidence, what is the point in having section 76 at all? Both questions must be answered if these provisions are to co-exist rationally.

Let us tackle the second question first. Section 76 merits a separate existence because it is declaratory of the effects of a particularly common and dangerous form of unreliability resulting from things said or done in the interrogation process. Common, because there is always a risk that defendants under interrogation might make unrealiable statements in order to halt the process, and dangerous because juries are believed to put too much faith in confessions obtained under interrogation. Thus it is provided that any suspicion of unreliability of this nature must lead to exclusion. The strength of the fear behind the provision can be seen from the fact that the section does not even concern itself with *actual* unreliability: the question to be put is a *hypothetical* one concerning the reliability of *any* confession made in those circumstances, and the question whether the actual statement is true may not be probed.

This leads us back to the first question, for there may be scope for a power to exclude evidence which may be unreliable and dangerous for reasons other than those covered by section 76. These will be cases where the unreliability cannot be causally linked with something 'said or done'. Because these cases will, like the cases of impropriety discussed above, inevitably fall along a spectrum, with at one end examples of evidence every bit as dangerous as that excluded automatically by section 76, the results of the division of functions between Act and discretion are bound to appear odd.

So, for instance, CR Williams has understandably taken the view that a confession by a defendant with a mental age of under five who is in the habit of telling people what he thinks they want to hear should be inadmissible in law, not subject to the checks and balances of discretionary exclusion. But (a) this is a case at the most serious end of the spectrum, and the existence of cases where the discretion will inevitably be exercised in the defence's favour does not of itself constitute an argument against the notion of a discretion to exclude, and (b) to apply to cases where the mentally ill or handicapped have been interviewed the hypothetical test for exclusion posed by section 76 might be to cross our wires of policy, for it can be argued that, provided the safeguards for interviewing such defendants have been complied with, we should concern ourselves with whether anything of value can be derived from *this* confession, not, as section 76 does, with '*any* confession' that D might have made. Take for example the facts of the case of *Miller* [1986] 1 WLR 1191, where D was quite convinced that 'small molecular people' had ordered him to kill his girlfriend. A test which required it to be proved that there was no likelihood that he would make an unreliable confession would probably have led to exclusion of his statement to the police. However Miller's account of the killing was clearly in line with scientific and other evidence and there was no threat to the fairness of the proceedings in putting the confession before a jury, who would have found no difficulty in distinguishing between the fantasy elements and the verifiable parts of the statement.

This is not to say that it is easy to distinguish between cases which fall to be dealt with under section 76 and those which are the proper province of section 78. An obvious question to begin with is to ask whether anything was 'said or done' to cause the confession so as to bring section 76 into play. But few confessions are entirely spontaneous, so the real question is whether the phrase is capable of referring to ordinary questioning and other happenings in the interrogation process, or whether it should be restricted to things said or done which are unusual (including things which are improper). Not surprisingly the courts seem to be opting only to exclude evidence under section 76 if something out of the ordinary has occurred. In *Waters* [1989] Crim LR 62 D made a number of separate confessions to different police officers after he had been charged. It is not generally permitted to question a suspect after charge, and the Court of Appeal scrupulously investigated the circumstances of each confession, admitting only those where no improper questioning had taken place. Similarly in *Doolan* [1988] Crim LR 747 where various breaches of the Code of Practice regarding cautioning and interviewing were broken, the Court of Appeal, excluding D's confession under section 76, held:

It is of course important that the Code of Practice should be complied with if possible, however difficult or inconvenient that may be. The Code should have been complied with here. There was no reason to depart from it.
. . . We take the view that [the breaches] . . . were likely, in the circumstances existing at the time, to render the evidence unreliable.

Thus it seems that not only is section 76 unlikely to be used in respect of ordinary proper questioning, but also that it is being seen as a positive weapon in the courts' armoury to ensure compliance with interrogation rules.

In the case of a mentally ill or handicapped defendant this is likely to mean that, whereas his condition is one of the 'circumstances existing at the time' referred to in section 76, the words 'anything said or done' will not include questions properly put to D in the presence of an independent adult as required by the Code of Practice. This is supported by *Everett* [1988] Crim LR 826, in which a mentally handicapped adult was interviewed on his own in breach of the Code. The trial judge had taken the view that he did not need to have regard to D's mental condition in reaching his decision under section 76. His approach was held by the Court of Appeal to be wrong: D's mental condition was one of the 'circumstances' to which the section directed the court to have regard and had the judge done this he would have concluded that the Code of Practice should have been complied with and would have excluded the confession. It seems likely that, had there been compliance with the Code, there would have been nothing 'said or done' to trigger the section.

Section 76 is further confined in its operation by *Goldenberg* (1988) 88 Cr App R 285. D, a drug addict, made a confession, possibly in order to get bail and feed his addiction. The Court of Appeal held that the words 'in consequence of anything said or done' exclude reference to the statements or acts of D himself, for in such cases the causal link between what was said or done and the confession could not be established. Self-induced unreliability will thus have to be dealt with, if at all, under section 78. This reasoning produces the odd result that where D is given a drug by a police doctor prior to confessing, the test for admissibility will be different from where the drug is self-administered. The reasoning of the Court does not, of course, necessarily hold good, for a confession might properly be said to be rendered potentially unreliable in consequence of D's own act, for example in the situation envisaged above where he took a drug before making it. Such cases are likely to be rare, but when they occur it is very much more debatable whether they ought to be dealt with under section 76 than the case of *Goldenberg* suggests. Whether that decision is right or wrong, however, unconvincing distinctions will have to be made. If it is wrong, a line would have to be drawn between unreliable statements 'caused' by a mentally disordered D's words and conduct, which would fall under section 76, and those which proceed directly from his mental condition with no intervening speech or acts by anyone, which would be governed by section 78.

When the duty to exclude in section 76 and the power to do so in section 78 are couched in such similar terms, it is almost inevitable that mistakes will be made by invoking principles relevant to one section while considering another. In *Doolan* the various breaches of the Code which occurred included the failure of the interviewer to take notes of the interview with D and show them to him afterwards. D's confession was, as we have seen, regarded as inadmissible under section 76. But the causal link required by that section can hardly be established by reference to a breach which took place after the confession was made!

The error arises because the type of unreliability in issue in *Doolan* is of a different sort from that at which section 76 is aimed. That section assumes that the confession was made, and is concerned with whether it can safely be acted on. The rules for showing suspects the notes of interviews are aimed instead at achieving an agreed and reliable record of what, if anything, was said — a completely different problem of reliability and one traditionally submitted to the good sense of the jury. There is, however, no reason why section 78 should not be invoked in some cases where it would be dangerous to put any weight on the notes at all, and yet there is a likelihood that a jury would do so.

In cases where only section 78 can be invoked, some guidelines for the exercise of the power need to be drawn up. It might, for example, be proper to take into account the existence of other evidence confirming the reliability of the confession under section 78 in a way that is not possible under section 76, where the confession remains inadmissible even if its accuracy can be established by evidence discovered as a result of it. The importance of the confession to the case might also be relevant in that the court could have regard to its probative value in the light of the weight which the prosecution seeks to put upon it. (Lest it be thought that any confession is bound to be an important part of the prosecution case it should be noted that the definition of 'confession' includes all partial admissions, which might be of tenuous relevance.)

In the light of the confusion that has already arisen the sooner such principles are articulated the better.

(iv) Miscellaneous matters

Note
Space precludes any detailed consideration of a number of matters associated with confession evidence, but for the sake of completeness they are noted below.

(a)   The voire dire

If the admissibility of a confession is challenged there will often take place a *voire dire* or 'trial within a trial'. The judge will, after hearing such evidence as the parties may wish to adduce, rule on the admissibility of the confession. The *voire dire* will normally take place in the absence of the jury, although it need not do so. If the *voire dire* takes place in the presence of the jury, the judge is still required to rule on the admissibility of the confession as a matter of law. The defendant may give evidence at the *voire dire* and the question arises as to what use, if any, the prosecution may make of such evidence.

R v Brophy
[1982] AC 477
House of Lords

LORD FRASER OF TULLYBELTON: My Lords, this appeal raises a question of importance to the administration of criminal justice, whether admissions made by an accused person in the course of giving evidence at a trial within a trial, or voir dire, can be used by the Crown at the substantive trial as evidence tending to prove that he is guilty of the offence charged in the indictment.

Once it has been held that the material part of the respondent's evidence was relevant to the issue at the voir dire, a necessary consequence is, in my opinion, that it is not admissible in the substantive trial. Indeed counsel for the Crown did not argue to the contrary. If such evidence, being relevant, were admissible at the substantive trial, an accused person would not enjoy the complete freedom that he ought to have at the voir dire to contest the admissibility of his previous statements. It is of the first importance for the administration of justice that an accused person should feel completely free to give evidence at the voir dire of any improper methods by which a confession or admission has been extracted from him, for he can almost never make an effective challenge of its admissibility without giving evidence himself. He is thus virtually compelled to give evidence at the voir dire, and if his evidence were admissible at the substantive trial, the result might be a significant impairment of his so-called 'right of silence' at the trial. The right means 'No man is to be compelled to incriminate himself; *nemo tenetur se ipsum prodere*' see *Reg.* v *Sang* [1980] AC 402, 455, *per* Lord Scarman. The word 'compelled' in that context must, in my opinion, include being put under pressure. So long as that right exists it ought not to be cut down, as it would be if an accused person, who finds himself obliged to give evidence at the voir dire, in order to contest a confession extracted by improper means, and whose evidence tends to show the truth of his confession, were liable to have his evidence used at the substantive trial. He would not receive a fair trial, as that term is understood in all parts of the United Kingdom.

I do not overlook or minimise the risk that accused persons may make false allegations of ill-treatment by the police; some of them undoubtedly do. But the detection of dishonest witnesses on this, as on other matters, is part of the ordinary duty of the courts and it should be left to them. The possibility, indeed the practical certainty, that some accused will give dishonest evidence of ill-treatment does not justify inhibiting their freedom to testify at the voir dire. The importance of the principle was explained by Lord Hailsham of St. Marylebone in the recent Privy Council case of *Wong Kam-ming* v *The Queen* [1980] AC 247, 261, where he said this:

> . . . any civilised system of criminal jurisprudence must accord to the judiciary some means of excluding confessions or admissions obtained by improper methods. This is not only because of the potential unreliability of such statements, but also, and perhaps mainly, because in a civilised society it is vital that persons in custody or

charged with offences should not be subjected to ill-treatment or improper pressure in order to extract confessions. It is therefore of very great importance that the courts should continue to insist that before extra-judicial statements can be admitted in evidence the prosecution must be made to prove beyond reasonable doubt that the statement was not obtained in a manner which should be reprobated and was therefore in the truest sense voluntary. For this reason it is necessary that the defendant should be able and feel free either by his own testimony or by other means to challenge the voluntary character of the tendered statement. If, as happened in the instant appeal, the prosecution were to be permitted to introduce into the trial the evidence of the defendant given in the course of the voir dire when the statement to which it relates has been excluded whether in order to supplement the evidence otherwise available as part of the prosecution case, or by way of cross-examination of the defendant, the important principles of public policy to which I have referred would certainly become eroded, possibly even to vanishing point.

The case of *Wong Kam-ming* differs from the present in two respects. First, the trial there was by a judge and jury. Secondly, the accused's admission had been elicited in cross-examination at the voir dire. The decision is therefore not directly in point, but neither of these features was essential to the observations by Lord Hailsham of St. Marylebone in the passage which I have quoted, which were quite wide enough to apply to the facts of this appeal. In my opinion they are applicable here also.

A submission was made by counsel for the Crown that the position of the accused could be adequately safeguarded if his evidence at the voir dire were admissible at the substantive trial, provided that the judge had a discretion to exclude at the trial any such evidence which would prejudice him unfairly. This was the approach favoured by Bray CJ in *Reg.* v *Wright* [1969] SASR 256 — a South Australian case, the actual decision in which cannot stand with *Wong Kam-ming* and was not supported by counsel for the Crown in this appeal. With all respect, I cannot regard that as a satisfactory solution. The right of the accused to give evidence at the voir dire without affecting his right to remain silent at the substantive trial is in my opinion absolute and is not to be made conditional on an exercise of judicial discretion.

Where an accused has admitted at the voir dire that he is guilty of a charge of such gravity as that contained in the 49th count in the instant appeal, no court can acquit him without most anxious consideration of the issues involved. The Court of Appeal evidently gave such consideration to the issues here, and I have endeavoured to do the same. Having done so, I feel no doubt that the Court of Appeal reached the right decision and that the respondent must be acquitted. . . .

I would dismiss this appeal.

LORD RUSSELL OF KILLOWEN: My Lords, I have had the advantage of reading in draft the speech of my noble and learned friend, Lord Fraser of Tullybelton. I agree with it and with the order that he proposes.

LORD KEITH OF KINKEL: My Lords, I have had the advantage of reading in draft the speech of my noble and learned friend, Lord Fraser of Tullybelton. I agree with it, and for the reasons stated by him I too would dismiss the appeal.

LORD ROSKILL: My Lords, I have had the advantage of reading in draft the speech of my noble and learned friend, Lord Fraser of Tullybelton. For the reasons he gives, I too would answer all the certified questions in the negative and would dismiss this appeal.

(b)   Editing a confession

A confession is evidence only against its maker. What is to happen if a confession implicates a co-accused or refers to some other inadmissible matter? If possible, the confession should be edited so as to remove the offending material. If the offending material relates to a co-accused and it is not possible to edit it out, then a number of choices present themselves. The judge may order separate trials, give a direction to the jury to ignore the reference to the co-accused, or perhaps exclude the whole confession even though this will benefit the maker.

(For examples see *R* v *Lake* (1976) 64 Cr App R 172; *R* v *Rogers and Tarran* [1971] Crim LR 413.)

(c)   Use of confession by a co-accused

Particular difficulties arise where a confession has been excluded from evidence and a co-accused then wishes to cross-examine the maker (his fellow co-accused) about the confession, in order to demonstrate the maker's previous inconsistency.

Lui Mei Lin v *The Queen*
[1989] 1 AC 288
Privy Council

LORD ROSKILL: At the conclusion of the hearing of this appeal on 25 July 1988 their Lordships stated that they would humbly advise Her Majesty that the appellant's appeal should be allowed and her conviction on 23 January 1987 in the High Court of Hong Kong on two counts of forgery quashed and that their Lordships' reasons for that advice would be given in due course. The Lordships now give those reasons.

The appellant was one of three defendants jointly charged on two counts (the first and second counts in the indictment), one of having forged dies with intent to defraud, the other of having forged valuable securities. The first defendant was named Liu Kan-por. The appellant was the third defendant. Yick Hak-kan was the second defendant. Yick Mai-ming was the fourth defendant. The third and fourth counts in the indictment were against the second defendant alone while a fifth count was against the first defendant alone. The first defendant, the appellant and the fourth defendant were all convicted on counts one and two. The second defendant was acquitted on counts three and four. The first defendant was also convicted on the fifth count. Substantial prison sentences were imposed upon all three defendants so convicted. Subsequent appeals to the Court of Appeal by the first and fourth defendants against their convictions on counts one and two succeeded on the ground of misdirection by the trial judge. Retrials were ordered. The appellant's application for leave to appeal against her convictions was dismissed.

The issue involved in the appellant's appeal to the Court of Appeal and now to this Board is entirely different from the issues involved in the appeals by the other defendants. On 11 June 1986 the first defendant was interviewed by and made a statement to the police. That statement, which their Lordships have read, beyond doubt incriminated the appellant. The prosecution sought to adduce that statement in evidence against its maker, the first defendant. The admissibility of the statement was challenged. At the outset of the trial a voire dire was held to determine whether or not the statement had been made voluntarily. The trial judge held that the statement was made as a result of inducements by a police officer. He accordingly excluded the statement on the ground that it was not made voluntarily. The first defendant in due course gave evidence in his own defence. He admitted that he had taken part in the arrangements for printing stamps, but had done so innocently, having been misled by the appellant. He was cross-examined on behalf of the second and fourth defendants. There is no doubt that his oral evidence differed in a number of material respects — the details do not now matter — from what he had said in the excluded statement. The appellant's counsel naturally cross-examined the first defendant on the basis that the oral evidence was false. He sought the leave of the trial judge further to cross-examine the first defendant upon the excluded statement as being an inconsistent statement previously made by the first defendant. Counsel for the Crown opposed the application relying on a previous decision of the Court of Appeal in *Yu Tit-hoi* v *The Queen* [1983] HKLR 7. The trial judge was of course bound by that decision and refused the application for leave to cross-examine the first defendant upon his statement. A further application on behalf of the appellant for a separate trial was also refused.

. . .

Counsel for the appellant placed great reliance upon the decision of the House of Lords in *Murdoch* v *Taylor* [1965] AC 574. The question there arose under section 1(f)(iii) of the Criminal Evidence Act 1898. The House decided that once a co-accused had 'given evidence against' another co-accused, the latter was under the statute entitled without restriction to cross-examine the former as to character and to put his previous convictions to him. In a passage, at p. 593, Lord Donovan emphasised the difference between the position of the prosecution and the position of a co-accused in this respect:

> But when it is the co-accused who seeks to exercise the right conferred by proviso (f)(iii) different considerations come into play. He seeks to defend himself; to say to the jury that the man who is giving evidence against him is unworthy of belief; and to support that assertion by proof of bad character. The right to do this cannot, in my opinion, be fettered in any way.

A similar view had earlier been expressed by Devlin J in an interlocutory ruling given in *Reg.* v *Miller* (1952) 36 Cr App R 169, 171. Their Lordships think it right to quote the relevant passage in full:

> The fundamental principle, equally applicable to any question that is asked by the defence as to any question that is asked by the prosecution, is that it is not normally relevant to inquire into a prisoner's previous character, and, particularly, to ask questions which tend to show that he has previously committed some criminal offence. It is not relevant because the fact that he has committed an offence on one occasion does not in any way show that he is likely to commit an offence on any subsequent occasion. Accordingly, such questions are, in general, inadmissible, not primarily for the reason that they are prejudicial, but because they are irrelevant. There is, however, this difference in the application of the principle. In the case of the prosecution, a question of this sort may be relevant and at the same time be prejudicial, and, if the court is of the opinion that the prejudicial effect outweighs its relevance, then it has the power, and indeed, the duty, to exclude the question. Therefore, counsel for the prosecution rarely asks such a question. No such limitation applies to a question asked by counsel for the defence. His duty is to adduce any evidence which is relevant to his own case and assists his client, whether or not it prejudices anyone else.

Counsel for the Crown invited their Lordships to distinguish *Murdoch* v *Taylor* [1965] AC 574 on the ground that the rights there in question arose under a statute and that what was there allowed to be put in cross-examination were the previous convictions of the co-accused. Their Lordships agree that this is so but find no sufficient ground of distinction in that fact. Ever since section 5 of the Criminal Procedure Act 1865 (28 Vict. c. 18) (Lord Denman's Act) was enacted — this section is exactly reproduced in section 14 of the Evidence Ordinance (Laws of Hong Kong, c. 8) — it has been permissible in every criminal and indeed in every civil trial to cross-examine a witness as to any previous inconsistent statement made by him in writing or reduced into writing subject, where the inconsistent statement is said to be in writing, to his attention first being called to those parts of any writing which were to be used in order to contradict him. The only limit on the right of a co-accused to cross-examine another co-accused in these circumstances is, in their Lordships' opinion, relevancy. If one co-accused has given evidence incriminating another it must be relevant for the latter to show, if he can, that the former has on some other occasion given inconsistent evidence and thus is unworthy of belief.

. . .

It was also suggested on behalf of the Crown that, if cross-examination upon the excluded statement were to be permitted, the trial judge might have to carry out what was described as a balancing exercise, balancing the interests of the maker of the statement against the interests of the co-accused on whose behalf it was sought to cross-examine before deciding whether or not to permit the proposed cross-examination. Their Lordships disagree. In their view the right to cross-examine is, as Lord Donovan stated in *Murdoch* v *Taylor* [1965] AC 574, 593, unfettered, the only limit being relevancy. If the statement contains irrelevant matter the trial judge would no doubt insist that the irrelevant matter should not be referred to and, if necessary, excised from any copies of the statement which the jury might be allowed to see.

. . .

Appeal allowed. Conviction quashed.

(d)   Statements partly adverse and partly favourable

R v Duncan
(1981) 73 Cr App R 359
Court of Appeal

The appellant made statements admitting the killing of a woman with whom he was living. At his trial for murder the appellant elected not to give evidence or call witnesses. The trial judge raised the question of provocation and invited submissions. The judge ruled that, in so far as the appellant's statements were self-serving, they could not be evidence of the facts and therefore provocation would not be left to the jury. The appellant was convicted and appealed on the ground that the ruling was wrong.

LORD LANE CJ: . . . The basic rules are as follows: (1) What a person says out of court is, generally speaking not admissible to prove the truth of what he says. (2) It may be admissible if — (a) it is an exception to the hearsay rule, in which case it is evidence of the truth of what is stated; (b) it falls outside the hearsay rule, that is to say if it is adduced for a purpose other than proving the truth of the statement — an example of this is to be found in *Subramaniam* v *Public Prosecutor* [1956] 1 WLR 965, where a statement was relevant to the question of whether there had been duress or not. The only relevant exception to the hearsay rule in the present circumstances is that relating to admissions against interest or confessions.

The issue between the parties here is the extent to which confessions are properly to be regarded as evidence of the truth of the facts which they state. Both parties are agreed that if a statement is adduced as an admission against interest, the whole of the statement must be admitted. Any other course would obviously be unfair.

It is contended on behalf of the Crown that this rule does not, however, make the contents of the statement evidence of the facts contained therein except in so far as those statements are admissions against interest. Mr Judge, on the other hand, on behalf of the appellant, contends that the whole statement is evidence of the truth of the facts contained therein. He, however, concedes that the judge is entitled to explain to the jury, if indeed it needs explanation, that the weight to be given to those parts of the statement which contain admissions against interest may be very different from the weight to be given to the parts which are self-exculpatory.

One is bound to observe that if the contentions of the Crown are correct, the judge would be faced with a very difficult task in trying to explain to the jury the difference between those parts of a 'mixed' statement (if we may call it such) which were truly confessions and those parts which were self-exculpatory. It is doubtful if the result would be readily intelligible. Suppose a prisoner had said 'I killed X. If I had not done so, X would certainly have killed me there and then.' If the judge tells the jury that the first sentence is evidence of the truth of what it states but that the second sentence is not; that it is merely something to which they are entitled to have regard as qualifying the first sentence and affecting its weight as an admission, they will either not understand or disregard what he is saying. Judges should not be obliged to give meaningless or unintelligible directions to juries.

We turn to examine the authorities. In *McGregor* (1967) 51 Cr App R 338; [1968] 1 QB 371 Lord Parker CJ, at p. 341 and p. 377, 378 respectively said this: 'As we understand it, Mr Dovener says and says rightly that, if the prosecution are minded to put in an admission or a confession, they must put in the whole and not merely part of it.' He later cited with approval a passage from the then current edition of *Archbold* (36th ed), para. 1128: '. . . the better opinion seems to be that as in the case of all other evidence the whole should be left to the jury to say whether the facts asserted by the prisoner in his favour be true.' Lord Parker went on to consider and reject out of hand a submission by counsel for the appellant that the jury should have been directed to give equal weight to both parts of the appellant's statement, those containing admissions and those containing excuses or explanations.

This case is clear authority for the proposition that in the case of a 'mixed' statement both parts are evidence of the facts they state, though they are obviously not to be regarded as having equal weight.

Sparrow (1973) 57 Cr App R 352; [1973] 1 WLR 488, seems to be inconsistent with the primary ruling in *McGregor* (*supra*), which was not cited to the Court, because Lawton LJ says this at p. 357 and p. 492 of the respective reports: 'The trial judge had a difficult task in summing up that part of the case which concerned the appellant. First, he had to try to get the jury to understand that the appellant's exculpatory statement to the police after arrest, which he had not verified in the witness box, was not evidence of the facts in it save in so far as it contained admissions. Many lawyers find difficulty in grasping this principle of the law of evidence. What juries make of it must be a matter of surmise, but the probabilities are they make very little.' He then turned to consider the extent to which the judge should comment on the way in which the case has been conducted and upon the failure of the accused man to go into the witness box.

Donaldson and Others (1976) 64 Cr App R 59 was another example of a 'mixed' statement. At p. 65 James LJ says this: 'In our view there is a clear distinction to be made between statements of admission adduced by the Crown as part of the case against the defendant and statements entirely of a self-serving nature made and sought to be relied by a defendant. When the Crown adduce a statement relied upon as an admission it is for the jury to consider the whole statement including any passages that contain qualifications or explanations favourable to the defendant, that bear upon the passages relied upon by the prosecution as an admission, and it is for the jury to decide whether the statement viewed as a whole constitutes an admission. To this extent the statement may be said to be evidence of the facts stated therein.'

Finally in *Pearce* (1979) 69 Cr App R 365, the Court gave directions on how three different factual situations should be approached. We are in this case only concerned with the first: '(1) A statement which contains an admission is always admissible as a declaration against interest and is evidence of the facts admitted. With this exception a statement made by an accused person is never evidence of the facts in the statement.' It is not clear from this what standing is to be given to the exculpatory parts of a 'mixed' statement, but since the Court expressly based themselves upon the principles in *Donaldson (supra)* one can assume that the statement is to be viewed as a whole by the jury.

We should add that we were referred to a number of other decisions: *Storey* (1968) 52 Cr App R 334 in which *McGregor (supra)* was not cited and which concerned the question of a purely exculpatory statement and its evidential weight upon a submission of no case; *Thompson* [1975] Crim LR 34; *Barbery Doney and Davis* (1975) 62 Cr App R 248 — which were cases of purely exculpatory statements.

Where a 'mixed' statement is under consideration by the jury in a case where the defendant has not given evidence, it seems to us that the simplest, and, therefore, the method most likely to produce a just result, is for the jury to be told that the whole statement, both the incriminating parts and the excuses or explanations, must be considered by them in deciding where the truth lies. It is, to say the least, not helpful to try to explain to the jury that the exculpatory parts of the statement are something less than evidence of the facts they state. Equally, where appropriate, as it usually will be, the judge may, and should, point out that the incriminating parts are likely to be true (otherwise why say them?), whereas the excuses do not have the same weight.

(The court held on the facts that there was nothing in the appellant's statements which amounted to a claim of provocation.)

Appeal dismissed.

Note

The principles in *Duncan* were later approved by the House of Lords in *R v Sharp* [1988] 1 WLR 7.

Question

Crook and Hook are arrested for allegedly committing a robbery. They are properly cautioned and separately interviewed by Sergeant Smith. Crook is refused access to his solicitor Mr Sharp, because Sergeant Smith honestly believes that Sharp was involved in planning the robbery. Crook then writes his own statement in which he admits his involvement and states that Hook

committed the offence with him. Hook is then interviewed, having refused
Sergeant Smith's offer of a solicitor. The interview is not written down
contemporaneously because Smith believes that making such records hampers the interview process. Crook and Hook are jointly tried for robbery. The
prosecution wish to rely on Crook's confession and Smith's testimony that
when interviewed, Hook admitted the offence.

Discuss.

(B)   Statements in the presence of the defendant

Admissions and confessions most usually follow a period of questioning by
the police, or are made in response to some suggestion or allegation put to
the defendant. With regard to some allegation or accusation, the accused
might respond in a variety of ways. He may fully admit the accusation, he
may deny it, he may remain silent or even respond with some kind of gesture.
Should the defendant respond with an admission then no particular problem
arises. Admissibility is, as we have seen, catered for by s. 76 of the Police and
Criminal Evidence Act 1984. Greater difficulty arises where the response is
ambiguous or where the response is mere silence. The common law approach
to this problem is dealt with at (*i*) below. The Criminal Justice and Public
Order Bill 1994 will also have an impact on this area of the law. Clauses 27,
29 and 30 propose changes in the law which will enable a jury to draw
inferences from an accused's failure or refusal to answer police questions in
certain circumstances. These clauses are dealt with at (*ii*) below.

(*i*)   *The common law*

R v Norton
[1910] 2 KB 496
Court of Criminal Appeal

The defendant was convicted of having unlawful sexual intercourse with a
girl under 13. The child was not called at the trial, but evidence was given
of statements made by her in the presence of the defendant and his answers
to them. The evidence was to the effect that, on being asked by the
defendant who had done it, she said, 'You', and, on being asked by another
person, she said, 'Stevie Norton,' and pointed to the defendant; that the
defendant said, 'No, Madge, you are mistaken'; that she then said, 'You
have done it, Stephen Norton', and pointed to him again. According to one
witness he then lifted his arms and said 'If I have done it I hope the Lord
will strike me dead,' and according to another witness, 'If you say so I
might as well put my clothes on and go home.' There was, therefore,
nothing in his answers necessarily amounting to an admission of the girl's
statements. The trial judge directed the jury to take into consideration the
girl's statement as evidence of the facts contained in it, and to consider
whether looking at all the circumstances they accepted it or the defendant's

denial. On appeal it was argued that they ought to have been directed that the statements were not evidence of the facts stated and that as they were denied by the defendant the jury should disregard them.

PICKFORD J: As a general rule, statements as to the facts of a case under investigation are not evidence unless made by witnesses in the ordinary way, but to this rule there are exceptions. One is that statements made in the presence of a prisoner upon an occasion on which he might reasonably be expected to make some observation, explanation, or denial are admissible under certain circumstances. We think it is not strictly accurate, and may be misleading, to say that they are admissible in evidence against the prisoner, as such an expression may seem to imply that they are evidence of the facts stated in them and must be considered upon the footing of other evidence. Such statements are, however, never evidence of the facts stated in them; they are admissible only as introductory to, or explanatory of, the answer given to them by the person in whose presence they are made. Such answer may, of course, be given either by words or by conduct, e.g., by remaining silent on an occasion which demanded an answer.

If the answer given amounts to an admission of the statements or some part of them, they or that part become relevant as showing what facts are admitted; if the answer be not such an admission, the statements are irrelevant to the matter under consideration and should be disregarded. This seems to us to be correctly and shortly stated in *Taylor on Evidence*, s. 814, p. 574: 'The statements only become evidence when by such acceptance he makes them his own statements.'

No objection was taken in this case to the admission of the statements in evidence, but as the prisoner may be tried again on an indictment on which that question may arise, we think it well to state in what cases such statements can be given in evidence. We think that the contents of such statements should not be given in evidence unless the judge is satisfied that there is evidence fit to be submitted to the jury that the prisoner by his answer to them, whether given by word or conduct, acknowledged the truth of the whole or part of them. If there be no such evidence, then the contents of the statement should be excluded; if there be such evidence, then they should be admitted, and the question whether the prisoner's answer, by words or conduct, did or did not in fact amount to an acknowledgment of them left to the jury.

In trials of prisoners on indictment, in which the most numerous and important of these cases arise, there is, as a rule, no difficulty in deciding whether there be such evidence or not, as the prisoner's answer appears upon the depositions, and the chance that the evidence with regard to it may be different on the trial is so small that it may be disregarded. When, however, the evidence of the prisoner's answer does not appear, there does not seem to be any practical difficulty in applying the rule above stated. The fact of a statement having been made in the prisoner's presence may be given in evidence, but not the contents, and the question asked, what the prisoner said or did on such a statement being made. If his answer, given either by words or conduct, be such as to be evidence from which an acknowledgment may be inferred, then the contents of the statement may be given and the question of admission or not in fact left to the jury; if it be not evidence from which such an acknowledgment may be inferred, then the contents of the statement should be excluded. To allow the contents of such statements to be given before it is ascertained that there is evidence of their being acknowledged to be true must be most prejudicial to the prisoner, as, whatever directions be given to the jury, it is almost impossible for them to dismiss such evidence entirely from their minds. It is perhaps too wide to say that in no case can the statements be given in evidence when they are denied by the prisoner, as it is possible that a denial may be given under such circumstances and in such a manner as to constitute evidence from which an acknowledgment may be inferred, but, as above stated, we think they should be rejected unless there is some evidence of an acknowledgment of the truth. Where they are admitted we think the following is the proper direction to be given to the jury — that if they come to the conclusion that the prisoner had acknowledged the truth of the whole or any part of the facts stated they might take the statement, or so much of it as was acknowledged to be true (but no more), into consideration as evidence in the case generally, not because the statement standing alone afforded any evidence of the matter contained in it, but solely because of the prisoner's acknowledgment of its truth; but unless they found as a fact that there was such an acknowledgment they ought to disregard the statement altogether: see *R v Smith* (1897) 18 Cox CC 470.

Conviction quashed.

R v Christie
[1914] AC 545
House of Lords

The respondent was convicted of an indecent assault upon a little boy. At the trial the boy's mother stated in evidence that, as she and her son came up to the respondent shortly after the act complained of, the little boy said in the respondent's hearing 'That is the man' and described what the respondent did to him, and that the respondent replied 'I am innocent.' The Court of Criminal Appeal quashed the conviction on the ground that evidence of a statement made in the presence of the accused was not admissible against him unless he acknowledged the truth of the statement. The Crown appealed.

LORD ATKINSON: . . . the rule of law undoubtedly is that a statement made in the presence of an accused person, even upon an occasion which should be expected reasonably to call for some explanation or denial from him, is not evidence against him of the facts stated save so far as he accepts the statement, so as to make it, in effect, his own. If he accepts the statement in part only, then to that extent alone does it become his statement. He may accept the statement by word or conduct, action or demeanour, and it is the function of the jury which tries the case to determine whether his words, action, conduct, or demeanour at the time when a statement was made amounts to an acceptance of it in whole or in part. It by no means follows, I think, that a mere denial by the accused of the facts mentioned in the statement necessarily renders the statement inadmissible, because he may deny the statement in such a manner and under such circumstances as may lead a jury to disbelieve him, and constitute evidence from which an acknowledgment may be inferred by them.

Of course, if at the end of the case the presiding judge should be of opinion that no evidence has been given upon which the jury could reasonably find that the accused had accepted the statement so as to make it in whole or in part his own, the judge can instruct the jury to disregard the statement entirely. It is said that, despite this direction, grave injustice might be done to the accused, in as much as the jury, having once heard the statement, could not, or would not, rid their mind of it. It is therefore, in the application of the rule that the difficulty arises. The question then is this: Is it to be taken as a rule of law that such a statement is not to be admitted in evidence until a foundation has been laid for its admission by proof of facts from which, in the opinion of the presiding judge, a jury might reasonably draw the inference that the accused had so accepted the statement as to make it in whole or in part his own, or is it to be laid down that the prosecutor is entitled to give the statement in evidence in the first instance, leaving it to the presiding judge, in case no such evidence as the above mentioned should be ultimately produced, to tell the jury to disregard the statement altogether?

In my view the former is not a rule of law, but it is, I think, a rule which, in the interest of justice, it might be most prudent and proper to follow as a rule of practice.

The course suggested by Pickford J in *R v Norton* [1910] 2 KB 496, where workable, would be quite unobjectionable in itself as a rule of practice, and equally effective for the protection of the accused.

LORD MOULTON: Now, in a civil action evidence may always be given of any statement or communication made to the opposite party, provided it is relevant to the issues. The same is true of any act or behaviour of the party. The sole limitation is that the matter thus given in evidence must be relevant. I am of opinion that, as a strict matter of law, there is no difference in this respect between the rules of evidence in our civil and in our criminal procedure. But there is a great difference in the practice. The law is so much on its guard against the accused being prejudiced by evidence which, though admissible, would probably have a prejudicial influence on the minds of the jury which would be out of proportion to its true evidential value, that there has grown up a practice of a very salutary nature, under which the judge intimates to the counsel for the prosecution that he should not press for the admission of evidence which would be open to this objection, and such an intimation from the tribunal trying the case is usually sufficient to prevent the evidence being pressed in all cases where the scruples of the tribunal in this respect are reasonable. Under the influence of this practice, which is based on an anxiety to secure for every one a fair trial, there has grown up a custom of not admitting certain kinds of evidence which is so constantly followed that it almost amounts to a rule of procedure. It is alleged on the part of the respondent that an instance of this is the case of the accused being charged with the crime and denying it, or not admitting it.

It is common ground that, if on such an occasion he admits it, evidence can be given of the admission and of what passed on the occasion when it was made. It seems quite illogical that it should be admissible to prove that the accused was charged with the crime if his answer thereto was an admission, while it is not admissible to prove it when his answer has been a denial of the crime, and I cannot agree that the admissibility or non-admissibility is decided as a matter of law by any such artificial rule. Going back to first principles as enunciated above, the deciding question is whether the evidence of the whole occurrence is relevant or not. If the prisoner admits the charge the evidence is obviously relevant. If he denies it, it may or may not be relevant. For instance, if he is charged with a violent assault and denies that he committed it, that fact might be distinctly relevant if at the trial his defence was that he did commit the act, but that it was in self-defence. The evidential value of the occurrence depends entirely on the behaviour of the prisoner, for the fact that someone makes a statement to him subsequently to the commission of the crime cannot in itself have any value as evidence for or against him. The only evidence for or against him is his behaviour in response to the charge, but I can see no justification for laying down as a rule of law that any particular form of response, whether of a positive or negative character, is such that it cannot in some circumstances have an evidential value. I am, therefore, of opinion that there is no rule of law that evidence cannot be given of the accused being charged with the offence and of his behaviour on hearing such charge where that behaviour amounts to a denial of his guilt. This is said to have been laid down as a rule of law in *R v Norton*, and to have been followed by the Courts since that decision. If this be so, I think that the decision was wrong, but I am by no means convinced that it was intended in that case to lay down any such rule of law.

But while I am of opinion that there is no such rule of law, I am of opinion that the evidential value of the behaviour of the accused where he denies the charge is very small either for or against him, whereas the effect on the minds of the jury of his being publicly or repeatedly charged to his face with the crime might seriously prejudice the fairness of his trial. In my opinion, therefore, a judge would in most cases be acting in accordance with the best traditions of our criminal procedure if he exercised the influence which he rightly possesses over the conduct of a prosecution in order to prevent such evidence being given in cases where it would have very little or no evidential value. Subject to these words of caution, I am of opinion that this appeal should be allowed upon this point, because we have to decide upon the admissibility as a matter of law, and so regarded I have no doubt that the evidence in question was rightly admitted.

LORD READING: A statement made in the presence of one of the parties to a civil action may be given in evidence against him if it is relevant to any of the matters in issue. And equally such a statement made in the presence of the accused may be given in evidence against him at his trial.

The principles of the laws of evidence are the same whether applied at civil or criminal trials, but they are not enforced with the same rigidity against a person accused of a criminal offence as against a party to a civil action. There are exceptions to the law regulating the admissibility of evidence which apply only to criminal trials, and which have acquired their force by the constant and invariable practice of judges when presiding at criminal trials. They are rules of prudence and discretion, and have become so integral a part of the administration of the criminal law as almost to have acquired the full force of law. . . .

Such practice has found its place in the administration of the criminal law because judges are aware from their experience that in order to ensure a fair trial for the accused, and to prevent the operation of indirect but not the less serious prejudice to his interests, it is desirable in certain circumstances to relax the strict application of the law of evidence. Nowadays, it is the constant practice for the judge who presides at the trial to indicate his opinion to counsel for the prosecution that evidence which, although admissible in law, has little value in its direct bearing upon the case, and might indirectly operate seriously to the prejudice of the accused, should not be given against him, and speaking generally counsel accepts the suggestion and does not press for the admission of the evidence unless he has good reason for it.

That there is danger that the accused may be indirectly prejudiced by the admission of such a statement as in this case is manifest, for however carefully the judge may direct the jury, it is often difficult for them to exclude it altogether from their minds as evidence of the facts contained in the statement.

In general, such evidence can have little or no value in its direct bearing on the case unless the accused, upon hearing the statement, by conduct and demeanour, or by the answer made by him, or in certain circumstances by the refraining from an answer, acknowledged the truth of the statement either in whole or in part, or did or said something from which the jury could infer such an acknowledgment, for if he acknowledged its truth, he accepted it as his own statement of the facts. If the accused denied the truth of the statement when it was made, and there was nothing in his conduct and demeanour from which the jury, notwithstanding his denial, could infer that he acknowledged its truth in whole or in part, the practice of the judges has been to exclude it altogether. In *R v Norton* Pickford J, in delivering the judgment of the Court of Criminal Appeal, said at p. 500: 'If there be no such evidence' (that is of acknowledgment by the accused), 'then the contents of the statement should be excluded; if there be such evidence, then they should be admitted.' If it was intended to lay down rules of law to be applied whenever such a statement is tendered for admission, I think the judgment goes too far; they are valuable rules for the guidance of those presiding at trials of criminal cases when considering how the discretion of the Court, with regard to the admission of such evidence, should be exercised, but it must not be assumed that the judgment in *R v Norton* exhausts all the circumstances which may have to be taken into consideration by the Court when exercising its judicial discretion.

It might well be that the prosecution wished to give evidence of such a statement in order to prove the conduct and demeanour of the accused when hearing the statement as a relevant fact in the particular case, notwithstanding that it did not amount either to an acknowledgment or some evidence of an acknowledgment of any part of the truth of the statement. I think it impossible to lay down any general rule to be applied to all such cases, save the principle of strict law to which I have referred.

Upon the whole, therefore, I come to the conclusion that the rules formulated in *R v Norton,* and followed in this and other cases, must be restricted in their application as above indicated, and cannot be regarded as strict rules of law regulating the admissibility of such evidence.

I think, therefore, that this statement was in law admissible as evidence against Christie.

(VISCOUNT HALDANE LC agreed with LORDS ATKINSON, MOULTON, and READING. LORD PARKER OF WADDINGTON agreed with LORD ATKINSON.)

The Court of Criminal Appeal's order quashing the conviction was affirmed on the ground of misdirection by the trial judge on the question of corroboration.

Hall v R
[1971] 1 WLR 298
Privy Council

The appellant was said to be living with G and T in a two-roomed building. During a search of the premises in his absence, police officers found 'ganja' in a shopping bag. T said that the appellant had brought the bag there. When a police officer told the appellant what T had said, he remained silent. 'Ganja' was also found in a grip and a brief-case in the room occupied by G, who admitted that the grip was hers but denied any knowledge of the drug. When the appellant, G and T were cautioned, they said nothing. They were charged with unlawful possession of 'ganja', and at their trial they neither gave evidence nor called witnesses, but the appellant and T made a statement from the dock denying all knowledge of the matter. They were convicted. The Court of Appeal for Jamaica, in dismissing the appellant's appeal, held that his silence, when told of the accusation made against him, amounted to an acknowledgment by him of the truth of the statement made by T against him. The appellant further appealed.

LORD DIPLOCK: In dealing with this question, the Court of Appeal cited the following paragraph from Archbold, *Criminal Pleading Evidence and Practice*, 37th ed (1969), para. 1126:

> A statement made in the presence of an accused person, accusing him of a crime, upon an occasion which may be expected reasonably to call for some explanation or denial from him, is not evidence against him of the facts stated, save in so far as he accepts the statement so as to make it in effect his own. If he accepts the statement in part only, then to that extent alone does it become his statement. He may accept the statement by word or conduct, action or demeanour and it is the function of the jury which tries the case to determine whether his words, action, conduct or demeanour at the time when the statement was made amount to an acceptance of it in whole or in part.

This statement in their Lordships' view states the law accurately. It is a citation from the speech of Lord Atkinson in *R* v *Christie* [1914] AC 545, 554. But their Lordships do not consider that in the instant case the Court of Appeal applied it correctly. It is not suggested in the instant case that the appellant's acceptance of the suggestion of Daphne Thompson which was repeated to him by the police constable was shown by word or by any positive conduct, action or demeanour. All that is relied upon is his mere silence.

It is a clear and widely known principle of the common law in Jamaica, as in England, that a person is entitled to refrain from answering a question put to him for the purpose of discovering whether he has committed a criminal offence. *A fortiori* he is under no obligation to comment when he is informed that someone else has accused him of an offence. It may be that in very exceptional circumstances an inference may be drawn from a failure to give an explanation or a disclaimer, but in their Lordships' view silence alone on being informed by a police officer that someone else has made an accusation against him cannot give rise to an inference that the person to whom this information is communicated accepts the truth of the accusation.

This is well established by many authorities such as *R* v *Whitehead* [1929] 1 KB 99 and *R* v *Keeling* [1942] 1 All ER 507. Counsel has sought to distinguish these cases on the ground that in them the accused had already been cautioned and told in terms that he was not obliged to reply. Reliance was placed on the earlier case of *R* v *Feigenbaum* [1919] 1 KB 431 where the accused's silence when told of the accusation made against him by some children was held to be capable of amounting to corroboration of their evidence. It was submitted that the distinction between *R* v *Feigenbaum* and the later cases was that no caution had been administered at the time at which the accused was informed of the accusation.

The correctness of the decision in *R* v *Feigenbaum* was doubted in *R* v *Keeling*. In their Lordships' view the distinction sought to be made is not a valid one and *R* v *Feigenbaum* ought not to be followed. The caution merely serves to remind the accused of a right which he already possesses at common law. The fact that in a particular case he has not been reminded of it is no ground for inferring that his silence was not in exercise of that right, but was an acknowledgment of the truth of the accusation.

Appeal allowed. Conviction quashed.

R v *Chandler*
[1976] 1 WLR 585
Court of Appeal

The defendant was convicted of conspiracy to defraud. He had been interviewed by the police in the presence of his solicitor. Both before and after being cautioned he answered some questions, but in relation to others either remained silent or refused to answer them. At the trial the judge in summing up said that a person who had been cautioned had a right to remain silent, but it was for the jury to decide whether the defendant remained silent before caution because of this right or because he might have thought, if he had answered, he would have incriminated himself.

LAWTON LJ: [Counsel] invited our attention to what Lord Diplock said in *Hall* v *The Queen* [1971] 1 WLR 298, 301:

> In their Lordships' view the distinction sought to be made - that is that no caution had been given - is not a valid one . . . The caution merely serves to remind the accused of a right which he already possesses at common law. The fact that in a particular case he has not been reminded of it is no ground for inferring that his silence was not in exercise of that right, but was an acknowledgment of the truth of the accusation.

Earlier he had said, at p. 301:

> It is a clear and widely known principle of the common law in Jamaica, as in England, that a person is entitled to refrain from answering a question put to him for the purpose of discovering whether he has committed a criminal offence. . . . It may be that in very exceptional circumstances an inference may be drawn from a failure to give an explanation or a disclaimer, but in their Lordships' view silence alone on being informed by a police officer that someone else has made an accusation against him cannot give rise to an inference that the person to whom this information is communicated accepts the truth of the accusation.

We have reservations about these two statements of law because they seem to conflict with *R* v *Christie* [1914] AC 545 and with earlier cases and authorities. For reasons which will appear later in this judgment, it is not necessary in this case to review the law relating to the so-called right of silence. The law has long accepted that an accused person is not bound to incriminate himself, but it does not follow that a failure to answer an accusation or question when an answer could reasonably be expected may not provide some evidence in support of an accusation. Whether it does will depend upon the circumstances. We could not improve on what Lord Atkinson said in *R* v *Christie*, at p. 554:

> . . . the rule of law undoubtedly is that a statement made in the presence of an accused person, even upon an occasion which should be expected reasonably to call for some explanation or denial from him, is not evidence against him of the facts stated save so far as he accepts the statement, so as to make it, in effect, his own. . . . He may accept the statement by word or conduct, action or demeanour, and it is the function of the jury which tries the case to determine whether his words,

action, conduct, or demeanour at the time when a statement was made amounts to an acceptance of it in whole or in part. It by no means follows, I think, that a mere denial by the accused of the facts mentioned in the statement necessarily renders the statement inadmissible, because he may deny the statement in such a manner and under such circumstances as may lead a jury to disbelieve him, and constitute evidence from which an acknowledgment may be inferred by them.

This statement of the law reflected legal opinion in the 19th century. Thus in *Phillips & Arnold on the Law of Evidence,* 10th ed (1852), vol. 1, p. 334, the law is stated as follows:

> In some cases, it is allowable to give evidence of written or verbal statements made, or of acts done, by others, and then to show how the party who heard or read the statements, or saw the acts done, was affected by them, - for the purpose of using his conduct, expressions or demeanour as evidence against him by way of admission. The evidence in such cases is altogether presumptive in its quality and character. . . . This species of evidence is very commonly used in criminal cases, although it appears to be somewhat inconsistent to hold, that the prisoner's silence on hearing an accusation is evidence against him, when his denial of the charge upon such an occasion would not be evidence for him.

This principle was applied in *Bessela v Stern* (1877) 2 CPD 265. In that case, which was an action for breach of promise of marriage, evidence from the plaintiff's sister was accepted as corroboration for the purpose of the statute 32 & 33 Vict. c. 68. This evidence was to the effect that the defendant had made no denial when the plaintiff had upbraided him for having promised to marry her and failing to do so. In *R v Mitchell* (1892) 17 Cox CC 503, 508, Cave J said:

> Undoubtedly, when persons are speaking on even terms, and a-charge is made, and the person charged says nothing, and expresses no indignation, and does nothing to repel the charge, that is some evidence to show that he admits the charge to be true.

As Professor Sir Rupert Cross commented in his book, *Evidence,* 4th ed, p. 189, in reference to *R v Mitchell,* this 'is a broad principle of common sense.' Indeed it is. It should not be forgotten that the law of evidence developed in the 18th century and the early part of the 19th century as a result of the search by the judges for rules which could be applied during a trial to obtain reliable testimony and to ensure a fair trial for the accused. The search had been made necessary by the disquiet and concern which had arisen after the perjury of Oates, Bedloe, Dugdale, Dangerfield and Turberville in the Popist Plot trials became known. Appeals such as Lord Diplock made in *Hall v The Queen* to the common law for support for a proposition in the law of evidence means seeking, at the earliest, an 18th century precedent. Between 1554 and 1640 a criminal trial bore little resemblance to a modern trial; indeed the examination of the accused in court by counsel for the Crown 'was the very essence of the trial': see Stephen, *History of the Criminal Law in England* (1883), vol. 1, p. 326. This went on until the beginning of the 18th century: see J H Wigmore, *Evidence in Trials at Common Law,* 2nd ed (1923), vol. 1, p. 604. It would be unfortunate if the law of evidence was allowed to develop in a way which was not in accordance with the common sense of ordinary folk. We are bound by *R v Christie,* not by *Hall v The Queen. R v Christie,* in our judgment, does accord with common sense.

When the judge's comments are examined against the principles enunciated in both *R v Mitchell* and *R v Christie* we are of the opinion that the defendant and the detective sergeant were speaking on equal terms since the former had his solicitor present to give him any advice he might have wanted and to testify, if needed, as to what had been said. We do not accept that a police officer always has an advantage over someone he is questioning. Everything depends upon the circumstances. A young detective questioning a local dignitary in the course of an inquiry into alleged local government corruption may be very much at a disadvantage. This kind of situation is to be contrasted with that of a tearful housewife accused of shoplifting or of a parent being questioned about the suspected wrongdoing of his son. Some comment on the defendant's lack of frankness before he was cautioned was justified provided the jury's attention was directed to the right issue, which was whether in the circumstances the defendant's silence amounted to an acceptance by him of what the detective sergeant had said. If he accepted what had been said, then the next question should have been whether guilt could reasonably be inferred from what he had accepted. To suggest, as the judge did, that the defendant's silence could indicate guilt was to short-circuit the intellectual process which has to be followed. Phillips in *A Treatise on the Law of Evidence* pointed out this very error, at p. 334:

> It very commonly happens, that evidence of the description referred to has the effect of misleading juries, who are frequently influenced by it . . . and are unable, notwithstanding any directions from a judge, to regard it solely as exhibiting demeanour and conduct. In many instances, especially where no observation has been made by the party on hearing it, the evidence is particularly liable to produce erroneous conclusions. An acquiescence in the truth of the statement is frequently inferred, though the inference may, from a variety of causes, be incorrect. Thus the evidence is not only fallacious with reference to its object, but in its collateral effect is prejudicial to the investigation of truth.

The same kind of error is seen in the comment which the judge made as to whether the defendant had been evasive in order to protect himself. He may have been; but that was not what the jury had to decide. It follows, in our judgment, that the comments made were not justified and could have led the jury to a wrong conclusion.

Appeal allowed.

Parkes v R
[1976] 1 WLR 1251
Privy Council

The defendant was charged with the murder of a woman who had died from stab wounds. At his trial the deceased's mother gave evidence that she had found her daughter injured and had gone to the defendant and said, 'What she do you - Why you stab her?'; that the defendant had made no answer and had tried to stab her when she threatened to hold him until the police came. The judge directed the jury that the defendant's failure to reply to the mother's accusation coupled with his conduct immediately afterwards was evidence from which the jury could infer that the defendant had accepted the truth of the accusation. The defendant was convicted and appealed.

LORD DIPLOCK: In support of the argument that the defendant's failure to answer Mrs Graham's accusation that he had stabbed her daughter was not a matter from which the jury were entitled to draw any inference that the defendant accepted the

truth of the accusation the defendant relied on the following passage in the judgment
of this Board in *Hall* v *The Queen* [1971] 1 WLR 298, 301:

> It is a clear and widely known principle of the common law in Jamaica, as in
> England, that a person is entitled to refrain from answering a question put to him
> for the purpose of discovering whether he has committed a criminal offence. *A*
> *fortiori* he is under no obligation to comment when he is informed that someone else
> has accused him of an offence. It may be that in very exceptional circumstances an
> inference may be drawn from a failure to give an explanation or a disclaimer, but
> in their Lordships' view silence alone on being informed by a police officer that
> someone else has made an accusation against him cannot give rise to an inference
> that the person to whom this information is communicated accepts the truth of the
> accusation.

As appears from this passage itself, it was concerned with a case where the person by
whom the accusation was communicated to the accused was a police constable whom
he knew was engaged in investigating a drug offence. There was no evidence of the
defendant's demeanour or conduct when the accusation was made other than the
mere fact that he failed to reply to the constable. The passage cited had been preceded
by a quotation from a speech of Lord Atkinson in *R* v *Christie* [1914] AC 545, 554,
in which it was said that when a statement is made in the presence of an accused
person:

> He may accept the statement by word or conduct, action or demeanour, and it is
> the function of the jury which tries the case to determine whether his words, action,
> conduct or demeanour at the time when the statement was made amount to an
> acceptance of it in whole or in part.

In the instant case, there is no question of an accusation being made by or in the
presence of a police officer or any other person in authority or charged with the
investigation of the crime. It was a spontaneous charge made by a mother about an
injury done to her daughter. In circumstances such as these, their Lordships agree
with the Court of Appeal of Jamaica that the direction given by Cave J in *R* v *Mitchell*
(1892) 17 Cox CC 503, 508 (to which their Lordships have supplied the emphasis)
is applicable:

> Now the whole admissibility of statements of this kind rests upon the consideration
> that if a charge is made against a person in that person's presence it is reasonable
> to expect that he or she will immediately deny it, and that the absence of such a
> denial is some evidence of an admission on the part of the person charged, and of
> the truth of the charge. *Undoubtedly, when persons are speaking on even terms,* and a
> charge is made, and the person charged says nothing, and expresses no indignation,
> and does nothing to repel the charge, that is some evidence to show that he admits
> the charge to be true.

Here Mrs Graham and the defendant were speaking on even terms. Furthermore, as
the Chief Justice pointed out to the jury, the defendant's reaction to the twice-
repeated accusation was not one of mere silence. He drew a knife and attempted to
stab Mrs Graham in order to escape when she threatened to detain him while the
police were sent for. In their Lordships' view, the Chief Justice was perfectly entitled
to instruct the jury that the defendant's reactions to the accusations including his
silence were matters which they could take into account along with other evidence in
deciding whether the defendant in fact committed the act with which he was charged.

Appeal dismissed.

Questions
1. Was Lawton LJ in *Chandler* right in saying that the words of Lord Diplock in *Hall* conflicted with *Christie*?
2. What are the practical implications of the decision in *Chandler*?

(ii) The effect of the Criminal Justice and Public Order Bill 1994 — inferences from the accused's silence

Criminal Justice and Public Order Bill 1994

Inferences from accused's silence
27. Effect of accused's silence when questioned or charged

(1) Where, in any proceedings against a person for an offence, evidence is given that the accused —

(a) at any time before he was charged with the offence, on being questioned by a constable trying to discover whether or by whom the offence had been committed, failed to mention any fact relied on in his defence in those proceedings; or

(b) on being charged with the offence or officially informed that he might be prosecuted for it, failed to mention any such fact,
being a fact which in the circumstances existing at the time the accused could reasonably have been expected to mention when so questioned, charged or informed, as the case may be, subsection (2) below applies.

(2) Where this subsection applies —

(a) the court, in determining whether to commit the accused for trial or whether there is a case to answer;

(b) a judge, in deciding whether to grant an application made by the accused under —

(i) section 6 of the Criminal Justice Act 1987 (application for dismissal of charge of serious fraud in respect of which notice of transfer has been given under section 4 of that Act); or

(ii) paragraph 5 of Schedule 6 to the Criminal Justice Act 1991 (application for dismissal of charge of violent or sexual offence involving child in respect of which notice of transfer has been given under section 53 of that Act); and

(c) the court or jury, in determining whether the accused is guilty of the offence charged,
may draw such inferences from the failure as appear proper.

(3) Subject to any directions by the court, evidence tending to establish the failure may be given before or after evidence tending to establish the fact which the accused is alleged to have failed to mention.

(4) This section applies in relation to questioning by persons (other than constables) charged with the duty of investigating offences or charging offenders as it applies in relation to questioning by constables; and in subsection (1) above 'officially informed' means informed by a constable or any such person.

(5) This section does not —

(a) prejudice the admissibility in evidence of the silence or other reaction of the accused in the face of anything said in his presence relating to the conduct in respect of which he is charged, in so far as evidence thereof would be admissible apart from this section; or

(b)   preclude the drawing of any inference from any such silence or other reaction of the accused which could properly be drawn apart from this section.

(6)   This section does not apply in relation to a failure to mention a fact if the failure occurred before the commencement of this section.

28.   Effect of accused's silence at trial
[See Chapter 4(A)(*ii*).]

29.   Effect of accused's failure or refusal to account for objects, substances or marks

(1)   Where —

(a)   a person is arrested by a constable, and there is —

(i)   on his person; or

(ii)   in or on his clothing or footwear; or

(iii)   otherwise in his possession; or

(iv)   in any place in which he is at the time of his arrest, any object, substance or mark, or there is any mark on any such object; and

(b)   that or another constable investigating the case reasonably believes that the presence of the object, substance or mark may be attributable to the participation of the person arrested in the commission of an offence specified by the constable; and

(c)   the constable informs the person arrested that he so believes, and requests him to account for the presence of the object, substance or mark; and

(d)   the person fails or refuses to do so,

then if, in any proceedings against the person for the offence so specified, evidence of those matters is given, subsection (2) below applies.

(2)   Where this subsection applies —

(a)   the court, in determining whether to commit the accused for trial or whether there is a case to answer; and

(b)   the court or jury, in determining whether the accused is guilty of the offence charged,

may draw such inferences from the failure or refusal as appear proper.

(3)   Subsections (1) and (2) above apply to the condition of clothing or footwear as they apply to a substance or mark thereon.

(4)   Subsections (1) and (2) above do not apply unless the accused was told in ordinary language by the constable when making the request mentioned in subsection (1)(c) above what the effect of this section would be if he failed or refused to comply with the request.

(5)   This section does not preclude the drawing of any inference from a failure or refusal of the accused to account for the presence of an object, substance or mark or from the condition of clothing or footwear which could properly be drawn apart from this section.

(6)   This section does not apply in relation to a failure or refusal which occurred before the commencement of this section.

30.   Effect of accused's failure or refusal to account for presence at a particular place

(1)   Where —

(a)   a person arrested by a constable was found by him at a place at or about the time the offence for which he was arrested is alleged to have been committed; and

(b)   that or another constable investigating the offence reasonably believes that the presence of the person at that place and at that time may be attributable to his participation in the commission of the offence; and

(c)   the constable informs the person that he so believes, and requests him to account for that presence; and

(d)   the person fails or refuses to do so,

then if, in any proceedings against the person for the offence, evidence of those matters is given, subsection (2) below applies.

(2)   Where this subsection applies —

(a)   the court, in determining whether to commit the accused for trial or whether there is a case to answer; and

(b)   the court or jury, in determining whether the accused is guilty of the offence charged,

may draw such inferences from the failure or refusal as appear proper.

(3)   Subsections (1) and (2) do not apply unless the accused was told in ordinary language by the constable when making the request mentioned in subsection (1)(c) above what the effect of this section would be if he failed or refused to comply with the request.

(4)   This section does not preclude the drawing of any inference from a failure or refusal of the accused to account for his presence at a place which could properly be drawn apart from this section.

(5)   This section does not apply in relation to a failure or refusal which occurred before the commencement of this section.

31.   Interpretation and savings for sections 27, 28, 29 and 30

(1)   In sections 27, 28, 29 and 30 of this Act —

'child' means a person under the age of fourteen;

'legal representative' means an authorised advocate or authorised litigator, as defined by section 119(1) of the Courts and Legal Services Act 1990; and

'place' includes any building or part of a building, any vehicle, vessel, aircraft or hovercraft and any other place whatsoever.

(2)   In sections 27(2), 28(4), 29(2) and 30(2), references to an offence charged include references to any other offence of which the accused could lawfully be convicted on that charge.

(3)   A person shall not be committed for trial, have a case to answer or be convicted of an offence solely on an inference drawn from such a failure or refusal as is mentioned in section 27(2), 28(4), 29(2) or 30(2).

(4)   A judge shall not refuse to grant such an application as is mentioned in section 27(2)(b) solely on an inference drawn from such a failure as is mentioned in section 27(2).

(5)   Nothing in sections 27, 28, 29 or 30 prejudices the operation of a provision of any enactment which provides (in whatever words) that any answer or evidence given by a person in specified circumstances shall not be admissible in evidence against him or some other person in any proceedings or class of proceedings (however described, and whether civil or criminal).

In this subsection, the reference to giving evidence is a reference to giving evidence in any manner, whether by furnishing information, making discovery, producing documents or otherwise.

(6)   Nothing in sections 27, 28, 29 or 30 prejudices any power of a court, in any proceedings, to exclude evidence (whether by preventing questions being put or otherwise) at its discretion.

Questions

Answer the following questions on the assumption that the Bill is enacted:

1. Do the clauses of the Bill mean that an accused person who remains silent under police questioning can now have that silence used against him as evidence of his guilt?

2. As regards clause 27, who will decide whether or not any particular fact might reasonably have been mentioned by the accused before he was charged?

3. Does clause 27 affect the *R* v *Chandler* line of cases?

4. For some time, MI5 suspected that information relating to SAS activities was being leaked to the IRA. It was decided that the informant was Oliver, an SAS sergeant, who passed messages to Peter, an elderly clergyman. One night, three MI5 officers, Roland, Stephen and Thomas, accompanied by four military policemen, followed Oliver and watched him place some papers in a broken tomb in Peter's churchyard. Roland's evidence is then as follows: 'The four policemen pounced on Oliver, then bundled him into a truck; I went with them: Oliver was shaking violently; he said "It's all Peter's fault — he's been blackmailing me for years". We took him to the police station and I cautioned him. He made a statement which he then signed.' The statement was to the effect that five years previously, Peter had caught Oliver molesting a child in the village; Peter promised not to report him provided he supplied information relating to SAS activities, which he had been doing ever since.

Stephen and Thomas remained in the churchyard, and about half an hour later Peter came and took the papers from the tomb. Stephen says: 'I challenged him. Peter said: "Caught at last: I've been doing this for fifty years; I'm a founder member". He invited us into the vicarage and showed us the paper. It appeared to refer to a wedding, but Peter said, "It's in code: it's a description of a new machine gun". I cautioned him and he then spent several hours writing out a statement in longhand.' The statement recounted how Peter joined Sinn Fein whilst at University, and named several distinguished people, dead and alive, who were Republican sympathisers; he said he frequently obtained information about the SAS, but the statement contained no reference to Oliver or other named members of the SAS.

Oliver and Peter are now on trial and have retracted their statements.

At the first trial-within-the-trial, Oliver gave evidence to the effect that he had been rendered unconscious and remembered nothing between leaving the barracks and waking up in the police station: he was interrogated for several days but never made a confession: eventually Roland wrote out a statement and asked him to sign it: when he refused, Roland forged his signature. In cross-examination, Roland agrees that Oliver was interrogated for several days, but otherwise denies Oliver's allegations.

At the second trial-within-the-trial, Peter said that as soon as he invited Stephen and Thomas into the vicarage, Stephen said: 'We'll do a Blunt: tell us all you know and name names, we won't prosecute.' Peter then explained that he lived alone and was addicted to spy stories; his statement was an invention from beginning to end, designed merely as a leg-pull. The cross-examination continued:

Counsel: You say your story is false?

Peter: Pure fantasy.
Counsel: Not one word of truth?
Peter: Well, I did join Sinn Fein at University.
Counsel: Why did you collect the papers from the tomb?
Peter: There's a crank in the village who always leaves messages about weddings there.

When Stephen was cross-examined, he said it was Peter who had initiated the conversation about Blunt and suggested making a deal.

(a)   Explain the steps which will be taken, and the factors the judge will consider, in deciding whether or not the statements are admissible.

(b)   On the available evidence, do you think the statements will be admitted?

(c)   If they are admitted, how is this likely to affect the rest of the trial?

(d)   Can the prosecution give evidence as to what was said at the trials-within-the-trial?

(e)   Are there any points which the judge should particularly mention during the summing-up?

5.   Sidney is arrested for allegedly raping Tina. Tina tells the police that a man jumped out from behind some bushes, held a knife to her throat and then committed the offence. She says she scratched her attacker on the face and he then ran away. She is unable to pick Sidney out at a subsequent identification parade. Sidney is interviewed by Sergeant Jones but refuses to answer any questions. Jones notices that Sidney has several scratch marks on his face, neck and hands. He asks Sidney to account for the marks after warning him that failure to do so may lead to a jury concluding he has got something to hide. Sidney remains silent. You are representing Sidney at his trial for rape. Sidney tells you that he received the scratch marks while pruning roses in his mother's garden. He says he did not tell Jones at the time because his mother was very ill and he realised that Jones would verify his story by questioning his mother. In any event, Sidney tells you that at the time of the alleged offence he was in bed with Mrs King, the wife of a prominent businessman. He tells you he was too embarrased to tell this to Jones and wished to protect Mrs King. Sidney proposes not to testify. Consider the evidential matters raised.

Further Reading
P. Murphy, *A Practical Approach to Evidence*, 4th ed. (1992), Ch. 7
P. Mirfield, *Confessions* (1985)

11 EVIDENCE OF CHARACTER — I

The word 'character' has a number of potential meanings in the law of evidence. It may refer to a person's disposition (i.e. his tendency to act in a particular way), his general reputation (good or bad), or perhaps his previous criminal record. It would, of course, be quite unfair to allow the prosecution complete freedom to reveal to the jury that the accused has, on a previous occasion or occasions, been convicted of criminal offences. Merely because D has been previously convicted of one, or two, or even a dozen burglaries, does not mean he must be guilty of the burglary with which he is now charged. It cannot credibly be disputed that a jury hearing of D's previous convictions is highly likely to reason, 'once a burglar always a burglar', convicting him not on the evidence in the case, but on his previous record. Therefore the law places restrictions upon what evidence concerning the accused's character can be adduced, and it generally limits the purpose to which such evidence, if admissible, may be put.

There may be occasions, however, where the previous conduct of the accused carries such a high degree of relevance and probative force, that to exclude it, or limit its use, would be an affront to justice. Accordingly, there are occasions where the law permits the prosecution to lead evidence of the accused's previous conduct for the purpose of proving he is guilty of the offence with which he is now charged. Such cases are generally known as 'similar fact' cases and are dealt with in Chapter 12.

This chapter is concerned with those aspects of the accused's character which fall outside the 'similar fact' principle.

(A) General admissibility and use of character evidence

Character evidence may be admitted if character itself is a fact in issue. Similarly, relevant evidence might incidentally reveal some aspect of a person's character but that will not, generally, impinge upon its admissibility.

The main difficulties arise in relation to evidence of the defendant's bad
character. This will be further examined in (B) below and Chapter 12. After
considering the general admissibility of character evidence, this section
considers the evidential value of the defendant's good character. Does the fact
that the defendant has a good character make it less likely that he has
committed the offence alleged, or does it merely reflect on his credit as a
witness?

(i)   Admissibility

R v Rowton
(1865) Le & Ca 520
Crown Cases Reserved

The defendant was charged with indecent assault on a boy and called
several witnesses to his character. The prosecution called a witness to give
evidence in rebuttal, and the witness was asked about the defendant's
general character for decency and morality of conduct. He replied: 'I know
nothing of the neighbourhood's opinion, because I was only a boy at school
when I knew him; but my own opinion, and the opinion of my brothers
who were also pupils of his, is that his character is that of a man capable
of the grossest indecency and the most flagrant immorality'.

COCKBURN CJ: There are two questions to be decided. The first is whether, when
evidence of good character has been given in favour of a prisoner, evidence of his
general bad character can be called in reply. I am clearly of opinion that it can be. It
is true that I do not remember any case in my own experience where such evidence
has been given; but that is easily explainable by the fact that evidence of good
character is not given when it is known that it can be rebutted; and it frequently
happens that the prosecuting counsel, from a spirit of fairness, gives notice to the other
side, when he is in a position to contradict such evidence. But, when we come to
consider whether the evidence is admissible, it is only possible to come to one
conclusion. It is said that evidence of good character raises only a collateral issue; but
I think that, if the prisoner thinks proper to raise that issue as one of the elements for
the consideration of the jury, nothing could be more unjust than that he should have
the advantage of a character which, in point of fact, may be the very reverse of that
which he really deserves.

Assuming, then, that evidence was receivable to rebut the evidence of good
character, the second question is, was the answer which was given in this case, in reply
to a perfectly legitimate question, such an answer as could properly be left to the jury?
Now, in determining this point, it is necessary to consider what is the meaning of
evidence of character. Does it mean evidence of general reputation or evidence of
disposition? I am of opinion that it means evidence of general reputation. What you
want to get at is the tendency and disposition of the man's mind towards committing
or abstaining from committing the class of crime with which he stands charged; but
no one has ever heard the question — what is the tendency and disposition of the
prisoner's mind? — put directly. The only way of getting at it is by giving evidence of
his general character founded on his general reputation in the neighbourhood in which
he lives. That, in my opinion, is the sense in which the word 'character' is to be taken,

when evidence of character is spoken of. The fact that a man has an unblemished reputation leads to the presumption that he is incapable of committing the crime for which he is being tried. We are not now considering whether it is desirable that the law of England should be altered — whether it is expedient to import the practice of other countries and go into the prisoner's antecedents for the purpose of shewing that he is likely to commit the crime with which he is charged, or, stopping short of that, whether it would be wise to allow the prisoner to go into facts for the purpose of shewing that he is incapable of committing the crime charged against him. It is quite clear that, as the law now stands, the prisoner cannot give evidence of particular facts, although one fact would weigh more than the opinion of all his friends and neighbours. So too, evidence of antecedent bad conduct would form equally good ground for inferring the prisoner's guilt, yet it is quite clear evidence of that kind is inadmissible. The allowing evidence of good character has arisen from the fairness of our laws and is an anomalous exception to the general rule. It is quite true that evidence of character is most cogent, when it is preceded by a statement shewing that the witness has had opportunities of acquiring information upon the subject beyond what the man's neighbours in general would have; and in practice the admission of such statements is often carried beyond the letter of the law in favour of the prisoner. It is, moreover, most essential that a witness who comes forward to give a man a good character should himself have a good opinion of him; for otherwise he would only be deceiving the jury; and so the strict rule is often exceeded. But, when we consider what, in the strict interpretation of the law, is the limit of such evidence, in my judgment it must be restricted to the man's general reputation, and must not extend to the individual opinion of the witness. Some time back, I put this question — suppose a witness is called who says that he knows nothing of the general character of the accused, but that he had had abundant opportunities of forming an individual opinion as to his honesty or the particular moral quality that may be in question in the particular case. Surely, if such evidence were objected to, it would be inadmissible.

If that be the true doctrine as to the admissibility of evidence to character in favour of the prisoner, the next question is, within what limits must the rebutting evidence be confined? I think that that evidence must be of the same character and confined within the same limits — that, as the prisoner can only give evidence of general good character, so the evidence called to rebut it must be evidence of the same general description, shewing that the evidence which has been given in favour of the prisoner is not true, but that the man's general reputation is bad.

ERLE CJ (dissenting): Now, what is the principle on which evidence of character is admitted? It seems to me that such evidence is admissible for the purpose of shewing the disposition of the party accused, and basing thereon a presumption that he did not commit the crime imputed to him. Disposition cannot be ascertained directly; it is only to be ascertained by the opinion formed concerning the man, which must be founded either on personal experience, or on the expression of opinion by others, whose opinion again ought to be founded on their personal experience. The question between us is, whether the Court is at liberty to receive a statement of the disposition of a prisoner, founded on the personal experience of the witness, who attends to give evidence and state that estimate which long personal knowledge of and acquaintance with the prisoner has enabled him to form? I think that each source of evidence is admissible. You may give in evidence the general rumour prevalent in the prisoner's neighbourhood, and, according to my experience, you may have also the personal judgment of those who are capable of forming a more real, substantial, guiding opinion than that which is to be gathered from general rumour. I never saw a witness examined to character without an inquiry being made into his personal means of knowledge of that character. The evidence goes to the jury depending entirely upon the personal experience of the witness who has offered his testimony. Suppose a witness to character were to say, 'This man has been in my employ for twenty years. I have had experience of his conduct; but I have never heard a human being express an opinion of him in my life. For my own part, I have always regarded him with the highest esteem and respect, and have had an abundant experience that he is one of the worthiest men in the world.' The principle the Lord Chief Justice has laid down would exclude this evidence; and that is the point where I differ from him. To my mind personal experience gives cogency to the evidence; whereas such a statement as, 'I have heard some persons speak well of him,' or 'I have heard general report in favour of the prisoner,' has a very slight effect in comparison. Again, to the proposition that general character is alone admissible the answer is that it is impossible to get at it. There is no such thing as general character; it is the general inference supposed to arise from hearing a number of separate and disinterested statements in favour of the prisoner. But I think that the notion that general character is alone admissible is not accurate. It would be wholly inadmissible to ask a witness what individual he has ever heard give his opinion of a particular fact connected with the man. I attach considerable weight to this distinction, because, in my opinion, the best character is that which is the least talked of.

(WILLES J also dissented. The other learned judges concurred in the judgment delivered by COCKBURN CJ.)

R v Redgrave
(1981) 74 Cr App R 10
Court of Appeal

The appellant was charged with persistently importuning for an immoral purpose contrary to section 32 of the Sexual Offences Act 1956. The appellant sought to tender detailed evidence of his heterosexual relationships with girls to rebut inferences from his conduct, as observed by police officers, that he had been making homosexual approaches to them. The judge ruled that evidence inadmissible and the appellant was convicted on a majority verdict. The appellant appealed on the ground, *inter alia*, that the judge's ruling was wrong.

LAWTON LJ: . . . In this court Mr Still put forward four propositions on behalf of his client. The first was that as the *mens rea* of the offence is an intention of a homosexual character, the defendant in a case of this kind is entitled to show that he is not of a homosexual disposition. Secondly, if the prosecution in this class of case, can, in order to rebut such defences as mistaken identity or innocent association, put in evidence showing that the defendant has homosexual tendencies, in the same way a defendant ought to be allowed to put in evidence showing that he has no homosexual tendencies, if his defence is that the prosecution have drawn wrong inferences from the proven facts. Thirdly he submitted that the decision in *R v Rowton* (1865) Le & Ca 520, which is now nearly 120 years old, has been overtaken by developments in the law and is no longer good law. Finally he submitted to the court that as the object of evidence is to obtain a just result, the law ought not to exclude any evidence which common sense says goes to prove that an offence has not been committed.

He developed these points citing well known cases. It is necessary to refer only to three: *R* v *Ferguson* (1909) 2 Cr App R 250; *R* v *Samuel* (1956) 40 Cr App R 8 and *R* v *Bellis* (1965) 50 Cr App R 88; [1966] 1 WLR 234. We do not consider it necessary to refer in detail to *R* v *Ferguson* (*supra*) as the matter which was canvassed in that case was considered more fully in *R* v *Samuel* (*supra*), which was heard in 1956 before Lord Goddard CJ, Hilbery and Stable JJ. The issue in that case was this: the accused had been charged with larceny by finding. He stated in his evidence that on two previous occasions he had restored property found by him. The prosecution took the view that what he was doing was putting in evidence of good character. They sought leave to cross-examine him about his previous convictions. Counsel was allowed to do so. The issue before the Court of Criminal Appeal was whether by saying what he did say about having returned property found by him on two previous occasions, he was giving evidence of his own good character. In the course of discussing that problem Lord Goddard in his judgment referred to the evidence which he had given about having returned goods found by him on two previous occasions as evidence clearly going to show that he was an honest man. The court was not concerned with the question as to whether what the defendant had said about his honest acts on other occasions was properly admissible. We get no help from this case. In *R* v *Bellis* (*supra*) the court was concerned with a direction by the judge about evidence as to character. The court decided that a jury should be directed that the possession of good character by a defendant is primarily a matter which goes to his credibility. But the judgment of the court, delivered by Widgery J (as he then was) said it could also go to probability.

On the basis of these cases Mr Still submitted that the law has altered since the decision in *R* v *Rowton* (*supra*) and if the law has altered, said Mr Still, it follows that any evidence going to show the improbability of the accused having committed the offence with which he was charged is evidence which a jury ought to consider, and even more so when common sense says that such evidence may tend to show that the accused has not committed the offence.

We make at this stage a comment about the so called common sense aspect of the case. It may well be that in many cases, perhaps in most cases, those who have homosexual dispositions and commit homosexual acts, do not have much inclination towards heterosexual activity, but this is not always so. It is a matter of both history and judicial experience that many who commit homosexual acts also indulge in heterosexual activity. Whether they do so because of genetic tendencies, or whether they do so out of what used to be called lust, is not a matter into which we need inquire. Some men and women do commit both kinds of acts.

Mr Smith's argument, on behalf of the Crown, was simple, clear and concise. It came to this: that the law of evidence has grown up over the centuries, largely as a result of the experience of the judges who have decided that certain types of evidence shall be admitted and certain types shall be excluded. The object has been to ensure that there is a fair trial before a jury and that there is a just verdict. Sometimes the rules which have evolved are not all that logical. But those are our rules and it is the duty of the courts to follow them. Parliament from time to time has intervened and has altered the law.

When everything has been taken into consideration, according to Mr Smith, the law is at present as follows. The prosecution can call evidence to prove directly that the accused committed the act. What they cannot do, save in special circumstances, is to call evidence to prove that the defendant had a propensity to commit the kind of crime with which he is charged. The exception either arises at common law, as set out in the well known case of *Makin* v *Attorney-General of New South Wales* [1894] AC 57;

17 Cox CC 704, or under statute, as in the circumstances referred to in the Criminal Evidence Act 1898. That is clear; and Mr Still did not seek to say that that was not the law so far as the prosecution was concerned. What he submitted was that the rules applying to the prosecution ought not to, and do not, apply to the defendant, because he is in a different situation to the prosecution and should not be bound by the same exclusions.

In our judgment the defendant is bound by the same rules as the prosecution. He can call evidence to show that he did not commit the acts which are alleged against him, but he is not allowed, by reference to particular facts, to call evidence that he is of a disposition which makes it unlikely that he would have committed the offence charged.

That this is the common law of England is shown clearly by the decision in *R v Rowton* (1865) Le & Ca 520. In the course of his judgment in that case Cockburn CJ said at p. 530: 'It is quite clear that, as the law now stands, the prisoner cannot give evidence of particular facts, although one fact would weigh more than the opinion of all his friends and neighbours.' That is what the appellant was trying to do in this case. He was trying, by his evidence about his relations with particular women and by the production of these letters and photographs, to show that he had had intimate heterosexual relationships with the writers of the letters and the girls in the photographs, and he was relying on those particular facts to show that he had not got a disposition to behave in the sort of way which the prosecution alleged.

The problem in this case is whether there is any exception in law to the general proposition laid down by Cockburn CJ nearly 120 years ago. The Court of Crown Cases Reserved in *R v Rowton* (*supra*), made up of no less than 12 judges, came to the conclusion, with two dissensions, that when a defendant wishes to show he has not got a disposition to commit the kind of offence with which he is charged, he is limited in what he can say. In 1866 he could call evidence to show that his general reputation made it unlikely that he would commit the kind of offence with which he was charged. He could do that by calling people who knew him, but beyond that he could not go.

It follows therefore, so it seems to us, that in this case, although disposition to commit the kind of offence charged was relevant, the law is as decided in *R v Rowton* (*supra*), viz that the defendant could do no more than say, or call witnesses to prove, that he was not by general repute the kind of young man who would have behaved in the kind of way that the Crown alleged.

The circumstances of this case show the undesirability of the law going further. Giving evidence and producing documents of this kind would be so easy for somebody who was putting a false defence forward. Clearly it would have been undesirable for this young man to have given evidence that he has had sexual intercourse with a number of named women who were not in court; and it would also not be in the public interest that he should be allowed to subpoena young women to give evidence on oath that they had had sexual intercourse with him. These are the sort of factors which no doubt before 1866 were taken into account by the judges when, during the seventeenth, eighteenth and early part of the nineteenth century, they formulated the rules dealing with evidence.

It seems to us that it is in the public interest generally that evidence of this kind should be limited as laid down in *R v Rowton* (*supra*). But it is not for us to consider whether the law is good law or bad law, unjust or fair law. We are here to apply the law.

It was brought to our attention by Mr Smith that nowadays, as a matter of practice in this class of case, defendants are often allowed to say that they are happily married and having a normal sexual relationship with their wives. We are not seeking to stop defending counsel putting that kind of information before a jury. It has long been the practice for judges to allow some relaxation of the law of evidence on behalf of defendants. Had this young man been a married man, or alternatively, had he confined his relationship to one girl, it might not have been all that objectionable for him to have given evidence in general terms that his relationship with his wife or the girl was satisfactory. That would have been an indulgence on the part of the court. It would not have been his right to have it said. Until such time as Parliament amends the law of evidence, it is the duty of this court, and of judges, to keep to the rules, and the rules are clear.

Appeal dismissed.

Question
Is the decision in *Redgrave* satisfactory? Why?

R v *Winfield*
[1939] 4 All ER 164
Court of Criminal Appeal

The defendant, who was charged with indecent assault on a woman, called a witness and asked her questions to establish his good character with regard to sexual morality. The witness and/or the defendant (there being a conflict between the two reports of the case, in [1939] 4 All ER 164 and in 27 Cr App R 139) were cross-examined on the defendant's previous convictions of offences involving dishonesty. On appeal against conviction, it was contended that the evidence as to his general character was improperly admitted.

HUMPHREYS J: . . . The deputy chairman knew, though probably the prisoner did not, that there is no such thing known to our procedure as putting half your character in issue and leaving out the other half. A man is not entitled to say, 'Well, I may have a bad character as a dishonest rogue, but at all events nobody has ever said that I have acted indecently towards women.' That cannot be done. If a man who is accused chooses to put his character in issue, he must take the consequences. It is quite clear that this man did. He asked questions about his character quite apart from the facts of this case. The result was that he was properly cross-examined as to character.

(The appeal was, however, allowed and conviction quashed on the ground of want of corroboration.)

Question
'If a man is charged with forgery, cross-examination as to his convictions for cruelty can have no purpose but prejudice.' (Noakes, *Introduction to Evidence*, 4th ed., p. 140)
Is this a sound criticism of the decision in *Winfield*?

(ii)   The evidential value of the accused's good character

R v Bryant and Oxley
[1979] QB 108
Court of Appeal

The defendants were jointly charged with robbery. One defendant, who did not testify, applied for leave to appeal against his conviction on the ground that the trial judge had misdirected the jury in stating that evidence given of his good character went to credibility and, in the circumstances, had little relevance to the issue whether he had committed the offence.

WATKINS J: . . . If . . . the judge was intending to convey to the jury the impression that a good character is relevant only when a defendant gives evidence and, therefore, is a matter only to be taken into consideration when the credibility of what he and other witnesses have said is being assessed, he was being too restrictive about its possible uses. The possession of a good character is a matter which does go primarily to the issue of credibility. This has been made clear in a number of recent cases. But juries should be directed that it is capable of bearing a more general significance which is best illustrated by what was said by Williams J in *R v Stannard* (1837) 7 C & P 673, 675:

> I have no doubt, if we are put to decide the unwelcome question, that evidence to character must be considered as evidence in the cause. It is evidence, as my brother Patteson has said, to be submitted to the jury, to induce them to say whether they think it likely that a person with such a character would have committed the offence.

The 'unwelcome question' related to counsel's right to sum up after defence evidence of character only had been given.

We have no doubt that the omission to direct the jury in this way in the present case could not possibly have had the effect of rendering the jury's verdict unsafe or unsatisfactory.

Application refused.

R v Berrada
(1990) 91 Cr App R 131
Court of Appeal

WATERHOUSE J: On November 4, 1987, in the Crown Court at Isleworth, this appellant was convicted of an offence of attempted rape and was sentenced to four years' imprisonment. He now appeals against his conviction for that offence with the leave of the Full Court and there is also an appeal against sentence by leave of the single judge.

[After reciting the facts of the case and considering other grounds of appeal, the court continued . . .]

The first of these points can be dealt with shortly because it relates to the direction given by the judge about the relevance of the previous good character of the appellant. The passage appears at p. 17 D-H of the transcript of the summing-up and was in the following terms:

Before I turn to the evidence in this case there are a number of matters about which I wish to speak. One is the defendant's character. I do not think it is right to say that he is wholly without convictions because, as we know, since the date of this incident he has been convicted of some offence under the drink/driving laws. So he has not got a completely clean character. But I do not doubt that you will be content for the purposes of this case to treat him as somebody who has no previous convictions, and you will doubtless want to give that some weight. How much weight you give it is a matter for you to decide. I only say this about it; that you must not give it too much weight in this sense; that it can never be a defence to a criminal charge. We are all born into this world without previous convictions and most of us hopefully leave it in the same state. But if there is to be a conviction, there is going to be a first time. You can and do get some people in that dock there with forty previous convictions who could, and doubtless did, say to a judge and jury at some stage: 'I have no previous convictions.' So by all means give it some weight, but you must not give it too much.

The striking omission in that passage is of any reference to the real and primary relevance of the appellant's previous good character. What the learned judge should have said was that it was primarily relevant to the question of the appellant's credibility. Moreover, this was clearly a case in which questions of credibility went to the heart of the matters that the jury had to decide, subject to the qualification that the burden of proof remained throughout on the prosecution. There was a decisive conflict of evidence between the complainant and the appellant and between him and the police so that it was necessary that the jury should be given proper guidance in relation to the appellant's credibility.

In the judgment of this Court, the appellant was entitled to have put to the jury from the judge herself a correct direction about the relevance of his previous good character to his credibility. That is a conventional direction and it is regrettable that it did not appear in the summing-up in this case. It would have been proper also (but was not obligatory) for the judge to refer to the fact that the previous good character of the appellant might be thought by them to be one relevant factor when they were considering whether he was the kind of man who was likely to have behaved in the way that the prosecution alleged. I think that the trial judge verged on saying something to that effect but she did not in fact say so in clear terms, because the point was submerged in other comment.

On behalf of the Crown, Mr Vagg has suggested that a direction to the effect that I have indicated is not mandatory and he has referred to a very abbreviated report of the case of *Smith* [1971] Crim LR 531. It is, of course, true that varying opinions have been expressed in the past about the need for a direction about a defendant's previous good character in the course of a summing-up. We have no doubt, however, that the modern practice is that, if good character is raised by a defendant, it should be dealt with in the summing-up. Moreover, when it is dealt with, the direction should be fair and balanced, stressing its relevance primarily to a defendant's credibility. The summing-up in the instant case was defective in that respect.

. . .

At the end of all this, each member of this Court has had to make his own assessment of the summing-up and each of us has read the transcript in full. We are satisfied in this case that, collectively, the comments of the trial judge went well beyond legitimate bounds in presenting the prosecution and the defence case. It was much too heavily weighted against this appellant and there were important omissions as I have indicated. We do not think that it would be right in these circumstances to uphold the appellant's conviction. There were weighty issues to be considered and the appellant was entitled to have impartial directions to the jury about them. The summing-up as a whole failed in that respect and, in our judgment, the conviction must be quashed.

R v Thanki
(1991) 92 Cr App R 12
Court of Appeal

LORD LANE CJ: On July 14, 1989 in the Crown Court at Snaresbrook, this applicant was convicted on retrial by a majority verdict of 10 to two on six counts of indecent assault on a male person. He was sentenced to four years' imprisonment to run concurrently on each of those counts. He now appeals against his conviction by leave of this Court. [After reciting the facts and considering another ground of appeal which was allowed, the court continued . . .]

Before departing from the case there is one further matter which was raised by Mr Arlidge. That is a passage in the summing up, where the judge is dealing with this appellant's good character. He first of all sets out the facts, the history of the appellant, how he came to this country although he was born in Kenya, got his degree and his Ph D at Thames Polytechnic. Then he said this:

> The good character of a defendant, members of the jury, is relevant primarily to his credibility, that is to say as to whether or not you believe his evidence.

He goes on to say how he has been teaching since having qualified.

Mr Arlidge submits that that direction is not sufficient. He draws our attention first of all to a passage in the judgment of another division of this court in *Berrada* (1990) 91 Cr App R 131, where Waterhouse J delivering the judgment of the court said this at p. 134:

> In the judgment of this Court, the appellant was entitled to have put to the jury from the judge herself a correct direction about the relevance of his previous good character to his credibility. That is a conventional direction and it is regrettable that it did not appear in the summing up in this case. It would have been proper also (but was not obligatory) for the judge to refer to the fact that the previous good character of the appellant might be thought by them to be one relevant factor when they were considering whether he was the kind of man who was likely to have behaved in the way that the prosecution alleged.

I think the trial judge verged on saying something to that effect, but she did not in fact say so in clear terms because the point was submerged in other comment. He further draws our attention to the case of *Marr* (1990) 90 Cr App R 154, which was a case coming from the same judge as did the case of *Berrada* (*supra*), in which I delivered the judgment of this Court, and cited the passage from Waterhouse J's judgment, which I have just read, including the words in brackets, namely, '(but was not obligatory).' I added this, having finished reading that passage,

> The judge, in the passage which we have read from her direction to the jury, was telling the jury what good character in the defendant cannot do, but nowhere did she go on to say what good character can do. The two items which she should have mentioned were set out by Waterhouse J in the case of *Berrada* which we have just cited.

It seems that that last passage has been the cause of subsequent decisions which would seem to indicate that a judge on every occasion, when the defendant's good character has to be drawn to the attention of the Court, must mention not only its effect on the defendant's credibility, but its effect on the likelihood of the defendant having committed the crime of which he is charged. The truth of the matter is that the phrase used by Waterhouse J is correct, namely:

> It would have been proper also (but was not obligatory) for the judge to refer to the fact that previous good character of the appellant might be thought by them to be one relevant factor when they are considering whether he was the kind of man who was likely to have behaved in the way that the prosecution alleged.

It is not obligatory for the judge to add that further concept. That therefore concludes the hearing of this appeal. The appeal is allowed and the conviction is quashed.

Note
The courts have not always adopted a consistent approach to the problem of whether or not good character might be treated by the jury as supporting the accused's innocence. In *R v Anderson* [1990] Crim LR 862, the Court of Appeal stressed that such a direction was important. The matter was again addressed by the Court of Appeal in *R v Vye* [1993] Crim LR 602, where it was stated that a direction as to the relevance of the accused's good character to the likelihood of his having committed the offences charged is to be given, whether or not he has testified. Moreover, where there are co-accused D1 and D2, and D1 has a good character but D2 does not, D1 is still entitled to have the judge direct the jury as to the effect of his good character. The trial judge should not mention D2's character at all or should direct the jury that they must not speculate about it.

Questions
1. Do you agree that a jury should be told that because the accused has a good character this makes it less likely that he committed the offence?
2. Where D1 and D2 are jointly tried for an offence, do you think it is realistic for a jury to obey a judge's instruction not to speculate about D2's character, where he has specifically emphasised D1's good character? What alternatives can you suggest?

(B)   Cross-examination of the defendant in criminal cases — Criminal Evidence Act 1898

Until the passing of the Criminal Evidence Act 1898, the defendant in a criminal case was not a competent witness. Accordingly, consideration now had to be given as to how far an accused person could be questioned during cross-examination about aspects of his character. The Act attempts to strike a balance between the two extremes of either (i) providing the accused person with complete immunity from questions about his character; or (ii) allowing the prosecution complete freedom to question the accused person about his character. It does this by providing the accused with 'a shield', preventing the disclosure of his character unless, generally, he behaves in such a way as to justify losing the shield. Whether or not the shield provided by the Act has been lost is a question of law for the trial judge, although loss of the shield does not necessarily mean the prosecution will be able to cross-examine the accused about his character. The trial judge retains a discretion to disallow the cross-examination in appropriate cases (see (B)(*iii*) below), although this discretion does not apply to cross-examination by a co-accused under s. 1(f)(iii) (see (B) (*iv*) below).

Criminal Evidence Act 1898

1. Competency of witnesses in criminal cases

(e)   A person charged and being a witness in pursuance of this Act may be asked any question in cross-examination notwithstanding that it would tend to criminate him as to the offence charged:

(f)   A person charged and called as a witness in pursuance of this Act shall not be asked, and if asked shall not be required to answer, any question tending to show that he has committed or been convicted of or been charged with any offence other than that wherewith he is then charged, or is of bad character, unless —

(i)   the proof that he has committed or been convicted of such other offence is admissible evidence to show that he is guilty of the offence wherewith he is then charged; or

(ii)   he has personally or by his advocate asked questions of the witnesses for the prosecution with a view to establish his own good character, or has given evidence of his good character, or the nature or conduct of the defence is such as to involve imputations on the character of the prosecutor or the witnesses for the prosecution; or

(iii)   he has given evidence against any other person charged in the same proceedings.

(i)   Sections 1(e) and 1(f)(i)

Maxwell v Director of Public Prosecutions
[1935] AC 309
House of Lords

The appellant was charged with manslaughter of a woman by performing upon her an illegal operation. He gave evidence of his good character. Thereupon counsel for the prosecution asked him the following questions:

'*Q* This is the second time that sudden death has come to a woman patient of yours, is it not? — *A* Yes.

Q The first time was in 1927? — *A* In 1927, yes . . ..

Q And were you tried for manslaughter? — *A* Something like that; I could not tell you exactly.

Q And you were acquitted by the jury? — *A* Yes.

The appellant was convicted of manslaughter and appealed unsuccessfully to the Court of Criminal Appeal. He further appealed to the House of Lords.

VISCOUNT SANKEY LC: The substantive part of proviso (f) is negative in form and as such is universal and is absolute unless the exceptions come into play. Then come the three exceptions: but it does not follow that when the absolute prohibition is superseded by a permission, that the permission is as absolute as the prohibition. When it is sought to justify a question it must not only be brought within the terms of the permission, but also must be capable of justification according to the general rules of evidence and in particular must satisfy the test of relevance. Exception (i) deals with the former of the two main classes of evidence referred to above, that is, evidence falling within the rule that where issues of intention or design are involved in the charge or defence, the prisoner may be asked questions relevant to these matters, even though he has himself raised no question of his good character. Exceptions (ii) and (iii) come into play where the prisoner by himself or his witnesses has put his character in issue, or has attacked the character of others. Dealing with exceptions (i) and (ii), it is clear that the test of relevance is wider in (ii) than in (i); in the latter, proof that the prisoner has committed or been convicted of some other offence, can only be admitted if it goes to show that he was guilty of the offence charged. In the former (exception (ii)), the questions permissible must be relevant to the issue of his own good character and if not so relevant cannot be admissible. But it seems clear that the mere fact of a charge cannot in general be evidence of bad character or be regarded otherwise than as a misfortune. It seemed to be contended on behalf of the respondent that a charge was *per se* such evidence that the man charged, even though acquitted, must thereafter remain under a cloud, however innocent. I find it impossible to accept any such view. The mere fact that a man has been charged with an offence is no proof that he committed the offence. Such a fact is, therefore, irrelevant; it neither goes to show that the prisoner did the acts for which he is actually being tried nor does it go to his credibility as a witness. Such questions must, therefore, be excluded on the principle which is fundamental in the law of evidence as conceived in this country, especially in criminal cases, because, if allowed, they are likely to lead the minds of the jury astray into false issues; not merely do they tend to introduce suspicion as if it were evidence, but they tend to distract the jury from the true issue — namely, whether the prisoner in fact committed the offence on which he is actually standing his trial. It is of the utmost importance for a fair trial that the evidence should be *prima facie* limited to matters relating to the transaction which forms the subject of the indictment and that any departure from these matters should be strictly confined.

It does not result from this conclusion that the word 'charged' in proviso (f) is otiose: it is clearly not so as regards the prohibition; and when the exceptions come into play there may still be cases in which a prisoner may be asked about a charge as a step in cross-examination leading to a question whether he was convicted on the charge, or in order to elicit some evidence as to statements made or evidence given by the prisoner in the course of the trial on a charge which failed, which tend to throw doubt on the evidence which he is actually giving, though cases of this last class must be rare and the cross-examination permissible only with great safeguards.

Again, a man charged with an offence against the person may perhaps be asked whether he had uttered threats against the person attacked because he was angry with him for bringing a charge which turned out to be unfounded. Other probabilities may be imagined. Thus, if a prisoner has been acquitted on the plea of *autrefois convict* such an acquittal might be relevant to his credit, though it would seem that what was in truth relevant to his credit was the previous conviction and not the fact that he was erroneously again charged with the same offence; again, it may be, though it is perhaps a remote supposition, that an acquittal of a prisoner charged with rape on the plea of consent may possibly be relevant to a prisoner's credit.

But these instances all involve the crucial test of relevance. And in general no question whether a prisoner has been convicted or charged or acquitted should be asked or, if asked, allowed by the judge, who has a discretion under proviso (f), unless it helps to elucidate the particular issue which the jury is investigating, or goes to credibility, that is, tends to show that he is not to be believed on his oath; indeed the question whether a man has been convicted, charged or acquitted ought not to be admitted, even if it goes to credibility, if there is any risk of the jury being misled into thinking that it goes not to credibility but to the probability of his having committed the offence of which he is charged. I think that it is impossible in the present case to say that the fact that the prisoner had been acquitted on a previous charge of murder or manslaughter, was relevant, or that it tended in the present case to destroy his credibility as a witness.

(LORDS ATKIN, BLANESBURGH, THANKERTON and WRIGHT agreed.)

Appeal allowed.

Stirland v *Director of Public Prosecutions*
[1944] AC 315
House of Lords

The appellant, on trial for forgery, put his character in issue and said in examination-in-chief that he had never been 'charged' with any offence. He was asked in cross-examination questions suggesting that on a previous occasion he had been 'questioned about a suggested forgery' by his former employers. The appellant was convicted and appealed.

VISCOUNT SIMON LC: It is necessary . . . to guard against a possible confusion in the use of the word 'charged'. In para (f) of s. 1 of the Act of 1898 the word appears five times and it is plain that its meaning in the section is 'accused before a court' and not merely 'suspected or accused without prosecution'. When the appellant denied that he had ever been 'charged', he may fairly be understood to use the word in the sense it bears in the statute and to mean that he had never previously been brought before a criminal court. Questions whether his former employer had suspected him of forgery were not, therefore, any challenge to the veracity of what he had said. Neither were they relevant as going to disprove good character. The most virtuous may be suspected, and an unproved accusation proves nothing against the accused, but the questions, while irrelevant both to the charge which was being tried and to the issue of good character, were calculated to injure the appellant in the eyes of the jury by suggesting that he had been in trouble before, and were, therefore, not fair to him. They should not have been put, and, if put, should have been disallowed . . .

It is most undesirable that the rules which should govern cross-examination to credit of an accused person in the witness box should be complicated by refined distinctions involving a close study and comparison of decided cases, when, in fact, these rules are few and can be simply stated. The following propositions seem to cover the ground (I am omitting the rule which admits evidence tending to prove other offences where this evidence is relevant to the issue being tried as helping to negative accident or to establish system, intent or the like): (i) The accused in the witness box may not be asked any question 'tending to show that he has committed or been convicted of or been charged with any offence other than that wherewith he is then charged, or is of bad character, unless' one or other of the three conditions set out in para (f) of s. 1 of the Act of 1898 is fulfilled. (ii) He may, however, be cross-examined as to any of the evidence he has given in chief, including statements concerning his good record, with a view to testing his veracity or accuracy or to showing that he is not to be believed on his oath. (iii) An accused who 'puts his character in issue' must be regarded as putting the whole of his past record in issue. He cannot assert his good conduct in certain respects without exposing himself to inquiry about the rest of his record so far as this tends to disprove a claim for good character. (iv) An accused is not to be regarded as depriving himself of the protection of the section, because the proper conduct of his defence necessitates the making of injurious reflections on the prosecutor or his witnesses: *R* v *Turner* [1944] KB 463. (v) It is no disproof of good character that a man has been suspected or accused of a previous crime. Such questions as 'Were you suspected?' or, 'Were you accused?' are inadmissible because they are irrelevant to the issue of character, and can only be asked if the accused has sworn expressly to the contrary. (vi) The fact that a question put to the accused is irrelevant is in itself no reason for quashing his conviction, though it should have been disallowed by the judge.

(LORDS RUSSELL OF KILLOWEN, THANKERTON, WRIGHT and POR-TER agreed.)

(The House applied the proviso to [s. 2(1) of the Criminal Appeal Act 1968] on the ground that there had been no miscarriage of justice.)

Appeal dismissed.

Jones v *Director of Public Prosecutions*
[1962] AC 635
House of Lords

The appellant was charged with the murder of a young girl guide in October 1960. He had previously been convicted of raping another girl guide during September 1960. Although the earlier conviction would have been relevant to the offence charged, in that both involved attacks on girl guides, the prosecution did not lead evidence of it because of a desire to spare the victim of the earlier crime the ordeal of giving evidence again. In statements to the police about the murder charge, the appellant gave an alibi which was false. Subsequently, he admitted that this alibi was false and put forward a second alibi. The second alibi was almost identical to an alibi which the appellant had advanced at his trial on the earlier rape charge. The similarity extended to details of conversations that the appellant alleged he had had with his wife, which were almost 'word for word' the same. At the trial, the appellant sought to explain his giving the first, false alibi by giving evidence that he had been 'in trouble' with the police. He was cross-examined about the suspicious similarity of his second alibi for the murder to his alibi on what was referred to as 'another occasion' — no details of the previous conviction being revealed to the jury. The appellant appealed on the ground that the cross-examination should not have been permitted.

LORD REID: It is well established that the 1898 Act has no application to evidence given by any person other than the accused: where it was competent before that Act for a witness to prove or refer to a previous conviction of the accused, that is still competent. What the Act does is to alter the old rules as regards the accused. It might merely have provided that the accused should be a competent witness; then the ordinary rules would have applied to him. But it goes on to afford to him protection which the ordinary rules would not give him: it expressly prohibits certain kinds of question being put to him. That must mean questions which would be competent and relevant under the ordinary rules, because there was no need to prohibit any question which would in any event have been excluded by the ordinary rules. So what must now be considered is what kinds of question, which would have been competent and relevant under the ordinary rules of evidence, does the Act prohibit. . . .

This raises at once the question what is the proper construction of the words in proviso (e), 'tend to criminate him, as to the offence charged.' Those words could mean 'tend to convince or persuade the jury that he is guilty,' or they could have the narrower meaning — 'tend to connect him with the commission of the offence charged.' If they have the former meaning, there is at once an insoluble conflict between provisos (e) and (f). No line of questioning could be relevant unless it (or the answers to it) might tend to persuade the jury of the guilt of the accused. It is only permissible to bring in previous convictions or bad character if they are so relevant, so, unless proviso (f) is to be deprived of all content, it must prohibit some questions which would tend to criminate the accused of the offence charged if those words are used in the wider sense. But if they have the narrower meaning, there is no such conflict. So the structure of the Act shows that they must have the narrower meaning.

So I turn to consider proviso (f). It is an absolute prohibition of certain questions unless one or other of three conditions is satisfied. It says the accused 'shall not be asked, and if asked shall not be required to answer,' certain questions. It was suggested that this applies to examination-in-chief as well as to cross-examination. I do not think so. The words 'shall not be required to answer' are quite inappropriate for examination-in-chief. The proviso is obviously intended to protect the accused. It does not prevent him from volunteering evidence, and does not in my view prevent his counsel from asking questions leading to disclosure of a previous conviction or bad character if such disclosure is thought to assist in his defence.

The questions prohibited are those which 'tend to show' certain things. Does this mean tend to prove or tend to suggest? Here I cannot accept the argument of the Attorney-General. What matters is the effect of the questions on the jury. A veiled suggestion of a previous offence may be just as damaging as a definite statement. In my judgment, 'tends to show' means tends to suggest to the jury. But the crucial point in the present case is whether the questions are to be considered in isolation or whether they are to be considered in the light of all that had gone before them at the trial. If the questions or line of questioning has to be considered in isolation I think that the questions with which this appeal is concerned would tend to show at least that the accused had previously been charged with an offence. The jury would be likely to jump to that conclusion, if this was the first they had heard of this matter. But I do not think that the questions ought to be considered in isolation. If the test is the effect the questions would be likely to have on the minds of the jury that necessarily implies that one must have regard to what the jury had already heard. If the jury already knew that the accused had been charged with an offence, a question inferring that he had been charged would add nothing and it would be absurd to prohibit it. If the obvious purpose of this proviso is to protect the accused from possible prejudice, as I think it is, then 'show' must mean 'reveal', because it is only a revelation of something new which could cause such prejudice.

I shall not detain your Lordships by analysing the questions to which objection is taken to see whether they contained any material revelation of anything which the jury were unlikely to infer from the evidence already given by the accused in chief. I need only refer to the speech about to be delivered by my noble and learned friend, Lord Morris of Borth-y-Gest, and to the judgment of the Court of Criminal Appeal. For the reasons which they give, I am of opinion that this appeal should be dismissed on the ground that these questions were not prohibited because they did not 'tend to show' any of the matters specified in proviso (f).

But, in case it should be thought that some of the views which I have expressed are not in accord with what was said by Lord Simon in *Stirland* v *Director of Public Prosecutions* [1944] AC 315, I must say something about that case. That was a case where the accused had put his character in issue and the questions which it was held ought not to have been put to him in cross-examination dealt with an occasion when a former employer had questioned him about a suspected forgery. But the case did not turn on proviso (f) because the second exception in the proviso was satisfied by the accused having given evidence of his good character and therefore the proviso was excluded.

Lord Simon did, however, state six rules which should govern cross-examination to credit of an accused person. First he set out proviso (f). Then comes the rule which gives rise to the difficulty: '(ii) He may, however, be cross-examined as to any of the evidence he has given in chief, including statements concerning his good record, with a view to testing his veracity or accuracy or to showing that he is not to be believed on his oath.' Applied to a case where the accused has put his character in issue I think that is correct, because then proviso (f) does not apply. But I do not think that Lord Simon can have meant it to apply in its general form to a case where proviso (f) does operate, because earlier in his speech he said [at p. 322]: 'This House has laid it down in *Maxwell* v *Director of Public Prosecutions* [1935] AC 309 that, while paragraph (f) of this section absolutely prohibits any question of the kind there indicated being put to the accused in the witness box unless one or other of the conditions (i), (ii) or (iii) is satisfied, it does not follow that such questions are in all circumstances justified whenever one or other of the conditions is fulfilled.' Thus he recognised the absolute character of the prohibition except where one or other of the conditions is satisfied, so he cannot have intended to say that there is another case, not covered by the conditions, where the proviso also does not apply, namely, where questions are put with a view to testing the veracity of the accused's evidence in chief. But if he did mean that it was certainly *obiter* and I would not agree with it. It would in effect be legislating by adding a fourth condition to proviso (f). The Attorney-General refused to take this point and I think he was perfectly right.

It is said that the views which I have expressed involve overruling two decisions of the Court of Criminal Appeal, *R* v *Chitson* [1909] 2 KB 945 and *R* v *Kennaway* [1917] 1 KB 25, CCA. I do not think so. I think the decisions were right but the reasons given for them were not. In the former case the accused was charged with having had carnal knowledge of a girl aged 14. Giving evidence, she said that the accused told her that he had previously done the same thing to another girl, who, she said, was under 16. No objection was taken to this evidence, I assume rightly. So before the accused gave evidence the jury already knew that he was alleged to have committed another offence. If the views which I have already expressed are right, cross-examining the accused about this matter disclosed nothing new to them and therefore did not offend against the prohibition in proviso (f). But the judgment of the court was not based on that ground: it was said that although the questions tended to prove that the accused was of bad character they also tended to show that he was guilty of the offence with which he was charged. For the reasons which I have given I do not think that that is sufficient to avoid the prohibition in proviso (f).

R v *Kennaway* was a prosecution for forgery. Accomplices giving evidence for the prosecution described the fraudulent scheme of which the forgery was a part and related a conversation with the accused in which he stated to them that some years earlier he had forged another will in pursuance of a similar scheme. Then in cross-examination the accused was asked a number of questions about this other forgery. Those questions were held to have been properly put to him. Here, again, these questions disclosed nothing new to the jury and I can see no valid objection to them. But again that was not the ground of the court's decision. Their ground of decision was similar to that in *Chitson's* case, and I need not repeat what I have said about that case.

LORD DENNING: My Lords, much of the discussion before your Lordships was directed to the effect of section 1(f) of the Criminal Evidence Act 1898: and, if that were the sole paragraph for consideration, I should have thought that counsel for the Crown ought not to have asked the questions he did. My reasons are these:

First: The questions *tended* to show that Jones had previously been charged in a court of law with another offence. True it is that they did not point definitely to that conclusion, but they conveyed that impression, and that is enough. Counsel may not have intended it, but that does not matter. What matters is the impression the questions would have on the jury. The Attorney-General said that, if the questions left the matter evenly balanced, so that there was some other conclusion that could equally well be drawn, as, for instance, that Jones had not been 'charged' in a court of law but had only been interrogated in a police station, there was no bar to the questions being asked. I cannot agree. If the questions asked by the Crown are capable of conveying two impressions — one objectionable and the other not — then they 'tend to show' each of them: and the questions must be excluded, lest the jury adopt the worse of the two impressions. I do not think that it is open to the prosecution to throw out prejudicial hints and insinuations — from which a jury might infer that the man had been charged before — and then escape censure under the cloak of ambiguity.

Second: I think that the questions tended to *show* that Jones had been charged with an offence, even though he had himself brought out the fact that he had been 'in trouble' before. It is one thing to confess to having been in trouble before. It is quite another to have it emphasised against you with devastating detail. Before these questions were asked by the Crown, all that the jury knew was that at some unspecified time in the near or distant past, this man had been in trouble with the police. After the questions were asked, the jury knew, in addition, that he had been very recently in trouble for an offence on a Friday night which was of so sensational a character that it featured in a newspaper on the following Sunday — in these respects closely similar to the present offence — and that he had been charged in a court of law with that very offence. It seems to me that questions which tend to reveal an offence, thus particularised, are directly within the prohibition in section 1(f) and are not rendered admissible by his own vague disclosure of some other offence. I do not believe that the mere fact that he said he had been in trouble before with the police — referring as he did to an entirely different matter many years past — let in this very damaging cross-examination as to recent events.

Third: The questions do not come within the exception (i) to section 1(f). There was no evidence before the court of any 'other offence' which would be admissible evidence to show that he had been guilty of this murder. If the prosecution had given evidence of the previous rape with its attendant circumstances, there might have been such similarities as to render the proof of that offence admissible to prove identity, see

R v *Straffen* [1952] 2 QB 911: but in the absence of such evidence, I do not see how these questions could be justified in cross-examination under exception (i). Before any cross-examination is permissible under exception (i), the prosecution must lay a proper foundation for it by showing some 'other offence which is admissible evidence to show that he is guilty.' The prosecution should normally do it by giving evidence in the course of their case; though there may be cases in which they might, with the leave of the judge, do it for the first time in cross-examination. No such foundation was laid here.

If the case rested solely on section 1(f), I would therefore have held that these questions were inadmissible. But I do not think it rests on section 1(f). In my judgment, the questions were admissible under section 1(e), which says that a person charged 'may be asked any question in cross-examination notwithstanding that it would tend to criminate him as to the offence charged.' As to this subsection, Viscount Sankey LC, speaking for all in this House in *Maxwell's* case, said that under section 1(e) 'a witness may be cross-examined in respect of the offence charged, and cannot refuse to answer questions directly relevant to the offence on the ground that they tend to incriminate him: thus if he denies the offence, he may be cross-examined to refute the denial.' I would add that, if he gives an explanation in an attempt to exculpate himself, he may be cross-examined to refute his explanation. And nonetheless so because it tends incidentally to show that he had previously been charged with another offence.

Let me first say why I think in this case the questions were directly relevant to the offence charged. They were directly relevant because they tended to refute an explanation which the accused man had given. He had given a detailed explanation of his movements on the crucial weekend, and so forth, all in an attempt to exculpate himself. The prosecution sought to show that this explanation was false: and I think it was of direct relevance for them to do so. From the very earliest times, long before an accused man could give evidence on his own behalf, the law has recognised that, in considering whether a man is guilty of the crime charged against him, one of the most relevant matters is this: What explanation did he give when he was asked about it? Was that explanation true or not? If he gives a true explanation, it tells in his favour. If he gives a false explanation, it tells against him. The prosecution have, therefore, always been entitled, as part of their own case, to give evidence of any explanation given by the accused and of its truth or falsity. Thus if a man, who is found in possession of a stolen watch, tells a policeman that he bought it for £5 from a tradesman whom he names, the prosecution can call that tradesman, as part of their case, to say whether that was true or not. If true, it is an end of the case against the accused. If false, it goes a long way to prove his guilt, see *R* v *Crowhurst* (1844) 1 Car & Kir 370 by Alderson B, *R* v *Henry Smith* (1845) 2 Car & Kir 207 by Lord Denman CJ. So also if a man, who is charged with murder at a specified time and place, tells a policeman that he was at the house of his sister-in-law at the time, as Jones did here, the prosecution can call the sister-in-law, as part of their case, to say it was false and that he was not at her house at all. So also if he tries, as Jones did, to get his sister-in-law to say that he was at her house at that time, contrary to the fact, the prosecution can call the sister-in-law to say that he tried to suborn her to give false testimony: for the simple reason that 'the recourse to falsehood leads fairly to an inference of guilt,' see *Moriarty* v *London, Chatham & Dover Railway Co.* (1870) LR 5 QB 314 by Cockburn CJ. In this very case Jones's sister-in-law, Mrs Eldridge, gave such evidence for the prosecution without any objection being taken to it, even though it tended to show that he was guilty of another offence, namely, the offence of attempting to pervert the course of justice.

Now, suppose the man does this further thing which Jones did here. He discards the story that he went to his sister-in-law's house and puts forward a different story. He says that he went up to London and was with a prostitute, but he does not identify her. So the prostitute cannot be called to falsify his story. Nevertheless the prosecution can falsify it by other evidence, if they have it available. They can call such evidence as part of their own case, even though it tends incidentally to show that he was guilty of another offence. For instance, they could prove that his finger-prints were on the window of a house that was broken into at Yateley that night. '. . . the mere fact that the evidence adduced tends to show the commission of other crimes does not render it inadmissible if it be relevant to an issue before the jury,' see *Makin v Attorney-General of New South Wales* [1894] AC 57. Evidence that he had committed burglary would not be admissible to prove that he had committed murder: but evidence that he was at Yateley would be admissible to prove that he was in the vicinity and had recourse to falsehood to explain his whereabouts. The prosecution would be entitled to call this evidence, even though it tended to show that he was guilty of burglary.

Such is the law as it is, and always has been, as to the evidence which can be called for the prosecution. They can, in the first place, give evidence of any explanation given by the accused of his movements and they can, in the second place, give evidence that his explanation is false, even though it tends incidentally to show the commission by him of some other offence. Now, when Parliament in 1898 enabled an accused man to give evidence on his own behalf, they did not cut down evidence of this kind for the prosecution. And when the prosecution gives such evidence, it must be open to the accused man himself to answer it. He must be able to give evidence about it and to be cross-examined upon it. He can be cross-examined as to any explanation he has given and as to its truth or falsity: and he can be cross-examined upon it nonetheless because incidentally it may tend to show that he has been guilty of some other offence.

No one, surely, can doubt the validity of *R v Chitson* [1909] 2 KB 945, and *R v Kennaway* [1917] 1 KB 25 at least to this extent, that when the prosecution have legitimately given in evidence any explanation or statement made by the accused relative to the offence charged, he can be cross-examined as to the truth or falsity of it, even though incidentally it may tend to show that he has been guilty of some other offence or is of bad character.

Now, the only difference is that, whereas in those cases the accused man made his explanation or statement *before* the trial, in the present case he made his explanation (about his conversations with his wife, and so forth) for the first time *at* the trial when he went into the witness box to give evidence on his own behalf. But this cannot give him any protection from a cross-examination to which he would otherwise be exposed. His explanation is not made sacrosanct, it is not made incapable of challenge, simply because he gives it at the trial instead of at an earlier stage. The prosecution are entitled to expose its falsity, no matter whether he gives it at the trial or beforehand. And they are not precluded from doing so merely because the exposure of it tends to show that he has been guilty of some other offence or is of bad character. The situation is precisely covered by the second proposition in *Stirland's* case [1944] AC 315 where Viscount Simon LC, in this House, with the assent of all present, said that, notwithstanding the prohibition in section 1(f), the accused man 'may, however, be cross-examined as to any of the evidence he has given in chief, including statements concerning his good record,' and including, I would add, any explanation offered by him, 'with a view to testing his veracity or accuracy or to showing that he is not to be believed on his oath.'

It is noteworthy that everyone at the trial of Jones acted on this view of the law. No one suggested that the questions were absolutely prohibited. All that was suggested was that it was a matter of discretion. And that is, I think, the true position. The judge was entitled in his discretion to exclude them if he thought they were so prejudicial as to outweigh their probative value. It was his discretion, not that of the prosecution. He did not exclude them but permitted them to be asked. They were, therefore, properly put.

In conclusion I would say that I view with concern the suggestion that the reasoning in *R v Chitson* and *R v Kennaway* was wrong and that what Viscount Simon LC said in *Stirland v DPP* is no longer a safe guide. Those cases have governed the practice in our criminal courts for years: and the result has been wholly beneficial. It is not, in my opinion, right to resort now to a literal reading of the Act so as to displace them.

LORD MORRIS OF BORTH-Y-GEST: My Lords, it seems to me that the clearest guidance as to provisos (e) and (f) was given in *Maxwell's* case. In his speech, Viscount Sankey LC said:

> In section 1, proviso (e), it has been enacted that a witness may be cross-examined in respect of the offence charged, and cannot refuse to answer questions directly relevant to the offence on the ground that they tend to incriminate him: thus if he denies the offence, he may be cross-examined to refute the denial. These are matters directly relevant to the charge on which he is being tried. Proviso (f), however, is dealing with matters outside, and not directly relevant to, the particular offence charged; such matters, to be admissible at all, must in general fall under two main classes: one is the class of evidence which goes to show not that the prisoner did the acts charged, but that, if he did these acts, he did them as part of a system or intentionally, so as to refute a defence that if he did them he did them innocently or inadvertently, as for instance in *Makin v Attorney-General for New South Wales* [1894] AC 57, where the charge was one of murder; another illustration of such cases is *R v Bond* [1906] 2 KB 389. This rule applies to cases where guilty knowledge or design or intention is of the essence of the offence.
>
> The other main class is where it is sought to show that the prisoner is not a person to be believed on his oath, which is generally attempted by what is called cross-examination to credit. Closely allied with this latter type of question is the rule that, if the prisoner by himself or his witnesses seeks to give evidence of his own good character, for the purpose of showing that it is unlikely that he committed the offence charged, he raises by way of defence an issue as to his good character, so that he may fairly be cross-examined on that issue, just as any witness called by him to prove his good character may be cross-examined to show the contrary. All these matters are dealt with in proviso (f) . . . .

In his speech in *Stirland v Director of Public Prosecutions* Viscount Simon LC said that he was disposed to think that in (f), where the word 'character' occurs four times, there is a combination of the conceptions of general reputation and of actual moral disposition.

Having regard to what has been laid down in *Maxwell's* case and in *Stirland's* case, I do not find it necessary to embark upon 'a close study and comparison' of earlier cases such as *R v Chitson* and *R v Kennaway*. If the results reached in those cases can be supported it must not be on any line of reasoning that runs counter to what has been laid down in *Maxwell's* case and in *Stirland's* case.

LORD DEVLIN: My Lords, I would dismiss this appeal on the short ground that the questions objected to were relevant to an issue in the case upon which the appellant had testified in chief. It is not disputed that the issue to which the questions related was a relevant one. It concerned the identification of the appellant as being at the material time at the scene of the crime. He testified that at the material time he was with a prostitute in the West End and he supported this alibi by giving evidence of a conversation which he had with his wife about it a day or two later. The purpose of the questions objected to was to obtain from the appellant an admission (which was given) that when he was being questioned about his movements in relation to another incident some weeks earlier he had set up the same alibi and had supported it with an account of a conversation with his wife in almost identical terms; the prosecution suggested that these similarities showed the whole story of the alibi to be an invented one. . . .

(VISCOUNT SIMONDS delivered a judgment agreeing with LORD REID and LORD MORRIS of BORTH-Y-GEST.)

Appeal dismissed.

Questions
1. Does the operation of s. 1(f)(i) depend on how the accused behaves at trial?
2. Referring to s. 1(e) and s. 1(f), Professor JC Smith in [1962] Crim LR 244 said:

Proviso (e) provides that the accused may be asked '*any question* in cross-examination notwithstanding that it would tend to criminate him as to the offence charged'. Proviso (f) provides that he shall not be asked, *inter alia*, any question tending to show that he has committed or been convicted of any other offence. Now it is apparent that a question which shows that the accused has committed or been convicted of some other offence may also tend to criminate him as to the offence charged. Proviso (e) apparently allows such a question, proviso (f) apparently forbids it. One or other must give way.

How did the House of Lords in *Jones* v *DPP* deal with this problem?

R v *Anderson*
[1988] QB 678
Court of Appeal

The appellant and the co-defendants, as members of the IRA, had planned to plant a number of bombs in London and south coast resorts. They were tried on a count of conspiracy to cause explosions likely to endanger life or cause serious injury to property. The appellant denied that she had taken part in the conspiracy charged and, without the prosecution being fore-warned, explained evidence against her by claiming that she had been concerned in attempting to smuggle IRA members, who had escaped from prison in Ireland, though Scotland to Denmark. To rebut her evidence the prosecution applied for leave to question her to establish that she had been 'wanted' by the police prior to her arrest in order to show that it was unlikely that as a wanted person she would have been chosen to help escaped prisoners or herself be willing to undertake a task with a double risk of identification. The judge exercised his discretion by granting leave and, on the questions being put, the appellant admitted she had been a wanted person. She was convicted of the conspiracy charged.

LORD LANE CJ: . . . The way in which the problem can be put is this: a defendant is faced with prosecution evidence which prima facie incriminates her of the offence charged. She puts forward in evidence an explanation of that prosecution case which is consistent with her innocence of the offence charged. The prosecution wish to cross-examine her about that explanation. Cross-examination necessarily involves questions which tend to show that she, the defendant, has committed a criminal offence, the nature of which the prosecution neither require nor intend to reveal. Are they allowed, by the terms of section 1 of the Criminal Evidence Act 1898 to ask those questions? I have no doubt the immediate reaction of the practitioner would be 'Of course they are allowed to ask the questions. If not it would be giving the dishonest defendant an unjust and ludicrous advantage.' The same practitioner would no doubt add 'In any event, the judge has an overriding discretion to reject the submission and disallow the questions if he thinks that they are going to produce unfairness to the defendant in the particular circumstances.'

Mr Mansfield will not mind us saying that it seems to have been his initial reaction, and indeed was the initial reaction of the court of first instance in a number of the reported cases, that this was a matter solely of discretion. To take one or two examples, *Rex v Kennaway* [1917] 1 KB 25 and *Rex v Chitson* [1909] 2 KB 945. Perhaps most surprisingly of all, also *Jones v Director of Public Prosecutions* [1962] AC 635, which we shall have to examine in more detail in a moment. In that case, in the court at first instance, the trial judge being Sachs J, the problem of the Criminal Evidence Act 1898 hardly raised its head if at all. It was only later when the matter came to be examined on appeal that the difficulties started to arise. This is, indeed, one of those situations where the criminal law in practice functions quite satisfactorily until one starts to subject the relevant statute to minute scrutiny.

Section 1 of the Criminal Evidence Act 1898 is a nightmare of construction. No doubt the reasons for its difficulty may be found in its Parliamentary history, but we are not allowed and nor do we wish to embark upon that sort of research. There is no need for me to read all the terms of the Act. Those have already been read to us and we can take them as read, but this appeal is yet another example of the perennial problem caused by the wording. Section 1(e) allows the accused person to be asked any question in cross-examination notwithstanding that it would tend to incriminate him as to the offence charged. Paragraph (f), however, provides that he shall not be asked 'any question tending to show that he has committed or been convicted of or been charged with any offence' subject to certain exceptions. Those two provisions are mutually contradictory, at least on the face of them, as has been said more than once by courts over the last 90 years. The reason for that is this: a question which tends to incriminate the defendant as to the offence charged, and so is relevant and admissible under paragraph (e), may very well tend to show, and often does, that the defendant has committed another offence and so is inadmissible under paragraph (f). This problem has been the subject of differing views, and those differing views are exemplified by the opinions of five of their Lordships in *Jones v Director of Public Prosecutions* [1962] AC 635.

The facts in that case are, very briefly, that Jones was charged with the murder of a young Girl Guide. He put forward an account of his movements which, to all intents and purposes, was the same, almost word for word, as an account he had put forward some three months earlier when he was charged with an offence of rape committed upon another young Girl Guide. Not surprisingly the prosecution wished to cross-examine Jones about this remarkable coincidence with a view to showing that his account was false. The question obviously indicated that he had committed another offence. The Court of Criminal Appeal held that the judge was correct to have allowed the questions because they said that Jones had, in his evidence-in-chief, said that he had 'been in trouble with the police.' Since the words 'tending to show' meant 'revealing,' the question asked of the defendant did not 'tend to show' the commission of a crime, because that crime had already been revealed to the jury. In other words, if the revelation as to a previous conviction has already been made to the jury, the prohibition does not apply.

This was the basis upon which the majority in the House of Lords, Viscount Simonds, Lord Reid and Lord Morris of Borth-y-Gest, dismissed the appeal. Their Lordships, however, did not leave the matter there. They ventured upon a discussion of the difficulties raised by the section, a discussion which is relevant to the present case. The majority supported the view that paragraph (e) is subordinate to and governed by paragraph (f)(i). Lord Reid's view was that the words of paragraph (e) have two possible interpretations. They could, first of all, mean 'tend to convince or persuade a jury that the defendant is guilty' or, secondly, 'tend to connect the defendant with the offence charged.' If they have the first meaning, the broader meaning, that, in his Lordship's view, produces the insoluble conflict with paragraph (f) which we mentioned a moment or two ago. If, on the other hand, they have the second meaning, the narrower meaning, there is no such conflict, because paragraph (f) could then apply to questions which tend to persuade a jury that the defendant is guilty.

That, of course, leaves the residual problem, not easy to answer, namely how close the connection must be with the offence to bring it within the narrower meaning of paragraph (e).

Lord Denning and Lord Devlin were in the minority and we do not feel it necessary to refer to their speeches save to say that they are interesting interpretations of the Act. Lord Reid seems to have thought that it was open to the House at some time or other to reconsider the matter if it should be directly raised.

In the present case there was, in the question, a clear tendency to show that Martina Anderson had committed an offence other than that with which she was charged — obviously so because otherwise she would not be 'wanted' by the police. So in the light of the decision in *Jones* the question would be admissible in any of the following circumstances, that is applying the reasoning which we have attempted to set out as explained by the House of Lords: first of all, if there was no tendency to reveal the commission of an offence as in *Jones*, for example, because the commission of an offence had already (properly) been made known to the jury. Secondly, if the proof of the commission tended to connect the appellant with the offence charged. Thirdly, if the appellant had given evidence of her own good character.

The third matter can be dealt with very shortly. Mr Mansfield on the appellant's behalf did persuade the prosecution to concede that the appellant was of good character, apart from being 'wanted' by the police, but that concession was only made after the judge had ruled upon the submission and consequently that would not, we are prepared to assume, be a ground for admitting the evidence under section 1(f) of the Act.

As to the tendency to reveal, the appellant had already revealed that it was likely that she had committed a number of offences in respect of any one of which she might well have been 'wanted' by the police. There was probably a conspiracy to assist the escape of a prisoner; probably forgery of documents; probably conspiracy to forge; possession of firearms and so on, as already set out when we detailed the evidence which she gave before the jury. Thus it was already revealed that she had committed offences, although it might be that she was not yet 'wanted' by the police in respect of them. The jury already knew, therefore, that she had committed a number of offences, and the fact that she was 'wanted' by the police in respect of an unspecified offence, and therefore was probably guilty of committing an unspecified offence was not, on the reasoning in *Jones*, in the view of this court, a revelation to the jury.

As to the second point, 'does evidence which tends to destroy the defendant's innocent explanation of prima facie damning circumstances, connect the defendant with the crime so as to come within Lord Reid's analysis of the meaning of paragraph (e)?' We are inclined to think that it may, but we prefer to base our conclusion primarily on the fact that the appellant had already revealed that she had committed crimes.

There is however a different approach which is perhaps less artificial than the reasoning in *Jones*, if we may say so.

Section 1 of the Act of 1898 did nothing to alter the pre-existing law as to what evidence the prosecution were entitled to adduce in order to prove their case. As Lord Reid said in Jones, at p. 590:

> It is well established that the 1898 Act has no application to evidence given by any person other than the accused: where it was competent before that Act for a witness to prove or refer to a previous conviction of the accused, that is still competent. What the Act does is to alter the old rules as regards the accused.

The extent of that pre-existing law had been examined only four years previously in *Makin* v *Attorney-General for New South Wales* [1894] AC 57. Lord Herschell LC said, at p. 65:

> It is undoubtedly not competent for the prosecution to adduce evidence tending to show that the accused has been guilty of criminal acts other than those covered by the indictment, for the purpose of leading to the conclusion that the accused is a person likely from his criminal conduct or character to have committed the offence for which he is being tried. On the other hand, the mere fact that the evidence adduced tends to show the commission of other crimes does not render it inadmissible if it be relevant to an issue before the jury, and it may be so relevant if it bears upon the question whether the acts alleged to constitute the crime charged in the indictment were designed or accidental, or to rebut a defence which would otherwise be open to the accused.

Thus, if the prosecution know that a particular defence is going to be advanced, they may (subject to the judge's discretion) call evidence to rebut it as part of their own substantive case even if that tends to show the commission of other crimes. The defendant can plainly then be cross-examined about the matter. If the prosecution do not know of the defence in advance, then they may call evidence to rebut it and the defendant can then be recalled, if that is desired, to deal with the rebutting evidence. The judge in the present case — wisely, the evidence not being in dispute — allowed that somewhat laborious process to be short-circuited. The result however was just as much in accordance with authority and the Act of 1898 as if the procedure had been carried out in extenso.

These considerations strengthen our view that the judge's decision in the present case was correct.

There only remains to deal with the question of discretion. We take the view that there is ample authority that the judge could exercise his discretion in the way that he did. Obviously he examined the matter very closely and we, in our judgment, feel he was not only entitled to exercise his discretion as he did, but was correct in doing so.

We wish to add further to this that, in view of the fact that we are dismissing this appeal on the grounds which I have indicated, there is no need for us to invite observations, nor indeed for ourselves to make observations, on the question of the proviso to which otherwise we should have had to address ourselves.

Question
Could the Court of Appeal in *Anderson* validly have reached any other conclusion?

(ii)   Section 1(f)(ii)

Note
Section 1(f)(ii) may operate in two distinct situations. First, if the accused puts his character in issue. This is usually referred to as 'the first limb of s. 1(f)(ii)'. Secondly, if the accused casts imputations on the prosecutor or his witnesses. This is usually referred to as 'the second limb of s. 1(f)(ii)'. Unlike s. 1(f)(i), s. 1(f)(ii) cannot operate without some action by or on behalf of the accused. Remember also, that the section cannot operate unless the accused *actually testifies*. If the *character* of the accused is put in issue and he does not testify, the prosecution can only rely on their common law right to call evidence in rebuttal, not the Act (see *R* v *Rowton*, (A)(*i*) above).

(a)   The first limb of s. 1(f)(ii)

R v *Redd*
[1923] 1 KB 104
Court of Criminal Appeal

The appellant was tried at the Northamptonshire Quarter Sessions upon a charge of breaking and entering a dwelling house at East Haddon and stealing therefrom the sum of about £140, the property of Agnes Weston, who was the grandmother of the appellant's wife. The appellant was also charged with receiving the property stolen. He was convicted upon the whole indictment and sentenced to seven years' penal servitude.

In the course of the trial the appellant, who undefended, called a witness named Williams for the sole purpose of producing certain letters. That witness, without any question being asked by the appellant, voluntarily made a statement that the appellant held a good position in the Army as a warrant officer and that so far as the witness knew he was quite all right. The counsel for the prosecution then said that as evidence had been given of the good character of the appellant he proposed to cross-examine the witness as to the real character of the appellant. He then proceeded to ask the witness whether he was aware that the appellant had been convicted eleven times, including two convictions in which the appellant had been sentenced to terms of penal servitude. The witness replied that he was not aware of that fact. No attempt was made by the prosecution to prove the previous convictions of the appellant, nor was any further reference to them made to the jury.

The appellant also gave evidence on his own behalf, but did not give evidence on his own good character. He was, however, asked in cross-examination by counsel for the prosecution as to the number of times he had deserted from the Army.

AVORY J: The question we have to determine is whether the suggestion of the previous bad character of the appellant was properly put before the jury. So far as the evidence given by the witness Williams is concerned the Criminal Evidence Act, 1898, has no application, but it does fall within the authority of *Reg.* v *Gadbury* (1838) 8 C & P 676. In the opinion of the Court the rule in that case is correctly stated in Archbold's Criminal Pleading, 26th ed., p: 366, as follows: 'If the prisoner endeavours to establish a good character, either by calling witnesses himself, or by cross-examining the witnesses for the prosecution, the prosecution is at liberty, in most cases, to give proof of the prisoner's previous convictions.' The question is whether the appellant was within the meaning of that rule endeavouring to establish a good character. In the opinion of the Court he was not endeavouring to establish a good character merely because a witness whom he called, voluntarily and probably against the appellant's own desire, made a statement as to the appellant's good character, and therefore the questions put to that witness in cross-examination by counsel for the prosecution were not admissible.

The matter does not stop there, because the appellant gave evidence on his own behalf, and he was cross-examined by counsel for the prosecution as to the number of times he had deserted from the Army, and he gave an answer which would convey to the jury that there was some truth in the question. The question put to the appellant in cross-examination as to his desertion from the Army does come directly within the provisions of the Criminal Evidence Act, 1898. That Act provides in s. 1(f) that 'a person charged and called as a witness in pursuance of this Act shall not be asked, and if asked shall not be required to answer, any question tending to show that he has committed or been convicted of or been charged with any offence other than that wherewith he is then charged, or is of bad character, unless . . . (ii.) he has personally or by his advocate asked questions of the witnesses for the prosecution with a view to establish his own good character, or has given evidence of his good character. . . .' In the opinion of the Court the appellant had not given evidence of good character within the meaning of the Act and therefore the cross-examination as to the appellant's desertion from the Army was not admissible.

Note

There are a number of authorities, some of them quite old, which deal with whether or not an accused has sought to 'establish his own good character'. Examples where the accused was held to have put character in issue include: *R* v *Ferguson* (1909) 2 Cr App R 250, where the accused stated he was a regular attender at Mass; *R* v *Coulman* (1927) 20 Cr App R 106, where the accused stated he was a 'family man in regular work'. A more recent example is provided by *R* v *Stronach* [1988] Crim LR 48, where it was held that evidence which, incidental to a description of the crime, demonstrated that the accused was a family man working for London Transport, was not sufficient to lose the accused his protection under the Act. The question of whether or not the accused has sought to establish his good character remains a question of law for the judge.

(b) The second limb of s. 1(f)(ii)

Selvey v Director of Public Prosecutions
[1970] AC 304
House of Lords

The appellant was charged with buggery. There was medical evidence that the complainant had been sexually interfered with by someone on the day in question, and also indecent photographs were found in the appellant's room. The defence was that the complainant had told him that he had already 'been on the bed' with a man for £1 and that he would do the same for him for £1. The appellant denied knowledge of the photographs and suggested that they had been planted on him by the complainant in annoyance at the rejection of the offer. The trial judge allowed the appellant to be cross-examined on his previous convictions for homosexual offences. The appellant was convicted and appealed on the ground, *inter alia*, that as the nature of his defence necessarily involved the imputation against the complainant, the judge in accordance with 'the general rule' should have exercised his discretion under s. 1(f)(ii) of the Criminal Evidence Act 1898, in his favour by excluding his previous record.

VISCOUNT DILHORNE: The cases to which I have referred, some of which it is not possible to reconcile, in my opinion finally establish the following propositions:
  (1)   The words of the statute must be given their ordinary natural meaning (*R v Hudson* [1912] 2 KB 464; *R v Jenkins* (1945) 31 Cr App R 1; *R v Cook* [1959] 2 QB 340).
  (2)   The section permits cross-examination of the accused as to character both when imputations on the character of the prosecutor and his witness are cast to show their unreliability as witnesses independently of the evidence given by them and also when the casting of such imputations is necessary to enable the accused to establish his defence (*R v Hudson*; *R v Jenkins*; *R v Cook*).
  (3)   In rape cases the accused can allege consent without placing himself in peril of such cross-examination (*R v Sheean*, 21 Cox CC 561; *R v Turner* [1944] KB 463). This may be because such cases are *sui generis* (per Devlin J in *R v Cook* [1959] 2 QB 340, 347), or on the ground that the issue is one raised by the prosecution.
  (4)   If what is said amounts in reality to no more than a denial of the charge, expressed, it may be, in emphatic language, it should not be regarded as coming within the section (*R v Rouse* [1904] 1 KB 184; *R v Grout* (1909) 3 Cr App R 64; *R v Jones* (1923) 17 Cr App R 117; *R v Clark* [1955] 2 QB 469).
  Applying these propositions to this case, it is in my opinion clear beyond all doubt that the cross-examination of the accused was permissible under the statute.
  I now turn to the question whether a judge has discretion to refuse to permit such cross-examination of the accused even when it is permissible under the section. Mr

Caulfield submitted that there was no such discretion and contended that a judge at a criminal trial had no power to exclude evidence which was admissible. He submitted that the position was correctly stated by Bankes J in *R v Fletcher* (1913) 9 Cr App R 53, 56, when he said:

> Where the judge entertains a doubt as to the admissibility of evidence, he may suggest to the prosecution that they should not press it, but he cannot exclude evidence which he holds to be admissible.

Since that case it has been said in many cases that a judge has such a discretion. In *R v Christie* [1914] AC 545 where the question was as to the admissibility of a statement made in the presence and hearing of the accused, Lord Moulton said, at p. 559:

> Now, in a civil action evidence may always be given of any statement or communication made to the opposite party, provided it is relevant to the issues. The same is true of any act or behaviour of the party. The sole limitation is that the matter thus given in evidence must be relevant. I am of opinion that, as a strict matter of law, there is no difference in this respect between the rules of evidence in our civil and in our criminal procedure. But there is a great difference in the practice. The law is so much on its guard against the accused being prejudiced by evidence which, though admissible, would probably have a prejudicial influence on the minds of the jury which would be out of proportion to its true evidential value, that there has grown up a practice of a very salutary nature, under which the judge intimates to the counsel for the prosecution that he should not press for the admission of evidence which would be open to this objection, and such an intimation from the tribunal trying the case is usually sufficient to prevent the evidence being pressed in all cases where the scruples of the tribunal in this respect are reasonable. Under the influence of this practice, which is based on an anxiety to secure for everyone a fair trial, there has grown up a custom of not admitting certain kinds of evidence which is so constantly followed that it almost amounts to a rule of procedure.

In *R v Watson*, 8 Cr App R 249, 254, the first case when the exercise of discretion in relation to cases coming within the section was mentioned, Pickford J said: 'It has been pointed out that to apply the rule' [in *R v Hudson* [1912] 2 KB 464] 'strictly is to put a hardship on a prisoner with a bad character. That may be so, but it does not follow that a judge necessarily allows the prisoner to be cross-examined to character; he has a discretion not to allow it, and the prisoner has that protection.' In *Maxwell* [1935] AC 309 and in *Stirland* [1944] AC 315 it was said in this House that a judge has that discretion. In *R v Jenkins*, 31 Cr App R 1, 15, Singleton J said:

> If and when such a situation arises [the question whether the accused should be cross-examined as to character] it is open to counsel to apply to the presiding judge that he may be allowed to take the course indicated . . . Such an application will not always be granted, for the judge has a discretion in the matter. He may feel that even though the position is established in law, still the putting of such questions as to the character of the accused person may be fraught with results which immeasurably outweigh the result of questions put by the defence and which make a fair trial of the accused person almost impossible. On the other hand, in the ordinary and normal case he may feel that if the credit of the prosecutor or his witnesses has been attacked, it is only fair that the jury should have before them material on which they can form their judgment whether the accused person is any more worthy to be believed than those he has attacked. It is obviously unfair that

the jury should be left in the dark about an accused person's character if the conduct of his defence has attacked the character of the prosecutor or the witnesses for the prosecution within the meaning of the section. The essential thing is a fair trial and that the legislature sought to ensure by section 1, subsection (f).

Similar views were expressed in *Noor Mohamed v The King* [1949] AC 182 by Lord du Parcq, in *Harris v Director of Public Prosecutions* [1952] AC 594, in *R v Cook* [1959] 2 QB 340, in *Jones v Director of Public Prosecutions* [1962] AC 635, and in other cases.

In the light of what was said in all these cases by judges of great eminence, one is tempted to say, as Lord Hewart said in *R v Dunkley* [1927] 1 KB 323 that it is far too late in the day even to consider the argument that a judge has no such discretion. Let it suffice for me to say that in my opinion the existence of such a discretion is now clearly established.

Mr Caulfield posed the question, on what principles should such a discretion be exercised. In *R v Flynn* [1963] 1 QB 729, 737 the court said:

> . . . where . . . the very nature of the defence necessarily involves an imputation, against a prosecution witness or witnesses, the discretion should, in the opinion of this Court, be as a general rule exercised in favour of the accused, that is to say, evidence as to his bad character or criminal record should be excluded. If it were otherwise, it comes to this, that the Act of 1898, the very Act which gave the charter, so to speak, to an accused person to give evidence on oath in the witness box, would be a mere trap because he would be unable to put forward any defence, no matter how true, which involved an imputation on the character of the prosecutor or any of his witnesses, without running the risk, if he had the misfortune to have a record, of his previous convictions being brought up in court while being tried on a wholly different matter.

No authority is given for this supposed general rule. In my opinion, the court was wrong in thinking that there was any such rule. If there was any such general rule, it would amount under the guise of the exercise of discretion, to the insertion of a proviso to the statute of the very kind that was said in *R v Hudson* [1912] 2 KB 464 not to be legitimate.

I do not think it possible to improve upon the guidance given by Singleton J in the passage quoted above from *R v Jenkins*, 31 Cr App R 1, 15, by Lord du Parcq in *Noor Mohamed* [1949] AC 182 or by Devlin J, in *R v Cook* [1959] 2 QB 340 as to the matters which should be borne in mind in relation to the exercise of the discretion. It is now so well established that on a charge of rape the allegation that the woman consented, although involving an imputation on her character, should not expose an accused to cross-examination as to character, that it is possible to say, if the refusal to allow it is a matter of discretion, that there is a general rule that the discretion should be so exercised. Apart from this, there is not, I think, any general rule as to the exercise of discretion. It must depend on the circumstances of each case and the overriding duty of the judge to ensure that a trial is fair.

It is desirable that a warning should be given when it becomes apparent that the defence is taking a course which may expose the accused to such cross-examination. That was not given in this case but the failure to give such a warning would not, in my opinion, justify in this case the allowing of the appeal.

LORD GUEST: If I had thought that there was no discretion in English law for a judge to disallow admissible evidence, as counsel for the Crown argued, I should have striven hard and long to give a benevolent construction to section 1(f)(ii), which would exclude such cases as *R v Rouse* [1904] 1 KB 184, 'liar,' *R v Rappolt* (1911) 6 Cr App R 156, 'horrible liar,' *R v Jones*, 17 Cr App R 117, 'fabricated evidence,' *R v Turner* [1944] KB 463, rape and other sexual offences, *R v Brown* (1960) 44 Cr App R 181, 'self defence.' I cannot believe that Parliament can have intended that in such cases an accused could only put forward such a defence at peril of having his character put before the jury. This would be to defeat the benevolent purposes of the 1898 Act which was for the first time to allow the accused to give evidence on his own behalf in all criminal cases. This would deprive the accused of the advantage of the Act. But I am not persuaded by the Crown's argument and I am satisfied upon a review of all the authorities that in English law such a discretion does exist. It was exercised for the first time in relation to this section in *R v Watson*, 8 Cr App R 249. Discretion as such has the general blessing of Lord Moulton in *R v Christie* [1914] AC 545 and thereafter it has been the uniform practice of judges to exercise it in this class of case. Discretion was recognised in this House in *Maxwell v Director of Public Prosecutions* [1935] AC 309; *Stirland* [1944] AC 315; *Harris v Director of Public Prosecutions* [1952] AC 694; and *Jones v Director of Public Prosecutions* [1962] AC 635. And in the Privy Council in *Noor Mohamed v The King* [1949] AC 182 and *Kuruma* [1955] AC 197. In face of this long established practice it is, in my opinion, now too late to say that the judge has no discretion. While I leave to others more versed than I am in English criminal law and practice to discuss the origin of this discretion, I would assume that it springs from the inherent power of the judge to control the trial before him and to see that justice is done in fairness to the accused . . .

I find it unnecessary to say much more on the principles upon which discretion should be exercised. The guiding star should be fairness to the accused. This idea is best expressed by Devlin J in *R v Cook* [1959] 2 QB 340. In following this star the fact that the imputation was a necessary part of the accused's defence is a consideration which will no doubt be taken into account by the trial judge. If, however, the accused or his counsel goes beyond developing his defence in order to blacken the character of a prosecution witness, this no doubt will be another factor to be taken into account. If it is suggested that the exercise of this discretion may be whimsical and depend on the individual idiosyncrasies of the judge, this is inevitable where it is a question of discretion; but I am satisfied that this is a lesser risk than attempting to shackle the judge's power within a straitjacket.

LORD PEARCE: My Lords, ever since the Criminal Evidence Act, 1898, came into force there has been difficulty and argument about the application of the words in section 1(f)(ii) 'the nature or conduct of the defence is such as to involve imputations on the character of the prosecutor or the witnesses for the prosecution.'

Two main views have been put forward. One view adopts the literal meaning of the words. The prosecutor is cross-examined to show that he has fabricated the charge for improper reasons. That involves imputations on his character. Therefore, it lets in the previous convictions of the accused. The practical justification for this view is the 'tit for tat' argument. If the accused is seeking to cast discredit on the prosecution, then the prosecution should be allowed to do likewise. If the accused is seeking to persuade the jury that the prosecutor behaved like a knave, then the jury should know the character of the man who makes these accusations, so that it may judge fairly between them instead of being in the dark as to one of them.

The other view would limit the literal meaning of the words. For it cannot, it is said, have been intended by Parliament to make a man liable to have his previous convictions revealed whenever the essence of his defence necessitates imputations on the character of the prosecutor. This revelation is always damaging and often fatal to a defence. The high-water mark of this argument is the ordinary case of rape. In this the vital issue (as a rule) is whether the woman consented. Consent (as a rule) involves imputations on her character. Therefore, in the ordinary case of rape, the accused cannot defend himself without letting in his previous convictions. The same argument extends in varying degrees to many cases.

The argument in favour of a construction more liberal to the accused is supported in two ways.

First, it is said that character is used in the sense in which it was used in *R* v *Rowton*, 10 Cox CC 25, where the full court ruled that evidence of good character must be limited solely to general reputation and not to a man's actual disposition; and no imputation on the prosecutor's general reputation is involved by allegations that he acted as a knave in matters relevant to the offence charged. So far as the meaning of 'character' is concerned, there is much force in this argument. It would accord with the word 'character' as used three times previously in the same subsection. See the judgment delivered by Lord Hewart CJ in *R* v *Dunkley* [1927] 1 KB 323, 329, where the argument was described as formidable but was rejected:

> Nevertheless, when one looks at the long line of cases beginning very shortly after the passing of the Criminal Evidence Act, 1898, it does not appear that that argument has ever been so much as formulated. It was formulated yesterday. One can only say that it is now much too late in the day even to consider that argument, because that argument could not now prevail without the revision, and indeed to a great extent the overthrow, of a very long series of decisions.

A similar view was expressed by Lord Denning in *Jones* v *Director of Public Prosecutions* [1962] AC 635, 671 (see also Lord Devlin, at p. 709), a case which dealt with a kindred problem under section 1(f)(i). Viscount Simon, however, in *Stirland* v *Director of Public Prosecutions* [1944] AC 315, 325, after discussing the two conceptions, that is reputation and real disposition, said 'I am disposed to think that in para (f) (where the word "character" occurs four times) both conceptions are combined.'

Late as it may be, it might be justifiable to consider whether 'character' means in the context solely general reputation, if a reassessment could lead to any clarification of the problem. But in my opinion it leads nowhere. For I cannot accept the proposition that to accuse a person of a particular knavery does not involve imputations on his general reputation. The words 'involve' and 'imputations' are wide. It would be playing with words to say that the allegation of really discreditable matters does not involve imputations on his general reputation, if only as showing how erroneous that reputation must be. The argument is, however, a valuable reminder that the Act is intending serious and not trivial imputations.

The second part of the argument in favour of a construction more liberal to the accused is concerned with the words 'the conduct or nature of the defence.' One should, it can be argued, read conduct or nature as something superimposed on the essence of the defence itself. In *O'Hara* v *HM Advocate* 1948 SC (J) 90, 98, the learned Lord Justice-Clerk (Lord Thomson), after a careful review of the English cases, construed 'conduct' as meaning the actual handling of the case by the accused or his advocate. He found difficulty with 'nature' but said: 'But the more general considerations which I have mentioned persuade me to the view that "nature" is to be read, not as meaning something which is inherent in the defence, but as referable to the mechanism of the defence; nature being the strategy of the defence and conduct the tactics.' This argument has obvious force, particularly in a case of rape, where the allegation of consent is in truth no more than a mere traverse of the essential ingredient which the Crown have to prove, namely, want of consent. But the argument does not, and I think cannot, fairly stop short of contending that all matters which are relevant to the crime, that is, of which rebutting evidence could be proved, are excluded from the words 'conduct or nature of the defence.'

To take the present case as an example, the evidence having established physical signs on the victim of the alleged offence, his admission that he had previously committed it with somebody else was relevant. So, too, was his admission that he had been paid £1 for it, since, when the conversation was relevant, it could not be right to bowdlerise it. And, therefore, it is said, the putting of the allegation in cross-examination and the evidence given by the accused was an essentially relevant part of the defence and therefore was not within the words 'the nature or conduct of the defence.' If Mr Jeremy Hutchison's forceful argument on the proper construction of the subsection is right, the story told by the accused did not let in the convictions.

So large a gloss upon the words is not easy to justify, even if one were convinced that it necessarily produced a fair and proper result which Parliament intended. But there are two sides to the matter. So liberal a shield for an accused is in many cases unfair to a prosecution. Provided it is all linked up to the defence put forward by an accused there would be no limit to the amount of mud which could be thrown against an unshielded prosecutor while the accused could still crouch behind his own shield.

(LORD HODSON delivered a concurring judgment. LORD WILBERFORCE agreed with LORD PEARCE.)

Appeal dismissed.

R v Bishop
[1975] QB 274
Court of Appeal

On a charge of burglary, the defendant sought to explain his presence in a room where his fingerprints were found by alleging that he had had a homosexual relationship with the occupier, who was a witness for the prosecution. The prosecution were allowed to cross-examine the defendant about his previous convictions for offences of dishonesty and he was convicted.

STEPHENSON LJ: . . . Mr Bate submitted that in these progressive (or permissive) days it was no longer an imputation on a man's character to say of him that he was a homosexual or that he practised homosexuality. Since 1967, when section 1 of the Sexual Offences Act 1967 became law, it was no longer an offence to commit a homosexual act with another man of full age in private. No reasonable person would now think the worse of a man who committed such acts; he might not wish to associate with him but he would not condemn him. We think that this argument goes too far and that the gap between what is declared by Parliament to be illegal and punishable and what the common man or woman still regards as immoral or wrong is not wide enough to support it. Most men would be anxious to keep from a jury in any case the knowledge that they practised such acts and many would be debarred from going to the police to charge another with any offence if they thought that he might defend himself by making such an allegation, whether baseless or not. If this is still true, we are not behind times in holding that Mr Price's character was clearly impugned by the allegation of homosexual conduct made against him by the defendant.

Then it is contended that even if the allegation reflects upon his character, it does not reflect upon his integrity, his honesty or his reliability so that he is thereby rendered less likely to be a truthful witness, or if in fact it has that effect it was not made with that intention.

Mr Bate says that the defendant's allegation against Mr Price was made not for the purpose of discrediting his testimony but for the purpose of explaining his presence in Mr Price's room.

We do not consider that this argument can succeed against the plain words of section 1(f)(ii) given their natural and ordinary meaning. If we give them that meaning, as we are now required to do by the House of Lords in *Selvey's* case (see for instance what Viscount Dilhorne said [1970] AC 304, 339), they cannot be restricted in the way suggested by the words of the judgment which we have just quoted. Though we agree that the general nature of the Act and the general principle underlying it are as there stated we do not accept the submission that an imputation of homosexual immorality against a witness may not reflect upon his reliability — generally or in the witness box; nor do we accept the submission that a defendant can attack the character of a witness without risk of the jury's learning that his own character is bad by disclaiming any intention to discredit the witness's testimony. Such a construction of the section would enable many guilty men to resort to variations of 'the Portsmouth defence' with success by unfairly keeping the jury in ignorance of their true character and would fly in the face of the decision in *Selvey's* case to strip the plain words of section 1(f)(ii) of the gloss put upon them in earlier cases.

. . . Once it is conceded, as Mr Bate rightly conceded, that an imputation on character covers charges of faults or vices, whether reputed or real, which are not criminal offences it is difficult to restrict the statutory exception of s. 1(f)(ii) in any such way as has been suggested on behalf of the defendant.

Appeal dismissed.

R v Britzmann and Hall
[1983] 1 WLR 350
Court of Appeal

A woman telephoned the police after she discovered that her writing bureau had been opened and damaged by one of two men who had entered her house, posing as water board employees. The police stopped and arrested Britzmann and Hall, who fitted the descriptions given by the woman, although at a subsequent identification parade she did not pick them out. Britzmann and Hall were charged with burglary. At their trial, police officers gave evidence of what Britzmann had said during interviews after his arrest, and when shouting to Hall while they were in their cells, from which guilt could be inferred. Britzmann's evidence was that those conversations had not taken place and that the officers must have been mistaken. The judge granted the prosecution leave to cross-examine Britzmann upon his previous convictions under section 1(f)(ii) of the Criminal Evidence Act 1898. Britzmann and Hall were convicted and appealed.

LAWTON LJ: . . . Mr Ingram, who appeared for Britzmann and who is an experienced advocate in criminal cases, appreciated that putting his client's case to these police officers in cross-examination, as he had to do, was like walking through a legal minefield, because of the provisions of section 1(f)(ii) of the Criminal Evidence Act 1898. It is clear from the way Britzmann gave his evidence that he too knew of the dangers, perhaps because his acquaintance with the criminal courts was longer than that of his counsel.

Any denial that the conversations had taken place at all necessarily meant by implication that the police officers had given false evidence which they had made up in order to get the appellants convicted. On the facts of this case there could be no question of mistake, misunderstanding or confusion. If Detective Inspector Whyte and Detective Constable Boal had made up this story, they had conspired together to commit perjury and had committed it. Detective Constable Self must have committed perjury when giving evidence about the alleged conversation on May 29, and Detective Constable Boal must have done the same about the cell conversation. The conversation on June 1 about which two officers gave evidence was long and of a kind which could have appeared in a television film script for a crime series.

A defence to a criminal charge which suggests that prosecution witnesses have deliberately made up false evidence in order to secure a conviction must involve imputations on the characters of those witnesses with the consequence that the trial judge may, in the exercise of his discretion, allow prosecuting counsel to cross-examine the defendant about offences of which he has been convicted. In our judgment this is what Parliament intended should happen in most cases. When allegations of the fabrication of evidence are made against prosecution witnesses, as they often are these days, juries are entitled to know about the characters of those making them.

The duty of the judge in such cases to exercise a discretion whether to allow prosecuting counsel to cross-examine a defendant about previous convictions puts defending counsel in a difficulty because some judges, so Mr Ingram told us and we accept from our own experience when we were at the Bar, will exercise their discretion in favour of the defendant if either he or his counsel avoids making specific allegations of misconduct. This practice has a long history and support for it can be found in *R v Clark* [1955] 2 QB 469 and *R v Jones (William)* (1923) 17 Cr App R 117. With such judges a suggestion that a witness is mistaken or has misunderstood usually attracts a favourable exercise of discretion.

Britzmann seems to have thought that Mr Recorder Titheridge might be such a judge, because he said in evidence that Detective Inspector Whyte had been mistaken in thinking that he had said what he was alleged to have done on June 1. Mr Ingram in cross-examination contented himself with suggesting to the officers that the alleged conversations had not taken place at all.

Mr Recorder Titheridge would have none of this delicate forensic language. When prosecuting counsel applied for leave to cross-examine Britzmann about his previous convictions he ruled that he could do so. He gave a reasoned ruling, the essence of which is contained in the following passage:

> In my judgment, the delicacy with which cross-examination was conducted on behalf of this defendant cannot hide the basic commonsense position, which is this; there is no room for error or mistake; it must be clear to the jury that the only real issue for their consideration, although, I repeat, it has never been so put to these police officers, that the only real issue for their consideration is whether the statements were made, or in the case of the conversation between the two defendants whether the conversation took place, or whether those officers have made them up: there is simply no other possibility.

Mr Ingram submitted that this ruling was wrong, because the defence amounted in reality to no more than a denial of the charge. In putting his case in that way he adopted what Viscount Dilhorne had said in *Selvey* v *DPP* [1970] AC 304, 339.

In our judgment the nature and conduct of the defence did involve imputations on the characters of the three officers, despite the delicacy of Britzmann's language and the forensic skill of Mr Ingram. The jury had to decide whether these officers had made up what they alleged had been said. If in any case that is the reality of the position and would be seen by a jury to be so, there is no room for drawing a distinction between a defence which is so conducted as to make specific allegations of fabrication and one in which the allegation arises by way of necessary and reasonable implication. Nor can any distinction be validly drawn between an allegation to commit perjury and one of conspiring to commit perjury; but when the allegation is one of perjury, discretion may have to be exercised in favour of the defendant more readily than with a conspiracy allegation, having regard to what was said by Viscount Dilhorne in *Selvey* v *DPP*.

This opinion is in accord with two decisions of this court, namely *R* v *Tanner* (1977) 66 Cr App R 56 and *R* v *McGee and Cassidy* (1980) 70 Cr App R 247. In *R* v *Tanner*, in a reserved judgment, Browne LJ said, at p. 64:

> In some cases the distinction may be a very narrow one, but that it exists in principle is clear. The decision whether a case is on one side of the line or the other must depend on the facts of each particular case. In our judgment, the nature and conduct of the defence in the present case did involve imputations on the character of the police officers. This was not a case of a denial of a single answer, nor was there any suggestion or possibility of mistake or misunderstanding. The appellant was denying not only his admission, but in the case of each interview a series of subsequent important answers attributed to him by the police. In spite of [defending counsel's] skilful handling of the cross-examination of the police officers, and of the defendant's evidence-in-chief, it necessarily followed, in the circumstances of this case, that the appellant was saying impliedly that the police officers had made up a substantial and vital part of their evidence and that [the two] had conspired together to do so. He also said expressly that one of the police officers said that if he admitted the offence he would get bail. The judge's interventions were, in our judgment, merely bringing into the open what was already necessarily implicit.

That passage applies aptly to this case.

In *R* v *Nelson (G)* (1978) 68 Cr App R 12, which was decided about 12 months after *R* v *Tanner*, this court came to a different conclusion. Two grounds for this decision were given, both purporting to be based on the second of the propositions set out in Viscount Dilhorne's speech in *Selvey* v *DPP* [1970] AC 304, 339. The first was that the attempt to demonstrate a detective constable's unreliability as to a disputed interview was not based on any matter independent of his evidence. That ground will not apply in this case to the interview of June 1, to which Detective Inspector Whyte and Detective Constable Boal spoke, since each gave evidence of what had happened. The second ground was that the appellant's case was that the cross-examination was only directed at supporting his denials of the contents of the disputed interview: it was not directed at casting imputations to establish a defence. Without the challenge he had no defence as he was alleged to have confessed. We prefer the decisions in *R* v *Tanner* and *R* v *McGee* to that in *R* v *Nelson (Gerrard)*. In our judgment the recorder's ruling was right.

In deciding as we have, we have not overlooked the potentiality of unfairness to defendants with previous convictions which a rigid application of section 1(f)(ii) of the Act of 1898 would cause and the difficulties in advising and deciding tactics which defending counsel have. No doubt it was appreciation of the potentiality of unfairness to defendants which led the House of Lords in *Selvey* v *DPP* [1970] AC 304 to reject the Crown's submission in that case that judges had no discretion to refuse leave to cross-examine about previous convictions.

We hope that it will be helpful for both judges and counsel if we set out some guidelines for the exercise of discretion in favour of defendants. First, it should be used if there is nothing more than a denial, however emphatic or offensively made, of an act or even a short series of acts amounting to one incident or in what was said to have been a short interview. Examples are provided by the kind of evidence given in pickpocket cases and where the defendant is alleged to have said: 'Who grassed on me this time?' The position would be different however if there were a denial of evidence of a long period of detailed observation extending over hours and just as in this case and in *R* v *Tanner*, 66 Cr App R 56 where there were denials of long conversations.

Secondly, cross-examination should only be allowed if the judge is sure that there is no possibility of mistake, misunderstanding or confusion and that the jury will inevitably have to decide whether the prosecution witnesses have fabricated evidence. Defendants sometimes make wild allegations when giving evidence. Allowance should be made for the strain of being in the witness box and the exaggerated use of language which sometimes results from such strain or lack of education or mental instability. Particular care should be used when a defendant is led into making allegations during cross-examination. The defendant who, during cross-examination, is driven to explaining away the evidence by saying it has been made up or planted on him usually convicts himself without having his previous convictions brought out. Finally, there is no need for the prosecution to rely upon section 1(f)(ii) if the evidence against a defendant is overwhelming.

Appeals dismissed.

Note
The Royal Commission on Criminal Procedure (Chairman: Viscount Runciman of Doxford, Cd 2263, 1993, para. 34) has recommended that the provisions of the Act be amended so that an accused person cannot avoid the consequences of s. 1(f)(ii) by not testifying. The Commission further recommend in para. 33 that s. 1(f)(ii) be amended so that where an accused person casts imputations on a prosecution witness as a necessary means of putting his defence, he should not lose the protection afforded by the Act.

Questions
1.   Would *Bishop* be decided in the same way today?
2.   If the purpose of cross-examination is to undermine credibility as a witness, why did the trial judge in *Selvey* v *DPP* allow the prosecution to cross-examine the accused about his previous convictions for sex offences but not about his previous convictions for offences of dishonesty? (Selvey had convictions for both types of offence.)
3.   Why did Lawton LJ in *Britzmann and Hall* state, 'there is no need for the prosecution to rely upon section 1(f)(ii) if the evidence against a defendant is overwhelming'? Does this not give tacit recognition to the fact that a jury will often treat cross-examination under s. 1(f)(ii) as relevant to guilt and not credit?
4.   Why should there be any difference between a denial of a brief incriminating statement and a denial of a long and detailed interrogation if, in both cases, the accused implies perjury by the police?

(iii)   Judicial discretion and s. 1 (f) (ii)

R v Watts
[1983] 3 All ER 101
Court of Appeal

The appellant, who was of low intelligence and had two previous convictions for sexual offences against children, was interviewed by the police after a young married woman was indecently assaulted near his home by a man whose description fitted the appellant. The appellant made plain admissions to the police both orally and in a statement and he was later charged with the indecent assault. At his trial he advanced an alibi defence and in effect claimed that the police had fabricated the admission evidence. The prosecution then sought, and was granted, leave pursuant to section 1(f)(ii) of the Criminal Evidence Act 1898 to cross-examine him as to his previous convictions. The jury found him guilty of the offence. The appellant appealed, contending that the judge had wrongly exercised his discretion by allowing the cross-examination as to previous convictions.

LORD LANE CJ: . . . There is no doubt that the law on this particular topic is in an unhappy state. There are numerous decisions of this court and of the House of Lords to the effect that the only relevance of the previous convictions of the defendant admitted by virtue of s. 1 of the Criminal Evidence Act 1898, is as to the credibility of the prisoner, and that the jury must not be asked to infer guilt from such convictions. This in many cases requires the jury to perform difficult feats of intellectual acrobatics. In the view of this court the present case is a good example.

We have been referred to a number of authorities, amongst them *R v France* [1979] Crim LR 48 and a further decision of this court, *R v Duncalf* [1979] 2 All ER 1116, [1979] 1 WLR 918. We have had the opportunity of seeing a transcript of the judgment in *R v France* and it is quite plain that the text is corrupt. There are a number of obvious misprints and mistakes. The transcript was not apparently approved by the judge who delivered the judgment, and we view *R v France* therefore with considerable suspicion.

In any event it seems to us that where the exercise of discretion is concerned, which is the problem here, each case is a case on its own and has to be considered on its own particular facts.

The jury in the present case was charged with deciding the guilt or innocence of a man against whom an allegation of indecent assault on a woman was made. They were told that he had previous convictions for indecent assaults of a more serious kind on young girls. They were warned that such evidence was not to be taken as making it more likely that he was guilty of the offence charged, which it seems it plainly did, but only as affecting his credibility, which it almost certainly did not.

The passage in which the judge directed the jury to that effect runs as follows:

And then his previous offences were put to him, members of the jury. And of course you will not use that knowledge in any way as being evidence against him of committing this offence. It is not. The fact that a person has committed an offence on a previous occasion does not make him any more or less likely to be guilty of committing an offence on a subsequent occasion. It is not evidence. It was only allowed to be brought to your knowledge because of the serious allegations of misconduct which are made by the defendant, albeit he is a man of low intelligence, against the police. You are entitled to know that a person has previous offences when such assertions are made, but not as evidence against him.

The direction was, of itself, sound in law but in the circumstances of this case it would have been extremely difficult, if not practically impossible, for the jury to have done what the judge was suggesting. The prejudice which the appellant must have suffered in the eyes of the jury when it was disclosed that he had previous convictions for offences against young children could hardly have been greater. The probative value of the convictions, on the sole issue on which they were admissible, was, at best, slight. The previous offences did not involve dishonesty. Nor were they so similar to the offence which the jury were trying that they could have been admitted as evidence of similar facts on the issue of identity. In short, their prejudicial effect far outweighed their probative value. We would not have allowed this particular man to have been cross-examined about these particular convictions in these particular circumstances. That is not, however, the end of the matter. This court will not simply substitute its own discretion for that of the judge. But in the present case it seems to us that the judge was not given an opportunity to exercise his discretion on a proper basis. In fairness to him neither counsel placed all the relevant considerations before him. It was all done in a hurry and in the presence of the jury. We cannot help feeling that if the matter had been argued before him in the absence of the jury and in the same care as that with which we have examined the case today, he would have exercised his discretion differently.

There is a passage in the opinion of their Lordships in *Maxwell* v *DPP* [1935] AC 309 at 321, [1934] All ER Rep 168 at 174 which seems to us to be appropriate. It is in the speech of Viscount Sankey LC. It relates, *inter alia,* to the exercise of the judge's discretion, and reads as follows: '. . . the question whether a man has been convicted . . . ought not to be admitted . . . if there is any risk of the jury being misled into thinking that it goes not to credibility but to the probability of his having committed the offence of which he is charged.' That exactly fits the present circumstances, and, for the reasons which we have endeavoured to indicate, this grave risk was overlooked by the judge.

Appeal allowed. Conviction quashed.

R v Powell
(1985) 82 Cr App R 167
Court of Appeal

The appellant owned premises consisting of a shop with residential accommodation above. He was charged with knowingly living wholly or in part on the earnings of prostitution contrary to section 30 of the Sexual Offences Act 1956. The Crown case was that police officers had kept watch on the premises and that they had seen the appellant take money from prostitutes who took their customers to the first floor of the premises; that prostitutes solicited passers-by in the presence of the appellant; and that the appellant was seen to warn them of the presence of police in the area. He was also seen to tell prostitutes where to stand for the purpose of soliciting; to separate prostitutes who were having an argument; and to give a prostitute the key to a side door leading to the first floor room. The defence was that

that evidence was a complete fabrication and the appellant put his own character in issue to show that he had no need to take money from prostitutes. At the conclusion of his evidence-in-chief the Crown applied to cross-examine him on his previous convictions since he had both put his own character in issue and attacked the police witnesses by alleging that they had lied on oath.

His previous convictions were for allowing his premises to be used for the purposes of prostitution. The judge ruled that although had the application been made solely on the ground of an attack on the police evidence, he would have refused it, yet since the appellant had gone further and put his own character in issue, then under section 1(f)(ii) of the Criminal Evidence Act 1898, in his discretion, the application would be allowed. The appellant was convicted and appealed on the ground that the judge had wrongly exercised his discretion in allowing the application.

LORD LANE CJ: . . . Much of the difficulty in the present case springs from two decisions of this Court, to each of which I was a party. They are *R v Watts* (1983) 77 Cr App R 126; [1983] 3 All ER 101 . . . and *R v John and Braithwaite* (unreported), decided on November 24, 1983. Both were *ex tempore* judgments. In neither case were the speeches of their Lordships in *Selvey v Director of Public Prosecutions* (1968) 52 Cr App R 443; [1970] AC 304 drawn to the attention of the Court, nor, regrettably, did the Court have them in mind when giving the judgment.

Giving the judgment of the Court in *Watts* (*supra*) I referred to the speech of Viscount Sankey LC, in *Maxwell v Director of Public Prosecutions* (1935) 24 Cr App R 152, 173; [1935] AC 309, 321. This is what he said:

> . . . in general no question as to whether a prisoner has been convicted or charged or acquitted should be asked or, if asked, allowed by the judge, who has a discretion under proviso (f), unless it helps to elucidate the particular issue which the jury is investigating, or goes to credibility, that is, tends to show that he is not to be believed on his oath; indeed the question whether a man had been convicted, charged or acquitted, even if it goes to credibility, ought not to be admitted, if there is any risk of the jury being misled into thinking that it goes not to credibility but to the probability of his having committed the offence with which he is charged.

In *Watts* (*supra*) the circumstances were somewhat special, and it may be that the decision would have been the same even if we had had the speeches of their Lordships in *Selvey v DPP* (*supra*).

The same cannot be said of *John Braithwaite* (*supra*). The facts in that case were these. The police saw two youths in Oxford Street jostle a woman and steal her purse. They chased and arrested the youths. The defence at trial was that the policemen had fabricated their evidence; they had not seen what they said. The judge gave leave to cross-examine the youths as to their convictions. Each of them had to admit a number of convictions for offences closely resembling that with which they were charged.

In allowing the appeal the judgment of the Court referred to the decision in *Watts* (*supra*) and to Viscount Sankey's observations in *Maxwell v DPP* (*supra*), and went on,

> It is necessary however to look to see precisely what their convictions were; for the reason that in fact, we are told, the precise nature of those previous convictions was put to them in cross-examination. . . . In the light of those records, it seems to us that a jury might think that these two young men had a specific disposition to snatch

bags from the person every bit as much as Mr Watts could be said to have a specific disposition to indecently assault females. In those circumstances, as in the case of *Watts* (*supra*), it would have been extremely difficult, if not practically impossible, for the jury to have done what the judge had suggested, namely use those convictions to judge the respective credibility of the appellants and the police officers, but not as evidence that they had committed the offence charged. However careful the direction, there was, to echo the words of Viscount Sankey LC, a very real risk of the jury being misled into thinking that they went not to credibility but to the probability of them having committed the offence with which they were charged.'

When one turns to consider *Selvey* v *Director of Public Prosecutions* (1968) 52 Cr App R 443; [1970] AC 304 decided by their Lordships 33 years after *Maxwell* v *Director of Public Prosecutions* (*supra*), the possible misapprehensions in *Watts* and *John Braithwaite* (*supra*) begin to emerge.

Selvey was indicted for buggery with a young man M. The prosecution at the trial before Stable J and a jury adduced evidence from M himself, police officers and a doctor who had examined M shortly after the alleged crime and said that M had been buggered within the previous six hours or so. The appellant in evidence stated that M had met him in the street and asked if he could see the appellant's room: when they got there M had asked for the loan of £1, and said that he was 'prepared to go on the bed', and that he had already been with a person for £1: that he, the appellant, was not interested and that M had then left.

The judge in the absence of the jury expressed the view that Selvey had alleged in effect that the incident was a blackmail operation which had involved an attack on M's character. Thereupon counsel for the prosecution applied for leave to put to Selvey his previous convictions. Leave was granted.

When the jury returned to court the judge told them that since it had been suggested that M should not be believed as he was a man of bad character, they were entitled to hear Selvey's record. The judge told them that they would not decide the case 'purely on matters of character'; that they would deal with the case upon the evidence they had heard; but at least they would not 'go into the jury room having heard what was put to M without knowing anything about the previous record of the man by whom those charges are now brought'.

Counsel for the Crown then put to Selvey that he had been in 1956 convicted of indecent assaults on two boys aged eight and six; in 1960 of two similar offences against other young boys; that he had been sentenced to two years' imprisonment in 1961 for persistently soliciting for an immoral purpose and in 1964 to six months' imprisonment on a similar offence. Thus the judge was permitting evidence to go before the jury which was at least as prejudicial to the defendant as that which was admitted in *Watts* (*supra*) and in *John and Braithwaite* (*supra*).

Their Lordships in *Selvey* v *DPP* (*supra*) examined the authorities on this difficult aspect of the law, including *Maxwell* v *Director of Public Prosecutions* (*supra*) but nowhere expressed disapproval of the course which Stable J had taken at the trial.

The results of their Lordships' opinions in *Selvey* v *DPP* (*supra*) in so far as they are relevant to the instant case were analysed by another division of the Court in *R* v *Burke* decided on June 21, 1985. We respectfully agree with the judgment in that case delivered by Ackner LJ and cannot improve upon his analysis, which was as follows:

> 1   The trial judge must weigh the prejudicial effect of the questions against the damage done by the attack on the prosecution's witnesses, and must generally exercise his discretion so as to secure a trial that is fair both to the prosecution and

the defence (thus approving the observations of Devlin J, as he then was, when giving the judgment of the full Court (five judges) of the Court of Criminal Appeal in *R v Cook* (1959) 43 Cr App R 138, 143; [1959] 2 QB 340, 345.

2   Cases must occur in which it would be unjust to admit evidence of a character gravely prejudicial to the accused, even though there may be some tenuous grounds for holding it technically admissible (thus approving the observation made by Lord du Parcq, giving the opinion of the Privy Council in *Noor Mohamed v R* [1949] AC 182, at 192). Thus, although the position is established in law, still the putting of the questions as to character of the accused person may be fraught with results which immeasurably outweigh the results of questions put by the defence and which make a fair trial of the accused almost impossible (thus approving the observations of Singleton J in *R v Jenkins* (1945) 31 Cr App R 1, 15).

3   In the ordinary and normal case the trial judge may feel that if the credit of the prosecutor or his witnesses has been attacked, it is only fair that the jury should have before them material on which they can form their judgment whether the accused person is any more worthy to be believed than those he has attacked. It is obviously unfair that the jury should be left in the dark about an accused person's character if the conduct of his defence has attacked the character of the prosecutor or the witnesses for the prosecution within the meaning of the section (thus approving the observations of Singleton J in *Jenkins* (*supra*) again at p. 15).

4   In order to see if the conviction should be quashed, it is not enough that the Court thinks it would have exercised its discretion differently. The Court will not interfere with the exercise of a discretion by a judge below unless he has erred in principle, or there is no material on which he could properly have arrived at his decision (see Lord Dilhorne at p. 469, quoting Pickford J in *R v Watson* (1913) 8 Cr App R 249, at p. 254 and Devlin J in *Cook* (*supra*) at p. 147).

It may be helpful to make particular reference to a passage in the judgment of Devlin J in *R v Cook* at p. 146 and pp. 347, 348 respectively as follows:

The cases on this subject-matter . . . indicate the factors to be borne in mind and the sort of question that a judge should ask himself. Is a deliberate attack being made upon the conduct of the police officer calculated to discredit him wholly as a witness? If there is, a judge might well feel that he must withdraw the protection which he would desire to extend as far as possible to an accused who was endeavouring only to develop a line of defence. If there is a real issue about the conduct of an important witness which the jury will inevitably have to settle in order to arrive at their verdict, . . . the jury is entitled to know the credit of the man on whose word the witness's character is being impugned.

In the light of all these considerations, it is clear that in *John and Braithwaite* (*supra*), and possibly to a lesser extent in *Watts* (*supra*), the Court fell into error. First of all, we interfered too lightly with the exercise of the judge's discretion, thereby overlooking the observations of Viscount Dilhorne already mentioned. Secondly, we overlooked the 'tit for tat' principle as enunciated by Devlin J in *Cook* (*supra*) and by Lord Pearce in *Selvey v DPP* at p. 485 and p. 353 of the respective reports, at the same time paying too much attention, at least in *Watts* (*supra*), to the question whether the previous offences did or did not involve dishonesty in the ordinary sense of that word. We further suggested that care should be taken to conceal from the jury that the previous convictions of the prisoner were of a similar nature to the offence being charged. We have said enough about the speeches of their Lordships in *Selvey v DPP* and the facts of that case to show that those views were wrong.

Moreover, the words used by Viscount Sankey, in *Maxwell v Director of Public Prosecutions (supra)*, which were largely the foundation of the judgment in *Watts (supra)*, cannot in the light of *Selvey's* case *(supra)* be interpreted as meaning that convictions for the same or kindred offences can never be admitted. A defendant with previous convictions for similar offences may indeed have a very great incentive to make false allegations against prosecution witnesses for fear of greater punishment on conviction. It does however require careful direction from the judge to the effect that the previous convictions should not be taken as indications that the accused has committed the offence.

In short, if there is a deliberate attack being made upon the conduct of a prosecution witness calculated to discredit him wholly; if there is a real issue about the conduct of an important witness which the jury will have to settle in order to reach their verdict, the judge is entitled to let the jury know the previous convictions of the man who is making the attack. The fact that the defendant's convictions are not for offences of dishonesty, the fact that they are for offences bearing a close resemblance to the offences charged, are matters for the judge to take into consideration when exercising his discretion, but they certainly do not oblige the judge to disallow the proposed cross-examination.

Applying these principles to the present appeal, we have no doubt that the learned judge rightly exercised his discretion in permitting cross-examination.

Appeal dismissed.

R v Owen
(1986) 83 Cr App R 100
Court of Appeal

The appellant was charged, *inter alia,* with theft of a purse. Police officers who arrested him said they had seen him reach inside his jacket and drop the purse. When interviewed, the appellant said the officers had lied; they had not seen him drop the purse. Evidence of that interview was given at his trial and was not challenged. The prosecution then applied for leave to cross-examine the appellant about his previous convictions, pursuant to s. 1(f)(ii) of the Criminal Evidence Act 1898 and that was granted to the extent that he could be asked if he had been found guilty of or had pleaded guilty to offences of dishonesty on previous occasions, without revealing that those offences were similar to the one charged. The appellant was convicted and appealed against conviction *inter alia,* on the ground that the judge had wrongly exercised his discretion in allowing him to be cross-examined about his previous convictions.

NEILL LJ: . . . In order to consider this aspect of the case it is necessary to bear the following points in mind:

(1) When an application is made on behalf of the Crown for leave to cross-examine the accused as to his previous convictions on the basis that the nature or conduct of the defence has been such as to involve imputations on the character of the prosecutor, or the witnesses for the prosecution, the judge at trial has two tasks to perform:

    (a) first he must form a judgment as to 'the nature or conduct of the defence' in order to decide whether the condition set out in paragraph (ii) of section 1(f) of the 1898 Act has been satisfied; and

(b)   if he is so satisfied, he must decide whether in the exercise of his discretion he should allow the cross-examination to take place.

(2)   In forming a judgment as to the nature and conduct of the defence the judge will have to consider the facts of the individual case. Where explicit allegations of the fabrication of evidence have been made against prosecution witnesses, his task will be easy. But it is clear that in many cases imputations on the character of the witnesses for the prosecution may be made even though no explicit allegation of fabrication is made and even though counsel for the accused has conducted his cross-examination with delicacy and restraint. A challenge to the evidence of a witness, where there can be no question of mistake or misunderstanding or confusion, may well bear the necessary implication that the evidence has been fabricated. If the reality of the position is that the jury will have to decide whether the evidence of the witness whose testimony has been challenged, has been made up, then, in the words of Lawton LJ in *R v Britzmann* (1983) 76 Cr App R 134, 138; [1983] 1 WLR 350, 354 'there is no room for drawing a distinction between a defence which is so conducted as to make specific allegations of fabrication and one in which the allegation arises by way of necessary and reasonable implication.' See also *R v Tanner* (1977) 66 Cr App R 56, 64.

(3)   Where the condition set out in paragraph (ii) of section 1(f) of the 1898 Act has been satisfied, the trial judge must weigh the prejudicial effect of the questions to be directed to the accused against the damage done by the attack on the prosecution's witness, and must generally exercise his discretion so as to secure a trial that is fair to the prosecution and the defence: see *R v Burke* [1985] Crim LR 660 and *R v Powell* (1985) 82 Cr App R 167; [1985] 1 WLR 1364 where the guidance to this effect given by the Court of Criminal Appeal in *Cook* (1959) 43 Cr App R 138,143; (1959) 2 QB 340, 348, was approved.

(4)   Cases must occur in which, although the grounds for putting questions to the accused about his previous convictions have been established, the effect of allowing such questions might be fraught with results which would unreasonably outweigh the result of the questions put by the defence and might make a fair trial of the accused almost impossible: see *Burke (supra)* and *Powell (supra)*, approving the observations of Singleton J in *Jenkins* (1945) 31 Cr App R 1, 15.

(5)   In the normal and ordinary case, however, the trial judge may feel that if the credit of the prosecutor or his witnesses has been attacked, it is only fair that the jury should have before them material on which they can form their judgment whether the accused person is any more worthy to be believed than those he has attacked: see *Burke (supra)* and *Powell (supra)*. If imputations on the character of a prosecution witness have been made and if there is a real issue about the conduct of that witness which the jury will inevitably have to settle in order to arrive at their verdict, then, in the words of Devlin J delivering the judgment of the full Court in *R v Cook (supra)* at p. 143 and p. 348 of the respective reports, '. . . the jury is entitled to know the credit of the man on whose word the witness's character is being impugned.' Devlin J was considering the case of a police officer whose evidence had been attacked, but it seems clear that the same principle is to be applied in the case of any important witness against whom such an imputation has been made and about whose conduct the jury will have to reach a conclusion.

(6)   The fact that the accused's convictions are not for offences of dishonesty, but may be for offences bearing a close resemblance to the offences charged, are matters for the judge to take into consideration when exercising his discretion, but they certainly do not oblige the judge to disallow the proposed cross-examination: see *Powell (supra)*.

(7)   An appellate court will not interfere with the exercise by the trial judge of his discretion unless he has erred in principle or there was no material on which he could properly arrive at his decision: see *Selvey* v *DPP* (1968) 52 Cr App R 443, 468; [1970] AC 304, 342 and *Powell* (*supra*). The Court will not quash a conviction merely because it would have exercised the discretion differently.

It seems to us that the judge was fully entitled to conclude that there could be no question of honest mistake and that despite the restraint which counsel exercised, there was a necessary implication in the questions which were addressed to the police officers that they had made their evidence up.

Counsel further submitted that even if imputations had been made against prosecution witnesses, the judge was wrong to exercise his discretion in the way that he did, because counsel had done his best to avoid making any imputation. We are unable to accept this submission. The effect and purport of the cross-examination must be judged objectively. We consider that there was ample material on which the judge could decide to allow cross-examination of the appellant on his previous convictions and it is to be noted that the judge restricted the cross-examination so that the prejudicial effect of the details of the previous offences should not be made known to the jury. We can see no basis for interfering with the exercise by the judge of his discretion.

Note
In *R* v *Khan* [1991] Crim LR 51, the Court of Appeal confirmed that cross-examination under s. 1(f)(ii) is relevant only to credibility and not to guilt. In most cases, therefore, counsel may only cross-examine as to the *fact* of previous convictions and must not further cross-examine about the circumstances of the previous convictions where this is not relevant to the credit of his testimony.

Question
In light of the recent cases on s. 1(f)(ii), does the jury still have to perform the 'intellectual acrobatics' referred to by Lord Lane in *Watts*?

(iv)   Section 1(f)(iii)

Murdoch v Taylor
[1965] AC 574
House of Lords

Murdoch, who had a criminal record, was jointly tried with Lynch, who was previously of good character. Each was charged with receiving stolen cameras. Lynch gave evidence implicating Murdoch and Murdoch gave evidence alleging that Lynch alone was in control and possession of a box containing the stolen cameras. The judge held that Lynch's counsel was entitled to take advantage of section 1(f)(iii) and cross-examine as to his previous convictions. Murdoch was convicted and appealed.

LORD REID: My Lords, two questions of law are before your Lordships in this case. On the question of the discretion of the court I entirely agree with the view expressed by my noble and learned friend, Lord Donovan. But on the other question I find great difficulty in agreeing with what I understand to be the unanimous view of your Lordships. The words which we have to construe are those of section 1(f)(iii) of the Criminal Evidence Act, 1898 — 'he has given evidence against any other person charged [in the same proceedings].' In proviso (e) of the same section there is reference to any question which 'would tend to criminate,' and I have difficulty in believing that the word 'against' in proviso (f)(iii) could have been used if the intention had been that this proviso should apply to all evidence which would tend to criminate the co-accused. If that had been the intention the obvious course would have been to say 'tending to criminate' instead of 'against.' And there are other reasons which tend to strengthen my doubts. If this provision has this wide meaning, an accused person with previous convictions, whose story contradicts in any material respect the story of a co-accused who has not yet been convicted, will find it almost impossible to defend himself, and. if he elects not to give evidence his plight will be just as bad. But I have been unable to find any satisfactory solution for the problem set by this proviso and therefore I shall not dissent.

LORD MORRIS OF BORTH-Y-GEST: If an accused person becomes a witness his sworn testimony, if admissible, becomes a part of the evidence in the case. What he says in cross-examination is just as much a part of that evidence as is what he says in examination-in-chief. The word 'against' is one that is well understood. It is a clear and robust word. It has more decisiveness than is possessed by such phrases as 'tending to show' or 'such as to involve.' It is a word that needs neither explanation nor translation. It calls for no synonym.

The Act does not call for any investigation as to the motives or wishes which may have prompted the giving of evidence against another person charged [in the same proceedings]. It is the nature of the evidence that must be considered. Its character does not change according as to whether it is the product of pained reluctance or of malevolent eagerness. If, while ignoring anything trivial or casual, the positive evidence given by the witness would rationally have to be included in any survey or summary of the evidence in the case which, if accepted, would warrant the conviction of the other person charged [in the same proceedings], then the witness would have given evidence against such other person. Such other person would then have that additional testimony against him. From his point of view that testimony would be just as damaging whether given with regret or whether given with relish. Such other person might then wish, in order to defend himself, to show that credence ought not to be attached to the evidence which had been given against him. In such circumstances the Act removes one barrier which would otherwise be in his way.

It may be noted that if A and B are jointly charged with the same offence and if A chooses to give evidence which is purely in defence of himself and is not evidence against B he may be asked questions in cross-examination by B notwithstanding that such questions would tend to criminate him (A) as to the offence charged. In similar circumstances B would be likewise placed. But questions of the kind denoted by section 1(f) could not be put. No doubt during any such cross-examination a judge would be alert to protect a witness from being cajoled into saying more than it was ever his plan or wish or intention to say.

LORD PEARCE (dissenting on the question of discretion): It is common ground that, until the case of *R v Ellis* [1961] 1 WLR 1064 decided briefly to the contrary, the practice and the general view of Bench and Bar alike was that a judge had a discretion whether to give leave to cross-examine under section 1(f)(iii). Moreover, it has long been established practice and law that the right to cross-examine under section 1(f)(ii) is subject to the judge's discretion (see the cases of *R v Jenkins* [1945] 114 LJ KB 425 and *R v Cook* [1959] 2 KB 340). Therefore, the right under section 1(f)(iii) would also seem, *prima facie* at least, to be subject to the judge's discretion. For there is nothing in the words of the Act which justifies any discrimination between the two subsections on the point in issue.

Admittedly the situation arising under section 1(f)(ii) differs from that arising under section 1(f)(iii). Under the former, an exercise of discretion could only deprive the prosecution of a right which they would otherwise have had; and the courts have always been ready to do that when fairness seemed to demand it. Under section 1(f)(iii), however, the judge, in using a discretion to refuse the introduction of a defendant's bad record, could only do so at the expense of a co-defendant. And how, it is argued, can he properly do this?

It is certainly not an easy problem. But the difficult burden of holding the scales fairly, not only as between the prosecution and defendants, but also as between the defendants themselves, and of doing his best thereby to secure a fair trial for all concerned, falls inevitably on the trial judge and is generally achieved in practice with considerable success. The use of a judicial discretion under section 1(f)(iii) as between co-defendants would be but an addition to the judge's existing burden.

The exercise of such a discretion would be within fairly narrow limits and the *prima facie* right could only be withheld for good judicial reasons. Two obvious examples occur to one of situations in which the judge ought to use a discretion to refuse a defendant's request to introduce a co-defendant's bad character. The first is where that defendant's counsel has deliberately led a co-defendant into the trap, or has, for the purpose of bringing in his bad record, put questions to him in cross-examination which will compel him, for the sake of his own innocence, to give answers that will clash with the story of the other defendant, or compel him to bring to the forefront implications which would otherwise have been unnoticed or immaterial. The second type of situation is where the clash between the two stories is both inevitable and trivial, and yet the damage by the introduction of a bad record (perhaps many years previous) will in the circumstances be unfairly prejudicial. Any attempt to deal with such a situation by means of the maxim *de minimis* is really to import some sort of discretion in disguise. For if a defendant is entitled to an absolute right, he can claim it on any technical ground that exists, whether it be large or small, fair or unfair: and however unfair or technical the ground may be, the right will be equally valuable to a defendant who can make his escape over the (perhaps innocent) body of a co-defendant.

In such a difficult matter which may not infrequently arise in borderline cases, the judge, who sees the general run of the case as it unfolds before him, can produce a fairer result by the exercise of a judicial discretion than by the strict and fettered application of an arbitrary rule of law. . . .

In my view, there should not be denied to the judges the discretion which in practice they exercised for so many years before the decision in the case of *Ellis* took it out of their capable hands.

LORD DONOVAN: It is now contended on behalf of Murdoch, first, that he had given no evidence against Lynch within the meaning of proviso (f)(iii). That expression in its context connotes, it is said, only evidence given in examination-in-chief and not evidence given in cross-examination. Alternatively, it refers only to evidence given with a hostile intent against a co-accused so that the test to be applied is subjective and not objective. In the further alternative, it is argued that, whatever be the true meaning of the expression, a trial judge has in all cases a discretion whether or not to allow questions to be put pursuant to proviso (f)(iii) just as he has in relation to proviso (f)(ii) of the section.

Prior to the Act of 1898 coming into force an accused person could not (speaking generally) give evidence in his own defence. The Act begins by enacting by section 1 that: 'Every person charged with an offence . . . shall be a competent witness for the defence at every stage of the proceedings. . . .' Then follow a number of provisos . . . An accused person was . . . given a new right of defending himself, if he wished, by his own sworn testimony. There is thus some initial impetus, at least, towards the view that when the legislature contemplated that he might give evidence against a co-accused, it was thinking of evidence produce directly by the testimony which the accused chose to give and not testimony which he might have preferred not to give but which was extracted from him under the pressure of cross-examination. Be that as it may, the words of the proviso are, in my opinion, too clear to admit of any such distinction. The object of proviso (f)(iii) is clearly to confer a benefit upon a co-accused. If evidence is given against him by another accused he may show, if he can, by reference to the latter's previous offences that his testimony is not worthy of belief. It is the effect of the evidence upon the jury which is material and which may be lessened or dissipated by invoking the proviso. The effect upon the jury is the same whether the evidence be given in examination-in-chief or in cross-examination; and the desirability of the co-accused being able to meet it by cross-examination as to credit is of the same importance, however the evidence is given. I feel no difficulty in holding that the first of the appellant's contentions must be rejected.

The like considerations also lead me to reject the argument that proviso (f)(iii) refers only to evidence given by one accused against the other with hostile intent. Again, it is the effect of the evidence upon the minds of the jury which matters, not the state of mind of the person who gives it. Were that the test, there would have to be something of the nature of a trial within a trial in order to determine the state of mind of the accused who gave the evidence, as was pointed out by the Court of Criminal Appeal in the case of R v Stannard [1965] 2 QB 1. The language of the Act gives no support for the view that this was the intention. In my opinion, the test to be applied in order to determine whether one accused has given evidence against his co-accused is objective and not subjective.

What kind of evidence is contemplated by proviso (f)(iii), that is, what is 'evidence against' a co-accused is perhaps the most difficult part of the case. At one end of the scale is evidence which does no more than contradict something which a co-accused has said without further advancing the prosecution's case in any significant degree. I agree with the view expressed by Winn J in giving judgment in Stannard that this is not the kind of evidence contemplated by proviso (f)(iii). At the other end of the scale is evidence which, if the jury believes it, would establish the co-accused's guilt, for example, in a case of theft: 'I saw him steal the purse' or in a case of assault, 'I saw him strike the blow.' It is this kind of evidence which alone, so the appellant contends, will satisfy the words 'has given evidence against.' Again, I regret I cannot share that view. There may well be evidence which regarded in isolation would be quite innocuous from the co-accused's point of view and, so regarded, could not be regarded as evidence 'against' him. For example, what would be proved if one co-accused said of his co-accused: 'He told me he knew of an easy job and persuaded me to help him'? If such evidence is kept unrelated to anything else it proves nothing criminal. But juries hear the whole of the evidence and they will consider particular parts of it, not in isolation but in conjunction with all the other evidence, and part of that other evidence may establish that 'job' meant a housebreaking job. Then the item of evidence I have taken as an example obviously becomes evidence 'against' the accused. If, therefore, the effect of the evidence upon the minds of the jury is to be taken as the test, it cannot be right to regard it in isolation in order to decide whether it is evidence against the co-accused. If Parliament had meant by proviso (f)(iii) to refer to evidence which was by itself conclusive against the co-accused it would have been easy to say so.

The test prescribed by the Court of Criminal Appeal in *Stannard* was whether the evidence in question tended to support the prosecution's case in a material respect or to undermine the defence. I have no substantial quarrel with this definition. I would, however, observe that some danger may lurk in the use of the expression 'tended to.' There will probably be occasions when it could be said that evidence given by one accused 'tended to' support the prosecution's case simply because it differed from the evidence of his co-accused; and the addition of the words 'in a material respect' might not wholly remove the danger. The difficulty is not really one of conception but of expression. I myself would omit the words 'tended to' and simply say that 'evidence against' means evidence which supports the prosecution's case in a material respect or which undermines the defence of the co-accused.

The evidence in the present case was clearly against Lynch in that sense. It was evidence which, if the jury accepted it, put Lynch in sole control and possession of property which according to the rest of the evidence had been stolen the day before, and which Lynch had tried to sell for a price which was a fraction of its real value. Murdoch's evidence thus supported the case of the prosecution in a material respect and none the less so because Coles had already given evidence to a somewhat similar effect.

On the question of discretion, I agree with the Court of Criminal Appeal that a trial judge has no discretion whether to allow an accused person to be cross-examined as to his past criminal offences once he has given evidence against his co-accused. Proviso (f)(iii) in terms confers no such discretion and, in my opinion, none can be implied. It is true that in relation to proviso (f)(ii) such a discretion does exist; that is to say, in the cases where the accused has attempted to establish his own good character or where the nature and conduct of the defence is such as to involve imputations on the character of the prosecutor or of a witness for the prosecution.

But in these cases it will normally, if not invariably, be the prosecution which will want to bring out the accused's bad character — not some co-accused; and in such cases it seems to me quite proper that the court should retain some control of the matter. For its duty is to secure a fair trial and the prejudicial value of evidence establishing the accused's bad character may at times wholly outweigh the value of such evidence as tending to show that he was guilty of the crime alleged.

These considerations lead me to the view that if, in any given case (which I think would be rare), the prosecution sought to avail itself of the provisions of proviso (f)(iii) then here, again, the court should keep control of the matter in the like way. Otherwise, if two accused gave evidence one against the other, but neither wished to cross-examine as to character, the prosecution could step in as of right and reveal the criminal records of both, if both possessed them. I cannot think that Parliament in the Act of 1898 ever intended such an unfair procedure. So far as concerns the prosecution, therefore, the matter should be one for the exercise of the judge's discretion, as it is in the case of proviso (f)(ii). But when it is the co-accused who seeks to exercise the right conferred by proviso (f)(iii) different considerations come into play. He seeks to defend himself; to say to the jury that the man who is giving evidence against him is unworthy of belief; and to support that assertion by proof of bad character. The right to do this cannot, in my opinion, be fettered in any way.

Finally, it is said that the decision in *Stannard* [1965] 2 QB 1, if upheld, will make it impossible for a person to defend himself at all effectively if he has a criminal record and is charged jointly with some other person. If he knows that the other person is guilty, and if in the witness box he speaks the truth, then he is liable to have his criminal past disclosed with fatal results.

This would, indeed, be a melancholy result, but I do not think the prospect is so gloomy. To test the matter, let me assume the case of two accused each charged with the same offence — No. 1 in fact being guilty but having no criminal record, No. 2 being in fact innocent but having such a record. No. 1 has nothing to lose by going into the witness box and accusing No. 2 of the crime; No. 2 quite truthfully in his evidence accuses No. 1, whereupon the past criminal record of No. 2 is disclosed to the jury by or on behalf of No. 1. It is said that No. 2 would have practically no hope of avoiding a conviction — hence the argument for an overriding discretion in the judge, although this would not necessarily cure the situation.

But in the case supposed, what would be the position in practice? In the first place, if No. 2 were in fact innocent, it would be in the highest degree unlikely that he would be found relying simply on his own denial. There would almost invariably be some evidence to support his defence. In the second place, his counsel or the judge or both would explain to the jury just how it was that accused No. 1 was able to force the revelation of No. 2's record. The judge would probably go on to exhort the jury not to let that revelation sway their minds and to consider the case against No. 2 primarily on the basis of the other evidence. The assistant recorder in the present case indeed went further and told the jury to ignore Murdoch's past altogether. It would be a very unusual jury which, in these circumstances, did not require cogent proof of guilt before convicting. Indeed, the effect of the disclosure of No. 2's past might have the result of causing the jury to give consideration to the case surpassing in carefulness even their usual high standard.

(LORD EVERSHED agreed with LORD DONOVAN.)

Appeal dismissed.

R v Hatton
(1976) 64 Cr App R 88
Court of Appeal

The appellant and two co-defendants were charged with stealing scrap metal. The first defendant (Hildon) denied that there was a plan to steal the metal, while the other two agreed there was such a plan but denied dishonesty. The trial judge allowed counsel for the first defendant to cross-examine the appellant as to his previous convictions on the ground that the appellant had given evidence against the first defendant, a person charged with the same offence pursuant to section 1(f)(iii) of the Criminal Evidence Act 1898, in that the appellant's evidence undermined the first defendant's story. All three were convicted. The appellant appealed on the ground that evidence which undermined part of a co-defendant's defence was not necessarily evidence 'against' him.

STEPHENSON LJ: . . . It is well known that in *Murdoch v Taylor* (1965) 49 Cr App R 119, the House of Lords (1) adopted in substance the interpretation — or gloss — put upon the statutory language in *Stannard* (1962) 48 Cr App R 81; [1965] 2 QB 1 and held that 'evidence against' means evidence, not necessarily given with hostile intent, which supports the prosecution's case in a material respect or which undermines the defence of the co-accused; (2) decided (by a majority) that, once the judge has ruled that the witness has given evidence against his co-accused, he has no discretion whether or not to allow him to be cross-examined on his past criminal offences. In *R v Bruce* (1975) 61 Cr App R 123; [1975] 1 WLR 1252 (which was decided a few months before this trial) this Court found it necessary to explain that interpretation — or to put a gloss upon that gloss — in 'wholly exceptional circumstances' and to hold that evidence which undermined part of a co-accused's defence and damaged his credibility was wrongly considered to be evidence against him, because on balance it was given more in his favour than against him and did more to undermine the prosecution's case than the co-accused's defence.

Before the judge it was submitted, both by counsel for Hildon and by counsel for the Crown, that the question whether the evidence of Hatton had provided a further defence for Hildon was irrelevant; by counsel for Hildon, that the test was whether the defence in fact put forward by him would be undermined; by counsel for the Crown, whether Hildon's credit would be undermined. In this Court the argument took account of what was said in *Bruce* (*supra*) that evidence which damaged a co-accused's credibility by contradicting his evidence, or which provided a co-accused with a different and possibly a better defence, does not thereby make it evidence given against him but only if it makes his acquittal less likely.

In *Bruce* (*supra*) the prosecution's case was that Bruce and seven others, including McGuinness, set out together to rob a Pakistani; they found a Burmese gentleman and robbed him. They were all acquitted of robbing him but convicted of stealing money from him. None of the defendants supported the prosecution's case of an agreement to rob except McGuinness. He admitted that there was such a plan but denied taking any part in it. Bruce gave evidence that there was no such plan and denied taking any money from the victim: he did not give evidence that McGuinness had taken any money from the victim. Yet the judge ruled that Bruce had given evidence against McGuinness because he had contradicted McGuinness's evidence that there was a plan to rob and so undermined his credit.

Hatton's evidence about Hildon is very different from Bruce's evidence about McGuinness. Bruce, as his counsel told the judge, had not said anything which directly involved McGuinness in the robbery or theft. He had merely denied a part of the prosecution's case which McGuinness had admitted. He had not supported the prosecution's case in any material respect. Hatton, on the other hand, had supported a material part of the prosecution's case which Hildon had denied, namely that Hildon had set out for the site with Hatton and Ripley to collect scrap for Hildon's step-brother and he had contradicted Hildon's evidence that he had only joined them later on the site. That evidence of Hatton, if believed, brought Hildon into a plan to collect scrap, albeit honest; and although it provided Hildon with another defence, it not merely undermined his credit but on balance did more to undermine his defence than to undermine the prosecution's case. Indeed it supported the prosecution's case in a material respect, that there was a plan to take scrap from the site, and thereby rendered Hildon's conviction more likely and reduced his chances of acquittal.

There being no discretion to exclude prejudicial evidence of other offences committed by a defendant who gives evidence against a co-accused, it is important that the evidence should be clearly given against the co-accused, as it was not in *Bruce's* case (*supra*) but was in this. Respectfully adopting the language of Lord Morris of Borth-y-Gest, to which we were referred in *Murdoch v Taylor* (*supra*) at pp. 124, 125 and p. 584B of the respective reports, we think that (unlike the evidence of Bruce) the positive evidence of Hatton (and Ripley) associating Hildon with them in their mission to the site 'would rationally have to be included in any survey or summary of the evidence in the case, which, if accepted, would warrant the conviction of' Hildon. The words 'if accepted' clearly refer to the survey or summary, not to the positive evidence, and Lord Morris is not saying that 'the positive evidence' must be accepted *in toto* or that it must by itself warrant the conviction of the other person charged [in the same proceedings].

For these reasons we are of opinion that the judge was right to admit the cross-examination of Hatton as to his previous convictions.

Appeal dismissed.

R v Varley
[1982] 2 All ER 519
Court of Appeal

The appellant and Dibble were jointly charged with robbery. At their trial Dibble admitted that they had both participated in the robbery but stated that he had been forced to do so by threats on his life by the appellant. The appellant denied that he had taken any part in the robbery and asserted that Dibble's evidence was untrue. On the basis that the appellant's evidence was evidence 'against' Dibble for the purposes of section 1(f)(iii) of the Criminal Evidence Act 1898, Dibble's counsel applied for and was granted leave to cross-examine the appellant as to his previous convictions. Dibble and the appellant were both convicted. The appellant appealed, contending that his evidence was not evidence 'against' Dibble and that leave to cross-examine him about his previous convictions should not have been granted.

KILNER BROWN J: . . . The operation of this particular part of the proviso seems to have given rise to no difficulty and no detailed analysis for well over 60 years. No doubt, as Lord Pearce indicated in his speech in *Murdoch* v *Taylor* [1965] 1 All ER 406 at 411, [1965] AC 574 at 586, 'the practice and the general view of Bench and Bar alike was that a judge had a discretion whether to give leave to cross-examine under s. 1(f)(iii)' and, in difficult cases where it was not easy to determine whether the evidence could be categorised as 'against' or where such questioning could well be unduly prejudicial, a judge would decline to rule that the proposed questions could be put. But this discretionary power was removed from trial judges by the Court of Criminal Appeal in *R* v *Ellis, R* v *Ellis* [1961] 2 All ER 928, [1961] 1 WLR 1064, when it was decided that cross-examination of a co-defendant who had given evidence against a person jointly charged with him was a matter of right and not of discretion.

The decision was approved by four of the Lords of Appeal (Lord Pearce dissenting) in *Murdoch's* case [1965] 1 All ER 406, [1965] AC 574. This decision created difficult problems in practice because either to establish or to destroy this right involved, in many cases, an acute analysis of whether or not the evidence which had been given was 'against' the other party charged. It sparked off a whole series of cases which have come before this court and at least the one *(Murdoch's* case) in the House of Lords. The instant case is a very good example of the additional burden placed on the trial judge. The application and the resistance to it occupied many hours of judicial time and took up no less than 57 pages of recorded transcript.

Although the judgment of the Court of Criminal Appeal in *R* v *Stannard* [1964] 1 All ER 34, [1965] 2 QB 1 was undoubtedly meant to have been of assistance to trial judges in their consideration of whether evidence was 'against' or not, in practice, it has in fact added to their burden and it has caused considerable anxiety to other divisions of this court as it did to Lord Reid and was tacitly ignored by Lord Morris in *Murdoch's* case. What was the nature of the guidance in *R v Stannard* [1964] 1 All ER 34, [1965] 2 QB 1? It was this, approved as amended by Lord Donovan in *Murdoch's* case [1965] 1 All ER 406 at 416, [1965] AC 574 at 592: '. . . "evidence against" means evidence which supports the prosecution's case in a material respect or which undermines the defence of the co-accused.' There are three reported cases in the Court of Appeal, Criminal Division, in which this interpretation has been considered and to which we were referred. They are *R v Davis (Alan Douglas)* [1975] 1 All ER 233, [1975] 1 WLR 345, *R v Bruce* [1975] 3 All ER 277, [1975] 1 WLR 1252 and *R v Hatton* (1976) 64 Cr App R 88. Now, putting all the reported cases together, are there established principles which might serve as guidance to trial judges when called on to give rulings in this very difficult area of the law? We venture to think that they are these and, if they are borne in mind, it may not be necessary to investigate all the relevant authorities. (1) If it is established that a person jointly charged has given evidence against the co-defendant that defendant has a right to cross-examine the other as to previous convictions and the trial judge has no discretion to refuse an application. (2) Such evidence may be given either in chief or during cross-examination. (3) It has to be objectively decided whether the evidence either supports the prosecution case in a material respect or undermines the defence of the co-accused. A hostile intent is irrelevant. (4) If consideration has to be given to the undermining of the other's defence care must be taken to see that the evidence clearly undermines the defence. Inconvenience to or inconsistency with the other's defence is not of itself sufficient. (5) More denial of participation in a joint venture is not of itself sufficient to rank as evidence against the co-defendant. For the proviso to apply, such denial must lead to the conclusion that if the witness did not participate then it must have been the other who did. (6) Where the one defendant asserts or in due course would assert one view of the joint venture which is directly contradicted by the other such contradiction may be evidence against the co-defendant.

We apply these principles to the facts of this case and particularly the latter two. Here was Dibble going to say, as he did, that he took part in the joint venture because he was forced to do so by Varley. The appellant, Varley, was saying that he was not a participant and had not gone with Dibble and had not forced Dibble to go. His evidence therefore was against Dibble because it amounted to saying that not only was Dibble telling lies but that Dibble would be left as a participant on his own and not acting under duress. In our view, the judge was right to rule that cross-examination as to previous convictions was permissible.

Appeal dismissed.

Note

If a co-accused gives evidence which, if believed, would tend to lead to the acquittal of a fellow co-accused, then this does not fall within s. 1(f)(iii) because it is not evidence 'against' the latter. This is so even though the evidence given is inconsistent with the co-accused's defence (*R v Bruce* [1975] 3 All ER 277).

Questions
1. What is the rationale underlying s. 1(f)(iii)?
2. Dennis and Eric are jointly tried for robbery. Dennis has previous convictions for both theft and robbery. Eric has no previous convictions. Eric testifies that he took part in the robbery but this was only because Dennis had threatened to injure his wife seriously if he did not. Dennis is furious about

this and maintains his innocence. He assumes that Eric is trying to frame him because Eric recently discovered that he (Dennis) once slept with Eric's wife. Would you advise Dennis to testify in these circumstances?

3.   You are acting for Charles, a man of 40, who is charged with two counts of indecent assault committed in May and August 1993 respectively. In both cases, it is alleged that Charles laid in wait behind some bushes on a university campus, seized a girl as she was returning to her hall of residence, and assaulted her. Charles has previous convictions: (i) for several indecent assaults; (ii) for several offences of theft.

The prosecution rely on a written confession signed by Charles. On one occasion Charles told you that he had made and signed a written statement, although he disputed the accuracy of its contents. On another occasion, he told you the statement was a fabrication and that his signature had been forged by one of the police officers who interviewed him. You do not know what version he will give in evidence should he choose to testify.

What factors will you consider when conducting the defence?

4.   Barry and Harry are being jointly tried for the attempted burglary of a shop. Barry has two previous convictions for burglary when, on each occasion, he gained entry to a shop using skeleton keys. Harry has a conviction for perjury. The prosecution assert that on this occasion, both Harry and Barry were using a set of skeleton keys to try and gain entry to the shop. Harry testifies that he was unaware that Barry had any keys and says that he was merely sheltering from the rain. When asked if he saw Barry try to gain entry to the shop he states that he saw him fiddling with the lock on the shop door. The trial judge then allows the prosecution to reveal Harry's previous conviction.

Barry's counsel accuses the police of planting the keys on his client. He also calls the Reverend Green who testifies that Barry is a regular attender at church. The trial judge then allows the prosecution to reveal the existence and nature of Barry's previous convictions.

Barry does not give evidence and the trial judge draws the attention of the jury to this.

Barry and Harry are convicted of the offence and seek your advice as to any grounds of appeal they might have.

Further Reading
P. Murphy, *A Practical Approach to Evidence*, 4th ed. (1992), Ch. 4
M. Cohen, 'Challenging Police Evidence of Interviews and the Second Limb of Section 1(f)(ii) — Another View' [1981] Crim LR 523
D. W. Elliott, 'Cut Throat Tactics: The Freedom of an Accused to Prejudice a Co-accused' [1991] Crim LR 5
R. Munday, 'Reflections on the Criminal Evidence Act 1898' [1985] 44 CLJ 377
R. Munday, 'Irregular Disclosure of Evidence of Bad Character' [1990] Crim LR 92
S. Seabrooke, 'Closing the Credibility Gap: A New Approach to Section 1(f)(ii) of the Criminal Evidence Act 1898' [1987] Crim LR 231

12 EVIDENCE OF CHARACTER — II SIMILAR FACT EVIDENCE

This chapter will consider those cases in which evidence of the prior conduct of the accused is admissible because it is directly relevant to the issue of the accused's guilt. In other words, evidence of the accused's character is admissible because that evidence is, in itself, the relevant evidence. Such evidence is usually referred to as 'similar fact evidence' though, as we shall see, the presence of similar facts may be just one way of demonstrating the true ground of admissibility namely, that the probative force yielded by admitting the evidence outweighs the prejudice caused. Many of the early cases on so called 'similar fact evidence' provide useful illustrations of how the rule operates, although the law has received some modification in modern times.

(A) Criminal cases

Although the similar fact rule has some application in civil cases (see (B) below), its principal importance relates to criminal cases. Imagine that D was convicted of several burglaries in 1990, his method being to enter houses at night by using a screwdriver to force a rear window. D is sentenced to a term of imprisonment and released in January 1994. A number of burglaries are then committed in D's locality, the offender gaining entry to houses at night by means of forcing a rear window with a screwdriver. If D is charged with these offences, could the prosecution lead evidence of D's earlier conduct which resulted in his convictions for burglary, as evidence that he committed the burglaries with which he is now charged? The likely answer would be 'no'. This would be inadmissible evidence of character. Merely because D has been convicted of similar burglaries in the past does not, as a matter of logic, mean he is guilty of the present offences. Whilst D's previous conduct might heighten suspicion about his involvement in the present offences, there is nothing particularly compelling in the prior conduct which would enable a jury safely to infer D's guilt on the present offences. After all, there must be many burglars who gain entry to houses at night by forcing windows. Indeed, a jury hearing of D's previous convictions might be extremely prejudiced against him, adopting what Lord Hailsham described as the 'forbidden reasoning', i.e. once a burglar always a burglar. There are occasions, however, where D's prior conduct is so similar to the present conduct, that both logic and the interests of justice demand the jury hear of it. It is these occasions with which similar fact evidence is concerned. The best examples are provided by the cases themselves, and it is worth bearing in mind that the more recent cases emphasise that the true ground for admitting such evidence is not necessarily 'striking similarity' between the prior conduct and the present conduct, but merely that the probative force of the evidence outweighs the prejudice caused.

Makin v Attorney-General for New South Wales
[1894] AC 57
Privy Council

The defendants were charged with the murder of a baby, whose body was found in the back yard of a house occupied by them. The defendants had 'adopted' it from its mother in return for a sum of money, stating that they wished to bring it up because they had lost their own child. The facts were consistent with an allegation that the defendants had killed the child for the maintenance, but equally were consistent with death by natural causes followed by an irregular burial. There was, however, evidence that the bodies of other babies, similarly adopted by the defendants, were found buried in the yards of houses occupied by the defendants. This evidence was held to be admissible, and the defendants were convicted. They appealed to the Supreme Court of New South Wales and from there to the Privy Council.

LORD HERSCHELL LC: . . . In their Lordships' opinion the principles which just govern the decision of the case are clear, though the application of them is by no means free from difficulty. It is undoubtedly not competent for the prosecution to adduce evidence tending to show that the accused has been guilty of criminal acts other than those covered by the indictment, for the purpose of leading to the conclusion that the accused is a person likely from his criminal conduct or character to have committed the offence for which he is being tried. On the other hand, the mere fact that the evidence adduced tends to show the commission of other crimes does not render it inadmissible if it be relevant to an issue before the jury, and it may be so relevant if it bears upon the question whether the acts alleged to constitute the crime charged in the indictment were designed or accidental, or to rebut a defence which would otherwise be open to the accused. The statement of these general principles is easy, but it is obvious that it may often be very difficult to draw the line and to decide whether a particular piece of evidence is on the one side or the other. . .

The leading authority relied on by the Crown was the case of *R v Geering* (1849) 18 LJMC 215, where on the trial of a prisoner for the murder of her husband by administering arsenic evidence was tendered, with the view of showing that two sons of the prisoner who had formed part of the same family, and for whom as well as for her husband the prisoner had cooked their food, had died of poison, the symptoms in all these cases being the same. The evidence was admitted by Pollock CB, who tried the case; he held that it was admissible, inasmuch as its tendency was to prove that the death of the husband was occasioned by arsenic, and was relevant to the question whether such taking was accidental or not. The Chief Baron refused to reserve the point for the consideration of the judges, intimating that Alderson B, and Talfourd J, concurred with him in his opinion.

This authority has been followed in several subsequent cases. And in the case of *R v Dossett* 2 C & K 306, which was tried a few years previously, the same view was acted upon by Maule J, on a trial for arson, where it appeared that a rick of wheatstraw was set on fire by the prisoner having fired a gun near to it. Evidence was admitted to show that the rick had been on fire the previous day, and that the prisoner was then close to it with a gun in his hand. Maule J, said: 'Although the evidence offered may be proof of another felony, that circumstance does not render it inadmissible, if the evidence be otherwise receivable. In many cases it is an important question whether a thing was done accidentally or wilfully.'

Under these circumstances their Lordships cannot see that it was irrelevant to the issue to be tried by the jury that several other infants had been received from their mothers on like representations, and upon payment of a sum inadequate for the support of the child for more than a very limited period, or that the bodies of infants had been found buried in a similar manner in the gardens of several houses occupied by the prisoners.

Appeal dismissed.

R v Ball
[1911] AC 47
House of Lords

A brother and sister were charged with incest between named dates in 1910. There was incontrovertible evidence that they had occupied the same bed in the house in which they were living. The trial judge admitted evidence that they had lived together as husband and wife in 1907 when incest was not a criminal offence. They were convicted and appealed successfully to the Court of Criminal Appeal. The prosecution appealed to the House of Lords.

LORD LOREBURN: My Lords, the law on this subject is stated in the judgment of Lord Chancellor Herschell in *Makin v Attorney-General for New South Wales* [1894] AC 57 PC; it is well known and I need not repeat it — the question is only of applying it. In accordance with the law laid down in that case, and which is daily applied in the Divorce Court, I consider that this evidence was clearly admissible on the issue that this crime was committed — not to prove the *mens rea*, as Darling J considered, but to establish the guilty relations between the parties and the existence of a sexual passion between them as elements in proving that they had illicit connection in fact on or between the dates charged. Their passion for each other was as much evidence as was their presence together in bed of the fact that when there they had guilty relations with each other.

My Lords, I agree that Courts ought to be very careful to preserve the time-honoured law of England, that you cannot convict a man of one crime by proving that he had committed some other crime; that, and all other safeguards of our criminal law, will be jealously guarded; but here I think the evidence went directly to prove the actual crime for which these parties were indicted.

(EARL OF HALSBURY and LORDS ASHBOURNE, ALVERSTONE CJ, ATKINSON, GORELL, SHAW OF DUNFERMLINE, MERSEY and ROBSON all concurred.)

Appeal allowed.

Question
Is it possible to reconcile the decision in *Ball* with Lord Herschell's first proposition in *Makin* v *Attorney-General for NSW*?

R v Sims
[1946] KB 531
Court of Criminal Appeal

The defendant was charged with sodomy with three men and gross indecency with a fourth. All the offences were alleged to have taken place on different occasions. At the trial the defendant made an application that the charges be tried separately in respect of each separate man. The application was refused and the defendant was convicted subsequently of sodomy on each of the three charges, but acquitted on the indecency charge.

LORD GODDARD CJ: We start with the general principle that evidence is admissible if it is logically probative, that is, if it is logically relevant to the issue whether the prisoner has committed the act charged. To this principle there are exceptions. One of the most important exceptions is this: Evidence that the accused has a bad reputation or has a bad disposition is not admissible unless he himself opens the door to it by giving evidence of good character or otherwise under the Criminal Evidence Act 1898. The reason for excluding evidence of bad character was said by Willes J to be policy and humanity. He thought that evidence of bad character was just as relevant as evidence of good character, but the unfair prejudice created by it was so great that more injustice would be done by admitting it than by excluding it: see *R v Rowton* (1865) Le & Ca 520. Lord Sumner, however, thought it was irrelevant: see *Thompson v R* [1918] AC 221. We do not stay to consider which view is correct. The exception is well settled. The question is what are its limits. In our opinion it does not extend further than the interests of justice demand. Evidence is not to be excluded merely because it tends to show the accused to be of a bad disposition, but only if it shows nothing more. There are many cases where evidence of specific acts or circumstances connecting the accused with specific features of the crime has been held admissible, even though it also tends to show him to be of bad disposition. The most familiar example is when there is an issue whether the act of the accused was designed or accidental or done with guilty knowledge, in which case evidence is admissible of a series of similar acts by the accused on other occasions, because a series of acts with the self-same characteristics is unlikely to be produced by accident or inadvertence: see *Makin* v *Attorney-General for New South Wales* [1894] AC 57.

Another example is where there is an issue as to the nature of an act done by the accused with or to another person, in which case evidence is admissible of a series of similar acts between them, because human nature has a propensity to repetition and a series of acts is likely to bear the same characteristics: see *R* v *Ball* [1911] AC 47. So also where there is an issue as to the identity of the accused, we think that evidence is admissible of a series of similar acts done by him to other persons, because, while one witness to one act might be mistaken in identifying him, it is unlikely that a number of witnesses identifying the same person in relation to a series of acts with the self-same characteristics would all be mistaken. In all these cases the evidence of other acts may tend to show the accused to be of bad disposition, but it also shows something more. The other acts have specific features connecting him with the crime charged and are on that account admissible in evidence. A similar distinction exists in respect of articles found in possession of the accused. If they have no connection with the crime except to show that the accused has a bad disposition, the evidence is not admissible; but if there are any circumstances in the crime tending to show a specific connection between it and the articles, the evidence is admissible; see per Lord Sumner in *Thompson* v *R*. Thus, in the case of burglary, evidence is admissible that housebreaking implements such as might have been used in the crime were found in the possession of the accused. In the case of abortion, evidence is admissible that the apparatus of an abortionist such as might have been used in the crime was found in the possession of the accused. The admissibility does not, however, depend on the circumstance that the articles might have been used in the crime. If there is any other specific feature connecting the articles with the crime, it will suffice. Thus, in the case of *Thompson*, there was no suggestion that the photographs were used in the crime charged, but the House of Lords found a connection between the crime and the photographs in that the criminal on the 16 March showed a propensity to unnatural practices by making an appointment for the 19 March and the accused showed a like propensity by the photographs found in his possession. In the cases of *R* v *Twiss* [1918] 2 KB 853 and *R* v *Gillingham* (1939) 27 Cr App R 143 there was also no suggestion that the photographs were used in the crime charged, but the court found a connection between the two in that the crime itself showed a propensity to unnatural practices and the photographs showed a like propensity. The specific feature in such cases lies in the abnormal and perverted propensity which stamps the individual as clearly as if marked by a physical deformity. We think that in all the cases where evidence has been admitted there have been specific features connecting the evidence with the crime charged as distinct from evidence that he is of a bad disposition. This is illustrated by the cases on false pretences where evidence can be given of other transactions when similar false pretences were used, because they have that specific feature in common; but not of different transactions which only show that the accused was of a generally fraudulent disposition.

It has often been said that the admissibility of evidence of this kind depends on the nature of the defence raised by the accused: see, for instance, the observations of Lord Sumner in *Thompson* v *R*, and of this court in *R* v *Cole* (1941) 28 Cr App R 43. We think that that view is the result of a different approach to the subject. If one starts with the assumption that all evidence tending to show a disposition towards a particular crime must be excluded unless justified, then the justification of evidence of this kind is that it tends to rebut a defence otherwise open to the accused; but if one starts with the general proposition that all evidence that is logically probative is admissible unless excluded, then evidence of this kind does not have to seek a justification but is admissible irrespective of the issues raised by the defence, and this we think is the correct view. It is plainly the sensible view. It is only fair to the prosecution, because the depositions have often to be taken and the evidence called before the nature of the defence is known. It is also only fair to the accused, so that he should have notice beforehand of the case he has to meet. In any event, whenever there is a plea of not guilty, everything is in issue and the prosecution have to prove the whole of their case, including the identity of the accused, the nature of the act and the existence of any necessary knowledge or intent. The accused should not be able, by confining himself at the trial to one issue, to exclude evidence that would be admissible and fatal if he ran two defences; for that would make the astuteness of the accused or his advisers prevail over the interests of justice. An attempt was made by the defence in R v *Armstrong* [1922] 2 KB 555 to exclude evidence in that way, but it did not succeed.

Applying these principles, we are of opinion that on the trial of one of the counts in this case, the evidence on the others would be admissible. The evidence of each man was that the accused invited him into the house and there committed the acts charged. The acts they describe bear a striking similarity. That is a special feature sufficient in itself to justify the admissibility of the evidence; but we think it should be put on a broader basis. Sodomy is a crime in a special category because, as Lord Sumner said [1918] AC 235, 'persons who commit the offences now under consideration seek the habitual gratification of a particular perverted lust, which not only takes them out of the class of ordinary men gone wrong, but stamps them with the hallmark of a specialised and extraordinary class as much as if they carried on their bodies some physical peculiarity.' On this account, in regard to this crime we think that the repetition of the acts is itself a specific feature connecting the accused with the crime and that evidence of this kind is admissible to show the nature of the act done by the accused. The probative force of all the acts together is much greater than one alone; for, whereas the jury might think one man might be telling an untruth, three or four are hardly likely to tell the same untruth unless they were conspiring together. If there is nothing to suggest a conspiracy their evidence would seem to be overwhelming. Whilst it would no doubt be in the interests of the prisoner that each case should be considered separately without the evidence on the others, we think that the interests of justice require that on each case the evidence on the others should be considered, and that, even apart from the defence raised by him, the evidence would be admissible.

In this case the matter can be put in another and very simple way. The visits of the men to the prisoner's house were either for a guilty or an innocent purpose: that they all speak to the commission of the same class of acts upon them tends to show that in each case the visits were for the former and not the latter purpose. The same considerations would apply to a case where a man is charged with a series of indecent offences against children, whether boys or girls: that they all complain of the same sort of conduct shows that the interest the prisoner was taking in them was not of a paternal or friendly nature but for the purpose of satisfying lust.

If we are right in thinking that the evidence was admissible, it is plain that the accused would not be prejudiced or embarrassed by reason of all the counts being tried together, and there was no reason for the judge to direct the jury that, in considering whether a particular charge was proved, they were to shut out other charges from their minds.

Appeal dismissed.

Harris v *Director of Public Prosecutions*
[1952] AC 694
House of Lords

A series of eight larcenies having common characteristics occurred in May, June and July 1951, in an office in an enclosed and extensive market at times when most of the gates were shut and in periods during part of which the defendant, a police officer, was on solitary duty there. The precise time of only one larceny, the last which occurred in July, was known and then the defendant was found to be in the immediate vicinity of the office. He was charged on indictment with all the larcenies and, having been tried on all eight counts simultaneously, he was acquitted on the first seven and convicted on the eighth, that relating to the larceny in July.

VISCOUNT SIMON LC: In my opinion, the principle laid down by Lord Herschell LC in *Makin's* case [1894] AC 57 remains the proper principle to apply and I see no reason for modifying it. *Makin's* case [1894] AC 57 was a decision of the Judicial Committee of the Privy Council, but it was unanimously approved by the House of Lords in *R v Ball* [1911] AC 47, 71, and has been constantly relied on ever since. It is, I think, an error to attempt to draw up a closed list of the sort of cases in which the principle operates: such a list only provides instances of its general application, whereas what really matters is the principle itself and its proper application to the particular circumstances of the charge that is being tried. It is the application that may sometimes be difficult, and the particular case now before the House illustrates that difficulty . . . When Lord Herschell speaks of evidence of other occasions in which the accused was concerned as being admissible to 'rebut' a defence which would otherwise be open to the accused, he is not using the vocabulary of civil pleadings and requiring a specific line of defence to be set up before evidence is tendered which would overthrow it. If it were so, instances would arise where magistrates might be urged not to commit for trial, or it might be ruled at the trial, at the end of the prosecution's case, that enough had not been established to displace the presumption of innocence, when all the time evidence properly available to support the prosecution was being withheld. 'In criminal cases, and especially in those where the justices have summary jurisdiction, the admissibility of evidence has to be determined in reference to all the issues which have to be established by the prosecution, and frequently without any indication of the particular defence that is going to be set up': *per* Avory J in giving the judgment of the Divisional Court in *Perkins v Jeffery* [1915] 2 KB 702, 707.

Lord du Parcq pointed out in *Noor Mohamed v The King* [1949] AC 182, 191 in commenting on what Lord Sumner had said in *Thompson v The King* [1918] AC 221, 232:

> An accused person need set up no defence other than a general denial of the crime alleged. The plea of not guilty may be equivalent to saying 'let the prosecution prove its case, if it can,' and having said so much the accused may take refuge in silence. In such a case it may appear (for instance) that the facts and circumstances of the particular offence charged are consistent with innocent intention, whereas further evidence, which incidentally shows that the accused has committed one or more other offences, may tend to prove that they are consistent only with a guilty intent. The prosecution could not be said, in their Lordships' opinion, to be 'crediting the accused with a fancy defence' if they sought to adduce such evidence.

Lord Herschell's statement that evidence of 'similar facts' may sometimes be admissible as bearing on 'the question whether the acts alleged to constitute the crime charged in the indictment were designed or accidental' deserves close analysis. Sometimes the purpose properly served by such evidence is to help to show that what happened was not an accident; if it was, the accused had nothing to do with it.

Sometimes the purpose is to help to show what was the intention with which the accused did the act which he is proved to have done. In a proper case, and subject to the safeguards which Lord Herschell indicates, either purpose is legitimate. Scrutton J points out the distinction very clearly in *R v Ball* [1911] AC 47. Sometimes the two purposes are served by the same evidence.

The substance of the matter appears to me to be that the prosecution may adduce all proper evidence which tends to prove the charge. I do not understand Lord Herschell's words to mean that the prosecution must withhold such evidence until after the accused has set up a specific defence which calls for rebuttal. Where, for instance, *mens rea* is an essential element in guilt, and the facts of the occurrence which is the subject of the charge, standing by themselves, would be consistent with mere accident, there would be nothing wrong in the prosecution seeking to establish the true situation by offering, as part of its case in the first instance, evidence of similar action by the accused at another time which would go to show that he intended to do what he did on the occasion charged and was thus acting criminally. *R v Mortimer* (1936) 25 Cr App R 150 is a good example of this. What Lord Sumner meant when he denied the right of the prosecution to 'credit the accused with fancy defences' (in *Thompson v The King*) was that evidence of similar facts involving the accused ought not to be dragged in to his prejudice without reasonable cause.

There is a second proposition which ought to be added under this head. It is not a rule of law governing the admissibility of evidence, but a rule of judicial practice followed by a judge who is trying a charge of crime when he thinks that the application of the practice is called for. Lord du Parcq referred to it in *Noor Mohamed v The King* [1949] AC 182, 192 immediately after the passage above quoted, when he said that

> in all such cases the judge ought to consider whether the evidence which it is proposed to adduce is sufficiently substantial, having regard to the purpose to which it is professedly directed, to make it desirable in the interest of justice that it should be admitted. If, so far as that purpose is concerned, it can in the circumstances of the case have only trifling weight, the judge will be right to exclude it. To say this is not to confuse weight with admissibility. The distinction is plain, but cases must occur in which it would be unjust to admit evidence of a character gravely prejudicial to the accused even though there may be some tenuous ground for holding it technically admissible. The decision must then be left to the discretion and the sense of fairness of the judge.

This second proposition flows from the duty of the judge when trying a charge of crime to set the essentials of justice above the technical rule if the strict application of the latter would operate unfairly against the accused. If such a case arose, the judge may intimate to the prosecution that evidence of 'similar facts' affecting the accused, though admissible, should not be pressed because its probable effect 'would be out of proportion to its true evidential value' *(per* Lord Moulton in *Director of Public Prosecutions v Christie* (1914) 24 Cox CC 249, 257). Such an intimation rests entirely within the discretion of the judge.

It is, of course, clear that evidence of 'similar facts' cannot in any case be admissible to support an accusation against the accused unless they are connected in some relevant way with the accused and with his participation in the crime. (See Lord Sumner in *Thompson v The King* [1918] AC 221, 234.) It is the fact that he was involved in the other occurrences which may negative the inference of accident or establish his *mens rea* by showing 'system.' Or, again, the other occurrences may sometimes assist to prove his identity, as, for instance, in *Perkins v Jeffery* [1915] 2 KB

702. But evidence of other occurrences which merely tend to deepen suspicion does not go to prove guilt. This is the ground, as it seems to me, on which the Judicial Committee of the Privy Council allowed the appeal in *Noor Mohamed* v *The King* [1949] AC 182. The Board there took the view that the evidence as to the previous death of the accused's wife was not relevant to prove the charge against him of murdering another woman, and if it was not relevant it was at the same time highly prejudicial. It is to be noted that the Judicial Committee did not question the decision in *R* v *Sims* [1946] KB 531.

It remains to examine certain reported cases dealing with admissibility of evidence of 'similar facts' decided since *Makin's* case, to which the Attorney-General referred us. Rightly understood, these cases do not seem to me to involve any enlargement of the area within which evidence of 'similar facts' might be admitted.

In *R* v *Smith* [1915] WN 309 the accused was charged with murdering a woman, immediately after going through a form of marriage with her, by drowning her in a bath in the lodging where they were staying. Evidence was held to be rightly admitted of very similar circumstances which connected the accused with the deaths at a later date of two other women who were drowned in their baths after the accused had gone through a form of marriage with each of them in turn. In all three cases it was shown that the accused benefited by the death. In all three cases the prisoner urged the woman to take a bath and was on the premises when she prepared to do so. The ground on which the evidence of the two later occurrences was admissible was that the occurrences were so alike and the part taken by the accused in arranging what the woman would do was so similar in each case as to get rid of any suggestion of accident. The decision in *R* v *Smith* therefore involved no extension of the principle laid down in *Makin's* case. The challenged evidence was admissible both to show that what happened in the case of the first woman was not an accident and also to show what was the intention with which the accused did what he did.

In *R* v *Armstrong* [1922] 2 KB 555 the accused was indicted for the murder of his wife by administering arsenic to her. The wife was shown to have died from arsenical poisoning, but the defence urged that it was not shown that the husband had administered the poison to her, but that she had committed suicide. The accused had purchased a quantity of arsenic and made it up into a number of small packets, each containing what would constitute a fatal dose, but offered the explanation that he had purchased the poison merely to use it as a weed-killer in his garden. The prosecution called evidence to show that, eight months after the death of his wife, he secretly administered arsenic to another person. The Court of Criminal Appeal held that this evidence was admissible because it went to disprove the suggestion that he had purchased and kept arsenic for an innocent purpose. The decision in *R* v *Armstrong* appears to me to involve no enlargement of the principle in *Makin's* case. Lord Hewart CJ rightly observed at p. 566: 'The fact that he was subsequently found not merely in possession of but actually using for a similar deadly purpose the very kind of poison that caused the death of his wife was evidence from which the jury might infer that that poison was not in his possession at the earlier date for an innocent purpose.'

In *R* v *Sims* there is a passage in the judgment of Lord Goddard CJ which appears to have raised doubts in some quarters as to whether the principle in *Makin's* case was being extended. The Lord Chief Justice there observed that one method of approaching the relevant problem is to start with the general proposition that all evidence that is 'logically probative' is admissible unless excluded by established rules, and that it would follow that evidence for the prosecution 'is admissible irrespective of the issues raised by the defence.' It is the words 'logically probative' which have raised doubts in some minds. Such a phrase may seem to invite philosophic discussion which would be ill-suited to the practical business of applying the criminal law with justice to all concerned. But I do not understand the Lord Chief Justice by the use of such a phrase to be enlarging the ambit of the principle in *Makin's* case at all or to be disregarding the restrictions which Lord Herschell indicated. In one sense, evidence of previous bad conduct or hearsay evidence, might be regarded as having, logically, a probative value, but, of course, the judgment in *Sims'* case is not opening the door to that. I understand the passage quoted to mean no more than what I have already formulated, viz., that the prosecution may advance proper evidence to prove its case without waiting to ascertain what is the line adopted by the defence. Lord du Parcq, in *Noor Mohamed* v *The King,* points out the possibility of misunderstanding the Lord Chief Justice's words and proceeds to put his own construction upon them. In substance, I agree with his interpretation. There is, however, this to be added. The proper working of the criminal law in this connection depends on the due observance of both the propositions which I have endeavoured to expound in this judgment. While the prosecution may adduce all proper evidence which tends to prove the charge, it must do so with due regard to the warnings contained in the judgments of Kennedy J in *R v Bond* [1906] 2 KB 389 and Lord Sankey LC in *Maxwell* v *Director of Public Prosecutions* [1935] AC 309. A criminal trial in this country is conducted for the purpose of deciding whether the prosecution has proved that the accused is guilty of the particular crime charged, and evidence of 'similar facts' should be excluded unless such evidence has a really material bearing on the issues to be decided. This, in my opinion, is the way in which Lord Sumner's observations in *Thompson* v *The King* should be regarded. It should be noted that in that case Lord Parker was careful to insist that it would be wrong to treat the decision as 'laying down any principle capable of general application.' With this explanation, I see no reason to differ from the conclusion in *R* v *Sims.*

(His Lordship held that as regards the larceny of July, the evidence of the previous larcenies, which occurred when he was not proved to have been near the office, should have been excluded from the consideration of the jury and, the judge having omitted to direct them to that effect, the conviction should be quashed. LORDS PORTER, TUCKER, and MORTON OF HENRYTON agreed. LORD OAKSEY agreed with the principles stated by the LORD CHANCELLOR as to the admissibility of evidence, but disagreed with the application of those principles to the facts of the case.)

Appeal allowed.

Questions
1. Does the admissibility of similar fact evidence depend on the nature of the defence raised?
2. How should a judge direct the jury where the accused is tried on two counts of rape if:

(a) similar fact evidence is admitted;
(b) similar fact evidence is not admitted?

Note
The decision in *Thompson* v *R* [1918] AC 221, approved in *Sims,* suggested that crimes involving homosexuality were a special type of offence which

allowed evidence of disposition to be admitted. This idea was dispelled in the case of *DPP* v *Boardman*, below.

Director of Public Prosecutions v *Boardman*
[1975] AC 421
House of Lords

The appellant, the headmaster of a boarding school for boys, was charged, *inter alia,* with buggery with S, a pupil aged 16, and inviting H, a pupil aged 17, to commit buggery with him. The defence was that S and H were lying and that the alleged incidents never took place. The trial judge ruled that the evidence of H was admissible on the count concerning S and *vice versa.* This was because, in each case, the homosexual conduct alleged by both boys against the appellant was of an unusual kind, in that it involved a request by a middle aged man to an adolescent to play the active role in buggery. There were, however, other similarities in the evidence of S and H. Both said that they were woken up by the appellant at about midnight whilst asleep in the dormitory; both said that he used similar words to induce their participation. The jury convicted the appellant, and his appeal against conviction on the ground, *inter alia,* that the judge's ruling had been wrong was dismissed by the Court of Appeal. A further appeal was made to the House of Lords. The point of law of general public importance certified was as follows: 'Whether on a charge involving an allegation of homosexual conduct where there is evidence that the accused person is a man whose homosexual proclivities take a particular form, that evidence is thereby admissible although it tends to show that the accused has been guilty of criminal acts other than those charged.'

LORD WILBERFORCE: My Lords, the question for decision in this appeal is whether, on a charge against the appellant of buggery with one boy, evidence was admissible that the appellant had incited another boy to buggery, and *vice versa.* The judge ruled that, in the particular circumstances of this case, the evidence was admissible. We have to decide whether this ruling was correct; for reasons which others of your Lordships have given, we cannot answer the question certified in the terms in which it is stated. Whether in the field of sexual conduct or otherwise, there is no general or automatic answer to be given to the question whether evidence of facts similar to those the subject of a particular charge ought to be admitted. In each case it is necessary to estimate (i) whether, and if so how strongly, the evidence as to other facts tends to support, i.e., to make more credible, the evidence given as to the fact in question, (ii) whether such evidence, if given, is likely to be prejudicial to the accused. Both these elements involve questions of degree.

It falls to the judge, in the first place by way of preliminary ruling, and indeed on an application for separate trials if such is made (see the opinion of my noble and learned friend Lord Cross of Chelsea), to estimate the respective and relative weight of these two factors and only to allow the evidence to be put before the jury if he is satisfied that the answer to the first question is clearly positive, and, on the assumption, which is likely, that the second question must be similarly answered, that on a combination of the two the interests of justice clearly require that the evidence be admitted.

Questions of this kind arise in a number of different contexts and have, correspondingly, to be resolved in different ways. I think that it is desirable to confine ourselves to the present set of facts, and to situations of a similar character. In my understanding we are not here concerned with cases of 'system' or 'underlying unity' (cf. *Moorov* v *HM Advocate,* 1930 JC 68), words whose vagueness is liable to result in their misapplication, nor with a case involving proof of identity, or an alibi, nor, even, is this a case where evidence is adduced to rebut a particular defence. It is sometimes said that evidence of 'similar facts' may be called to rebut a defence of innocent association, a proposition which I regard with suspicion since it seems a specious manner of outflanking the exclusionary rule. But we need not consider the validity or scope of this proposition. The Court of Appeal dealt with the case on the basis, submitted by the appellants's counsel, that no defence of innocent association was set up; in my opinion we should take the same course.

This is simply a case where evidence of facts similar in character to those forming the subject of the charge is sought to be given in support of the evidence on that charge. Though the case was one in which separate charges relating to different complainants were tried jointly, the principle must be the same as would arise if there were only one charge relating to one complainant. If the appellant were being tried on a charge relating to S, could the prosecution call H as a witness to give evidence about facts relating to H? The judge should apply just as strict a rule in the one case as in the other. If, as I believe, the general rule is that such evidence cannot be allowed, it requires exceptional circumstances to justify the admission. This House should not, in my opinion, encourage erosion of the general rule.

We can dispose at once of the suggestion that there is a special rule or principle applicable to sexual, or to homosexual, offences. This suggestion had support at one time — eminent support from Lord Sumner in *Thompson* v *The King* [1918] AC 221 — but is now certainly obsolete: see *per* Lord Reid (at p. 751) and the other learned lords in *R* v *Kilbourne* [1973] AC 729. Evidence that an offence of a sexual character was committed by A against B cannot be supported by evidence that an offence of a sexual character was committed by A against C, or against C, D and E.

. . .

If the evidence was to be received, then, it must be on some general principle not confined to sexual offences. There are obvious difficulties in the way of formulating any such rule in such a manner as, on the one hand, to enable clear guidance to be given to juries, and, on the other hand, to avoid undue rigidity. The prevailing formulation is to be found in the judgment of the Court of Criminal Appeal in *R* v *Sims* [1946] KB 531 where it was said, at pp. 539-540:

> The evidence of each man was that the accused invited him into the house and there committed the acts charged. The acts they describe bear a striking similarity. That is a special feature sufficient in itself to justify the admissibility of the evidence; . . . The probative force of all the facts together is much greater than one alone; for, whereas the jury might think that one man might be telling an untruth, three or four are hardly likely to tell the same untruth unless they were conspiring together. If there is nothing to suggest a conspiracy their evidence would seem to be overwhelming.

Sims has not received universal approbation or uniform commentary, but I think that it must be taken that this passage has received at least the general approval of this House in *R* v *Kilbourne* [1973] AC 529. For my part, since the statement is evidently related to the facts of that particular case, I should deprecate its literal use in other cases. It is certainly neither clear nor comprehensive. A suitable adaptation, and, if necessary, expansion, should be allowed to judges in order to suit the facts involved. The basic principle must be that the admission of similar fact evidence (of the kind now in question) is exceptional and requires a strong degree of probative force. This probative force is derived, if at all, from the circumstance that the facts testified to by the several witnesses bear to each other such a striking similarity that they must, when judged by experience and common sense, either all be true, or have arisen from a cause common to the witnesses or from pure coincidence. The jury may, therefore, properly be asked to judge whether the right conclusion is that all are true, so that each story is supported by the other(s).

I use the words 'a cause common to the witnesses' to include not only (as in *R v Sims* [1946] KB 531) the possibility that the witnesses may have invented a story in concert but also the possibility that a similar story may have arisen by a process of infection from media or publicity or simply from fashion. In the sexual field, and in others, this may be a real possibility: something much more than mere similarity and absence of proved conspiracy is needed if this evidence is to be allowed. This is well illustrated by *R v Kilbourne* [1973] AC 529 where the judge excluded 'intra group' evidence because of the possibility, *as it appeared to him,* of collaboration between boys who knew each other well. This is, in my respectful opinion, the right course rather than to admit the evidence unless a case of collaboration or concoction is made out.

If this test is to be applied fairly, much depends in the first place upon the experience and common sense of the judge. As was said by Lord Simon of Glaisdale in *R v Kilbourne,* at p 756, in judging whether one fact is probative of another, experience plays as large a place as logic. And in matters of experience it is for the judge to keep close to current mores. What is striking in one age is normal in another: the perversions of yesterday may be the routine or the fashion of tomorrow. The ultimate test has to be applied by the jury using similar qualities of experience and common sense after a fair presentation of the dangers either way of admission or of rejection. Finally, whether the judge has properly used and stated the ingredients of experience and common sense may be reviewed by the Court of Appeal.

The present case is, to my mind, right on the border-line. There were only two relevant witnesses, S and H. The striking similarity as presented to the jury was and was only the active character of the sexual performance to which the accused was said to have invited the complainants. In relation to the incident which was the subject of the second charge, the language used by the boy was not specific: the 'similarity' was derived from an earlier incident in connection with which the boy used a verb connoting an active role. I agree with, I think, all your Lordships in thinking that all of this, relating not very specifically to the one striking element, common to two boys only, is, if sufficient, only just sufficient. Perhaps other similarities could have been found in the accused's approaches to the boys (I do not myself find them particularly striking), but the judge did not rest upon them to direct the jury as to their 'similarity.' I do not think that these ought now to be relied upon. The dilution of the 'striking' fact by more prosaic details might have weakened the impact upon the jury rather than strengthened it. The judge dealt properly and fairly with the possibility of a conspiracy between the boys.

These matters lie largely within the field of the judge's discretion, and of the jury's task; the Court of Appeal has reviewed the whole matter in a careful judgment. I do not think that there is anything which justifies the interference of this House. But I confess to some fear that the case, if regarded as an example, may be setting the standard of 'striking similarity' too low.

LORD HAILSHAM OF ST MARYLEBONE: . . . In all these cases it is for the judge to ensure as a matter of law in the first place, and as a matter of discretion where the matter is free, that a properly instructed jury, applying their minds to the facts, can come to the conclusion that they are satisfied so that they are sure that to treat the matter as pure coincidence by reason of the 'nexus,' 'pattern,' 'system,' 'striking resemblances' or whatever phrase is used is 'an affront to common sense' [*R v Kilbourne* [1973] AC 729, *per* Lord Simon of Glaisdale, at p 759]. In this the ordinary rules of logic and common sense prevail, whether the case is one of burglary and the burglar has left some 'signature' as the mark of his presence, or false pretences and the pretences alleged have too many common characteristics to have happened coincidentally, or whether the dispute is one of identity and the accused in a series of offences has some notable physical features or behavourial or psychological charac-teristics or, as in some cases, is in possession of incriminating articles, like a jemmy, a set of skeleton keys or, in abortion cases, the apparatus of the abortionist. Attempts to codify the rules of common sense are to be resisted. The first rule in *Makin* [1894] AC 57, 65 is designed to exclude a particular kind of inference being drawn which might upset the presumption of innocence by introducing more heat than light. When that is the only purpose for which the evidence is being tendered, it should be excluded altogether, as in *R v Horwood* [1970] 1 QB 133. Where the purpose is an inference of another kind, subject to the judge's overriding discretion to exclude, the evidence is admissible, if in fact the evidence be logically probative. Even then it is for the jury to assess its weight, which may be greater or less according as to how far it accords with other evidence, and according as to how far that other evidence may be conclusive.

There are two further points of a general character that I would add. The 'striking resemblances' or 'unusual features,' or whatever phrase is considered appropriate, to ignore which would affront common sense, may either be in the objective facts, as for instance in *R v Smith, Notable British Trials Series*, or *R v Straffen* [1952] 2 QB 911, or may constitute a striking similarity in the accounts by witnesses of disputed transactions. For instance, whilst it would certainly not be enough to identify the culprit in a series of burglaries that he climbed in through a ground floor window, the fact that he left the same humorous limerick on the walls of the sitting room, or an esoteric symbol written in lipstick on the mirror, might well be enough. In a sex case, to adopt an example given in argument in the Court of Appeal, whilst a repeated homosexual act by itself might be quite insufficient to admit the evidence as confirmatory of identity or design, the fact that it was alleged to have been performed wearing the ceremonial head-dress of a Red-Indian chief or other eccentric garb might well in appropriate circumstances suffice.
. . .

It is fair to the appellant's argument to say that there is undoubted force in the criticism that, by fastening on the purely passive role said to have been adopted by the appellant towards the act of buggery suggested or performed as the sole element of 'striking resemblance' between S's testimony and that of H, the trial judge was on dubious ground, partly because it might be said that, as between two witnesses only, the fact, although perhaps unusual, was perhaps not so unusual as to render the evidence admissible, and partly because over the sequence of all the evidence, including that of A, it was not perhaps so unambiguously and consistently displayed as to render it a kind of signature which would make it an 'affront to common sense' (*R v Kilbourne* [1973] AC 729, 759) in the eyes of the jury to disregard it as coincidental. But I hope that I have exposed enough of the evidence to indicate that, if the learned judge erred here, he erred by giving too little weight to the case for a conviction. There were other points of resemblance sufficiently striking to have their value as corroboration whether in conjunction with or without the 'catamite' feature left to the jury and, in S's case, there was admittedly strong independent corroboration in the testimony of the police officer. If the jury convicted on a presentation of the case which may have been unduly favourable to the appellant, it cannot be doubted that they would have convicted if the matter had been exposed on its real, and stronger, impact.

So far as regards the question certified, I cannot say that the question admits of an absolutely categorical answer which would not be misleading. I therefore propose the following several points:

(1)   There is not, as the question rather suggests, a separate category of homosexual cases. The rules of logic and common sense must be the same for all trials where 'similar fact' or other analogous evidence is sought to be introduced. This can be inferred from *R v Kilbourne* [1973] AC 729.

(2)   The mere fact that the homosexual acts take a 'particular form' is not by itself enough to make the evidence admissible as a universal rule, as is rather suggested in the word 'thereby' as it appears in the question. The rule is as stated by Lord Herschell LC in *Makin v Attorney-General for New South Wales* [1894] AC 57, 65 and by Lord du Parcq in *Noor Mohamed v The King* [1949] AC 182, 192 in the passage quoted by Lord Simon in *Harris v Director of Public Prosecutions* [1952] AC 694, 707, and is subject also to the judge's discretion as defined by Lord Simon, at p. 707.

(3)   *R v Sims* [1946] KB 531 was rightly decided, but must be read subject to the criticisms of it in *Noor Mohamed v The King* and *R v Kilbourne* [1973] AC 729 and in paragraph (1) above, and to the rejection of the 'circular argument' heresy in *R v Manser* (1934) 25 Cr App R 18 as rejected in *R v Kilbourne* and *R v Hester* [1973] AC 296.

(4)   There is no ground for relaxing the 'cautious approach' recommended in *Ogg v HM Advocate* 1938 JC 152 by the Lord Justice-Clerk (Lord Aitchison), at p. 158, or for reducing the force of the first of Lord Herschell LC's rules in *Makin v Attorney-General for New South Wales* [1894] AC 57, 65. If this were done the result would be to admit a number of cases in which the forbidden type of inference would be the real reason for adducing the evidence.

(5)   The second of Lord Herschell's rules in *Makin* is not capable of codification into a series of tight propositions or categories of case. Each case must be looked at in the light of all the circumstances and of the sentence containing the rule and of the observations upon it of Lord du Parcq in *Noor Mohamed v The King* [1949] AC 182 and Lord Simon in *Harris v Director of Public Prosecutions* [1952] AC 694, and of the ordinary rules of logic and common sense.

(6)   Despite differences of pedigree and extent of application, there is no relevant difference in this context between the English doctrine of corroboration and the Scottish doctrine as defined in *Moorov v HM Advocate,* 1930 JC 68 and *Ogg v HM Advocate,* 1938 JC 152 and explained in *R v Kilbourne* [1973] AC 729.

LORD SALMON: My Lords, evidence against an accused which tends only to show that he is a man of character with a disposition to commit crimes, even the crime with which he is charged, is inadmissible and deemed to be irrelevant in English law. I do not pause to discuss the philosophic basis for this fundamental rule. It is certainly not founded on logic, but on policy. To admit such evidence would be unjust and would offend our concept of a fair trial to which we hold that everyone is entitled. Nevertheless, if there is some other evidence which may show that an accused is guilty of the crime with which he is charged, such evidence is admissible against him, notwithstanding that it may also reveal his bad character and disposition to commit crime.

I have no wish to add to the anthology of guidance concerning the special circumstances in which evidence is relevant and admissible against an accused, notwithstanding that it may disclose that he is a man of bad character with a disposition to commit the kind of crime with which he is charged. The principles upon which such evidence should be admitted or excluded are stated with crystal clarity in the celebrated passage from the judgment delivered by Lord Herschell LC in *Makin* v *Attorney-General for New South Wales* [1894] AC 57, 65. I doubt whether the learned analyses and explanations of that passage to which it has been subjected so often in the last 80 years add very much to it.

It is plain from what has fallen from your Lordships (with which I respectfully agree) that the principles stated by Lord Herschell are of universal application and that homosexual offences are not exempt from them as at one time seems to have been supposed: see *Thompson* v *The King* [1918] AC 221, *per* Lord Sumner, at p 232, and *R* v *Sims* [1946] KB 531, 537.

My Lords, whether or not evidence is relevant and admissible against an accused is solely a question of law. The test must be: is the evidence capable of tending to persuade a reasonable jury of the accused's guilt on some ground other than his bad character and disposition to commit the sort of crime with which he is charged? In the case of an alleged homosexual offence, just as in the case of an alleged burglary, evidence which proves merely that the accused has committed crimes in the past and is therefore disposed to commit the crime charged is clearly inadmissible. It has, however, never been doubted that if the crime charged is committed in a uniquely or strikingly similar manner to other crimes committed by the accused the manner in which the other crimes were committed may be evidence upon which a jury could reasonably conclude that the accused was guilty of the crime charged. The similarity would have to be so unique or striking that common sense makes it inexplicable on the basis of coincidence. I would stress that the question as to whether the evidence is capable of being so regarded by a reasonable jury is a question of law. There is no easy way out by leaving it to the jury to see how they decide it. If a trial judge wrongly lets in the evidence and the jury convict, then, subject to the proviso [to section 2(1) of the Criminal Appeal Act 1968], the conviction must be quashed. If, for example, A is charged with burglary at the house of B and it is shown that the burglar, whoever he was, entered B's house by a ground floor window, evidence against A that he had committed a long series of burglaries, in every case entering by a ground floor window, would be clearly inadmissible. This would show nothing from which a reasonable jury could infer anything except bad character and a disposition to burgle. The factor of unique or striking similarity would be missing. There must be thousands of professional burglars who habitually enter through ground floor windows and the fact that B's house was entered in this way might well be a coincidence. Certainly it could not reasonably be regarded as evidence that A was the burglar. On the other hand, if, for example, A had a long series of convictions for burglary and in every case he had left a distinctive written mark or device behind him and he was then charged with burglary in circumstances in which an exactly similar mark or device was found at the site of the burglary which he was alleged to have committed, the similarity between the burglary charged and those of which he had previously been convicted would be so uniquely or strikingly similar that evidence of the manner in which he had committed the previous burglaries would, in law, clearly be admissible against him. I postulate these facts merely as an illustration. There is a possibility but only, I think, a theoretical possibility that they might arise. In such a case, A would no doubt say, quite rightly, that, with his record it is inconceivable that he would have left the mark or device behind him had he been the burglar: he might just as well have published a written confession: the mark or device must have been made at the time of or just after the burglary by someone trying to implicate him. This, however, would be a question for the jury to decide.

(LORD MORRIS OF BORTH-Y-GEST and LORD CROSS OF CHELSEA delivered concurring judgments.)

Appeal dismissed.

Questions
1. What is the ratio of *DPP* v *Boardman*?
2. Would *Sims* be decided in the same way today?
3. Does the approach of the Law Lords in *Boardman* differ from the approach of Lord Herschell in *Makin*?
4. Do you think the decision in *Boardman* clarifies the approach trial judges should take when deciding upon the admissibility of similar fact evidence? What should that approach be?
5. The cases of *Novac* and *Johannsen* (below), were decided soon after *Boardman*. Can you offer any explanation for the differing decisions? Which case is to be preferred?

R v Novac
(1976) 65 Cr App R 107
Court of Appeal

The accused Novac, was jointly tried with others on an indictment containing 38 counts, mainly for sexual offences involving the procurement of boys. The question arose as to whether or not certain evidence satisfied the similar fact principle.

BRIDGE LJ: . . . The evidence relevant to the conspiracy and related counts can, for the purposes of this judgment, be very briefly summarised. It fell under three headings. The first and most voluminous category of evidence was that of police officers who between the dates mentioned in count 1 of the indictment had kept observation on the movements and activities of the first three appellants in and around an amusement arcade near Piccadilly Circus called Playland, which clearly was, upon the evidence, a favourite resort and meeting point for young male prostitutes and their customers. The second head of evidence was the evidence of nine or ten youths of various ages under 21 who spoke of acts of indecency between themselves and the first three appellants. Most of these were committed at an address in Garratt Lane, Wandsworth, where these three appellants were living together at the time. Finally there was evidence of lengthy written statements made by each of these three appellants and of interviews with police officers, all of which on the face of them contained important and damaging admissions. Without examining the evidence in detail it is no exaggeration to say that the evidence as a whole presented an overwhelming picture of these three appellants habitually consorting with young male prostitutes in the West End of London and frequently entertaining them at their flat in Wandsworth for immoral homosexual purposes.

. . .

Three of the boys called by the Crown to give evidence in connection with the conspiracy and related counts testified that Raywood had offered or attempted to bugger them. In each case he had met them in Playland or some similar amusement arcade and picked them up by offering them money to play the pin tables. In each case he had offered them shelter overnight at the place where he was living at the time and the offer or attempt to commit buggery had occurred when Raywood and the boy were sharing a bed. The boy P the subject of count 7, had similarly been picked up in an amusement arcade and offered shelter, but it is to be observed that he was first taken by Raywood to the house of a woman friend and it is not alleged that any offence was committed there. According to P he was subsequently taken to another address where the offence alleged in count 7 was committed when the boy and Raywood were sharing a bed. We cannot think that two or more alleged offences of buggery or attempted buggery committed in bed at the residence of the alleged offender with boys to whom he had offered shelter can be said to have been committed in a uniquely or strikingly similar manner. If a man is going to commit buggery with a boy he picks up, it must surely be a commonplace feature of such an encounter that he will take the boy home with him and commit the offence in bed. The fact that the boys may in each case have been picked up by Raywood in the first instance at amusement arcades may be a feature more nearly approximating to a 'unique or striking similarity' within the ambit of Lord Salmon's principle. It is not, however, a similarity in the commission of the crime. It is a similarity in the surrounding circumstances and is not, in our judgment, sufficiently proximate to the commission of the crime itself to lead to the conclusion that the repetition of this feature would make the boys' stories inexplicable on the basis of coincidence. It was for these reasons that we reached the conclusion that the evidence on the conspiracy count was inadmissible against Raywood on count 7 and that accordingly the refusal of his application to sever count 7 was reached on an erroneous basis. In the result his conviction on count 7 had to be quashed.

R v Johannsen
(1977) 65 Cr App R 101
Court of Appeal

LAWTON LJ: The judgment I am about to read is the judgment of the Court as constituted on the hearing of the appeal against conviction, which consisted of myself, Nield and Boreham JJ.

On April 8, 1976, at Norwich Crown Court, after a trial before Mars-Jones J, the appellant was convicted on five counts of buggery and five of gross indecency. He was sentenced to life imprisonment on each count of buggery and to five years' imprisonment concurrently on each count of gross indecency. He appeals against his conviction on grounds of law.

The indictment related to five schoolboys, aged 14 and 15. There were two counts in respect of each boy, one charging buggery, the other gross indecency. Save in the case of the boy C, who was named in counts 7 and 8, the boys each gave evidence about more than one incident.

After arraignment defending counsel moved the Court to sever the indictment so that there would be separate trials on each of the coupled counts. The ground put forward was that there were no striking similarities between each of the coupled counts so as to make the evidence on one admissible on the others.

. . .

Prosecuting counsel resisted the application for separate trials. He submitted that the evidence on the depositions did reveal striking similarities between each of the coupled counts. The judge agreed and ruled that all the counts should be tried together.

. . .

We do not find it necessary to set out in much detail the sordid evidence given in this case.

The appellant is 52 years of age. During most of 1975 he worked on oil rigs in the North Sea with regular periods of shore leave, which he spent in rented accommodation in Great Yarmouth. The prosecution's case was that between May and December 1975 he made a practice of accosting boys in amusement arcades and similar places, offering them money or a meal or treating them to a game, taking them to his accommodation or on to the beach and there committing the offences charged. His particular homosexual propensities were to handle the boys' penises and getting them to do the same with his, fellatio and buggery. On December 16, 1975, he was arrested. In the course of interviews he made oral statements, some of which were capable of being corroboration of T's evidence. He also made a written statement which was a confession of gross indecency with T.

. . .

We have no hesitation in deciding that there were striking similarities about what happened to each of the boys — the accostings in the same kind of places, the enticements, the visits to his accommodation, his homosexual propensities and his ways of gratifying them. It follows that the evidence of each boy was admissible to corroborate the evidence of the others: see *DPP* v *Kilbourne* (1973) 57 Cr App R 381; [1973] AC 729.

R v Scarrott
[1978] 1 All ER 672
Court of Appeal

The defendant was tried on an indictment, containing 13 counts, charging him with buggery, attempted buggery, assault with intent to commit buggery and indecent assault involving eight young boys over a period of four and a half years. Before arraignment, counsel for the defendant applied to sever the indictment and asked for separate trials in respect of each boy, as a multiple indictment would be prejudicial to the defendant. The application was refused. During the course of the trial the judge ruled that the evidence given by each boy relating to the count or counts concerning him had a striking similarity to the evidence given by the other boys, and was admissible on the other counts. The defendant was convicted on one count of buggery, one count of attempted buggery and eight counts of indecent assault on seven boys.

SCARMAN LJ: . . . To be admissible, the evidence by its striking similarity has to reveal an underlying link between the matters with which it deals and the allegations against the defendant on the count under consideration. Subject to one comment, which really goes only to choice of language, we would respectfully accept the way in which the general principle was put by Lord Salmon in *Boardman's* case ([1974] 3 All ER 887 at 913):

. . . whether or not evidence is relevant and admissible against an accused is solely a question of law. The test must be — is the evidence capable of tending to persuade a reasonable jury of the accused's guilt on some ground other than his bad character and disposition to commit the sort of crime with which he is charged? In the case of an alleged homosexual offence, just as in the case of an alleged burglary, evidence which proves merely that the accused has committed crimes in the past and is therefore disposed to commit the crime charged is clearly inadmissible. It has, however, never been doubted that if the crime charged is committed in a uniquely or strikingly similar manner to other crimes committed by the accused, the manner in which the other crimes were committed may be evidence on which a jury could reasonably conclude that the accused was guilty of the crime charged. The similarity would have to be so unique or striking that common sense makes it inexplicable on the basis of coincidence. I would stress that the question whether the evidence is capable of being so regarded by a reasonable jury is a question of law. There is no easy way out by leaving it to the jury to see how they decide it.

Thus, the admissibility of similar fact evidence, even when it is adduced as it is in this case as corroboration of direct evidence, does not depend on whether it is capable of corroborating the evidence of the victim or accomplice; it depends on its positive probative value. Its corroborative capability is a consequence of its probative value and not *vice versa*, for, if the evidence be admissible, it follows that it is capable of corroborating.

The point was succinctly put by Lord Cross in *Director of Public Prosecutions* v *Kilbourne* [1973] 1 All ER 440 where he said: 'Once the "similar fact" evidence is admitted — and it was common ground that it was properly admitted in this case — then of necessity it 'corroborates' — i.e., strengthens or supports — the evidence given by the boy an alleged offence against whom is the subject of the count under consideration.'

To succeed, therefore, in quashing these convictions counsel for the appellant has to persuade this court that the judge was wrong to treat the similar fact evidence in this case as strikingly similar. I now come to the one comment which this court would make on the statement of general principle made by Lord Salmon. Hallowed though by now the phrase 'strikingly similar' is (it was used by Lord Goddard CJ in *R v Sims* [1946] 1 All ER 699 in 1946 and has now received the accolade of use in the House of Lords in *Boardman* v *Director of Public Prosecutions*), it is no more than a label. Like all labels it can mislead; it is a possible passport to error. It is, we repeat, only a label and it is not to be confused with the substance of the law which it labels. We think that Lord Widgery CJ had the danger of a label in mind when, in a very different class of case, he made a comment on the passage from Lord Salmon's speech which we have quoted. In *R v Rance; R v Herron* (1975) 62 Cr App R 118 at 121, Lord Widgery CJ made this comment, and the court is grateful to counsel for the appellant for drawing our attention to it:

It seems to us that one must be careful not to attach too much importance to Lord Salmon's vivid phrase 'uniquely or strikingly similar'. The gist of what is being said both by Lord Cross and by Lord Salmon is that evidence is admissible as similar fact evidence if, but only if, it goes beyond showing a tendency to commit crimes of this kind and is positively probative in regard to the crime now charged. That, we think, is the test which we have to apply on the question of the correctness or otherwise of the admission of the similar fact evidence in this case.

Positive probative value is what the law requires, if similar fact evidence is to be admissible. Such probative value is not provided by the mere repetition of similar facts; there has to be some feature or features in the evidence sought to be adduced which provides a link, an underlying link as it has been called in some of the cases. The existence of such a link is not to be inferred from mere similarity of facts which are themselves so commonplace that they can provide no sure ground for saying that they point to the commission by the accused of the offence under consideration. Lord Cross put the matter, as we think, in its correct perspective at the end of the day when, in the course of his speech in *Boardman* v *Director of Public Prosecutions,* he said: 'The likelihood of such a coincidence obviously becomes less and less the more people there are who make the similar allegations and the more striking are the similarities in the various stories. In the end, as I have said, it is a question of degree. . .'

In this part of the case counsel for the appellant has referred us to two recent decisions of the Court of Appeal, one of which would appear to support his submission and the other of which would appear to support the assessment of the evidence made by the trial judge. . . .

In our view, we are here in that area of judgment on particular facts from which the criminal law can never depart. Plainly some matters, some circumstances may be so distant in time or place from the commission of an offence as not to be properly considered when deciding whether the subject-matter of similar fact evidence displays striking similarities with the offence charged. On the other hand, equally plainly, one cannot isolate, as a sort of laboratory specimen, the bare bones of a criminal offence from its surrounding circumstances and say that it is only within the confines of that specimen, microscopically considered, that admissibility is to be determined. Indeed, in one of the most famous cases of all dealing with similar fact evidence, 'the brides in the bath case', *R* v *Smith* (1915) 84 LJKB 2153, the court had regard to the facts that the accused man married the women and that he insured their lives. Some surrounding circumstances have to be considered in order to understand either the offence charged or the nature of the similar fact evidence which it is sought to adduce and in each case it must be a matter of judgment where the line is drawn. One cannot draw an inflexible line as a rule of law. We therefore observe that in *R* v *Novac* the line was drawn where Bridge LJ expressed it to be drawn. No doubt that was a line drawn after a full investigation and assessment of the particular facts of that case. It would be wrong, in our judgment, to elevate the passage which I have quoted from Bridge LJ's judgment into a statement of law. It is a judgment on the particular facts presented to the court for its consideration and decision and the same observations may be made in regard to *R* v *Johannsen* (1977) 65 Cr App R 101 the other case which, on a superficial view, might appear to be in conflict with *R* v *Novac*. *R* v *Johannsen,* on one view of it, could be said to be against counsel for the appellant; but, properly considered, it is no more against him than *R* v *Novac* is for him. Lawton LJ gave the judgment of the court in *R* v *Johannsen* and there is, I hesitate to say a striking similarity, but certainly a remarkable similarity between the salient facts of that case and the salient facts of *R* v *Novac*. Lawton LJ said: 'The prosecution's case was that between May and December 1975 he made a practice of accosting boys in amusement arcades and similar places, offering them money or a meal or treating them to a game, taking them to his accommodation or on to the beach and there committing the offences charged. His particular homosexual propensity was to handle the boys' penises and getting them to do the same with his . . .'.

Later Lawton LJ, with confidence, said: 'We have no hesitation in deciding that there were striking similarities about what happened to each of the boys — the accostings in the same kind of places, the enticements, the visits to his accommodation, his homosexual propensities and his ways of gratifying them. It follows that the evidence of each boy was admissible to corroborate the evidence of the others.' We therefore have to reach a judgment on the evidence of this particular case, and to determine whether the evidence adduced, that is the similar fact evidence adduced, possesses such features that it is a proper exercise of judgment to say that the evidence is logically probative, that it has positive probative value in assisting to determine the truth.

We have come to the conclusion that the evidence described by Judge Vowden in the terms which I have quoted does possess that positive, probative value, does possess striking similarities. It is necessary to repeat the features which are strikingly similar: the ages of the boys, the way in which their resistance was worn down, the location of the offences and the offences themselves. Taken together, these similarities are inexplicable on the basis of coincidence. We have come to the conclusion, therefore, that the judge was right to admit this evidence and that he was right to submit it to the jury in the way that he did.

That is not however quite the end of the appeal. I have referred already to the fact that counsel for the appellant did submit both before arraignment and later, at the end of the prosecution's case, that there was a real danger that the evidence of these boys was tainted by conspiracy or ganging up, the 'group' point as it is called. The judge had to consider this point first before arraignment, when the only material available to him was that contained in the depositions. He had to form a judgment at that stage whether it was, in all the circumstances, safe in the interests of justice to allow the trial to proceed on a multi-count indictment. Clearly there was a suggestion that some, or perhaps all, of these boys might have been party to a ganging up organised by the older brother of Peter B. He took the view that the matter could be dealt with by him in summing up, that whether or not there was such a ganging up should be considered by the jury. It was of course a matter for his discretion whether to accede to the application to sever the indictment or not and, in our judgment, he cannot be said to have erred in the exercise of his discretion in taking the view that in all the circumstances of this case the matter could properly be left to the jury, always assuming, as in the event occurred, that there was a full and proper direction and warning. There is therefore nothing in this point in our judgment. That really disposes of the points taken by counsel for the appellant.

We think, however, that, in this very difficult class of case where trial judges do face a very complex problem in both the conduct of the trial and in summing up, we should attempt to give some practical guidance to judges at certain stages of the trial. What we now say is not to be considered as any advance or development of the law; it is merely an attempt on the basis of *Director of Public Prosecutions* v *Kilbourne* [1973] 1 All ER 440 and *Boardman* v *Director of Public Prosecutions* [1974] 3 All ER 887 to give some guidance which may be helpful to judges who have this very difficult task to discharge.

The help that we can give deals really with a number of phases of the trial process. The first phase is before arraignment when a defendant submits that the indictment should be severed. Of course the question whether a judge should allow an indictment to contain a number of counts initially has to be dealt with under the discretion given to a judge by the Indictment Rules 1971 SI 1971 No 1253, and in particular rule 9 which only repeats the law as it has been ever since 1915:

Charges for any offences may be joined in the same indictment if those charges are founded on the same facts, or form or are a part of a series of offences of the same or a similar character.

It is not very difficult for a judge to reach a conclusion under that rule, but, having come to the conclusion, as Judge Vowden plainly did in this case, that the offences were of a similar character and a series, he then has to consider how to deal with the application to sever. It appears to us that when such an application at this stage is made a judge must, as Lawton LJ said in *R v Johannsen,* act not on some judicial speculation as to what may happen in the trial but on such factual material as is then available to him, i.e., the depositions or the statements, according to the nature of the committal proceedings. He must ask himself at that stage whether in his judgment it would be open to a jury, properly directed and warned, to treat the evidence available on a study of the depositions or statements as strikingly similar to the evidence to be adduced in respect of the various counts and he must, we think, be able even at that stage to take the matter a little further: he must be able to say that if this evidence is believed, it could be accepted as admissible similar fact evidence or, as in the circumstances of this class of case, as evidence capable of corroborating the direct evidence. Of course he will also at this stage, as at all stages of a criminal trial when a ruling is required of him, consider whether the evidence appears to be, on the information then available, independent or untainted evidence and whether there is a real chance that there is falsity or conspiracy to give false evidence and he must also consider at this stage, as at every stage when a ruling is sought, the balance, on the information then available to him, between the possible prejudicial effect of the evidence and its probative value.

If the judge takes all those well-known matters into account, and reaches his decision on the basis of the factual information which is available to him, it does not seem to us possible to fault the exercise of his discretion whichever way it goes. It is important to appreciate that at this stage, the pre-arraignment stage, the ultimate decision of the judge is an exercise of judicial discretion. So long as he does not err in law, takes into account all relevant matters and excludes consideration of irrelevant matters, his discretion will stand. Of course at this stage the judge is taking no final decision as to the admissibility of evidence. If he decides to allow the multi-count indictment to proceed, it will still be for his ruling whether the evidence, for instance, on counts 1 to 7 will be admitted as similar fact evidence to assist in the proof of the offence charged in count 8 and so on throughout the indictment. It does not follow that because a multi-count indictment has been allowed to proceed that therefore the evidence given will be evidence on all the counts contained in the indictment. Similarly, if he decides at that stage to sever and if the trial proceeds on the basis of only, let us say, one count, it will still be open to the prosecution, at the appropriate moment, to adduce evidence relating to the other (and now put aside) counts as similar fact evidence of that count and it will then be for the judge to rule, in accordance with the laws of evidence, whether the evidence is admissible or not.

The next phase of the trial process, on which we think, in the light of the authorities, we can give some practical guidance, is when the judge's ruling is sought as to the admissibility of the similar fact evidence. His task, though a difficult exercise of judgment, can be stated in simple terms. He first has to reach a view on what he then knows of the facts of the case and of the nature of the evidence to be adduced whether the evidence possesses the features of striking similarity or probative value which have been canvassed earlier in this judgment. If he reaches the view that it does, he then has to consider whether the evidence is such that it ought to be put to the jury. He may be impressed with the very real possibility that the evidence is tainted by conspiracy or ganging up, the group objection, or he may, because of the group objection or for some other reason, take the view that, though strikingly similar and therefore, *prima facie,* admissible, the evidence is so prejudicial that its prejudicial effect outweighs its probative value. If he admits the evidence, he will in his summing-up have to make sure that the jury is left with the task of deciding whether to accept the evidence and whether to treat the evidence as in fact corroboration or not. Here Judge Vowden, as I have already mentioned, very correctly did that, notwithstanding he had already made his ruling as to striking similarities.

Appeal dismissed.

Questions
1. How does 'positive probative value' differ, if at all, from 'striking similarity'? Which test is to be preferred?
2. Is Scarman LJ's treatment of the apparent conflict between *Novac* and *Johannsen* convincing?

P. Mirfield, 'Similar Facts — *Makin* Out?'
[1987] CLJ 83

In the first two or three years after *Boardman*, the attention of the Court of Appeal was largely focused, in cases involving evidence of bad character, upon the 'striking similarity' test of admissibility and upon a possible preference for a formulation of the test in terms of 'positive probative value.' However, since then, there has been an increasing tendency for Court of Appeal judgments to be reasoned in terms of Lord Herschell's statement in *Makin*, whether or not express reliance has been placed on that statement.

In *Seaman* (1978) 67 Cr App R 234, the accused's defence to a charge of shoplifting was that he had simply forgotten to pay. The court relied upon Lord Herschell's statement in deciding that evidence of two earlier occasions on which the accused had been guilty of conduct similar to that now alleged against him was admissible to rebut this defence (of accident). No reference was made to a need for high probative value or striking similarity. There are hints in *Barrington* [1981] 1 WLR 419, of the influence of *Makin*, though the actual decision in that case was based on the court's view that the tests of striking similarity and positive probative value were satisfied. It has already been noted that, in *Lewis* (1983) 76 Cr App R 33, the court, having taken the phrase 'similar fact evidence' at face value, went on to apply *Makin* rather than *Boardman*; the court did not apply any requirement of high probative value. In *Berry* (1986) 83 Cr App R 7, a murder case, though no reference was made to *Makin*, there is some indication that the purpose for which evidence is sought to be adduced is of decisive importance. However, it seems that the reason why the court decided that the trial judge had been wrong to allow evidence of the accused's violently jealous attitude towards his victim to be adduced was that that evidence concerned incidents too remote in time from the death of the victim. In other words, they were insufficiently probative, in any event, to be admissible.

Most recently, in *Butler* (1987) 84 Cr App R 12, the court, having stated that *Boardman* was 'the leading and most authoritative case on the subject,' went on to state the effect of the various authorities as follows:

1. Evidence of similar facts may be admissible in evidence, whether or not they tend to show the commission of other offences. This may be admitted:
   (a) if it tends to show that the accused has committed the particular crime of which he is charged,

(b) to support the identification of the accused as the man who committed a particular crime and, in appropriate cases, in order to rebut a defence of alibi, or

(c) to negative a defence of accident or innocent conduct.

2.   Admissibility is a question of law for the judge to decide. He must, in the analysis of the proferred evidence, be satisfied that:

(a) the nature and quality of the similar facts show a striking similarity or what Lord Justice Scarman . . . describes as being of 'positive probative value', and

(b) the evidence of a similar act goes well beyond a propensity to act in a particular fashion.

3.   Notwithstanding an established admissibility in law the judge in the exercise of discretion may refuse to admit the evidence if its prejudicial effect outweighs its probative value.

The remarkable feature of this passage is that it puts together virtually everything of significance which has been said, during the last hundred years, about the admission of evidence of bad character yet fails to acknowledge any incompatibility between the various things said. The third paragraph demonstrates the continuing influence of the notion that there can be both a special rule for evidence of bad character and a discretion to exclude such evidence available on the same facts. The first paragraph obviously derives from the second part of Lord Herschell's statement in *Makin* and does no obvious harm as long as it is realised that, to make sense of it in the light of the second paragraph, we must take it to be describing a necessary but not sufficient condition for the admissibility of such evidence. It must be added that it would be no less helpful if it simply stated that such evidence must be relevant to some issue in the case.

The second paragraph describes, in sub-paragraph (a), the special, high standard of relevance required of such evidence in terms which are very familiar. Paragraph 2(b) takes us back to the first part of Lord Herschell's statement and continues to be a misleading account of the position. Indeed, on the facts of *Butler* itself, it is quite clear that the similar fact evidence did not go beyond showing the accused to have a propensity to act in a particular fashion. He was charged with two offences of rape. His defence was simply that he had not committed the offences in question, though he elected not to testify. There was, from one of the complainants, some very weak direct evidence of identification of the accused as the rapist and some strong circumstantial evidence connecting him with both rapes. The judge allowed the prosecution to adduce evidence from another woman of certain incidents of consensual sexual behaviour between the accused and herself over a period of about two years, the last of these having taken place a similar period of time before the first of the rape offences. Apart from the consensual element present in relation to these incidents, they shared a number of similarities with the accusation made by the two complainants against the man who had raped them. It suffices here to say that the behaviour in question was assumed (by the court) to be of an unusual kind and would certainly be regarded by all but a tiny minority of jurors as morally highly reprehensible. In short, it showed the accused to be of bad character and was adduced in order to show that he had a propensity to behave in a way strikingly similar to the way in which the rapist had behaved before and after the rapes themselves. Though the importance of the circumstantial evidence of identity cannot be denied, there can be no doubt that the jury was also being invited to infer from the other woman's testimony that the accused must have been the man who had committed the rapes. The reasoning process was precisely the same as in *Straffen* and in *Thompson*.

Conclusion

It is submitted that the statement in *Butler* of the principles applicable in relation to the adducing of evidence of bad character by the prosecution more than amply demonstrates both the need finally to lay to rest the ghost of *Makin* and the need for an authoritative statement of a more simplified, helpful and logical structure for the admission of such evidence. The urgency of these needs is rendered the greater by the fact that both of the major practitioners' works dealing with the topic continue to give great prominence to Lord Herschell's statement in *Makin*. Sir Rupert Cross said of *Boardman* that it was a case of fourth time lucky in the House of Lords. Another commentator, LH Hoffman (now Hoffman J) was, perhaps, nearer the mark when he suggested that at least one more excursion to the House of Lords 'would probably be necessary before the law can be said to be established on a simple and rational basis.'

Director of Public Prosecutions v *P*
[1991] 3 WLR 161
House of Lords

LORD MACKAY OF CLASHFERN LC: My Lords, on 26 January 1988 the defendant was convicted in the Crown Court of two counts of rape and eight counts of incest. The indictment charged him with four offences of rape and four offences of incest in respect of each of two daughters, B and S. These were specimen counts. The defendant was convicted in the case of each girl on the first count of rape and all the counts of incest. He was acquitted of the later charges of rape. At the outset of the trial application was made on behalf of the defendant that the counts relating to the girl B should be tried separately from those relating to the girl S. The trial judge refused that application and the trial proceeded upon all the counts. The defendant appealed to the Court of Appeal (Criminal Division) against the judge's refusal. The Court of Appeal (Criminal Division) allowed the appeal and quashed the conviction.

The appellant, the Director of Public Prosecutions, applied for a certificate that a point of law of general public importance was involved in this decision and for leave to appeal to this House. The Court of Appeal granted these applications and certified the following questions for this House:

> 1. Where a father or stepfather is charged with sexually abusing a young daughter of the family, is evidence that he also similarly abused other young children of the family admissible (assuming there to be no collusion) in support of such charge in the absence of any other 'striking similarities?' 2. Where a defendant is charged with sexual offences against more than one child or young person, is it necessary in the absence of 'striking similarities' for the charges to be tried separately?

In giving the judgment of the court Lord Lane CJ after quoting from well known passages in the speeches in this House in *Reg.* v *Boardman* [1975] AC 421, said:

> The way in which this doctrine has developed has led, it seems, to courts requiring some features of the similarity beyond what has been described as the paederast's or the incestuous father's 'stock in trade,' before one victim's evidence can be properly admitted upon the trial of another: see for example *Reg.* v *Inder* (1978) 67 Cr App R 143, and more recently *Reg.* v *Brooks* (1990) 92 Cr App R 36.

After examining the features upon which the judge had founded as allowing the evidence of one girl to be properly admitted upon the trial of the counts relating to the other, Lord Lane CJ concluded that they could not properly be described in the light of the authorities to which he referred as unusual features such as to make the account given by one girl more credible because those features are mirrored by the statement of the other. He went on:

We have searched the committal papers to see whether there might be other matters which amounted to striking similarities between the girls' account of their father's behaviour towards them. Such incidents as we have been able to find do not, for one reason or another, fulfil the necessary requirements and were no doubt for that reason rejected by the prosecution as a possible ground for their arguments. It follows that there were, in the circumstances of this particular case, and in the light of the authorities as they now stand, no grounds for saying that the evidence of one girl was admissible so far as the other was concerned.

The court therefore felt compelled to allow the appeal and quash the conviction. Lord Lane CJ added:

> However, the prosecution might like to consider whether the time has not come for the House of Lords to be asked to look again at this branch of the law. We have said enough to indicate that it is an area which is difficult to understand and even more difficult to apply in practice. Mr Mansfield suggested, not without some force, that it is almost a lottery whether separate trials will be ordered or not. It seems to us absurd that counsel and judge should be spending time searching through committal papers, which may in the upshot not represent the evidence actually given, searching for 'striking similarities' such as to justify allowing the jury to hear evidence of that which they would naturally and rightly consider themselves entitled to know, namely that the defendant is charged with abusing not merely one but two or more of his young daughters. We see force in the suggestion adumbrated in the argument before us that where the father has allegedly shown himself to be someone prepared to abuse sexually girls who are no more than children, in this case under the age of 13, girls who are moreover his own children, and to use his position of power over them in their own home to achieve those ends, this might provide a sufficient hallmark to render the evidence of one girl admissible in the case of the other where the danger of collusion can be discounted. In the current state of decided cases we are, we think, inhibited from so deciding.

It is apparent that the particular difficulty which arose in this case is the development of the authorities in this area of the law requiring some feature of similarity beyond what has been described as the paederast's or the incestuous father's stock in trade before one victim's evidence can be properly admitted upon the trial of another that inhibited the Court of Appeal from deciding as otherwise they would have done. The question in this appeal therefore is whether this development is a sound one or not.

Consideration of this matter has normally begun with *Makin* v *Attorney-General for New South Wales* [1894] AC 57. In that case evidence was led that several infants had been received by the accused from their mothers on representations that they were willing to adopt the children and upon a payment of a sum inadequate for the support of the children for more than a very limited period and that the bodies of these children had been found buried in a similar manner in the gardens of several houses occupied by the accused and the question was whether this was relevant where another child was shown to have been received by the accused from its mother on similar representations as to their willingness to adopt it and upon payment of a sum similarly inadequate for its support for more than a very limited period. In giving the judgment of the Board Lord Herschell LC said, at p. 65:

> In their Lordships' opinion the principles which must govern the decision of the case are clear, though the application of them is by no means free from difficulty. It is undoubtedly not competent for the prosecution to adduce evidence tending to

show that the accused has been guilty of criminal acts other than those covered by the indictment, for the purpose of leading to the conclusion that the accused is a person likely from his criminal conduct or character to have committed the offence for which he has been tried. On the other hand, the mere fact that the evidence adduced tends to show the commission of other crimes does not render it inadmissible if it be relevant to an issue before the jury, and it may be so relevant if it bears upon the question whether the acts alleged to constitute the crime charged in the indictment were designed or accidental, or to rebut a defence which would otherwise be open to the accused. The statement of these general principles is easy, but it is obvious that it may often be very difficult to draw the line and to decide whether a particular piece of evidence is on the one side or the other.

This matter was very fully discussed in this House in *Reg.* v *Boardman* [. . . His Lordship then stated the facts of *Boardman* and cited from the speeches made in that case (see above) and then continued . . .]

As this matter has been left in *Reg.* v *Boardman* I am of opinion that it is not appropriate to single out 'striking similarity' as an essential element in every case in allowing evidence of an offence against one victim to be heard in connection with an allegation against another. Obviously, in cases where the identity of the offender is in issue, evidence of a character sufficiently special reasonably to identify the perpetrator is required and the discussion which follows in Lord Salmon's speech on the passage which I have quoted indicates that he had that type of case in mind.

From all that was said by the House in *Reg.* v *Boardman* I would deduce the essential feature of evidence which is to be admitted is that its probative force in support of the allegation that an accused person committed a crime is sufficiently great to make it just to admit the evidence, notwithstanding that it is prejudicial to the accused in tending to show that he was guilty of another crime. Such probative force may be derived from striking similarities in the evidence about the manner in which the crime was committed and the authorities provide illustrations of that of which *Reg.* v *Straffen* [1952] 2 QB 911 and *Rex* v *Smith* (1915) 11 Cr App R 229, provide notable examples. But restricting the circumstances in which there is sufficient probative force to overcome prejudice of evidence relating to another crime to cases in which there is some striking similarity between them is to restrict the operation of the principle in a way which gives too much effect to a particular manner of stating it, and is not justified in principle. *Hume on Crimes*, 3rd ed. (1844), vol. II, p. 384, said long ago:

> the aptitude and coherence of the several circumstances often as fully confirm the truth of the story, as if all the witnesses were deponing to the same facts.

Once the principle is recognised, that what has to be assessed is the probative force of the evidence in question, the infinite variety of circumstances in which the question arises, demonstrates that there is no single manner in which this can be achieved. Whether the evidence has sufficient probative value to outweigh its prejudicial effect must in each case be a question of degree.

The view that some feature of similarity beyond what has been described as the paederast's or the incestuous father's stock in trade before one victim's evidence can be properly admitted upon the trial of another seems to have been stated for the first time in those terms in *Reg.* v *Inder* (1977) 67 Cr App R 143. Although that case also contains a reference to a warning not to attach too much importance to Lord Salmon's vivid phrase 'uniquely or strikingly similar' I think in the context this is what has occurred. This trend has been followed in later cases, for example, *Reg.* v *Clarke* (1977) 67 Cr App R 398, *Reg.* v *Tudor* (unreported), 18 July 1988, and particularly

Reg. v *Brooks* (1990) 92 Cr App R 36. In so far as these decisions required, as an essential feature, a similarity beyond the stock in trade I consider they fall to be overruled.

In the present case the evidence of both girls describes a prolonged course of conduct in relation to each of them. In relation to each of them force was used. There was a general domination of the girls with threats against them unless they observed silence and a domination of the wife which inhibited her intervention. The defendant seemed to have an obsession for keeping the girls to himself, for himself. The younger took on the role of the elder daughter when the elder daughter left home. There was also evidence that the defendant was involved in regard to payment for the abortions in respect of both girls. In my view these circumstances taken together gave strong probative force to the evidence of each of the girls in relation to the incidents involving the other, and was certainly sufficient to make it just to admit that evidence, notwithstanding its prejudicial effect. This was clearly the view taken by the Court of Appeal and they would have given effect to it were it not for the line of authority in the Court of Appeal to which I have referred.

The approach which I have suggested is in accordance with the law of Scotland as described in *Moorov* v *HM Advocate*, 1930 JC 68, and the cases which followed it. These cases were referred to with approval by Lord Hailsham of St Marylebone in *Reg.* v *Boardman* [1975] AC 421, 450, 452. Although there is a difference between the law of Scotland, which requires corroboration generally in criminal cases, and the law of England, which does not, the principles which determine whether one piece of evidence can corroborate another are the same as those which determine whether evidence in relation to one offence is admissible in respect of another. The law of New Zealand, to which we were referred, also shows, in my opinion, a similar development. The latest of the cases from New Zealand to which we were referred is the decision of the Court of Appeal in *Reg.* v *Huijser* [1988] 1 NZLR 577. The crux of the judgment is set out succinctly, at pp. 578–579:

> In essence the argument for the appellant is that the evidence in question is no more than evidence of propensity. On the other hand the argument for the Crown is in essence, to quote from the written submissions by Mr Burston based on *Hsi En Feng's* case [1985] 1 NZLR 222: 'after hearing the four women in this case, the jury would be entitled to take the view that the appellant was operating his business in such a way as to create and take advantage of opportunities for sexual contact, not necessary for business purposes, with relatively young women shop employees. It would be contrary to the requirements of justice to deny the jury the advantage of the full picture.' Weighing the arguments and considering the depositions, we have concluded that the judge, in his conclusion, and the Crown are right. This is not a case like the more border-line one of *Reg.* v *McLean* [1978] 2 NZLR 358, where this court held the prejudicial effect clearly outweighed probative value. The evidence, if accepted, shows a practice established over a considerable number of years by the accused of subjecting women employees to minor sexual assaults and harassment during the course of their working relationships with him. It indicates a constant or continual attitude by him.

When a question of the kind raised in this case arises I consider that the judge must first decide whether there is material upon which the jury would be entitled to conclude that the evidence of one victim, about what occurred to that victim, is so related to the evidence given by another victim, about what happened to that other victim, that the evidence of the first victim provides strong enough support for the evidence of the second victim to make it just to admit it notwithstanding the prejudicial effect of admitting the evidence. This relationship, from which support is derived, may take many forms and while these forms may include 'striking similarity' in the manner in which the crime is committed, consisting of unusual characteristics in its execution the necessary relationship is by no means confined to such circumstances. Relationships in time and circumstances other than these may well be important relationships in this connection. Where the identity of the perpetrator is in issue, and evidence of this kind is important in that connection, obviously something in the nature of what has been called in the course of the argument a signature or other special feature will be necessary. To transpose this requirement to other situations where the question is whether a crime has been committed, rather than who did commit it, is to impose an unnecessary and improper restriction upon the application of the principle.

For the reasons which I have given, I am of opinion that there was sufficient connection between the circumstances spoken of by the two girls in the present case for their evidence mutually to support each other, that the appeal should be allowed, and the conviction restored.

I would answer the first question posed by the Court of Appeal by saying that the evidence referred to is admissible if the similarity is sufficiently strong, or there is other sufficient relationship between the events described in the evidence of the other young children of the family, and the abuse charged, that the evidence if accepted, would so strongly support the truth of that charge that it is fair to admit it notwithstanding its prejudicial effect. It follows that the answer to the second question is no, provided there is a relationship between the offences of the kind I have just described.

These matters raise questions of law but also involve judgments on matters of degree. Judgments properly made in the light of the appropriate principles should not, I think, yield results which could properly be described as a lottery.

(LORD KEITH OF KINKEL, LORD EMSLIE, LORD TEMPLEMAN and LORD ACKNER all agreed with the Lord Chancellor.)

Appeal allowed.

Questions
1.   P. Mirfield, in 'Similar Facts — *Makin* Out' (above), quotes Hoffman as saying 'at least one more excursion to the House of Lords will probably be necessary before the law can said to be established on a simple and rational basis'. Has *DPP* v *P* now put the law on that 'simple and rational basis'?
2.   Is there any specific role left for cases which reveal an accused's particular 'hallmark' or 'signature', or is it simply a question of the probative force needing to outweigh inevitable prejudice? If the former, what is that role? If the latter, how great does the probative force need to be?

(B)   Civil cases

The modern approach to similar fact evidence in civil cases reveals that such evidence is admissible according to the same principles as apply in criminal cases. As the vast majority of civil cases are heard by a judge alone, the dangers presented by the 'forbidden reasoning' are perhaps less acute. The most influential factor seems to be the degree of probative force which, if it is sufficiently high, will render the evidence admissible.

Mood Music Publishing Company Limited v De Wolfe Limited
[1976] Ch 119
Court of Appeal

The plaintiffs were the owners of the copyright in a musical work called '*Sogno Nostalgico*'. They alleged that the defendants had infringed such copyright by supplying for broadcasting a work entitled 'Girl in the Dark'. It was not disputed that the works were similar, but the defendants argued that the similarity was coincidental, and denied copying even though '*Sogno Nostalgico*' was composed prior to 'Girl in the Dark'. The plaintiffs were permitted to adduce evidence to show that on other occasions the defendants had reproduced works subject to copyright. The defendants appealed.

LORD DENNING MR: The admissibility of evidence as to 'similar facts' has been much considered in the criminal law. Some of them have reached the highest tribunal, the latest of them being *R* v *Boardman* [1975] AC 421. The criminal courts have been very careful not to admit such evidence unless its probative value is so strong that it should be received in the interests of justice: and its admission will not operate unfairly to the accused. In civil cases the courts have followed a similar line but have not been so chary of admitting it. In civil cases the courts will admit evidence of similar facts if it is logically probative, that is, if it is logically relevant in determining the matter which is in issue: provided that it is not oppressive or unfair to the other side: and also that the other side has fair notice of it and is able to deal with it. Instances are *Brown* v *Eastern & Midlands Railway Co.* (1889) 22 QBD 391: *Moore* v *Ransome's Dock Committee* (1898) 14 TLR 539 and *Hales* v *Kerr* [1908] 2 KB 601.

     The matter in issue in the present case is whether the resemblances which 'Girl in the Dark' bear to '*Sogno Nostalgico*' are mere coincidences or are due to copying. Upon that issue it is very relevant to know that there are these other cases of musical works which are undoubtedly the subject of copyright, but that the defendants have nevertheless produced musical works bearing close resemblances to them. Whereas it might be due to mere coincidence in one case, it is very unlikely that they would be coincidences in four cases. It is rather like *R* v *Sims* [1946] KB 531, 540, where it was said: 'The probative force of all the acts together is much greater than one alone.' So the probative force of four resemblances together is much better than one alone . . . It seems to me the judge was right.

     (ORR LJ and BROWNE LJ agreed.)

Appeal dismissed.

Thorpe v Chief Constable of Greater Manchester Police
[1989] 2 All ER 827
Court of Appeal

The plaintiff sued the Chief Constable for torts allegedly committed by two police officers. The judge granted the plaintiff an order for discovery of various documents concerning adjudications of guilt in police disciplinary proceedings following the plaintiff's arrest and further documents which, although not connected with that arrest, might be evidence of similar facts.

NEILL LJ: The plaintiff brings this action against the Chief Constable of the Greater Manchester Police for damages for assault, unlawful arrest, false imprisonment and malicious prosecution. So much is clear from the form of the writ. The claim arises out of an incident which took place on 1 March 1985 when the plaintiff was arrested during a demonstration at Manchester University on the occasion of a visit by the then Home Secretary.

. . .

Evidence of 'similar facts'
I have found this part of the case, which was not developed, even if it was mentioned, before the judge, more difficult.

The leading modern authority on 'similar fact' evidence in civil proceedings is *Mood Music Publishing Co Ltd* v *De Wolfe Ltd* [1976] 1 All ER 763, [1976] Ch 119. In that case the plaintiffs wished to adduce evidence of music which they claimed was very similar to music of which they owned the copyright. Lord Denning MR said ([1976] 1 All ER 763 at 766, [1976] Ch 119 at 127):

> The admissibility of evidence as to 'similar facts' has been much considered in the criminal law. Some of them have reached the highest tribunal, the latest of them being *Boardman* v *Director of Public Prosecutions* [1974] 3 All ER 887, [1975] AC 421. The criminal courts have been very careful not to admit such evidence unless its probative value is so strong that it should be received in the interests of justice and its admission will not operate unfairly to the accused. In civil cases the courts have followed a similar line but have not been so chary of admitting it. In civil cases the courts will admit evidence of similar facts if it is logically probative, that is if it is logically relevant in determining the matter which is in issue; provided that it is not oppressive or unfair to the other side; and also that the other side had fair notice of it and is able to deal with it . . . The matter in issue in the present case is whether the resemblances which 'Girl in the Dark' bears to '*Sogno Nostalgico*' are mere coincidences or are due to copying. On that issue it is very relevant to know that there are these other cases of musical works which are undoubtedly the subject of copyright, but yet the defendants have produced musical works bearing close resemblance to them. Whereas it might be due to mere coincidence in one case, it is very unlikely that there would be coincidences in four cases.

Evidence of 'similar facts' is relevant both in criminal and in civil cases to rebut defences such as accident or coincidence or sometimes to prove a system of conduct. Such evidence is not admissible, however, merely to show that the party concerned has a disposition to commit the conduct alleged. In the present case there is no reason to suppose that any defence of accident or coincidence is likely to be raised. Nor on the present material is there any basis for an argument that evidence or other convictions or adjudications might be relevant to prove a 'system' of, for example, violence towards demonstrators. It is also to be remembered that this is an application for specific discovery where a prima facie case of possession must be made out: see Ord 24, r 7.

I have therefore come to the conclusion that on the present pleadings it would be contrary to the established practice to make an order for disclosure which *might* provide evidence of 'similar facts' or lead to further inquiries on these lines.

DILLON LJ: . . . The test of the admissibility of evidence of similar facts is in general the same in civil and in criminal cases: see *Berger* v *Raymond Sun Ltd* [1984] 1 WLR 625 at 630 per Warner J. Lord Denning MR has suggested, in the passage from his judgment in *Mood Music Publishing Co Ltd* v *De Wolfe Ltd* [1976] 1 All ER 763, [1976] Ch 119 which is set out in the judgment of Neill LJ, which I have had the advantage of reading in draft, that in civil cases the courts have not been so chary of admitting such evidence as in criminal cases, but I apprehend that Lord Denning MR was thinking of civil cases tried by a judge alone. Where there is a jury the court must be more careful about admitting evidence which is in truth merely prejudicial than is necessary where there is a trial by a judge alone who is trained to distinguish between what is probative and what is not. By the test in criminal cases the evidence of similar facts should be excluded unless it has a really material bearing on the issues to be decided; to be admissible, therefore, the evidence must be related to something more than isolated instances of the same kind of offence: see *Boardman* v *DPP* [1974] 3 All ER 887 at 893, [1975] AC 421 at 439 per Lord Morris.

Applying these principles, my conclusion so far as regards adjudications of guilt in police disciplinary proceedings (as opposed to certificates of convictions in criminal courts) within heading (1) is that they do not lead to any train of inquiry, since the plaintiff will be getting the available statements of evidence under the undisputed part of the judge's order, and, being outside s. 11 of the 1968 Act, the adjudications of guilt are not probative of anything. It would indeed be quite wrong that they should be admitted in evidence in a jury trial because of the danger that the jury might regard them as probative of the matters which the jury themselves have to decide. These adjudications of guilt (if any) should not therefore be disclosed.

(MUSTILL LJ agreed.)

Questions
1.   Should the approach of the courts to similar fact evidence be the same in all cases, whether civil or criminal?
2.   Is Dillon LJ in the *Thorpe* case really arguing that the rule in civil cases should vary according to whether or not there is a jury?
3.   Dennis is charged with two counts of indecent assault, one against Fred, a boy of 12 years, and the other against Graham, a boy of 10 years. Both incidents allegedly occured in a local disused railway station, the one relating to Fred on Saturday, 1 November 1993, the one relating to Graham on Sunday, 23 November 1993. Fred and Graham attend the same school but are in different classes. They are both members of the school's athletics club, which meets every Tuesday evening after school classes have ended.

Fred will state in evidence that he was walking near the station when a man asked him if he had seen a puppy dog. The man asked Fred to help him search for the puppy, he agreed, and they both went into the station. The assault then took place in the waiting room. After the assault had taken place, the man gave Fred a fifty pence piece. Fred was unable positively to identify Dennis at a subsequent identification parade.

Graham will state in evidence that he was walking near the station when a man asked him if he had seen a kitten. The man asked Graham to help him search for the kitten, he agreed, and they both went into the station. The assault took place in the waiting room. The man then offered Graham money, but the offer was refused. Graham identified Dennis at a subsequent identification parade.

When Dennis's house was searched, the police found indecent photographs and a paedophile contact magazine. Dennis is also known to be a homosexual. Dennis denies both charges.

If the counts are tried together, will the evidence of each boy be admissible in respect of the count relating to the other? Will the prosecution be allowed to lead evidence of the photographs, magazine and Dennis's homosexuality?

Further Reading
P. Murphy, *A Practical Approach to Evidence*, 4th ed. (1992), Ch. 5
T. R. S. Allan, 'Similar Fact Evidence and Disposition: Law, Discretion and Admissibility' (1985) 48 MLR 253
P. B. Carter, 'Forbidden Reasoning Permissible: Similar Fact Evidence a Decade after *Boardman*' (1985) 48 MLR 29
R. Cross, 'Fourth Time Lucky — Similar Fact Evidence in the House of Lords' [1975] Crim LR 62
D. W. Elliott, 'The Young Person's Guide to Similar Fact Evidence' [1983] Crim LR 284
L. H. Hoffman, 'Similar Facts after *Boardman*' (1975) 91 LQR 193
R. Mahoney, 'Similar Fact Evidence and the Standard of Proof' [1993] Crim LR 185
R. Nair, 'Similar Fact Evidence — Prejudice and Irrelevance Revisited' [1993] Crim LR 432
A. A. S. Zuckerman, 'Similar Fact Evidence — the Unobservable Rule' (1987) 104 LQR 187

13 OPINION EVIDENCE

The function of the trier of the facts is to draw such inferences as seem proper based on the evidence admitted during the proceedings. Accordingly, it would be improper for a witness to be allowed to narrate his opinion on the facts in issue as by doing so he would be usurping the role given to the trier of the facts. Further, allowing witnesses to voice their opinions on the facts in issue would also raise questions about the reliability and relevance of those opinions. Therefore, the law does not generally admit opinion evidence but, as ever, there are exceptions to this general rule.

(A) Expert evidence: admissibility

There will be occasions where a witness testifies as to matters which fall outside the ordinary understanding of both the judge and the jury. In such cases, it is recognised that special help may be required in order that the jury are able to draw proper inferences from the facts. Perhaps the most common example would be the evidence of a medical expert. Jurors could not reasonably be expected to possess any detailed level of medical knowledge and, in the absence of special help, this might well hamper their ability to perform the task of drawing inferences in a proper manner. Accordingly, provided a witness is regarded as an 'expert', he will be allowed to state his opinion with regard to those matters which fall within his area of expertise.

Folkes v Chadd and Others
(1782) 3 Doug 157
King's Bench

In an action for trespass the question was whether an embankment erected by the plaintiff caused silting in the defendant's harbour. Mr Smeaton, a distinguished engineer, testified to his opinion as an expert that the silting was not caused by the embankment. The trial judge rejected the evidence on the ground that it was a matter of opinion and not of facts.

LORD MANSFIELD: . . . It is objected that Mr Smeaton is going to speak, not as to facts, but as to opinion. That opinion, however, is deduced from facts which are not disputed — the situation of banks, the course of tides and of winds, and the shifting of sands. His opinion, deduced from all these facts, is, that, mathematically speaking, the bank may contribute to the mischief, but not sensibly. Mr Smeaton understands the construction of harbours, the causes of their destruction, and how remedied. In matters of science no other witnesses can be called. An instance frequently occurs in actions for unskilfully navigating ships. The question then depends on the evidence of those who understand such matters; and when such questions come before me, I always send for some of the brethren of the Trinity House. I cannot believe that where the question is, whether a defect arises from a natural or an artificial cause, the opinions of men of science are not to be received. Handwriting is proved every day by opinion; and for false evidence on such questions a man may be indicted for perjury. Many nice questions may arise as to forgery, and as to the impressions of seals; whether the impression was made from seal itself, or from an impression in wax. In such cases I cannot say that the opinion of seal-makers is not to be taken. I have myself received the opinion of Mr Smeaton respecting mills, as a matter of science. The cause of the decay of the harbour is also a matter of science, and still more so, whether the removal of the bank can be beneficial. Of this such men as Mr Smeaton alone can judge. Therefore we are of opinion that his judgment, formed on facts, was very proper evidence.

Rule for a new trial made absolute.

R v Silverlock
[1894] 2 QB 766
Crown Cases Reserved

The defendant was charged with obtaining a cheque by false pretences. It became necessary to prove that certain documents were in the defendant's handwriting and the solicitor for the prosecution was called as an expert witness for this purpose. It was objected that the solicitor was not an expert, and could not give evidence as to his opinion. The solicitor said that he had since 1884, quite apart from his professional work, given considerable study and attention to handwriting and had on several occasions professionally compared evidence in handwriting. The objection was overruled, and the evidence was admitted. The jury convicted the defendant, who appealed.

LORD RUSSELL OF KILLOWEN CJ; It is true that the witness who is called upon to give evidence founded on a comparison of handwritings must be *peritus*; he must be skilled in doing so; but we cannot say that he must have become *peritus* in the way of his business or in any definite way. The question is, is he *peritus*? Is he skilled? Has he an adequate knowledge? Looking at the matter practically, if a witness is not skilled the judge will tell the jury to disregard his evidence. There is no decision which requires that the evidence of a man who is skilled in comparing handwriting, and who has formed a reliable opinion from past experience, should be excluded because his experience has not been gained in the way of his business. It is, however, really unnecessary to consider this point; for it seems from the statement in the present case that the witness was not only *peritus,* but was *peritus* in the way of his business. When once it is determined that the evidence is admissible, the rest is merely a question of its value or weight, and this is entirely a question for the jury, who will attach more or less weight to it according as they believe the witness to be *peritus.*

(MATHEW, DAY, VAUGHAN, WILLIAMS and KENNEDY JJ concurred.)

Conviction affirmed.

Question

Who may be classed as an 'expert' and who decides whether or not expert opinion evidence is admissible?

Note

As the following cases illustrate, merely because a witness is an expert, it does not follow that his evidence must be accepted by the jury. His evidence stands alongside all the other evidence in the case, and may be accepted or rejected by the jury performing their role as trier of the facts.

R v Lanfear
[1968] 2 QB 77
Court of Appeal

The appellant was charged with driving a motor vehicle on a road while unfit to drive through drink. The doctor who had examined him at the police station after the offence gave evidence at his trial. The appellant was convicted and appealed on the ground, *inter alia,* that the deputy recorder misdirected the jury in telling them that the doctor's evidence must be accepted unless the doctor showed by his own conduct that it ought not to be accepted.

DIPLOCK LJ: . . . In his notice of appeal he makes a number of complaints about the summing up by the deputy recorder. As regards all of the complaints but one I need say no more than that there is, in the view of this court, no substance in them. But he did complain, with justification, about the terms in which the deputy recorder instructed the jury about the attitude they should adopt towards the medical evidence. There is considerable excuse for the deputy recorder because he read out to them a passage which appears in the current volume of Archbold's Criminal Pleadings, Evidence and Practice 36th ed (1966) para 2849, under the heading 'Medical Witness,' which is in the following terms:

The evidence of any doctor, whether a police surgeon or not, should be accepted as the evidence of a professional man giving independent expert evidence with the sole desire of assisting the court, unless the doctor himself shows that his evidence ought not to be accepted.

The deputy recorder paraphrased that slightly. He said this:

Let me say immediately about medical evidence in general - this again, members of the jury, is a matter of law. The evidence of any doctor, whether a police surgeon or not, is to be accepted as the evidence of a professional man giving independent evidence with the sole desire of assisting the court unless the doctor by his own conduct shows that his evidence ought not to be accepted.

I think the only difference is that instead of 'himself' he has substituted the words 'by his own conduct.' Then he goes on subsequently to say this:

> . . . his evidence is to be accepted as the evidence of a professional man giving independent expert evidence with the sole desire of helping the court. This, then, puts him into a position in which, in the absence of reasons for rejecting his evidence, his evidence ought to be accepted.

In the view of this court that is an incorrect statement of the law and the passage which is cited in Archbold, which comes from *R* v *Nowell* (1948) 64 TLR 277, 278 is taken out of its context. In that case the argument before the court was based on the fact that a doctor who had examined a defendant had explained to him that it might be in his own interests to allow the doctor to examine him. The defendant eventually agreed to be examined and was examined by the doctor, who certified that owing to his consumption of alcohol, the defendant was unfit to drive a car. The argument was that the doctor should be treated as if he were an arm of the police and that there was an inducement held out to the defendant which made the evidence of the doctor as to the result of his examination inadmissible. That argument was sought to be supported by a decision of the Scots court, *Reid* v *Nixon* and *Dumigan* v *Brown* 1948 SC(J) 68, and the passage now incorporated in Archbold appeared at the end of the judgment in the Court of Criminal Appeal where they were dealing with that. After referring to the two cases, the court said (1948) 64 TLR 277, 278:

> It is not necessary to read the judgment of the court which was given by the Lord Justice-General, who made a number of general observations with regard to the principles on which he suggested police officers and doctors should act in examining persons who are charged with such an offence as this. The Lord Advocate, according to the judgment of the Lord Justice-General, had stated that in all such cases the police surgeon or other doctor summoned by the police to conduct an examination was acting as the hand of the police and not as an independent medical referee. This court can only say that it does not agree that that state of affairs, whether it exists in Scotland or not, exists in this country. Our view is that the evidence of a doctor, whether he be a police surgeon or anyone else, should be accepted, unless the doctor himself shows that it ought not to be, as the evidence of a professional man giving independent expert evidence with the sole desire of assisting the court.

What that passage meant in that context was that the evidence should be treated, as regards admissibility and other matters of that kind, like that of any other independent witness. But taken out of its context, the use of the word 'accepted' may well, we think, give to the jury a false impression of the weight to be given to a doctor's evidence. It is therefore desirable that in subsequent editions of Archbold that passage, which was read by the deputy recorder in this case, should be corrected.

Having said that, however, this, in the view of this court, is the clearest possible case in which to apply the proviso. On the evidence before the jury no jury properly directed could have possibly found the appellant otherwise than guilty of the offence.

Appeal dismissed.

Anderson v R
[1972] AC 100
Privy Council

The appellant was charged with murder. He put forward a defence of alibi but was convicted chiefly on circumstantial evidence and sentenced to death. He appealed against conviction to the Appeal Court of Jamaica on the ground, *inter alia,* that there had been a misdirection by the trial judge. The Court of Appeal held that there had been a misdirection but that no substantial miscarriage of justice had occurred and they applied the proviso to s. 13(1) of the Judicature (Appellate Jurisdiction) Law 1962 and dismissed the appeal. A further appeal was made to the Judicial Committee.

LORD GUEST: . . . The complaint which formed the basis of the Court of Appeal's judgment related to the trial judge's summing up in regard to the condition of the accused's boots. It should be explained that when the accused was arrested on December 25, his water boots were found and also a piece of cardboard from inside the boots. He admitted wearing the boots on the night of December 23. Mr Garriques a forensic expert examined the water boots and the cardboard on December 28. He found no human blood on the water boots. In his summing up the trial judge referred to the water boots in this way:

He [Mr Garriques] says there was no blood on the shoes — well, that is merely his opinion, members of the jury, you are not bound to accept it because he happens to be an expert in this particular field. An expert is brought before you merely to guide and assist you in evaluating evidence of a particular nature, he being trained in that particular field therefor. You will weigh well what an expert has said before you discard his evidence because neither you nor I is trained in that particular field in the same way that Mr Garriques would weigh well what I would have to say in the field of law, because he is not trained in that particular field. But you are still judges of the facts and you may accept or reject evidence of the expert.

The Court of Appeal considered that this was a serious misdirection because the judge was inviting the jury to disregard the evidence of the expert to the effect that there was no blood on the boots and form their own opinion as to whether there was blood upon the boots.

So far as the piece of cardboard is concerned this was found by Detective Constable Dwyer on his visit to the accused's home on December 25. It was in the right foot of the water boots which the accused said he was wearing on December 23. It had brown marks resembling blood stains. Mr Garriques said that on his examination on December 28 he found that those marks were human blood stains. The stains must have been about two weeks old but they could have been there before two weeks. In his opinion it was not more recent than two weeks. It might have been older. It was definitely not a fresh stain.

The trial judge in his summing up to the jury when dealing with Mr Garriques' evidence said that the witness found human blood. 'In his opinion they were then about two weeks old.' There is no doubt that in the summing up a confusion might have arisen in the jury's mind as to whether blood on the cardboard could have been of more recent origin than two weeks. Their Lordships are prepared to accept, following the Court of Appeal, that there were misdirections by the trial judge in regard to the boots and in regard to the cardboard.

Their Lordships do not agree with counsel for the respondent that these were subsidiary matters. These were serious misdirections as the Court of Appeal have held. There was no evidence of blood on the boots or the cardboard that could have implicated the accused. (His Lordship went on to consider the question of the proviso and affirmed the judgment of the Court of Appeal of Jamaica.)

Appeal dismissed.

Note

In the course of his research, the expert witness will often refer to the works of other experts in the same field. An expert will commonly base his own opinion on matters he has derived from the studies and works of others as well as his own experience and knowledge. The question then arises as to what extent, if at all, the expert witness may refer to the works of others which have influenced his own testimony. If the work of expert B is offered as evidence of the facts it contains by expert A during the course of his testimony, does this not infringe the rule against hearsay?

English Exporters (London) Limited v *Eldonwall Limited*
[1973] Ch 415
Chancery Division

By an originating summons the plaintiff tenants applied, pursuant to Part II of the Landlord and Tenant Act 1954, for the grant by the defendant landlords of a new tenancy of certain premises. By a summons the landlords applied under s. 24(A) of the Act for the determination of an interim rent while the tenancy continued under the provisions of the Act. During the hearing two valuers gave evidence as expert witnesses.

MEGARRY J: As is usual in these cases, a number of comparables was adduced. Eight were put forward by the landlords: the tenants put in none of their own. As is also far from unknown, some of the comparables were less comparable than others, and some turned out to be supported only by hearsay evidence, or by evidence that was in other respects less than cogent. There was no formal process of a ruling being made to exclude those comparables which were supported only by hearsay evidence; but I was discouraging, and in the event Mr Ibbotson, though rueful, did not seriously argue the point, or press it. I nevertheless think that I ought to make more explicit the reasons for my having been discouraging, for in my experience the status of hearsay evidence of comparables in valuation cases is a matter that is often misunderstood, and not only by valuers . . . .

Let me put on one side the cases in which exceptions to the rule excluding hearsay evidence have grown up, whether by case law or by statute (and sometimes almost by a side-wind; see, for example, *In re Koscot Interplanetary (UK) Ltd* [1972] 3 All ER 829); and in particular I exclude cases in which, subject to observing the statutory safeguards, hearsay evidence has been made admissible under the Civil Evidence Act 1968. Let me further ignore cases in which questions in cross-examination may have let in evidence that otherwise would be inadmissible, and confine myself to the admissibility of hearsay in chief and in re-examination in these valuation cases. In such circumstances, two of the heads under which the valuers' evidence may be ranged are opinion evidence and factual evidence. As an expert witness, the valuer is entitled to express his opinion about matters within his field of competence. In building up his opinions about values, he will no doubt have learned much from transactions in which he has himself been engaged, and of which he could give first-hand evidence. But he will also have learned much from many other sources, including much of which he could give no first-hand evidence. Textbooks, journals, reports of auctions and other dealings, and information obtained from his professional brethren and others, some related to particular transactions and some more general and indefinite, will all have contributed their share. Doubtless much, or most, of this will be accurate, though some will not; and even what is accurate so far as it goes may be incomplete, in that nothing may have been said of some special element which effects values. Nevertheless, the opinion that the expert expresses is none the worse because it is in part derived from the matters of which he could give no direct evidence. Even if some of the extraneous information which he acquires in this way is inaccurate or incomplete, the errors and omissions will often tend to cancel each other out; and the valuer, after all, is an expert in this field, so that the less reliable the knowledge that he has about the details of some reported transaction, the more his experience will tell him that he should be ready to make some discount from the weight that he gives it in contributing to his overall sense of values. Some aberrant transactions may stand so far out of line that he will give them little or no weight. No question of giving hearsay evidence arises in such cases; the witness states his opinion from his general experience.

Putting matters shortly, and leaving on one side the matters that I have mentioned, such as the Civil Evidence Act 1968 and anything made admissible by questions in cross-examination, in my judgment a valuer giving expert evidence in chief (or in re-examination): (a) may express the opinions that he has formed as to values even though substantial contributions to the formation of those opinions have been made by matters of which he has no first-hand knowledge; (b) may give evidence as to the details of any transactions within his personal knowledge, in order to establish them as matters of fact; and (c) may express his opinion as to the significance of any transactions which are or will be proved by admissible evidence (whether or not given by him) in relation to the valuation with which he is concerned; but (d) may not give hearsay evidence stating the details of any transactions not within his personal knowledge in order to establish them as matters of fact. To those propositions I would add that for counsel to put in a list of comparables ought to amount to a warranty by him of his intention to tender admissible evidence of all that is shown on the list.

R v Abadom
[1983] 1 WLR 126
Court of Appeal

The appellant was charged with robbery and it was alleged that he was one of four masked men armed with cudgels, who had entered an office, broken an internal window pane and demanded money from the occupants. A principal scientific officer gave evidence at the trial that he had analysed fragments of glass from a pair of shoes belonging to the appellant and glass from the office window and found that all the pieces of glass had the same refractive index. It was the practice of the Home Office Central Research Establishment to collate statistics of the refractive index of broken glass which had been analysed in forensic laboratories and, having consulted those statistics, he found that only four per cent of samples had the same refractive index as the glass he had analysed. He expressed the opinion that it was strong evidence that the fragments of glass on the appellant's shoes had come from the broken window pane. The appellant was convicted and appealed.

KERR LJ: . . .The point taken on this appeal was that the evidence of Mr Cooke, that the identical refractive index of the fragments of glass with that of the control sample occurred in only four per cent of all controlled glass samples analysed and statistically collated in the Home Office Central Research Establishment, was inadmissible because it constituted hearsay evidence. It was said to be hearsay because Mr Cooke had no personal knowledge of the analyses whose results were collated in these statistics, save possibly a few for which he may have been personally responsible. This submission was challenged on behalf of the Crown, but no point was taken, in our view clearly rightly, on the ground that the admissibility of this evidence had not been challenged on behalf of the defence at the trial. In our view, the evidence was not inadmissible as hearsay. It is convenient to deal with this issue first on the basis of general principle and then to consider the authorities.

Mr Cooke was admittedly an expert, and was giving evidence as an expert, on the likelihood or otherwise of the fragments of glass having come from the control sample, the broken window. As an expert in this field he was entitled to express an opinion on this question, subject to laying the foundation for his opinion and subject, of course, to his evidence being tested by cross-examination for evaluation by the jury. In the context of evidence given by experts it is no more than a statement of the obvious that, in reaching their conclusion, they must be entitled to draw upon material produced by others in the field in which their expertise lies. Indeed, it is part of their duty to consider any material which may be available in their field, and not to draw conclusions merely on the basis of their own experience, which is inevitably likely to be more limited than the general body of information which may be available to them. Further, when an expert has to consider the likelihood or unlikelihood of some occurrence or factual association in reaching his conclusion, as must often be necessary, the statistical results of the work of others in the same field must inevitably form an important ingredient in the cogency or probative value of his own conclusion in the particular case. Relative probabilities or improbabilities must frequently be an important factor in the evaluation of any expert opinion and, when any reliable statistical material is available which bears upon this question, it must be part of the function and duty of the expert to take this into account.

However, it is also inherent in the nature of any statistical information that it will result from the work of others in the same field, whether or not the expert in question will himself have contributed to the bank of information available on the particular topic on which he is called upon to express his opinion. Indeed, to exclude reliance upon such information on the ground that it is inadmissible under the hearsay rule, might inevitably lead to the distortion or unreliability of the opinion which the expert presents for evaluation by a judge or jury. Thus, in the present case, the probative value or otherwise of the identity of the refractive index as between the fragments and the control sample could not be assessed without some further information about the frequency of its occurrence. If all glass of the type in question had the same refractive index, this evidence would have virtually no probative value whatever. The extent to which this refractive index is common or uncommon must therefore be something which an expert must be entitled to take into account, and indeed must take into

account, before he can properly express an opinion about the likelihood or unlikelihood of the fragments of glass having come from the window in question. The
cogency or otherwise of the expert's conclusion on this point, in the light of, *inter alia,*
the available statistical material against which this conclusion falls to be tested, must
then be a matter for the jury.

We therefore consider that Mr Cooke's reliance on the statistical information
collated by the Home Office Central Research Establishment, before arriving at his
conclusion about the likely relationship between the fragments of glass and the control
sample, was not only permissible in principle, but that it was an essential part of his
function as an expert witness to take account of this material.

It was submitted that the present case was indistinguishable from the decision in
Myers v *Director of Public Prosecutions* [1965] AC 1001 since Mr Cooke had not been
personally responsible for the compilation of the Home Office statistics on which he
relied, so that the inferences which he drew from them must be inadmissible because
they were based on hearsay. In our view this conclusion does not follow, either as a
matter of principle or on the basis of authority. We are here concerned with the
cogency or otherwise of an opinion expressed by an expert in giving expert evidence.
In that regard it seems to us that the process of taking account of information
stemming from the work of others in the same field is an essential ingredient of the
nature of expert evidence. So far as the question of principle is concerned, we have
already explained our reasons for this conclusion. So far as the authorities are
concerned, the position can be summarised as follows.

First, where an expert relies on the existence or non-existence of some fact which
is basic to the question on which he is asked to express his opinion, that fact must be
proved by admissible evidence: see *English Exporters (London) Ltd* v *Eldonwall Ltd*
[1973] Ch 415, 421 *per* Megarry J and *R* v *Turner (Terence)* [1975] QB 834, 840.
Thus, it would no doubt have been inadmissible if Mr Cooke had said in the present
case that he had been told by somebody else that the refractive index of the fragments
of glass and of the control sample was identical, and any opinion expressed by him on
this basis would then have been based on hearsay. If he had not himself determined
the refractive index, it would have been necessary to call the person who had done so
before Mr Cooke could have expressed any opinion based on this determination. In
this connection it is to be noted that Mr Smalldon was rightly called to prove the
chemical analysis made by him which Mr Cooke was asked to take into account.
Secondly, where the existence or non-existence of some fact is in issue, a report made
by an expert who is not called as a witness is not admissible as evidence of that fact
merely by the production of the report, even though it was made by an expert: see for
instance *R* v *Crayden* [1978] 1 WLR 604, 607c.

These, however, are in our judgment the limits of the hearsay rule in relation to
evidence of opinion given by experts, both in principle and on the authorities. In other
respects their evidence is not subject to the rule against hearsay in the same way as
that of witnesses of fact: see *English Exporters* v *Eldonwall* [1973] Ch 415, 420d and
Phipson on Evidence, 12th ed (1976), para. 1207. Once the primary facts on which
their opinion is based have been proved by admissible evidence, they are entitled to
draw on the work of others as part of the process of arriving at their conclusion.
However, where they have done so, they should refer to this material in their evidence
so that the cogency and probative value of their conclusion can be tested and
evaluated by reference to it.

Thus, if in the present case the statistical tables of analyses made by the Home
Office forensic laboratories had appeared in a textbook or other publication, it could
not be doubted that Mr Cooke would have been entitled to rely upon them for the

purposes of his evidence. Indeed, this was not challenged. But it does not seem to us, in relation to the reliability of opinion evidence given by experts, that they must necessarily limit themselves to drawing on material which has been published in some form. Part of their experience and expertise may well lie in their knowledge of unpublished material and in their evaluation of it. The only rule in this regard, as it seems to us, is that they should refer to such material in their evidence for the reasons stated above.

We accordingly conclude that Mr Cooke's reliance on the Home Office statistics did not infringe the rule against hearsay . . .

Appeal dismissed.

H and Another v *Schering Chemicals Ltd and Another*
[1983] 1 WLR 143
Court of Appeal

BINGHAM J: . . . It is, as I have said, common ground that these articles can be referred to by experts as part of the general corpus of medical knowledge falling within the expertise of an expert in this field. That of course means that an expert who says (and I am looking at it from the plaintiffs' point of view for purposes of my example) 'I consider that there is a causal connection between the taking of the drug and the resulting deformity', can fortify his opinion by referring to learned articles, publications, letters as reinforcing the view to which he has come. In doing so, he can make reference to papers in which a contrary opinion may be expressed but in which figures are set out which he regards as supporting his contention. In such a situation one asks: Are the figures and statistics set out in such an article strictly proved? and I think the answer is no. I think that they are nonetheless of probative value when referred to and relied on by an expert in the manner in which I have indicated. If an expert refers to the results of research published by a reputable authority in a reputable journal the court would, I think, ordinarily regard those results as supporting inferences fairly to be drawn from them, unless or until a different approach was shown to be proper.

Let me apply that to this case. Mr Beldam submits that there are great dangers in relying on these results contained in this material. For example, he says that certain of them refer to pills having been prescribed but leave it uncertain whether the pills were taken. If the pills were taken the results as published often leave it unclear at what stage of a pregnancy they were taken. Were they, for example, taken at a stage when it was too late for the foetus to be affected by the pills, even if they were capable of having an injurious effect in other circumstances? How were the control cases matched? How were the histories taken? How were the cases identified, and so on? All of these are valid points which will fall to be considered and assessed when they are made and when they are put to and discussed with any expert who relies on the articles. It may be that some of the answers will be found in the papers themselves. It may be that other matters will be left in doubt. It may very well be that grounds will emerge for viewing the results of the research with caution or scepticism. But in my judgment the proper approach of this court is to admit the articles, in the sense of reading them, and to give the factual assertions in those articles such weight as appears to the court, having heard any cross-examination or other evidence, to be proper.

That this is the proper approach I think derives support from the judgment of Cooke J in *Seyfang* v *Searle (GD) & Co.* [1973] QB 148. That was a case in which there was litigation in the United States on a somewhat similar issue to the present issue, the issue in that case being whether there was a causative link between the taking of the contraceptive pill and thrombo-embolic disorder. One of the parties to the United States litigation sought to subpoena certain British experts who had published the results of their research on this subject, for the purpose of establishing the causative link on which they relied. In the course of giving his judgment, Cooke J said, at p. 151:

> Mr Baggott says in his affidavit that taking the testimony of the two doctors is the only way in which he can get the contents of the four articles into evidence in the action. While I accept that as a correct statement of Ohio law, in the absence of evidence to the contrary, I must confess that I find it surprising. The four articles now form part of the corpus of medical expertise on this particular subject. I apprehend that in England a medical expert witness with the proper qualifications would be allowed to refer to the articles as part of that corpus of expertise, even though he was not the author of the articles himself. It does appear to me with the greatest respect that a system which does not permit experts to refer in their expert evidence to the publications of other experts in the same field is a system which puts peculiar difficulties in the way of proof of matters which depend on expert opinion.

That seems to me with respect to be the right approach to the matter, and I say so with the greater diffidence having regard to the fact that I think the judge's observations reflect a submission made to him by counsel for the doctors in that case.

Accordingly the plaintiffs are, in my judgment, entitled by means of expert evidence to incorporate the contents of the articles in their evidence in this case, and it will be given such weight as in the light of any other evidence and of any cross-examination appears to be proper.

Civil Evidence Act 1972

1. Application of Part I of Civil Evidence Act 1968 to statements of opinion
    (1) Subject to the provisions of this section, Part I (hearsay evidence) of the Civil Evidence Act 1968, except section 5 (statements produced by computers), shall apply in relation to statements of opinion as it applies in relation to statements of fact, subject to the necessary modifications and in particular the modification that any reference to a fact stated in a statement shall be construed as a reference to a matter dealt with therein.
    (2) Section 4 (admissibility of certain records) of the Civil Evidence Act 1968, as applied by subsection (1) above, shall not render admissibile in any civil proceedings a statement of opinion contained in a record unless that statement would be admissible in those proceedings if made in the course of giving oral evidence by the person who originally supplied the information from which the record was compiled; but where a statement of opinion contained in a record deals with a matter on which the person who originally supplied the information from which the record was compiled is (or would if living be) qualified to give oral expert evidence, the said section 4, as applied by subsection (1) above, shall have effect in relation to that statement as if so much of subsection (1) of that section as requires personal knowledge on the part of that person were omitted.

3. Admissibility of expert opinion and certain expressions of non-expert opinion
    (1) Subject to any rules of court . . . where a person is called as a witness in any civil proceedings, his opinion on any relevant matter on which he is qualified to give expert evidence, shall be admissible in evidence . . .

Criminal Justice Act 1988

30. Expert reports

(1) An expert report shall be admissible as evidence in criminal proceedings, whether or not the person making it attends to give oral evidence in those proceedings.

(2) If it is proposed that the person making the report shall not give oral evidence, the report shall only be admissible with the leave of the court.

(3) For the purpose of determining whether to give leave the court shall have regard —

(a) to the contents of the report;

(b) to the reasons why it is proposed that the person making the report shall not give oral evidence;

(c) to any risk, having regard in particular to whether it is likely to be possible to controvert statements in the report if the person making it does not attend to give oral evidence in the proceedings, that its admission or exclusion will result in unfairness to the accused or, if there is more than one, to any of them; and

(d) to any other circumstances that appear to the court to be relevant.

(4) An expert report, when admitted, shall be evidence of any fact or opinion of which the person making it could have given oral evidence.

(5) In this section 'expert report' means a written report by a person dealing wholly or mainly with matters on which he is (or would if living be) qualified to give expert evidence.

Criminal Procedure Act 1865

8. Comparison of disputed writing with writing proved to be genuine
Comparison of a disputed writing with any writing proved to the satisfaction of the judge to be genuine shall be permitted to be made by witnesses; and such writings, and the evidence of witnesses respecting the same, may be submitted to the court and jury as evidence of the genuineness or otherwise of the writing in dispute.

R v Tilley
[1961] 1 WLR 1309
Court of Criminal Appeal

The appellants, G and L, were both charged with the larceny of a car. Their case was that they had bought it from a person claiming to be the owner and from whom they had obtained a receipt, which they produced. At the trial, in cross-examination, each appellant was asked to write out the words of the receipt. G's handwriting was plainly different, but there were similarities between L's writing and that on the receipt. Counsel for the prosecution did not pursue the matter, as it was the prosecution case that the receipt was a document devised by the appellants in order to explain their possession of the car if questioned, and that it was not of great importance whether they or someone else had written it. The matter was not mentioned again until the summing up, when the deputy chairman commented upon the similarities and invited the jury to decide whether or not the receipt was genuine, giving the jury the receipt and the handwriting exhibits to examine. G and L were convicted and appealed.

ASHWORTH J: . . . [C]riticism is now made by Mr Simpson on behalf of the two appellants that it was not right or fair that the defence should suddenly be met with this kind of address to the jury on a topic which had never been ventilated throughout the trial. Moreover, it was said that the topic was one on which the Crown had not relied, and in regard to it, if the defendants had had an opportunity they might have been in a position to call expert evidence. Those criticisms were, we think, of considerable force. But the matter goes even further. The question arises whether in any case it was proper for the deputy chairman to indulge in comments himself about these documents and then hand them to the jury for their consideration and decision without any evidence having been called to assist them on that issue.

The matter has come before the court in more than one previous case. One to which our attention was called was *R* v *Harvey* (1869) 11 Cox CC 546. The matter was also raised in *R* v *Rickard* (1918) 13 Cr App R 140. In that case Salter J, giving the judgment of this court, said this, after referring to section 8 of the Criminal Procedure Act, 1865 (Lord Denman's Act) ibid, 143:

That case [*R* v *Crouch* (1850) 4 Cox CC 163] does not decide what degree of preparation is necessary to constitute an expert, but it does decide that a person is not entitled to give such evidence if his only knowledge on the subject is that acquired in the course of the case. That was the position of the police officer, and the position of Busby is less satisfactory. Therefore no expert evidence at all was given in the case. This court does not decide that expert evidence in such cases is necessary, and the observations of Blackburn J in *Harvey* 11 Cox CC 546 do not so decide, but it is clear from the nature of things that to leave a question of handwriting to a jury without assistance is a somewhat dangerous course.

In the present case there was no evidence, not even questions directed to alleged similarities, and the matter only arose in the course of the summing up. This court endorses and reaffirms the statement of principle to be found in Salter J's judgment on behalf of this court in *Rickard's* case. A jury should not be left unassisted to decide questions of disputed handwriting on their own.

It is also to be noted that, although *R* v *Day* [1940] 1 All ER 402 raised in the main an utterly different issue, the question of handwriting did occur, and Croom-Johnson J ruled that the jury could not be asked to compare handwriting, without some assistance by way of expert evidence, and that ruling was once again in conformity with the decision in *Rickard's* case.

In these circumstances, in the view of this court, it is right to say that the course pursued by the deputy chairman was not in accordance with the principles previously laid down, and should not be followed in any other case.

Appeals allowed.

R v *O'Sullivan*
[1969] 1 WLR 497
Court of Appeal

The defendant, an employee of a firm whose custom it was to make overnight deposits in the night safe of their bank in wallets, was charged with the larceny as a servant of a wallet containing £411. The evidence was that a man had asked a bank official for the firm's wallet by number, and had signed for it on a register; that the bank official recognised the man as the defendant, whom she had seen several times, and later picked him out at an identification parade; and that only four people besides the defendant knew the number of the firm's wallet. Photostatic copies of the register on which appeared the signature of the man who had taken the wallet, as well as admittedly genuine signatures of the defendant, were given to the jury. At the outset of the trial the defence did not dispute, but later disputed that the signature of the man who had taken the wallet was that of the defendant, but no expert witness on handwriting gave evidence. The deputy chairman warned the jury of the dangers implicit in making comparisons of handwriting without the help of experts.

The defendant appealed against conviction, on the ground that the jury should not have been left to make the handwriting comparisons on their own.

WINN LJ: . . . It seems to this court that possibly there has been a misunderstanding from a very early date of what was said by Blackburn J in *R v Harvey* (1867) 11 Cox CC 546. That was a case where there had been an objection taken by the defence to certain evidence found in the house of the prisoner, certain copy books said to contain his handwriting, on the ground that police officers are not competent to give evidence as experts as to handwriting. The judge — and he has been accepted as one of the greatest judges this country has ever had the fortune to possess — said at p. 548:

> But the jury can inspect them and compare them with the forged document . . . they are only copy books . . . the evidence is very weak, and I do not think the jury ought to act upon it without the assistance of an expert. The policeman is certainly not a skilled witness.

and in three lines he gave his ruling: 'But here we have no expert, and I do not think it would be right to let the jury compare the handwriting without some such assistance. The evidence is very slight.' It seems to this court today that that was a ruling of a very narrow character indeed. The judge was saying 'in this particular case (a) we have no expert (b) the evidence is of very poor evidentiary value; therefore I am going to exercise my discretion in not allowing it to go to the jury.'

There has been a long sequence of authority and really it does not merit the time that otherwise would be taken that this court should go right through all those cases. The case of *R v Tilley* [1961] 1 WLR 1309 is undoubtedly the most important, most prominent, of the decisions and was a case where Ashworth J giving the judgment of the Court of Criminal Appeal, of which it happened that I was myself the junior member, used this expression which this court today, no longer the Court of Criminal Appeal but the Court of Appeal, Criminal Division, thinks has been not only misinterpreted to some extent but has been more widely applied and held to be of stricter restrictive effect than really is justified by the words of the court. This was said, at p. 1312: 'In the present case there was no evidence, not even questions directed to alleged similarities, and the matter only arose in the course of the summing up.' That point stresses the importance of what Mr Gale said to the court today in his submission, that it may very well be the proper practice where the prosecution does or should anticipate that there will be an issue as to the genuineness of some signature, that the prosecution should tender a witness who is properly expert to give evidence on that matter; in *R v Tilley*, as in the instant case, the matter only arose long after the trial had begun, at a time when even if the matter were dealt with by rebuttal, almost certainly there would have to be a second trial rather than such a long adjournment as would be required to obtain the expert advice. There was no evidence in *R* v *Tilley,* said the judge, and the matter only arose in the course of the summing up. He went on, at p. 1312:

> This court endorses and reaffirms the statement of principle to be found in Salter J's judgment on behalf of this court in *Rickard's* case ((1918) 13 Cr App R 140). A jury should not be left unassisted to decide questions of disputed handwriting on their own.

The question arises whether within the proper understanding of those words in the instant case the jury was 'left unassisted to decide questions of disputed handwriting.' The document had to go before the jury in the instant case since it formed part of the probative material establishing the visit by the man who took away the wallet and the fact that he had entered somebody's name in the register of the bank. The jury was not in the instant case invited to make any comparisons, as the jury had been in *R* v *Tilley.* The chairman in the instant case did not himself purport to make any comments of any kind about similarities or dissimilarities as had been done by the deputy chairman in *R* v *Tilley.* The jury were warned very, very carefully and stringently not to make these comparisons.

In the circumstances, it does not seem to this court that the jury in the instant case can be said to have been left to decide questions of disputed handwriting on their own. It is true they were not effectively prevented from doing it. What could possibly have been done effectively to prevent them from making the comparison passes the comprehension of this court. It can hardly be right to suppose that the documents already before them for a legitimate, proper and necessary purpose should have been snatched away from them since that could only have aroused dissatisfaction and grave doubt in their minds as to the fairness of the proceedings which were being conducted before them.

There have been subsequent references; it is right that I should say that one of them was a part of a judgment of mine in *R* v *Stannard* (1964) 48 Cr App R 81, a case which was quite a complicated and heavy appeal and I note on looking back at it — I well remember the burden of the judgment — that the judgment when reported extends over no less than twelve pages. A very subsidiary issue on the appeal was whether or not there had been any impropriety in the manner in which the jury were allowed to look at certain signatures. I attempted then, at p. 95, to give what, on looking at it again, I feel was not a very satisfactory paraphrase of the earlier case of *R* v *Tilley* [1961] 1 WLR 1309. I referred to the undoubtedly correct statement by Salter J in *R* v *Rickard* (13 Cr App R 140, 143) that the 'court does not decide that expert evidence in such cases is necessary and the observations of Blackburn J in *Harvey* (11 Cox CC 546, 548) do not so decide.' I referred to the danger involved. Then I said: 'The situation here was quite the obverse of the medal, because what [defending counsel] desired to have from the learned judge was a direction that they *should* make this comparison.'

It seems to the court that in the instant case the matter was properly dealt with. The fact remains that there is a very real danger where the jury make such comparisons, but as a matter of practical reality all that can be done is to ask them not to make the comparisons themselves and to have vividly in mind the fact that they are not qualified to make comparisons. It is terribly risky for jurors to attempt comparisons of writing unless they have very special training in this particular science. All possible was done, this court thinks, with great care and very fairly by the court in the instant case. It may well be that, despite it, the jury did try to make comparisons. That is really unavoidable and it should be accepted these days that *R v Tilley* [1961] 1 WLR 1309 cannot always be in its literal meaning exactly applied; nevertheless every possible step and regard should be had to what was said by the court in that case, inasmuch as never should it be deliberately a matter of invitation or exhortation to a jury to look at disputed handwriting. There should be a warning of the dangers; further than that, as a matter of practical reality, it cannot be expected that the court will go.

Appeal dismissed.

(B)   Functions of expert evidence

It has been suggested that by admitting expert evidence of opinion, the function of the jury may be usurped. An expert medical witness might testify as to the state of the defendant's mental health but should he be allowed to state further that, in his opinion, the defendant is insane? Is this not the very issue the jury have to decide upon? In civil cases, this problem of receiving opinion evidence on the 'ultimate issue' has been resolved by s. 3(3) of the Civil Evidence Act 1972 (see further (C) below). In criminal cases, the true position remains unclear although many writers suggest that, at least in practice, the courts do admit such evidence.

What seems to be clearer, is that where the matter in issue falls within the competence and understanding of the jury, expert evidence of opinion will remain inadmissible.

R v Chard
(1971) 56 Cr App R 268
Court of Appeal

The applicant was convicted of murder. His defence was provocation. He sought to call a doctor who had reported that there was nothing wrong with his mental state but was of the opinion that in the light of his personality he had no intent or *mens rea* to commit murder. The judge ruled that the evidence was inadmissible. The applicant applied for leave to appeal.

ROSKILL LJ: . . . Mr Back has not sought to say that that expression of Dr Mansbridge's opinion could have been admissible on the issue of provocation and plainly he was right to make that concession at the trial and to repeat it before this Court. But he has sought to say that Dr Mansbridge's opinion on the question of the supposed inability of the applicant to form any intent to kill or to do grievous bodily injury, which are, of course, the two relevant alternative constituents of murder, was admissible. He put the matter before us in this way. Whenever, he said, a mental element arises, whether the charge be murder or theft or for that matter grievous bodily harm with intent charged under section 18 of the Offences Against the Person Act 1861, and a question arises in which the decision of the jury is difficult because of their lack of experience, the jury is entitled to expert assistance. Mr Back was unable to cite any authority in support of that proposition, not altogether surprisingly, for with the greatest respect to his argument, it seems to this Court that his submission, if accepted, would involve the Court admitting medical evidence in other cases not where there was an issue, for example, of insanity or diminished responsibility but where the sole issue which the jury had to consider, as happens in scores of different kinds of cases, was the question of intent.

As Geoffrey Lane J said in the course of argument, one purpose of jury trials is to bring into the jury box a body of men and women who are able to judge ordinary day-to-day questions by their own standards, that is, the standards in the eyes of the law of theoretically ordinary reasonable men and women. That is something which they are well able by their ordinary experience to judge for themselves. Where the matters in issue go outside experience and they are invited to deal with someone supposedly abnormal, for example, supposedly suffering from insanity or diminished responsibility, then plainly in such a case they are entitled to the benefit of expert evidence. But where, as in the present case, they are dealing with someone who by concession was on the medical evidence entirely normal, it seems to this Court abundantly plain, on first principles of the admissibility of expert evidence, that it is not permissible to call a witness, whatever his personal experience, merely to tell the jury how he thinks an accused man's mind — assumedly a normal mind — operated at the time of the alleged crime with reference to the crucial question of what that man's intention was. As I have already said, this applicant was by concession normal in the eyes of the law.

Mr Back suggested that if this evidence were of no value, it could have been demolished by counsel for the Crown or perhaps by the learned trial judge in the summing-up. That submission, with respect, is of no relevance on the question whether or not the evidence was admissible. That consideration, if relevant at all, would go to weight, and questions of weight are in general irrelevant on questions of admissibility.

Application refused.

Lowery v The Queen
[1974] AC 85
Privy Council

The appellant and K were charged with the murder of a young girl. It was a sadistic killing and the only explanation put forward for it was that they had wanted to see what it was like to 'kill a chick'. The Crown's case was that they had been acting in concert but both the appellant's and K's defence was that the other had killed the girl. The appellant gave evidence of his good character, stressed the unlikelihood of his behaving in such a manner and said that, because of his fear of K, he had been unable to prevent the murder. K alleged that he had been unable to appreciate what was happening and had been powerless to prevent the appellant killing the girl as he had been under the influence of drugs. Despite the appellant's objection, the defence for K was allowed to call the evidence of a psychologist as to their respective personalities and, on that evidence, the jury were invited to conclude that the appellant was the more likely of the two to have killed the girl. They were both convicted and the appellant unsuccessfully appealed to the full Court of the Supreme Court of Victoria on the ground, *inter alia,* that the psychologist's evidence was inadmissible. He further appealed to the Privy Council.

LORD MORRIS OF BORTH-Y-GEST: . . . Having referred fully to the nature of the evidence given by Professor Cox the question as to its admissibility may now be considered. There was no doubt that Rosalyn Mary Nolte was killed in the bush area some 10 miles out of Hamilton when Lowery and King were present and when no one else was present. As was pointed out in the Court of Criminal Appeal the very nature of the killing showed that it was 'a sadistic and otherwise motiveless killing'. Any prospect of the acquittal of either of the two accused could only have been on the basis that one alone was the killer and that the other took no part whatsoever. That was what Lowery alleged when he said that King alone was the killer and that he (Lowery) was powerless to save the girl. In *R v Miller* (1952) 36 Cr App R 169, Devlin J referred to the duty of counsel for the defence to adduce any admissible evidence which is strictly relevant to his own case and assists his client whether or not it prejudices anyone else. The case for King was that Lowery had alone been the killer and that King had been heavily under the influence of drugs and had been powerless to stop Lowery. It was furthermore the evidence of each of them, in spite of what they said in their statements, that the idea or suggestion of seeing 'what it would be like to kill a chick' emanated from the other. In all these circumstances it was necessary on behalf of King to call all relevant and admissible evidence which would exonerate King and throw responsibility entirely on Lowery. If in imaginary circumstances similar to those of this case it was apparent that one of the accused was a man of great physical strength whereas the other was a weakling it could hardly be doubted that in forming an opinion as to the probabilities it would be relevant to have the disparity between the two in mind. Physical characteristics may often be of considerable relevance: see *R v Toohey* [1965] AC 595. The evidence of Professor Cox was not related to crime or criminal tendencies: it was scientific evidence as to the respective personalities of the two accused as, and to the extent, revealed by certain well known tests. Whether it assisted the jury is not a matter that can be known. All that is known is that the jury convicted both the accused. But in so far as it might help in considering the probabilities as to what happened at the spot to which the girl was taken it was not only relevant to and indeed necessary for the case advanced by King but it was made relevant and admissible in view of the case advanced by Lowery and in view of Lowery's assertions against King.

The case being put forward by counsel on behalf of King involved posing to the jury the question 'which of these two men is the more likely to have killed this girl?' and inviting the jury to come to the conclusion that it was Lowery. If the crime was one which was committed apparently without any kind of motive unless it was for the sensation experienced in the killing then unless both men acted in concert the deed was that of one of them. It would be unjust to prevent either of them from calling any evidence of probative value which could point to the probability that the perpetrator was the one rather than the other.

Appeal dismissed.

R v Turner
[1975] QB 834
Court of Appeal

The defendant, who was charged with murder, admitted that he had killed his girl friend by hitting her with a hammer, but pleaded that he had been provoked by her statement that she had had affairs with other men and that he was not the father of her expected child. The defence sought to call a psychiatrist to give his opinion that the defendant was not suffering from a mental illness, that he was not violent by nature but that his personality was such that he could have been provoked in the circumstances and that he was likely to be telling the truth. The judge ruled the psychiatric evidence inadmissible. The defendant was convicted and appealed.

LAWTON LJ: Before this court Mr Mildon submitted that the psychiatrist's opinion as to the defendant's personality and mental make-up as set out in his report was relevant and admissible for three reasons: first, because it helped to establish lack of intent; secondly, because it helped to establish that the defendant was likely to be easily provoked; and thirdly, because it helped to show that the defendant's account of what had happened was likely to be true. We do not find it necessary to deal specifically with the first of these reasons. Intent was not a live issue in this case. The evidence was tendered on the issues of provocation and credibility. The judge gave his ruling in relation to those issues. In any event the decision which we have come to on Mr Mildon's second and third submissions *would also apply to* his first.

The first question on both these issues is whether the psychiatrist's opinion was relevant. A man's personality and mental make-up do have a bearing upon his conduct. A quick-tempered man will react more aggressively to an unpleasing situation than a placid one. Anyone having a florid imagination or a tendency to exaggerate is less likely to be a reliable witness than one who is precise and careful. These are matters of ordinary human experience. Opinions from knowledgeable persons about a man's personality and mental make-up play a part in many human judgments. In our judgment the psychiatrist's opinion was relevant. Relevance, however, does not result in evidence being admissible; it is a condition precedent to admissibility. Our law excludes evidence of many matters which in life outside the courts sensible people take into consideration when making decisions. Two broad heads of exclusion are hearsay and opinion. As we have already pointed out, the psychiatrist's report contained a lot of hearsay which was inadmissible. A ruling on this ground, however, would merely have trimmed the psychiatrist's evidence: it would not have excluded it altogether. Was it inadmissible because of the rules relating to opinion evidence?

The foundation of these rules was laid by Lord Mansfield in *Folkes v Chadd* (1782) 3 Doug 157 and was well laid: the opinion of scientific men upon proven facts may be given by men of science within their own science. An expert's opinion is admissible to furnish the court with scientific information which is likely to be outside the experience and knowledge of a judge or jury. If on the proven facts a judge or jury can form their own conclusions without help, then the opinion of an expert is unnecessary. In such a case if it is given dressed up in scientific jargon it may make judgment more difficult. The fact that an expert witness has impressive scientific qualifications does not by that fact alone make his opinion on matters of human nature and behaviour within the limits of normality any more helpful than that of the jurors themselves; but there is a danger that they may think it does.

What, in plain English, was the psychiatrist in this case intending to say? First, that the defendant was not showing and never had shown any evidence of mental illness, as defined by the Mental Health Act 1959, and did not require any psychiatric treatment; secondly, that he had had a deep emotional relationship with the girl which was likely to have caused an explosive release of blind rage when she confessed her wantonness to him; thirdly, that after he had killed her he behaved like someone suffering from profound grief The first part of his opinion was within his expert province and outside the experience of the jury but was of no relevance in the circumstances of this case. The second and third points dealt with matters which are well within ordinary human experience. We all know that both men and women who are deeply in love can, and sometimes do, have outbursts of blind rage when discovering unexpected wantonness on the part of their loved ones; the wife taken in adultery is the classical example of the application of the defence of 'provocation'; and when death or serious injury results, profound grief usually follows. Jurors do not need psychiatrists to tell them how ordinary folk who are not suffering from any mental illness are likely to react to the stresses and strains of life. It follows that the proposed evidence was not admissible to establish that the defendant was likely to have been provoked. The same reasoning applies to its suggested admissibility on the issue of credibility. The jury had to decide what reliance they could put upon the defendant's evidence. He had to be judged as someone who was not mentally disordered. This is what juries are empanelled to do. The law assumes they can perform their duties properly. The jury in this case did not need, and should not have been offered, the evidence of a psychiatrist to help them decide whether the defendant's evidence was truthful.

Mr Mildon submitted that such help should not have been rejected by the judge because in *Lowery* v *The Queen* [1974] AC 85 the Privy Council had approved of the admission of the evidence of a psychologist on the issue of credibility. We had to consider that case carefully before we could decide whether it had in any way put a new interpretation upon what have long been thought to be the rules relating to the calling of evidence on the issue of credibility, *viz.*, that in general evidence can be called to impugn the credibility of witnesses but not led in chief to bolster it up. In *Lowery* v *The Queen* evidence of a psychologist on behalf of one of two accused was admitted to establish that his version of the facts was more probable than that put forward by the other. In every case what is relevant and admissible depends on the issues raised in that case. In *Lowery* v *The Queen* the issues were unusual; and the accused to whose disadvantage the psychologist's evidence went had in effect said before it was called that he was not the sort of man to have committed the offence. In giving the judgment of the Board, Lord Morris of Borth-y-Gest said, at p. 103:

> The only question now arising is whether in the special circumstances above referred to it was open to King in defending himself to call Professor Cox to give the evidence that he gave. The evidence was relevant to and necessary for his case which involved negativing what Lowery had said and put forward; in their Lordships' view in agreement with that of the Court of Criminal Appeal the evidence was admissible.

We adjudge *Lowery* v *The Queen* [1974] AC 85 to have been decided on its special facts. We do not consider that it is an authority for the proposition that in all cases psychologists and psychiatrists can be called to prove the probability of the accused's veracity. If any such rule was applied in our courts, trial by psychiatrists would be likely to take the place of trial by jury and magistrates. We do not find that prospect attractive and the law does not at present provide for it.

In coming to the conclusion we have in this case we must not be taken to be discouraging the calling of psychiatric evidence in cases where such evidence can be helpful within the present rules of evidence. These rules may be too restrictive of the admissibility of opinion evidence. The Criminal Law Revision Committee in its eleventh report thought they were and made recommendations for relaxing them: see paragraphs 266-271. The recommendations have not yet been accepted by Parliament and until they are, or other changes in the law of evidence are made, this court must apply the existing rules: see *Myers v Director of Public Prosecutions* [1965] AC 1001 *per* Lord Reid at pp. 1021-1022. We have not overlooked what Lord Parker CJ said in *Director of Public Prosecutions* v *A and BC Chewing Gum Ltd* [1968] 1 QB 159, 164 about the advance of science making more and more inroads into the old common law principle applicable to opinion evidence; but we are firmly of the opinion that psychiatry has not yet become a satisfactory substitute for the common sense of juries or magistrates on matters within their experience of life.

Appeal dismissed.

Question
Can the decisions in *Lowery* and *Turner* be sensibly reconciled?
(See also *R* v *Rimmer* [1983] Crim LR 250.)

R v *Smith*
[1979] 1 WLR 1445
Court of Appeal

The applicant occupied rooms in the same house as the victim and his wife. The victim arrived home late one evening, having been drinking heavily, and was told by his wife that she had had an altercation with the applicant. The victim went up to the room where the applicant was asleep. A quarrel and fight took place during which the applicant stabbed the victim to death with a knife. While in custody the applicant was examined by two psychiatrists. At his trial for murder the applicant raised the defence of automatism while asleep. The prosecution, who contended that the applicant had recently thought of that defence, sought and obtained leave to cross-examine him about his interviews with the psychiatrists and to call the psychiatrists to give their views on automatism. The applicant was convicted of murder and applied for leave to appeal against conviction on the ground, *inter alia,* that the judge erred in allowing the psychiatrists to give their opinions as to whether the applicant's evidence was consistent with a defence of automatism.

GEOFFREY LANE LJ: . . . The next point Mr Blom-Cooper made is this: as a matter of discretion these reports should not be admitted. In effect, he says this: that in order to be admissible at all the reports must be relevant; that is to say, relevant to some issue which the jury have to determine. He submits that since there was no question of insanity or diminished responsibility, automatism or not was a matter which could and should be decided by the jury in the light of their own experience and they should not be assisted by medical or expert evidence as to the state of mind of the defendant. That being so, he suggests the doctors' evidence was irrelevant and, on that basis, should not have been admitted. Here, again, he cites a number of authorities. First was the decision of this court in *R* v *Chard* (1971) 56 Cr App R 268:

> Where no issue of insanity, diminished responsibility or mental illness has arisen, and it is conceded on the medical evidence that the defendant is entirely normal, it

is not permissible to call a medical witness to state how, in his opinion, the defendant's mind operated at the time of the alleged crime with regard to the question of intent.

He referred to a passage of Roskill LJ's judgment, at p. 270:

Mr Back was unable to cite any authority in support of the proposition, not altogether surprisingly, for with the greatest respect to his argument, it seems to this court that his submission, if accepted, would involve the court admitting medical evidence in other cases not where there was an issue, for example, of insanity or diminished responsibility but where the sole issue which the jury had to consider, as happens in scores of different kinds of cases, was the question of intent . . . .. One purpose of jury trials is to bring into the jury box a body of men and women who are able to judge ordinary day-to-day questions by their own standards, that is, the standards in the eyes of the law of theoretically ordinary reasonable men and women. That is something which they are well able by their ordinary experience to judge for themselves. Where the matters in issue go outside that experience and they are invited to deal with someone supposedly abnormal, for example, supposedly suffering from insanity or diminished responsibility, then plainly in such a case they are entitled to the benefit of expert evidence.

There is a further decision very much to the same effect which we do not find it necessary to cite in detail. I mention it simply for the purpose of completeness. That is *R v Turner (Terence)* [1975] QB 834. So, the question seems to be whether or not the applicant exhibited the type of abnormality in relation to automatism that would render it proper and, indeed, desirable for the jury to have expert help in reaching their conclusion. It seems to us without the benefit of authority that that is clearly the case. This type of automatism — sleepwalking — call it what you like, is not something, we think, which is within the realm of the ordinary juryman's experience. It is something on which, speaking for ourselves as judges, we should like help were we to have to decide it and we see not why a jury should be deprived of that type of help . . .

Accordingly, it seems to us this was a case where the jury were entitled to have the benefit of medical evidence and the judge was right on that basis at any rate to admit the evidence in question as he did.

(His Lordship decided that there was no reason to exclude the evidence because of possible unfairness to the applicant. The court granted leave to appeal, treating the hearing as the appeal.)

Appeal dismissed.

(C)   Non-expert opinion evidence: admissibility

Sometimes, the distinction between fact and opinion is difficult to discern. If W testifies that he saw a bicycle being ridden on the wrong side of the road then this would clearly be a statement of fact. If the witness testified that the bicycle was being ridden in a careless manner then this would be a statement of opinion. But what if the witness testifies that the bicycle was being ridden at high speed? Is this fact or opinion? In civil cases, provision has been made to enable a non-expert witness to testify on such matters if the statement is made as a way of conveying facts (see below). Whether this provision accurately reflects the position in criminal cases is unclear, although most writers suggest it does.

Civil Evidence Act 1972

3. Admissibility of expert opinion and certain expressions of non-expert opinion

(2) It is hereby declared that where a person is called as a witness in any civil proceedings, a statement of opinion by him on any relevant matter on which he is not qualified to give expert evidence, if made as a way of conveying relevant facts personally perceived by him, is admissible as evidence of what he perceived.

(3) In this section 'relevant matter' includes an issue in the proceedings in question.

R v *Davies*
[1962] 1 WLR 1111
Courts-Martial Appeal Court

At a court-martial in Germany the driver of a car involved in a collision was charged with having driven a vehicle on a road while unfit to drive through drink or drugs. Three witnesses were allowed to give evidence about the facts they had observed and also to give their opinions as to the defendant's ability or fitness to drive. The driver was convicted and appealed.

LORD PARKER CJ: . . . The defence had strongly taken the stand that the witness should be allowed to speak only as to facts he had seen, because it was for the court to say what was the appellant's condition. Apparently the judge advocate advised the court that the witness could state the impression he formed as to the appellant's condition at the time he saw him if he was a witness who knew what was entailed in the driving of a car.

It is to be observed that the witness was allowed to speak about two matters which are quite distinct; one is what his impression was as to whether drink had been taken by the appellant, and the second was his opinion as to whether as the result of that drink he was fit or unfit to drive a car.

The court has come clearly to the conclusion that a witness can quite properly give his general impression as to whether a driver had taken drink. He must describe of course the facts upon which he relies, but it seems to this court that he is perfectly entitled to give his impression as to whether drink had been taken or not. On the other hand, as regards the second matter, it cannot be said, as it seems to this court, that a witness, merely because he is a driver himself, is in the expert witness category so that it is proper to ask him his opinion as to fitness or unfitness to drive. That is the very matter which the court itself has to determine. Accordingly, in so far as this witness and two subsequent witnesses, the lance-corporal and the regimental sergeant-major gave their opinion as to the appellant's ability or fitness to drive, the court was wrong in admitting that evidence. [His Lordship considered the evidence as a whole and continued:] This court has come quite clearly to the conclusion that there was ample evidence here to support the verdict and that so far as the wrongful admission of certain evidence is concerned the court would have been bound to come to the same conclusion even if that evidence had not been admitted.

Appeal dismissed.

Questions
1. The following is an extract from the summing-up of a trial judge in a criminal case:

Members of the jury, I now turn to deal with the subject of the handwritten evidence which forms exhibits SC1 and SC2. The prosecution called no evidence from any handwriting expert in order to prove to you that the defendant is the author of exhibit SC1. The defence on the other hand called a Mr Allen, in order to prove the contrary. Now you may think that the reason why the prosecution did not call such a witness is that the documents speak for themselves. You have seen them on several occasions during the trial and you are free to take them into the jury room when you retire to consider your verdict. You will be able to study the exhibits and, bearing in mind it is for the prosecution to prove authorship of the documents, consider where the truth lies. If you wish, you will be provided with a magnifying glass to enable you to study them more carefully. But with regard to Mr Allen let me say this. Mr Allen claims an expertise in the field of handwriting although his profession is one of barrister. He has, it is true, out of interest over the past 13 years, spent a good deal of time examining various documents and handwriting and accordingly, has developed a degree of expertise in this area. That is why I allowed you to hear his evidence. You may think however, that his expertise is really no greater than your own. Mr Mansfield stated that he was sure the defendant was not the author of the documents SC1 and SC2. That is for you to decide and, if you follow my advice, you will not place too much emphasis on opinion evidence in this type of case. There is no reason why you should not trust your own observations.

Criticise this passage.
2. Would an expert astrologer be permitted to testify as to the behaviour of the defendant on a certain day, assuming that the astrologer had prepared an astrological chart in strict compliance with the principles of astrology?
3. You are acting for George, who is jointly tried with Harry on a charge of murdering Ivan. The case for the prosecution is that both George and Harry committed the offence together. Harry, who has pleaded not guilty, has given evidence to the effect that George was the ringleader and that he, Harry, although present, never touched Ivan. You have in your presence statements from two doctors: Dr James says that George, although physically large, is a timid young man and easily led, and is not as strong as he looks; Dr Kay says that Harry is mentally unbalanced, prone to fits of violence and a pathological liar. What use, if any, can you make of this evidence in defence of George?

Further Reading
P. Murphy, *A Practical Approach to Evidence*, 4th ed. (1992), Ch. 9
J. D.Jackson, 'The Ultimate Issue Rule: one rule too many' [1984] Crim LR 75
A. Kenny, 'The Expert in Court' (1983) 99 LQR 197
R. D. Mackay, 'Excluding Expert Evidence: a tale of ordinary folk and common experience' [1991] Crim LR 800
R. Munday, 'Excluding the Expert Witness' [1981] Crim LR 688
R. Pattenden, 'Expert Opinion Evidence Based on Hearsay' [1982] Crim LR 85
R. Pattenden, 'Conflicting Approaches to Psychiatric Evidence in Criminal Trials: England, Canada and Australia' [1986] Crim LR 92

14   PUBLIC POLICY AND PRIVILEGE

It is in the public interest that legal proceedings are conducted in a frank and open manner with access being available to all the relevant evidence. It follows from this that witnesses should be required to answer all relevant questions and any material documents should be made available for use in litigation. However, there may well be occasions where two competing interests clash; one interest may favour disclosure of a document for use in litigation, while the other interest favours the document remaining confidential. Such a conflict of interest provides the basis for the law relating to public policy and privilege. The similarity between public policy and privilege lends itself to their being treated together in the same chapter, but the rules governing the two concepts are quite distinct. For a full treatment of the distinction see P. Murphy, *A Practical Approach to Evidence*, 4th ed. (1992), Ch. 11.

(A)   Public policy

There may be occasions when public policy dictates that certain matters of public interest outweigh the need to present the court with all the relevant evidence, leading the court to conclude that certain evidence should be excluded. A party to a case might argue that certain evidence, often in the form of a document, should not be presented in evidence because the public interest in keeping that document confidential outweighs the need to make full disclosure of the facts to the court. This topic often, but not always, arises at the discovery stage of the trial process, i.e. where one party to an action is seeking to discover certain evidence, often in the form of a document, which he knows or believes to be in the possession of the other.

There are a large number of situations which might attract the application of the public policy doctrine. For example, revealing the contents of a particular document might jeopardise national security, leading the court to conclude that the document should not be revealed to a particular party. Another example would be where a person has given information to the authorities which has resulted in a prosecution. Should the identity of the person who has supplied the information be revealed? If it is revealed, will this not jeopardise the continued supply of valuable information to the authorities in the future? As a matter of public policy the courts have generally taken the view that it is in the public interest to prevent the identity of certain informants from being revealed. These, and other examples, are considered in the following cases.

Conway v *Rimmer*
[1968] AC 910
House of Lords

The plaintiff, a probationary police constable, was prosecuted for theft by the defendant, a superintendent in the same force. The jury stopped the case. The plaintiff now brought an action for malicious prosecution against the defendant. In the course of discovery, the defendant disclosed a list of documents in his possession, admittedly relevant to the plaintiff's action, which included four reports made by him about the plaintiff during his period of probation, and a report in connection with his prosecution. The Home Secretary objected to production of all five documents on the grounds that each fell within a class of documents the production of which would be injurious to the public interest.

LORD REID: The question whether such a statement by a Minister of the Crown should be accepted as conclusively preventing any court from ordering production of any of the documents to which it applies is one of very great importance in the administration of justice. If the commonly accepted interpretation of the decision of this House in *Duncan* v *Cammell, Laird & Co. Ltd* [1942] AC 624 is to remain authoritative the question admits of only one answer — the Minister's statement is final and conclusive. Normally I would be very slow to question the authority of a unanimous decision of this House only 25 years old which was carefully considered and obviously intended to lay down a general rule. But this decision has several abnormal features.

Lord Simon thought that on this matter the law in Scotland was the same as the law in England and he clearly intended to lay down a rule applicable to the whole of the United Kingdom. But in *Glasgow Corporation* v *Central Land Board* 1956 SC (HL) 1 this House held that this was not so, with the result that today on this question the law is different in the two countries. There are many chapters of the law where for historical and other reasons it is quite proper that the law should be different in the two countries. But here we are dealing purely with public policy — with the proper relation between the powers of the executive and the powers of the courts — and I can see no rational justification for the law on this matter being different in the two countries.

Secondly, events have proved that the rule supposed to have been laid down in *Duncan's* case is far from satisfactory. In the large number of cases in England and elsewhere which have been cited in argument much dissatisfaction has been expressed and I have not observed even one expression of whole-hearted approval. Moreover a statement made by the Lord Chancellor in 1956 on behalf of the Government, to which I shall return later, makes it clear that that Government did not regard it as consonant with public policy to maintain the rule to the full extent which existing authorities has held to be justifiable.

I have no doubt that the case of *Duncan* v *Cammell, Laird & Co. Ltd* was rightly decided. The plaintiff sought discovery of documents relating to the submarine Thetis including a contract for the hull and machinery and plans and specifications. The First Lord of the Admiralty had stated that 'it would be injurious to the public interest that any of the said documents should be disclosed to any person'. Any of these documents might well have given valuable information, or at least clues, to the skilled eye of an agent of a foreign power. But Lord Simon LC took the opportunity to deal with the whole question of the right of the Crown to prevent production of documents in a litigation. Yet a study of his speech leaves me with the strong impression that throughout he had primarily in mind cases where discovery or disclosure would involve a danger of real prejudice to the national interest. I find it difficult to believe that his speech would have been the same if the case had related, as the present case does, to discovery of routine reports on a probationer constable.

Early in his speech Lord Simon quoted with approval the view of Rigby LJ, in *Attorney-General* v *Newcastle-upon-Tyne Corporation* [1897] 2 QB 384 that documents are not to be withheld 'unless there be some plain overruling principle of public interest concerned which cannot be disregarded'. And, summing up towards the end, he said:

> . . . the rule that the interest of the state must not be in jeopardy by producing documents which would injure it is a principle to be observed in administering justice, quite unconnected with the interests or claims of the particular parties in litigation.

Surely it would be grotesque to speak of the interest of the state being put in jeopardy by disclosure of a routine report on a probationer. Lord Simon did not say very much about objections 'based upon the view that the public interest requires a particular class of communications with, or within, a public department to be protected from production on the ground that the candour and completeness of such communications might be prejudiced if they were ever liable to be disclosed in subsequent litigation rather than on the contents of the particular document itself.' But at the end he said that a Minister 'ought not to take the responsibility of withholding production except in cases where the public interest would otherwise be damnified, for example, where disclosure would be injurious to national defence, or to good diplomatic relations, or where the practice of keeping a class of documents secret is necessary for the proper functioning of the public service'. I find it difficult to believe that he would have put these three examples on the same level if he had intended the third to cover such minor matters as a routine report by a relatively junior officer. And my impression is strengthened by the passage at the very end of the speech:

> . . . the public interest is also the interest of every subject of the realm, and while, in these exceptional cases, the private citizen may seem to be denied what is to his immediate advantage, he, like the rest of us, would suffer if the needs of protecting the interests of the country as a whole were not ranked as a prior obligation.

Would he have spoken of 'these exceptional cases' or of 'the needs of protecting the interests of the country as a whole' if he had intended to include all manner of routine communications? And did he really mean that the protection of such communications is a 'prior obligation' in a case where a man's reputation or fortune is at stake and withholding the document makes it impossible for justice to be done?

It is universally recognised that here there are two kinds of public interest which may clash. There is the public interest that harm shall not be done to the nation or the public service by disclosure of certain documents, and there is the public interest that the administration of justice shall not be frustrated by the withholding of documents which must be produced if justice is to be done. There are many cases where the nature of the injury which would or might be done to the nation or the public service is of so grave a character that no other interest, public or private, can be allowed to prevail over it. With regard to such cases it would be proper to say, as Lord Simon did, that to order production of the document in question would put the interest of the state in jeopardy. But there are many other cases where the possible injury to the public service is much less and there one would think that it would be proper to balance the public interests involved. I do not believe that Lord Simon really meant that the smallest probability of injury to the public service must always outweigh the gravest frustration of the administration of justice.

It is to be observed that, in a passage which I have already quoted, Lord Simon referred to the practice of keeping a class of documents secret being '*necessary* [my italics] for the proper functioning of the public interest'. But the certificate of the Home Secretary in the present case does not go nearly so far as that. It merely says that the production of a document of the classes to which it refers would be 'injurious to the public interest:' it does not say what degree of injury is to be apprehended. It may be advantageous to the functioning of the public service that reports of this kind should be kept secret — that is the view of the Home Secretary — but I would be very surprised if anyone said that that is necessary.

There are now many large public bodies, such as British Railways and the National Coal Board, the proper and efficient functioning of which is very necessary for many reasons including the safety of the public. The Attorney-General made it clear that Crown privilege is not and cannot be invoked to prevent disclosure of similar documents made by them or their servants even if it were said that this is required for the proper and efficient functioning of that public service. I find it difficult to see why it should be *necessary* to withhold whole classes of routine 'communications with or within a public department' but quite unnecessary to withhold similar communications with or within a public corporation. There the safety of the public may well depend on the candour and completeness of reports made by subordinates whose duty it is to draw attention to defects. But, so far as I know, no one has ever suggested that public safety has been endangered by the candour or completeness of such reports having been inhibited by the fact that they may have to be produced if the interests of the due administration of justice should ever require production at any time . . .

In my judgment, in considering what it is 'proper' for a court to do we must have regard to the need, shown by 25 years' experience since *Duncan's* case [1942] AC 624, that the courts should balance the public interest in the proper administration of justice against the public interest in withholding any evidence which a Minister considers ought to be withheld.

I would therefore propose that the House ought now to decide that courts have and are entitled to exercise a power and duty to hold a balance between the public interest, as expressed by a Minister, to withhold certain documents or other evidence, and the public interest in ensuring the proper administration of justice. That does not mean that a court would reject a Minister's view: full weight must be given to it in every case, and if the Minister's reasons are of a character which judicial experience is not competent to weigh, then the Minister's view must prevail. But experience has shown that reasons given for withholding whole classes of documents are often not of that character. For example a court is perfectly well able to assess the likelihood that, if the writer of a certain class of document knew that there was a chance that his report might be produced in legal proceedings, he would make a less full and candid report than he would otherwise have done.

I do not doubt that there are certain classes of documents which ought not to be disclosed whatever their content may be. Virtually everyone agrees that Cabinet minutes and the like ought not to be disclosed until such time as they are only of historical interest. But I do not think that many people would give as the reason that premature disclosure would prevent candour in the Cabinet. To my mind the most important reason is that such disclosure would create or fan ill-informed or captious public or political criticism. The business of government is difficult enough as it is, and no government could contemplate with equanimity the inner workings of the government machine being exposed to the gaze of those ready to criticise without adequate knowledge of the background and perhaps with some axe to grind. And that must, in my view, also apply to all documents concerned with policy making within departments including, it may be, minutes and the like by quite junior officials and correspondence with outside bodies. Further it may be that deliberations about a particular case require protection as much as deliberations about policy. I do not think that it is possible to limit such documents by any definition. But there seems to me to be a wide difference between such documents and routine reports. There may be special reasons for withholding some kinds of routine documents, but I think that the proper test to be applied is to ask, in the language of Lord Simon in *Duncan's* case, whether the withholding of a document because it belongs to a particular class is really 'necessary for the proper functioning of the public service'.

It appears to me that, if the Minister's reasons are such that a judge can properly weigh them, he must, on the other hand, consider what is the probable importance in the case before him of the documents or other evidence sought to be withheld. If he decides that on balance the documents probably ought to be produced, I think that it would generally be best that he should see them before ordering production and if he thinks that the Minister's reasons are not clearly expressed he will have to see the documents before ordering production. I can see nothing wrong in the judge seeing documents without their being shown to the parties. Lord Simon said (in *Duncan's* case) that 'where the Crown is a party . . . this would amount to communicating with one party to the exclusion of the other'. I do not agree. The parties see the Minister's reasons. Where a document has not been prepared for the information of the judge, it seems to me a misuse of language to say that the judge 'communicates with' the holder of the document by reading it. If on reading the document he still thinks that it ought to be produced he will order its production.

But it is important that the Minister should have a right to appeal before the document is produced. This matter was not fully investigated in the argument before your Lordships. But it does appear that in one way or another there can be an appeal if the document is in the custody of a servant of the Crown or of a person who is willing to co-operate with the Minister. There may be difficulty if it is in the hands of a person who wishes to produce it. But that difficulty could occur today if a witness wishes to give some evidence which the Minister unsuccessfully urges the court to prevent from being given. It may be that this is a matter which deserves further investigation by the Crown authorities.

The documents in this case are in the possession of a police force. The position of the police is peculiar. They are not servants of the Crown and they do not take orders from the Government. But they are carrying out an essential function of Government, and various Crown rights, privileges and exemptions have been held to apply to them. Their position was explained in *Coomber* v *Berkshire Justices* [1883] 9 AC 61 (HL) and cases there cited. It has never been denied that they are entitled to Crown privilege with regard to documents, and it is essential that they should have it.

The police are carrying on an unending war with criminals many of whom are today highly intelligent. So it is essential that there should be no disclosure of anything which might give any useful information to those who organise criminal activities. And it would generally be wrong to require disclosure in a civil case of anything which might be material in a pending prosecution: but after a verdict has been given or it has been decided to take no proceedings there is not the same need for secrecy. With regard to other documents there seems to be no greater need for protection than in the case of departments of Government.

It appears to me to be most improbable that any harm would be done by disclosure of the probationary reports on the appellant or of the report from the police training centre. With regard to the report which the respondent made to his chief constable with a view to the prosecution of the appellant there could be more doubt, although no suggestion was made in argument that disclosure of its contents would be harmful now that the appellant has been acquitted. And, as I have said, these documents may prove to be of vital importance in this litigation.

In my judgment, this appeal should be allowed and these documents ought now to be required to be produced for inspection. If it is then found that disclosure would not, in your Lordships' view be prejudicial to the public interest, or that any possibility of such prejudice is, in the case of each of the documents, insufficient to justify its being withheld, then disclosure should be ordered.

(LORDS MORRIS OF BORTH-Y-GEST, HODSON, PEARCE and UPJOHN delivered concurring judgments.)

Appeal allowed. Documents ordered to be produced.

Question
Was *Duncan* v *Cammell Laird* correctly decided?

D v *National Society for the Prevention of Cruelty to Children*
[1978] AC 171
House of Lords

The National Society for the Prevention of Cruelty to Children received and investigated complaints from members of the public about cases of ill-treatment or neglect of children under an express pledge of confidentiality and was authorised under s. 1(1) of the Children and Young Persons Act 1969 to bring care proceedings in respect of children. The society received a complaint from an informant about the treatment of a 14-month-old girl, and an inspector of the society called at the parents' home. The mother subsequently brought an action against the society for damages for personal injuries alleged to have resulted from the society's negligence in failing properly to investigate the complaint and the manner and circumstances of the inspector's call which she said had caused her severe and continuing shock. The society denied negligence and applied for an order that there should be no discovery or inspection ordered under RSC Order 24 rule 2(1), of any documents which revealed or might reveal the identity of the complainant, on the grounds, *inter alia*, that the proper performance by the society of its duties under its charter and the Act of 1969 required that the absolute confidentiality of information given in confidence should be preserved, that if disclosure were ordered in the mother's action its sources of information would dry up and that that would be contrary to the public interest, and it also claimed that disclosure of the informant's identity was not necessary for disposing fairly of the action. Master Jacob ordered that the relevant documents be disclosed. On appeal by the society Croom-Johnson J reversed the master's order. On appeal by the mother the Court of Appeal by a majority restored it. The society appealed to the House of Lords.

LORD HAILSHAM OF ST MARYLEBONE: The appellant society argued, in effect, for a general extension in range of the nature of the exceptions to the rule in favour of disclosure. This, it was suggested, could be summarised in a number of broad propositions, all in support of the view that, where an identifiable public interest in non-disclosure can be established, either there is a firm rule against disclosure (for example, legal professional privilege or state secrets) or the court has a discretion whether or not to order disclosure, and that this discretion must be exercised against disclosure in all cases where, after balancing the relevant considerations, the court decides that the public interest in non-disclosure outweighs the ordinary public interest in disclosure. The appellants contended that new cases will arise from time to time calling for a protection from disclosure in classes of case to which it was not previously extended, and that the courts had in practice shown great flexibility in adapting these principles to new situations as and when these arise. The appellants contended that some of those entitled to the benefits of protection had, and some had not, been subject to statutory or common law duties or been clothed with government authority or been answerable to Parliament or the executive. This contention was aimed at the majority judgments in the Court of Appeal which in substance disallowed the appellants' claim to immunity on the grounds that they are a private society clothed arguably with authority to fulfil a function but not a duty which they are compelled to perform, and that they are not in any sense either an organ of central government or part of the public service. The appellants noted that the dissenting judgment of Lord Denning MR, which was in their favour, largely relied on the confidentiality which the appellants had pledged to potential informants. Their own contention was that, while the mere fact that a communication was made in confidence did not of itself justify non-disclosure, the fact of confidentiality was relevant to reinforce the view that disclosure would be against the public interest. In this connection the appellants cited *Alfred Crompton Amusement Machines Ltd* v *Customs and Excise Commissioners (No. 2)* [1974] AC 405. Lastly the appellants contended that there was no reported case in which the court, once it had identified a public interest in non-disclosure, had ever regarded itself as debarred from taking it into consideration or from weighing its importance against the damage to be apprehended from excluding relevant evidence.

These contentions have at least the merit of propounding a lucid and coherent system. Nevertheless, I am compelled to say that, in the breadth and generality with which they were put forward, I do not find them acceptable.

They seem to me to give far too little weight to the general importance of the principle that, in all cases before them, the courts should insist on parties and witnesses disclosing the truth, the whole truth, and nothing but the truth, where this would assist the decision of the matters in dispute. In the second place, I consider that the acceptance of these principles would lead both to uncertainty and to inconsistency in the administration of justice. If they were to be accepted, we should remember that we should be laying down a large innovation not merely in the law of discovery but equally in the law of evidence, which has to be administered not merely in the High Court, but in the Crown Courts, the county courts and the magistrates' courts throughout the land. What is the public interest to be identified? On what principles can it be defined? On what principles is the weighing-up process to proceed? To what extent, if at all, can the right to non-disclosure be waived? Can secondary or extraneous evidence of the facts not disclosed be permitted? To what extent should the Crown be notified of the fact that the issue has been raised? These questions are all manageable if the categories of privilege from disclosure and public interest are considered to be limited. Indeed, reported authority, which is voluminous, shows that largely they have been solved. But to yield to the appellants' argument on this part of the case would be to set the whole question once more at large, not merely over the admitted categories and the existing field but over a much wider, indeed over an undefined, field.

Thirdly, and perhaps more important, the invitation of the appellants seems to me to run counter to the general tradition of the development of doctrine preferred by the English courts. This proceeds through evolution by extension or analogy of recognised principles and reported precedents. Bold statements of general principle based on a review of the total field are more appropriate to legislation by Parliament which has at its command techniques of inquiry, sources of information and a width of worldly-wise experience far less restricted than those available to the courts in the course of contested litigation between adversaries.

On the other hand, I find equally unattractive the more restricted and even, occasionally, pedantic view of the authorities advanced on behalf of the respondent. This was based on a rigid distinction, for some purposes valuable, between privilege and public interest, and an insistance on a narrow view of the nature of the interest of the public, reflected in the reasoning of the majority in the Court of Appeal, which would virtually have restricted the public interest cases to the narrower interests of the central organs of the state, or what might be strictly called the public service. The effect of the argument would not merely limit the ambit of possible categories of exception to the general rule. In my view, it would virtually ensure that the categories would now have to be regarded as effectively closed. In her printed case the respondent contended that:

> No party is protected from his obligation to disclose documents on the grounds of public interest unless there is some connection between the claim for protection and the functions of central government or the public service of the state: . . . The expression 'Crown privilege' has been criticised but . . . it accurately reflects the basic requirement that there must be a connection with the Crown or public service of the state.

In support of this contention the respondent referred *inter alia* to *Conway* v *Rimmer* [1968] AC 910, to *R* v *Lewes Justices, ex parte Secretary of State for the Home Department* [1973] AC 388 and to *Alfred Crompton Amusement Machines Ltd* v *Customs and Excise Commissioners (No. 2)* [1974] AC 405. There is, of course, a sense, which will become apparent as I proceed, in which the appellants' claim can be brought squarely within the respondent's principle. But the principle is itself, as I shall show, open to criticism.

In particular the argument was based on what was described as a fundamental principle that the exceptions to the general rule requiring disclosure all come within one or the other of two rigidly confined categories, one described as privilege, when secondary evidence could be given or the privilege could be waived, and the other as 'public interest' where these possible escapes were excluded. But this, it was contended, was virtually restricted to the category formerly, but inaccurately, referred to as 'Crown privilege'.

The result of this is that I approach the problem with a caution greater than that contended for the appellants, but with a willingness to extend established principles by analogy and legitimate extrapolation more flexible than was admitted by the respondent.

I am emboldened to do so by the reflection that, quite apart from legislation like the Civil Evidence Act 1968, the law of evidence has steadily developed since my own practice at the Bar began in 1932. This can be seen by a consideration of cases like *McTaggart* v *McTaggart* [1949] P 94, *Mole* v *Mole* [1951] P 21, *Theodoropoulas* v *Theodoropoulas* [1964] P 311, which undoubtedly developed from the long recognised category of 'without prejudice' negotiations but which in my opinion has now developed into a new category of a public interest exception based on the public interest in the stability of marriage. I think the case, widely canvassed in argument, of *R* v *Lewes Justices, ex parte Secretary of State for the Home Department* [1973] AC 388 was a clear extension of the previous 'Crown privilege' type of case by which, for the first time, communications to the Gaming Board were recognised as a suitable object of such 'privilege'. Possibly *In re D (Infants)* [1970] 1 WLR 599 is another example, for it decided, I think, for the first time, that local authority records of child care investigations were immune from disclosure in wardship proceedings to which they would otherwise be relevant. I believe that traces of similar evolution, for instance in the field of legal professional privilege, can be found in the 19th century authorities.

I find it also interesting to note that the report (Law Reform Committee Sixteenth Report (Privilege in Civil Proceedings) (1967) (Cmnd. 3472) to which judges of every Division of the High Court were signatories, which was referred to extensively by counsel for both sides, shows a definite development in the law and practice in the precise field now under discussion from what it was generally considered to be when I entered the profession in 1932.

According to paragraph 1 of that report, which is before us, but which represents no more than contemporary textbook authority:

> Privilege in the main is the creation of the common law whose policy, pragmatic as always, has been to limit to a minimum the categories of privileges *(sic)* 'which a person has an absolute right to claim, *but to accord to the judge a wide discretion to permit a witness, whether a party to the proceedings or not, to refuse to disclose information where disclosure would be a breach of some ethical or social value and non-disclosure would be unlikely to result in serious injustice in the particular case in which it is claimed* (emphasis mine).

This doctrine was not merely an incidental statement at the beginning of the report. It runs right through it, and forms the basis of some of the most notable conclusions (see, for example, paragraph 3, paragraph 7, paragraphs 36, 37, paragraphs 41, 43, paragraphs 48-52).

Counsel for the respondent, who was himself, as he candidly confessed, signatory to the report, was constrained to argue that the report, the authors of which included Lords Pearson and Diplock, Winn and Buckley LJJ, Orr J and the present Vice-

Chancellor (Megarry V-C), was an inaccurate representation of the then existing state of the law, and that the two cases (*Attorney-General* v *Clough* [1963] 1 QB 773 and *Attorney-General* v *Mulholland; Attorney-General* v *Foster* [1963] 2 QB 477) cited in the report to support the proposition did not in truth do so, were wrong if they did and, being modern, departed from legal principle. Speaking for myself, I am sure that the law has in fact developed in this field during my lifetime, and I find it incredible that paragraph 1 of the report cited, bearing the weight of judicial authority I have described, does not represent the current practice of the courts in 1967, although in fact it goes plainly beyond the current practice of my youth.

For these reasons, I feel convinced that I am entitled to proceed more boldly than counsel for the respondent argued, though more timidly than the robust counsels of the appellants' counsel urged.

The authorities, therefore, seem to me to establish beyond doubt that the courts have developed their doctrine in this field of evidence. An example of this is seen in the privilege extended to editors of newspapers in the 19th century, before the present Order 82, rule 6 was passed, to refuse to answer interrogatories in defamation cases where the issue was malice and the plaintiff desired to discover their sources (cf. *Hope* v *Brash* [1897] 2 QB 188; *Hennessy* v *Wright* (1888) 21 QBD 509; *Plymouth Mutual Co-operative and Industrial Society Ltd* v *Traders' Publishing Association Ltd* [1906] 1 KB 403). This practice, robustly developed by the judges of the Queen's Bench Division (in contrast with the contemporary Chancery Division practice even after 1873), can only have been based on public policy. It has been stressed that these cases relate to discovery and not to questions to witnesses at the trial. This may well be so, at least at present, but certainly they illustrate the use of the court of a discretion, and its sensitiveness to public policy where discretion exists. Until the introduction of the new rules it is within my recollection that interrogatories and discovery on the lines disallowed in the newspaper cases were frequently allowed in other defamation cases where malice was in issue, although it was pointed out in argument that the newspaper principle was, at least once, applied, rather strangely, to MP's in *Adam* v *Fisher* (1914) 30 TLR 288.

In all this argument, however, two facts stand out unmistakably as true beyond dispute. The first is that the welfare of children, particularly of young children at risk of maltreatment by adults, has been, from the earliest days, a concern of the Crown as *parens patriae*, an object of legal charities and in latter years the subject of a whole series of Acts of Parliament, of which the Act of 1969 is only an example, and that not the latest. The second is that the information given by informants to the police or to the Director of Public Prosecutions, and now, since *R* v *Lewes Justices, ex parte Secretary of State for the Home Department* [1973] AC 388, to the Gaming Board, is protected from disclosure in exactly the manner demanded by the appellants. The question, and it is I believe the only question, necessary to be decided in this appeal, is whether an extension of this established principle to information relating to possible child abuse supplied to the appellants is a legitimate extension of a known category of exception or not. For this purpose it is necessary to consider the position of the appellants in relation to the enforcement provisions of the Children and Young Persons Act 1969 . . . .

Of the three classes with *locus standi* to initiate care proceedings, it is common ground that information given to the police is protected to the extent demanded by the society. This is clear from many cases including *Marks* v *Beyfus,* 25 QBD 494 (which applied the principle to the Director of Public Prosecutions), and many of the recent cases in your Lordships' House. The rule relating to the immunity accorded to police informants is in truth much older, so old and so well established, in fact, that it was not and could not be challenged in the instant case before your Lordships.

Once, however, it is accepted that information given to the police in the instant case would have been protected, it becomes, in my judgment, manifestly absurd that it should not be accorded equally to the same information if given by the same informant to the local authority (who would have been under a duty to act on it) or to the appellant society, to whom, according to the undisputed evidence, ordinary informants more readity resort.

The last point seems to have been realised, at least to some extent, by Sir John Pennycuick: see, for instance, the passage in his judgment, [1978] AC at p. 203. But I cannot see the sense of allowing the immunity where care proceedings actually result, but not in cases where the society or the local authority, after sifting the information, and assessing the credentials of the informants, decide in the event upon an alternative course. It is not for the informant to predict what course the recipient of the information may take, nor does his (or her) right to anonymity depend upon the outcome. The public interest is that the parties with *locus standi* to bring care proceedings should receive information under a cloak of confidentiality. It may well be that neither the police, nor the local authority, nor the society, can give an absolute guarantee. The informant may in some cases have to give evidence under *subpoena*. In other cases their identity may come to light in other ways. But the police, the local authority and the society stand on the same footing. The public interest is identical in relation to each. The guarantee of confidentiality has the same and not different values in relation to each. It follows that the society is entitled to succeed upon the appeal.

Lord Denning MR, in his dissenting judgment, places his own reasoning on the pledge of confidentiality given by the society, and seeks to found the immunity upon this pledge. I do not think that confidentiality by itself gives any ground for immunity (cf., for example, *per* Lord Cross of Chelsea in *Alfred Crompton Amusement Machines Ltd* v *Customs and Excise Commissioners (No. 2)* [1974] AC 405, 433). Confidentiality is not a separate head of immunity. There are, however, cases when confidentiality is itself a public interest and one of these is where information is given to an authority charged with the enforcement and administration of the law by the initiation of court proceedings. This is one of those cases, whether the recipient of the information be the police, the local authority or the NSPCC. Whether there be other cases, and what these may be, must fall to be decided in the future. The categories of public interest are not closed, and must alter from time to time whether by restriction or extension as social conditions and social legislation develop.

LORD EDMUND-DAVIES: In the result, I believe that the law applicable to all civil actions like the present one may be thus stated:

(1)   In civil proceedings a judge has no discretion, simply because what is contemplated is the disclosure of information which has passed between persons in a confidential relationship (other than that of lawyer and client), to direct a party to that relationship that he need not disclose that information even though its disclosure is (a) relevant to and (b) necessary for the attainment of justice in the particular case. If (a) and (b) are established, the doctor or the priest must be directed to answer if, despite the strong dissuasion of the judge, the advocate persists in seeking disclosure. This is also true of all other confidential relationships in the absence of a special statutory provision, such as the Civil Evidence Act 1968, regarding communications between patent agents and their clients.

(2)   But where (i) a confidential relationship exists (other than that of lawyer and client) *and* (ii) disclosure would be in breach of some ethical or social value involving the public interest, the court has a discretion to uphold a refusal to disclose relevant evidence provided it considers that, on balance, the public interest would be better served by excluding such evidence.

(3)   In conducting the necessary balancing operation between competing aspects of public interest, the presence (or absence) of involvement of the central government in the matter of disclosure is *not* conclusive either way, though in practice it may affect the cogency of the argument against disclosure. It is true that in *Blackpool Corporation v Locker* [1948] 1 KB 349 the Court of Appeal dismissed a local authority's claim to exclude their interdepartmental communications in the public interest, Scott LJ saying, at p. 380: 'No such privilege has yet, so far as I know, been conceded by the courts to any local government officer when his employing authority is in litigation'. But it is worthy of note that he went on to observe that, although:

> Public interest is, from the point of view of English justice, a regrettable and sometimes dangerous form of privilege, though at times unavoidable; . . . *no such ground was put forward in the plaintiffs' affidavit.* (The italics are mine.)

We therefore cannot be sure how that case would otherwise have been decided, but we do know from *Conway v Rimmer* [1968] AC 910 and *In re D (Infants)* [1970] 1 WLR 599 that an organ of central government does not now necessarily have to be involved before a claim for non-disclosure can succeed. In my judgment, Scarman LJ therefore went too far in asserting in the Court of Appeal in the present case [1976] 3 WLR 124, 139 that '. . . state interest alone can justify the withholding of relevant documents . . .' So to assert is, in the wise words of one commentator, '. . . to place too high a value on the arbitrary factor of the status of the possessor of the information. It also assumes that organisations can be classified into those which have the status of a "central organ of government" . . . and those which do not. Such a classification is surely impracticable'. (Joseph Jacob, 'Discovery and Public Interest' [1976] PL 134, 138.)

(4)   The sole touchstone is the public interest, and not whether the party from whom disclosure is sought was acting under a 'duty' — as opposed to merely exercising 'powers'. A party who acted under some duty may find it easier to establish that public interest was involved than one merely exercising powers, but that is another matter.

(5)   The mere fact that relevant information was communicated in confidence does not necessarily mean that it need not be disclosed. But where the subject matter is clearly of public interest, the *additional* fact (if such it be) that to break the seal of confidentiality would endanger that interest will in most (if not all) cases probably lead to the conclusion that disclosure should be withheld. And it is difficult to conceive *of any* judicial discretion to exclude relevant and necessary evidence save in respect of confidential information communicated in a confidential relationship.

(6)   The disclosure of all evidence relevant to the trial of an issue being at all times a matter of considerable public interest, the question to be determined is whether it is clearly demonstrated that in the particular case the public interest would neverthe-less be better served by excluding evidence despite its relevance. If, on balance, the matter is left in doubt, disclosure should be ordered.

(LORD KILBRANDON, LORD DIPLOCK and LORD SIMON delivered speeches in favour of allowing the appeal.)

Appeal allowed.

Science Research Council v Nasśe; Leyland Cars v Vyas
[1979] QB 144 (Court of Appeal)
[1980] AC 1028 (House of Lords)

The two appeals were heard together. The complainants alleged that refusal of promotion by their employers was motivated by unlawful discrimination. They sought discovery of confidential reports by their employers concerning both themselves and the other employees who were considered for promotion at the same time. The employers in each case did not object to disclosure of the reports relating to the applicants, but did object to discovery of those dealing with the rivals. The Employment Appeal Tribunal ordered disclosure in both cases. The employers appealed successfully to the Court of Appeal. The complainants appealed to the House of Lords.

LORD WILBERFORCE: . . . On these points my conclusions are as follows:

1   There is no principle of public interest immunity, as that expression was developed from *Conway v Rimmer* [1968] AC 910, protecting such confidential documents as those with which these appeals are concerned. That such an immunity exists, or ought to be declared by this House to exist, was the main contention of Leyland. It was not argued for by the SRC; indeed that body argued against it.

2   There is no principle in English law by which documents are protected from discovery by reason of confidentiality alone. But there is no reason why, in the exercise of its discretion to order discovery, the tribunal should not have regard to the fact that documents are confidential, and that to order disclosure would involve a breach of confidence. In the employment field, the tribunal may have regard to the sensitivity of particular types of confidential information, to the extent to which the interests of third parties (including their employees on whom confidential reports have been made, as well as persons reporting) may be affected by disclosure, to the interest which both employees and employers may have in preserving the confidentiality of personal reports, and to any wider interest which may be seen to exist in preserving the confidentiality of systems of personal assessments.

3   As a corollary to the above, it should be added that relevance alone, though a necessary ingredient, does not provide an automatic sufficient test for ordering discovery. The tribunal always has a discretion. That relevance alone is enough was, in my belief, the position ultimately taken by counsel for Mrs Nassé thus entitling the complainant to discovery subject only to protective measures (sealing up, etc.). This I am unable to accept.

4   The ultimate test in discrimination (as in other) proceedings is whether discovery is necessary for disposing fairly of the proceedings. If it is, then discovery must be ordered notwithstanding confidentiality. But where the court is impressed with the need to preserve confidentiality in a particular case, it will consider carefully whether the necessary information has been or can be obtained by other means, not involving a breach of confidence.

5   In order to reach a conclusion whether discovery is necessary notwithstanding confidentiality the tribunal should inspect the documents. It will naturally consider whether justice can be done by special measures such as 'covering up' substituting anonymous references for specific names, or, in rare cases, hearing in camera.

6   The procedure by which this process is to be carried out is one for tribunals to work out in a manner which will avoid delay and unnecessary applications. I shall not say more on this aspect of the matter than that the decisions of the Employment Appeal Tribunal in *Stone v Charrington & Co. Ltd* (unreported), February 15, 1977, *per* Phillips J, *Oxford v Department of Health and Social Security* [1977] ICR 884, 887, *per* Phillips J and *British Railways Board v Natarajan* [1979] ICR 326 *per* Arnold J well indicate the lines of a satisfactory procedure, which must of course be flexible.

7   The above conclusions are essentially in agreement with those of the Court of Appeal. I venture to think however that the formula suggested, namely [1979] QB 144, 173, 182:

The industrial tribunals should not order or permit the disclosure of reports or references that have been given and received in confidence except in the very rare cases where, after inspection of a particular document, the chairman decides that it is essential in the interests of justice that the confidence should be overridden: and then only subject to such conditions as to the divulging of it as he shall think fit to impose — both for the protection of the maker of the document and the subject of it.

may be rather too rigid. For myself I prefer to rest such rule as can be stated upon the discretion of the court.

LORD EDMUND DAVIES: Learned counsel for the appellants went so far as to submit that the confidential nature of the documents here in question is totally irrelevant to the matter of discovery, and that the tribunal or court should therefore wholly ignore the protests of third parties against the disclosure of information furnished by them in the belief that neither it nor its sources would ever be revealed. Reliance for that submission was placed on cases ranging from *Hopkinson* v *Lord Burghley* (1867) LR 2 Ch App 447 to *McIvor* v *Southern Health and Social Services Board* [1978] 1 WLR 757; and the Industrial Relations Act 1971, section 158(1), and the Employment Protection Act 1975, section 18, were adverted to as illustrating Parliament's ability to provide express safeguards for the preservation of confidences when it thinks this is desirable. But for myself I am wholly unable to spell out from the absence of corresponding statutory provisions applicable to the present cases the conclusion that confidentiality is an irrelevance. It is true that it cannot of *itself* ensure protection from disclosure (*Alfred Crompton Amusement Machines Ltd* v *Customs and Excise Commissioners* (No. 2) [1974] AC 405; *D* v *National Society for the Prevention of Cruelty to Children* [1978] AC 171), but confidentiality may nevertheless properly play a potent part in the way in which a tribunal or court exercises its discretion in the matter of discovery.

There was ample evidence supporting the view expressed by the Court of Appeal that the disclosure to inspection of confidential reports could well create upsets and unrest which would have a general deleterious effect. And a court, mindful of that risk may understandably — and properly — think it right to scrutinise with particular care a request for their inspection. That is not to say, however, that the fear of possible unrest should deter the court from ordering discovery where the demands of justice clearly require it, but it serves to counsel caution in such cases.

LORD FRASER OF TULLYBELTON: The argument based on the need for candour in reporting echoes the argument which was presented in *Conway* v *Rimmer* [1968] AC 910 and I do not think that it has any greater weight now than it had then. The objections by and on behalf of employees other than the complainers to having their confidential reports disclosed, readily understandable as they are, do not create a public interest against disclosure. They are based on a private interest which must yield, in accordance with well-established principles, to the greater public interest that is deemed to exist in ascertaining the truth in order to do justice between the parties to litigation. I am not satisfied that disclosure of the contents of confidential reports of the kind in question here would have serious consequences upon the efficiency of British industry. In any event, the possibility of industrial unrest is not a sufficient reason for the courts to fail to give full effect to the intentions of Parliament; the courts cannot refuse to apply the law between litigants because of threats by third parties. Much reliance was placed in argument on a passage in the speech of Lord Hailsham of St. Marylebone in *D* v *National Society for the Prevention of Cruelty to Children* [1978] AC 171, 230 as follows:

> The categories of public interest are not closed, and must alter from time to time whether by restriction or extension as social conditions and social legislation develop.

Speaking for myself I fully accept that proposition, but any extension can only be made by adding new categories analogous to those already existing, just as in that case immunity was extended to a new category of informers to the NSPCC by analogy with informers to the police who were already entitled to immunity. There is no analogy between the suggested public interest in the present cases and the kinds of public interest that have so far been held to justify immunity from disclosure. Such public interest as there is in withholding the documents from disclosure is not enough to justify the creation of a new head of immunity for a whole class of documents.

Two other considerations point against immunity. One is that in some cases immunity would make it impossible for an employee to enforce his rights under the Acts. The confidential information is almost always in the possession of the employer, and, in cases where discrimination cannot be inferred from the bare fact that someone other than the complainer has been selected for preferment, it may be of vital importance to the complainer to have access to the reports on the preferred individual. This is particularly true where the complaint is based on discrimination on grounds of race or sex, because in those cases the onus of proof is on the complainer. But even where the complaint is of discrimination for trade union activities, and the onus is on the employer, disclosure may be essential in order to do justice between the parties.

The second consideration is that, if public interest immunity applied, it could not be waived either by the employer alone, or by the employer with the consent of the individual who is the subject of a report and of the person who made it. That would be inconvenient, and, in my opinion, quite unnecessarily restrictive.

LORD SCARMAN: For myself, I regret the passing of the currently rejected term 'Crown privilege'. It at least emphasised the very restricted area of public interest immunity. As was pointed out by Mr Lester QC who presented most helpful submissions on behalf of the two statutory bodies as well as specifically for the appellant, Mr Vyas, the immunity exists to protect from disclosure only information the secrecy of which is essential to the proper working of the government of the state. Defence, foreign relations, the inner workings of government at the highest levels where ministers and their advisers are formulating national policy, and the prosecution process in its pre-trial stage are the sensitive areas where the Crown must have the immunity if the government of the nation is to be effectually carried on. We are in the realm of public law, not private right. The very special case of *D v National Society for the Prevention of Cruelty to Children* [1978] AC 171 is not to be seen as a departure from this well established principle. Immunity from disclosure existed in that case because the House recognised the special position of the NSPCC in the enforcement process of the provisions of the Children Act 1969: a position which the House saw as comparable with that of a prosecuting authority in criminal proceedings. But I would not, with respect, go as far as my noble and learned friend, Lord Hailsham of St Marylebone, when he said in that case, at p. 230: 'The categories of public interest are not closed;' nor can I agree with the *dictum* of my noble and learned friend, Lord Edmund-Davies, at p. 245 that, where a confidential relationship exists and disclosure would be in breach of some ethical or social value involving the public interest, the court may uphold a refusal to disclose relevant evidence, if, on balance, the public interest would be better served by excluding it.

I do not find anything in *Conway v Rimmer* [1968] AC 910 or the cases therein cited which would extend public interest immunity in this way. On the contrary, the theme of Lord Reid's speech is that the immunity arises only if 'disclosure would involve a danger of real prejudice to the national interest' (p. 939). The public interest protected by the immunity is that 'harm shall not be done to the nation or the public service by disclosure': Lord Reid at p. 940. Whatever may be true generally of the categories of public interest, the 'public interest immunity', which prevents documents from being produced or evidence from being given is restricted, and is not, in my judgment, to be extended either by demanding ministers or by the courts. And, though I agree with my noble and learned friend, Lord Edmund-Davies, in believing that a court may refuse to order production of a confidential document if it takes the view that justice does not require its production, I do not see the process of decision as a balancing act. If the document is necessary for fairly disposing of the case, it must be produced, notwithstanding its confidentiality. Only if the document should be protected by public interest immunity, will there be a balancing act. And then the balance will not be between 'ethical or social' values of a confidential relationship involving the public interest and the document's relevance in the litigation, but between the public interest represented by the state and its public service, i.e., the executive government, and the public interest in the administration of justice: see Lord Reid. Thus my emphasis would be different from that of my noble and learned friends. 'Public interest immunity' is, in my judgment, restricted to what must be kept secret for the protection of government at the highest levels and in the truly sensitive areas of executive responsibility.

(LORD SALMON delivered a concurring judgment.)

Appeals dismissed.

Burmah Oil Co. Ltd v Governor and Company of the Bank of England
[1980] AC 1090
House of Lords

The company sought a declaration against the Bank that a sale by the company to the Bank of certain stock at a price required by the government, pursuant to an agreement made in 1975, was inequitable and unfair, and claimed an order for the transfer back of the stock at the 1975 price. The company had, at the time of the agreement, been in dire financial straits because of an international oil crisis, and the agreement had been designed to 'rescue' the company, under the very close control of the government, working through the Bank. The company sought discovery of all relevant documents. The Crown intervened and objected to the production of some sixty-two documents, which for this purpose were divided into three categories. Categories A and B both related to the formulation of government economic policy, at ministerial level and at a lower level. By a majority, the Court of Appeal upheld the Crown's objection. The company appealed.

LORD SCARMAN: It is said — and this view commended itself to the majority of the Court of Appeal — that the bank has given very full discovery of the documents directly relevant to the critical issue in the action, namely, the conduct by the bank of the negotiations with Burmah: that Burmah knows as much about this issue as does the bank: and that it can be fully investigated and decided upon the documents disclosed and the evidence available to Burmah without recourse to documents noting or recording the private discussions between the bank and the government. Upon this view, Burmah's attempt to see these documents is no more than a fishing expedition.

I totally reject this view of the case. First, as a matter of law, the documents for which immunity is claimed relate to the issues in the action and, according to the *Peruvian Guano* formulation, 11 QBD 55, may well assist towards a fair disposal of the case. It is unthinkable that in the absence of a public immunity objection and without a judicial inspection of the documents disclosure would have been refused. Secondly, common sense must be allowed to creep into the picture. Burmah's case is not merely that the bank exerted pressure: it is that the bank acted unreasonably, abusing its power and taking an unconscionable advantage of the weakness of Burmah. Upon these questions the withheld documents may be very revealing. This is not 'pure speculation'. The government was creating the pressure: the bank was exerting it upon the government's instructions. Is a court to assume that such documents will not assist towards an understanding of the nature of the pressure exerted? The assumption seems to me as unreal as the proverbial folly of attempting to understand Hamlet without reference to his position as the Prince of Denmark. I do not understand how a court could properly reach the judge's conclusion without inspecting the documents: and this he refused to do. The judge in my opinion wrongly exercised his discretion when he refused to inspect unless public policy (of which public interest immunity is a manifestation) required him to refuse.

It becomes necessary, therefore, to analyse closely the public interest immunity objection made by the minister and to determine the correct approach of the court to a situation in which there may be a clash of two interests — that of the public service and that of justice.

In *Conway* v *Rimmer* [1968] AC 910 this House had to consider two questions. They were formulated by Lord Reid in these terms, at p. 943:

> . . . first, whether the court is to have any right to question the finality of a minister's certificate and, secondly, if it has such a right, how and in what circumstances that right is to be exercised and made effective.

The House answered the first question, but did not, in my judgment, provide, nor was it required to provide, a complete answer to the second.

As I read the speeches in *Conway* v *Rimmer* the House answered the first question by establishing the principle of judicial review. The minister's certificate is not final. The immunity is a rule of law: its scope is a question of law: and its applicability to the facts of a particular case is for the court, not the minister, to determine. The statement of Lord Kilmuir LC of June 6, 1956 (all that is relevant is quoted in *Conway* v *Rimmer* at p. 922) that: 'The minister's certificate on affidavit setting out the ground of the claim must in England be accepted by the court . . .' is no longer a correct statement of the law. Whether *Conway* v *Rimmer* be seen as a development of or a departure from previous English case law is a matter of no importance. What is important is that it aligned English law with the law of Scotland and of the Commonwealth. It is the heir apparent not of *Duncan* v *Cammell, Laird & Co. Ltd* [1942] AC 624 but of *Robinson* v *State of South Australia (No. 2)* [1931] AC 704 and of *Glasgow Corporation* v *Central Land Board*, 1956 SC (HL) 1.

Having established the principle of judicial review, the House had in *Conway* v *Rimmer* [1968] AC 910 a simple case on the facts to decide. The question was whether routine reports, albeit of a confidential character, upon a former probationary police constable should in the interests of justice be disclosed in an action brought by him against his former superintendent in which he claimed damages for alleged malicious prosecution. There was a public interest in the confidentiality of such reports, but the Home Secretary, in his affidavit objecting to production on the ground of injury to the public interest, did not go so far as to say that it was necessary for the proper functioning of the public service to withhold production. On the other hand, the reports might be of critical importance in the litigation. Granted the existence of judicial review, here was a justiciable issue of no great difficulty. The House decided itself to inspect the documents, and, having done so, ordered production.

In reaching its decision the House did indicate what it considered to be the correct approach to the clash of interests which arises whenever there is a question of public interest immunity. The approach is to be found stated in two passages of Lord Reid's speech: pp. 940 and 952. The essence of the matter is a weighing, on balance, of the two public interests, that of the nation or the public service in non-disclosure and that of justice in the production of the documents. A good working, but not logically perfect, distinction is recognised between the contents and the classes of documents. If a minister of the Crown asserts that to disclose the contents of a document would, or might, do the nation or the public service a grave injury, the court will be slow to question his opinion or to allow any interest, even that of justice, to prevail over it. Unless there can be shown to exist some factor suggesting either a lack of good faith (which is not likely) or an error of judgment or an error of law on the minister's part, the court should not (the House held) even go so far as itself to inspect the document. In this sense, the minister's assertion may be said to be conclusive. It is, however, for the judge to determine whether the minister's opinion is to be treated as conclusive. I do not understand the House to have denied that even in 'contents' cases the court retains its power to inspect or to balance the injury to the public service against the risk of injustice, before reaching its decision.

In 'class' cases the House clearly considered the minister's certificate to be more likely to be open to challenge. Undoubtedly, however, the House thought that there were certain classes of documents, which ought not to be disclosed however harmless the disclosure of their contents might be, and however important their disclosure might be in the interest of justice. Cabinet minutes were cited as an example. But the point did not arise for decision. For the documents in *Conway* v *Rimmer* [1968] AC 910, though confidential, were 'routine', in no way concerned with the inner working of the government at a high level; and their production might well be indispensable to the doing of justice in the litigation.

The point does arise in the present case. The documents are 'high level'. They are concerned with the formulation of policy. They are part of the inner working of the government machine. They contain information which the court knows does relate to matters in issue in the action, and which may, on inspection, prove to be highly material. In such circumstances the minister may well be right in his view that the public service would be injured by disclosure. But is the court bound by his view that it is *necessary* for the proper functioning of the public service that they be withheld from production? And, if non-disclosure is necessary for that purpose, is the court bound to hold that the interest in the proper functioning of the public service is to prevail over the requirements of justice?

If the answer to these two questions is to be in the affirmative as Lord Reid appears to suggest in *Conway* v *Rimmer*, I think the law reverts to the statement of Lord Kilmuir. A properly drawn minister's certificate, which is a *bona fide* expression of his opinion, becomes final. But the advance made in the law by *Conway* v *Rimmer* was that the certificate is not final. I think, therefore, that it would now be inconsistent with principle to hold that the court may not — even in a case like the present — review the certificate and balance the public interest of government to which alone it refers, against the public interest of justice, which is the concern of the court.

I do not therefore accept that there are any classes of document which, however harmless their contents and however strong the requirement of justice, may never be disclosed until they are only of historical interest. In this respect I think there may well be a difference between a 'class' objection and a 'contents' objection — though the residual power to inspect and to order disclosure must remain in both instances. A Cabinet minute, it is said, must be withheld from production. Documents relating to the formulation of policy at a high level are also to be withheld. But is the secrecy of the 'inner workings of the government machine' so vital a public interest that it must prevail over even the most imperative demands of justice? If the contents of a document concern the national safety, affect diplomatic relations or relate to some state secret of high importance, I can understand an affirmative answer. But if they do not (and it is not claimed in this case that they do), what is so important about secret government that it must be protected even at the price of injustice in our courts?

The reasons given for protecting the secrecy of government at the level of policy-making are two. The first is the need for candour in the advice offered to ministers: the second is that disclosure 'would create or fan ill-informed or captious public or political criticism'. Lord Reid in *Conway* v *Rimmer* [1968] AC 910, 952, thought the second 'the most important reason'. Indeed, he was inclined to discount the candour argument.

I think both reasons are factors legitimately to be put into the balance which has to be struck between the public interest in the proper functioning of the public service (i.e., the executive arm of government) and the public interest in the administration of justice. Sometimes the public service reasons will be decisive of the issue: but they should never prevent the court from weighing them against the injury which would be suffered in the administration of justice if the document was not to be disclosed. And the likely injury to the cause of justice must also be assessed and weighed. Its weight will vary according to the nature of the proceedings in which disclosure is sought, the relevance of the documents, and the degree of likelihood that the document will be of importance in the litigation. In striking the balance, the court may always, if it thinks it is necessary, itself inspect the documents.

Inspection by the court is, I accept, a power to be exercised only if the court is in doubt, after considering the certificate, the issues in the case and the relevance of the documents whose disclosure is sought. Where documents are relevant (as in this case they are), I would think a pure 'class' objection would by itself seldom quieten judicial doubts — particularly if, as here, a substantial case can be made out for saying that disclosure is needed in the interest of justice.

I am fortified in the opinion which I have expressed by the trend towards inspection and disclosure to be found both in the United States and in Commonwealth countries. Of course, the United States have a written constitution and a Bill of Rights. Nevertheless both derive from the common law and British political philosophy. *Mutatis mutandis,* I would adopt the principle accepted by the Supreme Court in *Nixon* v *United States,* 418 US 683 which is summarised in 41 LEd 2d 1039, 1046:

Neither the doctrine of separation of powers, nor the need for confidentiality of high level communications, without more, can sustain an absolute unqualified presidential privilege of immunity from judicial process under all circumstances; although the President's need for complete candor and objectivity from advisers calls for great deference from the courts, nevertheless when the privilege depends solely on the broad, undifferentiated claim of public interest in the confidentiality of such conversations, a confrontation with other values arises; absent a claim of need to protect military, diplomatic or sensitive national security secrets, it is difficult to accept the argument that even the very important interest in confidentiality of Presidential communications is significantly diminished by production of such material for in camera inspection with all the protection that a United States District Court will be obliged to provide.

In Australia the High Court had to consider the problem in a recent case where the facts were, admittedly, exceptional. In *Sankey v Whitlam*, 53 ALJR 11 [(1978) 21 ALR 505] the plaintiff sought declarations that certain papers and documents, to which the magistrate in criminal proceedings instituted by the plaintiff against the defendants had accorded privilege, should be produced. The offences alleged against Mr Whitlam, a former Prime Minister, and others were serious — conspiracies to act unlawfully in the conduct of official business. Gibbs ACJ dealt with the issue of Crown privilege as follows:

For these reasons I consider that although there is a class of documents whose members are entitled to protection from disclosure irrespective of their contents, the protection is not absolute, and it does not endure for ever. The fundamental and governing principle is that documents in the class may be withheld from production only when this is necessary in the public interest. In a particular case the court must balance the general desirability that documents of that kind should not be disclosed against the need to produce them in the interests of justice. The court will of course examine the question with especial care, giving full weight to the reasons for preserving the secrecy of documents of this class, but it will not treat all such documents as entitled to the same measure of protection — the extent of protection required will depend to some extent on the general subject matter with which the documents are concerned. If a strong case has been made out for the production of the documents, and the court concludes that their disclosure would not really be detrimental to the public interest, an order for production will be made. In view of the danger to which the indiscriminate disclosure of documents of this class might give rise, it is desirable that the government concerned, Commonwealth or State, should have an opportunity to intervene and be heard before any order for disclosure is made. Moreover no such order should be enforced until the government concerned has had an opportunity to appeal against it, or test its correctness by some other process, if it wishes to do so (cf. *Conway v Rimmer* [1968] AC 910, 953).

Both *Nixon's* case, 418 US 683 and *Sankey v Whitlam*, 53 ALJR 11 are far closer to the Scottish and Commonwealth stream of authority than to the English. In the *Glasgow Corporation* case, 1956 SC (HL) 1, Viscount Simonds said, at p. 11; 'that there always has been and is now in the law of Scotland an inherent power of the court to override the Crown's objection to produce documents on the ground that it would injure the public interest to do so'.

In *Robinson v State of South Australia (No. 2)* [1931] AC 704 the Privy Council reminded the Supreme Court of South Australia of the existence of this power. The power must be exercised judicially, and all due weight must be given to the objections of the Crown: that is all.

Something was made in argument about the risk to the nation or the public service of an error at first instance. Injury to the public interest — perhaps even very serious injury — could be done by production of documents which should be immune from disclosure before an appellate court could correct the error. The risk is inherent in the principle of judicial review. The House in *Conway* v *Rimmer* [1968] AC 910 recognised its existence, but, nevertheless, established the principle as part of our law. Gibbs J also mentioned it in *Sankey* v *Whitlam*, 53 ALJR 11. I would respectfully agree with Lord Reid's observations on the point in *Conway* v *Rimmer* [1968] AC 910, 953: '. . . it is important that the minister should have a right to appeal before the document is produced'.

In cases where the Crown is not a party — as in the present case — the court should ensure that the Attorney-General has the opportunity to intervene before disclosure is ordered.

For these reasons I was one of a majority of your Lordships who thought it necessary to inspect the 10 documents. Having done so, I have no doubt that they are relevant and, but for the immunity claim, would have to be disclosed, but their significance is not such as to override the public service objections to their production. Burmah will not suffer injustice by their non-disclosure, while their disclosure would be, in the opinion of the responsible minister, injurious to the public service. I would, therefore, dismiss the appeal.

LORD KEITH OF KINKEL: In my opinion, it would be going too far to lay down that no document in any particular one of the categories mentioned should never in any circumstances be ordered to be produced . . . Something must turn upon the nature of the subject matter, the persons who dealt with it, and the manner in which they did so. In so far as a matter of government policy is concerned, it may be relevant to know the extent to which the policy remains unfulfilled, so that its success might be prejudiced by disclosure of the considerations which led to it. In that context the time element enters into the equation. Details of an affair which is stale and no longer of topical significance might be capable of disclosure without risk of damage to the public interest. The ministerial certificate should offer all practicable assistance on these aspects. But the nature of the litigation and the apparent importance to it of the documents in question may in extreme cases demand production even of the most sensitive communications at the highest level. Such a case might fortunately be unlikely to arise in this country, but in circumstances such as those of *Sankey* v *Whitlam*, 53 ALJR 11 or *Nixon* v *United States* (1974) 418 US 683 to which reference is made in the speech of my noble and learned friend Lord Scarman, I do not doubt that the principles there expounded would fall to be applied. There can be discerned in modern times a trend towards more open governmental methods than were prevalent in the past. No doubt it is for Parliament and not for courts of law to say how far that trend should go. The courts are, however, concerned with the consideration that it is in the public interest that justice should be done and should be publicly recognised as having been done. This may demand, though no doubt only in a very limited number of cases, that the inner workings of government should be exposed to public gaze, and there may be some who would regard this as likely to lead, not to captious or ill-informed criticism, but to criticism calculated to improve the nature of that working as affecting the individual citizen. I think that considerations of that nature were present in the mind of Lord Denning MR when delivering his dissenting judgment in the Court of Appeal in this case, and in my opinion they correctly reflect what the trend of the law should be.

There are cases where consideration of the terms of the ministerial certificate and of the nature of the issues in the case before it as revealed by the pleadings, taken with the description of the documents sought to be recovered, will make it clear to the court that the balance of public interest lies against disclosure. In other cases the position will be the reverse. But there may be situations where grave doubt arises, and the court feels that it cannot properly decide upon which side the balance falls without privately inspecting the documents. In my opinion the present is such a case.

(LORDS SALMON and EDMUND-DAVIES agreed that the documents should be inspected. LORD WILBERFORCE dissented on that issue. After inspecting them the majority found (LORD KEITH *dubitante)* that none was of such evidential value as to justify an order for disclosure for the purpose of disposing fairly of the case.)

Appeal dismissed.

Campbell v *Tameside Metropolitan Borough Council*
[1982] QB 1065
Court of Appeal

The prospective plaintiff, a school teacher employed by the defendant education authority, was violently assaulted by an 11-year-old boy in her classroom and suffered severe injuries. Before commencing proceedings against the defendants, the plaintiff applied for an order for disclosure of all documents in their possession relating to the boy including the reports of teachers and of psychologists and psychiatrists. The defendants contended that they were confidential documents of a class which was protected by public interest immunity. Russell J, after he had inspected the relevant documents ordered the defendants to disclose documents in their possession concerning the educational and psychological welfare of the boy. The defendants appealed.

LORD DENNING MR: We have many cases about children in the care of local authorities. One side or the other ask to see the reports which the children's officers have made on the children. They are always confidential. Never, I think, have we ordered them to be disclosed. They are privileged — not because of their actual contents — but because as a class they should be kept confidential. We have always found that justice can be done in the individual case without compelling disclosure of these documents.

The first case was *In re D (Infants)* [1970] 1 WLR 599, which was approved by the House of Lords in *D* v *National Society for the Prevention of Cruelty to Children* [1978] AC 171. Another is *Gaskin* v *Liverpool City Council* [1980] 1 WLR 1549. The latest is *R* v *Birmingham City Council, ex parte O* [1982] 1 WLR 679. In every case our task was to hold the balance between the interests involved. On the one hand the public interest in keeping the reports confidential. On the other hand the public interest in seeing that justice is done.

Mr Clegg for the education authority relied on those cases. But in addition he relied particularly on a recent case in this court of *Neilson* v *Laugharne* [1981] QB 736. *Neilson* v *Laugharne* was considered by the court a few weeks ago in *Hehir* v *Commissioner of Police of the Metropolis* [1982] 1 WLR 715. The court doubted its correctness but felt it was bound by it. . . . I do not think that *Neilson* v *Laugharne* [1981] QB 736 compelled the result. This court was not referred to the line of cases where a man has made a statement in a confidential document and then afterwards goes into the witness box and gives evidence contrary to what he said in the confidential document. It has always been held that he can be cross-examined on the confidential document, in which case the whole document is to be made available: see

North Australian Territory Co. v *Goldsborough, Mort and Co.* [1893] 2 Ch 381; *Burnell* v *British Transport Commission* [1956] 1 QB 187 and more fully in [1955] 2 Lloyd's Rep 549 and *Alfred Crompton Amusement Machines Ltd* v *Customs and Excise Commissioners (No. 2)* [1974] AC 405, 434, where Lord Cross of Chelsea said: 'No doubt it will form part of the brief delivered to counsel for the commissioners and may help him to probe the appellants' evidence in cross-examination.'

The reasoning behind it is that the maker of a confidential document can always waive the privilege which attaches to it, or by his conduct become disentitled to it. When he goes into the box and gives evidence which is contrary to his previous statement — then the public interest in the administration of justice outweighs the public interest in keeping the document confidential. He can be cross-examined to show that his evidence in the box is not trustworthy.

I know that in the days of the old Crown privilege it was often said that it could not be waived. That is still correct when the documents are in the vital category spoken of by Lord Reid in *Conway* v *Rimmer* [1968] AC 910, 940. This category includes all those documents which must be kept top secret because the disclosure of them would be injurious to national defence or to diplomatic relations or the detection of crime (as the names of informers). But not where the documents come within Lord Reid's lower category. This category includes those documents which are kept confidential in order that subordinates should be frank and candid in their reports, or for any other good reason. In those cases the privilege can be waived by the maker and recipients of the confidential document. It was so held by Lord Cross of Chelsea in *Alfred Crompton Amusement Machines Ltd* v *Customs and Excise Commissioners (No. 2)* [1974] AC 405, 434H, when he said: 'if any of them is in fact willing to give evidence, privilege in respect of any documents or information obtained from him will be waived.'

I am still of opinion, therefore, that *Neilson* v *Laugharne* [1981] QB 736 was correctly decided. It is worth noticing that the House of Lords [1981] 2 WLR 553 refused leave to appeal in it. I would, therefore, stand by the principle, at p. 748:

> This modern development shows that, on a question of discovery, the court can consider the competing public interests involved. The case is decided by the court holding the balance between the two sides. One of them is asserting that, in the interest of justice, the documents should be disclosed. The other is asserting that in the public interest they should not be disclosed. Confidentiality is often to be considered. So is the need for candour and frankness. So is the desirability of co-operation. Or any other factors which present themselves. On weighing them all the judge decides according to which side the balance comes down. Once it is decided that the public interest is in favour of non-disclosure, the decision is regarded as a precedent for later situations of the same kind. So the body of law is built up. As Lord Hailsham of St Marylebone said in *D* v *National Society for the Prevention of Cruelty to Children* [1978] AC 171, 230: 'The categories of public interest are not closed, and must alter from time to time whether by restriction or extension as social conditions and social legislation develop.'

In holding the balance, I would add an additional factor. It applies especially to the lower category spoken of by Lord Reid in *Conway* v *Rimmer* [1968] AC 910, 940. In these cases the court can and should consider the *significance* of the documents in relation to the decision of the case. If they are of such significance that they may well affect the very decision of the case, then justice may require them to be disclosed. The public interest in justice being done — in the instant case — may well outweigh the public interest in keeping them confidential. But, if they are of little significance, so that they are very unlikely to affect the decision of the case, then the greater public interest may be to keep them confidential. In order to assess their significance, it is open to the court itself to inspect the documents. If disclosure is necessary in the interest of justice in the instant case, the court will order their disclosure. But otherwise not. That is the basic reason why the Burmah Oil Company did not get discovery of the documents of the Bank of England. It was not necessary for fairly disposing of the matter: see *Burmah Oil Co. Ltd* v *Governor and Company of the Bank of England* [1980] AC 1090, 1121 and 1122, *per* Lord Salmon; pp. 1129 and 1130, *per* Lord Edmund-Davies; p. 1136, *per* Lord Keith of Kinkel; pp. 1145 and 1147 *per* Lord Scarman.

Like the judge, I have looked at the documents. I think that they may be of considerable significance, They go to show whether or not he was of a violent disposition. They go to show whether he should have been allowed to go into this class or not. And so forth. I see no difference between this case and any other school case where a child is injured in the playground by defective equipment, or by want of supervision by the teacher. Full discovery would be ordered there. There is no difference in principle between a child being injured and a teacher being injured. Nor indeed do I see any difference between this case and the ordinary case against a hospital authority for negligence. The reports of nurses and doctors are, of course, confidential; but they must always be disclosed: subject to the safeguard that they are only for use in connection with the instant case and not for any other purpose: see *Riddick* v *Thames Board Mills Ltd* [1977] QB 881 and *Home Office* v *Harman* [1982] 2 WLR 338.

So here, I am quite clear that these documents must be disclosed for use in this litigation. They must not, of course, be used for any other purpose.

ACKNER LJ: Despite the apparent conflict in the able submissions addressed to us, the basic principles which we must apply in the resolution of this dispute do not seem to me to be much in issue. These are:

1   The exclusion of relevant evidence always calls for clear justification. All relevant documents, whether or not confidential, are subject to disclosure unless upon some recognised ground, including the public interest, their non-disclosure is permissible.

2   Since it has been accepted in this court that the documents for which the respondent seeks discovery are relevant to the contemplated litigation, there is a heavy burden upon the appellants to justify withholding them from disclosure; see in particular *Conway* v *Rimmer* [1968] AC 910 and *R* v *Lewes Justices, ex parte Secretary of State for the Home Department* [1973] AC 388, 400, *per* Lord Reid.

3   The fact that information has been communicated by one person to another in confidence is not, of itself, a sufficient ground for protection from disclosure in a court of law, either the nature of the information or the identity of the informant if either of these matters would assist the court to ascertain facts which are relevant to an issue upon which it is adjudicating: *Alfred Crompton Amusement Machines Ltd* v *Customs and Excise Commissioners (No. 2)* [1974] AC 405, 433-443. The private promise of confidentiality must yield to the general public interest, that in the administration of justice truth will out, unless by reason of the character of the information or the relationship of the recipient of the information to the informant a more important public interest is served by protecting the information or identity of the informant from disclosure in a court of law: *per* Lord Diplock, *D* v *National Society for the Prevention of Cruelty to Children* [1978] AC 171, 218. Immunity from disclosure was permitted in that case because the House of Lords recognised the special position of

the NSPCC in the enforcement process of the provisions of the Children and Young Persons Act 1969, a position which the House saw as comparable with that of a prosecuting authority in criminal proceedings. It applied the rationale of the rule as it applies to police informers, that if their identity was liable to be disclosed in a court of law, this source of information would dry up and the police would be hindered in their duty of detecting and preventing crime.

4   Documents in respect of which a claim is made for immunity from disclosure come under a rough but accepted categorisation known as a 'class' claim or a 'contents' claim. The distinction between them is that with a 'class' claim it is immaterial whether the disclosure of the particular contents of particular documents would be injurious to the public interest — the point being that it is the maintenance of the immunity of the 'class' from disclosure in litigation that is important. In the 'contents' claim, the protection is claimed for particular 'contents' in a particular document. A claim remains a 'class' even though something may be known about the documents; it remains a 'class' even if part of documents are revealed and part disclosed: per Lord Wilberforce in *Burmah Oil Co. Ltd* v *Governor and Company of the Bank of England* [1980] AC 1090, 1111.

5   The proper approach where there is a question of public interest immunity is a weighing, on balance, of the two public interests, that of the nation or the public service in non-disclosure and that of justice in the production of the documents. Both in the 'class' objection and the 'contents' objection the courts retain the residual power to inspect and to order disclosure: *Burmah Oil* case [1980] AC 1090, 1134, *per* Lord Keith of Kinkel; pp. 1143-1144, *per* Lord Scarman.

6   A judge conducting the balancing exercise needs to know whether the documents in question are of much or little weight in the litigation, whether their absence will result in a complete or partial denial of justice to one or other of the parties or perhaps to both, and what is the importance of the particular litigation to the parties and the public. All these are matters which should be considered if the court is to decide where the public interest lies: *per* Lord Pearce in *Conway* v *Rimmer* [1968] AC 910, 987, quoted by Lord Edmund-Davies in the *Burmah Oil* case [1980] AC 1090, 1129. Lord Edmund-Davies commented that a judge may well feel that he cannot profitably embark on such a balancing exercise without himself seeing the disputed documents and cited in support of that view the observations of Lord Reid and Lord Upjohn in *Conway* v *Rimmer* [1968] AC 910, 953, 995.

(O'CONNOR LJ also delivered a judgment dismissing the appeal.)

Appeal dismissed

A.W. Bradley, 'Justice, Good Government and Public Interest Immunity'
(1992) *Public Law* 514, pp. 517–20

At least since *Duncan* v *Cammell Laird* [1942] AC 624, the common law relating to what is now termed public interest immunity (PII) has raised vexing questions about the division of functions (or separation of powers) between government and the courts. In 1956, Lord Radcliffe said, 'The interests of government, for which the Minister should speak with full authority, do not exhaust the public interest.' Although these words are applicable in many situations, their relevance to the law of official secrecy was ignored by McCowan J in his direction to the jury in *R* v *Ponting*.

As regards the Matrix Churchill trial, it appears that four ministers signed certificates claiming PII for documents relating to communications between ministers, civil servants and the security service about the government's policy on arms for Iraq and the handling of applications for export licences. The trial judge (Judge Smedley, QC) having considered the certificates and the defence submissions admitted the evidence. Once the trial had collapsed, it was alleged that the government had kept secret its real policy on arms for Iraq, and that the certificates of PII had been given to cover up the truth. Replying to the latter allegation, two of the ministers, Mr Kenneth Clarke and Mr Heseltine, stated that they had been advised by the Attorney-General that it was their duty to sign the certificates and that they had no discretion in the matter.

The opinions of law officers are in principle confidential unless a minister deems it expedient to make them known in Parliament or elsewhere. The stance taken by the ministers here raises the issue of whether the Attorney-General's advice was correct and whether it took account of the exceptional circumstances of the trial to which the documents were relevant.

So long as *Duncan* v *Cammell Laird* prevailed, and the courts were deemed to have no power to overrule the executive's claims for Crown privilege, in practice ministers and departments did at their discretion choose when to claim privilege. This power was exercised in a quasi-legislative manner when the Lord Chancellor twice indicated that privilege would not be claimed for certain classes of document.

In *Conway* v *Rimmer* [1968] AC 910, the House of Lords declared that the courts had power in the interests of the administration of justice to overrule executive claims to Crown privilege. This opened the way for the transformation of that privilege into an exclusionary rule of evidence, founded upon public policy, which must if necessary be applied directly by the court.

Recent decisions by the Court of Appeal confirm that PII is not a privilege that can be waived by the litigant who holds the documents. In *Neilson* v *Laugharne* [1981] QB 736, the Court of Appeal held, in an action for damages against the police, that public interest privilege was properly claimed on a 'class' basis in respect of statements made to the police during their investigation of a complaint by the plaintiff arising from the same events. Oliver LJ said:

> Every case of this kind depends ultimately on balancing the public interest in the administration of justice, which demands the disclosure of all relevant material, against a competing public interest in withholding that material . . . If public policy prevents disclosure, it prevents it . . . *in all circumstances except to establish innocence in criminal proceedings.*

This decision was followed in 1989 in an appeal on somewhat similar facts, *Makanjuola* v *Commissioner of Police* [1989] NLJ 468. Bingham LJ, with the approval of Lord Donaldson MR, summarised the law by emphasising that PII:

> is an exclusionary rule, imposed on parties in certain circumstances, even where it is to their disadvantage in litigation. *This does not mean that in any case where a party holds a document in a class prima facie immune he is bound to persist in an assertion of immunity* even where it is held that, on any weighing of the public interest in withholding the document against the public interest in disclosure for . . . furthering the administration of justice, there is a clear balance in favour of the latter.

PII could not 'in any ordinary sense' be waived. Where a litigant held documents that were prima facie immune he should '*save perhaps in a very exceptional case*' assert immunity and decline to disclose them, leaving the court to decide where the ultimate balance lies.

Where a senior woman police officer had taken proceedings against the police for sex discrimination, the Court of Appeal in *Halford* v *Sharples* by a majority arrived at the same result as in *Neilson* and *Makanjuola*, holding that there was an overriding public interest in maintaining the integrity of police complaints and disciplinary files even where the files were directly relevant to the allegations of discrimination. Dissenting, Ralph Gibson LJ took the view that the court was obliged 'in the circumstances of the case' to consider whether it was necessary for the proper functioning of the public service or for the proper fulfilment of the purpose of the legislation, to exclude the documents in question. While being aware of possible unfairness caused by the doctrine of immunity, he considered that the person possessing the documents (there, the chief constable) was as much entitled to ask the court to order the documents to be produced as the opposite party.

It is likely that the Attorney-General's advice to ministers was based on the principles emerging from these decisions. It does not follow that the ministers had a duty merely to sign standard-form certificates claiming PII. One important consideration is that these decisions of the Court of Appeal concerned civil actions, brought against the police, in which the adversary context of the actions was foremost in the judges' analysis of the competing interests before them. While PII is certainly capable of applying in criminal cases, the prosecutor can hardly seek a conviction and at the same time prevent a court from considering whether documents that might be subject to PII are in fact necessary for justice to be done. If damage to the public interest from disclosure of essential documents would be too great, the prosecutor has in that dilemma the option of not prosecuting.

Questions
1.   Considering the preceding cases, by what criteria should an assertion by a minister that documents should be withheld on grounds of public policy be judged?
2.   Should the courts' approach vary as between 'class claims' and 'contents claims'?
3.   Should the court ever inspect the document privately?
4.   Is confidentiality by itself ever sufficient to create public interest immunity?
5.   May public policy immunity ever be waived?

(B)   Private privilege

In addition to evidence being excluded on policy grounds, certain evidence may also be excluded on the ground that it is privileged. There are several categories of private privilege, the principal ones being: (i) the privilege against self-incrimination; (ii) legal professional privilege; and (iii) negotiations conducted 'without prejudice'.

The privilege against self-incrimination is concerned with the situation in which a person's truthful answers to questions may incriminate him, or give support to the bringing of a charge against him. For example, if W is testifying for a particular party in a case, is he required to answer a question put to him, the answer to which may incriminate him in the commission of a criminal offence?

Legal professional privilege is concerned with the extent to which communications between (i) lawyer and client, or (ii) lawyer and client and a third party, can be used in any subsequent litigation. In both cases, subject to certain conditions, the client may exercise a privilege preventing any such communications from being used in evidence.

Lastly in this section, consideration is given to that privilege known as 'without prejudice'. Any negotiations which take place with an opposing party with a view to reaching a settlement may be made 'without prejudice'. The law takes the view that it is in the interests of both parties and the public to reach a compromise agreement. Consequently, any communications made 'without prejudice' in the course of these negotiations may not be referred to at trial, either on the issue of liability, or as an indication of a party's willingness to settle.

(i)   Privilege against self-incrimination

Blunt v Park Lane Hotel Ltd and Briscoe
[1942] 2 KB 253
Court of Appeal

This was an action for slander based on an allegation that the plaintiff had committed adultery. The plaintiff objected to answering interrogatories which the defendants wished to administer in support of their plea of justification. The defendants were given leave to administer the interrogatories. The plaintiff appealed on the ground, *inter alia,* that an affirmative answer to the interrogatories would expose her to the risk of ecclesiastical penalties.

GODDARD LJ: [T]he rule is that no one is bound to answer any question if the answer thereto would, in the opinion of the judge, have a tendency to expose the deponent to any criminal charge, penalty, or forfeiture which the judge regards as reasonably likely to be preferred or sued for. This rule was laid down by the Queen's Bench in *R* v *Boyes* 1 B&S 311, and the words in which I have stated it are those of Stephen J in *Lamb* v *Munster* (1882) 10 QBD 110. A party can also claim privilege against discovery of documents on the like ground: see *Hunnings* v *Williamson* (1883) 10 QBD 459. Is there, then, except in a case of a clerk in holy orders, any reasonable likelihood that such interrogatories would expose a person to ecclesiastical penalties? It is purely fantastic to suppose anything of the sort. When Lord Hardwicke decided *Finch* v *Finch* 2 Ves Sen 493 and *Chetwynd* v *Lindon* 2 Ves Sen 450, there was, no doubt, a real risk of such proceedings. In those days the courts of the Church exercised a very active jurisdiction over the laity in criminal causes. Heresy, simony, defamation, brawling in church or churchyard, and all forms of immorality and not merely adultery were within their cognisance, *pro reformatione morum et pro salute animae* . . . Such jurisdiction has long been obsolete, so far as the laity are concerned, when it has not been expressly taken away by legislation.

. . . One other argument that was adduced was that an admission of adultery might result in the refusal of the sacrament to the offender. There is a complete air of unreality about such an argument in a case of this sort, and I will only say that, assuming that acts of adultery (of which the offender may have repented) as distinct from living in adultery would furnish 'lawful cause' within the Statute 1 Edward 6, C 1, for a minister's refusal to administer the sacrament, that is not a penalty within the rule to which I referred at the beginning of this judgment.

(LORD CLAWSON delivered a judgment to the same effect.)

Appeal dismissed.

Civil Evidence Act 1968

14. Privilege against incrimination of self or spouse

(1) The right of a person in any legal proceedings other than criminal proceedings to refuse to answer any question or produce any document or thing if to do so would tend to expose that person to proceedings for an offence or for the recovery of a penalty —

(a) shall apply only as regards criminal offences under the law of any part of the United Kingdom and penalties provided for by such law; and

(b) shall include a like right to refuse to answer any question or produce any document or thing if to do so would tend to expose the husband or wife of that person to proceedings for any such criminal offence or for the recovery of any such penalty.

(2) In so far as any existing enactment conferring (in whatever words) powers of inspection or investigation confers on a person (in whatever words) any right otherwise than in criminal proceedings to refuse to answer any question or give any evidence tending to incriminate that person, subsection (1) above shall apply to that right as it applies to the right described in that subsection; and every such existing enactment shall be construed accordingly.

(3) In so far as any existing enactment provides (in whatever words) that in any proceedings other than criminal proceedings a person shall not be excused from answering any question or giving any evidence on the ground that to do so may incriminate that person, that enactment shall be construed as providing also that in such proceedings a person shall not be excused from answering any question or giving any evidence on the ground that to do so may incriminate the husband or wife of that person.

(4) Where any existing enactment (however worded) that —

(a) confers powers of inspection or investigation; or

(b) provides as mentioned in subsection (3) above,

further provides (in whatever words) that any answer or evidence given by a person shall not be admissible in evidence against that person in any proceedings or class of proceedings (however described, and whether criminal or not), that enactment shall be construed as providing also that any answer or evidence given by that person shall not be admissible in evidence against the husband or wife of that person in the proceedings or class of proceedings in question.

(5) In this section 'existing enactment' means any enactment passed before this Act; and the references to giving evidence are references to giving evidence in any manner, whether by furnishing information, making discovery, producing documents or otherwise.

(ii)   Legal professional privilege

Minter v *Priest*
[1930] AC 558
House of Lords

The respondent refused to act as a solicitor in a transaction relating to land, and was alleged to have defamed the plaintiff in the course of giving his reasons for so refusing. The respondent pleaded that the slander was uttered on a privileged occasion and under such circumstances as to make it a privileged communication. The jury found for the appellant, but the Court of Appeal upheld the claim of privilege and set aside the judgment.

LORD BUCKMASTER: I am not prepared to assent to a rigid definition of what must be the subject of discussion between a solicitor and his client in order to secure the protection of professional privilege. That merely to lend money, apart from the existence or contemplation of professional help, is outside the ordinary scope of a solicitor's business is shown by the case of *Hagart and Burn-Murdoch* v *Inland Revenue Commissioners* [1929] AC 386. But it does not follow that, where a personal loan is asked for, discussions concerning it may not be of a privileged nature . . . .

The relationship of solicitor and client being once established, it is not a necessary conclusion that whatever conversation ensued was protected from disclosure. The conversation to secure this privilege must be such as, within a very wide and generous ambit of interpretation, must be fairly referable to the relationship, but outside that boundary the mere fact that a person speaking is a solicitor, and the person to whom he speaks is his client affords no protection.

LORD ATKIN: It is I think apparent that if the communication passes for the purpose of getting legal advice it must be deemed confidential. The protection of course attaches to the communications made by the solicitor as well as by the client. If therefore the phrase is expanded to professional communications passing for the purpose of getting or giving professional advice, and it is understood that the profession is the legal profession, the nature of the protection is I think correctly defined. One exception to this protection is established. If communications which otherwise would be protected pass for the purpose of enabling either party to commit a crime or a fraud the protection will be withheld. It is further desirable to point out, not by way of exception but as a result of the rule, that communications between solicitor and client which do not pass for the purpose of giving or receiving professional advice are not protected. It follows that client and solicitor may meet for the purpose of legal advice and exchange protected communications, and may yet in the course of the same interview make statements to each other not for the purpose of giving or receiving professional advice but for some other purpose. Such statements are not within the rule: see per Lord Wrenbury in *O'Rourke* v *Darbishire* [1920] AC 581, 629.

(VISCOUNT DUNEDIN, and LORDS THANKERTON and WARRINGTON of CLIFFE agreed.)

Appeal allowed.

R v *Central Criminal Court, ex parte Francis & Francis*
[1989] 1 AC 346
House of Lords

The police obtained an order *ex parte* under the Drug Trafficking Offences Act 1986, s. 27 for the production of G's client files held by a firm of solicitors. The police believed that G had been supplied with money to purchase property by a suspected drug trafficker. The solicitors applied for judicial review of the order on the ground, *inter alia*, that the material was subject to legal privilege as defined in the Police and Criminal Evidence Act 1984, s. 10. The Divisional Court dismissed the application and the solicitors appealed to the House of Lords.

LORD BRANDON OF OAKBROOK: My Lords, Part II of the Police and Criminal Evidence Act 1984, which comprises sections 8 to 22, is headed 'Powers of entry, search and seizure.' Under section 8 a justice of the peace, if satisfied of certain specified matters, may issue a warrant authorising a constable to enter and search premises for material likely to be of evidential value in relation to a serious arrestable offence, and a constable, acting on such a warrant, may seize and retain any such material. Items subject to legal privilege, however, are expressly excluded from the ambit of material which may be the subject matter of such a warrant.

The expression 'items subject to legal privilege' as used in section 8 is defined in section 10. The section provides:

(1) Subject to subsection (2) below, in this Act 'items subject to legal privilege' means — (a) communications between a professional legal adviser and his client or any person representing his client made in connection with the giving of legal advice to the client; (b) communications between a professional legal adviser and his client or any person representing his client or between such an adviser or his client or any such representative and any other person made in connection with or in contemplation of legal proceedings and for the purposes of such proceedings; and (c) items enclosed with or referred to in such communications and made — (i) in connection with the giving of legal advice; or (ii) in connection with or in contemplation of legal proceedings and for the purposes of such proceedings, when they are in the possession of a person who is entitled to possession of them. (2) Items held with the intention of furthering a criminal purpose are not items subject to legal privilege.

It is clear that the person by whom items are held in terms of subsection (2) is the person in whose possession they are and who is entitled to possession of them in terms of subsection (1). That person is the holder of the items and will in most cases be a solicitor.

The question for decision in this appeal is to whose intention the expression 'with the intention of furthering a criminal purpose' contained in subsection (2) refers. Does it refer to the intention of the holder only ('the first meaning')? Or does it refer to the intention of any person including the holder ('the second meaning')?

It has been suggested that the first meaning is the literal meaning of the expression, and even that it is the only meaning which the expression is, as a matter of grammar, capable of having. With great respect to those of your Lordships who are of that opinion, I do not agree with it. It would have been possible for the draftsman to have inserted the qualifying words 'of the holder' between the word 'intention' and the words 'of furthering.' Subsection (2) would then have read 'Items held with the intention of the holder of furthering a criminal purpose are not items subject to legal privilege,' and the first meaning would then with certainty have been the meaning intended. The draftsman could on the other hand have inserted the qualifying words 'of the holder or any other person' in the same place. Subsection (2) would then have read 'Items held with the intention of the holder or any other person of furthering a criminal purpose are not items subject to legal privilege.' There would have been nothing ungrammatical in making the latter insertion, and the result of it would have been that the second meaning would with certainty have been intended.

What then is the consequence of the draftsman having inserted no qualifying words between the word 'intention' and the words 'of furthering?' It is not, in my view, that the expression is only capable of having the first meaning. It is rather that the expression is capable of having either the first meaning or the second meaning, and that a choice between the two meanings has to be made by reference to the purpose of Part II of the Act.

That purpose is to give the police the power, when so authorised on proper grounds by the appropriate judicial authority to enter premises, search for material likely to be of evidential value in relation to a serious offence, and to seize and retain such material. That power is conferred on the police in the public interest, so that serious crimes may be more easily and effectively investigated and the perpetrators of them more easily and effectively prosecuted. If the first meaning of the expression 'with the intention of furthering a criminal purpose' is adopted, the result will be that items held by a solicitor will only be subject to search, seizure and retention if the solicitor himself has the intention concerned. If the second meaning of the expression is adopted, the result will be that items held by a solicitor will be subject to search, seizure and retention not only in cases where a solicitor himself has the intention concerned, but also in cases where a client, or another person making use of a client as an intermediary, has the intention concerned.

Because cases of solicitors having the intention of furthering a criminal purpose are happily rare, the first result referred to above would do little to assist in achieving the purpose of Part II of the Act, and would allow the principle of legal privilege to be used to protect the perpetrators of serious crimes. By contrast, the second result referred to above would materially assist in achieving the purpose of Part II of the Act, and would prevent the principle of legal privilege being used to protect the perpetrators of serious crimes.

The conclusion to which I am led by these considerations is that the legislature must have intended to bring about the second result rather than the first, and that the expression 'with the intention of furthering a criminal purpose' should therefore be given the second meaning rather than the first.

I would therefore answer the certified question as follows:

On the true construction of section 10(2) of the Police and Criminal Evidence Act 1984 items which would otherwise come within the definition of 'items subject to legal privilege' contained in section 10(1) are excluded from that definition if they are held with the intention of either the holder or any other person of furthering a criminal purpose.

and I would dismiss the appeal accordingly.

LORD BRIDGE OF HARWICH: . . . If the decision of the majority of your Lordships stopped short at construing section 10(2) of the Act of 1984 as embracing the intention of a client who has deceived his solicitor, and thus bringing the statute into line with the common law as expounded in *Reg.* v *Cox and Railton*, 14 QBD 153, I should be content to indicate my dissent for the reasons I have already sought to explain. But your Lordships take the very large further step of deciding that otherwise privileged communications between an innocent solicitor and his innocent client may lose their privilege, both under the statute and at common law, by reference to the intention of some third party to further a criminal purpose. As the case has been presented throughout, this is a necessary step if the decision of the Divisional Court is to be upheld and I well understand your Lordships' concern to give every assistance to the police in pursuit of drug traffickers, who are rightly regarded as enemies of society scarcely less deadly than terrorists. But this development of the law goes well beyond any previous authority and, if it is a legitimate extension of a previously accepted principle, it should be capable of being expressed in language sufficiently precise to make clear the boundary within which the new principle is to apply that the criminal intention of one party may operate to deprive another innocent party seeking legal advice of the protection of legal professional privilege. The answer proposed by your Lordships to the certified question in terms suggests that the relevant intention for the purposes of section 10(2) may be that of 'any other person' without limitation. The only other language which I find in any of your Lordship's speeches to indicate the required nexus between the criminal party and the innocent party, who is to be deprived of legal professional privilege for communications with his legal adviser, is that the latter is the 'innocent tool' of the former. If this is intended to serve as a sufficient definition of a new legal principle, I must say, with all respect, that I find it totally inadequate.

As I have earlier pointed out the facts on which we are required to decide this appeal are exiguously stated. All that is certain is that we are required to assume that Mrs G was the innocent beneficiary of the suspected drug trafficker's unconditional largesse. On this basis I can see that Mrs G may be described as the 'innocent tool' of the drug trafficker in receiving his ill gotten gains which he wished to 'launder.' I find it much more difficult to say that she acted as his 'innocent tool' in seeking legal advice in relation to the details of the property transaction effected with the proceeds. Be that as it may, the result in the instant case is of minor importance compared to the use which will be made of your Lordships' decision in future unforeseen and unforesee-able circumstances. Mr Worsley, in his forceful submissions for the respondent, made no secret of the fact that the police regard this as a test case of crucial importance and seek to open a very wide door in favour of criminal investigation at the expense of privilege. If section 10(2) were to be construed as embodying his suggested implied terms at their widest, it would seem to give the police unlimited access to privileged material which they could plausibly suggest to be intended to serve a criminal purpose irrespective of any connection between the party claiming privilege and the party whose criminal purpose was alleged to be served.

It is for these reasons that I am apprehensive that your Lordships' decision will open the door to a spate of applications to obtain access to privileged material on the ground that the privilege is vitiated by a criminal intention on the part of some third party. It will then fall to circuit judges, on a case by case basis, to seek to define the limits of application of the new principle in the absence of guidance from your Lordships. It is for their benefit that I feel obliged to sound this note of warning. Whilst loyally accepting the authority of your Lordships' decision on the facts, I cannot for a moment accept the wide terms of your Lordships' answer to the certified question as a satisfactory statement of the law without further limitation and definition.

For my part, I would allow the appeal and remit the case to the Divisional Court to determine which, if any, of the documents listed in schedule A to Otton J's order are items subject to legal privilege under section 10(1) of the Act of 1984. I would answer the certified question as follows:

> Upon the true construction of section 10(2) of the Police and Criminal Evidence Act 1984 items which would otherwise fall within the definition of 'items subject to legal privilege' are excluded from that definition if, but only if, the solicitor or other person holding the item in question has the intention of furthering a criminal purpose.

[LORD GRIFFITHS and LORD GOFF delivered speeches dismissing the appeal and LORD OLIVER delivered a speech allowing the appeal.]

Appeal dismissed with costs.

Question
In *Central Criminal Court, ex parte Francis & Francis*, whose reasoning do you find more convincing — Lord Brandon's or Lord Bridge's?

Waugh v *British Railways Board*
[1980] AC 521
House of Lords

The plaintiff's husband, an employee of the British Railways Board, was killed in an accident while working on the railways. In accordance with the board's usual practice a report on the accident, called an internal enquiry report, was prepared by two of the board's officers two days after the accident. The report was headed 'For the information of the Board's solicitor'. However, it appeared from an affidavit produced on behalf of the board that the report was prepared for two purposes: to establish the cause of the accident so that appropriate safety measures could be taken and to enable the board's solicitor to advise in the litigation that was almost certain to ensue. Although the first purpose was more immediate than the second, they were described in the affidavit as being of equal importance. The report contained statements by witnesses and was probably the best evidence available as to the cause of the accident. The plaintiff commenced an action against the board under the Fatal Accidents Act 1846 to 1959 and applied for discovery of the report to assist in preparing and conducting her case. The board resisted discovery on the ground that the report was protected by legal professional privilege. The master ordered disclosure but on appeal the judge reversed the order. The plaintiff appealed to the Court of Appeal which held that a report which came into existence or was obtained for the purpose of anticipated litigation was privileged from production even though it might serve some other even more important purpose, and dismissed her appeal. The plaintiff appealed to the House of Lords.

LORD WILBERFORCE: My Lords, before I consider the authorities, I think it desirable to attempt to discern the reason why what is (inaccurately) called legal professional privilege exists. It is sometimes ascribed to the exigencies of the adversary system of litigation under which a litigant is entitled within limits to refuse to disclose the nature of his case until the trial. Thus one side may not ask to see the proofs of the other side's witnesses or the opponent's brief or even know what witnesses will be called: he must wait until the card is played and cannot try to see it in the hand. This argument cannot be denied some validity even where the defendant is a public corporation whose duty it is, so it might be thought, while taking all proper steps to protect its revenues, to place all the facts before the public and to pay proper compensation to those it has injured. A more powerful argument to my mind is that everything should be done in order to encourage anyone who knows the facts to state them fully and candidly — as Sir George Jessel MR said, to bare his breast to his lawyer: *Anderson* v *Bank of British Columbia* (1876) 2 ChD 644, 699. This he may not do unless he knows that his communication is privileged.

But the preparation of a case for litigation is not the only interest which calls for candour. In accident cases '. . . the safety of the public may well depend on the candour and completeness of reports made by subordinates whose duty it is to draw attention to defects': *Conway* v *Rimmer* [1968] AC 910, *per* Lord Reid, at p. 941. This however does not by itself justify a claim to privilege since, as Lord Reid continues:

'. . . no one has ever suggested that public safety has been endangered by the candour or completeness of such reports having been inhibited by the fact that they may have to be produced if the interests of the due administration of justice should ever require production at any time.'

So one may deduce from this the principle that while privilege may be required in order to induce candour in statements made for the purposes of litigation it is not required in relation to statements whose purpose is different — for example to enable a railway to operate safely.

It is clear that the due administration of justice strongly requires disclosure and production of this report: it was contemporary; it contained statements by witnesses on the spot; it would be not merely relevant evidence, but almost certainly the best evidence as to the cause of the accident. If one accepts that this important public interest can be over-ridden in order that the defendant may properly prepare his case, how close must the connection be between the preparation of the document and the anticipation of litigation? On principle I would think that the purpose of preparing for litigation ought to be either the sole purpose or at least the dominant purpose of it: to carry the protection further into cases where that purpose was secondary or equal with another purpose would seem to be excessive, and unnecessary in the interest of encouraging truthful revelation. At the lowest such desirability of protection as might exist in such cases is not strong enough to outweigh the need for all relevant documents to be made available.

There are numerous cases in which this kind of privilege has been considered. A very useful review of them is to be found in the judgment of Havers J in *Seabrook* v *British Transport Commission* [1959] 1 WLR 509 which I shall not repeat. It is not easy to extract a coherent principle from them. The two dominant authorities at the present time are *Birmingham and Midland Motor Omnibus Co.* v *London and North Western Railway Co.* [1913] 3 KB 850 and *Ogden* v *London Electric Railway Co.* (1933) 49 TLR 542, both decisions of the Court of Appeal. These cases were taken by the majority of the Court of Appeal in the present case to require the granting of privilege in cases where one purpose of preparing the document(s) in question was to enable the defendants' case to be prepared whether or not they were to be used for another substantial purpose. Whether in fact they compel such a conclusion may be doubtful — in particular I do not understand the *Birmingham* case to be one of dual purposes at all: but it is enough that they have been taken so to require. What is clear is that, though loyally followed, they do not now enjoy rational acceptance: in *Longthorn* v *British Transport Commission* [1959] 1 WLR 530 the manner in which Diplock J managed to escape from them, and the tenor of his judgment, shows him to have been unenthusiastic as to their merits. And in *Alfred Crompton Amusement Machines Ltd* v *Customs and Excise Commissioners (No. 2)* [1974] AC 405 Lord Cross of Chelsea, at p. 432, pointedly left their correctness open, while Lord Kilbrandon stated, at p. 435, that he found the judgment of Scrutton LJ in *Ogden* v *London Electric Railway Co.*, 49 TLR 542, 543-544, 'hard to accept'. Only Viscount Dilhorne (dissenting) felt able to follow them in holding it to be enough if one purpose was the use by solicitors when litigation was anticipated.

The whole question came to be considered by the High Court of Australia in 1976: *Grant* v *Downs*, 135 CLR 674. This case involved reports which had 'as one of the material purposes for their preparation' submission to legal advisers in the event of litigation. It was held that privilege could not be claimed. In the joint judgment of Stephen, Mason and Murphy JJ, in which the English cases I have mentioned were discussed and analysed, it was held that 'legal professional privilege' must be confined to documents brought into existence for the sole purpose of submission to legal advisers for advice or use in legal proceedings. Jacobs J put the test in the form of a question, at p. 692: '. . . does the purpose' — in the sense of intention, the intended use — 'of supplying the material to the legal adviser account for the existence of the material?' Barwick CJ stated it in terms of 'dominant' purpose. This is closely in line with the opinion of Lord Denning MR in the present case that the privilege extends only to material prepared 'wholly or mainly for the purpose of preparing [the defendant's] case'. The High Court of Australia and Lord Denning MR agree in refusing to follow *Birmingham and Midland Motor Omnibus Co.* v *London and North Western Railway Co.* [1913] 3 KB 850 and *Ogden* v *London Electric Railway Co.*, 49 TLR 542, as generally understood.

My Lords, for the reasons I have given, when discussing the case in principle, I too would refuse to follow those cases. It appears to me that unless the purpose of submission to the legal adviser in view of litigation is at least the dominant purpose for which the relevant document was prepared, the reasons which require privilege to be extended to it cannot apply. On the other hand to hold that the purpose, as above, must be the sole purpose would, apart from difficulties of proof, in my opinion, be too strict a requirement, and would confine the privilege too narrowly: as to this I agree with Barwick CJ in *Grant* v *Downs*, 135 CLR 674, and in substance with Lord Denning MR.

(LORDS EDMUND-DAVIES, SIMON, RUSSELL and KEITH delivered concurring speeches.)

R v *Ataou*
[1988] 1 QB 798
Court of Appeal

FRENCH J: On 13 November 1986 in the Crown Court at Southwark the appellant was found guilty of conspiracy to supply a controlled drug (count 1) and of supplying a controlled drug (count 9). He was sentenced to five years' imprisonment on each count to run concurrently. On count 1, conspiracy, he was charged jointly with two others, Harvey and Christodoulou, both of whom pleaded guilty to that count, so that on it the appellant stood trial alone. He was also sentenced to 12 months' imprisonment for breach of a suspended sentence which his convictions constituted. He now appeals against conviction on a point of law.

The point taken on appeal arises out of the following facts. As we have stated, Harvey pleaded guilty to count 1 of the indictment. He pleaded not guilty to two other counts and these were allowed to lie on the file marked in the usual way. Harvey then elected to give evidence for the prosecution. While he was in the witness-box it was sought on behalf of the appellant to cross-examine Harvey on a previous and allegedly inconsistent statement made to his, Harvey's, solicitor. Harvey claimed privilege successfully. The question is whether that claim to privilege should have succeeded, or was otherwise correctly dealt with.

. . .

Our attention has been drawn to authorities in this country and in Commonwealth jurisdictions bearing on the topic. The first in order of date was *Reg.* v *Barton* [1973] 1 WLR 115. The short facts were that the defendant was charged with fraudulent conversion, theft and falsification of accounts, all alleged to have been committed in the course of his employment as a legal executive with a firm of solicitors. The defence served on a partner in the firm, who was already in attendance as a prosecution witness, notice to produce documents which had come into existence in the solicitors' office in the administration or winding up of estates in which his firm were acting or had acted. The defence contended that production of the documents was necessary for the proper defence of Barton. The solicitor, having consulted The Law Society, took the point that the documents were privileged and that he was not obliged to produce them. It appears that the objection was taken on general principles rather than on any contention that the interests of the clients in question would suffer from disclosure of the documents.

The trial judge, Caulfield J, ruled in favour of production of the documents, and said, at p. 118:

> I think the correct principle is this, and I think it must be restricted to these particular facts in a criminal trial, and the principle I am going to enunciate is not supported by any authority that has been cited to me, and I am just working on what I conceive to be the rules of natural justice. If there are documents in the possession or control of a solicitor which, on production, help to further the defence of an accused man, then in my judgment no privilege attaches. I cannot conceive that our law would permit a solicitor or other person to screen from a jury information which, if disclosed to the jury, would perhaps enable a man either to establish his innocence or to resist an allegation made by the Crown. I think that is the principle that should be followed.

It is noteworthy that, as one would expect, Caulfield J was careful, in an uncharted sea, to confine himself to the facts before him.

Barton's case was considered by Cooke J, a New Zealand judge of high distinction, in *Reg. v Craig* [1975] 1 NZLR 597. In that case the defendant had been indicted for perjury alleged to have been committed in a civil action brought against an insurance company in which the defendant had been a witness for the plaintiff. The Crown wished to call the solicitor who, when acting for the plaintiff in the civil action, had taken a proof of evidence from the defendant. The Crown sought to rely on the proof of evidence in support of their case that the defendant had perjured herself in the civil proceedings.

The judge heard argument as to the admissibility of the solicitor's evidence, in the absence of a jury. He ruled against the admission of the evidence. In dealing with the question whether privilege properly extended to a witness from whom a solicitor had taken a proof as well as to the actual client he said, at p. 598:

> In that situation of indecisive authority one must look to first principles. A convenient statement is that of Stirling J in *Goldstone's* case: 'These decisions appear to be based on the necessity of allowing full and free communication for the purposes of litigation, not only between a solicitor and his client, but between the solicitor and persons whose assistance he requires, or with whom he communicates in order to enable him properly to conduct the litigation, [1899] 1 Ch 47, 52. With regard to both classes of case the privilege is the client's. If the solicitor were called as a witness it would be his duty to claim privilege on behalf of his client unless instructed otherwise . . . It is common ground that here the client has instructed the solicitor to claim the privilege. Further, the client's privilege is not confined to the original litigation. How far it extends in other litigation is apparently unsettled . . . I think that the plaintiff in [the civil] action, on such information as is before the court, appears to have a sufficiently substantial interest in the present trial for the privilege to attach. The same result may be reached by an approach which, in the absence of clear authority, attracts me as general principle. When a communication was originally privileged and in criminal proceedings the privilege is claimed,

against the prosecution, in respect of evidence by the client originally concerned or his solicitor, the onus should be on the prosecution to show that the claim cannot be sustained. That might be done either by demonstrating that there is no ground on which the client could any longer be reasonably regarded as having a recognisable interest in asserting the privilege or that an established exception applies. Here the first of those things could not be said.

Also cited to us was *Reg.* v. *Dunbar and Logan* (1982) 138 DLR (3d) 221, a decision of the Ontario Court of Appeal. The facts of the case were complex, but for present purposes suffice it to say that B and two others were jointly tried for murder. After the other two accused had testified, B also testified and gave evidence incriminating his co-accused. Counsel for one of the accused had acted for a period for both that accused and for B, and during this period B had prepared certain documents which in part indicated that his, B's, former lawyer had attempted to persuade B to change his story and incriminate the accused. Counsel for the accused wished to cross-examine B on these documents and also on a third document, which appeared to be a note prepared by B's former lawyer and which had been found by one of the accused in B's cell.

The trial judge ruled that all three documents were subject to solicitor-client privilege and that B could not be cross-examined on them, since he was not waiving privilege. During cross-examination B on several occasions testified that his first lawyer attempted to 'make a deal' with the Crown which required B to perjure himself. B further testified that when the present lawyer of one of the co-accused was representing both him, B, and the accused he had directed the accused as to what B should write in certain documents.

Counsel for one of the accused (not B) sought to re-open his case to call the two lawyers against whom the imputations had been made. This was refused. On appeal by the accused from their conviction the appeal was allowed and a new trial ordered.

Martin JA, giving the judgment of the court, cited the passage quoted above from the judgment of Caulfield J in *Reg.* v *Barton* [1973] 1 WLR 115 and continued, 138 DLR (3d) 221, 251, 252:

> Sir Rupert Cross, in commenting on the principle enunciated by Caulfield J, states that the merits of the doctrine are obvious but its precise implications and limitations, if any, have not been worked out . . . One limitation of the wide principle enunciated by Caulfield J that suggests itself is that an accused ought not to be required to disclose privileged information, the disclosure of which might assist a co-accused to the detriment of the accused who is required to disclose the privileged communication. Assuming for the present purpose that the privilege protecting communications by Bray to his solicitors was not destroyed by his subsequent imputations against them, the removal of the privilege, while it may assist his co-accused, might be damaging to Bray. The interests of Bray as well as his co-accused must be balanced in deciding whether the privilege must yield in the interests of the co-accused. . . . Bray having been acquitted, a balancing of interests at a new trial of the appellants favours the admission of the communications of Bray to his former solicitors, notwithstanding that privilege initially attached to the communications (and even if, contrary to the view I have already expressed, the privilege was not lost by Bray's imputation of fraud against his former solicitors), where the admission of the communications assists the appellants in resisting the allegations made against them. The principle enunciated in *Reg.* v *Barton* (*supra*) is, in my view, properly involved in those circumstances.

We would observe, first, that in each of the cases cited the result was in favour of the man standing trial: secondly, that the resolution of the problem in each individual case involves balancing the competing interests of the public in the due and orderly administration of justice, on the one hand, and of the public and the accused, in ensuring that all evidence supportive of his case is before the court, on the other hand.

Discussing the duration of the privilege, Sir Rupert Cross said in his work, *Cross on Evidence*, 5th ed. (1979), p. 286:

A time may come when the party denying the continued existence of the privilege can prove that the party relying on it no longer has any interest to protect, as where the solicitor for the unsuccessful plaintiff in a civil action takes a statement from a witness who is subsequently prosecuted for perjury and the prosecution wish to ask the solicitor what the witness said to him.

This is clearly a reference to *Reg.* v *Craig* [1975] 1 NZLR 597.

Basing ourselves on the principle which attracted Cooke J, as cited above, and on the passage from *Cross on Evidence* and amended for the purposes of the issues raised in this appeal, we would set out the principle as follows: 'When a communication was orginally privileged and in criminal proceedings privilege is claimed against the defendant by the client concerned or his solicitor, it should be for the defendant to show on the balance of probabilities that the claim cannot be sustained. That might be done by demonstrating that there is no ground on which the client could any longer reasonably be regarded as having a recognisable interest in asserting the privilege. The judge must then balance whether the legitimate interest of the defendant in seeking to breach the privilege outweighs that of the client in seeking to maintain it.'

Applying this test, there are only two factors which might have tended to show that Harvey continued to have a recognisable interest in asserting the privilege, and if so that his interest outweighed that of the appellant in seeking to breach the privilege. These were that the statement, if disclosed, might have an adverse influence on the judge when he came to sentence him, that disclosure of the statement might expose him to a risk of prosecution for perjury. The first risk could have been avoided by the judge arranging for another judge to sentence Harvey or someone in Harvey's position, in the rare cases where this proved necessary, undesirable though such a course is in most circumstances.

The second risk we regard as too theoretical to carry much weight. However that may be, the judge did not apply his mind at all to the balancing of competing interests. He is not to be blamed for this, since he was not invited to do so; nor, it would appear, were the authorities of which we have had the advantage cited to him.

This leads us to the second question: was the procedure adopted at the trial to resolve this problem the proper one? In our judgment, the answer is that it was not. It was, we consider, essential, in order for the judge to decide both whether Harvey could reasonably be regarded as having a recognisable interest in asserting the privilege and, if so, whether the interests of Harvey outweighed those of the appellant in seeking to breach it, for him to have heard argument on the point and to have carried out such investigation as the circumstances required in order to determine it. It is our view that had this been done it is very likely that the judge would have resolved the conflict in favour of the appellant. Putting the matter at its lowest from the appellant's point of view he was, as matters turned out, deprived of the opportunity to impugn the credit of an important witness for the Crown.

We consider that the foregoing renders the conviction, in all the circumstances of the case, unsafe or unsatisfactory, and that this is not a case in which it would be proper to apply the proviso to section 2 of the Criminal Appeal Act 1968.

Accordingly, the appeal is allowed.

(iii)   Without prejudice negotiations and media sources

Contempt of Court Act 1981

10.   Sources of information
No court may require a person to disclose, nor is any person guilty of contempt of court for refusing to disclose, the source of information contained in a publication for which he is responsible, unless it be established to the satisfaction of the court that disclosure is necessary in the interest of justice or national security or for the prevention of disorder or crime.

Note
Considerations of space preclude a treatment of the cases concerning the application of s. 10 but reference may be made, *inter alia*, to *Secretary of State for Defence* v *Guardian Newspapers Ltd* [1985] AC 339, *Maxwell* v *Pressdram Ltd* [1987] 1 WLR 298, and *X Ltd* v *Morgan-Grampian (Publishers) Ltd* [1991] 1 AC 1.

Rush & Tomkins v *Greater London Council*
[1989] AC 1280
House of Lords

The plaintiff settled an action brought by D1 but not an action brought by D2. D2 sought discovery of the without prejudice negotiations that had taken place between D1 and the plaintiff. It was admitted that these negotiations were relevant to D2's case. The Court of Appeal held that D2 was entitled to discovery on the ground that once the negotiations with D1 had been concluded, the reason for the privilege attatching to without prejudice negotiations had ended. The plaintiff appealed to the House of Lords.

LORD GRIFFITHS: . . . The 'without prejudice' rule is a rule governing the admissibility of evidence and is founded upon the public policy of encouraging litigants to settle their differences rather than litigate them to a finish. It is nowhere more clearly expressed than in the judgment of Oliver LJ in *Cutts* v *Head* [1984] Ch 290, 306:

That the rule rests, at least in part, upon public policy is clear from many authorities, and the convenient starting point of the inquiry is the nature of the underlying policy. It is that parties should be encouraged so far as possible to settle their disputes without resort to litigation and should not be discouraged by the knowledge that anything that is said in the course of such negotiations (and that includes, of course, as much the failure to reply to an offer as an actual reply) may be used to their prejudice in the course of the proceedings. They should, as it was expressed by Clauson J in *Scott Paper Co.* v *Drayton Paper Works Ltd* (1927) 44 RPC 151, 156, be encouraged fully and frankly to put their cards on the table. . . . The public policy justification, in truth, essentially rests on the desirability of preventing statements or offers made in the course of negotiations for settlement being brought before the court of trial as admissions on the question of liability.

The rule applies to exclude all negotiations genuinely aimed at settlement whether oral or in writing from being given in evidence. A competent solicitor will always head any negotiating correspondence 'without prejudice' to make clear beyond doubt that in the event of the negotiations being unsuccessful they are not to be referred to at the subsequent trial. However, the application of the rule is not dependent upon the use of the phrase 'without prejudice' and if it is clear from the surrounding circumstances that the parties were seeking to compromise the action, evidence of the content of those negotiations will, as a general rule, not be admissible at the trial and cannot be used to establish an admission or partial admission. I cannot therefore agree with the Court of Appeal that the problem in the present case should be resolved by a linguistic approach to the meaning of the phrase 'without prejudice.' I believe that the question has to be looked at more broadly and resolved by balancing two different public interests namely the public interest in promoting settlements and the public interest in full discovery between parties to litigation.

Nearly all the cases in which the scope of the 'without prejudice' rule has been considered concern the admissibility of evidence at trial after negotiations have failed. In such circumstances no question of discovery arises because the parties are well aware of what passed between them in the negotiations. These cases show that the rule is not absolute and resort may be had to the 'without prejudice' material for a variety of reasons when the justice of the case requires it. It is unnecessary to make any deep examination of these authorities to resolve the present appeal but they all illustrate the underlying purpose of the rule which is to protect a litigant from being embarrassed by any admission made purely in an attempt to achieve a settlement. Thus the 'without prejudice' material will be admissible if the issue is whether or not the negotiations resulted in an agreed settlement, which is the point that Lindley LJ was making in *Walker* v *Wilsher* (1889) 23 QBD 335 and which was applied in *Tomlin* v *Standard Telephones & Cables Ltd* [1969] 1 WLR 1378. The court will not permit the phrase to be used to exclude an act of bankruptcy: see *In re Daintrey, Ex parte Holt* [1893] 2 QB 116 nor to suppress a threat if an offer is not accepted: see *Kitcat* v *Sharp* (1882) 48 LT 64. In certain circumstances the 'without prejudice' correspondence may be looked at to determine a question of costs after judgment has been given: see *Cutts* v *Head* [1984] Ch 290. There is also authority for the proposition that the admission of an 'independent fact' in no way connected with the merits of the cause is admissible even if made in the course of negotiations for a settlement. Thus an admission that a document was in the handwriting of one of the parties was received in evidence in *Waldridge* v *Kennison* (1794) 1 Esp 142. I regard this as an exceptional case and it should not be allowed to whittle down the protection given to the parties to speak freely about all issues in the litigation both factual and legal when seeking compromise and, for the purpose of establishing a basis of compromise, admitting certain facts. If the compromise fails the admission of the facts made for the purpose of the compromise should not be held against the maker of the admission and should therefore not be received in evidence.

I cannot accept the view of the Court of Appeal that *Walker* v *Wilsher*, 23 QBD 335, is authority for the proposition that if the negotiations succeed and a settlement is concluded the privilege goes, having served its purpose. In *Walker* v *Wilsher* the Court of Appeal held that it was not permissible to receive the contents of a 'without prejudice' offer on the question of costs and no question arose as to the admissibility

of admissions made in the negotiations in any possible subsequent proceedings. There are many situations when parties engaged upon some great enterprise such as a large building construction project must anticipate the risk of being involved in disputes with others engaged on the same project. Suppose the main contractor in an attempt to settle a dispute with one subcontractor made certain admissions it is clear law that those admissions cannot be used against him if there is no settlement. The reason they are not to be used is because it would discourage settlement if he believed that the admissions might be held against him. But it would surely be equally discouraging if the main contractor knew that if he achieved a settlement those admissions could then be used against him by any other subcontractor with whom he might also be in dispute. The main contractor might well be prepared to make certain concessions to settle some modest claim which he would never make in the face of another far larger claim. It seems to me that if those admissions made to achieve settlement of a piece of minor litigation could be held against him in a subsequent major litigation it would actively discourage settlement of the minor litigation and run counter to the whole underlying purpose of the 'without prejudice' rule. I would therefore hold that as a general rule the 'without prejudice' rule renders inadmissible in any subsequent litigation connected with the same subject matter proof of any admissions made in a genuine attempt to reach a settlement. It of course goes without saying that admissions made to reach settlement with a different party within the same litigation are also inadmissible whether or not settlement was reached with that party.
. . .

(LORDS OLIVER, GOFF, BRANDON and BRIDGE all agreed with LORD GRIFFITHS.)

Appeal allowed with costs.

Questions

1. If documents are not headed 'without prejudice', does this mean they are not privileged? What does determine if the documents are privileged?
2. Is there a case for extending the English rules of privilege to other relationships, for example, doctor and patient, or priest and penitent?
3. Pete was employed by the Ministry of Defence at a research laboratory which was exploring new applications for the use of nuclear energy. Pete brings an action alleging that he has suffered eye damage by constant exposure to radiation. He has requested disclosure of reports detailing the levels of radiation at the laboratory at the relevant times but the MOD have refused to disclose the documents on the ground of national security.

Pete's friend, Julie, still works at the laboratory and passes to Pete a memorandum marked 'Strictly Private' which details that levels of radiation have now been reduced to lower levels. The memo was sent by the head of the research section to the head of the personnel section. Julie found the memo lying by the photocopier and assumed it had been left there in error.

If the matter goes to trial it is understood that counsel for the MOD will seek to question Pete about his breaching certain health and safety regulations, thereby suggesting that Pete caused his own injuries. Such breaches constitute criminal offences under a statute.

Discuss.

Further Reading
P. Murphy, *A Practical Approach to Evidence*, 4th ed. (1992), Ch. 11
P. Allen, 'Legal Privilege and the Principles of Fairness in the Criminal Trial'
[1987] Crim LR 449
J. D. Heydon, 'Legal Professional Privilege and Third Parties' (1974) 37
MLR 601
C. Tapper, 'Privilege and Confidence' (1972) 35 MLR 83
A. A. S. Zuckerman, 'Privilege and Public Interest' in *Crime, Proof and Punishment* (ed. Tapper) (1981)

15 PREVIOUS JUDGMENTS AS EVIDENCE

The general rule is that a previous judgment should not be admitted into evidence in order to demonstrate the truth of the facts on which it is based, at least as against strangers to the judgment. The issue may arise in one of three situations, and each of these situations must be distinguished:

(a) Where it is sought to admit the judgment as evidence of its own existence, content and legal effect.

(b) Where it is sought to admit the judgment as evidence of the truth of the facts on which it is based, as between the parties to the case which resulted in the judgment, and their privies.

(c) Where it is sought to admit the judgment as evidence of the truth of the facts on which it is based, as between strangers to the case which resulted in the judgment, or as between parties to the case and strangers.

This chapter will concern itself with situation (c) only. For a general discussion of situations (a) and (b), see P. Murphy, *A Practical Approach to Evidence*, 4th ed. (1992), Chapter 10.

(A) Previous judgments as evidence of the facts — civil cases

Here we are concerned with the extent to which the prior findings of a court are admissible in subsequent civil proceedings as evidence of the facts on which they are based. The rule at common law was clearly stated in *Hollington v Hewthorn & Co. Ltd* [1943] KB 587. The plaintiff sued for negligence following a collision between him and the defendant's car. The driver of the defendant's car was subsequently convicted of driving without due care and attention. The plaintiff wished to introduce evidence of the other driver's conviction to demonstrate negligence. The Court of Appeal held that evidence of the conviction was inadmissible on the grounds that:

(a)   the opinion of the previous tribunal was irrelevant;
(b)   findings of fact in magistrates' courts might be qualitatively different from those which should prevail in a contested High Court action; and
(c)   it would be almost impossible to identify which facts the earlier tribunal found proved and which they did not find proved.

Despite these cogent reasons, the rule has now been reversed by statute.

Civil Evidence Act 1968

11.   Convictions as evidence in civil proceedings

(1)   In any civil proceedings the fact that a person has been convicted of an offence by or before any court in the United Kingdom or by a court-martial there are elsewhere shall (subject to subsection (3) below) be admissible in evidence for the purpose of proving, where to do so is relevant to any issue in those proceedings, that he committed that offence, whether he was so convicted upon a plea of guilty or otherwise and whether or not he is a party to the civil proceedings; but no conviction other than a subsisting one shall be admissible in evidence by virtue of this section.

(2)   In any civil proceedings in which by virtue of this section a person is proved to have been convicted of an offence by or before any court in the United Kingdom or by a court-martial there or elsewhere —

(a)   he shall be taken to have committed that offence unless the contrary is proved; and
(b)   without prejudice to the reception of any other admissible evidence for the purpose of identifying the facts on which the conviction was based, the contents of any document which is admissible as evidence of the conviction, and the contents of the information, complaint, indictment or charge-sheet on which the person in question was convicted, shall be admissible in evidence for that purpose.

(3)   Nothing in this section shall prejudice the operation of section 13 of this Act or any other enactment whereby a conviction or a finding of fact in any criminal proceedings is for the purposes of any other proceedings made conclusive evidence of any fact.

(4)   Where in any civil proceedings the contents of any document are admissible in evidence by virtue of subsection (2) above, a copy of that document, or of the material part thereof, purporting to be certified or otherwise authenticated by or on behalf of the court or authority having custody of that document shall be admissible in evidence and shall be taken to be a true copy of that document or part unless the contrary is shown.

(5)   Nothing in any of the following enactments, that is to say —

(a)   [section 1C of the Powers of Criminal Courts Act 1973] (under which a conviction leading to discharge is to be disregarded except as therein mentioned);
(b)   section 9 of the Criminal Justice (Scotland) Act 1949 (which makes similar provision in respect of convictions on indictment in Scotland); and
(c)   section 8 of the Probation Act (Northern Ireland) 1950 (which corresponds to the said section 12) or any corresponding enactment of the Parliament of Northern Ireland for the time being in force,

shall affect the operation of this section; and for the purposes of this section any order made by a court of summary jurisdiction in Scotland under section 1 or section 2 of the said Act of 1949 shall be treated as a conviction.

(6)   In this section 'court-martial' means a court-martial constituted under the Army Act 1955, the Air Force Act 1955 or the Naval Discipline Act 1957 or a disciplinary court constituted under section 50 of the said Act of 1957, and in relation to a court-martial 'conviction', as regards a court-martial constituted under either of the said Acts of 1955, means a finding of guilty which is, or falls to be treated as, a finding of the court duly confirmed and, as regards a court-martial or disciplinary court constituted under the said Act of 1957, means a finding of guilty which is, or falls to be treated as, the finding of the court, and 'convicted' shall be construed accordingly.

12.   Findings of adultery and paternity as evidence in civil proceedings

(1)   In any civil proceedings —

(a)   the fact that a person has been found guilty of adultery in any matrimonial proceedings; and

(b)   the fact that a person has been found to be the father of a child in relevant proceedings before any court in England and Wales or has been adjudged to be the father of a child in affiliation proceedings before any court in the United Kingdom shall (subject to subsection (3) below) be admissible in evidence for the purpose of proving, where to do so is relevant to any issue in those civil proceedings, that he committed the adultery to which the finding relates or, as the case may be, is (or was) the father of that child, whether or not he offered any defence to the allegation of adultery or paternity and whether or not he is a party to the civil proceedings; but no finding or adjudication other than a subsisting one shall be admissible in evidence by virtue of this section.

(2)   In any civil proceedings in which by virtue of this section a person is proved to have been found guilty of adultery as mentioned in subsection (1)(a) above or to have been found or adjudged to be the father of a child as mentioned in subsection (1)(b) above —

(a)   he shall be taken to have committed the adultery to which the finding relates or, as the case may be, to be (or have been) the father of that child, unless the contrary is proved; and

(b)   without prejudice to the reception of any other admissible evidence for the purpose of identifying the facts on which the finding or adjudication was based, the contents of any document which was before the court, or which contains any pronouncement of the court, in the other proceedings in question shall be admissible in evidence for that purpose.

(3)   Nothing in this section shall prejudice the operation of any enactment whereby a finding of fact in any matrimonial or affiliation proceedings is for the purposes of any other proceedings made conclusive evidence of any fact.

(4)   Subsection (4) of section 11 of this Act shall apply for the purposes of this section as if the reference to subsection (2) were a reference to subsection (2) of this section.

. . .

13.   Conclusiveness of convictions for purposes of defamation actions

(1)   In an action for libel or slander in which the question whether a person did or did not commit a criminal offence is relevant to an issue arising in the action, proof that at the time when that issue falls to be determined, that person stands convicted

of that offence shall be conclusive evidence that he committed that offence; and his conviction thereof shall be admissible in evidence accordingly.

(2) In any such action as aforesaid in which by virtue of this section a person is proved to have been convicted of an offence, the contents of any document which is admissible as evidence of the conviction, and the contents of the information, complaint, indictment or charge-sheet on which that person was convicted, shall, without prejudice to the reception of any other admissible evidence for the purpose of identifying the facts on which the conviction was based, be admissible in evidence for the purpose of identifying those facts.

(3) For the purposes of this section a person shall be taken to stand convicted of an offence if but only if there subsists against him a conviction of that offence by or before a court in the United Kingdom or by a court-martial there or elsewhere.

(4) Subsection (4) to (6) of section 11 of this Act shall apply for the purposes of this section as they apply for the purposes of that section, but as if in the said subsection (4) the reference to subsection (2) were a reference to subsection (2) of this section.

(5) The foregoing provisions of this section shall apply for the purposes of any action begun after the passing of this Act, whenever the cause of action arose, but shall not apply for the purposes of any action begun before the passing of this Act or any appeal or other proceedings arising out of any such action.

Note

Section 11 provides that the conviction is admissible for the purpose of proving that a person committed the offence 'unless the contrary is proved'. Where a conviction is admitted into evidence what weight, if any, should be attached to it? Does it merely reverse the burden of proof? If so, what standard of evidence must be adduced to discharge the burden of proof?

Taylor v *Taylor*
[1970] 1 WLR 1148
Court of Appeal

On 11 September 1969, the wife filed a petition for divorce on the grounds of adultery and cruelty against the husband. The husband cross prayed for a divorce on the grounds of the wife's adultery with three men. Both grounds of the wife's petition consisted of allegations of incest on the 14-year-old daughter of the parties. In November 1962, the husband had been convicted of incest at Newport Assizes before Thesiger J and a jury and had been sentenced to three years' imprisonment concurrent on each count. On 5 March 1963, his application for leave to appeal against his conviction was refused by the Court of Criminal Appeal (Lord Parker CJ, Ashworth and Winn JJ) who directed that 42 days of the time he had been in prison should not count against his sentence. At the hearing of the divorce suit the commissioner found that the husband had not committed incest, granted him a divorce on the ground of the wife's adultery and rejected the prayer of the wife's petition. The wife appealed on the grounds, *inter alia*, that the commissioner had erred in law in deciding that the husband had discharged the burden of proof under s. 11 of the Civil

Evidence Act 1968, that he had wrongly been convicted of incest, and that the commissioner had conducted the case in such a determined and emphatic manner that the witnesses and the wife were intimidated and deterred from giving evidence freely.

DAVIES LJ: [After citing s. 11 His Lordship continued . . .] That section obviously, in contradistinction to section 13 of the same Act, which deals with the effect of convictions when they fall to be considered in an action of defamation, means that the onus of proof of upsetting the previous conviction is on the person who seeks to do so. It is probable, though I do not want to make any particular [pronouncement] about it at the moment, that that is an onus of proof on balance of probabilities. But, having said that, it nevertheless is obvious that, when a man has been convicted by 12 of his fellow countrymen and countrywomen at a criminal trial, the verdict of the jury is a matter which is entitled to very great weight when the convicted person is seeking, in the words of the statute, to prove the contrary.

[His Lordship concluded that the respondent had not discharged the onus placed on him by s. 11 and the appeal was allowed.]

Stupple v Royal Insurance Co. Ltd
[1971] 1 QB 50
Court of Appeal

The plaintiff had been convicted of armed robbery, a major piece of evidence against him being the discovery of a substantial amount of stolen money in his flat. The plaintiff claimed the return of the money from the insurance company who had paid off the robbery victim. The plaintiff sought to demonstrate that he was not guilty of the robbery and had been wrongly convicted. The High Court found in favour of the defendant. The plaintiff appealed to the Court of Appeal.

LORD DENNING MR: . . . Mr Hawser, for Mr Stupple, submitted that the only effect of the Act was to shift the burden of proof. He said that, whereas previously the conviction was not admissible in evidence at all, now it was admissible in evidence, but the effect was simply to put on the man the burden of showing, on the balance of probabilities, that he was innocent. He claimed that Mr Stupple had done so.

I do not accept Mr Hawser's submission. I think that the conviction does not merely shift the burden of proof. It is a weighty piece of evidence of itself. For instance, if a man is convicted of careless driving on the evidence of a witness, but that witness dies before the civil action is heard (as in *Hollington* v *F Hewthorn & Co. Ltd* [1943] 1 KB 587), then the conviction itself tells in the scale in the civil action. It speaks as clearly as the witness himself would have done, had he lived. It does not merely reverse the burden of proof. If that was all it did, the defendant might well give his own evidence negativing want of care, and say: 'I have discharged the burden. I have given my evidence and it has not been contradicted.' In answer to the defendant's evidence, the plaintiff can say to him: 'But your evidence is contradicted. It is contradicted by the very fact of your conviction.'

In addition, Mr Hawser sought, as far as he could, to minimise the effect of shifting the burden. In this, too, he did not succeed. The Act does not merely shift the evidential burden, as it is called. It shifts the *legal* burden of proof. I explained the difference long ago, in 1945, in an article in the Law Quarterly Review 61 LQR 379. Take a running-down case where a plaintiff claims damages for negligent driving by the defendant. If the defendant has not been convicted, the legal burden is on the plaintiff throughout. But if the defendant has been convicted of careless driving, the legal burden is shifted. It is on the defendant himself. At the end of the day, if the judge is left in doubt the defendant fails because the defendant has not discharged the legal burden which is upon him. The burden is, no doubt, the civil burden. He must show, on the balance of probabilities, that he was not negligent: see *Public Prosecutor v Yuvaraj* [1970] 2 WLR 226, 231, in the Privy Council quite recently. But he must show it nevertheless. Otherwise he loses by the very force of the conviction.

How can a man, who has been convicted in a criminal trial, prove his innocence in a subsequent civil action? He can, of course, call his previous witnesses and hope that the judge will believe them now, even if they were disbelieved before. He can also call any fresh witnesses whom he thinks will help his case. In addition, I think he can show that the witnesses against him in the criminal trial were mistaken. For instance, in a traffic accident he could prove that a witness who claimed to have seen it was miles away and committed perjury. This would not, of course, prove his innocence directly, but it would do so indirectly by destroying the evidence on which he was convicted. So in this case Mr Stupple could prove that Mr Ford was mistaken.

In any case, what weight is to be given to the criminal conviction? This must depend on the circumstances. Take a plea of guilty. Sometimes a defendant pleads guilty in error: or in a minor offence he may plead guilty to save time and expense, or to avoid some embarrassing fact coming out. Afterwards, in the civil action, he can, I think, explain how he came to plead guilty.

Take next a case in the magistrates' court when a man is convicted and bound over or fined a trifling sum, but had a good ground of appeal, and did not exercise it because it was not worth while. Can he not explain this in a civil court? I think he can. He can offer any explanation in his effort to show that the conviction was erroneous: and it is for the judge at the civil trial to say how far he has succeeded.

In my opinion, therefore, the weight to be given to a previous conviction is essentially for the judge at the civil trial. Just as he has to evaluate the oral evidence of a witness, so he should evaluate the probative force of a conviction.

If the defendant should succeed in throwing doubt on the conviction, the plaintiff can rely, in answer, on the conviction itself; and he can supplement it, if he thinks it desirable, by producing (under the hearsay sections) the evidence given by the prosecution witnesses in the criminal trial, or, if he wishes, he can call them again. At the end of the civil case, the judge must ask himself whether the defendant has succeeded in overthrowing the conviction. If not, the conviction stands and proves the case.

[His lordship held that the plaintiff had not discharged the onus placed on him by s. 11 and dismissed the appeal.]

BUCKLEY LJ: If, before 1968, A sued B for an act of B's of which B had earlier been convicted in criminal proceedings, evidence of B's conviction was inadmissible in A's action. It merely demonstrated that another court had, on the material and arguments before it, concluded that B was guilty of the act with which he was charged in the criminal proceedings. It did not prove any of the matters proved in the criminal proceedings, nor anything which A would need to prove to make good his civil claim. Proof of B's conviction was accordingly irrelevant to A's action, and so was inadmissible: *Hollington* v *F Hewthorn & Co. Ltd* [1943] 1 KB 587.

The Civil Evidence Act, 1968, has changed this. Section 11(1) makes proof of B's conviction admissible in evidence for the purpose of proving that B did the act of which he has been convicted. If section 11(1) stood alone it would be clear that proof of the conviction would be some evidence of B's act: it would not be clear what weight it should be given. Under section 11(2)(a), however, if in A's action B is proved to have been convicted he is to be taken to have committed the offence of which he was convicted unless the contrary is shown. The effect of proof of the conviction under this subsection is, as my Lord, the Master of the Rolls, has said, to shift the 'legal' burden of proof in respect of B's act or alleged act from A, who would otherwise have to prove it to make good his claim, to B who must disprove it to avoid the presumption of his having committed the offence prevailing. Once the conviction has been proved the task of the court, instead of being, as would otherwise be the case, to decide whether A has successfully shown that on a balance of probability B did the act, becomes to decide whether B has successfully shown that, on a balance of probability, he did *not* do the act.

The judge in the present case rightly recognised that this was his function.

There remains, however, the problem of what weight, if any, should be accorded to the proved fact of conviction in deciding whether any other evidence adduced is sufficient to discharge the onus resting on B. In my judgment no weight is in this respect to be given to the mere fact of conviction.

If, as seems to be the case, I differ from Lord Denning MR in this respect, I do so with the greatest diffidence.

The effect of the bare proof of conviction is, I think, spent in bringing section 11(2)(a) into play. But very much weight may have to be given to such circumstances of the criminal proceedings as are brought out in the evidence in the civil action. Witnesses called in the civil proceedings may give different evidence from that which they gave in the criminal proceedings. Witnesses may be called in the civil proceedings who might have been but were not called in the criminal proceedings, or vice versa. The judge may feel that he should take account of the fact that the judge or jury in the criminal proceedings disbelieved a witness who is called in the civil proceedings, or that the defendant pleaded guilty or not guilty, as the case may be. Many examples could be suggested of ways in which what occurred or did not occur in the criminal proceedings may have a bearing on the judge's decision in the civil proceedings: but the judge's duty in the civil proceedings is still to decide that case on the evidence adduced to him. He is not concerned with the evidence in the criminal proceedings except so far as it is reproduced in the evidence called before him, or is made evidence in the civil proceedings under the Civil Evidence Act, 1968, section 2, or is established before him in cross-examination. He is not concerned with the propriety of the conviction except so far as his view of the evidence before him may lead him incidentally to the conclusion that the conviction was justified or is open to criticism: but even if it does so, this must be a consequence of his decision and cannot be a reason for it. The propriety or otherwise of the conviction is irrelevant to the steps leading to his decision.

It was suggested in argument that so to view section 11 would result in the issues in the criminal proceedings being retried in the civil proceedings, and that this would be contrary to an intention on the part of the legislature to avoid this sort of duplication.

I do not myself think that this would be the result in most cases, and I do not discern any such general intention in the section. If the fact of conviction were meant to carry some weight in determining whether the convicted man has successfully discharged the onus under section 11(2)(a) of proving that he did not commit the offence, what weight should it carry? I cannot accept that this should depend on such considerations as, for instance, the status of the court which convicted, or whether the decision was a unanimous or a majority verdict of a jury. I cannot discover any measure of the weight which the unexplored fact of conviction should carry. Although the section has made proof of conviction admissible and has given proof of conviction a particular statutory effect under section 11(2)(a), it remains, I think, as true today as before the Act that mere proof of conviction proves nothing relevant to the plaintiff's claim, and it clearly cannot be intended to shut out or, I think, to mitigate the effect of any evidence tending to show that the convicted person did not commit the offence. In my judgment, proof of conviction under this section gives rise to the statutory presumption laid down in section 11(2)(a), which, like any other presumption, will give way to evidence establishing the contrary on the balance of probability, without itself affording any evidential weight to be taken into account in determining whether that onus has been discharged.

With respect to the judge, I think that he was unnecessarily alarmed at the possibility of his reaching a different conclusion from the conclusion reached at the criminal trial, where both the burden of proof and the standard of proof differed from those in the action, and by the Court of Criminal Appeal. The conclusion which he did reach was one which, I think, was clearly open to him on the evidence before him, and I see no reason to disturb it.

I agree that the appeal should be dismissed.

Question
Lord Denning says the conviction is 'a weighty piece of evidence in itself', whereas Buckley LJ states that the conviction merely raises a presumption against the convicted person which may be displaced by evidence establishing the contrary on a balance of probabilities. Buckley LJ further denies that the conviction has any evidential weight. Whose view is to be preferred? Why?

Note
In *Hunter v Chief Constable of the West Midlands Police* [1982] AC 529, Lord Diplock was unable to agree with Lord Denning's observation that evidence adduced to disprove a conviction must be decisive. Lord Diplock confirmed that the standard of proof which applies is the normal civil standard, a balance of probabilities.

(B) Previous judgments as evidence of the facts — criminal cases

In criminal cases as with civil cases, statute has also abrogated the rule in *Hollington v Hewthorn* by providing that a person's conviction is admissible evidence to prove the convicted person committed the offence, and that person is taken to have committed that offence unless the contrary is proved. The statute does not alter the existing law which governs the admissibility of character evidence, thus it is not open to the prosecution to introduce evidence of the defendant's previous convictions for the purpose of demonstrating his guilt on the present charge. This course may only be taken where the 'similar fact' principle applies (see Chapter 12). A defendant's previous conviction will only be admissible in limited circumstances, if it is *relevant* to show he was convicted of that offence.

Police and Criminal Evidence Act 1984

73. Proof of convictions and acquittals

(1)   Where in any proceedings the fact that a person has in the United Kingdom been convicted or acquitted of an offence otherwise than by a Service court is admissible in evidence, it may be proved by producing a certificate of conviction or, as the case may be, of acquittal relating to that offence, and proving that the person named in the certificate as having been convicted or acquitted of the offence is the person whose conviction or acquittal of the offence is to be proved.

(2)   For the purposes of this section a certificate of conviction or of acquittal —

(a) shall, as regards a conviction or acquittal on indictment, consist of a certificate, signed by the clerk of the court where the conviction or acquittal took place, giving the substance and effect (omitting the formal parts) of the indictment and of the conviction or acquittal; and

(b) shall, as regards a conviction or acquittal on a summary trial, consist of a copy of the conviction or of the dismissal of the information, signed by the clerk of the court where the conviction or acquittal took place or by the clerk of the court, if any, to which a memorandum of the conviction or acquittal was sent;

and a document purporting to be a duly signed certificate of conviction or acquittal under this section shall be taken to be such a certificate unless the contrary is proved.

(3)   References in this section to the clerk of a court include references to his deputy and to any other person having the custody of the court record.

(4)   The method of proving a conviction or acquittal authorised by this section shall be in addition to and not to the exclusion of any other authorised manner of proving a conviction or acquittal.

74. Conviction as evidence of commission of offence

(1)   In any proceedings the fact that a person other than the accused has been convicted of an offence by or before any court in the United Kingdom or by a Service court outside the United Kingdom shall be admissible in evidence for the purpose of proving, where to do so is relevant to any issue in those proceedings, that that person committed that offence, whether or not any other evidence of his having committed that offence is given.

(2)   In any proceedings in which by virtue of this section a person other than the accused is proved to have been convicted of an offence by or before any court in the United Kingdom or by a Service court outside the United Kingdom, he shall be taken to have committed that offence unless the contrary is proved.

(3)   In any proceedings where evidence is admissible of the fact that the accused has committed an offence, in so far as that evidence is relevant to any matter in issue in the proceedings for a reason other than a tendency to show in the accused a disposition to commit the kind of offence with which he is charged, if the accused is proved to have been convicted of the offence —

(a)   by or before any court in the United Kingdom; or

(b)   by a Service court outside the United Kingdom,

he shall be taken to have committed that offence unless the contrary is proved.

(4)   Nothing in this section shall prejudice —

(a)   the admissibility in evidence of any conviction which would be admissible apart from this section; or

(b)   the operation of any enactment whereby a conviction or a finding of fact in any proceedings is for the purposes of any other proceedings made conclusive evidence of any fact.

75. Provisions supplementary to section 74

(1) Where evidence that a person has been convicted of an offence is admissible by virtue of section 74 above, then without prejudice to the reception of any other admissible evidence for the purpose of identifying the facts on which the conviction was based —

(a) the contents of any document which is admissible as evidence of the conviction; and

(b) the contents of the information, complaint, indictment or charge-sheet on which the person in question was convicted,

shall be admissible in evidence for that purpose.

(2) Where in any proceedings the contents of any document are admissible in evidence by virtue of subsection (1) above, a copy of that document, or of the material part of it, purporting to be certified or otherwise authenticated by or on behalf of the court or authority having custody of that document shall be admissible in evidence and shall be taken to be a true copy of that document or part unless the contrary is shown.

(3) Nothing in any of the following —

(a) section 13 of the Powers of Criminal Courts Act 1973 (under which a conviction leading to probation or discharge is to be disregarded except as mentioned in that section);

(b) section 392 of the Criminal Procedure (Scotland) Act 1975 (which makes similar provision in respect of convictions on indictment in Scotland); and

(c) section 8 of the Probation Act (Northern Ireland) 1950 (which corresponds to section 13 of the Powers of Criminal Courts Act 1973) or any legislation which is in force in Northern Ireland for the time being and corresponds to that section,

shall affect the operation of section 74 above; and for the purposes of that section any order made by a court of summary jurisdiction in Scotland under section 182 or section 183 of the said Act of 1975 shall be treated as a conviction.

(4) Nothing in section 74 above shall be construed as rendering admissible in any proceedings evidence of any conviction other than a subsisting one.

R v O'Connor
(1987) 85 Cr App R 298
Court of Appeal

TAYLOR J: On May 23, 1986 in the Crown Court at St Albans, the appellant was convicted and sentenced as follows: on count 1 of the indictment, conspiracy to obtain property by deception, he was fined £1,000, to be paid within three months, with 90 days' imprisonment in default. He was also ordered to pay £300 prosecution costs.

He now appeals against conviction by leave of the single judge.

The history of the matter is as follows. The prosecution contended that the appellant and his co-accused, a man called Beck, had agreed falsely to report a van as stolen, thereby to claim under an insurance policy for the loss. The appellant was in business as an electrical contractor. Beck worked for him as a self-employed sub-contractor. The appellant provided a Vauxhall van for Beck, which he, the appellant, leased. An agreement was made between the men that if Beck met the payments for the van as well as maintaining it, then when all the payments had been made the van would be his, Beck's. Beck insured the van. He substituted it on his insurance for a car which was already thereon.

On the evening of January 17, 1985 at Vine Street Police Station, Beck reported that van stolen. A claim was subsequently made on Beck's insurance policy. In the event the insurers refused to pay on the ground, unconnected with matters in this case, that Beck had falsely described himself as the owner and keeper of the car.

Subseqently on May 22, 1985 the police found the van near Wheathamstead. It bore a false registration number, a number in fact of a similar van owned by a mutual acquaintance of the appellant and Beck. When the van was found Beck was standing nearby. He admitted the offence when questioned by the police.

The appellant was then seen on May 23. He admitted that he had agreed with Beck to report the van stolen and to make an insurance claim. The reasons he gave were these; that Beck was no longer in a position to make payments on the van, the appellant could not afford to take it back, having since bought some new vehicles, and so the appellant agreed to have new plates made for the van, copying the number from a similar van belonging to an acquaintance. The intention was that the appellant and Beck would repay the leasing company from the insurance money and then split the balance between themselves. That obviously was a complete confession to the offence of conspiracy which was charged in the first count of the indictment.

On August 1 however the appellant was interviewed again in the presence of his solicitor. He told a different story, that there was no dishonest agreement between himself and Beck to report the van stolen. According to this story Beck told him that the van had gone and they both reported the matter to the police. It was only a month later that the appellant saw Beck in a similar looking van. Beck admitted that this was the same van with different number plates and that he was making a false insurance claim. The appellant explained that the reasons for his making admissions on the first interview was that he had spoken to Beck when they were both in the cells and he had agreed to go along with Beck's story in order both to help Beck and, as he thought, to get himself released from the police station.

The matter came before the Court first on March 14, 1986. There were five counts on the indictment. Beck pleaded guilty to the conspiracy charge in count 1. This appellant pleaded not guilty. The other counts were not put to Beck, but count 4 of the indictment was put to this appellant. That was a charge of conspiring to assist in the retention and disposal of stolen goods. The appellant pleaded guilty to that, but the Crown did not accept his plea, which was made on the basis of the appellant only having come into this matter at a late stage, and having then given some assistance to Beck when the scheme to obtain money from the insurance company was well under way. Accordingly the matter came on for trial on May 22, 1986, and the appellant was tried on count 1 of the indictment.

He gave evidence at the trial in accordance with his second statement to the police. He said as to his first admissions that he did not remember making some of them, and that the others he made because he thought that he would be able to go home if he did.

The substance of this appeal is the decision of the learned Judge to admit before the jury evidence of the conviction of Beck on his own confession at the first hearing of the case. The evidence was given by a police officer that Beck had pleaded guilty to count 1, and the evidence was admitted pursuant to section 74(1) of the Police and Criminal Evidence Act 1984. The contention on this appeal is that the learned judge ought not to have admitted that evidence, and that to do so was unfair to the appellant.

It is therefore necessary to look at the relevant provisions of the Police and Criminal Evidence Act 1984. Section 74(1) provides:

[His Lordship then cited from s.74(1), s.75(1) and s.78(1) of the Police and Criminal Evidence Act 1984 and then continued . . .]

The submissions which have been made to this Court by Mr Lewis on behalf of the appellant are first, that section 74 did not permit evidence of the kind admitted here to be put before a jury. Alternatively he contends that if the strict wording of section 74(1) did render the evidence admissible, then the learned judge ought, pursuant to section 78 of the Act, to have excluded it on the ground that it would have such an adverse effect on the fairness of the proceedings that he ought so to do.

We have been greatly assisted by the very helpful arguments which have been addressed to the Court by counsel, both for the appellant and for the Crown.

The terms of section 74 clearly were designed, in the judgment of this Court, to deal with the situation where it was necessary as a preliminary matter for is to be proved that a person other than the accused had been convicted of an offence. The object, it would seem, of the section is to avoid that matter having to be proved twice where the other person had already pleaded guilty to the offence it was necessary to prove. In effect therefore the object of the section, in our view, was to deal with cases where it was necessary to prove the conviction of another as a condition precedent to the conviction of the defendant of the charge laid against him. The most obvious example would be a case where it is necessary to prove against another that he was guilty of theft before the person before the court could be convicted of handling or harbouring.

The question raised in this case is as to whether the wording of the section is apt to cover the rather different situation which applies here. Here the conviction which was proved before the Court, the conviction of Beck, related to the very charge which was also levelled against this appellant. Mr Lewis cogently argued in this Court that the effect of that was to enable the prosecution to put a statement made by a co-accused in the absence of the defendant to the jury, which would not normally, in accordance with the rules of evidence, be permissible. Furthermore it enabled that to be done without the co-accused being before the Court to be cross-examined, tested or challenged as to the admission which he had made. In other words here Beck's admission was before the Court, but Beck was not.

Mr Lewis seeks to argue that this was not the object of section 74, and that in the particular circumstances of this case the previous conviction should not have been allowed to be proved in evidence. His argument on that point was to this effect, that when Beck pleaded guilty on March 14, all he was saying was that he, Beck, had conspired with the appellant. That was all that the court was interested in at that stage and that was the extent of the evidential effect of his plea. It was not open, says Mr Lewis, to the jury in this case to infer from Beck's plea that necessarily O'Connor, the appellant, had conspired with Beck.

The difficulty about that argument, apart from the obvious one that it is repugnant to common sense that A should be guilty of conspiring with B where B is not guilty of conspiring with A, is the wording of section 75, which makes it clear that where the conviction is admitted in evidence, it is not admitted as a bare plea of guilty, it is admitted with all the detail that is contained in the relevant count on the indictment. That appears from the citation I have already made from section 75.

Accordingly here the indictment, in count 1, read as to particulars of offence: 'Howard Richard Beck and Peter Stephen O'Connor between 26th day of December 1984 and 18th January, 1985 conspired together to obtain by deception insurance monies from the Mitre Assurance Association and Provincial Insurance plc by falsely reporting and claiming that a Vauxhall Astra motor vehicle . . . and its contents had been stolen.'

Once the conviction was put in evidence, all those details went in as being admitted by Beck. It would be very difficult to contend realistically that a jury would not be entitled to draw the inference from that admission and those details that not only had Beck conspired with O'Connor, but also the converse had taken place.

We find this a difficult point, and, without deciding the full scope of section 74, for the purposes of this case, it is sufficient to say that if it was appropriate within the section to admit the conviction of Beck in the proceedings, we take the view that it would have resulted in a very unfair state of affairs. For the reasons already given, it was not open to the defence to challenge what had been said by Beck. The result was that not only was what he had said in the appellant's absence admitted, but it was not exposed to any kind of challenge or test. In those circumstances we take the view that section 78 ought to have been brought into play by the learned judge. This was a case in which the admission of the evidence would have such an adverse effect on the fairness of the proceedings that the court ought not to have admitted it.

The learned judge rejected the submission to that effect at the time when the evidence was sought to be adduced. But it is clear from the way in which he summed the case up, that he himself came to the view that Beck's conviction was evidence which the jury ought not to take into account. In a long passage in the summing up, which it is necessary to recite, the learned judge, having admitted the evidence, in effect invited the jury to disregard it.

In his summing up he said this: 'The next piece of evidence which the Crown pray in aid is Beck's plea of guilty to precisely this charge. That evidence, it is important, should not be overvalued.'

The learned judge then went on to indicate that if Beck had been called, it would have been necessary to view his evidence as that of an accomplice with all the dangers attendant upon accomplice evidence.

He went on to say:

As it is of course he has not given evidence and as Mr Lewis points out you have not had the opportunity to see him in the witness box and even more important perhaps you have not had the opportunity of seeing his evidence tested by Mr Lewis in cross-examination. Mr Lewis has had no opportunity to put what Mr O'Connor says to Mr Beck. You have not heard his motives probed as no doubt they would have been by Mr Lewis had he had the opportunity. So by adopting the course which they have adopted, by simply proving the conviction and not tendering Mr Beck for cross-examination, the Crown have really faced Mr Lewis with a blank wall, a bare plea and he has not had the chance on behalf of Mr O'Connor to look behind it and to test it. It may be superficially attractive to say to yourselves if Mr Beck admits conspiring with Mr O'Connor then Mr O'Connor must have conspired with Mr Beck, but when you come to value that piece of evidence you may think in the end it would be wrong to place much if any reliance upon it. Much better as Mr Lewis suggested to you in the course of his speech to look at the evidence of what the officers said and look alongside that at what the defendant said in the witness box and make up your minds whether he was telling the truth then or whether he may be telling the truth now.

We therefore have come to the conclusion that this evidence ought not to have been admitted, pursuant to section 78 of the Act, and to that extent there was an irregularity in the course of this trial.

However we now have to consider the effect of the evidence which was adduced before the jury against this appellant, leaving aside the conviction of Beck. This court is of the view that that evidence is overwhelming. The appellant himself had made a complete confession. Indeed he had written out a voluntary statement himself in circumstantial detail indicating his participation in the conspiracy with Beck. The story that he gave as to why he had made those admissions when he was withdrawing them was one which, in the judgment of this Court, the jury would have been certain to reject. Bearing in mind also the passage which I have cited from the learned judge's summing up, in which he effectively told the jury to disregard evidence of Beck's conviction, we consider that the result of this case, had the evidence not been admitted, would necessarily have been the same as in fact it was.

In those circumstances this court is prepared to apply the proviso, and for those reasons this appeal must be dismissed.

Appeal dismissed. Proviso applied

Question
Does s. 74(1) create a risk that the jury will conclude that because D1 has been convicted of an offence then D2 must be guilty? If so, how can this risk be eliminated or minimised?

R v Robertson
[1987] 1 QB 920
Court of Appeal

The defendant was charged with conspiring with P and L to commit burglary. P and L were convicted of a number of burglaries following guilty pleas. R was tried some time later and the prosecution were allowed to admit evidence of P and L's convictions of the burglaries.

LORD LANE CJ: . . . After a five-day trial the appellant was convicted of the conspiracy. The jury were discharged from returning verdicts on counts 21 to 23. The appellant was sentenced to three years' imprisonment. His application for leave to appeal against that sentence was refused by the single judge, and has not been renewed.

Mr Tansey on behalf of the appellant submits that the verdict was unsafe and unsatisfactory by reason of, what he submits was, a serious irregularity in the course of the trial, and two more in the course of the summing up. The irregularity in the trial relates to the admissibility of evidence. The Crown sought to prove the existence of the conspiracy between Poole and Long by proving, inter alia, that within the relevant period Poole and Long had committed a number of burglaries at different Comet premises and had stolen television sets and video recorders. The inference was that they must have conspired together. To do this the Crown sought the leave of the judge to adduce evidence of the convictions of Poole and Long of 16 relevant counts of burglary. Their case was that they were entitled to adduce that evidence by virtue of the provisions of section 74(1) of the Police and Criminal Evidence Act 1984. The judge heard argument and ruled in favour of the Crown.

Mr Tansey challenges that ruling on a number of grounds. To put his submissions into perspective, it is necessary to refer to section 74 and the related sections of the Police and Criminal Evidence Act 1984.

[After citing the relevant parts of ss. 74 and 75 and s. 78 of the Police and Criminal Evidence Act 1984, His Lordship continued . . .]

Mr Tansey's criticism of the judge's ruling may be summarised as follows. (1) Section 74 did not apply for the following reasons: (a) there was no issue that many burglaries had been committed at Comet premises within the relevant period, because that fact was conceded by the appellant; (b) the mischief against which the section was directed did not exist or apply here; (c) the section has a restricted application: it only applies where the defendant on trial has played no part in the offences of which the third party has been convicted — for instance on a charge of handling stolen goods. The conviction of the thief of the same goods may properly be given in evidence. (2) Even if the Crown could bring themselves within the ambit of section 74, the evidence should have been excluded in accordance with section 78(1) because of its adverse effect on the fairness of the proceedings.

In support of his submission that section 74 had no application, Mr Tansey relies on paragraph 218 of the Criminal Law Revision Committee 11th Report (1972) (Cmnd. 4991) for the background of the law as it was. The relevant part reads:

> There is no doubt that the principle of *Hollington* v *Hewthorn* [1943] KB 587 applies to criminal cases, although there is very little authority. For example, in *Rex* v *Turner* (1832) 1 Mood CC 347, 349, 'many of [the judges] appeared to think' that in a case of receiving stolen property the conviction of the thief 'would not have been any evidence of her guilt, which must have been proved by other means.' This is always taken to be the law. In our opinion it is clearly right that convictions of persons other than the accused should be made admissible in criminal proceedings as evidence of the fact that the person convicted was guilty of the offence charged and that on proof of the conviction that person should be taken to have committed the offence charged unless the contrary is proved. Clause 24 provides accordingly. It seems quite wrong, as well as being inconvenient, that the prosecution should be required to prove again the guilt of the person concerned. The clause will be helpful to the prosecution in various cases where the guilt of the accused depends on another person's having committed an offence. Examples are handling stolen goods, harbouring offenders and the offences under sections 4 and 5 of the Criminal Law Act 1967 of assisting offenders and concealing offences.

The terms of clause 24 of the committee's draft bill are in all material respects identical to those of section 74.

The matter has already been considered by this court in *Reg.* v *O'Connor* [(1987)]. O'Connor was charged with conspiring with a man named Beck to obtain property by deception. He pleaded not guilty and was tried. Beck pleaded guilty and evidence of that plea was admitted at O'Connor's trial. On appeal it was submitted (1) that section 74 did not permit evidence of Beck's plea to be put before the jury, alternatively (2) that even if the strict wording of section 74(1) did render the evidence admissible, then the judge ought, pursuant to section 78, to have excluded it on the ground that it would have such an adverse effect on the fairness of the proceedings. The court held that the disputed evidence ought to have been excluded, but applied the proviso to section 2(1) of the Act of 1968 and dismissed the appeal.

The following is an extract from the judgment in that case:

> The terms of section 74 clearly were designed, in the judgment of this court, to deal with the situation where it was necessary as a preliminary matter for it to be proved that a person other than the accused had been convicted of an offence. The object, it would seem, of the section is to avoid that matter having to be proved twice where the other person had already pleaded guilty to the offence it was necessary to prove. In effect therefore the object of the section, in our view, was to deal with cases where it was necessary to prove the conviction of another as a condition precedent to the conviction of the defendant of the charge laid against him. The most obvious example would be a case where it is necessary to prove against another that he was

guilty of theft before the person before the court could be convicted of handling or harbouring.

Mr Tansey's case is that this view of the restricted application of section 74(1) is in accordance with the views of the Criminal Law Revision Committee and entirely supports his submission that section 74 had no application to the instant case.

For the Crown Mr Patterson contends that the judge's ruling was correct. His case is that the words of section 74(1) are clear and unambiguous, and should be given their natural meaning; that being so they are wide enough to cover the instant case. Had Parliament intended to restrict the application of the section, they could, and would, have done so in clear terms: for instance, by substituting for the words 'where to do so is relevant to any issue in those proceedings' some such expression as 'where it is necessary to prove the guilt of another.' Parliament has not chosen to do so.

The heart of the problem is the correct interpretation of the expression 'issue in the proceedings.' Only when that is determined can the court decide what in the particular circumstances is relevant and thus admissible. That is the very question left open in O'Connor's case. There, in the passage already cited, the court gave its view of the primary object of section 74. It expressly left open the limits or scope of the section in the following terms:

> We find this a difficult point, and, without deciding the full scope of section 74, for the purposes of this case, it is sufficient to say that if it was appropriate within the section to admit the conviction of Beck in the proceedings, we take the view that it would have resulted in a very unfair state of affairs.

Despite the assistance of counsel, the difficulty remains.

We think the time has come to attempt to provide some guidance for courts who have the task of applying section 74. The word 'issue' in relation to a trial is apt to cover not only an issue which is an essential ingredient in the offence charged, for instance in a handling case the fact that the goods were stolen (that is the restricted meaning), but also less fundamental issues, for instance evidential issues arising during the course of the proceedings (that is the extended meaning). Section 74 by using the words 'any issue in those proceedings' does not seek to limit the word 'issue' to the restricted meaning indicated above. Although the Report of the Criminal Law Revision Committee is an indication that the committee may have been regarding the matter at least primarily in the restricted sense, it seems to us that we are not entitled to use that possibility as showing that the words of the section mean other than what they plainly state.

On any view we find no support for Mr Tansey's submission that the section applies only to proof of conviction of offences in which the defendant on trial played no part. It may well be that the section will be at its most useful in dealing with the type of situation exemplified by the Law Revision Committee, but it is not restricted to that kind of case. Provided that there is an issue before the jury to which the conviction is relevant, the conviction, subject to what we say hereafter, is admissible.

So far as the present case is concerned, there was certainly an issue. Indeed it was probably an issue in the restricted sense, namely, the issue of whether there was a conspiracy between Poole and Long (of which their joint conviction of burglary was the clearest evidence). It was that conspiracy to which the prosecution sought to prove the appellant was a party. It is true that the appellant was prepared to accept that there had been a series of burglaries at Comet's premises during the material times, but that would not preclude the prosecution from relying on section 74 as the words of subsection (1) of that section make clear.

The judge gave his ruling as follows:

in a conspiracy case where there is only one defendant being tried, but it is alleged that he conspired with two other named persons and others unknown, it is relevant that those named persons committed a number of burglaries which the Crown allege were acts done by those named persons in furtherance of the common design. If the fact of committing those burglaries is relevant, then section 74 . . . facilitates the manner in which their participation in those events may be proved. I think that the evidence of their conviction is relevant to an issue in these proceedings, namely, was there a conspiracy.

That in our judgment, was a correct approach.

It remains to consider the submissions based on section 78. The complaint here is that by relying on section 74 to prove the convictions of Poole and Long, the prosecution deprived the appellant of the opportunity to cross-examine them. Mr Tansey points out that this was a prominent feature in the *O'Connor* case already referred to.

The circumstances there however were quite different. O'Connor and Beck were jointly indicted in one count with having conspired together and with no one else. It followed that Beck's admission of guilt of that very offence might well lead the jury to infer that O'Connor in his turn must have conspired with Beck.

That situation did not exist here. The pleas and consequent convictions of Poole and Long did not on the face of them involve the appellant whose name did not appear in the relevant counts at all. Consequently, even if Poole and Long had given evidence in accordance with their pleas, counsel would have been unlikely to cross-examine them or, if he had, to have achieved anything except disaster for his client.

The judge was, in our view, correct to admit the evidence.

It only remains to add this. Section 74 is a provision which should be sparingly used. There will be occasions where, although the evidence may be technically admissible, its effect is likely to be so slight that it will be wiser not to adduce it. This is particularly so where there is any danger of a contravention of section 78. There is nothing to be gained by adducing evidence of doubtful value at the risk of having the conviction quashed because the admission of that evidence rendered the conviction unsafe or unsatisfactory. Secondly, where the evidence is admitted, the judge should be careful, as Judge Owen Stable was here, to explain to the jury the effect of the evidence and its limitations.

. . . This appeal is dismissed.

Question

Frank, George and Harry are accused of commiting an act of gross indecency together in a public toilet. Frank and George plead guilty and are sentenced to a period of probation. Harry pleads not guilty and the matter is adjourned and a date set for trial. At the subsequent trial, the prosecution seek permission from the trial judge to lead evidence of the convictions of Frank and George.

Should the trial judge grant the prosecution's request? If so, what direction(s), if any, should the judge give to the jury?

Further Reading

P. Murphy, *A Practical Approach to Evidence*, 4th ed. (1992), Ch. 10
R. Munday, 'Proof of Guilt by Association under Section 74 of the Police and Criminal Evidence Act 1984' [1990] Crim LR 236

INDEX